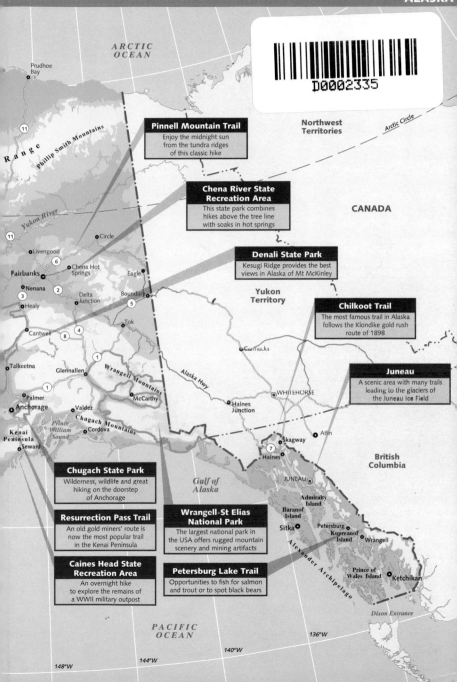

D0002335

Pinnell Mountain Trail
Enjoy the midnight sun from the tundra ridges of this classic hike

Chena River State Recreation Area
This state park combines hikes above the tree line with soaks in hot springs

Denali State Park
Kesugi Ridge provides the best views in Alaska of Mt McKinley

Chilkoot Trail
The most famous trail in Alaska follows the Klondike gold rush route of 1898

Juneau
A scenic area with many trails leading to the glaciers of the Juneau Ice Field

Chugach State Park
Wilderness, wildlife and great hiking on the doorstep of Anchorage

Resurrection Pass Trail
An old gold miners' route is now the most popular trail in the Kenai Peninsula

Caines Head State Recreation Area
An overnight hike to explore the remains of a WWII military outpost

Wrangell-St Elias National Park
The largest national park in the USA offers rugged mountain scenery and mining artifacts

Petersburg Lake Trail
Opportunities to fish for salmon and trout or to spot black bears

ARCTIC OCEAN

Prudhoe Bay

Northwest Territories

Arctic Circle

CANADA

Range

Phillip Smith Mountains

Yukon River

Circle

Livengood

Chena Hot Springs

Fairbanks

Nenana

Healy

Delta Junction

Eagle

Boundary

Yukon Territory

Tok

Carmacks

Cantwell

Talkeetna

Glennallen

Wrangell Mountains

Alaska Hwy

WHITEHORSE

Palmer

Anchorage

Valdez

McCarthy

Haines Junction

Atlin

Chugach Mountains

Prince William Sound

Cordova

Skagway

Haines

Kenai Peninsula

Seward

Gulf of Alaska

British Columbia

JUNEAU

Admiralty Island

Baranof Island

Sitka

Petersburg

Kupreanof Island

Wrangell

Alexander Archipelago

Prince of Wales Island

Ketchikan

Dixon Entrance

PACIFIC OCEAN

136°W

140°W

144°W

148°W

Hiking in Alaska
2nd edition – November 2000
First published – April 1995

Published by
Lonely Planet Publications Pty Ltd A.C.N. 005 607 983
192 Burwood Rd, Hawthorn, Victoria 3122, Australia

Lonely Planet Offices
Australia PO Box 617, Hawthorn, Victoria 3122
USA 150 Linden St, Oakland, CA 94607
UK 10a Spring Place, London NW5 3BH
France 1 rue du Dahomey, 75011 Paris

Photographs
All of the images in this guide are available for licensing from
Lonely Planet Images.
email: lpi@lonelyplanet.com.au

Front cover photograph
Hiker on Mt McKinley, Denali National Park (Stone/Paul Souders)

ISBN 1 86450 038 7

Contents

2 Contents

FAIRBANKS REGION   297

GLOSSARY   317

INDEX   320

MAP LEGEND   back page

METRIC CONVERSION   inside back cover

The Trails	Miles	Duration	Difficulty
Southeast Alaska			
Deer Mountain & John Mountain Trails	12	2 days	Medium to Hard
Petersburg Lake Trail	10.5	2–3 days	Medium
Gavan Hill & Harbor Mountain Trails	11	1–2 days	Medium
Mt Edgecumbe Trail	13.4	2–3 days	Medium to Hard
Perseverance Trail	11	1–2 days	Medium to Hard
Dan Moller Trail	6.6	1–2 days	Easy
West Glacier Trail	6.8–10.2	1–2 days	Medium to Hard
Montana Creek & Windfall Lake Trails	11.5	1–2 days	Easy to Medium
Amalga Trail	15	1–2 days	Medium
Mt Riley Loop	9–10.7	5–6 hours	Easy
Chilkoot Trail	30–35	3–4 days	Medium to Hard
Upper Dewey Lake Trail	6	1–2 days	Easy to Hard
Laughton Glacier Trail	3–8	1–2 days	Easy to Hard
Anchorage Region			
Flattop Mountain Trail	3.4	3–5 hours	Easy to Medium
Williwaw Lakes Loop	16	2 days	Medium
McHugh Lake Trail	16	2 days	Medium to Hard
Historic Iditarod Trail	26	2–3 days	Hard
Eklutna Lakeside Trail	25.7	1–3 days	Easy
Kenai Peninsula			
Johnson Pass Trail	23	2–3 days	Medium
Resurrection Pass Trail	38.5	4 days	Easy
Russian Lakes & Resurrection River Trails	21.6	2 days	Easy
Primrose & Lost Lake Trails	15	2 days	Medium
Coastal Trail	9–22	2–3 days	Easy
Glacier Lake & Lagoon Trails	16.5–30	3–4 days	Easy to Hard
Copper River Region			
Dixie Pass Route	22	4–5 days	Hard
Nugget Creek Trail	29	3–4 days	Medium
Bonanza Mine Trail	8	7.5–11.5 hours	Easy to Medium
Power Creek & Crater Lake Trails	12–15	2–3 days	Medium to Hard
McKinley Lake & Pipeline Lakes Trails	6	1 day	Easy to Medium
Denali			
Mt Healy Overlook Trail	5	3–4 hours	Medium
Polychrome Pass Circuit	8	1–2 days	Medium to Hard
East Branch of the Toklat River Route	12–16	2–3 days	Medium to Hard
Mt Eielson Loop	14	2 days	Medium
Little Coal Creek Trail & Kesugi Ridge Route	6.2–27.4	2–4 days	Medium to Hard
Fairbanks Region			
Pinnell Mountain Trail	27.3	3 days	Medium to Hard
Granite Tors Trail	15	2 days	Medium
Chena Dome Trail	29.5	3–4 days	Hard

Transportation	Shelter	Features	Page
Bus	Yes	Ketchikan's most scenic alpine hike	114
Boat/Plane	Yes	Excellent salmon fishing and lots of bears	120
Taxi	Yes	Overnight alpine hike or day hike	126
Boat	Yes	A climb to the top of an extinct volcano	127
Not Needed	No	Great alpine scenery and gold rush artifacts	135
Bus	Yes	Excellent day hike to the alpine area above Juneau	138
Bus	No	Best glacier hike in the Southeast	140
Bus/Rental Car	No	Good fishing during salmon runs	142
Rental Car	Yes	Scenic setting overlooking glacier	144
Not Needed	No	Easy climb to great views of Haines	148
Bus/Train	No	Historic gold rush trail	153
Not Needed	Yes	An alpine escape from bustling Skagway	158
Train	Yes	Historic gold rush train provides transportation	160
Taxi	No	Alaska's most popular mountain to climb	177
Taxi	No	Best overnight hike from Anchorage	179
Bus	No	Day hike or overnight hike into Chugach Mountains	181
Rental Car	No	Alpine crossing once used by gold miners	183
Rental Car	Yes	Easy hike along beautiful lake	187
Bus	No	Popular two-day alpine crossing	200
Rental Car	Yes	Easy alpine hike on old gold rush route	204
Bus	Yes	Easy overnight hike in Chugach National Forest	211
Bus	Yes	Scenic alpine hike along bus routes	215
Not Needed	Yes	Overnight hike to WWII military base	221
Boat	Yes	Excellent glacial and coastal scenery	226
Bus	No	Trail-less wilderness adventure	242
Bus	Yes	Moderate hike along old mining pack trail	246
Not Needed	No	Steep climb to old copper mine	248
Bus	Yes	Cordova's best alpine traverse	256
Rental Car	Yes	Day hike to old gold mine	259
Bus	No	A climb to views of Alaska Range and Mt McKinley	280
Bus	No	A trail-less hike past multicolored mountains	281
Bus	No	Possibilities for seeing caribou and Dall sheep	284
Bus	No	Popular route with excellent views of Mt McKinley	286
Bus	No	An alternative to busy Denali National Park	291
Bus	Yes	Scenic hike along tundra ridges	301
Bus	Yes	Unusual granite rock formations	307
Bus	Yes	Ridge walk past military plane crash	311

MAP INDEX

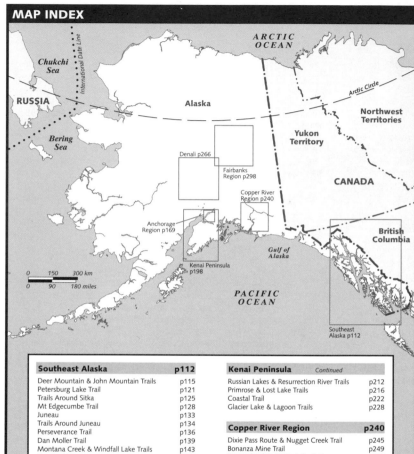

The Author

Jim DuFresne

Jim is a former sports and outdoors editor of the *Juneau Empire* and the first Alaskan sportswriter to win a national award from the Associated Press. He is presently a freelance writer, specializing in outdoor adventure and travel writing. He is the author of the Lonely Planet guidebooks *Tramping in New Zealand* and *Alaska,* and he contributed a story about a death on an Alaskan raft trip to *Lonely Planet Unpacked.* His other books include wilderness guides to Isle Royale, Voyageurs and Glacier Bay National Parks.

FROM THE AUTHOR

After meeting them on a trail in Ketchikan, I somehow convinced Nadine Caisley, Samantha Thompson, Alistair Davidson and Bob Storey to join me for a hike in Petersburg. I had reserved the Petersburg Lake Cabin for two nights. The cabin has six bunks, and I was planning to use only one of them. The hike in was long and wet, but late in the afternoon, we finally arrived at the prettiest wilderness cabin you'll ever see in Alaska – at least it was to us, five tired backpackers with sore shoulders and soaked feet.

Once we were in the cabin, we inventoried our supplies. Storey and Davidson had hauled in a roll of aluminum foil, some dried dill and two lemons. I had a fishing rod and a handful of lures. Somebody else had carried in a box of wine. For the next three days, we caught rainbow trout and sockeye salmon, feasted on sweet fillets sprinkled with fresh lemon juice, watched black bears across the river, drank cheap wine, talked late into the night and realized that, in the middle of nowhere with only what we could carry in on our backs, we had found paradise. It never ceases to amaze me how little we need sometimes to be so totally content: red wine, good conversation and a large salmon.

As always when researching any book to Alaska, I deeply appreciate all the assistance and accommodations my old Alaskan mates have provided during my many travels to the state. Thanks especially to Jeff and Sue Sloss, Ken Leghorn and Susan Warner, Ed Fogel, Frank and Janie Homan and Todd and Geri Hardesty.

I received considerable assistance from Karen Lundquist and Mandie Lewis of the Fairbanks Convention & Visitor Bureau, Ken Morris of the Anchorage Convention & Visitor Bureau, John Beiler of the Alaska Division of Tourism, Jon and Karin Nierenberg of Earthsong Lodge and Kathy Hedges of Chena Hot Springs Resort.

This book would not have been possible without the assistance of my editors and assorted bosses at Booth News Service: Meegan Holland, Dennis Tanner and Phil Moldenhauer. Most of all I want to thank my traveling and hiking partners: Caisley, Thompson, Davidson, Storey, Pattie Zwers, Brian Leigh, Ricardo and Rachel Miller, Martin McCaffery, Trish and Julia Finn and my son, Michael.

This Book

FROM THE PUBLISHER

This 2nd edition of *Hiking in Alaska* is a product of Lonely Planet's office in Oakland, California. Wade Fox and Erin Corrigan edited and proofed the text, under the supervision of senior editor Laura Harger. Ken DellaPenta created the index.

Shelley Firth laid out the book and Henia Miedzinski created the colorwraps, both with direction from Wendy Yanagihara and Susan Rimerman. The cover was designed by Jamieson Gross in Melbourne, Australia.

Beca Lafore coordinated the illustrations, and illustrations were drawn by Hugh D'Andrade, Shelley Firth, Hayden Foell, Beca Lafore, Justin Marler, Anthony Phelan, Tamsin Wilson, and Wendy Yanagihara.

Colin Bishop was the lead cartographer. Heather Haskell and Kat Smith edited maps, and Chris Gillis, Guphy, Chris Howard, Tessa Rottiers, and Ed Turley drew and edited maps. Senior cartographer Tracey Croom Power and cartography manager Alex Guilbert supervised map production.

THANKS

Many thanks to the travelers and hikers who used the last edition and wrote to us with their corrections, advice, hints and suggestions:

Paul Connelly, Robert Cregan, Andrew Reback, Roland Spencer-Jones.

Foreword

ABOUT LONELY PLANET GUIDEBOOKS

The story begins with a classic travel adventure: Tony and Maureen Wheeler's 1972 journey across Europe and Asia to Australia. Useful information about the overland trail did not exist at that time, so Tony and Maureen published the first Lonely Planet guidebook to meet a growing need.

From a kitchen table, then from a tiny office in Melbourne (Australia), Lonely Planet has become the largest independent travel publisher in the world, an international company with offices in Melbourne, Oakland (USA), London (UK) and Paris (France).

Today Lonely Planet guidebooks cover the globe. There is an ever-growing list of books, and there's information in a variety of forms and media. Some things haven't changed. The main aim is still to help make it possible for adventurous travelers to get out there – to explore and better understand the world.

At Lonely Planet we believe travelers can make a positive contribution to the countries they visit – if they respect their host communities and spend their money wisely. Since 1986 a percentage of the income from each book has been donated to aid projects and human-rights campaigns.

Updates Lonely Planet thoroughly updates each guidebook as often as possible. This usually means there are around two years between editions, although for more unusual or more stable destinations the gap can be longer. Check the imprint page (following the color map at the beginning of the book) for publication dates.

Between editions, up-to-date information is available in two free newsletters – the paper *Planet Talk* and email *Comet* (to subscribe, contact any Lonely Planet office) – and on our website at www.lonelyplanet.com. The *Upgrades* section of the website covers a number of important and volatile destinations and is regularly updated by Lonely Planet authors. *Scoop* covers news and current affairs relevant to travelers. And, lastly, the *Thorn Tree* bulletin board and *Postcards* section of the site carry unverified, but fascinating, reports from travelers.

Correspondence The process of creating new editions begins with the letters, postcards and emails received from travelers. This correspondence often includes suggestions, criticisms and comments about the current editions. Interesting excerpts are immediately passed on via newsletters and the website, and everything goes to our authors to be verified when they're researching on the road. We're keen to get more feedback from organizations or individuals who represent communities visited by travelers.

Lonely Planet gathers information for everyone who's curious about the planet – and especially for those who explore it firsthand. Through guidebooks, phrasebooks, activity guides, maps, literature, newsletters, image library, TV series and website, we act as an information exchange for a worldwide community of travelers.

Research Authors aim to gather sufficient practical information to enable travelers to make informed choices and to make the mechanics of a journey run smoothly. They also research historical and cultural background to help enrich the travel experience and allow travelers to understand and respond appropriately to cultural and environmental issues.

Authors don't stay in every hotel because that would mean spending a couple of months in each medium-size city and, no, they don't eat at every restaurant because that would mean stretching belts beyond capacity. They do visit hotels and restaurants to check standards and prices, but feedback based on readers' direct experiences can be very helpful.

Many of our authors work undercover; others aren't so secretive. None of them accept freebies in exchange for positive write-ups. And none of our guidebooks contain any advertising.

Production Authors submit their raw manuscripts and maps to offices in Australia, the USA, the UK or France. Editors and cartographers – all experienced travelers themselves – then begin the process of assembling the pieces. When the book finally hits the shops, some things are already out of date, we start getting feedback from readers and the process begins again....

WARNING & REQUEST

Things change – prices go up, schedules change, good places go bad and bad places go bankrupt – nothing stays the same. So, if you find things better or worse, recently opened or long since closed, please tell us and help make the next edition even more accurate and useful. We genuinely value all the feedback we receive. Julie Young coordinates a well-traveled team that reads and acknowledges every letter, postcard and email and ensures that every morsel of information finds its way to the appropriate authors, editors and cartographers for verification.

Everyone who writes to us will find their name in the next edition of the appropriate guidebook. They will also receive the latest issue of *Planet Talk*, our quarterly printed newsletter, or *Comet*, our monthly email newsletter. Subscriptions to both newsletters are free. The very best contributions will be rewarded with a free guidebook.

Excerpts from your correspondence may appear in new editions of Lonely Planet guidebooks, the Lonely Planet website, *Planet Talk* or *Comet*, so please let us know if you *don't* want your letter published or your name acknowledged.

Send all correspondence to the Lonely Planet office closest to you:

Australia: PO Box 617, Hawthorn, Victoria 3122
USA: 150 Linden St, Oakland, CA 94607
UK: 10A Spring Place, London NW5 3BH
France: 1 rue du Dahomey, 75011 Paris

Or email us at: talk2us@lonelyplanet.com.au

For news, views and updates, see our website: www.lonelyplanet.com

Introduction

You can visit Alaska, tour Alaska, or you can experience Alaska. The best way to really appreciate this magnificent land is on foot; get off the bus, out of the car, away from the road and onto a trail. More than any other activity, hiking allows you to escape the crowds, dodge the monstrous RVs on George Parks Hwy and sneak away from the cities, fast-food chains and high prices – to really see and experience what Alaska is all about, pristine wilderness.

Alaska draws backpackers, hikers and other wilderness seekers like few other places in the world. This 'Last Frontier' is the first place that comes to mind for those tempted by the North Country, evoking images of mountains, icy blue glaciers, brown bears feeding on salmon runs and treeless

tundra valleys uncluttered by buildings, billboards or other signs of so-called 'progress.'

Alaska is home to the highest peak in North America (Mt McKinley, 20,320ft), has a glacier (Bering Glacier complex) larger than the US state of Delaware, boasts a lake with a surface area of over 1000 sq mi (Iliamna) and has more coastline than the rest of the US states put together. At 570,374 sq mi (a fifth of the size rest of the USA), Alaska is a vast land of extraordinary dimensions.

More than three-quarters of Alaska is land 'locked up' as parks, wildlife preserves, wild rivers and national forests. The National Park Service (NPS) alone oversees 70,313 sq mi of land, including Denali and Wrangell–St Elias National Parks. These

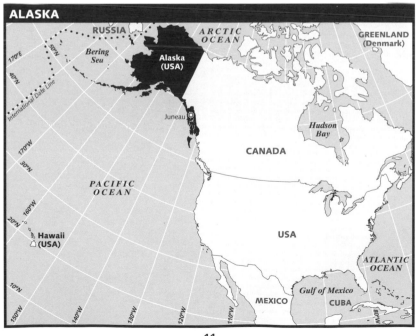

and other parks have endless hiking and roaming possibilities.

This book is a detailed guide to 37 trails and routes in regions ranging from Ketchikan in Southeast Alaska to north of Fairbanks, near the Arctic Circle. The trails include an afternoon day hike along the edge of the Mendenhall Glacier in Juneau, a 10-day journey across the Kenai Peninsula on the Resurrection Pass trail system, and an adventure in Denali Wilderness, where there are no trails at all. Dozens of other trails in six regions of the state – Southeast, Anchorage, Kenai Peninsula, Copper River, Denali and Fairbanks – are mentioned and briefly described, with information on transportation to the area and the trailheads, special concerns, permits and places to stay off the trail.

Each hike is rated in terms of difficulty. 'Easy' trails are well maintained, with bridges over all major streams and planking over many bog areas. Paths are easy to locate and follow, primarily because they are well used by hikers and other groups like mountain bikers and equestrians. Often junctions are posted with mileage signs or even maps. Some climbing may be necessary, but switchbacks make the ascents easier.

'Medium' trails are still beaten paths in the woods, but they are not posted as often as the easy trails. These trails require you to ford small streams or negotiate short stretches along ridges or other alpine areas.

The hiking is more demanding, involving greater elevation gains, longer days and 'bouldering' (stepping from one large rock to the next) rocky slopes around peaks.

'Hard' treks are often combinations of several hiking trails, frequently following the natural route of a ridgeline or the gravel bars of a river. Hikers will often use animal trails to make their way from one valley to another in an area that may not have maintained trails. The challenging hikes in this guidebook often involve fording rivers – a difficult, if not impossible task when water levels are high – and alpine crossings with little protection from weather that may suddenly turn foul. These hikes demand that you be in good walking condition, have previous backcountry experience and possess a sound understanding of both maps and compasses.

Don't let the fear of bears and bugs dictate where or when you go hiking in Alaska. These are minor concerns; the great dangers in the Alaska wilderness are hypothermia, underestimating swollen rivers and getting lost. Eliminate these risks by being properly equipped, choosing the right hike for your ability and scheduling enough days so that exhaustion doesn't lead to an accident.

Be prepared, and you will enjoy hiking in Alaska. Only through the soles of your boots will you unlock the wonders of this land and experience the wilderness and wildlife that have been so carefully protected.

Facts about Alaska

HISTORY

Alaska's history is a strange series of spurts and sputters, booms and busts. Although today Alaska is viewed as a wilderness paradise and an endless source of raw materials, in the past it has often been regarded as a frozen wasteland, a suitable home only for Inuit and polar bears. Once some natural resource was uncovered, however, a short period of prosperity and exploitation followed: first with sea-otter skins; then gold, salmon and oil; and most recently, untouched wilderness. After each resource was exhausted, some would say raped, the land slipped back into oblivion.

The First Alaskans

The first Alaskans migrated from Asia to North America between 30,000 and 40,000 years ago, during an ice age that lowered the sea level and created a 900mi land bridge linking Siberia and Alaska. The nomadic groups who crossed the bridge were not bent on exploration but on following the animal herds that provided them with food and clothing. Although many tribes wandered deep into North and South America, four ethnic groups – the Athabascans, Aleuts, Inuit and the coastal tribes of Tlingit and Haida – remained in Alaska and made the harsh wilderness their homeland.

The First Europeans

Thanks to the cold and stormy North Pacific, Alaska was one of the last places in the world to be mapped by Europeans. Because of this, several countries explored the region and then attempted to lay a claim to the land and its resources by establishing a fort or two. Spanish admiral Bartholeme de Fonte is credited by many with making the first trip into Alaskan waters when, in 1640, he sailed from Mexico up the western coast of North America to Alaska. There he explored a network of rivers looking for the Northwest Passage, a water route between the Pacific and Atlantic Oceans, before returning south.

The first written record of the state was made by Vitus Bering, a Danish navigator sailing for the Russian tsar. Bering's trip, in 1728, proved that America and Asia were two separate continents, and 13 years later, commanding the ship *St Peter,* he went ashore near Cordova, becoming the first European to set foot in Alaska. Bering and many of his crew died from scurvy during that journey, but his lieutenant (aboard the ship *St Paul*) sailed all the way to the site of present-day Sitka before turning around. Despite all the hardships, the survivors brought back fur pelts and tales of fabulous seal and otter colonies – Alaska's first boom was under way. Russian fur merchants wasted little time in overrunning the Aleutian Islands and quickly established a settlement on Kodiak Island. Chaos followed, as bands of Russian hunters robbed and murdered each other for furs while the peaceful Aleuts, living near the hunting grounds, were almost annihilated through disease and forced labor.

By the 1790s, Russia had organized the Russian-American Company to regulate the fur trade and ease the violent competition. However, tales of the enormous wealth to be gained in the Alaskan wildlife trade brought representatives of several other countries to the frigid waters. Spain claimed the entire western coast of North America, including Alaska, and sent several explorers to the Southeast region. These early visitors took boatloads of furs but left neither settlers nor forts, only a few Spanish place names.

The British arrived when Captain James Cook also began searching the area for the Northwest Passage. From Vancouver Island, Cook sailed north to Southcentral Alaska in 1778, anchoring at what is now Cook Inlet for a spell before continuing on to the Aleutian Islands, Bering Sea and even the Arctic Ocean. The French sent Jean-Françoise

Galaup, comte de La Pérouse, who in 1786 made it as far as Lituya Bay on the southern coast of Alaska. The wicked tides within the long, narrow bay caught the exploration party off guard, capsizing three longboats, killing 21 sailors and discouraging the French from colonizing the area.

Cook's shipmate George Vancouver, returning on his own in the 1790s, finally charted the complicated waters of the Southeast's Inside Passage. Aboard his ship, HMS *Discovery,* Vancouver surveyed the coastline from California to Alaska's Panhandle, producing maps so accurate they were still being used a century later.

Having depleted the sea otter colonies in the Aleutians, Aleksandr Baranov, who headed the Russian-American Company, moved his territorial capital from Kodiak to Sitka in the Southeast. After ruthlessly subduing the Tlingit Indians with cannons and soldiers, Baranov built a stunning city, 'an American Paris in Alaska,' with the immense profits from furs. At one point, Baranov oversaw, or some would say ruled, a fur empire that stretched from Bristol Bay to Northern California. When the British began pushing north into Southeast Alaska, he built a second fort near the mouth of the Stikine River in 1834. That fort, which was named St Dionysius at the time, eventually evolved into the small lumbering and fishing town of Wrangell.

When a small trickle of US adventurers began to arrive, four nations had a foot in the Panhandle of Alaska: Spain, France, Britain and Russia. However, Spain and

Russia established early colonies in Southeast Alaska.

France were squeezed out of the area by the early 1800s, and the British were reduced to leasing selected areas from the Russians.

The Sale of Alaska

By the 1860s, the Russians found themselves badly overextended. Their involvement in Napoleon's European wars, a declining fur industry and the long lines of shipping between Sitka and the heartland of Russia were draining their national treasury. The country made several overtures to the USA for the sale of Alaska, and commercial fishing companies from the state of Washington pushed for the sale. The American Civil War delayed the negotiations, and it wasn't until 1867 that Secretary of State William H Seward, with extremely keen foresight, signed a treaty to purchase the state for $7.2 million – less than 2¢ an acre.

Gold

What brought Alaska into the world limelight, however, was gold. The promise of quick riches and the adventure of the frontier became the most effective lure Alaska ever had. Gold was discovered in the Gastineau Channel in the 1880s, and the towns of Juneau and Douglas sprang up overnight, living off the very productive Treadwell and Alaska-Juneau Mines. Circle City, in the Interior, suddenly emerged in 1893, when gold was discovered in nearby Birch Creek. Three years later, one of the world's most colorful gold rushes took place in the Klondike region of Canada's Yukon Territory.

Often called 'the last grand adventure,' the Klondike gold rush occurred when the country and much of the world was suffering a severe recession. When the banner headline of the *Seattle Post-Intelligencer* bellowed 'GOLD! GOLD! GOLD! GOLD!' on July 17, 1897, thousands of people began quitting their jobs and selling their homes to finance a trip through Southeast Alaska to the newly created boomtown of Skagway. From this tent city, almost 30,000 prospectors tackled the steep Chilkoot Trail to Lake Bennett, where they built crude rafts to float the rest of the way to the goldfields; an equal number of people returned home along the route, broke and disillusioned.

The number of miners who made fortunes was small, but the tales and legends that emerged were endless. The Klondike stampede, though it only lasted from 1896 to the early 1900s, was Alaska's most colorful era and earned Alaska the reputation of being the country's last frontier.

Statehood

The USA experienced its only foreign invasion on home soil when the Japanese attacked the Attu Islands and bombed Dutch Harbor in the Aleutian Islands during WWII. Congressional and military leaders panicked and rushed to develop and protect the rest of Alaska. Large army and air-force bases were built throughout the state at places that included Anchorage, Fairbanks, Sitka, Whittier and Kodiak, and thousands of military personnel were sent to Alaska. But the famous Alcan (also known as the Alaska Hwy) was the single most important project of the military buildup. The 1520mi road was a major engineering feat and became the only overland link between Alaska and the rest of the USA.

The road was built by the military, but Alaska's residents benefited, as the Alcan stimulated the development of Alaska's natural resources. The growth led to a new drive for statehood, to fix what many felt was Alaska's '2nd-class citizenship.' Early in 1958, Congress approved a statehood act, which Alaskans quickly accepted, and on January 3, 1959, President Dwight Eisenhower proclaimed Alaska the USA's 49th state.

The Modern State

Alaska entered the 1960s full of promise, and then disaster struck: The most powerful earthquake ever recorded in North America (registering 9.2 on the Richter scale) hit Southcentral Alaska on Good Friday morning in 1964. If the natural catastrophe left the newborn state in a shambles, then it was another gift from nature that soon rushed Alaska to recovery and beyond. Alaska's next boom took place in 1968, when

Atlantic Richfield discovered massive oil deposits underneath Prudhoe Bay in the Arctic Ocean. The oil's value doubled after the Arab oil embargo of 1973, but the oil couldn't be tapped until there was a pipeline to transport it to the warm-water port of Valdez. The pipeline, in turn, couldn't be built until the US Congress, which still administered most of the land, settled the intense controversy between industry, environmentalists and Native Alaskans with historical claims to the land.

The Alaska Native Claims Settlement Act of 1971 was an unprecedented piece of legislation that opened the way for a consortium of oil companies to undertake the construction of the 789mi pipeline. The Trans-Alaska Pipeline took three years to build, cost more than $8 billion in 1977 dollars and, at the time, was the most expensive private construction project ever undertaken. At the peak of construction, the pipeline employed 28,000 people, doing '7-12s' (seven 12-hour shifts a week) and receiving weekly paychecks that topped $1,500.

For a decade or more, oil gave Alaska an economic base that was the envy of every other state, accounting for as much as 80% of state government revenue. In the explosive growth period of the mid-1980s, Alaskans enjoyed the highest per-capita income in the country. The state's budget was in the billions. Legislators in Juneau transformed Anchorage into a stunning city, with sports arenas, libraries and performing-arts centers, and virtually every bush town has a million-dollar school. From 1980 to 1986, this state of only a half million residents generated revenue of $26 billion.

For most Alaskans, it was hard to see beyond the gleam of the oil dollar. Their first rude awakening came in 1986, when world oil prices dropped. Their second dose of reality was even harder to swallow. In March 1989, the *Exxon Valdez*, a 987ft Exxon oil supertanker, rammed Bligh Reef a few hours out of the port of Valdez. The ship spilled almost 11 million gallons of North Slope crude into the bountiful waters of Prince William Sound. Alaskans and the rest of the country watched in horror as the spill quickly became far too large for booms to contain the oil, spreading 600mi from the grounding site. Within months, miles of tainted coastline began to appear throughout the Gulf of Alaska as currents dispersed streamers of oil and tar balls.

In the end, the oil, like resources exploited in the past, is simply running out. That pot of gold called Prudhoe Bay began its decline in production in 1989, and in 1995

Who Owns the Land?

Alaska is the largest state in the USA, with 570,374 sq mi, yet it has just over 600,000 residents, giving it a population density of just over one person per square mile. The national average is 76 persons per square mile, and New Jersey, the most crowded state, has 1085 persons per square mile. So there's lots of land for everybody in Alaska, right?

Well, not really. Two-thirds of the land in the state, or 372,031 sq mi, is owned by the federal government and set aside as national parks, wild rivers, designated wilderness areas and wildlife refuges. To put it in better perspective, the USA has 1,034,375 sq mi of national parks, national forests, and Bureau of Land Management holdings, and a third of this land is in Alaska.

The state of Alaska also owns its share of land, just over 137,656 sq mi, the result of its statehood compact. The Alaska state park system alone totals 5156 sq mi. The state park systems in the other 49 states total 14,375 sq mi. Native corporations control 56,406 sq mi, the result of the Alaska Native Claims Settlement Act that was passed in 1971 to pave the way for the Trans-Alaska Pipeline.

Less than 1% of the land in Alaska is in private, non-Native corporation ownership, and many Alaskans demand that they be given an opportunity to purchase, own and develop more of the state's acreage. On the other hand, the greatest, and some say last, true wilderness areas in the USA are protected for future generations of hikers and backpackers to enjoy.

alone, North Slope oil output decreased by more than 4%. Arco, the state's second largest employer, laid off almost a third of its 2350 employees in Alaska. Other related companies, which move the oil and maintain the Trans-Alaska Pipeline, also began to slash jobs. The end of the Cold War and the subsequent downsizing of the US military in the early 1990s was more economic bad news for Alaska. Fort Greely, Delta Junction's largest employer, was closed in 1994, with more Alaskan bases on the chopping block. Alaskan state revenues went tumbling along with the declining oil royalties, forcing state legislators to slash services and programs in an attempt to balance the budget.

The Battle over the Wilderness

Many Alaskans see another North Slope oil field as the solution to their problems. Large mining projects are being pushed as Alaska faces its greatest debate – over the exploitation of its remaining wilderness. The issue first emerged when industry, conservation groups and the government came head to head over a single paragraph in the Alaska Native Claims Settlement Act, known simply as 'd-2,' that called for the preservation of 125,000 sq mi of Alaskan wilderness. To most residents, this paragraph evoked the issue of federal interference with the state's resources and future.

The resulting battle was a tug of war over how much land the US Congress would preserve, to what extent industries such as mining and logging would be allowed to develop, and what land permanent residents would be allowed to purchase. The fury over wilderness reached a climax when, on the eve of his departure from office in 1980, President Jimmy Carter signed the Alaska National Interest Lands Conservation Act into law, setting aside 84,375 sq mi for national parks and preserves with a single stroke of the pen.

The problems of managing the USA's remaining true wilderness areas are far from over, and presently the debate is centered on the Arctic National Wildlife Refuge (ANWR). Oil-company officials and Alaskan politicians in particular are pushing hard to open up this 2344-sq-mi refuge, one of the last great wilderness areas in the USA, to oil and gas drilling. A bill to open up the refuge in the US Congress, backed by then-President George Bush, was believed to be headed for passage when the *Exxon Valdez* ran aground in 1989.

After several years of hibernation, the effort was revived again when the Republicans took control of the US Congress in 1992 and members of Alaska's long-term Republican delegation suddenly had key leadership roles.

President Bill Clinton has since vowed to veto any bill opening up the ANWR to pipelines and oil rigs. But many Alaskans believe it's only a matter of time before the inevitable happens in a state where 80% of the revenue comes from the oil industry.

History of Hiking

Native Americans and miners dreaming of gold and wealth were as responsible for hiking and trails in Alaska today as any other groups. Many of the state's best-known trails were originally Native Alaskan routes that were then used by miners during the various gold rushes from the late 1800s to the early 1900s. The Chilkoot Trail was the result of 30,000 prospectors eager to reach the Klondike fields in 1898–1900. The lure of gold was also responsible for many other trails, including Resurrection Pass, Iditarod and Juneau's Perseverance Trail.

These boom-and-bust times resulted in widespread resource abuse, which ultimately lead to an early conservation movement in Alaska. The US Forest Service (USFS) was created in 1905, and two years later Tongass National Forest was formed. Its original boundaries resembled those of present-day Misty Fjords National Monument. A year later, Chugach National Forest was established. The first national park in the USA, Yellowstone, was created in 1872, but by 1925 Alaska, not even a state yet, had four national parks: Sitka (1910), Denali (1917), Katmai (1918) and Glacier Bay (1925).

Hiking and outdoor recreation in Alaska received a boost during the Great Depression. From 1933 to 1941, members of the Civilian Conservation Corps worked under the direction of the USFS to restore historic trails, cut new ones and construct roads into the national forests. They also built the original Forest Service cabins. Many are still in use more than a half century later.

The back-to-nature, backpacking boom of the 1970s also shaped outdoor recreation in Alaska. The state's Division of Parks and Outdoor Recreation was created in 1970 and included five parks (Chugach, Denali, Kachemak Bay, Chilkat and Nancy Lake) that totaled 1459 sq mi. In 1972, Alaska Discovery was formed as a response to plans for increased logging on Admiralty Island. By guiding people across the wilderness island, the outfitter was able to raise public support for preserving it. Within six years, there were more than 30 recreational companies guiding clients on hikes and paddles in regions from Glacier Bay to the Arctic National Wildlife Refuge, proving that ecotourism can be profitable.

The event most significant to outdoor recreation in Alaska, however, occurred in 1980, when the Alaska National Interest Lands Conservation Act was signed into law. This single act created 14 wilderness areas, established 10 new national parks and expanded four others. With a stroke of his pen, President Jimmy Carter doubled the size of the national park system in the USA, increasing the units in Alaska to 84,375 sq mi, or 14% of the state's 570,374 sq mi. In Alaska there's room to play.

GEOGRAPHY

The word 'Alaska' is derived from the Aleut word *Alyeshka,* meaning 'great land,' an appropriate name. The state measures 1400mi north to south, 2300mi east to west and covers 570,374 sq mi. The land's diversity is mind-boggling. The landscape ranges from lush rain forests in the Southeast to drifting sand dunes in the dry Arctic coastal plain, from glaciers and the highest peaks in the country to muskeg and tundra.

Southeast Alaska, also known as the Panhandle, is a 500mi coastal strip that extends from Dixon Entrance, north of Prince

Rupert, to the Gulf of Alaska. In between are the hundreds of islands (including Prince of Wales Island, the third largest island in the USA) of the Alexander Archipelago and a narrow strip of coast separated from Canada's mainland by the glacier-filled Coast Mountains. The major parks and preserves of the Southeast are Glacier Bay National Park, Admiralty Island National Monument and Misty Fjords National Monument. Nearly every town in this region has trails that go into the surrounding mountains or remote valleys.

Southcentral Alaska curves 650mi from the Gulf of Alaska, past Prince William Sound to Kodiak Island. Like the Southeast, this area is a mixture of rugged mountains, glaciers, steep fjords and virgin forests, and includes the Kenai Peninsula – a superb recreational area for backpacking, day hiking and escaping into the wilderness – and the Copper River region. The major parks and preserves include Chugach National Forest, Kenai Fjords National Park, Kenai National Wildlife Refuge and Kachemak Bay State Park and Wilderness.

With almost half the state's population living in the Anchorage Bowl, Alaska's largest city is a region unto itself. Anchorage has the luxury of mountains above its skyline and wilderness at its doorstep, as it is practically surrounded by Chugach State Park. Surrounding the state park is Chugach National Park.

The Interior is the heartland of Alaska. With the Alaska Range to the north, the Wrangell and Chugach Mountains to the south and the Talkeetna Mountains cutting through the middle, the Interior has a rugged appearance matching that of either Southeast or Southcentral Alaska, but without much of the rain and cloudy weather. It also has three roads – the George Parks, Glenn, and Richardson Hwys – that provide access to a number of forests, state parks and recreational areas, including Denali National Park and Preserve, Alaska's number one attraction, Denali State Park and Wrangell–St Elias National Park and Preserve.

Farther north is Alaska's second largest city. Fairbanks is located in the flat valley floor formed by the Tanana and Chena Rivers. The Alaska Range and Mt McKinley are off in the distance, but the surrounding area is typified by rolling mountains and ridges and much thermal activity. On the Pinnell Mountain Trail and in Chena River State Recreation Area, hikers end their long walks by recuperating in nearby natural hot springs.

Alaska's Bush is a vast region that includes the Brooks Range, Arctic Alaska, Western Alaska on the Bering Sea, the Alaska Peninsula and also the Aleutian Islands, which make up the western arm of the state. The Bush is larger than the other five regions put together and is separated from them by mountains and rivers.

GEOLOGY

Horizontally Alaska is spread over 570,374 sq mi, but vertically it is even more impressive, with elevations ranging from the Aleutian Trench, which lies 25,000ft below the sea, to the highest mountain in North America, Mount McKinley at 20,320ft. This is a range of almost 9mi.

Three impressive mountain systems arch across the state. The Coast Range sweeps along the southern edge of Alaska as a continuation of Washington State's Olympic Range and includes the St Elias Range and the Chugach and Kenai Mountains before dipping into the sea southwest of Kodiak Island. The Alaska and Aleutian Ranges parallel these mountains in the same arc, and the Brooks Range skirts the Arctic Circle. In between the Alaska Range and the Brooks Range is Interior Alaska, an immense plateau rippled by foothills, low mountains and great rivers. North of the Brooks Range is the North Slope, which gently descends to the Arctic Ocean.

In geologic time, the Alaskan landmass is relatively new and still very active. The result of plate tectonics, where the Pacific Plate (the ocean floor) drifts under the North American Plate, Alaska is the northern rim of the chain of Pacific Ocean volcanoes known as the Ring of Fire. The state is also the most seismically active region of North America. It's estimated that 10% of the world's earthquakes occur in Alaska. Almost half of the state is susceptible to an earthquake, and the town of Valdez on Prince William Sound experiences a major one – 5.0 or higher on the Richter scale – almost annually. In 1964, Valdez was wiped out from the tsunamis produced by the Good Friday Earthquake. At 9.2 on the Richter scale, this earthquake was the strongest ever recorded in North America.

Glaciers

Glaciers form whenever the snowfall in the mountains exceeds the rate of melting. As the snow builds up, it becomes a solid cap of ice that, because of gravity, flows like a frozen river. Because glacial ice absorbs all the colors of the spectrum except blue, which it reflects, glacial ice often appears blue. The more overcast the day, the bluer glacial ice appears. If it's raining on the day you are to view a glacier, rejoice; the blues will never be more intense.

Alaska is one of the few places in the world where active glaciation occurs on a grand scale. There are an estimated 100,000 glaciers in Alaska, covering 29,000 sq mi, or 5% of the state, and containing three-fourths of all its fresh water.

The largest glacier is the Bering Glacier, which stretches more than 100mi, from the St Elias Range to the Gulf of Alaska. If you include the Bagley Ice Field, where the Bering Glacier begins, this glacial complex covers 2250 sq mi, making it larger than the state of Delaware. Just to the east is the Malaspina Glacier complex, which covers an area of 2000 sq mi.

Tidewater glaciers calve (icebergs break off the glacier) directly into a body of water. The southernmost tidewater glacier in North America is the Le Conte Glacier, near Petersburg in the Southeast. La Perouse Glacier, in Glacier Bay National Park, is the only one that discharges icebergs directly into the Pacific Ocean. The largest collection of tidewater glaciers is in Prince William Sound, where 20 of them are active.

The longest tidewater glacier is Hubbard, which begins in Canada and stretches 76mi

to Russell Fjord near Yakutat. It might also be one of the most active. In 1986, Hubbard rapidly advanced across the fjord, reaching the shoreline on the other side. For most of the year, Russell Fjord was technically a lake, until the ice dam dramatically broke.

Active tidewater glaciers can be easily viewed from tour boats. The best places to go for such a day cruise are Glacier Bay National Park, Kenai Fjords National Park or Prince William Sound out of Whittier. Alaska's most popular roadside glaciers are Worthington (Richardson Hwy), Matanuska (Glenn Hwy), Exit (Seward Hwy), Portage (Seward Hwy) and Mendenhall (off of Glacier Hwy in Juneau).

CLIMATE & THE 24-HOUR DAY

It only makes sense that a place as large and diverse as Alaska would have a climate to match. The oceans surrounding 75% of the state, the mountainous terrain and the low angle of the sun give Alaska an extremely variable climate and daily weather that is famous for being unpredictable.

The Interior can top 90°F during the summer, yet six months later in the same region the temperature can drop to -60°F. Fort Yukon holds the state record for maximum temperature at 100°F in June 1915, yet it once recorded a temperature of -78°F.

For the most part, Southeast and Southcentral Alaska have high rainfall and temperatures that only vary 40°F during the year. Anchorage, shielded by the Kenai Mountains, has an annual rainfall of 15 inches and average temperatures of 60° to 70°F from June to August. Juneau averages 57 inches of rain or snow annually, and Ketchikan gets 154 inches a year, most of which is rain, as the temperatures are extremely mild even in the winter. A good week in Southcentral and Southeast Alaska during the summer will include three sunny days, two overcast ones and two when you need to pull your rain gear out or duck for cover.

In the Interior and up around Fairbanks, precipitation is light, but temperatures can fluctuate by more than 100°F during the year. In summer, the average daytime tem-

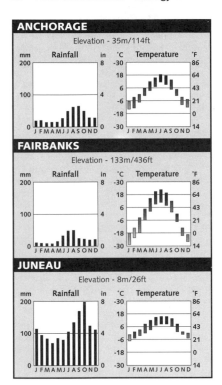

ANCHORAGE
Elevation - 35m/114ft

FAIRBANKS
Elevation - 133m/436ft

JUNEAU
Elevation - 8m/26ft

perature can range from 55° to 75°F, with a brief period in late July to early August when temperatures will top 80°F or even 90°F. At night, temperatures can drop sharply to 45°F or even lower, and freak snowfalls can occur in the valleys during July or August, with the white stuff lasting a day or two.

The climate in the Bush varies. The region north of the Arctic Circle is cool most of the summer, with temperatures around 45°F, and annual rainfall is less than 4 inches. This far north, fall colors begin appearing in mid-August. Other areas are a mixed bag, with long periods of strong winds and foul weather in the summer.

In most of Alaska, summers are a beautiful mixture of long days and short nights, making activities in the great outdoors even more appealing. At Point Barrow, Alaska's northernmost point, the sun never sets for 2½ months, from May to August. The longest day is on June 21 (the solstice), when the sun sets for only two hours in Fairbanks, for four hours in Anchorage and five to six hours in the Southeast. Even after the sun sets in late June and July, it is replaced not by night but by a dusk that still allows good visibility.

To obtain weather forecasts for Alaska before and during your trip, see Weather Information in the Facts for the Hiker chapter.

ECOLOGY & ENVIRONMENT

Due to Alaska's size and the huge tracts of remaining wilderness, its environmental concerns are not just regional conflicts but, more often than not, national debates. Whether to open up the coastal plain of the Arctic National Wildlife Refuge to oil drilling is just one of the prominent issues. Another heated controversy was the state's decision in the mid-1990s to embark on a program of 'wolf management' in a Connecticut-size chunk of spruce forests and foothills south of Fairbanks. This is the home of the Fortymile caribou herd, whose numbers have bounced between 6,000 and 500,000 in the past century and have hovered around 20,000 since the early 1990s. In 1993, local hunters successfully urged the state to undertake the snaring and shooting of up to 80% of the wolves in the area, as a way to build up the herd. One state official even suggested that wolves could be killed more efficiently by using helicopters and automatic weapons. Outraged Alaskan environmentalists and national organizations like the Sierra Club turned the issue into a national debate, which led to a brief tourism boycott of Alaska. The program was permanently canceled in 1995, after photographs of a biologist repeatedly shooting wolves that had been trapped live appeared in papers across the country. The stormy issue, however, has not gone away. A citizen planning team studying the issue has recommended sterilizing wolves as a way to control their numbers. Environmentalists argue that the wolf control program isn't necessary, because caribou herds naturally fluctuate in size.

Meanwhile, impatient Fairbanks-area hunters have started a private bounty program on Fortymile wolves, offering trappers $400 per hide, twice the market value.

Other environmental concerns range from clear-cutting of the Tongass National Forest to overfishing by fleets of factory ships. In 1996, the Sierra Club announced a hard-line stance against commercial logging on federal lands, ensuring the battle over Alaska timber would rage on well into the 21st century. In the same year, Greenpeace launched a campaign to put factory trawlers out of business. Larger than football fields, these ships haul up hundreds of tons of fish in a single netting and are plundering the ecosystem, Greenpeace claims, in waters like the Bering Sea.

Perhaps the environmental issue that affects hikers and backpackers the most is Alaska's desire to build roads. Politicians and pro-development Alaskans have been pushing for years to expand the state's meager system of highways. The issue came to climax in 1997, when Alaska senator Ted Stevens tacked a rider onto a disaster-relief bill for flood-ravaged North Dakota. The rider would give Alaska the right to build roads through federal lands, including designated wilderness areas. Environmentalists promptly organized a campaign against what they dubbed the 'pave the parks' rider.

Stevens backed down, but road building remains a sensitive issue in Alaska. More pavement would provide low-cost transportation into remote areas of the state, which in turn would lower prices for everything from food to fuel, but roads threaten Alaska's most abundant resource, wilderness. The ability to escape the crowds and the fast pace of urbanization is not only a lifestyle in this state but often the main attraction for visitors. Once Alaska is bisected with highways, that ability is lost forever.

Conservation

Tourism, especially ecotourism, is booming in Alaska and is inevitably impacting the state's sensitive environment. Too many cruise ships in Glacier Bay, too many tour buses on the highways and too many people in wilderness areas like Denali National Park are having a negative effect on the land, the wildlife and Native cultures.

In 1992, the Alaska Wilderness Recreation and Tourism Association was formed in an effort to balance tourism with 'environmentally sustainable economic growth.' Members of AWRTA are often tour companies and outfitters that are committed to responsible tourism and minimizing visitor impact. When looking for a guide company, a charter operator or lodging, an AWRTA member should be given serious consideration. You can get a complete list of members by requesting the AWRTA's Alaska Adventure Sourcebook. Contact the AWRTA (☎ 907-463-3038), PO Box 22827, Juneau, AK 99802, or check for information on their Web site (www.awrta.org).

NATIONAL & STATE PARKS, FORESTS & REFUGES
National Parks

One of the main attractions of Alaska is the 84,375 sq mi administered by the National Park Service as national parks, national preserves and national monuments, by far the most national park land of any state in the USA. Much of the land is the result of the Alaska National Interest Lands Conservation Act of 1980, which created 10 new parks and upgraded the status of three others – Denali, Glacier Bay and Katmai – to national parks and preserves and substantially increased their size.

In 1997, Alaska's 15 national park units topped 2 million visitors for the first time, marking an 80% increase in visitors in the 10-year period since 1987. The most popular unit that year was Klondike Gold Rush National Historical Park, followed by Glacier Bay National Park and Preserve. Both units have experienced a jump in visitors in the 1990s, due primarily to an increased number of large cruise ships into Southeast Alaska. Other popular parks include Denali and Kenai Fjords National Park, in Seward, which recorded more than 300,000 visitors in 1997. The least crowded park is the Yukon–Charley Rivers National Preserve, northwest of Eagle, with just 1,825 people visiting the area in 1997.

For information on all the parks before your trip, contact the Alaska Public Lands Information Center (☎ 907-271-2737), 605 W 4th St, Suite 105, Anchorage, AK 99501, or check the National Park Service Web site (www.nps.gov/parklists/ak.html).

Aniakchak National Monument and Preserve (☎ 907-246-3305), PO Box 7, King Salmon, AK 99613. This 942-sq-mi preserve is on the Alaska Peninsula and has no developed facilities. The main activities are wilderness backpacking and kayaking.

Bering Land Bridge National Preserve (☎ 907-443-2522), PO Box 220, Nome, AK 99762. Located about 100mi north of Nome, this 4219-sq-mi unit is known for its lava fields, archaeological sites and migratory waterfowl.

Cape Krusenstern National Monument (☎ 907-442-8300), PO Box 1029, Kotzebue, AK 99752. This 1031-sq-mi unit has no developed facilities and attracts a small number of visitors interested in archaeological sites, birding and kayaking.

Denali National Park and Preserve (☎ 907-683-2290), PO Box 9, Denali Park, AK 99755. Alaska's best-known park, Denali is a 9375-sq-mi unit in the heart of the Alaska Range. Well developed with facilities, the park features the highest peak in North America (Mt McKinley) and an abundance of wildlife.

Gates of the Arctic National Park and Preserve (☎ 907-456-0281), PO Box 74680, Fairbanks, AK 99707. Preserving a large slice of the Brooks Range is this 13,125-sq-mi park above the Arctic Circle. Floating wild rivers, backpacking and climbing are the main activities in the park. Gates of the Arctic has no developed facilities but is well served by guiding companies and outfitters.

Glacier Bay National Park and Preserve (☎ 907-697-2232), PO Box 140, Gustavus, AK 99826. Glacier Bay is a 5000-sq-mi park that includes 16 tidewater glaciers and some of the highest peaks in Southeast Alaska. Kayaking, whale watching and boat tours are the main activities.

Katmai National Park and Preserve (☎ 907-246-3305), PO Box 7, King Salmon, AK 99613. This 6250-sq-mi park on the Alaska Peninsula is renowned for volcanoes, the Valley of 10,000 Smokes and giant brown bears. Kayaking, bear watching and wilderness backpacking are the most popular activities.

Kenai Fjords National Park (☎ 907-224-3175), PO Box 1727, Seward, AK 99664. The number of visitors has tripled in the past five years at this 906-sq-mi park on the southeast corner of the Kenai Peninsula. Kenai Fjords is popular for glacier tours, whale watching and wilderness kayak trips.

Klondike Gold Rush National Historical Park (☎ 907-983-2921), PO Box 517, Skagway, AK 99840. This small unit covers only 2,271 acres but includes the historic gold rush town of Skagway and the American portion of the famous Chilkoot Trail that miners followed in 1898 to reach the Klondike goldfields.

Kobuk Valley National Park (☎ 907-442-8300), PO Box 1029, Kotzebue, AK 99752. Located 75mi east of Kotzebue, this 2656-sq-mi Arctic park attracts a small number of visitors for river running and exploring the Great Kobuk Sand Dunes.

Lake Clark National Park and Preserve (☎ 907-271-3751), 4230 University Drive, Suite 311, Anchorage, AK 99508. Spreading across 6250 sq mi, Lake Clark is only a short flight from Anchorage, making it a popular park for wilderness backpacking, fishing and river running.

Noatak National Preserve (☎ 907-442-8300), PO Box 1029, Kotzebue, AK 99752. Protecting much of the Noatak River, this 10,156-sq-mi Arctic unit has no facilities but attracts visitors for river running and to witness the great caribou migrations in late summer and early fall.

Sitka National Historic Park (☎ 907-747-6281), PO Box 738, Sitka, AK 99835. Alaska's smallest unit at only 107 acres, this national historic park in Southeast Alaska is famous for its collection of totems.

Wrangell–St Elias National Park and Preserve (☎ 907-822-5235), PO Box 29, Glennallen, AK 99588. The largest unit in Alaska at 20,469 sq mi, this park is a crossroads of mountains and includes the second highest peak in the USA (St Elias). Accessible by road, the park attracts backpackers, rafters and kayakers.

Yukon–Charley Rivers National Preserve (☎ 907-246-3305), PO Box 164, Eagle, AK 99738. Straddling the Yukon and Charley Rivers, this 3906-sq-mi park attracts a small number of river rafters and canoers.

National Forests

Most of the Southeast and practically all of the eastern Kenai Peninsula, including Prince William Sound, is preserved as

Tongass and Chugach National Forests. Some of the best trails in Alaska are in the national forests, where hiking is free and permits are not required.

The USFS provides hiking information and maintains 190 public-use cabins and campgrounds. Most USFS campgrounds charge $6 to $8 per day, depending on the facilities, and have a 14-day stay limit. Many of the cabins are on the trail system and cost $25 to $45 a night. They are heavily booked throughout the summer, however, so advance reservations are recommended.

The Tongass National Forest maintains more than 150 cabins in the Southeast and trails in almost every major town, including the extensive systems in Juneau and Sitka. For more information about the Tongass National Forest, contact the USFS office in the area you plan to visit:

Forest Service Information Center
  (☎ 907-586-8751) 101 Egan Dr, Juneau,
  AK 99801

Petersburg Visitor Information Center
  (☎ 907-772-4636) PO Box 1328, Petersburg,
  AK 99833-1328

Southeast Alaska Visitor Center
  (☎ 907-228-6214) 50 Main St, Ketchikan,
  AK 99901-6559

Chugach National Forest, located in South-central Alaska features some of the best long-distance trails in the state and 39 cabins, including seven along the Resurrection Trail and three on the Russian Lakes Trail. You can also reach a couple cabins in the Cordova area by foot. For a complete list of cabins and trails in the Chugach National Forest, contact the following offices in Alaska:

Alaska Public Lands Information Center
  (☎ 907-271-2737) 605 W Fourth Ave, Suite 105,
  Anchorage, AK 99501

Cordova Ranger District
  (☎ 907-424-7661) PO Box 280, Cordova,
  AK 99574

Seward Ranger District
  (☎ 907-224-3374) PO Box 390, Seward, AK
  99664-0390

The Forest Service also maintains a Web site for the Alaska region (www.fs.fed.us/

recreation/states/ak.html), allowing you to access information on trails, rustic cabins, fishing opportunities and wilderness areas in Tongass and Chugach National Forests.

State Parks

The Alaska Division of Parks and Outdoor Recreation controls 4688 sq mi in almost 120 units in the Alaska state park system, ranging from the 2344-sq-mi Wood-Tikchik State Park, north of Dillingham on Bristol Bay, to small parks along the highways. The division also controls state trails, campgrounds, wilderness parks and historical sites.

Tongass National Forest

Tongass National Forest received its name from the Tongass clan of the Tlingit Indians, who lived near its southern edge. This area's preservation dates back to 1902, when President Theodore Roosevelt created the Alexander Archipelago Forest Reserve. Five years later, Tongass Reserve was placed in the national forest system, and the following year, the two reserves were consolidated to form Tongass National Forest.

Today, at 26,406 sq mi in area, Tongass is the largest national forest in the country. It stretches from the Pacific Ocean to the vast inland ice fields that border British Columbia and from the southern tip of Prince of Wales Island to Malaspina Glacier, 500mi to the north. More than 90% of Southeast Alaska is in Tongass National Forest. Even more amazing is that Tongass, with its thousands of islands, bays and fjords, has 11,000mi of coastline (about half that of North America).

As a result of the Alaska National Interest Lands Conservation Act, which was enacted in 1980, more than 7813 sq mi were set aside in Tongass as 14 separate wilderness areas. The largest is Misty Fjords National Monument, a 3281-sq-mi wilderness area 22mi south of Ketchikan. The smallest wilderness area is Maurelle Islands, a 4937-acre wilderness area off the northwest coast of Prince of Wales Island.

The more popular parks for hikers are Chugach State Park, which surrounds Anchorage; Denali State Park, south of Mt McKinley; Nancy Lake Recreational Area, just south of Willow; and Chilkat State Park, south of Haines. Hiking is free, but in the mid-1990s user fees, in the form of daily parking permits of $3 to $5 per vehicle, were implemented. Most campgrounds cost $8 a night, with the more popular ones charging $15.

If you plan to spend a summer camping in Alaska, it's possible to purchase a state park camping pass as a nonresident for $200, allowing unlimited camping for a year. The state parks division also rents out recreational cabins in the Southeast, the Southcentral and the Interior regions for $25 to $50 a night, depending on the cabin. To obtain an annual Alaska Camping Pass in advance, send a check or money order to one of the following offices: Alaska Division of Parks, 3601 C St, Suite 200, Anchorage, AK 99503-5929, or the Alaska Division of Parks, 400 Willoughby Center, Juneau, AK 99801.

The Division of Parks has an excellent Web site (www.dnr.state.ak.us/parks) that provides information on individual cabins and other recreational opportunities.

National Refuges

The US Fish & Wildlife Service (USF&WS) is an arm of the Department of the Interior that administers 16 wildlife refuges in Alaska which total more than 120,313 sq mi. The largest refuge, Yukon Delta, surrounding Bethel in Western Alaska, is almost 31,250 sq mi.

The purpose of wildlife refuges is to protect habitats; visitor use and developed recreational activities are strictly an afterthought. Most of the refuges are in remote areas of the Bush with few, if any, developed facilities. Guide companies are the only means by which most travelers visit them. The one exception is Kenai National Wildlife Refuge, which can be reached by road from Anchorage. This preserve has 14 campgrounds, with the Kenai-Russian River Campground by far the most popular, and

over 200mi of hiking trails and water routes, including the popular Swanson River canoe route.

The Kodiak National Wildlife Refuge, although considerably more remote and more expensive to reach than Kenai, does offer eight wilderness cabins similar to USFS cabins for $20 per night. For general information contact the US Fish & Wildlife Service Regional Office (☎ 907-786-3487), 1011 East Tudor Rd, Anchorage, AK 99503. You can also access information through its Web site (www.r7.fws.gov).

Bureau of Land Management Lands

The Bureau of Land Management (BLM) is the federal agency that maintains much of the wilderness around and north of Fairbanks. The BLM has developed almost 30 camping areas and a dozen public-use cabins in the Interior, as well as two popular trails (Pinnell Mountain and White Mountain), both off the highways north of Fairbanks. Most of the cabins are in the White Mountains National Recreation Area, whose trails are primarily winter routes and are often impassable during the summer. The exception is the Summit Trail, which was built for summer use. Camping, free in most BLM campgrounds, is handled on a first-come, first-served basis. The cabins are $20 a night, and most are within 100mi of Fairbanks.

The BLM offices have good publications on paddling national wild rivers such as the Gulkana, Fortymile and Delta. For more information, contact the BLM Alaska State Office (☎ 907-271-5076), 222 W 7th Ave, Suite 13, Anchorage, AK 99513, or the BLM district office in Fairbanks (☎ 907-474-2200), 1150 University Ave, Fairbanks, AK 99709. You can also get information through the BLM Web site (www.ak.blm.gov).

POPULATION & PEOPLE

Alaska, the largest state in the USA, has the third smallest population and is the most sparsely populated state. Permanent residents, not including the large influx of seasonal workers in the fishing and tourist industries, number 609,311 in a state of 570,374 sq mi. There is just under a square mile for every resident in Alaska, compared to 71.2 people per square mile in the rest of the USA. Alaska is actually even more sparsely populated when you consider that almost half of its population lives in the Anchorage area.

An estimated 30% of the state's population was born in Alaska. Of the rest, 25% has moved there in the last five years. The average resident is young (average age between 26 and 28 years), mobile and mostly from the US West Coast. Inuit and other indigenous groups make up only 15% of the total population, and ethnic groups of Japanese, Filipinos and African Americans represent less than 5%.

The five largest cities in Alaska are Anchorage (population 259,391), Fairbanks (population 31,697 in the city, 83,773 in the surrounding borough), Juneau (population 30,852), Sitka (population 8681) and Ketchikan (population 8320, 13,961 in the surrounding borough).

Native Alaskans

Long before Bering's journeys to Alaska, other groups of people had made their way there and established a culture and lifestyle in one of the world's harshest environments. The first major invasion, which came across the land bridge from Asia, was by the Tlingits and the Haidas, who settled throughout the Southeast and British Columbia, and the Athabascans, a nomadic tribe that lived in the Interior. The other two major groups were the Aleuts of the Aleutian Islands and the Inuit (Eskimos) who settled on the coast of the Bering Sea and the Arctic Ocean; both groups are believed to have migrated only 3000 years ago but were well established by the time the Europeans arrived.

The Tlingit and Haida cultures were advanced; the tribes had permanent settlements, including large clan houses that housed related families. These tribes were noted for their excellent wood carving, particularly carved poles, called *totems,* which can still be seen today in most Southeast communities. The Tlingits were spread throughout the Southeast in large numbers and occasionally went as far south as Seattle in their large dugout canoes. Both groups had few problems gathering food, as fish and game were plentiful in the Southeast.

Life was not so easy for the Aleuts and the Inuit. With much colder winters and cooler summers, both groups had to develop a highly effective sea-hunting culture to sustain life in the harsh regions of Alaska. This was especially true for the Inuit, who could not have survived the winters without their skilled ice-hunting techniques. In the spring, armed with only jade-tipped harpoons, the Inuit, in skin-covered kayaks called *bidarkas* and *umiaks,* stalked and killed 60-ton bowhead whales.

The Aleuts were known for some of the finest basket weaving in North America, using the highly prized Attu grass of the Aleutian Islands. The Inuit were unsurpassed carvers of ivory, jade and soapstone; many support themselves today by continuing the art.

The indigenous people, despite their harsh environment, were numerous until non-Natives, particularly fur traders and whalers, brought guns, alcohol and disease that destroyed the Native Alaskans' delicate relationship with nature and wiped out entire villages. At one time, an estimated 20,000 Aleuts lived throughout the islands of the Aleutian chain. In only 50 years, the Russians reduced the Aleut population (mainly through deaths caused by forced labor) to less than 2000. The whalers who arrived at Inuit villages in the mid-19th century were similarly destructive, introducing alcohol, which devastated the lifestyles of entire villages. Even when the 50th anniversary of the Alcan was celebrated in October 1992, many Native Alaskans and Canadians called the event a 'commemoration' and not a 'celebration,' due to the things that the highway brought (disease, alcohol and a cash economy) that further changed a nomadic lifestyle.

More than 85,000 indigenous people (half of whom are Inuit) live in Alaska. Native Alaskans are no longer tribal nomads but live in permanent villages ranging in size from less than 30 people to almost 4000 in Barrow, the largest center of indigenous people in Alaska.

Most indigenous people in the Bush still depend on some level of subsistence, but today their houses are constructed of modern materials and often heated by electricity or oil. Visitors are occasionally shocked when they fly hundreds of miles into a remote area only to see TV antennae sticking out of cabins, community satellite dishes, people drinking Coca-Cola or children listening to the latest pop songs on boom boxes.

All indigenous people received a boost in 1971, when Congress passed the Alaska Native Claims Settlement Act in an effort to allow oil companies to build a pipeline across the Native peoples' traditional lands. The act created the Alaska Native Fund and formed 13 regional corporations, controlled and administered by the local tribes, that invested and developed the $900 million and 44 million acres received for their historical lands.

Native Alaskans face serious challenges, however, as they enter the 21st century. Many live at or below the poverty level, as creating sustainable economic opportunities and jobs in small, isolated communities is especially difficult. Drug and alcohol abuse in rural Alaska is also rampant, leading to a high death rate. The rate of suicide for Native males is seven times higher than the national average, and it's estimated that one Native Alaskan dies every 12 days directly from alcohol abuse. This has led to a Native sobriety movement in recent years, and tempers have flared over whether communities should be dry or not. Dry communities are rarely dry; instead they usually have a thriving black market for liquor in which a $10 bottle of whiskey can sell for as much as $120. The alternative for 14 communities, including Barrow, Bethel and Kotzebue, is to be damp, allowing alcohol to be consumed but not sold. In these damp communities, the local government operates delivery centers

where residents go to pick up alcohol orders, as a way to put at least some bootleggers out of business.

SOCIETY & CONDUCT
Traditional Culture

Despite the modernization of the Native Alaskans' lifestyles and the rapid advances of communications into what has been a remote region of the world, Natives still cling to their culture and practice traditional ceremonies. In recent years, there has even been a movement to resurrect Native languages before they are forever lost with the few elders that still speak them. Of the 20 Native languages, 16 are in danger of becoming extinct.

Perhaps the best-known Native ceremony is the potlatch, a village gathering to celebrate a major passage in a family's life. Usually the focal point of Native society, potlatches often involved the host family giving away most of its possessions in an effort to demonstrate wealth to the rest of the village. A funeral potlatch would result in the family giving away the deceased's worldly possessions. The USA and Canada outlawed potlatches in the 1880s, which resulted in a disintegration of all aspects of Native culture. That law was repealed in 1951.

The most commercialized Native custom is the blanket toss. Originally, groups of villagers would grab a walrus hide in a circle to form a trampoline. Then, a hunter standing on the hide would be tossed high in the air, to spot game on the flat, treeless terrain of the Arctic tundra. Depending on the number of people gripping the blanket, a hunter could be thrown 20 feet or higher. Today the ceremony is a popular one with tour-bus groups.

Travelers interested in experiencing a slice of Native culture should plan on attending the World Eskimo-Indian Olympics, held annually on the second-to-last weekend in July in Fairbanks. The four-day competition attracts several hundred Native athletes from Alaska and other circumpolar nations, who compete, usually dressed in authentic Native costumes, in such events as ear-weighted pull, knuckle hop, fish cutting, blanket toss and dancing. For information, write to World Eskimo-Indian Olympics, PO Box 2433, Fairbanks, AK 99707.

Dos & Don'ts

As with the indigenous people in any country, Native Alaskans deserve the respect of travelers, who basically are trespassing through the Natives' traditional homeland. Try to understand their cultures and the delicate situation their societies face as they confront the growing influence of modern society.

Don't just pick out a village and fly to it. It is wise to either have a contact there or travel with somebody who does. Although Native Alaskans, especially the Inuit, are very, very hospitable people, there can be much tension and suspicion of strangers in small, isolated Bush communities.

Also be conscious of the most widespread problem, the rip-off of Native arts, which have become extremely valuable and are a lucrative business with tourists. Much of what is being passed on as authentic art has in reality been mass-produced in China, Taiwan or Bali. If you're considering purchasing Native art, try to search out a legitimate shop and look for the *Authentic Native Handicraft from Alaska* symbol. If the price of a soapstone carving seems too good to be true, it probably is.

Flora & Fauna of Alaska

The main attraction for many visitors to Alaska is the state's abundance of wildlife. From the road, most people see more wildlife in Alaska than they do in a lifetime elsewhere. From the trails, such encounters are often the highlight of an entire trip; you can spot an animal, watch it quietly and marvel at the experience when the creature moves on leisurely.

With a relatively small human population that's concentrated in a handful of cities, Alaska is one of the few places in the USA where entire ecosystems are still intact and ancient migratory routes uninterrupted. Some species that are threatened or endangered elsewhere – browns bears and bald eagles, to name but two – are thriving in the 49th state. More caribou live in Alaska (900,000) than people (609,000), and birds are in no short supply either. More than 400 species have been spotted in the state, with 20 million shorebirds and waterfowl migrating through the Copper River Delta near Cordova every spring. Pods of humpback whales spend summers in the Icy Straits of Southeast Alaska. Come August, streams and rivers are choked with millions of spawning salmon.

While the numbers are impressive, it's important to remember that Alaska's wildlife is spread over an area the size of a small continent. Some species, particularly large land mammals, need a vast territory to survive the harsh climactic conditions and short growing season of their food supply. Many species migrate as the seasons change, and others are concentrated in specific locations across the state.

If the main intent of your trip to Alaska is to see as much wildlife as possible, take the time to research particular species in advance of arriving. You'll increase your chances of encountering wild animals if you know the habitats they prefer, the best places to encounter them and the months when they are most active. An excellent resource guide is the 'Wildlife Notebook Series' by the Alaska Department of Fish and Game, which covers the life history, habitat, foods and range for 88 species of mammals, birds and fish. The collection of loose-leaf notebook pages is $10 and can be purchased at any Alaska Public Lands Information Center or ordered in advance from the Alaska Natural History Association (☎ 907-274-8440).

FLORA

The flora of Alaska, like everything in the state, is diverse, changing dramatically from one region to the next. In the coastal regions of Southeast and Southcentral Alaska, mild temperatures in winter and summer and frequent rains produce lush coniferous forests of Sitka spruce (the state tree) and western hemlock. Any opening in the forest is often a bog or an area filled with alder or spiny devil's club, a mildly poisonous plant. The tree line is often between 2000 and 3000ft, where thick alder takes over before giving way to alpine meadows.

In the Alaskan Interior region, the large area of plains and hills between the Alaska Range and the Brooks Range is dominated by boreal forests of white spruce, cottonwood and paper birch, while on north-facing slopes and in moist lowlands you'll find a stunted forest of scrawny black spruce. Continue traveling north and you'll enter a zone known as taiga, characterized by muskeg, or bog, willow thickets and more stunted spruce, before you reach the tundra of the Arctic coastal region.

The Arctic tundra is a bizarre world, a treeless area except for a few small stands on gravel flood plains of rivers. Plant life hugs the ground – even pussy willows that only grow 6 inches in height still produce catkins. Other plants, including grasses, mosses and a variety of tiny flowers, provide a carpet of life for a short period in July and August, despite little precipitation and a harsh climate.

Tundra can make for tough hiking for those who travel this far north in Alaska. Wet and moist tundra sits on top of permanently frozen ground known as permafrost. The tundra thaws in the summer but remains waterlogged because the permafrost prevents drainage. The caribou can navigate these soggy conditions because their dew claws and spreading cleft hooves help support their weight on the soft ground. Hikers are not so lucky.

Trees

There are 33 native species of trees, the fewest of any state in the USA, and only 12 of these are classified as large trees (more than 70ft in height). Not surprisingly, nine of these species live in the coastal regions of Southeast and Southcentral Alaska.

Sitka Spruce Alaska's state tree, the Sitka spruce *(Picea sitchensis)*, thrives in the coastal regions of Southcentral and Southeast Alaska. The largest species of spruce in the USA, Sitka spruce grows quickly and can reach heights of 225ft and diameters of 8ft. The short, sharp needles are dark green on top, silvery blue underneath.

The tree's lumber is strong and lightweight, making it ideal for the construction of aircraft, gliders and boats. It is also a popular tonewood for guitar bodies. Native Alaskans used its roots for basket weaving. Commercially, the Sitka spruce is the most valuable species in Alaska.

Sitka spruce

Western Hemlock Occupying the same regions as the Sitka spruce is the western hemlock *(Tsuga heterophylla)*. In Southeast Alaska, the western hemlock makes up more than 70% of the trees in coastal spruce/hemlock forests. Hemlocks can grow to 190ft in height and 5ft in diameter and live to be 500 years old. Their needles are short, soft and rounded at the tip. Needles grow on only two sides of a twig, giving the branches a flat, feathery appearance.

Like the Sitka spruce, hemlock is commercially harvested, with much of the wood used for construction lumber. Poor quality hemlock goes into pulp to make paper; the bark was once used extensively for tanning leather.

Western hemlock

White Spruce Found primarily in Interior Alaska, white spruce *(Picea glauca)* is considerably smaller than the Sitka spruce, rarely exceeding 50ft in height and 1 to 2ft in diameter. Needles are less than an inch long and yellow to blue-green in color. Moose and sheep occasionally feed on the white spruce twigs, and porcupines gnaw the inner bark.

Black Spruce This subarctic species of spruce can withstand severe winds and extreme cold. Pockets of dwarfed black spruce *(Picea mariana)* exist in the Brooks Range, and in bogs, wetlands and tundra areas farther south.

Paper Birch Widely found in the Interior and Southcentral regions, paper birch *(Betula papyrifera)* is easily identified by its dull white, peeling bark. The tree reaches heights of 70ft and diameters of 1 to 3ft. Its green, pointed leaves range from 1 to 4 inches long. Birch is an important food source for wildlife, as the twigs are eaten by moose and mountain goats, the seeds by songbirds and the inner bark by porcupines and beavers.

Alder Ranging from the size of a shrub to a small tree, alder is found in the southern half of the state and is the most common broadleaf tree in the Southeast. The dark green leaves are 1 to 3 inches wide with serrated edges, and the gray bark is smooth. The species produces a small, nutmeg-shaped nut.

Alder is a pioneer species, a rapid invader of bare soil that has been newly exposed by glaciers, avalanches or loggers clear-cutting a track of hemlock. There are three species of alder in Alaska: red alder *(Alnus rubra)*, the largest, lives predominantly in the Southeast; Sitka alder *(Alnus sinuata)* is more widespread; mountain alder *(Alnus tenuifolia)* exists at higher elevations in the Interior.

Willow Various species of willow can be found alongside alder in stream beds or in newly scarred areas. It's the tangle of willow and alder that makes cross-country trekking such a nightmare in many parts of Alaska. Willow has light, gray-green leaves that are 2 to 5 inches long, smooth and oblong. The telltale signs of willow are the caterpillar-shaped catkins that explode with white fluff in the spring. The three main species of willow are the Sitka willow *(Salix sitchensis)*, feltleaf willow *(Salix alaxensis)* and scouler willow *(Salix scoulerana)*.

Black Cottonwood Commonly found mixed with alder, the black cottonwood *(Populus trichocarpa)* lives throughout Southeast and Southcentral Alaska, often in river valleys. It's one of the tallest of Alaska's broadleaf trees, often reaching heights of 80ft; one cottonwood found near Haines in 1965 measured 101ft. Cottonwood leaves are dark green on top and silvery white beneath, with smooth edges (unlike the alder's toothed leaves).

Wild Berries

From a hiker's point of view, Alaska's wild berries may be the most interesting flora. Blueberries *(Vaccinium uliginosum)*, which grow throughout much of the state, can reach heights of 6ft in the Southeast. Thickets of salmonberries

(Rubus spectablis) thrive in moist woods and lower mountain slopes from the Alaskan Peninsula to Southcentral and Southeast Alaska. A cousin of the raspberry, the fruit looks similar but can range in color from red to yellow to orange.

You'll encounter raspberries *(Rubus idaeus)* in fields and thickets in the Interior, Southcentral and Southeast regions. Wild strawberries *(Fragaria chiloensis)* grow in

Wild strawberry

scattered clumps throughout Southeast and Southcentral Alaska and the Aleutian Islands, particularly on beaches. Other edible species worth learning to identify include red huckleberries *(Vacciium parvifolium)*, lowbush and highbush cranberries *(Vaccinium vitis idaea* and *Vaccinium edule)* and red currants or gooseberries *(Ribes triste)*, which have an excellent flavor without the skunklike smell associated with many species of currants.

If you plan to feast on berries, take the time to learn which ones are inedible. The most common poisonous variety is the baneberry *(Actaea rubra)*, which often appears as a white berry in the Southeast and the Interior.

Wildflowers

Alaska's state flower is the forget-me-not *(Myosotis sylvatica)*, a delicate, sky-blue flower with a yellow eye. It grows 6 to 20 inches in height. Blue-violet wild lupine *(Lupinus perennis)* can reach heights of 4ft; it thrives along coastal shores and in alpine areas. Even more impressive is fireweed *(Epilobium angustifolium)*, whose pink blossoms can be found throughout much of subarctic Alaska, in open areas such as meadows, riverbanks and clear-cuts. If conditions are right, fireweed can grow up to 7ft tall.

Forget-me-not

In the bogs and wetlands of Southeast and Southcentral Alaska, you'll undoubtedly see – and smell – skunk cabbage *(Lysichitum americanum)*. The yellow-brown flower often appears while snow is still on the ground, and the leaves soon follow. Prickly wild rose *(Rosa acicularis)* features five pink petals, which you may spot anywhere from Sitka north to the Alaska Range and as far west as Unalaska. Its fruit, rose hips, are often collected in the fall and are an excellent source of vitamin C.

Other common wildflowers in Alaska are pink and red primrose *(Oenothera)*, yellow mountain marigold *(Caltha leptosepala)*, blue mountain harebell *(Campanula lasiocarpa)*, white Arctic daisy *(Chrysanthemum arcticum)* and the dark blue monkshood *(Aconitum leptosepala)*, a member of the buttercup family.

Fireweed

A good identification guide to bring along is *A Field Guide to Alaskan Wildflowers* by Verna Pratt. It's available through the Alaska Natural History Association (☎ 907-274-8440), Mail Order Services, 605 W 4th Ave, Suite 85, Anchorage, AK 99501.

Lupine

FAUNA
Bears

Bears and visitors to Alaska have a love-hate relationship. Nothing makes you more afraid in the backcountry than the thought of encountering a bear, but you would hate to leave the state without having seen a bear in the wild. After a handful of bear encounters, most people develop a healthy respect for these magnificent animals. There are three species of bear in Alaska – brown, black and polar bears – and you're most likely to see the brown bears, since these have the greatest range.

Brown Bears At one time, brown and grizzly bears were listed as separate species, but now both are classified as *Ursus arctos*. The difference isn't so much genetics but size. Browns live along the coast where abundant salmon runs help them grow to a large size (often exceeding 800lb). The famed Kodiak brown bear has been known to stand 10ft tall and tip the scales at 1500lb. Grizzlies are browns found inland, away from the rich salmon runs. Normally a male ranges from 500 to 700lb, and females weigh half to three-quarters as much.

Brown bear

The color of a brown bear can range from almost black to blond, with the darker individuals resembling black bears. One way biologists tell them apart is by measuring the upper rear molar. The length of the crown of this tooth in a brown bear is always more than an inch and a quarter. A less dangerous approach is to look for the prominent shoulder hump, easily seen behind the neck when a brown bear is on all fours.

In June and July, you can see brown bears fishing along rivers. In late summer and early fall, bears will often move to the tundra area and to open meadows to feed on berries. Browns occasionally act like predators, but only in the spring, when the young are most vulnerable.

There are more than 40,000 brown bears in Alaska. They live everywhere in the state except for some islands in Frederick Sound in the Southeast, the islands west of Unimak in the Aleutian chain and some Bering Sea islands. One famous place to watch them is Brooks River in Katmai National Park, but brown bears are also common in Denali National Park, on Admiralty Island in the Southeast and in Wrangell–St Elias National Park.

Black Bears Though black bears *(Ursus americanus)* are the most widely distributed of the three bear species in the USA, their range is more limited in Alaska than that of their brown cousin. They usually live in most forested areas of the state, but not north of the Brooks Range, on the Seward Peninsula or on many large islands like Kodiak and Admiralty.

The average male weighs 180 to 250lb and can range in color from black to a rare creamy white color. A brown or cinnamon black bear often appears in

Southcentral Alaska, leaving many backpackers confused about what the species is. Aside from measuring that upper rear molar, look for the straight facial profile to confirm it's a black bear.

Black bears, as well as brown, are creatures of opportunity when it comes to eating. Bears are omnivorous, and their common foods include berries, grass, sedge, salmon and any carrion they happen to find in their travels.

Bears don't hibernate but enter a stage of 'dormancy' – basically a deep sleep while denning up during the winter. Black bears usually enter their dens in November or December and reemerge in April or May. In the more northern areas of the state, some bears may be dormant for as long as seven or eight months a year.

Polar Bears Polar bears *(Ursus maritimus)* have always captured our interest because of their large size and white color, but they're not easy to encounter in person. Plan on stopping at the zoo in Anchorage if you want to see one in Alaska. Polar bears occur only in the Northern Hemisphere and almost always in association with Arctic Sea ice. Past studies have shown that few polar bears make their dens along the north Alaska coast.

A male usually weighs between 600 and 1200lb but occasionally tops 1400lb. The polar bear's adaptations to a life on the sea ice include its white, water-repellent coat, dense underfur, specialized teeth for a carnivorous diet (primarily seals), and hair that almost completely covers the bottom of its feet.

Moose

Moose *(Alces alces)* are improbable-looking mammals: long-legged to the extreme but short-bodied, with a huge rack of antlers and a drooping nose. Standing still, they look uncoordinated until you watch them run or, better still, swim – then their speed and grace are astounding. They're the largest members of the deer family in the world, and the Alaskan species is the largest of all moose. A newborn weighs in at 35lb and can grow to more than 300lb within five months. Cows range from 800 to 1200lb and bulls from 1000lb to more than 1500lb.

In the wild, moose may live to be more than 20 years old and often travel 20 to 40mi to find their main forage of birch, willow, alder and aspen saplings. In the spring and summer, you often encounter them feeding in lakes, ponds and muskegs, with those huge noses below the water as they grab for aquatic plants and weeds.

The population ranges from an estimated 120,000 to 160,000 animals, and historically moose have always been the most important game animal in Alaska. Athabascan Indians survived by utilizing the moose as a source of food, clothing and implements, and professional hunters in the 19th century made a living by supplying moose meat to mining camps. Today, some 35,000 Alaskans and nonresidents harvest 9000 moose, or a total of five million pounds of meat, during the hunting season each year.

Moose are widespread throughout the state and range from the Stikine River in the Southeast to the Colville River on the North Slope. They're most abundant in second-growth birch forests, on timberline plateaus and along the major rivers of Southcentral Alaska and the Interior. Moose are frequently sighted along the Alcan, and Denali National Park and Preserve is an excellent place to watch them. But the best place to see the biggest moose is the Kenai Peninsula, especially if you take time to paddle the Swanson River or Swan Lake canoe routes in the Kenai National Wildlife Refuge. The refuge even maintains a Moose Research Center 50mi from Soldotna, and you can often see the animal there.

Caribou

Although an estimated 900,000 caribou *(Rangifer tarandus)* live in Alaska's 32 herds, these animals are relatively difficult to view as they travel from the Interior north to the Arctic Sea. Often called the 'nomads of the north,' caribou range in weight from 150lb to more than 400lb. They migrate hundreds of miles annually between their calving grounds, rutting areas and winter home. In the summer, they feed on grasses, grasslike sedges, berries and small shrubs of the tundra. In the winter, they eat a significant amount of lichen called 'reindeer moss.'

The principal predators of caribou are wolves, and some wolf packs on the North Slope have been known to follow caribou herds for years, picking off the young, old and victims of disabling falls caused by running in tightly massed herds. Bears, wolverines, foxes and eagles will also prey on calves, and every year several thousand non-resident hunters come to Alaska in search of a bull. The caribou, however, are most important to the Inuit and other Native Alaskans, who hunt more than 30,000 a year to support their subsistence lifestyle.

The best place for the average visitor to see caribou is Denali National Park. Occasionally,

Caribou

you can see them from the park road, but if the day is warm and still, you'll often encounter them above the tree line, where they head to seek relief from insects. In late spring, look for them around the remaining patches of snow.

Perhaps one of the greatest wildlife events left in the world today is the migration of the Western Arctic herd of caribou, the largest such herd in North America, with 450,000 animals. The herd uses the North Slope for its calving area, and in late August many of the animals begin to cross the Noatak River on their journey southward. During that time, the few visitors lucky enough to be on the river are often rewarded with the awesome experience of watching 20,000 or more caribou crossing the tundra toward the Brooks Range.

Deer

The Sitka black-tailed deer *(Odocoileus hemionus sitkensis)* is native to the coastal rain forests of Southeast Alaska, but its range has expanded to Prince William Sound and Kodiak Island. The deer is a favorite target of hunters, but it's not the abundant source of meat that the moose is. The largest black-tailed deer weighs 212lb, but most weigh an average of 100lb, with bucks around 150lb.

The deer's coat is reddish-brown in summer and gray in winter. The antlers are small, usually with three points on each side, and the deer's tail is indeed black. Sitka black-tailed deer respond readily to calls. Most 'calls' consist of a thin strip of rubber or plastic stretched between two pieces of wood; they're held between the teeth and blown. The high-pitched note they produce simulates a fawn's cry and can stop a deer in its tracks and turn the animal around. Some old-time hunters can make the call by simply blowing on a leaf.

Mountain Goats

The mountain goat *(Oreamnos americanus)* is the single North American species in the widespread group of goat-antelopes. All are characterized by short horns and a fondness for the most rugged alpine terrain.

Although goats are often confused with Dall sheep, they are easily identified by their longer hair, black horns and deep chest. They're quite docile, making them easy to watch in the wild, and their gait, even when they're approached too closely, is a deliberate pace. In the summer, they normally frequent high alpine meadows, grazing on grasses and herbs, while in the winter they often drop down to the tree line to graze.

In Alaska, the goats range through most of the Southeast, fanning out north and west into the coastal mountains of Cook Inlet as well as the Chugach and Wrangell Mountains. Good places to spot them include Glacier Bay National Park, Wrangell–St Elias National Park and many of the alpine trails in Juneau. But you have to climb to see them.

Mountain goat

Dall Sheep

Dall sheep *(Ovis dalli dalli)* are more numerous and widespread than mountain goats. They number close to 80,000 in Alaska and live principally in the Alaska, Wrangell, Chugach and Kenai mountain ranges. Often, sheep are spotted in Denali National Park when the park shuttle bus crosses Polychrome Pass on its way to Wonder Lake.

Rams are easy to spot thanks to their massive curling horns, which grow throughout the life of the sheep, unlike deer antlers, which are shed and regrown annually. The horns – like claws, hooves and your fingernails – grow from the skin, and as rams mature, the horns continue their ever-increasing curl, reaching a three-quarters curl in four to five years and a full curl in seven years.

It's spectacular to watch two rams in a horn-clashing battle, but contrary to popular belief, they are not fighting for a female, just for social dominance. Dall sheep do not clash as much as their big-horn cousins to the south, but you can spot the activity throughout the summer and into fall.

Dall sheep prefer rocky, open alpine tundra regions. In the spring and fall, however, they tend to move to lower slopes where the grazing is better. The best time to spot rams and see them clash is right before the rut (their mating period), which begins in November. At that time, they are moving among bands of ewes and often encountering other unfamiliar rams.

Wolves

While the wolf *(Canis lupus)* is struggling to survive throughout most of the USA, its natural distribution and population numbers still seem to be unaffected by human undertakings in Alaska. Throughout history no animal has been more misunderstood than the wolf. Unlike human hunters, who seek out the outstanding physical specimens, wolves can usually only catch and kill the weak, injured or young, thus strengthening the herd they are stalking. A pack of wolves is no match for a healthy 1200lb moose.

Eight thousand wolves live in packs scattered throughout Alaska, in almost every region except for some islands in the Southeast and Prince William Sound and in the Aleutian chain.

Gray wolf

Most adult males average 85 to 115lb, and their pelts can be gray, black, off-white, brown and yellow, with some tinges approaching red. Wolves travel, hunt, feed and operate in the social unit of a pack. In the Southeast, their principal food is deer; in the Interior, it's moose; in Arctic Alaska, it's caribou.

Even if you're planning to spend a great deal of time away from the road wandering in the wilderness, your chances of seeing wolves are slight. You might, however, find evidence of them in their doglike tracks, their howls at night and the remains of their wild kills.

Other Land Mammals

In the lowlands, hikers have a chance to view red fox *(Vulpes vulpes)*. A shy animal, the fox can occasionally be seen darting across roads or meadows into woody, bushy areas. Other lowland mammals you might see include pine marten *(Martes americana)*, snowshoe hare *(Lepus americanus)*, red squirrel *(Tamiasciurus hudsonicus)*, porcupine *(Erethizon dorsatum)* and, on very rare occasions, wolverines *(Gulo gulo)*.

Around lakes and rivers you stand a good chance of spotting river otters *(Lutra canadensis)* and beavers *(Castor canadensis)*. Both live throughout the state with the exception of the North Slope. Often larger than their relatives farther south, otters range from 15 to 35lb, and beavers weigh between 40 and 70lb, although 100lb beavers have been recorded in Alaska. In alpine areas, look for the ever-curious hoary marmot *(Marmota caligata)*, a large ground squirrel.

Porcupine

Marine Mammals

The most commonly spotted marine mammals are seals, often seen basking in the sun on an ice floe. Six species of seal exist in Alaska, but most visitors will encounter just the harbor seal *(Phoca vitulina)*, the only seal whose range includes the Southeast, Prince William Sound and the rest of the Gulf of Alaska. The average weight of a male is 200lb – achieved through a diet of herring, flounder, salmon, squid and small crabs.

Two other species, ringed seals *(Phoca hispida)* and bearded seals *(Erignathus barbatus)*, occur for the most part in the northern Bering, Chukchi and Beaufort Seas where sea ice forms during the winter. Although travel on land or ice is laborious and slow for seals, they're renowned divers.

Orca or killer whale

During a dive, their heartbeat may slow from a normal 55 to 120 beats per minute to 15. This allows them to stay underwater for more than five minutes, often reaching depths of 300ft or more. Harbor seal dives of 20 minutes or longer have been recorded by biologists.

Many visitors also see dolphins and harbor porpoises *(Phocaena vomerina)*, even from the decks of the ferries. Occasionally, ferry travelers spot a rare treat: a pod of killer whales or orcas *(Orcinus orca)*, whose high black-and-white dorsal fins make them easy to identify from a distance. Orcas, which can exceed 20ft in length, are actually the largest members of the dolphin family, which also includes the beluga *(Delphinapterus leucas)* or white whale. Belugas range in length from

Humpback whale

11 to 16ft and often weigh more than 3000lb. The 57,000 belugas that live in Alaskan waters travel in herds of more than 100. Their range includes the Arctic waters north of Bristol Bay and also Cook Inlet, where most visitors will spot them, especially in Kenai, which has a beluga observation area.

The three most common whales seen in coastal waters are the 50ft-long humpback *(Magaptera novaeangliae)*, with its humplike dorsal fin and long flippers; the smaller bowhead whale *(Balaena mysticetus)*; and the gray whale *(Eschrichtius robustus)*. Other marine mammals include Steller's sea lions *(Eumetopias jubatus)*, sea otters *(Enhydra lutris)* and walruses *(Odobenus rosmarus divergens)*.

The best-known destination for sighting marine mammals, particularly whales, is Glacier Bay National Park in the Southeast. If you can spare a few days to kayak the glaciated sections of the bay, you'll increase your chances of seeing a whale. Kayak and boat tours in Prince William Sound, particularly around Kenai Fjords National Park near Seward, should result in encounters with marine mammals. Just a trip on the ferry from Seward to Kodiak offers an opportunity to see a colony of sea lions.

Sea otter

FLORA & FAUNA

Salmon

The salmon runs (when thousands of fish swim upstream to spawn) rank among Alaska's most amazing sights and are common throughout much of the state. From late July to mid-September, many coastal streams are choked with salmon. You won't see just one fish here and there, but thousands – so many that they have to wait their turn to swim through narrow gaps of shallow water. The salmon are famous for their struggle against the current and their magnificent leaps over waterfalls, as well as for the density of salmon carcasses that cover stream banks after the spawning ends. Five kinds of salmon populate Alaskan waters: sockeye *(Oncorhynchus nerka;* also referred to as red salmon), king or chinook *(Oncorhynchus tshawytscha)*, pink or humpie *(Oncorhynchus gorbuscha)*, coho or silver *(Oncorhynchus kisutch)* and chum *(Oncorhynchus keta)*.

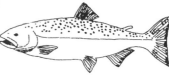

King (chinook) salmon

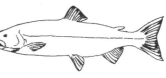

Sockeye (red) salmon

Birds

More than anything, Alaska is a haven for winged wildlife. Biologists have identified 437 species of bird in the state, and only 65 of them are accidental visitors.

The most impressive bird in Alaska's wilderness is the bald eagle *(Haliaeetus leucocephalus)*, whose white tail and head – and wingspan that often reaches 8ft – have become the symbols of a nation. While elsewhere the bird is on the endangered species list, in Alaska it thrives. The eagle can be sighted almost daily in most of the Southeast and is common in Prince William Sound. It also migrates once a year in a spectacle that exceeds even the salmon runs. As many as 3500 bald eagles gather along the Chilkat River north of Haines from late October to December. They come to feed on the late chum salmon run and create an amazing scene during the bleakness of early winter. Bare trees, without a leaf remaining, support 80 or more white-headed eagles, four or five to a branch.

Bald eagle

The state bird of Alaska is the ptarmigan *(Lagopus)*, a cousin of the prairie grouse. Three species of the ptarmigan can be found throughout the state in high treeless country. The birds are easy to spot during the summer, as their wings remain white while their head and chest turn brown. In the winter, they sport pure white plumage.

Alaskan seabirds include the playful horned puffin *(Fratercula corniculata)*, six species of auklet *(Aethia)* and three species of albatross *(Diomedea)*, which boost a wingspan of up to 7ft. The best way to see a variety of seabirds, including the rare black-footed albatross, is to board the Alaska Marine Hwy ferry for its special run along the Alaska

Ptarmigan

Peninsula to Unalaska in the Aleutian Islands. Shorter and much more affordable is the tour of Gull Island in Kachemak Bay. It's offered daily in the summer, departing from Homer.

An amazing variety of waterfowl also migrate to Alaska, including the trumpeter swans *(Cygnus buccinator)*. The swan is the world's largest member of the waterfowl family and occasionally tips the scales at 30lb. Other waterfowl include Canada geese *(Branta canadensis)*, of which more than 130,000 nest in Alaska; all four species of eider *(Somateria)* in the world; the colorful Harlequin duck *(Histrionicus histrionicus)*; and five species of loons *(Gavia)*.

Horned puffin

The Pribilof Islands in the Bering Sea attract birders from around the world. If you can't afford that trip, visit Potter Marsh south of Anchorage, a sanctuary that attracts more than 100 species annually. If you're serious about birding, then try to come to Alaska during the spring migration in May and attend either the Copper River Delta Shorebird Festival in Cordova or the Kachemak Bay Shorebird Festival in Homer.

ENDANGERED SPECIES

Species that are threatened or endangered in the Lower 48 – brown bears, wolves and bald eagles, to name but three – are usually thriving in Alaska in healthy numbers. But occasionally an animal will become threatened in a region of the state. The cause is usually overconsumption and rarely lost habitat, the most common reason for endangered species elsewhere in the country.

The classic example is the Cook Inlet belugas, the unique white whale. Throughout Alaska the beluga population is stable at 45,000 whales, but in the Cook Inlet the population has dropped 50% since the mid-1990s, from approximately 1000 animals to as few as 500. Biologists suspect legal hunting by Alaskan Natives is a huge part of the problem, as they kill close to 100 whales a year.

The situation is so dire that in 1999 the National Marine Fisheries Service was studying whether Cook Inlet belugas should be protected under the Endangered Species Act or the Marine Mammal Protection Act. If the species does qualify for a protective listing, it may be the first time that Alaskan Natives have overharvested a marine mammal stock, something that, up to now, only Outsiders could claim.

Facts for the Hiker

SUGGESTED ITINERARIES
If your aim is to hike as many trails in Alaska as possible and you have the whole summer, have fun. You have the time to do whatever you want. If you have less time and still want to hike, then you need to plan carefully. Alaska is a big state.

With three to four weeks in the state, you can travel to three regions and do overnight hikes in each one of them. Such an itinerary might include flying into Anchorage and walking the Historic Iditarod Trail or the Williwaw Lakes Loop and then venturing south to Seward by bus or train. At Seward, you could combine a hike at Caines Head State Recreation Area or Lost Lake Trail with some whale watching or kayaking in Kenai Fjords National Park. Jump on the Alaska Marine Hwy ferry for Homer and a hike in Kachemak Bay State Park and then backtrack to Anchorage and

continue north to hike in either Denali State Park or Denali National Park and Preserve.

With two weeks or less, you should seriously consider just one region of the state. An excellent choice would be Southeast Alaska. You could jump on the Alaska Marine Hwy ferry in either Bellingham, Washington, or Prince Rupert, British Columbia, and disembark at a handful of ports for a few days of hiking at each. You might hike the Deer Mountain Trail near Ketchikan, Petersburg Lake Trail and the Chilkoot Trail from Skagway. You could then backtrack to Juneau and hike the Dan Moller or West Glacier Trail before jumping on a plane for the trip home.

Two weeks would also be enough time to fly into Anchorage for an extended hike in Chugach State Park. You could then continue north to Denali National Park for a

Highlights

I have lived, worked and hiked in Alaska for almost a quarter of a century. What follows are my favorite hikes.

- The Chilkoot Trail is one of the most remarkable trails in the USA, a link to the past where you can relive the great Klondike gold rush of 1898.

- The Pinnell Mountain Trail is a three-day hike in the sub-Arctic, treeless world north of Fairbanks. The adventure begins at Eagle Summit, where you can witness the midnight sun, and ends with a possible side trip to Circle Hot Springs, where you can soak away those sore leg muscles.

- Denali National Park and Preserve, despite the crowds at the entrance area and the long waits for backcountry permits, is still the best destination for a true wilderness adventure, with great mountain scenery and an excellent chance to encounter wildlife.

- Petersburg Lake Trail, in the Southeast, is an interesting hike through lush rain forest, with good trout and salmon fishing.

- Hop on the historic White Pass & Yukon Route railroad in Skagway to get to an easy hike to the stunning amphitheater of Laughton Glacier.

- Little Coal Creek Trail, in Denali State Park, is a wonderful hike above the tree line, with the best views of Mt McKinley in the state.

- Williwaw Lakes Loop, the best overnight hike out of Anchorage, combines great alpine scenery with a chance to spot some wildlife.

week or head south to the Kenai Peninsula to hike the Resurrection Pass Trail, Russian Lakes Trail or in Kachemak Bay State Park.

The other option for travelers with only two weeks is to fly into Anchorage, Juneau or Fairbanks (Chena Mountain or Pinnell Trail) for some an extended hiking and then join an outfitter for a wilderness trip (see Guided Hikes later in this chapter). Such a trip would combine independent trekking with a once-in-a-lifetime adventure into one of Alaska's great wilderness areas. A little more expensive? Sure. Memorable? You better believe it.

PLANNING
The Nature of Hiking in Alaska
Hiking – or 'trekking,' 'tramping' or 'bush-walking,' as it is called in other countries – is the best way to soak in Alaska's incredible natural beauty and spot its abundant wildlife. Hiking allows you to escape the crowds, the noisy RVs on the highway and the overflowing campgrounds, to enjoy the peace and tranquility that only the wilderness can provide.

Hiking in Alaska can be divided between following marked trails and exploring trail-less wilderness areas such as Denali National Park and Preserve. Because of the vast tracts of undeveloped public land in Alaska, the number of hikes possible is almost unlimited. The National Park Service (NPS) alone oversees 84,375 sq mi of land, and the 119 units in the Alaska state park system total 5000 sq mi in area. That's a lot of land to roam with a hiking stick in your hand and a pack on your back.

The state, the NPS, the Bureau of Land Management (BLM), the US Forest Service (USFS) and the US Fish and Wildlife Service (USFWS) maintain hundreds of miles of trails. The vast majority of the developed trails are located in the Southeast and Southcentral regions or near Fairbanks and Anchorage and can be reached by car. Depending on who you talk to, the hiking capital in Alaska is either Anchorage or Juneau. You could spend a month in either city and not walk a fraction of the trails that begin at its doorstep.

Trails in Alaska range from gravel, handicapped-accessible nature paths with interpretive signs to easy-to-follow footpaths through the woods to alpine routes marked by only rock cairns. Most trails provide opportunities to overnight in the backcountry, and a growing number of trails feature rustic cabins. Alaskan backcountry cabins, however, are not community huts like those found in New Zealand or in many European countries. They are rented and used by a single hiking party, and usually are reserved months in advance of the hike (see Cabins later in this chapter). Thus, for most hikers, overnight adventure in Alaska means bedding down in a tent.

The most popular walk in Alaska is the Chilkoot Trail, starting near Skagway. Annually, more than 2,000 backpackers hike the 33mi Klondike route. Other popular trails include the Resurrection Pass, Russian Lakes and Coastal Trails in the Kenai Peninsula, the Williwaw Lakes Loop and the Historic Iditarod Trail near Anchorage, Deer Mountain Trail in Ketchikan and Perseverance and West Glacier Trails near Juneau.

The majority of Alaska's vast wilderness, however, is both trail-less and treeless. On such hikes, backpackers use a map and compass to read land formations and choose a route into the backcountry and back out again. In such situations, streambeds, ridgelines and even wildlife trails replace manmade trails. This type of hiking is challenging but rewarding, often allowing hikers to escape everybody and everything for days at a time.

The best-known destination for this type of trekking adventure is Denali National Park and Preserve, but other parks also offer true wilderness experiences without the costs, crowds or complications that must be dealt with before you can enter the backcountry of Denali. Such national parks include Gates of the Arctic, Wrangell–St Elias or Lake Clark, to name but a few.

When to Hike
The hiking season in Alaska generally runs from May through September, possibly later in some regions. In October, a steady

Watching Wildlife

The Bureau of Land Management (BLM) says that, to see wildlife in Alaska, the first thing you have to do is to not pack high expectations. Every year visitors arrive thinking they will see herds of wildlife, only to go home with a photo of a squirrel that was raiding their picnic table.

To see a variety of wildlife, you have to leave the roads, travel into the backcountry and learn how to 'watch wildlife.' Here's what the BLM recommends:

• Keep your distance. Don't try to get too close with camera in hand. Most wild animals react with alarm when approached by humans on foot or in vehicles. Repeated disturbances may cause animals or birds to leave the area for good. Also learn animal behavior patterns that will tip you off when you are too close. Mammals often raise their heads high with ears pointed in your direction if you are closing in too fast. They might also exhibit signs of skittishness or display aggressive behavior. You are too close to birds if they also seem skittish or raise their heads to watch you. They may preen excessively, give alarm calls, flush repeatedly or even feign a broken wing when threatened by your presence.

• Don't hurry. The more time you take in the backcountry, the greater the opportunity to observe wildlife. Instead of moving camp every day, set up a base camp and do nothing at dawn or dusk but scan areas for wildlife.

• Use proper equipment. You will see more by carrying high-quality binoculars or even a spotting scope. If you're set on photographing wildlife, make sure you have a telephoto lens, tripod and the right film for low-light conditions to deliver those close-up shots.

• Blend in. Wear muted colors, sit quietly and even avoid using scented soaps and perfumes.

• Look for wildlife signs. There's added enjoyment in recognizing animals by their tracks, droppings or vocalizations. To do that, you might want to carry a field guide or two (see the Books section later in this chapter).

drizzle begins in the Southeast that lasts until late November or December. The weather also deteriorates in Southcentral at this time of year, and farther north, especially in Fairbanks, the snow begins falling and doesn't stop until April.

Because most hikers like to avoid below-zero temperatures, the peak season for hiking is early July through mid-August, a time when you might have to wait three or four days to get into the backcountry of Denali National Park and many of the campgrounds in the Kenai Peninsula will be filled nightly. During the peak of the summer tourist season, it's worth it to hike longer trails to get away from the road traffic and day hikers or pay the expense of bush-plane travel to reach more remote parks.

You might also consider traveling and hiking during the 'shoulder season.' May and September offer mild weather and off-season discounts on motels and transporta-tion. At this time, the backcountry in most parks is usually empty of hikers and other travelers. However, if you arrive early or stay late, make sure you equip yourself for some cold, rainy weather and possibly even snow.

Maps

A good topographical map, known to hikers as simply a 'topo' or 'quad,' is indispensable when hiking in Alaska. For most trails, especially multiday hikes, you should have the corresponding topos.

US Geological Survey (USGS) topographical maps come in a variety of scales, but hikers prefer the smallest scale available for most of Alaska (1:63,360), on which each inch equals a mile. USGS maps cost $4 for each section (or 'quad') of the 1:63,360 series.

A growing number of commercial hiking maps are often much more up to date than

USGS quads. Trails Illustrated, a National Geographic mapping company, publishes more than 50 maps that cover US national parks and recreational areas. Some, like *Wrangell–St Elias* and *Denali National Park,* do not provide enough detail for backpackers, but others, such as *Chugach National Forest* or *Chilkoot Trail,* are more accurate and cheaper than the corresponding USGS topos. The maps are printed on waterproof paper and cost $10. Call Trails Illustrated (☎ 800-962-1643) for a complete list or check out its Web site (www.trailsillustrated .com) for more information.

USGS maps and trail maps can be purchased at the Public Lands Information Centers in Anchorage, Fairbanks and Ketchikan, and at many bookstores and backpacking shops (see the regional chapters for addresses and phone numbers). Most tend to carry only the maps for their area of the state. For topos and other maps that cover the complete state, stop at the main USGS offices in Alaska, either in Fairbanks (Geophysical Institute Map Office on the University of Alaska campus) or Anchorage (Grace Hall on the Alaska Pacific University campus). You can also order maps in advance by writing and asking for a free index of maps for Alaska from the USGS Western Distribution Branch (Denver Federal Center, PO Box 25286 Denver, CO 80225). The USGS also maintains a Web site (www.usgs.gov) that lists all the dealers who sell topos.

What to Bring

For longer hikes into the Alaska wilderness you will need suitable equipment: appropriate clothing, a tent, sleeping bag, camp stove, maps and a compass. But also be equipped for a spur-of-the-moment, three-hour day hike. In addition to your large backpack, take a soft day pack or rucksack. Some expedition packs, such as Dana Designs, allow you to convert the top pouch and hip belt into a fanny pack that is ideal for an afternoon hike up a mountain trail. Otherwise, carry a small, compressible, nylon knapsack.

On day hikes you should always carry a waterproof parka, woolen mittens and a hat if you are climbing above the tree line. Also pack a knife, high-energy food (chocolate, energy bars or nuts), matches, maps and a compass, insect repellent and water.

Clothing The only way to dress for a climate as varied as Alaska's and to accommodate the many exertion levels of backpacking is in layers. Generally, you will have three layers – underwear, insulating layer and shell layer – and will remove or add layers according to the weather conditions.

Begin with a set of lightweight underwear of polypropylene or some other high-tech synthetic fabric. Synthetic underwear, as opposed to wool, silk or cotton, will do the best job of 'wicking' moisture away from the skin to the surface of the garment. In summer, an increasingly common form of dress in the backcountry is synthetic long underwear under baggy hiking shorts. Such an outfit, though it might seem strange, provides comfort in cold temperatures and protection from too much sun and bugs, while allowing for maximum freedom of movement.

The insulating layer provides essential warmth. For that layer, many hikers use a jersey of pile or fleece fabric such as Polartec rather than a wool sweater. Like wool, the pile will keep you warm when wet, but it dries much faster. Avoid cotton, as it will not insulate when wet and takes forever to dry.

The final layer – parka and overpants – must protect you against wind, snow or rain. Some overpants and parkas are windproof and water resistant but will not hold up in an all-day rain. Waterproof but 'breathable' garments will provide the most protection and comfort. Gore-Tex is the best-known of the breathable materials, but others are available. A parka and pants set made of Gore-Tex can cost $300 to $500 but will be a worthwhile investment.

On any trip longer than two days, you should also have two to three pairs of woolen socks, a pair of woolen mittens, a knitted hat, spare shirt, walking shorts and long pants (preferably light wool or Supplex nylon, never blue jeans).

Equipment Checklist

The following list is only a general guide to what is needed for hiking in Alaska. The area you plan to walk in and the size and level of experience of your party will affect what you toss in your backpack:

❏ **Alternative footwear** Sandals or running or tennis shoes.

❏ **Boots** Light to medium boots are recommended.

❏ **Shorts, light shirt** Remember clothes for everyday wear.

❏ **Socks** Three pairs heavy polypropylene or woolen socks are a good idea. Wear two pairs at once to reduce the chance of blisters. Frequent changes of socks during the day can also reduce blisters.

❏ **Rain gear** Parka and overpants.

❏ **Long underwear** Shirt and leggings of polypropylene.

❏ **Insulating clothing** Take a sweater or jersey of wool, fiber pile or polar fleece.

❏ **Wool hat and mittens** These are important any time you are in Alaska, but especially when you are above the tree line.

❏ **Tent** Bring a lightweight tent with a rain fly if you plan to overnight in the backcountry. For the most part, there is not a hut system along Alaska's trails.

❏ **Sleeping bag** Bring a three-season bag made of synthetic fibers. Avoid down bags.

❏ **Backpack** The popular choice is an internal-frame pack, but an external-frame pack works just as well. Bring a waterproof rain cover for it and then make sure everything inside is stored in resealable plastic bags.

❏ **Camping stove** Pack one stove for every four people.

❏ **Water purifier** A filter is the easiest way to make sure the water you drink is safe. See the Health & Safety chapter for more information.

❏ **First-aid kit** See the 'First-Aid Kit for Hikers' boxed text in the Health & Safety chapter.

❏ **Tableware** Pack a large cup, a spoon and a bowl.

❏ **Cooking pot** Two pots with a capacity of 1½ to 2 quarts and a secure lid are adequate for two people. Preferably the pots should fit into each other and be made of aluminum for lightness.

❏ **Pot scrubber and wash cloth** Washing up is usually done in cold water, making pot cleaning difficult.

❏ **Pocket knife** A pocket knife with several tools, such as a Swiss Army knife, is handy for emergency repairs.

❏ **Flashlight** This is essential for nocturnal toilet visits and late arrivals at camp.

❏ **Map and compass** See the Maps section in this chapter.

❏ **Matches or lighter** Needed for cooking and lighting candles.

❏ **Playing cards** Brush up on hearts, cribbage and euchre.

❏ **Pen or pencil and paper**

❏ **Sun protection** A hat, block and sunglasses are essential.

❏ **Toilet paper, Band-Aids, insect repellent**

❏ **Towel** Choose a small one that will dry quickly.

❏ **Candle** Calculate on half to one candle per day.

❏ **Binoculars** Compact, high-powered binoculars are easy to carry and great for wildlife and birding.

❏ **Camera** See Photography later in this chapter.

❏ **Useful books** Books on birding, plant identification and wildlife tracks may be worth carrying. See Books later in this chapter.

Footwear Many recreational backpackers opt for the new lightweight nylon boots made by sport-shoe companies like Nike, Vasque or Hi-Tec. These 'day-hiking boots,' designed for hiking on easy terrain and carrying light loads, are fine for easy, bridged trails like Resurrection Pass in the Kenai Peninsula. For more difficult trails like the Chilkoot or trail-less areas like Denali National Park, the traditional leather hiking boots are a much wiser choice. Such boots offer more support with a stiff leather upper, a more durable sole and protective shanks. These boots are more suitable for hiking on rocky and unstable ground and for carrying heavier packs over longer hikes in the backcountry. Which style of boot you bring to Alaska will depend on where and for how long you're planning to hike.

You should also pack a spare pair of shoes for fording rivers or to wear once you have reached camp. Most hikers still choose tennis shoes, but a growing number now use rafter sandals. These heavy rubber-soled sandals, held onto your feet by straps, are lighter to carry, dry more quickly and can be just as comfortable and warm as tennis shoes when worn with wool socks. They also strap onto the outside of your pack nicely.

Tent Your tent is one of the most essential items you'll carry in your pack. Generally, in Alaska, hikers use one of three types. The most popular tent by far is the dome tent. They're light, and the curved design and crisscrossed poles provide plenty of room. More importantly, these tents are freestanding, so they don't have to be staked out to be set up.

Tunnel tents are an elongated variation of the dome tent. They usually require two or three stakes but are lighter than dome tents and are far more stable in strong winds or heavy storms – important if you plan to spend a great deal of time above the tree line. Bivy or 'ultralight' tents are extremely small units that provide shelter for one person. They are often used by cyclists and rock climbers.

Your choice of a tent will be depend on how much space you need and your budget.

Some models exceed $500, providing such features as a vestibule for your equipment, drying lofts for wet clothes and ultralight aluminum poles (instead of the heavier fiberglass type). Whatever you spend, the tent should have a good rain fly that can double as a shade provider during those Alaskan summer days when the sun is still shining long after you've gone to bed. Make sure the netting around the doors and windows is bugproof, so you aren't a nightly smorgasbord for any mosquito that passes by. If your present tent is more than four years old, waterproof the floor and the rain fly before you leave home.

Sleeping Bag Many backpackers have debated the qualities of down versus synthetic fibers. What can't be argued, though, is down's quality of clumping when wet. In rainy Southeast and Southcentral Alaska, this means trouble during most wilderness trips. Synthetics are also easier to wash and dry; an advantage if you plan to spend the summer trekking in Alaska.

Try to choose a three-season bag, which suits temperatures between -10°F and 40°F. A mummy bag will fit closer to your body. If you like to roll around in your bag, the slightly wider modified mummy bag is more suitable but weighs more.

Along with a sleeping bag, bring an insulated foam pad to sleep on. It will reduce much of the ground chill. In the Interior, you will often be sleeping just inches away from permafrost, permanently frozen ground. If you'll be spending a considerable amount of time sleeping in the wilderness, skip the foam and invest in a self-inflating sleeping pad, such as the Thermarest. It may cost $80, but once you're out there, you'll be thankful for having purchased it.

Also consider packing one of the new backpacker's pillows. It's one more thing to carry, but if it helps you get a good night's sleep, it's well worth it.

Camp Stove Cooking dinner over a crackling campfire may be a romantic notion while you're planning your trip, but it is an inconvenience and often a major headache when you're actually on the trail. Bring a reliable stove and make life simple in the woods. Rain, strong winds and a lack of available wood will hamper your efforts to build a fire, and some preserves like Denali won't even allow campfires in the backcountry. Many stove brands are on the market today, but stoves like the MSR WhisperLite, which can be 'field repaired,' are the most dependable.

White gas (also known as 'white spirits' or 'Shellite') is widely available throughout Alaska and will cost $5 to $11 a gallon in Bush communities like Nome and Kotzebue. Gas cartridges, particularly Coleman's Peak 1 brand, can be purchased at most major towns that support a backpacking shop or large sports store. Other fuels, such as kerosene and methylated spirits, are more difficult to find outside of Anchorage, Fairbanks and Juneau. Remember, you cannot carry white gas or other camp stove fuels on airline flights.

Backpack Finally, you will need a backpack to carry all this clothing and gear in. The overwhelmingly popular choice in Alaska is the internal frame pack. Whatever you bring – internal or a pack with an external frame – make sure it is a high-quality pack with a waist belt, padded shoulder straps and a chest strap. Avoid glorified day packs or backpacks that are designed to be converted into a piece of luggage. Also bring a pack cover, for protection against the rain, or store everything in the pack in plastic bags.

Map & Compass Hikers should carry a compass into the wilderness and know how to use it correctly. Also pack the correct USGS topographical map for the area in which you are planning to travel. (See Maps earlier for more information.)

Sun Protection Alaska has long hours of sunlight during the summer, and the sun's

Finding Your Way with a Compass

When following a well-maintained and posted trail, you often won't need a compass. However, in wilderness areas like Denali National Park and Preserve and Wrangell–St Elias National Park, where you follow natural routes, a compass is necessary to determine your direction of travel, or bearing, from one point to the next (especially if you cannot judge your location from land formations alone). To take a compass bearing from a map, follow these steps:

1. On a USGS quad, draw a straight line on the map from your location to your destination and extend the line across any one of the borders. Borders on the topos are oriented in true north-south and east-west directions.

2. Center the compass on the line, where it intersects the border, and then align the compass housing north-south or east-west, to whichever border you chose. Read the true bearing of your drawn line from the compass circle.

3. To use the bearing, you must compensate for magnetic declination. A compass never points to true north. The needle shows magnetic north, because the needle is attracted by the earth's magnetic field (which varies in different parts of the world). In Alaska, the difference between true north and magnetic north ranges from 12° in the Aleutian Islands to almost 30° in the Southeast. All USGS quads have a magnetic declination diagram showing the difference between true north and magnetic north. If the magnetic north arrow is to the right of the true north line, as it is on Alaska maps, subtract the degrees from the figure on the compass circle. If it is to the left, then you add the degrees.

4. You can now set the direction-of-travel arrow on the compass to the bearing. Keep the magnetic needle inside the house on 'N' and the arrow will point to the proper line of travel.

rays are even more intense when they are reflected off snow or water. Bring a cap with a visor and a small tube of sunblock to save at least one layer of skin on your nose. If you plan to do any alpine hiking around snowfields, you should bring a pair of dark sunglasses, known by many locals as 'glacier goggles,' with UV protection.

Food You can buy food in almost any town or village, but the smaller and more remote the town, the more you'll have to pay. (See the Food section later in this chapter for more information.) For information on water purification, see the Health & Safety chapter.

Buying & Renting Locally Purchase your backpacking equipment before leaving home. Although most major towns in Alaska will have at least one store with a wall full of camping supplies, prices will be high, and by mid- to late summer certain items will be out of stock. The best place to purchase equipment is Anchorage, and the best store is REI (☎ 272-4565), 1200 W Northern Lights Blvd. Juneau and Fairbanks also have good backpacking stores (see regional chapters for names and addresses).

Renting equipment is even harder than purchasing it. A few places rent tents, stoves and sleeping bags, but for what you pay, you might as well purchase the gear when passing through Anchorage or Juneau.

Physical Preparation
For an enjoyable wilderness adventure, most people should spend some time preparing physically before arriving in Alaska and heading out on a trail. The preparation could be as simple as walking 3 to 6mi three or four times a week. Choose an area with a number of hills or ridges, as backpacking in Alaska often means climbing. How far in advance you prepare depends on your age and endurance level, but shortchanging yourself will mean a week of painful walking, until your body gets in shape.

The main areas of concern are your feet and shoulders. When exercising, wear the footwear you plan to wear on the hike, to ensure the boots are well broken in and your feet are adjusted to them. Carrying a half-loaded pack a few times just before your trip is also not a bad idea. The ultimate nightmare on your first hike is to have burning shoulders and blistered heels.

HIKES IN THIS BOOK
Route Descriptions
The trails and routes described in this book are broken into stages. Each stage is a one-day walk for the average hiker, and for the most part, the hike ends at a suitable campsite or trailhead. Most stages require four to six hours of walking, and it has been noted where stronger backpackers can combine two stages to skip a night on the trail.

Trails and routes can be walked in either direction; however, following a trail in a certain direction often has advantages (getting transportation, ease of crossing a pass, etc), which have been spelled out in the text.

Level of Difficulty
Each trail or route is rated according to difficulty in the Trail Standards & Seasons table and again in the facts box that precedes each trail description.

'Easy' trails are well maintained and frequently used, with planking over most wet areas, footbridges over major streams and directional signs. These tracks present few if any navigational difficulties and can be attempted by families and visitors with just day-hiking experience.

'Medium' trails are well cut and usually well marked but are more strenuous than easy trails, with numerous stream crossings and greater changes in elevation. They require a greater degree of physical stamina and better map-reading skills than easy trails.

'Hard' hikes are either very lightly marked trails or suggested routes in a trailless park. These trips should be attempted only by experienced backpackers with the right equipment and a good knowledge of Alaska's weather patterns and experience with wildlife encounters, particularly with bears.

Times & Distances

Approximate hiking times are also provided for each hike, usually from one camping area to the next. These are only average walking times based on a hiker with a 30lb pack covering 1mi of well-marked and somewhat level trail in 30 to 40 minutes. The times do not include major rest periods, lunch stops or that hour break you took to fish a stream. Swollen streams, muddy trails, bad weather or a heavy pack will slow you down. Even in good conditions, your hiking time will probably be different. What one person thinks is a backbreaking trudge will be judged as a pleasant stroll by others. Determine your own endurance and speed and then adjust the times in this book accordingly.

The distances given are also approximate. This is especially true of routes without an exact trail to follow. On these routes, the path followed and the distances covered will differ from one party to the next.

Maps in This Book

While the maps in this book show contour lines, the trail or route and notable features, such as cabins, rivers and peaks, they are not meant to replace topos. The maps in this book should be used in conjunction with the more detailed maps recommended for use in each section.

Altitude Measurements

Alaska has been well mapped by the USGS. All altitude measurements in this book are based on USGS topographical maps.

Place Names & Terminology

Alaskan hikers and trail descriptions in this book use a number of terms that are common in the USA but possibly not known by overseas visitors. You should understand the difference between a 'trail,' a 'route' and a 'two-track.' A trail is a developed and maintained footpath or track built for hiking. A route is a natural direction of travel in the backcountry, such as along a river or ridge, but *is not a developed path* that is marked or features signposts. A two-track is a rough road that might also be used by all-terrain or

four-wheel-drive vehicles to reach remote areas. In Alaska, hikers often will use all three – trail, route and two-track – during extended backpacking trips.

You should also understand the 'true left' and 'true right' sides of a river. The true left bank of a river is the left bank when you are looking downstream. The true right side is obviously the other bank. The glossary at the back of this book contains most of the terminology that might be encountered as you read or while hiking.

GUIDED HIKES

Much of Alaska's wilderness is inaccessible to the first-time visitor; travelers either don't know about wilderness areas or don't know how to get to them, which makes guide companies very useful. Guides are not only for novice campers. Their clients can be experienced backpackers who want to explore the far reaches of Alaska's wilderness but don't have the time or money to put together an expedition on their own. Guides can arrange the many details of a large-scale trip into the backcountry – everything from food and equipment to air charter.

Guided expeditions cost money, and most budget travelers prefer unguided trips. However, many guide companies offer adventures to areas that are only visited by a few people each year, an inviting prospect. Trips can range from a day hike on a glacier to a 12-day raft trip or a three-week ascent of Mt McKinley, and costs range from $175 to more than $250 per day, depending upon the amount of air travel involved. Expeditions usually have five to 12 clients; guide companies are extremely hesitant to take larger groups because of the environmental impact. The tour season extends from late May to September, and a select group of guide companies specialize in winter Nordic (cross-country) skiing or dogsledding expeditions.

Although most companies begin taking reservations in April, don't hesitate to call one after you've arrived in Alaska. Often, you can score a discount of 30% to 50% on a trip in the middle of the summer, as guide companies are eager to fill any remaining places on a scheduled trip.

The following is a list of recreational guide companies in Alaska. Don't confuse them with hunting or fishing guides, whose main interest is to make sure that their client gets a trophy to hang on the wall of the family room. Also don't confuse expeditions with fishing camps or wilderness lodges. The camps and lodges are established rustic resorts in the wilderness where travelers have many of the comforts of home but see little beyond the immediate area.

Southeast Alaska

Southeast Exposure (☎ 907-225-8829, ✉ burd@ptialaska.net), PO Box 9143, Ketchikan, AK 99901, rents kayaks and offers guided trips to Misty Fjords National Monument. A four-day paddle to the heart of Rudyerd Bay – the most scenic part of Misty Fjords – Manzanita Bay and Behm Canal is $700 per person and includes the boat trip from Ketchikan. A six-day trip that includes Walker Cove is $950.

Alaska Discovery (☎ 800-586-1911, ✉ akdisco@alaska.net), 5449 Shaune Drive, Suite 4, Juneau, AK 99801, was organized in 1972 and is one of the oldest and largest guide companies in Alaska. It used to operate mainly in the Southeast but now has raft trips down the Kongakut River in the Arctic National Wildlife Refuge. Still, kayak trips in Glacier Bay and Russell Fjord, home of Hubbard Glacier, are the company's specialty. Among its expeditions are a five-day paddle in Glacier Bay for $1675 per person and a seven-day Hubbard Glacier adventure for $1775. It also offers 10- to 12-day raft trips down the spectacular Tatshenshini River for $2250.
Web site: www.akdiscovery.com

Chilkat Guides (☎ 907-766-2491, ✉ raftalaska@aol.com), PO Box 170, Haines, AK 99827, offers a handful of raft trips from its base in Haines and is best known for its expeditions down the Tatshenshini and Alsek Rivers. Both are spectacular trips past dozens of glaciers. The 'Tat' is a 10-day float that costs $1975, and the Alsek, with a helicopter flight to bypass Turnback Canyon, is a 13-day trip for $2400.

Spirit Walker Expeditions (☎ 907-697-2266, 800-529-2537, ✉ 72537.555@compuserve.com), PO Box 240, Gustavus, AK 99826, is based near Glacier Bay and offers sea-kayaking trips along the coastline of Chichagof Island, just south of

the national park, and to Hubbard Glacier near Yakutat. The company prides itself on sighting whales and on providing memorable dinners that range from halibut kebabs to fresh Dungeness crabs. Prices range from $685 for a two-night paddle to $1875 for a seven-day trip along Chichagof Island.

Anchorage Area & Southcentral

Wilderness Alaska (☎ 907-345-3567, ✉ macgill@alaska.net), PO Box 113063, Anchorage, AK 99511, is an Anchorage-based company that runs trips throughout the state, from backpacking in the Arctic National Wildlife Refuge to kayaking in Prince William Sound. A seven-day float on the John River in the Gates of the Arctic National Park is $1995, and a six-day kayak trip to view the glaciers of Harriman Fjord in Prince William Sound is $1095.
Web site: www.gorp.com/wildak

Alaska World Wide Adventures (☎ 888-842-2964, ✉ akwildj@alaska.net), PO Box 220204, Anchorage, AK 99522, is a highly respected company that also runs trips throughout the state. A six-day float down the Copper River in Wrangell–St Elias National Park is $1175, and a six-day rafting and base camp hiking adventure in the Talkeetna Mountains costs $1825. One of the more unusual trips is an eight-day volcano hike and paddle in Aniakchak National Monument for $2725.
Web site: www.alaska.net/~akwildj

Hugh Glass Backpacking Co (☎ 907-344-1340), PO Box 110796, Anchorage, AK 99511, is a small but long-established guide company that offers kayak trips in Kenai Fjords National Park and Arctic wilderness fishing expeditions. Among its outings is a seven-day trip on the Stuyahok River for salmon, trout, char and grayling for $1995 and an eight-day trip on the Goodnews River for silver salmon and trout for $2395.

Sunny Cove Sea Kayaking (☎ 907-345-5339, 800-770-9119, ✉ kayakak@alaska.net), PO Box 111283, Anchorage, AK 99511, specializes in paddling trips in Resurrection Bay and Kenai Fjords National Park near Seward. Its five-day trip into the national park's Northwestern Fjord includes charter transportation to cut down on the long paddle out of Seward and costs $1195.

Anadyr Adventures (☎ 907-835-2814, 800-865-2925, ✉ anadyr@alaska.net), PO Box 1821, Valdez, AK 99686-1812, offers trips, paddling classes and kayak rentals for use in Prince William Sound. Guided trips range from one-day paddles and a three-day trip to the Columbia Glacier for $499 to an eight-day tour in the Sound that includes charter boat drop-off for $1499.

Web site: www.alaska.net/~anadyr

Alaska Wildtrek (☎ 907-235-6463, ✉ aktrek@xyz.net), PO Box 1741, Homer, AK 99603, offers guided tours throughout the state, from the Brooks Range to the Alaska Peninsula. Directed by Chlaus Lotscher, a German transplant in Alaska, the company caters almost entirely to Europeans, especially Germans. Among the wilderness trips it offers is a 10-day rafting adventure down the Hulahula River in the Arctic National Wildlife Refuge for $2495 and a five-day float along the Chilikadrotna in Lake Clark National Park for $1495.

Alaskan Wilderness Sailing Safaris (☎ 907-835-5175, ✉ awss@alaska.net), PO Box 1313, Valdez, AK 99686, offers kayaking and sailing trips from its Growler Island camp, a wilderness island south of Columbia Glacier. Accommodations and food at the camp are $100 a night; a full-day kayak rental is $89.

Web site: www.alaskanwilderness.com

St Elias Alpine Guides (☎ 907-277-6867, 888-933-5427), PO Box 111241, Anchorage, AK 99511-1241, specializes in mountaineering and glacier-skiing adventures at Wrangell–St Elias National Park. It also offers a 13-day trip down the Copper River to Cordova for $2275 and an 11-day backpacking trip around Chitistone Canyon of the Wrangell–St Elias National Park for $2175. Want to climb a mountain? The 17-day ascent of Mt Blackburn (elevation 16,390ft) is only $2900.

Web site: www.steliasguides.com

Mt McKinley, Denali & the Interior

Alaska Wilderness Journeys (☎ 800-349-0064, ✉ journeys@alaska.net), PO Box 743, Talkeetna, AK 99676, runs a variety of float trips, glacier treks and backpacking adventures around Denali National Park and Brooks Range above the Arctic Circle. A unique two-day raft trip begins on the flag-stop train of the Alaska Railroad and includes overnighting in a rustic cabin. The cost is $465. The company also has a three-day South Denali base camp trip featuring day hiking high in the Talkeetna Mountains for $650.

Web site: www.alaskajourneys.com

Denali Raft Adventures (☎ 907-683-2234, 888-683-2234, ✉ denraft@mtaonline.net), Drawer 190, Denali Park, AK 99755, offers a variety of day-rafting trips down the Nenana River near Denali National Park. Some are in calm waters, but others involve two hours of white-water rafting. Prices are $50 to $70 per person for two-to four-hour trips. The company also has a full-day trip.

Nova (☎ 907 745-5753, 800-746-5753, ✉ nova@alaska.net), PO Box 1129, Chickaloon, AK 99674-1129, specializes in river rafting. Its trips range from a day run down the Matanuska River for $60 per person to a three-day journey along the Talkeetna River that involves flying to the heart of the Talkeetna Mountains and grade IV white water for $950. The company handles trips to the Copper River in Wrangell–St Elias National Park (six days for $1450) as well as sea-kayaking adventures and glacier hikes.

Web site: www.novalaska.com

Fairbanks Area & Brooks Range

CanoeAlaska (☎ 907-479-5183, ✉ canoeak@mosquitonet.com), PO Box 81750, Fairbanks, AK 99708-1750, specializes in canoeing trips that teach boating skills and explore scenic rivers. Throughout the summer, the guide company runs trips on the Chena, Delta, Gulkana and Fortymile Rivers that last three to 10 days. The cost is $150 to $250 per person per day, depending on the river and the length of the trip.

Alaska Fish & Trails Unlimited (☎ 907-479-7630), 1177 Shypoke Dr, Fairbanks, AK 99709, runs backpacking, kayaking and canoeing trips in the Gates of the Arctic National Park that include a 14-day backpack and raft trip from Anaktuvak Pass in the Brooks Range to Bettles for $1800. The company also offers an unguided raft-and-backpack trip from Summit Lake along the Koyukuk River for $1000.

Arctic Treks (☎ 907-455-6502), PO Box 73452, Fairbanks, AK 99707, is a family operation that specializes in treks and rafting in the Gates of the Arctic National Park and the Arctic National Wildlife Refuge. A 10-day backpacking trip to the high mountain valleys of the Brooks Range is $2050 per person, and a 10-day float down the Hulahula River through the Arctic North Slope costs $2875.

Sourdough Outfitters (☎ 907-692-5252, ✉ info@sourdoughoutfitters.com), PO Box 26066, Bettles, AK 99726, runs canoe, kayak and backpacking trips to the Gates of the Arctic National Park, Noatak and Kobuk Rivers and other areas. The outfitters also provide unguided trips for individuals who have the experience to make an independent journey but want a guide company to handle the logistics (such as trip planning, transportation and canoe or raft rental) of a major expedition. Unguided trips throughout the Brooks

Range are $420 to $960 per person, depending on the number of people in your party. Guided trips include a 12-day combination float/backpacking trek in the Gates of the Arctic National Park for $1950, a 10-day canoe trip along the Noatak River for $2000 and a five-day paddle of the Wild River in the Brooks Range for $1350.
Web site: www.sourdoughoutfitters.com

ABEC's Alaska Adventures (☎ 907-457-8907, ✆ abec@polarnet.com), 1550 Alpine Vista Court, Fairbanks, AK 99712, is another outfitter that concentrates on trips in the Arctic National Wildlife Refuge and Gates of the Arctic National Park. Its 12-day Hulahula River raft trip is $2650, and a 12-day backpack trek to witness the caribou migration is $1800.

Arctic Wild (☎ 907-479-8203, ✆ arctic@willowbud .com), PO Box 80562, Fairbanks, AK 99708, offers a range of floats and treks in the Brooks Range and Arctic National Wildlife Refuge. The 11-day Hulahula float in the ANWR is $2600, and a six-day caribou migration backpack is $1875. Other rivers floated include the Noatak, the Aichlik on the border of the ANWR and the Alanta on the south side of the Brooks Range.

RESPONSIBLE HIKING

Check in with the USFS office or national park headquarters before entering the backcountry. By letting them know your intentions, you'll get the peace of mind of knowing that someone knows you're out there. If there is no ranger office in the area, advise the air charter service responsible for picking up your party of your travel plans.

Do not harass wildlife while traveling in the backcountry. Avoid startling an animal, as it will most likely flee, leaving you with a short and forgettable encounter. If you flush a bird from its nest, leave the area quickly, as an unattended nest leaves the eggs vulnerable to predators. Never attempt to feed wildlife; it is not healthy for you or the animal.

Be thoughtful when in the wilderness; it is a delicate environment. Carry in your supplies and carry out your trash. Never litter or leave garbage to smolder in a fire pit. Always put out your fire and cover it with natural materials, or better still, don't light a fire in heavily traveled areas. Use biodegradable soap and do all washing away from water sources. In short, practice low-impact no-trace camping and leave no evidence of your stay. Only then can these areas remain true wilderness.

WOMEN HIKERS

Perfumes or scented cosmetics, including deodorants, should not be worn in areas where you are likely to encounter bears, as the smell will attract them. Women who are menstruating should also be cautious. Women should also be alert to the dangers of hitchhiking, especially when they are traveling alone. Use common sense and don't be afraid to say no to lifts.

In general, women are safe traveling, hiking and camping in Alaska. The combination of a booming tourist industry, low crime rate and small towns and cities, allow women to have fewer worries traveling without male companions in Alaska than in almost any other state in the USA.

HIKING WITH CHILDREN

Alaska is a great destination for children. Children ages two through 11 years old receive a 50% discount on the Alaska Marine Hwy ferry, and the Alaska Railroad, bus companies and national parks also extend hefty discounts to kids.

If your family enjoys the outdoors, then Alaska can be a relatively affordable destination once you have arrived. A campsite is cheap compared to a motel room, and hiking, backpacking and wildlife watching are free. Even fishing is free for children, as the state does not require anglers under the age of 16 years to purchase a fishing license.

The key to any Alaskan wilderness adventure with children is to match the hike or activity to your child's ability and level of endurance. Children lacking outdoor experience will struggle with a weeklong kayak trip in Glacier Bay or hiking the Chena Dome Trail near Fairbanks. On the other hand, the easy Resurrection Pass Trail can be handled by most children, even those as young as six or seven if their packs are light and the children are in good walking shape.

If your child is younger than five years old, and you still want to take them on a wilderness trip, consider a rental cabin in either Tongass or Chugach National Forest (see Accommodations later in this chapter). Most cabins are reached via a floatplane, an exciting beginning to any adventure for a child, allowing you to bypass long hikes in with heavy backpacks, yet offering a remote location and good opportunities to see wildlife or catch fish.

When backpacking with children, make sure their gear will hold up in Alaska's weather. This is particularly true with their parka and rain pants. If you're wearing a fleece jersey and a high-tech Gore-Tex parka, why shouldn't they? The other important thing to remember is to make sure you pack enough food. After a full day of hiking, parents are always shocked to see their children consume twice as much as they would at home.

OTHER ACTIVITIES
Blue-Water Paddling

'Blue water,' in Alaska, refers to the coastal areas of the state, which are characterized by extreme tidal fluctuations, cold water and the possibility of high winds and waves. Throughout Southeast and Southcentral Alaska, the open canoe gives way to the kayak, and blue-water paddling is the means of escape into the beauty of the coastal wilderness.

Don't confuse white-water kayaking with ocean touring. River running, wearing helmets and wet suits, in light, streamlined kayaks and executing Eskimo rolls has nothing to do with paddling coastal Alaska in ocean-touring kayaks. Every year, hundreds of backpackers with canoeing experience arrive in the North Country and undertake their first blue-water kayak trip in such protected areas as Muir Inlet in Glacier Bay National Park or Tracy Arm Fjord, south of Juneau.

Tidal fluctuations are the main concern in blue water areas. Paddlers should always pull their boats above the high-tide mark and secure them by tying a line to a rock or tree. A tide book for the area should be in the same pouch as the topographic map – paddlers schedule days around the changing tides, traveling with the tidal current or

during slack tide for easy paddling. Check with local rangers for the narrow inlets or straits where riptides or whirlpools might form, and always plan to paddle these areas during slack tides.

Cold coastal water, rarely above 45°F in the summer, makes capsizing more than unpleasant. Even with a life jacket, survival time in the water is less than two hours; without one, the time is considerably less. Plan your trip to run parallel with the shoreline and arrange your schedule so you can sit out rough weather without missing your pickup date. If you do flip, stay with the boat and attempt to right it and crawl back in. Trying to swim to shore in Arctic water is risky at best.

Give a wide berth to marine mammals such as sea lions, seals and especially any whales. Glacial ice should also be treated with respect. Don't get closer than a half mile to a glacier face, as icebergs can calve suddenly and create a series of unmanageable waves and swells. Never try to climb onto floating icebergs. They are extremely unstable and can roll without warning.

Framed backpacks are almost useless in kayaks; gear is better stowed in duffel bags or small day packs. Carry a large supply of assorted plastic bags, including several garbage bags. All gear, especially sleeping bags and clothing, should be stowed in plastic bags, as water tends to seep in even when you seal yourself in with a cockpit skirt. For getting in and out of kayaks and pulling them across muddy tidal flats, over-the-calf rubber boots, so-called Southeast sneakers, are the best footwear to have. You might also want to invest in a pair of felt liners to help keep your toes warm. For any blue-water paddling, include an extra paddle, a large sponge for bailing the boat, sunglasses and sunscreen, extra lines and a repair kit of duct tape and a tube of silicone sealant for fiberglass cracks.

White-Water Paddling

Throughout Alaska's history, rivers have been the traditional travel routes through the rugged terrain. Many rivers can be paddled in canoes; others, due to extensive white water, are better handled in rafts or kayaks. If access is available by road, hard-shell canoes and kayaks can be used. If not, you might have to arrange for a folding boat, such as a Klepper kayak, or an inflatable canoe or raft. Or you can pay for an additional bush flight so a hard-shell canoe can be carried in on the floats.

Alaska's rivers vary from one end of the state to the other, but you will find they share characteristics not found on many rivers in the Lower 48. Water levels tend to change rapidly in Alaska. Due to temperature changes, rainfall and other factors, a river's depth and character can change noticeably even within a day. Many rivers are heavily braided and boulder-strewn and require a careful eye in picking out the right channel to avoid spending most of the day pulling your boat off gravel. And count on there being cold water, especially in any glacial-fed river, where the temperatures will be in the mid-30s (F). You can survive flipping your canoe in an Alaskan river, but you'll definitely want a plan of action in case you ever do.

North Slope rivers in the Arctic tend to be extremely braided, swift and free-flowing by mid-June. They remain high and silty for several weeks after that, but by mid-July even the sea ice is open enough to permit paddling in coastal lagoons.

Rivers flowing from the south slope of the Brooks Range are moving by early June and have good water levels through mid-August, and rivers in Fairbanks and Interior areas can usually be run from late May to mid-September. Farther south, around Anchorage and the Southcentral region, the paddling season lasts even longer – from May to September.

Much of the equipment for canoeists is the same as it is for blue-water paddlers. You want all gear in dry storage bags, especially extra clothing, sleeping bag and tent. Tie everything into the canoe; you never know when a whirlpool or a series of standing waves will be encountered. Wear a life jacket at all times. Many paddlers stock their life jacket with insect repellent, waterproof matches and other survival gear in case they flip and get separated from their boat.

Always make a float plan before you depart and leave it with either the bush pilot who flies you in or the nearest BLM or USFS office. Most importantly, research the river you want to run and make sure you have the ability to handle whatever class of water it's rated. Descriptions of paddling conditions follow:

Class I – easy
The river ranges from flat water to occasional series of mild rapids.

Class II – medium
The river has frequent stretches of rapids with waves up to 3ft high and easy chutes, ledges and falls. The best route is easy to identify, and the entire river can be run in open canoes.

Class III – difficult
The river features numerous rapids with high, irregular waves and difficult chutes and falls that often require scouting. These river are for experienced paddlers who either use kayaks and rafts or have a spray cover for their canoe.

Class IV – very difficult
Rivers with long stretches of irregular waves, powerful eddies and even constricted canyons. Scouting is mandatory, and rescues can be difficult in many places. Suitable in rafts or whitewater kayaks with paddlers equipped with helmets.

Class V – extremely difficult
Rivers with continuous violent rapids, powerful rollers and high, unavoidable waves and haystacks. These rivers are only for white-water kayaks and paddlers who are proficient in the Eskimo roll.

Class VI – highest level of difficulty
These rivers are rarely run except by very experienced kayakers under ideal conditions.

Wilderness Fishing

Many people have a 'fish-per-cast' vision of angling in Alaska. They expect every river, stream and lake, no matter how close to the road, to be bountiful, but often go home disappointed when their fishing efforts produce little to brag about. Serious anglers visiting Alaska carefully research the areas to be fished and are equipped with the right gear and tackle. They often pay for guides or book a room at remote camps or lodges where rivers are not 'fished out' by every passing motorist.

If, however, you plan to undertake a few wilderness trips, by all means pack a rod, reel and some tackle. You can purchase a backpacking rod that breaks down into five sections and has a light reel; it takes up less room than soap, shaving cream and a wash rag. In the Southeast and Southcentral regions, backpackers can catch cutthroat trout, rainbow trout and Dolly Varden (a fish similar to the other two). Farther north, especially around Fairbanks, you'll get grayling, with its sail-like dorsal fin, and arctic char; during August, salmon seem to be everywhere.

If angling is just a second thought, load an open-face spinning reel with light line, something in the four to six-pound range, and take along a small selection of spinners and spoons. After you arrive, you can always purchase the lures used locally, but in most wilderness streams, I've rarely had a problem catching fish on Mepps spinners, sizes No 1 to No 3. Other lures that work well are Pixies, Dardevles and Krocodiles.

For fly fishing, a No 5 or No 6 rod with a matching floating line or sinking tip is well suited for Dolly Vardens, rainbows and grayling. For species of salmon, a No 7 or No 8 rod and line are better choices. For ease of travel, rods should break down and be carried in a case.

A nonresident's fishing license costs $50 a year ($15 for residents), or you can purchase a three-day license for $20 or a 14-day one for $30; every bait shop in the state sells them.

The Alaska Department of Fish and Game puts out a variety of material for fishers, including the *Alaska Sport Fishing Guide*. You can obtain the brochure by contacting the Department of Fish & Game (☎ 907-465-4180), PO Box 25526, Juneau, AK 99802-5526. You can also request one through the state Web site (www.state.ak.us) by clicking on Alaska Fish and Game under Departments.

Perhaps the most comprehensive angler's guide to the state is *Alaska Fishing* by Gunnar Pedersen and Rene Limeres. The authors begin with a detailed look at the different species of Alaskan fish, including the best fishing techniques, and then follow with a review of each region and major river system throughout the state.

Equally good for fly fishing is *Flyfishing Alaska* by Anthony Route. Route writes a fly fishing column for the *Anchorage Daily News* and does a particularly good job covering the species found in Alaska's rivers, streams and lakes and the tackle and equipment you need to catch them.

For those who want to combine a cabin rental with fishing there is *Fishing Alaska on Dollars a Day* by Christopher and Adela Batin. The guide describes Forest Service cabins that can be rented for $25 to $45 per day, fishing in the immediate area and gateway cities.

Here is a brief synopsis of the most common non-salmon species you find in lakes and streams all summer long.

Rainbow Trout This is without a doubt the best fighting fish and the most sought after by most anglers. Fishing from shore in lakes is best in late spring and early summer, just after ice breakup, and again in the fall when water temperatures are cooler. During the height of the summer, rainbows move into deeper water in lakes, and you usually need a boat to fish them.

Fish them at dawn and dusk when, on calm days, they can be

seen surfacing for insects. Use spinners, size No 1 to No 3, and flashy spoons, but avoid treble hooks (or clip one or two of the hooks on them), as they make releasing fish hard. The workhorse fly is the lake leech, in either purple or olive, fished with a slow retrieve on sinking-tip lines.

Cutthroat Trout The cutthroat picks up its name from the reddish-orange slash along the inner edge of the fish's lower jaw. Outside Southeast Alaska, most traveling anglers end up casting for resident cutthroats that spend their entire lives in the streams and lakes, as opposed to larger anadromous (those migrating upstream to breed) cutthroats that migrate to saltwater where food is more abundant. This trout likes to stay around submerged logs, aquatic vegetation or near other cover and is an aggressive feeder.

In most lakes, you can take them on small spinners, size No 0 up to No 2, but they also will hit on larger spoons, especially red-and-white Dardevles. For fly fishing, a floating line with a 9ft leader and a slowly twitching mosquito-larva fly can be very effective. The best time to fish is early morning and at dusk when light is low and cutthroats are often cruising the shallows for food.

Dolly Varden One of the most widespread varieties of fish in Alaska, Dolly Varden's aggressive behavior makes them easy to catch. Dolly Varden are often caught near the entrances of streams or along weed beds near shore, making them accessible to backpacking anglers. With spinning gear, use spinners in sizes No 1 and No 2 or small spoons. Fly fishers often use a blue smolt fly on a sinking-tip line and a short leader and use an erratic strip retrieve. Other streamers work as well, and a pinhead muddler and a floating line are often used in shallow rivers or when Dolly Varden are holding in shallow water.

Arctic Char A closely related cousin to the Dolly Varden, the arctic char is not quite as widespread in Alaska. Often anglers will confuse the two species. Arctic char will be encountered predominantly in the Alaska Peninsula and Bristol Bay areas, on Kodiak Island, in some lakes in the Kenai Peninsula and in the Brooks Range and to the north. Spawning male char turn brilliant red or gold with red or orange spots, while Dolly Varden are just as brightly colored but only on their lower body. For the most part, anglers use the same tackle and techniques for catching both species.

Grayling There can be no mistaking the grayling. Its long dorsal fin allows hikers to identify the fish even if they have never hooked one. Grayling in streams feed at the surface or in midwater drift and almost exclusively on insects or larvae. In other words, they are a fly fisher's dream. They are extremely receptive to dry flies and rarely are so selective as to choose one pattern over another. Generally small flies (sizes No 16 to No 18) will produce more rises than larger ones. Even if you have spinning gear, tie on a clear plastic bubble 4 to 6ft above a dry fly and fish for grayling with that.

Mountain Biking

The mountain bike's durable design, knobby tires and suspension is ideal for Alaska. With such a bike you can explore an almost endless number of dirt roads, miners' two-tracks and even some hiking trails that you would never consider with a road bike. By exploring rough 4WD roads, you not only can escape those monster RVs but will see more wildlife.

Always pick your route carefully before heading out. Make sure the length of the ride and the ruggedness of the terrain are within your ability and the equipment you are carrying. Stay away from trails and areas that ban mountain bikes. If you choose a route already dedicated to vehicle use, such as an ATV trail, your trip is unlikely to contribute to erosion.

There is much mountain bike activity around Anchorage, with several places to rent bikes (see the Anchorage chapter). One of the more popular trails is the Powerline Pass Trail, an 11mi roundtrip into the mountains of Chugach State Park. Within the Kenai Peninsula, the Resurrection Pass, Russian River and Johnson Pass Trails in the Chugach National Forest have become popular among off-road cyclists. There are also many two-tracks along Glenn Hwy that can be explored on a mountain bike.

If you have the ability to carry equipment on your bike (sleeping bag, food and tent) you can enjoy a variety of overnight trips. The 92mi Denali park road is closed to vehicles, but you can explore it on a mountain bike. Another excellent dirt road for such an adventure is the 135mi Denali Hwy from Paxson to Cantwell.

For additional information before your trip, write to Arctic Bicycle Club, PO Box 140269, Anchorage, AK 99514, or check their Web site (www.arcticbike.alaska.net).

Rock Climbing

Rock climbing has been growing in popularity in Alaska in recent years. On almost any summer weekend, you can watch climbers working bolt-protected sport routes just above Seward Hwy along Turnagain Arm. Canyons in nearby Portage are also capturing the attention of rock climbers. Off Byron Glacier, several routes grace a slab of black rock polished smooth by the glacier. Not far from Portage Lake, a short hike leads to the magnificent slate walls of Middle Canyon.

Fairbanks climbers head north of town to the limestone formations known as Grapefruit Rocks or else pack along a tent and sleeping bag for the Granite Tors Trail off the Chena Hot Springs Rd. A 7mi hike from the trailhead brings them to the tors, a series of 100ft granite spires in a wilderness setting.

For equipment and more information in Anchorage, contact REI (☎ 907-272-4565), 1200 Northern Lights Blvd, Anchorage, AK 99503. In Fairbanks, contact Beaver Sports (☎ 907-479-2494), 3480 College Rd, Fairbanks AK 99709.

USEFUL ORGANIZATIONS

There are a number of useful organizations in Alaska for people interested in the outdoors and outdoor activities.

The Alaska Natural History Association (ANHA) promotes a better understanding of Alaska's natural, cultural and historical resources by working with the agencies that manage them. This group runs most of the bookstores in the national parks and another 30 located around the state. By joining the association (605 W 4th Ave, Suite 85, Anchorage, AK 99501), you can get a 10% discount on their books and on goods at Public Lands Information Centers that sell, among other things, USGS topos.

The Artic Bicycle Club, Alaska's largest bicycle club, can provide information on mountain biking, racing, road routes and tours. Call their hot line (☎ 907-566-0177) for details on road conditions, mountain bike races and organized bike tours. You can also write to Arctic Bicycle Club at PO Box 140269, Anchorage, AK 99514, or check their Web site (www.arcticbike.alaska.net).

For information about scaling peaks or other climbs, contact the Anchorage-based Mountaineering Club of Alaska (☎ 907-272-1811) at PO Box 102037, Anchorage, AK 99501. If they cannot help you, they will know the outfitter who can.

For a local bird list or schedule of field trips during the summer, birders can contact the regional office of the National Audubon Society in Anchorage (☎ 907-276-7034) at 308 G St, Suite 219, Anchorage, AK 99501-2134.

The Sierra Club, the oldest and best-known environmental group in the country today, has a chapter in Anchorage (☎ 907-276-4048) at 241 E 5th Ave, Suite 205, Anchorage, AK 99501.

The Southeast Alaska Conservation Council (SEACC) is the environmental watchdog of Southeast Alaska. There would be a lot more clear cuts and strip mines without SEACC (☎ 907-586-6942, ✉ info@seacc.org). For more information, write to them at 419 6th St, Suite 328, Juneau, AK 99801, or check out the SEACC Web site (www.seacc.org).

The Wilderness Society lobbies for the preservation of the remaining wilderness areas in the USA. Contact its Alaska office (☎ 907-272-9453) at 430 W 7th Ave, Suite 205, Anchorage, AK 99501.

TOURIST OFFICES

The first place to contact while planning your adventure is the Alaska Division of Tourism (☎ 907-465-2010, fax 907-465-2287), Dept 901, PO Box 110801, Juneau, AK 99811-0801, where you can request a copy of the *Alaska State Vacation Planner,* a 120-page annually-updated tourist magazine, a state highway map, and schedules for the Alaska Marine Hwy and the Alaska Railroad. You can also check its Web site (www.travelalaska.com).

Travel information is easy to obtain once you are on the road, as almost every city, town and village has a tourist contact center, whether it be a visitor center, a chamber of commerce or a hut near the ferry dock. These places are good sources of free maps, information on local accommodations, and directions to the nearest campground or hiking trail.

For information on national parks, refuges and other public lands, contact one of the Alaska Public Lands Information Centers (APLIC). These centers are clearinghouses for outdoor recreation information on all public land in Alaska, no matter who controls the land. You can also get information or request material through the APLIC Web site (www.nps.gov/aplic/center/index.html). There are four APLIC centers in Alaska, with the main one in Anchorage:

Anchorage
   Alaska Public Lands Information Center, (☎ 907-271-2737), 605 W 4th Ave, Anchorage, AK 99501

Ketchikan
   Southeast Alaska Discovery Center, (☎ 907-228-6214), 50 Main St, Ketchikan, AK 99901

Fairbanks
   Alaska Public Lands Information Center, (☎ 907-456-0527), 250 Cushman St, Suite 1A, Fairbanks, AK 99701

Tok
   Alaska Public Lands Information Center, (☎ 907-883-5667), PO Box 359, Tok, AK 99780

Anchorage, Fairbanks and Juneau are the three main cities visitors fly into and often use as a base for their wilderness adventures.

Each has a visitor center that you can contact in advance for more information on transportation, lodging or a city map:

Anchorage Convention & Visitors Bureau
   (☎ 276-4118, fax 278-5559),
   524 W 4th Ave, Anchorage,
   AK 99501
   Web site: www.anchorage.net

Fairbanks Convention and Visitors Bureau
   (☎ 456-5774, 800-327-5774),
   550 First Ave, Fairbanks, AK 99701
   Web site: www.fairbanks.polarnet.com

Juneau Convention and Visitors Bureau
   (☎ 586-2201, 888-581-2201),
   134 Third St, Juneau, AK 99801
   Web site: www.juneau.com

VISAS & DOCUMENTS
Passports

If you are traveling to Alaska from overseas, you will need a passport. Only US and Canadian citizens can cross the borders to Alaska without one. Even they should carry valid identification, such as a driver's license and a voter registration card. Often a driver's license or a social security card alone is not enough to satisfy some customs officials.

Make sure your passport does not expire halfway through the trip, and if traveling with children, it's best to bring a photocopy of their birth certificates.

Visas

Overseas travelers also need at least one visa, possibly two. Obviously, a US visa is needed, but if you're taking either the Alcan or the Alaska Marine Hwy ferry from Prince Rupert in British Columbia, you will also need a Canadian visa. The Alcan begins in Canada, requiring travelers to pass from the USA into Canada and back into the USA again.

Travelers from Western Europe and most Commonwealth nations do not need a Canadian visa and can get a six-month travel visa to the USA without too much paperwork or waiting.

Vaccinations are not required for either country. However, the form for nonimmigrant visas into the US asks if you have 'ever been afflicted with a communicable disease of public health significance.'

Exploring Alaska Online

At home, you're only a few keystrokes away from many of Alaska's national parks, state parks and other recreation areas. Here are the most useful Web sites for hikers and backpackers planning a trip to Alaska:

Alaska Marine Hwy:	www.akferry.com
Alaska Public Lands Information Center:	www.nps.gov.aplic/center/index.html
Alaska State Parks:	www.dnr.state.ak.us/parks
Chilkoot Trail:	www.nps.gov/klgo
Denali National Park:	www.nps.gov/dena
Gates of the Arctic National Park:	www.nps.gov/gaar
Glacier Bay National Park:	www.nps.gov/glba
Katmai National Park:	www.nps.gov/katm
Kenai Fjords National Park:	www.nps.gov/kefj
Lake Clark National Park:	www.nps.gov/lacl
Tongass and Chugach National Forests:	www.fs.fed.us/recreation/states/ak.html
US Fish & Wildlife Service – Alaska Region:	www.r7.fws.gov
White Mountain Recreation Area:	www.ndo.ak.blm.gov
Wrangell–St Elias National Park:	www.nps.gov/wrst

Answering 'yes' to this question can cause the Immigration and Naturalization Service (INS) to try to exclude you. This is of particular import to those with HIV. In addition, people who have been on a farm during the previous 30 days will be detained by immigration officials.

Onward Tickets

All visitors must have an onward or return ticket to enter the USA and sufficient funds to pass into Canada. No set amount constitutes 'sufficient funds,' but most customs officials suggest around $500, and anybody arriving at the Canadian border with less than $250 will likely be turned back.

A word of warning: Overseas travelers should be aware of the procedures to re-enter the USA. Occasionally visitors get stuck in Canada because they had a single-entry visa into the USA and used it passing through the Lower 48. Canadian immigration officers often caution people whom they feel might have difficulty returning to the USA. Some information about visa or other requirements for entering the USA is available on the US Department of State home page (www.state.gov/index.html), which, among other things, lists foreign embassies and consulates in the US.

Hiking Permits

In some national parks, including Denali, Glacier Bay and Katmai, you must register and obtain a backcountry permit. The permits allow you to spend the night in the parks; they're free and easy to obtain from ranger stations near the trailheads.

For trails in state parks and national forests, no backcountry or hiking permit is required. However, at most trailheads there is an 'intentions book,' and it is a wise practice to add your name, address, the number of days you plan to hike and your route.

Entry Fees

For the most part trekking and backpacking is still free in Alaska, but the trend is moving towards charging permit and entry fees. Canada Parks now requires a permit to hike the Chilkoot Trail and charges $35. Denali National Park charges an entrance fee, and a growing number of state parks have instituted daily parking fees.

Travel Insurance

Travel agents can provide a traveler's insurance policy. Coverage varies from policy to policy but usually includes loss of baggage, sickness and accidental injury or death. Most policies also cover the reimbursement of cancellation fees and other costs if you must cancel your trip because of accident or illness or the illness or death of a family member. Many travelers feel it's worth purchasing this inexpensive protection, especially if you are traveling on nonrefundable advance purchase plane tickets.

Be sure that the policy does not exclude wilderness trekking, mountaineering, kayaking, white-water rafting or any other activities you might be participating in while traveling in Alaska, or you may have a difficult time settling a claim. Also be sure that the policy specifically covers helicopter evacuation, the most common way of reaching troubled backpackers in Alaska's wilderness areas.

If you purchase insurance and have a loss, you must submit proof of this loss when you make an insurance claim. If you have a medical problem, you should save all your bills and get a physician's certificate stating that you were sick. If you lose something covered by insurance, you must file a police report, no matter how remote the location. No insurance company considers a claim without such documentation.

Other Documents

Next to your passport, a picture driver's license is the best piece of identification you can carry. Most national driver's licenses are valid in Canada, or you can obtain an international driving permit before leaving home. If you plan to take a vehicle rented in the USA into Canada, make sure the rental company issues you a contract that stipulates the vehicle's use in Canada.

US citizens traveling extensively through Canada to reach Alaska should look into obtaining a Canadian Nonresident Interprovincial Motor Vehicle Liability Insurance Card. Such a card provides proof of insurance and can be obtained in the USA through insurance companies.

Occasionally in Alaska, especially around the University of Alaska campuses in Anchorage and Fairbanks, student discounts are available, in which case your university identification or Hostelling International card is a handy thing to have. The hostel card is especially useful, as there are a growing number of businesses that feed off the Alaskan hostels (see the Accommodations section later in this chapter) by targeting such travelers with discounts.

In the USA, you can get a Hostelling International membership by contacting Hostelling International. In Anchorage, the HI office (☎ 907-276-3635) is located at 700 H St, Anchorage, AK 99501. You can locate other offices or join online at www.hiayh .org. Adult memberships are $25 a year, or $250 for a lifetime.

EMBASSIES & CONSULATES
US Embassies

Here is a list of US embassies in other countries:

Australia
(☎ 02-6214 5600)
Moonah Place, Yarralumla ACT 2600

Canada
(☎ 613-238-5335)
490 Sussex Drive, Ottawa,
Ontario K1N 1GB

France
(☎ 01 43 12 22 22)
2 Ave Gabriel, 75008 Paris

Germany
(☎ 30-832-9233)
Neustädtische Kirchstrasse, 10117 Berlin

Japan
(☎ 0990-5-26160)
10-5 Akasaka 1-Chome, Minato-ku,
Tokyo 107-8420

Netherlands
(☎ 70-310-9209)
Lange Voorhout 102, 2514 EJ The Hague

New Zealand
(☎ 644-472-2068)
29 Fitzherbert Terrace, Thorndon,
Wellington

UK
(☎ 020-7499-9000)
24 Grosvenor Square, London W1A 1AE

Consulates in Alaska

There are 11 foreign consulates in Anchorage to assist overseas travelers with unusual problems. They include:

Belgium
(☎ 276-5617)
1031 W 4th Ave, Room 400, Anchorage,
AK 99501-7502

Denmark
(☎ 261-7600)
3111 C St, Suite 100, Anchorage,
AK 99503-3915

Finland
(☎ 279-6607)
1529 P St, Anchorage, AK 99501-4923

France
(☎ 277-4770)
2605 Denali St, Suite 101, Anchorage,
AK 99503

Germany
(☎ 274-6537)
425 G St, Suite 650, Anchorage,
AK 99501-2176

Italy
(☎ 762-7664)
12840 Silver Spruce Drive, Anchorage,
AK 99516-2603

Japan
(☎ 279-8428)
550 W 7th Ave, Suite 701, Anchorage,
AK 99501

Korea
(☎ 561-5488)
101 W Benson Blvd, Suite 304, Anchorage,
AK 99503-3997

Norway
(☎ 279-6942)
203 W 15th Ave, Suite 105, Anchorage,
AK 99501-5128

Sweden
(☎ 265-2930)
301 W Northern Lights Blvd, Anchorage,
AK 99503

UK
(☎ 786-4848)
3211 Providence Drive, Room 362, Anchorage,
AK 99508-4614

CUSTOMS

Travelers are allowed to bring all personal goods (including camping gear or hiking equipment) into the USA and Canada free of duty, along with food for two days and up to 50 cigars, 200 cigarettes and 40oz of liquor or wine.

There are no forms to fill out if you are a foreign visitor bringing a vehicle into Alaska, whether it is a bicycle, motorcycle or a car, nor are there forms for hunting rifles or fishing gear. Hunting rifles (handguns and automatic weapons are prohibited) must be registered in your own country, and you should bring proof of registration. There is no limit to the amount of money you can bring into Alaska, but anything over $5000 must be registered with customs officials.

Keep in mind that endangered-species laws prohibit transporting products made of bone, skin, fur, ivory, etc, through Canada without a permit. Import and export of such items into the USA is also prohibited. If you have any doubt about a gift or item you want to purchase, call the US Fish & Wildlife Service in Anchorage (☎ 786-3311).

Hunters and anglers who want to ship home their salmon, halibut or the rack of a caribou can easily do so. Most outfitters and guides will make the arrangements for you, including properly packaging the game. In the case of fish, most towns have a storage company that will hold your salmon or halibut in a freezer until you are ready to leave Alaska. When frozen, seafood can usually make the trip to any city in the Lower 48 without spoiling.

MONEY
Currency

All prices quoted in this book are in US dollars unless otherwise stated. The US dollar is divided into 100 cents (¢). Coins come in denominations of 1¢ (penny), 5¢ (nickel), 10¢ (dime), 25¢ (quarter) and the seldom seen 50¢ (half dollar). In 1999, the USA introduced a $1 coin. Notes, commonly called 'bills,' come in $1, $2, $5, $10, $20, $50 and $100 denominations – $2 bills are rare, but perfectly legal.

Keep in mind that the Canadian system is also dollars and cents but is a separate currency and worth considerably less than American dollars.

Exchange Rates

The following currencies convert at these approximate rates:

country	unit		dollars
Australia	A$1	=	US$0.59
Canada	C$1	=	US$0.68
euro	€1	=	US$0.95
France	1FF	=	US$0.15
Germany	DM1	=	US$0.49
Japan	¥100	=	US$0.93
New Zealand	NZ$1	=	US$0.46
UK	UK£1	=	US$1.51

Exchanging Money

The National Bank of Alaska (NBA) is the largest bank in the state, with offices in most towns on the heavily traveled routes. The NBA can meet the needs of most visitors, including changing currency. Though opening hours vary from branch to branch, you can usually count on it being open 10 am to 3 pm Monday to Friday, with evening hours on Wednesday and Friday.

Cash Cash works. It may not be the safest way to carry funds, but nobody will hassle you when you purchase something with US dollars. Most businesses along the Alcan in Canada will also take US dollars, and to a lesser degree, many merchants in Alaska will accept Canadian money. Keep in mind, however, they often burn you on the exchange rate.

Traveler's Checks Other ways to carry your funds include the time-honored method of traveler's checks. The popular brands of US traveler's checks, such as American Express and VISA, are widely used around the state and will be readily cashed at any store, motel or bank in the major tourist areas of Alaska.

ATMs Pack along your ATM card from home to access ATMs in Alaska. The NBA, which has offices throughout the state, is connected to both the Plus and Cirrus ATM networks. Chances are that any bank in the USA is connected to one or the other.

Credit Cards Probably some stores or hotels in some isolated Bush communities somewhere in Alaska don't accept any type of credit card, but not many. Like in the rest of the USA, Alaskan merchants are ready and willing to accept just about all major credit cards. Visa and MasterCard are the most widely accepted cards, but American Express and Discover are not far behind. In short, having some plastic money is good security for the unexpected on any major trip, and some travelers say it's now even better to take a credit card than haul a wad of traveler's checks.

International Transfers You can also have money wired to Alaska from more than 100 countries through Western Union. Money transfers can also be sent and usually received in 15 minutes at any Western Union branch office in the state. If you're in Alaska, call ☎ 800-325-6000 to locate the nearest office and a complete list of services.

On the Hike

Once on the trail, there is little use for money as there often nothing to purchase.

Due to a lack of large cities and its small population, Alaska is a relatively safe place in terms of carrying your money, credit cards and traveler's checks. This includes the wilderness areas and national parks. When you are hiking, you should be more concerned with keeping your money and other important papers dry than having them stolen. Use a heavy resealable plastic bag to safeguard funds from foul weather.

Costs

Alaskans use the same currency as the rest of the USA, American dollars, only they tend to use a little more of it. The state is traditionally known for having the highest cost of living in the country, though places like Southern California, San Francisco and New York City have caught up with Alaska, if not surpassed it. There are two reasons for the high prices in Alaska: the long distances needed to transport everything and the high cost of labor.

A rule of thumb for Alaskan prices is that they are lowest in Ketchikan and increase gradually as you go north. Overall, the Southeast is generally cheaper than most places in the Interior or elsewhere because barge transport from Seattle (the supply center for the area) is only one to two days away. Anchorage, and to a lesser extent Fairbanks, are the exceptions to the rule, as they have competitive prices due to their large populations and business communities. Anchorage, which also receives most of its goods on oceangoing barges, can be extremely affordable if you live there, outrageous if you are a tourist. Gas prices often hover around $1.20 a gallon, and apples in a supermarket could cost less than 90¢ a pound. But it's hard to find a motel room under $80, and the price of other tourist-related services, such as taxis and restaurants, seems to be inflated as well.

Outside of Anchorage, a loaf of bread will cost $2 to $2.50, a can of tuna fish 90¢ to $1.60, apples from $1.50 to $2 per pound and hamburger anywhere from $2 per pound in the large cities to over $4 per pound in outlying communities. Generally, the cost of dairy products, even in Anchorage, will get you to swear off them forever, or at least until the end of your trip. A gallon of milk will be priced anywhere from $4 to over $5 (in Bettles, it will cost $8). The cost of gas here is surprisingly reasonable, far cheaper than it is in Canada. A gallon in Anchorage will cost anywhere from $1.30 to $1.40, and in many secondary cities, such as Seward and Valdez, gas will cost $1.60 or so. Only at some deserted station will you pay more than $2.50 a gallon. A single in the cheapest motels or hotels costs $60 to $70. Many state and federal campgrounds charge $6 to $10 per tent site, and privately owned campgrounds charge anywhere from $12 to $20 a night.

When entering remote parks, be prepared: Stock up on supplies before reaching such places as McCarthy in the Wrangell–St Elias National Park or even Denali National Park. You'll save a bundle by hauling in a week's worth of Lipton noodle dinners, instant oatmeal and a six-pack of beer.

Tipping & Bargaining

Tipping in Alaska, like in the rest of the USA, is expected. The going rate for restaurants, hotels and taxi drivers is about 15%. Bargaining is not accepted when purchasing items in stores in Alaska.

Taxes & Refunds

There is no national sales tax in the USA and no state sales tax in Alaska, but individual cities and boroughs are allowed to have a city sales tax. They might also have a bed tax used to support local tourist bureaus. When both taxes are applied to your hotel bill, it can raise the price anywhere from 4% to a whopping 11.5% in Ketchikan.

Canada does have a national sales tax called the Goods and Services Tax (GST), but travelers are often eligible for a rebate on certain purchases and short-term accommodations, like motel rooms. The purchase must be for a minimum of C$100 to qualify for the refund. Check with customs officials at the border for more information or refund forms.

POST & COMMUNICATIONS
Post

Planning to write home or to friends? Send your mail 1st class by sticking a 33¢ stamp on the envelope or by using a 50¢ aerogram for overseas destinations. For travelers, especially those from overseas tripping through Canada into Alaska, it's best to wait until you're in the USA to mail home packages. Generally, you'll find the US postal service is half as expensive and twice as fast as its Canadian counterpart. Don't send packages from Alaska, however, since surface mail can take up to a month moving to or from Alaska.

To receive mail while traveling in Alaska, have it sent c/o General Delivery to any post office that has its own five-digit zip (postal) code. Although everybody passes through Anchorage (zip code 99501), it's probably better to have mail sent to smaller towns like Juneau (99801), Ketchikan (99901), Seward (99664), Tok (99780) or Delta Junction (99737). Post offices are supposed to keep letters for 30 days before returning them, although smaller places may keep letters longer, especially if your letters have 'Please Hold Forever!!' written on the front in big red crayon. If you are planning to stay at hostels, theirs are the best addresses to leave with letter writers.

Telephone

Telephone area codes are simple in Alaska: The entire state shares ☎ 907, except Hyder, which uses ☎ 604.

Every little town and village in Alaska has public pay phones that you can use to call home if you have a phone card or a stack of quarters. There's a wide range of international and local phone cards. For local calls, you're usually better off with a local card. These cards are sold in amounts of $5, $10 and $20 and are available at airports, in many drugstores or at shipping companies like Mail Boxes Etc. The best way to make international calls is to first purchase a phone card. Lonely Planet's eKno Communication Card is aimed specifically at travelers and provides cheap international calls, a range of messaging services and free email. You can join online at www.ekno.lonelyplanet.com; to join by phone from the areas covered in this book, dial the relevant registration number. Once you have joined, to use eKno, dial the access number:

country	customer service	access numbers
Lower 48 US States	800-707-0031	800-706-1333
Alaska	800-294-3676	800-318-7039
Canada	800-294-3676	800-808-5773

Fax

Facsimile machines, or 'fax' for short, are very common in Alaska. Within this book, the fax numbers of government offices or businesses are listed right after the phone number. Many lodges, hotels and print shops like Kinko's will also have fax machines for hire, charging a per page price to send or receive faxes.

Email & Internet Access

Alaska is very much a high-tech state and email is very common. Again, email addresses are listed in this book with telephone and fax numbers, and a growing numbers of places, including hostels, coffee shops and libraries, are equipped to send and retrieve email.

INTERNET RESOURCES

Highly computer literate, extremely remote – Alaska was made for the Internet and electronic mail. Small, isolated schools in the Bush were some of the first in the country to get online in the classroom and use the Internet for a peek at the outside world.

As a traveler, you can access a great deal of information about the state if your computer at home is online. You can research your trip, hunt down bargain airfares, book hotels, check on weather conditions or chat with locals and other travelers about the best places to visit (or avoid!). There's no better place for you to start your Web explorations than on the Lonely Planet Web site (www.lonelyplanet.com). Here you'll find succinct summaries on traveling to most places on Earth, postcards from other travelers and the Thorn Tree bulletin board, where you can ask questions before you go or dispense advice when you get back. You can also find travel news and updates to many of our most popular guidebooks, and the subWWWay section links you to the most useful travel resources elsewhere on the Web.

Although many Alaskan Web pages are university and government sites, a large number are dedicated to travel in the state. The State of Alaska maintains a large Web site (www.state.ak.us/) that includes a link to its Division of Tourism, where you can use its vacation planner or click into a listing of more than 200 B&Bs. One of the most interesting features of the Web site is the Alaska Communities Online section, which has Web pages for more than 100 towns, from Anchorage to Eagle. The Alaska Tourism Marketing Council (www.travelalaska.com) maintains its own page

Backpacking in the New Millennium

Some say hiking and backpacking in the new millennium will mean using digitized, interactive mapping on computers. If so, the future has arrived. In recent years, mapping companies have begun marketing computerized programs in which a single compact disc holds hundreds of topographical maps. But digital mapping is more than just a topo on the screen of your computer. The base map that they digitize is often the same USGS quad that you can purchase for $4. And the accompanying software, called a 'map engine,' makes the program interactive and allows you to customize a map for an upcoming hike.

One of the leaders in the field of digital maps is Maptech. The New Hampshire–based software company has now produced a series of CDs that cover all 54 national parks in the US, including the eight in Alaska: Denali, Gates of the Arctic, Katmai, Kenai Fjords, Kobuk Valley, Lake Clark, Wrangell–St Elias and Glacier Bay.

Each CD begins with an overview map of the park. Tools then allow you to zoom in to four levels of detail, the most detailed being the scale of 1:24,000, at which 2½ inches on paper equals a mile on the ground. With a mouse, you can mark a route along the park's trail system, and the map engine will inform you how many miles you'll be hiking and the elevation gained each day. Click the Profile button to see a cross section of the terrain and just how steep the climb will be.

The Place Finder tool allows you to type in the name of any creek, lake, campground, trail or swamp, and the map engine will automatically find and display it. You can mark a route, print the sections you need and then grab your boots, backpack and compass.

Or you can forget the compass. Most digital mapping programs can be integrated with a global positioning system (GPS) unit. You mark a route on your digital map and connect your GPS unit to

with similar information. For other useful Internet sites, see 'Exploring Alaska Online' earlier in this chapter.

The Alaskan Center Web site (www .alaskan.com/) features background on the state and bus, ferry, air and train schedules. The Alaskan Center also serves as a link to many other Web pages, including the Juneau Web, Alaskan Visitors and Information Center and the State of Alaska page. The Alaska Internet Travel Guide (www .AlaskaOne.com) includes lists of accommodations throughout the state, many guide companies and links to the Alaska Railroad, Alaska Marine Highway and bus companies such as Seward Bus Lines.

The National Park Service has a Web site (www.nps.gov/parklists/ak.html) for Alaskan parks. From a list of the national park units, you can click on the particular park you're interested in and its Web page will appear. The US Forest Service also maintains a Web site for the Alaska region (www.fs.fed.us/ recreation/states/ak.html), allowing you to access information on trails, rustic cabins, fishing opportunities and wilderness areas in Tongass and Chugach National Forests.

The travel sections of both AOL and CompuServe also have Alaskan message boards and chat rooms and are always popular. Be wary of the information posted, however. A great deal of it is misleading or simply incorrect.

Other Web sites and email addresses will appear throughout this guidebook, allowing you to contact everything from a B&B in Anchorage and a wilderness outfitter in Bettles to Alaska Airlines, all for the cost of a local phone call.

BOOKS

The following publications will aid hikers heading north to Alaska. An increasing number of books today are published in different editions by different publishers in different countries. For that reason, only the

Backpacking in the New Millennium

your computer, and the map engine will then download all the coordinators you'll need to keep from getting lost in the wilderness.

There are some drawbacks. The technology may be new, but the maps being digitized are not. Many of the USGS quads for Alaska were surveyed in the 1950s and 1960s. A bigger concern is printing your customized map. What appears on the screen is not what your $200 ink-jet printer is going to spit out, and neither image will be as sharp as the $4 quad you can purchase at the park headquarters.

But that might be irrelevant. Some day, you won't need a map at all, at least not a paper one. Industry experts predict that some time soon hikers will be packing along a lightweight, palm-sized computer with a built-in GPS receiver. Hikers will be able to stop anywhere along the trail, turn on the computer and immediately see their position on the proper quad. The mapping program will also tell how far away the next campground is and which route is the easiest.

Many of Maptech's National Park Digital Guides show campgrounds, trails and other park features and come with a database of information on the park's history, wildlife and weather. Single parks are $30 each. A set of CDs for all eight Alaskan national parks is $70. To order, call Maptech (☎ 800-627-7236) or check out its Web site (www.maptech.com).

Trails Illustrated, best known for its waterproof hiking maps, is also producing a series of CDs that will cover trails and national parks. The best one in the collection is *The Definitive Alaska* ($140), which includes six national parks and such prime hiking areas as Kachemak Bay State Park, Chugach National Forest and the Chilkoot Trail. Like Maptech, the maps are digitized USGS quads that have been updated and are compatible with most GPS receivers. For more information, call Trails Illustrated (☎ 800-962-1643) or check out its Web site (www.trailsillustrated.com).

title and the author of the following recommendations have been given, but that should be enough to enable any library or bookstore to locate it. A few of the more popular books mentioned can be found in any good bookstore, but many are available only in Alaska.

To obtain them before your trip request a catalog from the Alaska Natural History Association (☎ 907-274-8440), ANHA, Mail Order Services, 605 West 4th Ave, Suite 85, Anchorage, AK 99501, which distributes more than 50 Alaskan titles. Most of the books can also be ordered through Adventurous Traveler Bookstore (☎ 800-282-3963), PO Box 64769, Burlington, VT 05406-4769, or from the company's Web site (www.AdventurousTraveler.com).

Lonely Planet

Alaska, 6th edition, by Jim DuFresne, is Lonely Planet's 520-page guide to visiting Alaska. This comprehensive guidebook has extensive details on accommodations, places to eat, sights, transportation, and activities such as hiking and paddling.

Canada, 6th edition, is Lonely Planet's 970-page guidebook to Canada. The guide includes British Columbia and Yukon Territory, which many travelers pass through to reach Alaska.

Hiking Guidebooks

55 Ways to the Wilderness in Southcentral Alaska, by Helen Nienhueser and John Wolfe, is a hiking guide covering popular trails around the Kenai Peninsula, the Anchorage area and from Palmer to Valdez.

Juneau Trails (Alaska Natural History Association) is a bible for Juneau hikers, describing 26 trails around the capital city – perhaps the best area for hiking in Alaska. The guidebook includes basic maps, distances, rating of the trails and location of trailheads, along with brief descriptions of the route.

Sitka Trails (Alaska Natural History Association) is similar to *Juneau Trails* and covers 30 hiking trails around Sitka and its nearby coastline.

Petersburg Hiking Trails (USFS) is another trail guide for Southeast Alaska. The Petersburg booklet covers more than 20 trails and a handful of portages that kayakers would use when paddling Kuiu Island.

Discover Southeast Alaska with Pack and Paddle, by Margaret Piggott, a longtime guidebook to a dozen water routes and 58 trails of the Southeast, was out of print for years before the author finally updated the first edition in 1990. Its downfall is the weak, hand-drawn maps. Make sure you pack the topos.

Backcountry Companion for Denali National Park, by Jon Nierenberg, is a general guide to wilderness trekking in the popular national park. It's not a trail guide, but rather provides short synopses to each of Denali's backcountry zones to help backpackers pick the right area to travel in.

Katmai, by Jean Bodeau, is a general guide to Katmai National Park on the Alaska Peninsula. It will assist you in understanding this special park and help you arrange a trip here, but it won't necessarily lead you through the Valley of 10,000 Smokes.

Chilkoot Pass, by Archie Satterfield, is a historical guide for hikers following Alaska's most famous gold rush trail. The book includes a mile-by-mile description of the trail and history and stories of every segment of the route that Klondike stampeders followed at the turn of the century.

Travel & Exploration

The Milepost, unquestionably the most popular travel guide, is put out every year. While it has good information, history and maps of Alaska and western Canada, its drawbacks include its large size – at 8 by 11 inches, it is impossible to slip into the side pocket of a backpack – and that its listings of hotels, restaurants and other businesses are limited to advertisers.

The Alaska Wilderness Milepost used to be a slim section in *The Milepost* but is now the most comprehensive guide to Bush Alaska, the parts of Alaska that can't be reached by road. This *Milepost* covers more than 250 remote towns and villages in a much smaller format.

Adventuring in Alaska, by Peggy Wayburn, is a good general guidebook to the many new national parks, wildlife preserves and other remote regions of Alaska. It also contains excellent how-to information on undertaking wilderness expeditions in the state, whether the mode of travel is canoeing, kayaking or hiking.

Alaska's Southeast: Touring the Inside Passage, by Sarah Eppenbach, offers some of the most comprehensive accounts of the Southeast's history and culture, although it lacks detailed travel information.

Alaska's Wilderness Highway, by Mike Jensen, is a guide to traveling the Dalton Hwy, which climbs over the Brooks Range en route to Prudhoe Bay on the Arctic Sea. The book includes a history of the area, a primer for those driving the road and then a mile-by-mile description of the road itself.

Alaska's Parklands, The Complete Guide, by Nancy Simmerman, is the encyclopedia of Alaskan wilderness, covering over 110 state and national parks and wilderness areas. It lacks detailed travel information and guides to individual canoe and hiking routes but does a thorough job of covering the scenery, location and activities available in each preserve.

Alaska Bicycle Touring Guide, by Pete Praetorius and Alys Culhane, is the first guide put together for touring Alaska on two wheels. It's been called the 'bicycling equivalent of *The Milepost*' for its thorough description of routes throughout the state, including two that go north of the Arctic Circle.

Mountain Bike Alaska, by Richard Larson, is a guide to 49 trails for mountain bikers. They range from the Denali Hwy and the Denali park road to many of the traditional hiking trails situated on the Kenai Peninsula.

Natural History

Mammals of Alaska, edited by Penny Rennick, is a well-illustrated, concise and easy-to-carry guide that covers all of the mammals in the 49th state, from bears and beavers to marmots and lemmings. Each animal is discussed in a two-page mini-essay that includes habitat, range, eating habits and the best places for viewing.

Alaska Pocket Guides, by Alaska Northwest Books, are a series of slender pocket guidebooks to a variety of Alaskan species, including bears, birds, mammals, fish, mushrooms and wild plants. Each book includes color photos, natural history about the animals or plants and where to go for wildlife-viewing opportunities.

Roadside Geology of Alaska, by Cathy Connor and Daniel O'Haire, does an excellent job of covering the geology of Alaska you see from the road and explaining how it shaped the state's history and development. Every road and sea route is covered, even dead-end roads in the Southeast. Along the way you learn what happened during the Good Friday Earthquake and why miners turned up gold on the beaches of Nome – not dull reading by any means.

Alaska Wildlife Viewing Guide, by Michelle Sydeman and Annabell Lund, is a slender volume that briefly describes 68 places in the state to watch wildlife. The various sites were selected by state, federal and other wildlife experts in Alaska.

To ornithologists, Alaska is the ultimate destination. More than 400 species of birds have been spotted in the state, and the above guide has information on identification, distribution and habitat of 335 of them. Along with text, *Guide to the Birds of Alaska,* by Robert H Armstrong, contains color photographs of the species, drawings and a bird checklist.

A Guide to Alaskan Seabirds (Alaska Natural History Association) is a thin guide to the birds that thrive in coastal Alaska. It has excellent drawings for easy identification.

Alaska-Yukon Wild Flowers Guide, edited by Helen A White, uses both illustrations and color photos to help you identify what's blooming.

Wildflowers along the Alaska Highway, written by Verna Pratt for the amateur botanist, has species keyed by color and includes 497 color photographs and a checklist for each 300mi section of the road.

Wild, Edible & Poisonous Plants of Alaska, by Dr Christine Heller, is an excellent companion on any hike, as it contains both drawings and color photos of Alaskan flora, including edible plants, berries and wildflowers.

Animal Tracks of Alaska, by Chris Stall, is a must for any traveler who plans to do a fair amount of hiking or beachcombing in Alaska. You'll see wildlife tracks everywhere.

WEATHER INFORMATION

Before your trip or while you're in Alaska you can call the National Weather Service Weather Line (☎ 907-458-3745, 800-472-0391) for both an immediate and long-range forecast in different regions of the state. You can also use the Internet. The Anchorage Daily News (www.adn.com) will have a blurb on the conditions in Anchorage, but for a statewide weather forecast go to a meteorological Web site like Weather Underground (www.wunderground.com).

PHOTOGRAPHY
Film & Equipment

The most cherished items you can take home from your trip are pictures and slides of Alaska's powerful scenery. Much of the state is a photographer's dream, and your shutter finger will be tempted by mountain and glacier panoramas, bustling waterfronts and the diverse wildlife encountered during paddling and hiking trips. Even if you have never toted a camera before, seriously consider taking one to Alaska.

A small, fixed-lens, point-and-shoot 35mm camera is OK for a summer of backpacking in the North Country. For a step up, however, purchase a 35mm camera with a built-in zoom lens. The Nikon Lite-Touch 110 is such a camera, providing a lens that zooms from a 38mm-wide angle to a 110mm telephoto. The camera is still compact and easy to use but will greatly increase your variety of shots.

If you want to get serious about photography, you need a full 35mm camera with a couple of interchangeable lenses and maybe even a second body. To photograph wildlife in its natural state, a 135mm or larger telephoto lens is needed to make the animal the main object in the picture. Any lens larger than 135mm will probably also require a tripod to eliminate camera shake, especially during low-light conditions. A wide-angle lens of 35mm, or better still 28mm, adds considerable dimension to scenic views, and a fast (f1.2 or f1.4) 50mm 'normal' lens will provide you with more opportunities for pictures during weak light. If you want simplicity, check out today's zoom lenses. They are much smaller and compact than they have been in the past and provide a sharpness that's more than acceptable to most amateur photographers. A zoom from 35mm to 105mm would be ideal. And keep in mind the rainy weather that you'll encounter on your trip; a waterproof camera bag is an excellent investment, especially if a great deal of your time will be spent in the woods.

Photographers find that Kodachrome ISO 64 or Fujichrome ISO 100 (older cameras and film refer to ASA, but the ASA number is the same as the ISO number) are the best all-around films for slides, especially when you're photographing glaciers or snowfields where the reflection off the ice and snow is strong. A few rolls of high-speed film (ISO 200 or 400) are handy for nature photography, as the majority of wildlife will be encountered at dusk and dawn, periods of low light. For print film, try to use Kodak Select series Royal Gold 100 or 200 or Fujicolor 100.

Bring all your own film if possible; in the large Alaskan cities and towns, film will generally be priced around $9 to $11 for a roll of Kodachrome (36 exposures), and in smaller communities you may have a hard time finding the type of film you want.

Technical Tips

If you take enough shots, you're bound to end up with a few good ones, but here are a few tips to shooting better pictures in Alaska:

- Take time to compose your shots; don't just point and shoot. Experiment with different distances and angles – vertical, horizontal or from the ground shooting up.

- Get close to your subject and avoid what professional photographers call middle-distance shots: photos with too much foreground and clutter.

- Be aware that the best light for the most vivid colors is just after sunrise and before sunset. Shooting at midday, with its harsh light, is not as bad in Alaska as it would be in a place like Arizona, but you still want to take advantage of late afternoon sunlight.

- If shadows are inevitable, make use of your flash (even in daytime) to brighten objects in the shade. You might also consider bracketing your photos, by reducing or adding to the exposure time over several frames, to ensure that one picture is at the right setting. Remember that film is cheap when compared to the cost of your trip to Alaska.

- Don't try to hold a camera for an exposure time longer than the focal length of your camera. If you're shooting with a 200mm lens, any exposure longer than $\frac{1}{200}$ second will require a tripod. Consider purchasing a mini-tripod for the trip, one that will easily fit into a side pocket of a backpack but features a Velcro strap so you can attach the tripod to a tree for an extended exposure or self-portrait.

Airport Security

When flying to and around Alaska, pack your film in your carry-on luggage and have the airport security person visually inspect it. Security personnel at US airports are required by law to honor such requests and are usually very accommodating if you have the film out and ready. I've only met a handful who made me uncap all 48 rolls of film I was hauling along. Airport X-ray machines are supposed to be safe for film, but why take the chance? Remember the higher the film speed, the more susceptible the film is to damage by X rays.

TIME

With the exception of several Aleutian Island communities and Hyder, a small community on the Alaska/British Columbia border, the entire state shares the same time zone, Alaska Time, which is one hour earlier than Pacific Standard Time – the zone in which Seattle, Washington, falls. When it is noon in Anchorage, it is 9 pm in London, 4 pm in New York and 7 am the following day in Melbourne, Australia.

ELECTRICITY

Voltage in Alaska is 110V – the same as everywhere else in the USA. The plugs have two (flat) or three (two flat, one round) pins. Plugs with three pins don't fit into a two-hole socket, but adapters are easy to buy at hardware or drugstores.

WEIGHTS & MEASURES

In the USA, distances are in feet (ft), yards (yd) and miles (mi). Three feet equal 1yd (.914m); 1760yd or 5280ft equal 1mi. Dry weights are in ounces (oz), pounds (lb) and tons (16oz are 1lb; 2000lb are 1 ton), but liquid measures differ from dry measures. One pint equals 16 fluid oz; 2 pints equal 1 quart, a common measure for liquids like milk, which is also sold in half gallons (2 quarts) and gallons (4 quarts). The US gallon is about 20% less than the imperial gallon. Pints and quarts are also 20% less than the imperial measure. There is a conversion chart on the inside back cover of this book.

LAUNDRY

Virtually every town with more than 100 residents in Alaska has a Laundromat, the place to go to clean your clothes or take a shower. A small load of clothes is going to cost at least $3, plus you'll need another $1 to dry your clothes in the dryer. A shower and clean towel costs around $3. Many hostels and a motels also provide laundry facilities for a fee.

BUSINESS HOURS

Banks and post offices in Alaska are generally open 9 am to 5 pm Monday to Friday. Other business hours are variable, but many shops are open 9 am to 10 pm during the week, 10 am to 6 pm Saturday and noon to 5 pm Sunday.

Most national and state park visitor centers are open daily June to September but will have drastically reduced hours before and after the summer tourist season.

PUBLIC HOLIDAYS

Alaskans do their fair share of celebrating, much of it during the summer. One of the biggest celebrations in the state is the summer solstice on June 21, the longest day of the year. Fairbanks holds the best community festival, with a variety of events, including midnight baseball games (played without the use of artificial light) and hikes to local hills to view the midnight sun. Nome stages a weeklong Midnight Sun Festival, and Barrow stages a 'sun will not set for 83 days' festival. If you are in Anchorage or the Kenai Peninsula, head over to Moose Pass for its Summer Solstice Festival, where the barbecued chicken dinner alone is worth the trip.

Independence Day (July 4) is a popular holiday around the state. The larger communities of Ketchikan, Juneau, Anchorage and Fairbanks sponsor well-planned events. Perhaps even more enjoyable during this time of year is a visit to a small settlement such as Gustavus, Seldovia or McCarthy, where you cannot help but be swept along with the local residents in an afternoon of old-fashioned celebrating that usually ends with a square dance in the evening.

Salmon and halibut derbies that end with cash prizes for the heaviest fish caught are regular events around the coastal regions of Alaska, with Juneau and Seward having the largest. Although most travelers are ill-prepared to compete in such fishing contests, watching the boats returning to the marina with their catch makes for an interesting afternoon.

State fairs, though small compared to those in the Lower 48, are worth attending if for no other reason than to see what a 70lb cabbage, a 20lb stalk of celery or a 200lb pumpkin looks like. The fairs all take place in August and include the Alaska State Fair at Palmer, the Tanana Valley Fair at Fairbanks, the Southeast State Fair at Haines and smaller ones at Kodiak, Delta Junction and Ninilchik.

State & National Holidays

Public holidays for Alaska include the following:

New Year's Day January 1

Martin Luther King Day Third Monday in January

Presidents' Day Third Monday in February

Seward's Day Last Monday in March

Easter Sunday in late March or early April

Memorial Day Last Monday in May

Independence Day July 4

Labor Day First Monday in September

Columbus Day Second Monday in October

Alaska Day October 18

Veterans' Day November 11

Thanksgiving Day Fourth Thursday in November

Christmas Day December 25

ACCOMMODATIONS
In Cities & Towns

When booking a room at a B&B, hotel, lodge or even a hostel, you will most likely be hit with a city tax and possibly a bed tax. Almost every town of any size in Alaska has these taxes, ranging from as low as 4% to as high as 9% for both city tax and bed tax in Seward and 11.5% in Ketchikan. Bed prices in this book do not include the taxes, but towns with the highest taxes are clearly noted.

Camping Bring a tent. Then you will never be without inexpensive accommodations in Alaska. Alaska doesn't have cheap B&Bs like those in Europe, and the number of hostels is limited, but there are state, federal and private campgrounds from Ketchikan to Fairbanks. Nightly fees range from $6 for the walk-in Morino Campground in Denali National Park to $25 to park your 30ft RV in some of the more deluxe private campgrounds. It is also a widely accepted practice among backpackers to just wander into the woods and find a spot to pitch a tent. With the exception of Anchorage, Fairbanks and

a few other cities, you can walk a mile or so from most towns and find yourself in an isolated wooded area.

Hostels The Alaska Council of American Youth Hostels has 10 hostels scattered around the state that are stable, having been in operation for years at the same location. The mainstays of the system are the hostels in Anchorage, Juneau, Ketchikan, Delta Junction and Tok. The first hostel you check into is the best source of information on which hostels are open and which need reservations in advance. You should always plan on reserving your bed at Anchorage, Juneau and Ketchikan.

The hostels range from a huge house in Juneau (four blocks from the capitol building) with a common room with a fireplace, cooking facilities and showers to a church basement in Ketchikan. Perhaps the most important hostel for many budget travelers is the Anchorage International Hostel, which is now closer to the city center and the bus terminal.

The hostel fees are $10 for members for a one-night stay and $20 for nonmembers. Some hostels accept reservations and others don't; each hostel's particulars will be discussed later in this guide. Be aware that hostelling means separate male and female dormitories, house parents, chores assigned for each day you stay and curfews. Also, the hostels are closed during the day – even when it rains. The hostels are strict about these and other rules. No smoking, drinking or illegal drugs are allowed. Still, hostels are the best bargains for accommodations in Alaska and the best place to meet other budget travelers and backpackers. For more information on Alaska's hostels before you depart on your trip, write or call Hostelling International – Anchorage (☎ 907-276-3635), 700 H St, Anchorage, AK 99501-3417, or visit its Web site at www.alaska.net/~hianch.

Alaska also finally has some offbeat backpackers' hostels that offer cheap accommodations, without all the rules and regulations of an official youth hostel. More than 20 backpacker hostels are scattered from Haines and Homer to Anchorage, the

Denali Park area and Talkeetna. Fairbanks alone has six. Rates range from $12 to $25 per person.

B&Bs Some B&Bs are in small, out-of-the-way communities such as Angoon, Gustavus, McCarthy or Talkeetna, where staying in a private home can be a unique and interesting experience. All recommend making reservations in advance, but it is often possible, in cities like Anchorage, Juneau and Fairbanks where there are many B&Bs, to obtain a bed the day you arrive by calling around. Many visitor centers now have sections devoted entirely to the B&Bs in their area and even courtesy phones for booking a room. Details about B&Bs will be covered in the regional chapters. You can also contact the following B&B reservation services to book rooms in advance of your trip:

Southeast Alaska
Bed & Breakfast Association of Alaska (☎ 907-789-8822), PO Box 22800, Juneau, AK 99802 Web site: www.wetpage.com/bbaaip
Ketchikan Reservation Service (☎ 800-987-5337), 412 D-1 Loop Rd, Ketchikan, AK 99901

Anchorage & Southcentral
Alaska Available (☎ 907-337-3414, ✉ akavailable@juno.com), 1325 O St, Anchorage, AK 99501
Alaska Private Lodging (☎ 907-258-1717, ✉ apl@alaska.net), 704 W 2nd Ave, Anchorage, AK 99520-0047; send $5 for a descriptive directory
Alaska Sourdough B&B Association (☎ 907-563-6244, ✉ aksbba@alaska.net), 889 Cardigan Circle, Anchorage, AK 99503-7027
Mat-Su Chapter of Bed and Breakfast Association of Alaska (☎ 800-401-7444, ✉ akhosts@alaska.net), PO Box 873507, Wasilla, AK 99687-3507

Fairbanks
Fairbanks Bed & Breakfast (☎ 907-452-7700), PO Box 73334, Fairbanks, AK 99707-3334

Hotels Hotels and motels are the most expensive lodgings you can book. Although there are a few bargains, the average single room in an 'inexpensive' hotel costs $50 to $60, and a double costs $60 to $70 (these are the places down by the waterfront with shared bathrooms). Better hotels will even be close to $100 for a double, and Anchorage's best places exceed $200 per night.

The other problem with hotels and motels is that they tend to be full during much of the summer. Without being part of a tour or having advance reservations, you may have to search for an available bed in some cities. In small villages, you could be out of luck, as they may only have one or two places to choose from.

Wilderness Lodges These are off the beaten path and usually require a bush plane or boat to reach them. The vast majority of places need advance booking and offer rustic cabins with saunas and ample opportunities to explore the nearby area by foot, canoe or kayak (they provide the boats). The lodges are designed for people who want to 'escape into the wilderness' without having to endure the 'hardship' of a tent, freeze-dried dinners or a small camp stove. The prices range from $150 to $250 per person per day and include all meals.

On the Hike
Campgrounds Some trails begin or end along campgrounds that can be reached by vehicles and usually feature drinking water, toilets, tables and fire grills.

Free-Use Shelters Free-use shelters can be three-sided shelters, old miner's huts or new, completely enclosed cabins with windows and woodstove. Shelters vary greatly but are used on a first-come, first-served basis. In many areas, such as on the Pinnell Mountain Trail, the shelters are designed as emergency shelters during foul weather and as escapes from the wind when cooking. They are not free lodging for the night. Even if there is a shelter on the trail, you should always plan on packing along a tent.

Backcountry Campsites Some trails, like Resurrection Pass or the Historic Iditarod Trail, have posted campsites, which may feature tent pads and fire grills.

Backcountry Camping In the backcountry, sites are not posted and there are no facilities such as tables, fire rings or vault toilets (outhouses). Take your time when searching for a spot to pitch a tent in the wilderness. Throughout much of Alaska, especially the Interior, sandbars are the best places to pitch a tent. Strips of sand or small gravel patches along rivers provide good drainage and a smoother surface on which to pitch a tent than tussock grass.

Take time to check out the area before unpacking your gear. Avoid animal trails (whether the tracks be moose or bear), areas with bear scat and berry patches with ripe fruit. In late summer, stay away from streams choked with salmon runs.

In the Southeast and other coastal areas of Alaska, search out beaches and ridges with southern exposures; they provide the driest conditions in these rainy zones. Old glacier and stream outwashes (sand or gravel deposits) make ideal campsites as long as you stay well above the high-tide line. Look for the last ridge of seaweed and debris on the shore and then pitch your tent another 20 to 30yd above that to avoid waking up with salt water flooding your tent. Tidal fluctuations along Alaska's coast are among the largest in the world – up to 30ft in some places.

Cabins Built and maintained by the US Forest Service, these cabins are scattered throughout the Tongass National Forest (practically the entire Southeast), the Chugach National Forest on the Kenai Peninsula and in Prince William Sound. For the most part, the cabins are rustic log cabins or A-frames with woodstoves, plywood bunks, pit toilets and often a rowboat if the cabins are on a lake.

Some of the cabins can be reached by hiking. In Chugach National Forest, trails covered in this guidebook that have rental cabins include the Resurrection Pass, Russian Lakes, Lost Lake and Historic Iditarod Trails. In Tongass National Forest, Deer Mountain, Petersburg Creek, Dan Moller, Mt Edgecombe, Amalga, Upper Dewey Lake and Laughton Glacier Trails feature cabins.

Most USFS cabins require arranging a bush plane or chartered boat to drop you off and then return for you. Staying in the cabins is an ideal way to sneak into the woods and separate yourself from the world without having to undertake rigorous backcountry travel.

During the summer, the cabins are heavily used by both locals and travelers, and stays are limited to seven consecutive nights per party, or three days for hike-in cabins.

The cabins provide excellent shelter from bad weather, but you have to bring your own bedding (sleeping bag and ground pad), food and cooking gear, including a small backpacker's stove for when the woodpile is wet. Other items that come in handy are insect repellent, matches, candles, a water filter and a topographic map of the surrounding area.

Of the 190 USFS public-use cabins, almost 150 of them are in the Southeast and are accessible from Ketchikan, Petersburg, Juneau or Sitka. If you haven't made reservations but have a flexible schedule, it is still possible to rent a cabin. During the summer, USFS offices in the Southeast maintain lists of the cabins and dates still available. A few cabins are usually available for a couple of days in the middle of the week, although they will most likely be the remote ones requiring more flying time (and thus money) to reach.

USFS cabins cost $25 to $40 per night to rent but can comfortably hold parties of six or more people. You can reserve the cabins 180 days in advance by calling the National Recreation Reservation Service (☎ 877-444-6777, 518-885-3639 for international calls) or through its Web site (www.reserveusa.com). For a reservation less than 20 days in advance, you need a credit card to secure the booking. For dates more than 20 days out, you may use a credit card, money order or a cashier's check.

Once in Alaska, you can reserve the cabins through Forest Service visitor centers and district offices. Addresses and phone numbers for these offices are listed in the regional chapters. For a complete list and description of cabins, check out the Alaska Region Web site for the USFS (www.fs .fed.us/r10/) and then click on either Tongass or Chugach National Forest on the map.

For the Tongass National Forest, you can also write to the following USFS offices in Alaska, which will forward a booklet describing each cabin in its district, along with details about the surrounding terrain and the best way to travel to the cabin.

Forest Service Information Center (☎ 907-586-8751), 101 Egan Drive, Juneau, AK 99801
Southeast Alaska Visitor Center (☎ 907-228-6214), 50 Main St, Ketchikan, AK 99901
Web site: www.ktn.net/usfs/ketchikan/

The Chugach National Forest in Southcentral Alaska has 40 cabins. For a complete list of cabins and for bookings in the Chugach National Forest, write to the following Alaska Public Lands Information Center or USFS district offices in Alaska:

Alaska Public Lands Information Center
(☎ 907-271-2737), 605 W 4th Ave, Suite 105, Anchorage, AK 99501-5162
Cordova Ranger District (☎ 907-424-7661), PO Box 280, Cordova, AK 99574
Seward Ranger District (☎ 907-224-3374), PO Box 390, Seward, AK 99664

The BLM, USFWS and the Alaska Division of Parks also maintain rustic cabins in remote areas. There are 17 state parks and recreation areas with cabins, from Point Bridget in Juneau to Chena River near Fairbanks. Trails described in this book with state park cabins include Chena Dome Trail near Fairbanks and Kachemak Bay State Park and Caines Head State Recreation Area in the Kenai Peninsula. State park cabins rent for $35 to $50 per night and are rented through any state park office or the DNR Public Information Center. For descriptions of cabins in advance, contact the DNR Public Information Center (☎ 907-269-8400), 3601 C St, Suite 200, Anchorage,

AK 99503-5929, or check its Web site (www.dnr.state.ak.us/parks/).

The BLM has nine cabins in the White Mountain National Recreational Area north of Fairbanks. The cabins cost $20 a night. Contact White Mountain National Recreation Area (☎ 907-474-2200, 800-437-7021), 1150 University Ave, Fairbanks, AK 99709-3899, or check out the BLM Web site (www.ak.blm.gov/WhiteMtns/).

FOOD
Local Food
While shopping for your trail food, keep an eye out for fresh Alaskan seafood, especially in Southeast and Southcentral markets. Local seafood is not cheap, but it is renowned throughout the country for its superb taste. The most common catches are king salmon steaks, at $10 per pound and halibut fillets, at $6 per pound. Whole Dungeness crabs cost $4 to $5 per pound, and prawns cost $9 to $10 per pound. The larger markets will also have smoked salmon and cooked king crab.

Fast-food restaurants are usually the cheapest restaurants in Alaskan towns. Alaska is no longer so remote that the US fast-food restaurants have not reached it. Back in the late 1970s, only Anchorage and Fairbanks had a McDonald's franchise. Now you can order a Big Mac in Ketchikan, Juneau and Kodiak, Homer and Eagle River, and other chains, such as Pizza Hut, Burger King, Wendy's and Taco Bell, are almost as widespread. There is even a Burger King in Nome.

Another option for those on a budget are the large supermarket chains: Carrs, Fred Meyer and Safeway. Most of them have espresso bars, bakeries, counters serving ready-to-eat items and hot soup, salad bars and dining areas. Salad and soup is priced around $3.50 a pound.

The smaller towns you pass through will usually have a local coffee shop or cafe. Breakfast, which many places serve all day, is the best bargain; a plate of eggs, toast and hash browns will cost $5 to $7, and a cup of coffee will cost 75¢ to $1.

An influx of Asian people immigrating to Alaska has resulted in most midsize towns having at least one Chinese restaurant, if not two. Some towns, like Homer (population 3900), support three. Many of these places have a lunch buffet that runs from 11 am to 3 pm or so and is an all-you-can-eat affair that costs $7 to $10. Eat a late lunch here, and you can make it through to breakfast the next morning.

One popular eating event during the summer in most of the state, but especially the Southeast, is the salmon bake. The salmon is caught locally, grilled, smothered with somebody's home-made barbecue sauce and often served all-you-can-eat-style. A dinner costs $15 to $20, but it is worth trying at least once. One of the best bakes is at Alaskaland in Fairbanks.

On the Hike

The food you eat while backpacking needs to be filling, nourishing and lightweight. It also needs to cook quickly. The overwhelming majority of hikers in Alaska carry a small stove (see What to Bring, earlier in this chapter) to prepare meals. If every dish needs to simmer for 30 or 40 minutes, you are going to have to carry a lot of fuel.

For any hike under a week in length, you don't need to outfit your food bag exclusively with pricey freeze-dried meal packets that can be prepared with very little simmering time, but when selecting noodle dinners, hot cereals and other staples, choose those with a cooking time of 10 minutes or less.

Instant hot cereals, such as Quaker Instant Oatmeal and Cream of Wheat, along with dried fruit and instant coffee or tea are excellent for breakfast. Such a menu is lightweight and quick to prepare but will get you going in the morning and keep your stomach from growling before lunch.

You can create quick lunches from hard cheeses, canned meat spreads (Spreadables) or peanut butter on crackers, bagels or pocket bread. Round out the meal with a variety of dried fruits (raisins, peaches, apricots), trail mix (nuts, raisins, M&Ms; commonly called 'gorp') and a packet of

Kool-Aid that will make 2 quarts of flavored drink. Keep your lunch bag at the top of your pack for easy access, along with trail snacks, such as chocolate or hard candy, that will give you an instant energy boost while hiking.

Dinner should be hot and substantial. Instant soup is an excellent starter, and you can eat it while you wait for something else to cook. Cup-A-Soup is a common choice, but many new gourmet instant soups are on the market. Try any of the flavors by Knorr or Harvest Valley.

Rice, noodle or macaroni dinners (Rice-A-Roni, Kraft) make good entrees. Most require less than 2 cups of water and cook in as little as five minutes. If you're hauling a block of cheese for lunch, toss a few slices in your noodle dinner for a rich, thick sauce. Top off the meal with a pot of instant pudding or a quick-cooking custard and a mug of hot chocolate.

Don't forget to pack any ingredient you might need to prepare a meal: butter, dry milk, oil or brown sugar. Also carry a few extra packets of noodle soups such as Ramen, just in case you get stuck out in the backcountry longer than planned.

Buying Food You'll be able to stock up for your next hike in supermarkets in every major town. Occasionally, fresh fruits, vegetables and dairy products might be limited or simply unavailable in small, remote towns, but there will always be a good stock of dried and canned food. The major chains (Carrs, Safeway, Fred Meyer) have bulk food sections, where you can purchase as much or as little as you need of everything from raisins and instant cereal to trail mix and dried milk.

DRINKS
Coffee

The coffee craze that began in Seattle and the Northwest has extended into Alaska. Espresso shops are everywhere – even in towns as small as McCarthy, you can find somebody with an espresso machine. In the cities, especially Anchorage, there are dozens of these places plus drive-through espresso shops so you can enjoy a latte without even getting out of the car. Alaskans take their coffee seriously.

Alcoholic Drinks

The legal drinking age in Alaska is 21 years, and only the churches outnumber the bars. Except for 70 Native Alaskan towns that are dry (alcohol is prohibited) or that are damp (the sale of alcohol is prohibited), finding an open bar or liquor store is never very difficult. That and the long, dark winters explain why Alaska has the highest alcoholism rate in the USA, especially among the indigenous people. Bar hours vary, but there are always a few places that open their doors at 9 am and don't close until 5 am. All bars serve the usual US beer found in the Northwest (Miller, Rainier) and usually one or two places have that fine Canadian brew, which is darker and richer than US beer, costing around $4 for a 12oz bottle. Alaska also has a growing number of microbreweries, the largest being Juneau's Alaskan Brewing Co. Its Alaska Ambler is now seen all over the state and sold in stores for around $8 a six-pack.

Health & Safety

Camping, hiking and backpacking in Alaska are more dangerous than in most other places. The weather is more unpredictable, the climate harsher, and encounters with wildlife a frequent occurrence. Unpredictable situations such as getting lost, snowstorms in the middle of the summer or being 'socked in' by low clouds and fog for days while waiting for a bush plane happen annually to hundreds of backpackers in Alaska. This is not intended to alarm. With proper precautions and knowledge of potential hazards, thousands of hikers enjoy safe and healthy hiking adventures in Alaska each year.

Predeparture Planning

HEALTH INSURANCE
Alaska is largely a clean, healthy, disease-free state, and medical attention is of high quality, even in the Bush. But the cost of health care in the USA is extremely high, and Alaska is no exception. A travel insurance policy to cover theft, loss and medical problems is therefore a wise idea. A wide variety of policies are available, and your travel agent will have recommendations. See the Facts for the Hiker chapter for some details. The international student travel policies handled by the Student Travel Association (STA) or other student travel organizations are usually a good value. Some policies offer lower and higher medical expense options, but the higher option is chiefly for countries like the USA, which have extremely high medical costs. Check the small print.

IMMUNIZATIONS
There are no vaccination requirements to enter the USA. No matter where you are, it's always a good idea to keep your tetanus immunization up to date – boosters are necessary every 10 years – but even this is not strictly required.

HIKING HEALTH GUIDES
Numerous health guides on the market today are geared toward hiking and wilderness travel. *Wilderness 911,* by Eric Weiss, MD, is a guidebook for medical emergencies and care in the backcountry with an easy-to-follow format. The drawback is its size; 240 pages is a lot to haul around. *First Aid Pamphlet: Quick Information for Mountaineering and Backcountry Use,* by Mountaineer Books, is much smaller. This 36-page reference guide covers basics and life-threatening emergencies and costs less than $2.

Staying Healthy

NUTRITION
If your food is poor or limited in availability, if you're traveling hard and fast and therefore missing meals, or if you simply lose your appetite, you can soon start to lose weight and place your health at risk.

Make sure your diet is well balanced on and off the trail. Beans, lentils, nuts and peanut butter are all good ways to get protein while hiking. Fruit you can peel (bananas, oranges or mandarins, for example) is safe and a good source of vitamins but doesn't travel well in a backpack. Toss a few apples in the pack or carry dried fruit. Try to eat plenty of grains (including rice and oatmeal) and bread. If your diet isn't well balanced or if your food intake is insufficient, it's a good idea to take vitamin and iron pills.

Make sure you drink enough on hot days or while exercising heavily – don't rely on feeling thirsty to indicate when you should drink. Not needing to urinate or small amounts of very dark yellow urine are danger signs. Always carry a water bottle with you on long trips. Excessive sweating can lead to salt loss and therefore muscle cramping. Salt tablets are not a good idea as a preventative, but in places where salt is not used much, adding salt to food can help.

FOOD
In recent years, paralytic shellfish poisoning (PSP) has become a problem in Alaska. Since 1990, an average of eight people a year have become ill from eating untested shellfish, and in 1995 one Alaskan died from PSP. State officials warn people not to eat mussels, clams or snails gathered from unmonitored beaches in Alaska. PSP is possible anywhere in Alaska, and within 12 hours of consuming the infected shellfish, victims experience symptoms of tingling or numbness in the lips and tongue (which can spread to the fingers or toes), loss of muscle coordination, dizziness, weakness and drowsiness. To get an update on the PSP situation, or to find out which beaches in the state are safe to clam, call the Division of Environmental Health (☎ 907-465-5280).

WATER
Tap water in Alaska is safe to drink, but you need to purify surface water that is to be used for cooking and drinking. Alaska's water is affected by *Giardia lamblia,* or 'beaver fever' as it is known among hikers. The parasite is found in surface water, particularly beaver ponds, and is transmitted between humans and animals. Giardia is an intestinal parasite that causes stomach cramps, nausea, a bloated stomach, watery, foul-smelling diarrhea and frequent gas (see Giardia in Medical Problems & Treatment).

Often, in the backcountry you'll encounter glacially fed streams, distinguished by a gray color. You may drink glacial water, if necessary, in small quantities, although drinking too much of it tends to clog up the internal plumbing. The murk is actually fine particles of silt scoured from the rock by the glacier. Avoid glacial water if possible, and if you have to drink from such a stream, let the water sit overnight in a bottle to allow the particles to settle.

Water Purification
The simplest way to purify water is to boil it for more than a minute. Filtering is acceptable, if you use giardia-rated filters, which are widely available from outdoor equipment retailers. Filters such as First Need, SweetWater or MSR's Waterworks are designed to take out whatever you shouldn't be drinking, including *Giardia lamblia.* The filters cost $50 to $80 and are well worth it.

If you cannot boil or filter water, you should treat it chemically. Iodine is very effective and is available in tablet form (such as Potable Aqua), but follow the directions carefully and remember that too much iodine can be harmful. Before buying iodine tablets, check the manufacturer's specifications on the packet to ensure that the tablets will kill the giardia parasite.

If you can't find tablets, tincture of iodine (2%) or iodine crystals can be used. Two drops of tincture of iodine per liter of clear water is the recommended dosage; the treated water should be left to stand for half an hour before drinking. Iodine crystals can also be used to purify water, but this is a more complicated process, because you have to first prepare a saturated iodine solution. Iodine loses its effectiveness if exposed to air or damp, so keep it in a tightly sealed container. Flavoring powder (like Kool-Aid) will disguise the taste of treated water and is a good idea if you are traveling with children.

COMMON AILMENTS
Blisters
Probably the most common medical problem among hikers is blisters on the feet. While not serious, a blister on a heel or toe can be a painful ordeal. Prevent blisters by breaking in your boots before embarking on a hike and by using thick wool socks or two pairs of socks to eliminate friction.

As soon as you feel a tender spot on your feet, what is commonly referred to as a 'hot spot', stop and treat it. Either apply moleskin, a cushioned, adhesive pad, or Spenco 2nd Skin, a water-based pad that is kept in place with an adhesive dressing. If a blister

A First-Aid Kit for Hikers

A small medical kit is a wise thing to carry. A possible kit list includes:

❑ Antihistamine (such as Benadryl), which is useful as a decongestant for colds and allergies, to ease the itch from insect bites or stings and to help you prevent motion sickness

❑ Antiseptic, mercurochrome and antibiotic powder or similar 'dry' spray for cuts and grazes

❑ Aspirin or ibuprofen for pain or fever

❑ Bandages and Band-Aids for use with minor injuries

❑ Calamine lotion or anti-itch cream to ease irritation from bites or stings

❑ Insect repellent (DEET), sunscreen, lip balm

❑ Kaolin preparation (Pepto-Bismol), Imodium or Lomotil for stomach upsets

❑ Rehydration mixture for treatment of severe diarrhea (particularly important if traveling with children)

❑ Scissors, tweezers and a thermometer (note that mercury thermometers are prohibited by airlines)

❑ Moleskin or 2nd Skin for the treatment of blisters on the feet while hiking

❑ Water-purification tablets (Potable Aqua) for emergency use

has already formed, do not cover it with moleskin. Cut the padded dressing so it surrounds the blister or broken skin. Don't put the dressing directly on the blister, or you might tear the blister when removing the bandage. Large blisters can be pricked with a sterile needle, drained and covered with a dressing.

Knee Pain

Sometimes, while climbing and descending long, steep slopes, hikers experience knee pain. This is especially true while descending, as you are placing a lot of weight on your knees at what is often a rapid pace.

If you anticipate such a problem, seriously consider using a pair of trekking poles (also referred to as walking sticks). Poles are very popular in Europe and are becoming more common in the USA. A pair of poles is estimated to reduce the strain and impact on knees and thigh muscles while hiking by 20%.

Also, while descending, take plenty of breaks to give your knees a chance to recover. Maintain a slow pace; don't allow gravity to induce you to running downhill. And never shortcut switchbacks. Always follow the trail when it weaves back and forth to gradually descend a ridge.

Motion Sickness

Since a great deal of travel in Alaska is done by boat or small charter planes, motion sickness can be a real problem for those prone to it. Eating lightly before and during a trip will reduce the chances of motion sickness. If you are prone to motion sickness, try to find a place that minimizes disturbance – near the wing on aircraft, close to midships on boats and near the center of buses. Fresh air or watching the horizon while on a boat usually helps; reading or cigarette smoke doesn't. Commercial motion-sickness preparations, which can cause drowsiness, have to be taken before the trip commences; when you're feeling sick it's too late. Ginger (available in capsule form) is a natural preventative.

Medical Problems & Treatment

The information included here is for hikers and is intended to supplement information widely available in guidebooks.

ENVIRONMENTAL HAZARDS
Hypothermia

Too much cold can be dangerous and lead to hypothermia, a serious problem in Alaska. A number of backpackers, caught in bad weather without adequate equipment, die from hypothermia every year. Always be prepared for cold, wet or windy conditions, even if you're just out walking or hitching; this is especially important if you're participating in a multiple-day hike in a remote area.

Hypothermia occurs when you lose heat faster than your body can produce it, leading to a drop in your core temperature. It is surprisingly easy to progress from very cold to dangerously cold due to a combination of wind, wet clothing, fatigue and hunger, even if the air temperature is above freezing. Symptoms of mild hypothermia are exhaustion, numbness in limbs (particularly fingers and toes), shivering and clumsiness. Symptoms of more severe cases include slurred speech, irrational or violent behavior, lethargy, stumbling, dizzy spells and muscle cramps. Irrationality may take the form of sufferers claiming they are warm and trying to take off their clothes.

Decreased consciousness occurs when the core body temperature falls from a normal 98.6°F down to 86° to 90°F. Unconsciousness often occurs below 86°F. At this point, the victim has bluish-gray skin, a weak pulse (if one can be found at all) and no apparent breathing. Death, usually by heart failure, is just around the corner.

Prevention of hypothermia includes dressing in layers; silk, wool and synthetic pile fibers are all good insulating materials. A hat is important, because a lot of heat is lost through the head. A strong, waterproof outer layer is essential, since keeping dry is vital. Be sure to carry food containing simple sugars, to generate heat quickly, and lots of fluid to drink.

To treat mild hypothermia, get the patient out of the wind and rain and replace wet clothing with dry, warm clothing. Give the patient warm liquids – not alcohol – and some high-calorie, easily digestible food like chocolate, trail mix or energy bars. Apply mild heat to the chest region only, using hot water bottles or warm moist towels. Gentle exercise will also generate heat.

In more severe cases, it may be necessary to place the victim in a warm sleeping bag and get in. Do not rub the patient. Place the patient near a fire or give the victim hot liquids. Rapid warming may be fatal in severe cases and, at the very least, causes complications. Treat for shock by making the victim lay immobile in the bunk and by elevating his or her feet. Then seek medical help, if possible.

Frostbite

Frostbite refers to the freezing of extremities, including the fingers, toes and nose. Signs and symptoms of frostbite include a whitish or waxy cast to the skin, sometimes with crystals on the surface, itching, numbness and pain. Warm the affected areas by immersion in warm (not hot) water or with blankets or clothes, only until the skin becomes flushed. *Frostbitten parts should not be rubbed.* Pain and swelling are inevitable. Blisters should be broken. Seek medical attention immediately.

Sunburn & Windburn

Alaska has long hours of sunlight during the summer, and the sun's rays are even more intense when they are reflected off snow or water. Sunburn and windburn should be primary concerns for anyone planning to spend time outdoors. The sun will burn you even if you feel cold, and the wind will cause dehydration and skin chafing. Use a good sunscreen and a moisture cream on exposed skin, even on cloudy days. A hat provides added protection, and zinc oxide or some other barrier cream for your nose and lips is recommended for people spending any time on the ice or snow.

Reflection and glare off ice and snow can cause snow blindness, so high-protection sunglasses, known by many locals as 'glacier goggles,' should be considered essential for any sort of visit on or near glaciers.

Altitude Sickness

Acute mountain sickness (AMS) occurs at high altitudes and can be fatal. In the thinner atmosphere of the high mountains, lack of oxygen causes many individuals to suffer headaches, nausea, nosebleeds, shortness of breath, physical weakness and other symptoms that can lead to very serious consequences, especially if combined with heat exhaustion, sunburn or hypothermia. There is no hard and fast rule as to how high is too high: AMS has been fatal at altitudes of 10,000ft, although it is much more common above 11,500ft. For mild cases, everyday painkillers such as aspirin will relieve symptoms until the body adapts. Avoid smoking, drinking alcohol, eating heavily or exercising strenuously. Most people recover within a few hours or days. If the symptoms persist, it is imperative to descend to lower elevations. The drugs acetazolamide (Diamox) and dexamethasone are recommended by some doctors for the prevention of AMS, but their use is controversial. They can reduce the symptoms, but they may also mask warning signs; severe and fatal AMS has occurred in people taking these drugs. In general, we do not recommend them for travelers. A number of other measures can prevent or minimize AMS:

- Ascend slowly. Have frequent rest days, spending two to three nights at each rise of 3000ft. If you reach a high altitude by hiking, acclimatization takes place gradually, and you are less likely to be affected by AMS than if you fly directly to high altitude.

- It is always wise to sleep at a lower altitude than the greatest height reached during the day, if possible. Also, once above 10,000ft, care should be taken not to increase the sleeping altitude by more than 1000ft per day.

- Drink extra fluids. The mountain air is dry and cold, and moisture is lost as you breathe. Evaporation of sweat may occur unnoticed and result in dehydration.

- Eat light, high-carbohydrate meals for more energy.

- Avoid alcohol, as it may increase the risk of dehydration.

- Avoid sedatives.

INFECTIOUS DISEASES
Giardia
This intestinal parasite has been found in water supplies in Alaska, so it's important to know about it. The symptoms are stomach cramps, nausea, a bloated stomach, watery, foul-smelling diarrhea and frequent gas. Giardiasis can appear several weeks after you have been exposed to the parasite. The symptoms may disappear for a few days and then return; this can go on for several weeks. As long as you are carrying the parasite, you risk spreading it to the environment and to other people.

Metronidazole (known as Flagyl) is the recommended drug but should only be taken under medical supervision. Treatment is simple and acts quickly. You might want to carry Flagyl in your first-aid kit, if you plan to be in the backcountry for a while. Antibiotics are of no use. If you suspect you have giardiasis, see a doctor as soon as practical.

Diarrhea
A change of water, food or climate can all cause the runs; diarrhea caused by contaminated food or water is more serious. Despite all your precautions you may still have a bout of mild travelers' diarrhea, but a few rushed toilet trips with no other symptoms is not indicative of a serious problem.

Moderate diarrhea, involving a half-dozen loose movements in a day, is more of a nuisance. Dehydration is the main danger with any diarrhea, particularly for children. Fluid replacement remains the mainstay of management. Weak black tea with a little sugar, soda water, or soft drinks allowed to go flat and diluted 50% with water are all good. With severe diarrhea, a rehydrating solution is necessary to replace minerals and salts. Commercially available ORS (oral rehydration salts) are very useful; add the contents of one packet to a quart of boiled or bottled water. In an emergency, you can make up a solution of 8 teaspoons of sugar to a quart of boiled water. You should stick to a bland diet as you recover.

Fungal Infections
When hiking – especially if you're backpacking – it's easy to forget to wash or change clothing as often as you would normally. This can lead to fungal infections. Hikers are most commonly affected by athlete's foot (tinea), which occurs between the toes. Another common complaint is 'crotch rot,' a painful rash between the groin and the buttocks that is caused by the

combination of sweating and rubbing as you walk. Moisture, most commonly in the form of sweat, encourages these infections.

To prevent fungal infections, wear loose, comfortable clothes, avoid artificial fibers, wash frequently and dry carefully. If you get an infection, wash the infected area at least daily with a disinfectant or medicated soap and water, and rinse and dry well. Apply an antifungal cream or powder like Tinaderm. Try to expose the infected area to sunlight as much as possible and wash all towels and underwear in hot water. Change them often and let them dry in the sun.

HIV & AIDS

The human immunodeficiency virus (HIV) may develop into acquired immune deficiency syndrome (AIDS). HIV is a major problem in many countries. Any exposure to blood, blood products or bodily fluids may put an individual at risk. The disease is often transmitted through sexual contact, or via contaminated needles shared by intravenous drug users. Apart from abstinence from sex, the most effective preventative is always to practice safe sex by using condoms.

HIV/AIDS can also be spread by dirty needles – vaccinations, acupuncture, tattooing and body piercing can be potentially as dangerous as intravenous drug use if the equipment is not clean. If you do need an injection, ask to see the syringe unwrapped in front of you, or take a needle and syringe pack with you.

Fear of HIV infection should never preclude treatment for serious medical conditions. A good resource for help and information is the US Centers for Disease Control AIDS hotline (☎ 800-342-2437, 800-344-7432 in Spanish).

Rabies

Rabies is found in Alaska, especially among small rodents such as squirrels and chipmunks in wilderness areas; it is caused by a bite or scratch from an infected animal. Any bite, scratch or even lick from a mammal should be cleaned immediately and thoroughly. Scrub with soap and running water and then clean with an alcohol or iodine solution. If there is any possibility that the animal is infected, medical help should be sought immediately.

Even if the animal is not rabid, all bites should be treated seriously, as they can become infected or can result in tetanus. A rabies vaccination is now available and should be considered if you are in a high-risk category – for instance, handling or working with animals.

Tetanus

This disease is caused by a germ that lives in the soil and in the feces of horses and other animals. It enters the body via breaks in the skin. The first symptom may be discomfort in swallowing, or stiffening of the jaw and neck; this is followed by painful convulsions of the jaw and whole body. The disease can be fatal. It can be prevented by vaccination, so make sure you are up to date with this vaccination before you leave.

TRAUMATIC INJURIES
Sprains

Ankle and knee sprains can occur when backpacking, particularly in rugged areas that require extensive bouldering or traversing scree slopes at an angle. If you anticipate such conditions, pass up ultralight, low-cut hiking boots, which are basically glorified tennis shoes. Choose an all-leather boot with adequate ankle support.

Mild sprains should be wrapped immediately with a crepe bandage to prevent swelling. Often, a day spent in camp elevating the leg will allow you to continue on with the hike without too much pain. For more serious sprains, when the victim cannot walk, seek medical assistance.

Head Injuries & Fractures

A serious fall, resulting in head injuries or fractures, is always a possibility when hiking, especially if you are climbing around steep slopes above the tree line.

If a person suffers a head injury but is conscious, they are probably OK but should be closely monitored for at least 24 hours. For unconscious victims, check their airway and breathing immediately and attend to them while they are lying down, without moving them much. Bleeding from the nose or ear may indicate a fractured skull. If so, lay the victim so the bleeding ear is downwards and avoid carrying the victim if at all possible.

Indications of a fracture are pain, swelling, loss of function in a limb or irregularities in the shape of the bones. Fractures of unconscious victims may be detected by gently attempting to bend each bone in turn. If the bone moves it is broken, and you should not try to move it any farther. Immobilize a fracture by securing one limb to another or by splinting. Suspected broken bones should be immobilized in the position they are found. In the backcountry, splints may be made from sticks, ski or walking poles, foam pads, backpack frames or any other firm, supportive material. A splint should immobilize the joint above and below the break, and padding should be added to fit the deformities. Never manipulate the injured part to fit a splint.

CUTS & SCRATCHES

Skin punctures can easily become infected while you are traveling and may take time to heal. Treat any cut with an antiseptic solution and mercurochrome. Whenever possible, avoid bandages and Band-Aids, which can keep wounds wet; if you have to keep a bandage on during the day to protect the wound from dirt, take the bandage off while you sleep, to let it get air.

BITES & STINGS
Insects

Alaska is notorious for its biting insects. In the cities and towns you have few problems, but out in the woods you'll have to contend with a variety of insects, including mosquitoes, blackflies, white-socks, no-see-ums and deer flies. Coastal areas, with their cool summers, have smaller numbers of insects than the Interior. Generally, camping on a beach where there is some breeze is better than pitching a tent in the woods. In the end, just accept the fact that you will be bitten.

Mosquitoes Mosquitoes can often be the most bothersome pest. They emerge from hibernation before the snow has entirely melted away, peak in late June and are around until the first frost. Saliva from the mosquito is injected into your skin, and the reaction to this saliva is what causes the bite to itch. The severity ranges from a barely noticeable raised circle of skin that is gone within an hour to bites that turn into welts (due to excessive scratching) that last into the next day. You can combat mosquitoes by wearing light colors and a snug-fitting parka and by tucking the legs of your pants into your socks or boots.

Blackflies These flies, members of the Simuliidae family, begin their assault during the middle of the summer, and the assault intensifies until freezing temperatures in late August or early September begin to diminish the blackfly numbers. Their bite – which you won't feel until its too late to stop – is far more annoying than a mosquito's. The resultant welt has a red dot in the middle and can last for days on some people.

No-see-ums The tiny no-see-um is a member of the Ceratopgonidae family and follows the same seasonal schedule as blackflies. Its bite is a prolonged prick, after which the surrounding skin becomes inflamed and itches intermittently for up to a week or more. The problem with no-see-ums is that they usually travel en masse, and a cloud of them can leave you looking as though you have a bad rash. Unlike the mosquito, these insects will crawl into your hair, slip under a collar or up a pant leg in search of bare skin. To your advantage is the fact that no-see-ums are notoriously weak fliers and you can usually escape them by simply walking away.

Insect Protection The best protection, and a fact of life in Alaska's backcountry, are long-sleeved shirts, socks that will allow you to tuck your pants into them and a snug cap or woolen hat. Another fact of life in Alaska is insect repellent. You have to have it. The most potent, long-lasting repellents by far contain a high percentage of DEET (diethyltoluamide), the active ingredient. A little bottle of Musk Oil or Cutter can cost $6 or $7 (they contain high percentages of DEET), but it's one of the best investments you will make. Unfortunately, repellents that work with mosquitoes are less effective, and some say useless, against blackflies and no-see-ums.

Some people are leery about spreading DEET on their skin, a chemical compound that can dissolve wood finishes, fishing lines and watch crystals. If that's the case, then just apply it to the cuffs and collars of your shirt and on the outside of your hat. Or use a repellent with citronella, a natural product derived from plants. Keep in mind, however, that citronella is not as effective as DEET.

Many backcountry travelers also pack head nets. They're not something you wear a lot – it drives you crazy looking through mesh all day – but when you really need one a head net is a lifesaver. Since they are relatively light and inexpensive, you might as well pack one if you are doing extensive wilderness travel.

Other items you might consider are bug jackets and an after bite medication. The mesh jackets are soaked in insect repellent and kept in a resealable plastic bag until you wear them. Some people say they are the only effective way to keep no-see-ums at bay. After-bite medications contain ammonia and are rubbed on the bite. The smell might drive away your tent partner, but the medication will soothe the craving to scratch the assortment of bites on your arms and neck.

To avoid insects as much as possible, you also want to avoid their favorite habitats. For mosquitoes and no-see-ums that's low-lying, brushy swamp, muskeg and bogs. Blackflies, on the other hand, need cold, clear, oxygen-rich streams to survive. When stopping for an extended break or for the night, search out a dry area that is elevated enough to catch a bit of breeze. You'll quickly discover in that wind, which prevents insects from even taking flight, is much more effective than an entire bottle of DEET.

Poisonous Plants

The one plant you should learn to recognize and avoid at all costs is devil's club, or *Opolopanax horridus*. Devil's club is found throughout the Southeast and in parts of Southcentral and can grow to 10ft. It has huge maple-shaped leaves and stems covered with sharp barbed spines. When a spine punctures your skin, it feels like a bee sting, and swelling often occurs. The spines are difficult to remove, due to their barbs. Wear gloves and long-sleeved shirts when you encounter heavy areas of devil's club.

A few poisonous berries are also found in Alaska. The most common one, the baneberry *(Acteaea rubra)*, is also the most poisonous. As few as six berries can cause dizziness, burning in the stomach and colicky pains. Baneberries are usually found in forests and thickets of the Southeast, Southcentral Alaska, including the Kenai Peninsula and Kodiak, and some areas of the Yukon River and Bristol Bay. The plant ranges in height from 2 to 3ft. Its leaves are large, lobed and coarsely toothed, and its berries can be either white or red.

See the Books section in the Facts for the Hiker chapter for recommended guides to Alaskan plants.

WOMEN'S HEALTH

Antibiotic use, synthetic underwear, sweating and contraceptive pills can lead to fungal vaginal infections, especially when you're traveling in hot climates. Fungal infections are characterized by a rash, itch and discharge and can be treated with a diluted vinegar, lemon-juice or yogurt douche. Nystatin, miconazole or clotrimazole suppositories or vaginal cream are the usual treatments. Maintaining good personal hygiene and wearing loose-fitting clothes and cotton underwear may help prevent these infections.

Cystitis, or inflammation of the bladder, can be a common problem for women. Symptoms include burning on urination and having to urinate frequently and urgently. Blood can sometimes be seen in the urine. Sexual activity with a new partner or with an old partner who has been away for a while can trigger an infection.

The first line of treatment is to drink plenty of fluids, particularly unsweetened cranberry juice, which may resolve the problem. If symptoms persist, they should be treated with an antibiotic, because a simple infection can spread to the kidneys, causing a more severe illness. You'll need a prescription for antibiotics, which can be obtained from doctors at walk-in clinics or from the emergency rooms of public hospitals in Alaska.

Safety on the Hike

If you're planning to wander beyond roadside parks, don't take your adventure lightly. You must be totally independent in the wilderness – a new experience for most city dwellers. You need the knowledge and equipment to sit out bad weather, find your way through a trail-less area or assist an injured member of your party. For that information consult a survival manual such as *Walking Softly in the Wilderness,* by John Hart, or *Wilderness Basics: The Complete Handbook for Hikers & Backpackers,* by Jerry Schad. The most important thing is to be prepared before you enter the Alaskan wilderness.

When hiking in Alaska, you should also be aware of the extreme range of weather that can be experienced any time during the summer. In the afternoon, temperatures in the mountains can approach 80°F and then drop below freezing at night. Heavy rain, snow and high winds can hit at any time – and quickly – even on a warm, sunny day. Always be mentally and physically prepared for all kinds of weather. Take along enough warm clothes, waterproof rain gear (raincoat and overpants) and a waterproof pack liner. If you find your clothing and footwear inadequate for the conditions, turn back.

Far more backpackers lose their lives to hypothermia in Alaska than bear attacks. Be aware of what causes it so you can avoid it, and know what to do about it if it does occur. (Hypothermia is covered in the Medical Problems & Treatment section of this chapter.)

Other safety rules include:

• Choose a trail that suits your level of fitness and experience.
• Find out what to expect on a trip. Always seek local advice about current track and weather conditions – from the local Forest Service office, national park headquarters, etc – before you set out.
• Travel with at least one other person, and stay on the track.
• Purify river or lake water before drinking it.
• Take a first-aid kit and proper equipment – water purifier, warm clothes, etc.
• If you encounter heavy rain and rivers in your path have risen, stay where you are until the rivers go down, retrace your tracks or take another route. Don't cross a swollen river unless you are absolutely certain you can get across safely.

BEARS

Bears are a fact of life in the Alaska backcountry and wilderness areas and the best way to avoid bears is to follow a few commonsense rules. Bears do not roam the backcountry looking for hikers to maul; bears only charge when they feel trapped, when a hiker comes between a sow and her cubs or when enticed by food. Sing or clap when traveling through thick bush, so you don't surprise a bear. That has happened, and usually the bear feels threatened and has no choice but to defend itself. Don't camp near bear food sources or in the middle of an obvious bear path. Stay away from thick berry patches, streams choked with salmon or beaches littered with bear scat.

Leave the pet at home; a frightened dog only runs back to its owner, and most dogs are no match for a bear. Set up the spot where you will cook and eat 30 to 50yd away from your tent. In coastal areas, many backpackers eat in the tidal zone, knowing that when the high tide comes in all evidence of food will be washed away.

At night, try to place your food sacks 10ft or more off the ground by hanging them in a tree, placing them on top of a tall boulder or putting them on the edge of a rock cliff. In a treeless, flat area, cover up the food sacks with rocks. A bear is not going to see the food bags; it's going to smell them.

By packaging all food items in resealable plastic bags, you greatly reduce the animal's chances of getting a whiff of your next meal. Avoid odoriferous foods such as bacon or sardines in areas with many bears.

And please, don't take food into the tent at night. Don't even take toothpaste, hand lotion, suntan oils or anything with a smell. If a bear smells a human, it will leave; anything else might encourage it to investigate.

Encountering a Bear

If you do encounter a bear on the trail, *do not* turn and run. Stop, make no sudden moves, and begin talking calmly to it. Bears have extremely poor eyesight, and speaking helps them understand that you are there. If it doesn't take off right away, back up slowly before turning around and leaving the area. A bear standing on its hind legs is not on the verge of charging; it's only trying to see you better. When a bear turns sideways or begins making a series of woofing sounds, it is only challenging you for space. Just back away slowly and leave. If the animal follows you, *stop* and hold your ground.

Most bear charges are bluffs, with the animal veering off at the last minute. Experienced backpackers handle a charge in different ways. Some people throw their packs

Hiking without Bridges

More so in Alaska than in more developed areas of the USA, backpackers must know how to ford a river correctly. Crossing rivers is inevitable in a region as wild as Alaska. Ford a river haphazardly, and you're courting a disaster that has probably claimed more lives in the wilderness than bear attacks.

River crossing involves picking the best time and the right place and using the proper technique. Knowing when to ford is especially important. In the summer, glacial rivers are usually at their lowest levels in the early morning, before the heat of the sun has made them swell. Be aware of approaching storms and cross before heavy rainfall turns a stream into a raging river. If a stream has turned into white water, simply wait for it to drop to its normal level.

Never cross a river barefoot. The cold temperatures of a mountain stream can cause numbness in your feet, and you're likely to stub a toe on rocks and boulders and slip. Carry a pair of tennis shoes or neoprene booties with hard soles for fording rivers. Sport sandals with thick rubber soles are becoming popular. Just remember that many sandals use Velcro to hold the straps in place, and in water Velcro quickly loosens and releases. If you don't have a spare pair of shoes, take off your socks and wear your boots.

Before crossing the river, release all the waist belts and chest straps on your pack. If you fall, you must be able to ditch your pack, as it will fill with water and become a deadly anchor. If you are making a solo crossing, you might also want to use a long sturdy stick.

Choosing the right place to cross a river is the key to fording it safely. Wide sections of a river are the shallowest. Avoid areas of cut banks; a deep current will be eroding the shoreline. Look for a spot where the river is braided, having divided into several manageable channels. If you are unsure about the depth of the river, toss a big rock into it. A hollow 'kathump' indicates deep water.

When you cross the river, look at the opposite shore, never at the mesmerizing rushing current. Face slightly downstream and move diagonally in that direction, probing each step as you cross. This is where a sturdy stick is useful. If you are in a group, put the largest and strongest person at the upstream end and then sandwich the smaller people in between. Link arms and enter the river together.

If the water is deeper than your thighs, turn back and look for another place to cross. If the stream is especially swift, turn back when it reaches your knees. If you do fall, ditch your pack and roll over on your back, pointing your feet downstream. This will allow you to fend off approaching boulders. Swim towards the shore by waving or 'flippering' with your arms.

3ft in front of them, which will often distract the bear long enough for the person to back away. Other backpackers fire a handheld signal flare over the bear's head (but never at it) in an attempt to use the noise and sudden light to scare it away. If an encounter is imminent, drop into a fetal position, place your hands behind your neck and play dead. If a bear continues biting you after you have assumed a defensive posture, then you must fight back vigorously.

Some people carry guns to fend off bear charges. Shooting a charging bear is a skilled operation if you are a good shot, a foolish one if you are not. You must drop the bear with one or two shots, as a wounded bear is extremely dangerous. Other people are turning to defensive aerosol sprays that contain red pepper extract. These sprays cost $40 to $50 each and have been used with some success for protection against bears. They are effective at a range of 10 to 15ft but must be discharged downwind. If not, you will just disable yourself. See the boxed text 'Pepper Spray: Bearproof or a Bad Bet?' for more about this.

Be extremely careful in bear country, but don't let the bears' reputation keep you out of the woods.

GETTING LOST

Because so much of Alaska is still trail-less wilderness, the danger of getting lost is far greater than in many other places in the USA. Backpackers and hikers, used to following trails, can get hopelessly turned around when relying only on their map-and-compass skills.

Before heading out, always make sure that someone responsible knows where you're going, what route you intend to take and when you expect to come out, so they can notify rangers or police if you are missing. Fill out a backcountry intention form, when they are available, at national park headquarters or ranger stations at the

---

Pepper Spray: Bearproof or a Bad Bet?

Although Alaska has more bears than any state in the USA, attacks by bruins are still few and far between. From 1990 to 1996, bears in Alaska mauled 26 people. Three maulings were by polar bears, four by black bears and the rest by brown bears.

Fortunately, only four people died. Still, backpackers must always be prepared for an encounter with a bear. For a growing number of hikers, that means carrying a small aerosol can of pepper spray. Pepper spray is made of 10% to 15% capsaicin, an active cayenne ingredient. In theory, the spray irritates the bear's nasal passages and makes its eyes tear so uncontrollably that it scampers away frightened and half blind.

In reality, that hasn't quite been the case. In a 1995 study, Canadian researchers discovered that a quarter of the 26 black bears they sprayed proved to be immune to the effects of capsaicin. Researchers said black bears respond to the spray by generating a protective mucus in their eyes and nasal passages that prevents further irritation.

The spray seems to be much more effective on brown bears. Out of 16 documented cases in Canada of people using pepper spray, 15 at least temporarily stopped the brown bear's aggressive behavior. But in 38% of those cases the aggressive brown bear returned.

The best bear deterrent is still avoidance. Watch for bears and go around them if you see any. Avoid areas of obvious bear concentrations, such as salmon spawning streams, and make lots of noise to warn bears you are in the area.

If you choose to carry pepper spray, remember it is not a cure-all but a last-ditch effort for self-preservation. Pepper sprays are only effective at close range, no more than 10 to 15ft, will not shoot in strong wind and require the operator to aim at a charging bear. Also, many sprays don't work in low temperatures.

start of the trip. Then remember to let rangers know when you've come out safely!

Pack along a compass and have the proper USGS topographical map for every trail you walk. Do not depend on the ones that are in this book, as they do not contain enough detail.

If you do get lost:

• Stop, stay calm and carefully plan what to do.
• If you think you can retrace your footsteps then do so. Otherwise, stay put or move to an open area, such as clearing or a riverbank. The last thing you want to do is be hopelessly wandering in the wilderness.
• Help searchers find you by building arrows or cairns out of rocks and wood, laying out brightly colored items that can be easily seen from the air or burning green wood and leaves to produce smoke.

RESCUE & EVACUATION

If a member of your party is lost or needs assistance in the backcountry, you begin a rescue or emergency evacuation by calling the local Alaska State Trooper post. There is a post in every major town and city throughout the state. State troopers will organize a helicopter evacuation and any other rescue service that might be needed. If you are in a national park, however, call a ranger station or park office for assistance. For any ambulance service in Alaska, call ☎ 911.

Getting There & Away

Many travelers from the Lower 48 mistak
enly think that a trip to Alaska is like visit
ing another state of the USA. It isn't; getting
to the North Country is as costly and com
plicated as traveling to a foreign country.
Plan ahead and check around for the best
possible deal, especially on airline flights.

If you're coming from the US mainland,
there are three ways of getting to Alaska: by
driving the Alcan (also known as the Alaska
Hwy), taking a ferry or cruise up the Inside
Passage waterway or flying in from a
number of cities.

If you're coming from Asia or Europe, it's
become harder to fly directly to Anchorage.
Many international airlines, including British
Airways and Japan Air Lines, have dropped
their service to Anchorage. Now, most inter
national travelers come through the gateway
cities of Seattle, Los Angeles, Detroit and
Vancouver en route to Anchorage.

AIR

The quickest and easiest way to reach
Alaska is to fly. A number of major US do
mestic carriers and a few international air
lines offer regular service to Alaska,
primarily to Anchorage International
Airport. Unfortunately, thanks to the steady
consolidation of the US airline industry in
the 1990s, ticket wars and travel promotions
aren't nearly as common as they were
during the height of airline deregulation in
the 1970s. But in the all-important Seattle-
to-Anchorage market, the 1995 demise of
MarkAir, once the largest Alaska-based
airline, created a void that the discount air
lines Reno Air and America West soon
filled, and the added competition has
brought down the price of that ticket.

On intrastate routes, though, Alaska Air
lines is now your only choice, which ulti
mately means higher prices. In the
Southeast, Alaska Airlines has cornered the
Anchorage-to-Juneau and the Seattle-to-
Juneau markets, ever since Delta Air Lines
dropped its Juneau service in 1998.

Also in 1998, Northwest Airlines bought a
controlling stake in Continental Airlines;
American Airlines bought Reno Air the fol
lowing year. Both Continental and Ameri
can Airlines are important carriers to
Alaska, and it remains to seen how these de
velopments will affect ticket prices.

Unfortunately the number of interna
tional airlines that serve Alaska continue to
dwindle. In 2000, both Aeroflot and Korean
Air suspended direct service to Anchorage.
Now, only China Airlines has a direct flight
from Asia and only Swissair offers a direct
flight from Europe, with nonstop service
from Zurich.

Airports & Airlines

The vast majority of visitors to Alaska fly
into Anchorage International Airport,
which handles 5 million passengers annu
ally. Anchorage was once called the 'Air
Crossroads of the World,' and practically

Warning

The information in this chapter is particularly
vulnerable to change: Prices for international
travel are volatile, routes are introduced and
canceled, schedules change, special deals
come and go, and rules and visa require
ments are amended. Airlines and govern
ments seem to take a perverse pleasure in
making price structures and regulations as
complicated as possible. You should check di
rectly with the airline or a travel agent to
make sure you understand how a fare (and
ticket you may buy) works. In addition, the
travel industry is highly competitive and there
are many lurks and perks.

The upshot of this is that you should get
opinions, quotes and advice from as many
airlines and travel agents as possible before
you part with your hard-earned cash. The
details given in this chapter should be re
garded as pointers and are not a substitute
for your own careful, up-to-date research.

every great foreign carrier made a stop here to refuel. But the introduction of new long-range jets led the international airlines to begin dropping the Anchorage stopover in the mid-1980s.

Those few international flights that still come to Anchorage arrive at the north terminal; domestic flights arrive at the south terminal. A complimentary shuttle service runs between the two terminals and all parking lots. You'll find taxis and car rental companies at both terminals.

The airport has the usual services of any major travel center, including gift shops, restaurants, bars, pay phones, ATMs, currency exchange and baggage storage – $3 a day per bag (ground level of south terminal; ☎ 907-266-2437).

Visitors flying into Southeast Alaska will arrive at the Ketchikan or Juneau airport. Both are extremely small facilities with only a handful of gates and one carrier – Alaska Airlines. A few visitors also fly directly from Seattle to the Fairbanks airport, which is bigger than the airports in Southeast Alaska but nowhere near the size of Anchorage International Airport.

The following airlines have scheduled services into and out of Anchorage. The phone numbers listed are either local Anchorage numbers or toll-free numbers good for anywhere in the USA and Canada.

Alaska Airlines (☎ 800-426-0333)
   Web site: www.alaskaair.com
American Airlines (☎ 800-882-8880)
   Web site: www.imaa.com
America West Airlines (☎ 800-235-9292)
   Web site: www.americawest.com
Canada 3000 (☎ 877-658-3000)
   Web site: www.canada3000.com
China Airlines (☎ 800-227-5118)
   Web site: www.china-airlines.com
Continental Airlines (☎ 800-525-0280)
   Web site: www.flycontinental.com
Delta Air Lines (☎ 800-221-1212)
   Web site: www.delta-air.com
ERA Aviation (☎ 800-478-1947)
   Web site: www.era-aviation.com
Northwest Airlines (☎ 800-225-2525)
   Web site: www.nwa.com

PenAir (☎ 800-448-4226)
   Web site: www.penair.com
Reeve Aleutian Airways (☎ 907-243-4700)
   Web site: www.reeveair.com
TWA (☎ 800-221-2000)
   Web site: www.twa.com
United Airlines (☎ 800-241-6522)
   Web site: www.ual.com

Buying Tickets

Airfare Report once tracked down 58 different published fares for the same Northwest Airlines flight, with prices ranging from $129 to $629. Keep this in mind when purchasing a ticket. Even if you're using a travel agent, comparison shop to see who comes up with the best price. Ticket consolidators receive wholesale rates from airlines that fly to Alaska, including America West, then pass on the savings to travel agents.

Basically, tickets fall into two groups: regular fares, which no budget traveler would ever be caught purchasing; and Advance Purchase Excursion (Apex), or 'Supersavers' as they are known domestically, which require 14- to 30-day advance reservations and limit your stay to a maximum number of days. The wide variety of prices results from an array of promotional gimmicks. US domestic airlines may offer a special price to passengers traveling on Tuesday and Wednesday – off-peak days for the airline industry – and most have off-season rates for travel to Alaska between December and May. Many airlines also offer senior citizens and students a 10% discount, but you have to ask for it when booking the ticket.

'Nonrefundable' tickets are often the best deal. These are great if you make the flight, bad if you change your plans after you booked it. Airlines frequently charge penalties ($50 and up) for making any changes.

If you're traveling internationally, Round-the-World tickets allow you to fly on the combined routes of two or more airlines in one direction for a more economic journey around the globe. Several major airlines, including TWA and Continental, offer such tickets, but unfortunately Anchorage is not one of the possible stopovers.

In recent years, the growth of Internet e-commerce has made it easier for travelers to seek out the lowest fares. Practically every major airline now has a Web site that allows you to check flight schedules, browse fares and purchase tickets with a credit card. Alaska Airlines and a number of other carriers entice customers with Internet specials – Alaska has a special site for these offers (see www.alaskair.com/webspecials/start.asp) – but these fares are pretty restrictive. When they're posted, you practically have to have your bags packed and be ready to leave within days. But if traveling on a whim suits you, the savings can be substantial, with roundtrip fares from Los Angeles to Anchorage for $239; from Boise, Idaho to Juneau for $279; or from Seattle to Fairbanks for $239.

While the Internet is a great way to comparison shop, you still might want to call the airline's toll-free numbers before booking the ticket. The sales representative will often know how to modify the ticket (and lower its price) by changing departure days or rerouting stopovers.

When you leave Alaska, there are no additional state or airport departure taxes to worry about, so a departure tax won't be added to the price of your airline ticket.

The USA

Domestic airfares are constantly moving up and down and will vary with the season, the days you want to travel, the length of stay and how rigid the ticket is in terms of changes and refunds after purchase. Many tickets allow you to stay in Alaska for three months to a year. Some only allow a stay of 21 days or less, which makes for a challenge when you're planning weeklong treks into the Alaskan wilderness.

The airfare to Alaska from most of the USA is far more affordable now than it was 15 years ago; occasionally, you can pick up a roundtrip ticket from the Midwest or East Coast to Anchorage for under $500. But most of those economy fares have tight restrictions, are for off-season travel or apply to a limited number of seats. Airlines don't offer economy fares during July, since the summer travel season in Alaska is short and demand for seats is high.

Seattle, Washington serves as the major hub for flights into Alaska. Alaska Airlines owns the lion's share of the market, with more than two dozen flights daily between Seattle and Anchorage, as well as direct flights to Ketchikan, Juneau and Fairbanks.

A discount roundtrip fare between Seattle and Anchorage is now creeping toward $300. For the lowest possible fare, purchase your ticket 21 days in advance and book one of the red-eye flights that depart Seattle between 9 pm and 2 am and leave Anchorage between 12:45 am and 2 pm (Alaskan time) on the return leg. Alaska Airlines has five such flights daily; United, Delta and Continental also offer middle-of-the-night trips. Shop around and you might be able to pick up a ticket for $200 to $250.

An advance-purchase, roundtrip ticket between Seattle and Juneau on Alaska Airlines is $325. The Seattle-to-Fairbanks route costs $380 to $430. During the profitable summer season, you can add $100 to $150 for every stop you make along the way.

You can now book a nonstop flight to Anchorage from a number of other US cities, including San Francisco, Salt Lake City, Detroit, Minneapolis, Reno, Portland, Chicago, Atlanta and Los Angeles. Northwest Airlines flies nonstop between Minneapolis and Anchorage; advance-purchase tickets usually cost $600 to $700. A similar ticket from Detroit is $700 to $800. Delta Air Lines flies from Salt Lake City to Anchorage for a roundtrip fare of $696 and from Los Angeles for $300 to $400. United Airlines has two daily, nonstop flights from Chicago to Anchorage for $679 and similar flights from San Francisco for $454.

Continental Airlines offers a one-stop flight from Houston to Anchorage for $704 during the summer if booked 14 days in advance. TWA flies nonstop to Anchorage from St Louis daily during the summer for $575 roundtrip. From Boston, you can fly to Anchorage on Delta, United, Northwest or Continental, which often offers the lowest fare. Still, a roundtrip, advance-purchase ticket usually exceeds $800.

America West moved into the Alaska market in the mid-1990s with a $300 Phoenix-to-Anchorage nonstop flight, but dropped out in 1997. In 1999, it was considering resuming service to the 49th state from its major hubs of Phoenix and Las Vegas.

Another strategy for saving money is to reserve a cheap flight to Seattle with such discount carriers as Southwest Airlines (☎ 800-435-9792) or America West and then book a second ticket to Anchorage with a different airline. In 1999, Southwest was offering a special $99 one-way, cross-country fare.

In short, air travel is the best way to go if you plan to spend three weeks or less touring Alaska. But if you are planning to spend a month or more venturing through the state, you see more and pay less by combining the Alaska Marine Hwy ferry out of Bellingham, Washington, with a bus ride from Haines.

Canada

Canadian Airlines does not service Alaska but will fly you to Seattle, where you can pick up a domestic US carrier for the second leg of your journey. The roundtrip fare from Toronto to Seattle, for a ticket purchased 14 days in advance, is $351. Contact Canadian Airlines toll-free from Canada (☎ 800-665-1177) and from the USA (☎ 800-426-7000) or visit the Web site (www.cdnair.ca).

You can also fly to Vancouver on Canadian Airlines and then take either an Alaska Airlines or Canada 3000 flight to Anchorage. Alaska Airlines charges $383 for the roundtrip ticket if purchased 21 days in advance. Another option is to fly to Whitehorse on Canadian Airlines and then jump on an Air North Flight headed for Juneau or Fairbanks. You can book that entire ticket through Canadian Airlines; a roundtrip flight to Juneau costs $500 to $536.

A roundtrip Air North flight from Whitehorse to Juneau is C$237; to Fairbanks, it's C$460. The Whitehorse-based airline also offers a Klondike Explorer Pass for C$654. This allows unlimited air travel for 21 days between the five cities Air North serves:

Juneau, Whitehorse, Dawson City, Old Crow and Fairbanks. In Alaska, contact the airline at ☎ 800-764-0407; in northern British Columbia and the Yukon Territory, call ☎ 403-668-2228.

Australia & New Zealand

In Australia, STA and Flight Centres are the major dealers in cheap airfares. They have branches in all the major cities. You can also contact the travel agents in the Yellow Pages. Qantas Airways has flights from Sydney to Los Angeles with direct connections on Alaska Airlines to Anchorage. A roundtrip, advance-purchase ticket starts at A$2741 and allows you to stay up to two months.

Air New Zealand has a similar agreement with Alaska Airlines. Most flights go through Los Angeles, where you pick up an Alaska Airlines flight. Such a roundtrip ticket is NZ$2986 if purchased seven days in advance and is good for up to two months of travel.

The UK

British Airways no longer flies into Anchorage. It does have nonstop flights from London (Heathrow) to Seattle, where you continue north on a domestic carrier. The roundtrip fare is UK£584; the ticket must be booked 21 days in advance, and your stay in the USA can't exceed 45 days.

Northwest has a London-to-Anchorage flight that begins at Gatwick Airport and changes planes in Detroit. A roundtrip economy fare is UK£635. Both Delta and United offer similar flights from Gatwick and Heathrow, respectively.

Continental Europe

The usual route to Anchorage from Europe is to head west with a stop in New York and then Seattle. From Paris, Continental offers a daily flight to Anchorage with a change of planes in Houston and an additional stop before reaching Alaska. A roundtrip fare, purchased 14 days in advance, is $1222. Northwest also has a daily Paris-to-Anchorage flight that changes planes in Detroit. The roundtrip fare is $1237, but the ticket must be booked 21 days in advance, can only be used in July and August and limits your stay in Alaska to 30 days. You also have to travel between Monday and Thursday.

Similar flights can be arranged from Frankfurt through Delta, Northwest and United. Northwest charges $1384 for a roundtrip ticket with a 21-day advance purchase; this allows you to stay up to three months. Travel must take place between Monday and Friday. Delta offers a similar ticket for $1376. Also, check Condor Airlines (www.condor.de), a carrier that began offering nonstop, semiweekly service between Anchorage and Frankfurt in 1999, with roundtrip fares around $1000. Balair/CTA, a division of Swissair, offers a nonstop Zurich-to-Anchorage flight every Wednesday from May through September for $1100 roundtrip.

Asia

In 2000, Northwest suspended its summer nonstop service between Anchorage and Tokyo. Now travel to Alaska is via daily flights from Tokyo to Seattle or Los Angeles, where travelers can pick up a second flight to Alaska.

Northwest flies into Seattle and onto Anchorage daily for a roundtrip fare of $2686. Delta offers daily flights that change at either Salt Lake City or Seattle; the roundtrip fare is $2700, with no requirements for length of stay.

Japan Air Lines has discontinued its service to Anchorage and does not fly into Seattle. On JAL, the best you can do is fly to San Francisco and then pick up an Alaska Airlines flight to Anchorage.

The daily service from Seoul to Anchorage is far cheaper than departing from Tokyo. United Airlines offers a daily flight with a change of planes at San Francisco. Or, you can fly nonstop four days a week with Korean Air. Its roundtrip fare is $1160 and requires only a four-day advance purchase.

There is also nonstop service between Taipei, Taiwan and Anchorage with China Air. United offers daily service from Taipei with a change of planes in San Francisco.

When booking a flight from Asia, remember that the fares of US-based airlines like Northwest and Delta fluctuate wildly with the rise and fall of the dollar against the yen.

LAND

What began in April 1942 as an unprecedented construction project during WWII ended eight months later as the first overland link between the Lower 48 and Alaska. Known formally as the Alaska-Canada Military Hwy, it's affectionately called the Alcan. Today, the Alcan (also known as the Alaska Hwy) is a road through the vast wilderness of northwest Canada and Alaska, starting at Dawson Creek in British Columbia and ending at Delta Junction.

For those with the time, the Alcan is a unique way to travel north. The trip is an adventure in itself; the 1520mi road is a legend among highways, and completing the journey along the Alcan is a feather in anyone's cap. Each summer, thousands of travelers enjoy the spectacular drive.

The Alcan is now entirely paved, and although sections of jarring potholes, frost heaves (the rippling of the pavement caused by freezing and thawing) and loose gravel still exist, the infamous rough conditions of 20 years ago no longer prevail. The era of lashing spare fuel cans to the side of the car because gasoline stations are 250mi apart is also gone. Food, gas and lodging can be found every 20 to 50mi along the highway, with 100mi being the longest stretch between fuel stops.

There are several ways to get to the Alcan: you can begin in the US states of Washington, Idaho or Montana and pass through Edmonton or Jasper in Alberta or Prince George in British Columbia, Canada. There are also several ways of traveling the highway: bus, car or a combination of Alaska Marine Hwy ferry and bus.

Bus

A combination of buses will take you from Seattle via the Alcan to Anchorage, Fairbanks, Skagway or Haines for a moderate cost. There are no direct bus services from the Lower 48 to Alaska; travelers have to be patient, as services here are more limited than in the rest of the country. Be fore-warned that a roundtrip ride on a bus from Seattle to Anchorage will end up costing you more than flying.

Greyhound Using this major US bus company, the closest you can get to Alaska is Whitehorse in British Columbia, and this involves purchasing two tickets. You begin at the Seattle Greyhound station (☎ 206-628-5530), on the corner of 8th Ave and Stewart St, where you can buy a one-way ticket to Vancouver for $20. The bus departs at least five times a day, more often if the demand is high during the summer. At Pacific Central Station on Main St in Vancouver, you switch to a Greyhound Lines of Canada bus for the rest of the journey, which includes a two-hour layover at Prince George and another at Dawson Creek in British Columbia. The Vancouver bus departs at 7:30 am daily except Saturday and arrives in Whitehorse at 4:30 am, 44 hours later – an epic journey that takes its toll. If you plan to continue your travels on an Alaska Direct bus and don't want to stay overnight in Whitehorse, you must catch the Monday morning bus from Vancouver.
Web site: www.greyhound.com

The one-way fare from Vancouver to Whitehorse is C$298. For C$450, you can purchase a Canadian Pass that allows 30 days of travel within 40 days. When planning your trip, remember that most Greyhound special offers, such as Ameripass (unlimited travel for seven days), do not apply to Yukon or Alaska destinations.

There is also a more pleasant way to reach Alaska than spending two days on a Greyhound bus. Once in Vancouver, you can buy a ticket to Prince Rupert, where you can hop on a delightful Alaska Marine Hwy ferry. There are two buses a day, at 7:30 am and 8:30 pm, and they arrive in Prince Rupert some 20 hours later. The roundtrip fare is C$173. Call Greyhound Lines of Canada (☎ 800-661-8747) or try their Web site (www.greyhound.ca) for information.

Alaskon Express Once you've reached Whitehorse, you change to an Alaskon Express bus for the next leg of the journey. Gray Line of Alaska operates these buses from May to September, from either Westmark Whitehorse, at 2nd Ave and Steele St, or the Greyhound Bus Terminal at the north end of 2nd Ave.

Buses depart the Yukon capital for Anchorage on Tuesday, Thursday and Sunday at noon, stay overnight at Beaver Creek in the Yukon and then continue to Anchorage the next day, reaching the city at 7:30 pm. You can get off the bus earlier at Tok, Glennallen or Palmer. On Monday, Wednesday and Saturday, buses depart Whitehorse at noon for Haines, reaching the Southeast Alaska town and ferry terminal port at 5:30 pm.

As a testimony to the popularity of the Chilkoot Trail, an Alaskon Express bus departs daily from Whitehorse at 4:30 pm for Skagway, stopping along the way to pick up backpackers coming off the popular trek.

You can also go overland to Fairbanks, something that was hard to do in the past. An Alaskon Express bus departs at noon on Tuesday, Thursday and Sunday for Fairbanks with a stopover in Beaver Creek. A nice thing about these buses is that you can flag them down along the road, which is good if you've been sitting around for most of the morning trying to thumb a ride out of a town like Haines Junction.

The one-way fare from Whitehorse to Anchorage is $195, to Fairbanks $165, to Haines $85 and to Skagway $56; these fares do not include lodging at Beaver Creek. In Whitehorse, call ☎ 867-667-2223 for current bus information. If you're still in the planning stages of your trip, contact Gray Line of Alaska (☎ 800-544-2206, fax 206-281-0621); by January, the company can provide schedules, departure times and rates for the following summer.

Alaska Direct Bus Line Much smaller and slightly cheaper than Gray Line's Alaskon Express is Alaska Direct Bus Line, based in Anchorage. On Tuesday, Friday and Sunday, an Alaska Direct bus departs Whitehorse at

7 am, reaching Tok around 3 pm. From there, you can continue on to Fairbanks or transfer to a bus for Anchorage.

The one-way fare from Whitehorse to Tok is $80, to Fairbanks $120 and Anchorage $145. In the USA, call Alaska Direct at ☎ 800-770-6652; in Whitehorse, call ☎ 867-668-4833. Make sure you call to find out where the pickup point is or if the company is even still in business.

Car

Without a doubt, driving your own car to Alaska allows you the most freedom. You can leave when you want, stop where you feel like it and pretty much make up your itinerary as you go along. It's not exactly cheap driving to Alaska, and that's not even considering the wear and tear and thousands of miles you'll put on your vehicle.

If you're contemplating this car trip, remember that the condition of your tires is most important. The Alcan may be paved, but it's constantly under repair, and stretches of frost heaves and potholes are common, especially on the Canadian side; worn tires don't last long here.

Even your spare – and you *must* have one – should be fairly new. You should also avoid the newer 'space-saver' spares and carry a full-size spare as your extra tire.

Replace windshield wipers before you depart and carry an extra set along with a gallon of solvent for the windshield-washer reservoir. Dust, dirt and mud make good visibility a constant battle while driving. Also bring a jack, wrenches and other assorted tools, spare hoses, fan belts and a quart of oil or two; even an extra headlight or air filter is not being too extreme. Carry them and hope you never have to use them.

Some travelers use an insect screen, some put plastic headlight covers or a wire-mesh screen over the headlights, and others place a rubber mat or piece of carpet between the gas tank and securing straps. These measures can protect the vehicle from the worst danger on the road – flying rocks that are kicked up by truck-and-trailer rigs passing you.

By far the worst problem on the Alcan and many other roads in Alaska and the Yukon is dust – that's why even on the hottest days you see most cars with their windows up. To control dust in an RV or trailer, reverse the roof vent on your rig so it faces forward. Then, keep it open a few inches while driving, creating air pressure inside to combat the incoming dust.

Those traveling the route in small or compact vehicles often face another problem – an overloaded car. Stuffing the trunk and the backseat and then lashing on a car-top carrier in order to take along extra boxes of macaroni-and-cheese dinners could do you in, miles from anywhere. It's been said that the biggest single cause of flat tires and broken suspension systems along the Alcan is an overloaded car.

Since almost 80% of the Alcan is in Canada, it's best to brush up on the metric system or have a conversion chart taped to the dashboard. On the Canada side, you'll find kilometer posts (as opposed to the mileposts found in Alaska) which are placed every 5km after the zero point in Dawson Creek. (With more than 1000 vehicles passing through Dawson Creek daily during the summer, it's the one place where you might want to book a room or a campsite in advance.) Most Alcan veterans say 300mi a day is a good pace – one that will allow for plenty of stops to see the scenery or wildlife.

The best stretch? That's tough, but some will argue it's the 330mi from Fort Nelson (British Columbia) to Watson Lake (Yukon). As you wind around hairpin turns, you'll enjoy panoramas of the Rocky Mountains and you'll stand a good chance of spotting wildlife, especially if you leave early in the morning.

It's always good to have Canadian currency or a major credit card on hand to purchase gasoline. One or two of the major gasoline credit cards will also come in handy, especially if you have a major breakdown. Along the way, Tourism Yukon operates a number of visitor reception centers that provide a wealth of information and maps for drivers. These include the following:

Beaver Creek
(☎ 867-862-7321) Visitor Center, at Mile 1202 of the Alcan in the heart of Beaver Creek

Haines Junction
(☎ 867-634-2345) Visitor Center, at Kluane National Park Headquarters

Watson Lake
(☎ 867-536-7469) Alaska Highway Interpretive Center, at the junction of the Alcan and Campbell St

Whitehorse
(☎ 867-667-2915) Visitor Center, downtown at 2nd St and Hanson Ave

Hitchhiking

Hitchhiking is probably more common in Alaska than it is in the rest of the USA, and more so on rural dirt roads like the McCarthy Rd and the Denali Hwy than on the major paved routes. But this doesn't mean it's a totally safe way of getting around. Hitchhiking is never entirely safe in any country in the world, and we don't recommend it. Travelers who decide to hitchhike should understand that they are taking a small but potentially serious risk. If you do choose to do this, you'll be safer if you travel in pairs and let someone know where you're planning to go. That said, if you're properly prepared and have sufficient time, thumbing the Alcan can be an easy way to see the country, meet people and save money.

The Alcan seems to inspire the pioneer spirit in travelers who drive it. Drivers are good about picking up hitchhikers, much better than those across the Lower 48 – the only problem is that there aren't as many of them. In places along the route, you may have to wait 30 minutes or longer before a car passes by. During the summer, the number of vehicles increases significantly, but if you're attempting the trip in early spring or late fall, be prepared to wait hours or even overnight at one of a handful of junctions along the way.

All hitchhikers should be patient and self-sufficient, with a tent, some food, water, warm clothing and a good book or two. Moving through the USA and southern Canada, you'll get the usual short and long rides from one city to the next. Once you make it to Dawson Creek, it will probably only take you one or two longer rides to reach your destination.

Any part of the Alcan can be slow, but some sections are notorious. The worst can be Haines Junction, the crossroads in the Yukon where southbound hitchhikers occasionally have to stay overnight before catching a ride to Haines in Southeast Alaska. Longer waits may also occur if you're heading home in late summer or early fall and thumbing out of Glennallen, Tok or Delta Junction back into Canada and the Lower 48. A sign with your destination on it helps, as does displaying your backpack, which tells drivers you're a summer traveler.

The hardest part of the trip for many is crossing the US-Canadian border. Canadian officials usually pull cars over if the passengers are not of the same nationality as the driver, and they will ask to see proof of sufficient funds. Anybody without prearranged transport is required to have $80 per day to travel through Canada or a total of $200 to $250.

The Canadians are not hassling hitchhikers when they do this; they're just making sure that visitors don't get stuck somewhere for a week because they've run out of money. On the way to Alaska, most travelers will have these funds; on the way back, however, it may be difficult if you're at the end of your trip and without money.

Three places to make contacts for a ride back to the Lower 48 are the Anchorage International Hostel; the Wood Center in the middle of the University of Alaska campus in Fairbanks, where there's a bulletin board for students offering or needing rides; and the Chamber of Commerce hospitality center in Tok, where the free coffee pulls in many drivers before they continue into Canada. If you're heading north, the bulletin board outside the tourist office in Dawson Creek is worth checking, as it often contains messages from people looking for somebody to help with fuel costs.

With luck, it can take you less than a week to hitchhike from Seattle to Fairbanks or Anchorage, but to be on the safe side, plan on the trip taking seven to eight days. The route from Seattle to Alaska is the most direct and sees the most traffic to Dawson Creek. This route involves hitchhiking along I-5 in Washington to the Canadian border, then on the Trans-Canada Hwy 1 to Cache Creek and finally on Hwy 97 north to Dawson Creek and the Alcan.

If you'd rather not hitchhike the entire Alcan, take the Alaska Marine Hwy ferry from Bellingham, Washington, to Haines and start hitchhiking from there; you'll cut the journey in half but still travel along the highway's most spectacular parts. Haines, however, is a town of about 1150 people, and traffic is light on the road to the Alcan at Haines Junction. It's best to hustle off the ferry and begin thumbing as vehicles unload, so you can catch a driver heading north. Or, seek out a lift while you're still on the boat by taping a notice outside the ship's cafeteria or showers.

AlaskaPass

A concept that has been hugely popular with travelers in Europe for years finally arrived in the North Country in 1989, when a small company in Haines (of all places) organized nine major carriers and offered an unlimited travel pass. AlaskaPass Inc, now with headquarters in Vashon, Washington, offers the only all-inclusive ground transportation pass that will get you from Washington into Canada into Alaska and even as far north as Dawson City in the Yukon for a set price.

The carriers include Alaska Marine Hwy, Greyhound Lines of Canada, Vancouver Island Coach Lines, British Columbia Rail, British Columbia Ferries, Alaskon Express, Norline Coaches and the Alaska Railroad.

After you purchase your pass, choosing the number of days you want to travel, you make your own reservations with the individual carriers. Each time you pick up a ticket, you simply show your AlaskaPass.

On the plus side, you can save money with such a pass. On the down side, you have to plan carefully to do so, and the pass does not include any air travel.

The passes are offered for either continuous or flexible travel, which allows travel on a number of days during a time period. The latter is a much better choice, as it leaves you time to enjoy an area or take side trips before moving on.

The 15-day pass is $699, but there's a $50 surcharge if you use it to board the Alaska Marine Hwy ferry in Bellingham. The 30-day pass, at $949, covers the longest time period. Still better over the long haul is the 8–12-day pass (travel eight out of 12 days) for $499 and the 12–21-day pass for $799. Discounts for children ages three to 11 are available, and there's a cheaper off-season pass for travel between October and April.

You can purchase a pass ahead of time from most travel agents or directly from the company by calling ☎ 800-248-7598 in the US and Canada or ☎ 206-463-6550 overseas. You can also visit the Web site (www.alaskapass.com).

SEA
Ferry

As an alternative to the Alcan, you can travel the Southeast's Inside Passage, a waterway made up of thousands of islands, fjords and mountainous coastlines. To many, the Southeast is the most beautiful area in the state, and the Alaska Marine Hwy ferries are the country's best public transportation bargain.

With its leisurely pace, travel on the ferries is a delightful experience. The midnight sun is warm, and the possibility of sighting whales, bald eagles or sea lions keeps most travelers at the side of the ship. This is also an excellent way to meet other independent travelers heading for a summer in the North Country.

The ferries to Alaska begin at either Bellingham, Washington, or Prince Rupert in British Columbia and then continue on to Ketchikan in Alaska. Most ferries then depart for Wrangell, Petersburg, Sitka, Juneau, Haines and Skagway before heading back. A trip from Bellingham to Juneau takes 2½ to four days, depending on the route. Most ferry terminals are a few miles out of town, and the short in-port time

Northern fur seal

Horned puffin

Bald eagles

Moose out for a stroll

Brown bear eyeing its lunch

Hiking boots after a long day

doesn't allow passengers to view the area without making a stopover.

If you intend to use the ferries to tour the Southeast, obtain a current schedule and keep it handy at all times. The ferries stop almost every day at larger centers like Juneau, but the smaller villages may only have one ferry every three or four days; many places won't have service at all.

Seven ships ply the waters of Southeast Alaska, but only the M/V *Columbia* sails the entire route from Bellingham to Skagway. The M/V *Matanuska*, M/V *Taku* and M/V *Kennicott* depart from Prince Rupert and reach Skagway before turning around.

The M/V *Kennicott* is the newest boat in the fleet and in 1998 began a special run from Southeast Alaska across the Gulf of Alaska to Seward. This marks the first time that the Southeast routes of the Alaska Marine Hwy ferry have been connected with a Southcentral portion that includes such ports as Homer, Valdez, Kodiak and Cordova. These trips are offered only once a month during the summer, departing Juneau and reaching Seward three days later. The one-way fare is $128. Because it allows travelers to skip the long haul over the Alcan, this sailing is extremely popular and should be booked before you arrive in Alaska.

The M/V *Malaspina* sails only North Lynn Canal during the summer, connecting Juneau with Haines and Skagway. The other two ships are smaller and serve out-of-the-way villages from Juneau or Ketchikan. In the summer, the M/V *Aurora* sails between Ketchikan, Metlakatla, Hollis and Hyder. The M/V *Le Conte* stops at Juneau, Hoonah, Angoon, Sitka, Kake, Tenakee Springs, Skagway, Haines and Petersburg; it makes a special run to Pelican once a month.

The large 'blue canoes' of the Alaska Marine Hwy are equipped with observation decks, food services, lounges and solariums with deck chairs. You can rent a stateroom for overnight trips, but most backpackers head straight for the solarium and sleep in one of the deck chairs or on the floor with a sleeping pad.

When boarding, it's best to scramble to the solarium and either stake out a lounge chair or at least an area on the floor. The solarium and observation deck are the best places to sleep, as the air is clean and the nighttime peace is unbroken. The other places to crash are the indoor lounges, which can be smoky, noisy or both.

On the long haul from Bellingham, backpackers are still allowed to pitch freestanding tents outside the solarium, and the ferry staff even designate the correct area for doing so. Bring duct tape to attach the tent to the floor, but remember that during a busy summer tents tend to take up more space than two people really need in an already crowded section of the ship.

Food on board is reasonably priced compared to what you will pay on shore, with breakfast and lunches costing around $4 to $6 and dinner $7 to $10. Still, it's cheaper to bring your own grub and eat it in the solarium or the cafeteria. Some backpackers bring their own tea bags, coffee or instant soup and then just purchase the cup of hot water. The pursers, however, do not allow any camp stoves to be used on board and are very strict about enforcing this.

The only thing cheaper than the food on board is the shower. Showers are free on all ferries except the M/V *Tustumena*, where they cost only 25¢ for 10 minutes. They're the best bargain you'll find in Alaska.

There is a tariff for carrying on bicycles or kayaks, but compared to the cost of bringing a car or motorcycle, it's very reasonable. The cost is only $41 to take what ferry officials call an 'alternative means of conveyance' from Bellingham to Haines. A bicycle can be a handy way to see at least part of a town without disembarking for a few days, while a summer (or even a lifetime) can be spent using the ferry system to hop from one wilderness kayak trip to another.

Above all else, when using the Alaska Marine Hwy system, check and double-check the departures of ferries once you have arrived in the Southeast. It's worth a phone call to the terminal to find out actual arrival and departure times; the ferries are notorious for being late or breaking down and having their departures canceled. It's something that happens every summer.

Reservations The ferries are extremely popular during the peak season from June to August. You must make reservations if you want a cabin or vehicle space and if you're a walk-on passenger boarding at Bellingham. Space for summer trips from Bellingham is often filled by April, forcing walk-on passengers to wait on standby for an available spot.

The Alaska Marine Hwy's reservation office will take written requests any time and telephone requests from the first working day of January for the following summer. As telephone lines are jammed most of the time after the first day of the year, it's wise to send in a written or email request as soon as you can figure out your itinerary. When writing or faxing in the reservation, provide the port of embarkation; names and ages of all travelers; width, height and overall length of vehicle including trailers; mailing address; telephone numbers; alternative travel dates; and the date you will be leaving home.

The summer sailing schedule comes out in December; to obtain one, contact the Alaska Marine Hwy (☎ 907-465-3941), PO Box 25535, Juneau, AK 99802-5535. There are also toll-free telephone numbers (☎ 800-642-0066, 800-526-6731 from the Lower 48) to handle schedule requests, or you can view the schedule online at www.akferry.com.

Once you're ready to make a reservation, call the toll-free numbers, fax your request (fax 907-277-4829) or book your passage through the Alaska Marine Hwy Web site.

When you book a passage on the ferry, you must have an idea of what ports you want to visit along the route, with exact dates, before purchasing the ticket. Stopovers are not free; rather, tickets are priced on a port-to-port basis. From Bellingham to Haines, you can generally count on each stopover adding 2 percent to the fare.

Once on the boat, you can still arrange a stopover but will be charged an additional fee. If you plan to spend a good deal of time or the entire summer in the region, purchase a ticket to Juneau and then use that as your base, taking shorter trips to other towns on the M/V *Le Conte*. The fare for walk-on passengers from Bellingham to

Haines is $244, while the ticket from Bellingham to Juneau is $226.

All fares listed in this book are for adults (ages 12 and older). Fares for children ages two to 11 are about half the price of an adult fare, and children under two travel free. The ferry system also offers 50% discount passes to both senior citizens and disabled persons. Both are restricted to travel between Alaskan ports when space is available and can be used only for the M/V *Le Conte*, M/V *Aurora*, M/V *Bartlett* and M/V *Tustumena*. Applications for a disabled pass must be filed in advance by writing to Alaska Marine Highway System Pass Desk, PO Box 25535, Juneau, AK 99802-5535.

Bellingham, Washington Bellingham is the southern terminus of the Alaska Marine Hwy and includes an information center, a ticket office, luggage lockers and an outdoor seating area with a nice view of Bellingham Bay and the surrounding hills. It's 10 minutes south of the Bellingham International Airport in the historic Fairhaven shopping district, 87mi north of Seattle. From I-5, go west on Fairhaven Parkway (exit 250) for 1.1mi and then turn right onto 12th St, where signs will direct you to the terminal at the end of Harris Ave.

Prince Rupert, British Columbia If the Alaska Marine Hwy ferries are full in Bellingham, one alternative is to begin your cruise in Seattle, utilizing two ferry systems before switching to the Alaska line in Prince Rupert, in Canada.

At Pier 69, off Alaskan Way in the heart of Seattle, catch the *Victoria Clipper* to Victoria on Vancouver Island. During the summer, boats depart at least four times daily – at 7:30, 8 and 8:30 am and 3:30 pm – for a trip that takes 2½ to three hours. The one-way fare for walk-on passengers is $58. For reservations, call ☎ 800-888-2535 from the USA.

Once you land on Vancouver Island, head north to Port Hardy and catch one of the BC Ferries to Prince Rupert. From this Canadian city, you have a much better chance of boarding the Alaska Marine Hwy ferry because there are three vessels that connect Prince Rupert to Southeast Alaska. Port Hardy can be reached by bus from Victoria on Laidlaw Coach Lines (☎ 800-318-0818 in Canada, ☎ 800-663-8390 in the USA), which leaves once a day at 6:15 am; the one-way fare is C$82. The bus depot is at 700 Douglas St, behind the Empress Hotel in the center of Victoria.

At Port Hardy, the BC Ferries dock is at Bear Cove, about 5mi from town, but there is a shuttle van service from the Island Coach Line bus terminal on Main St. At Bear Cove, the *Queen of the North* departs at 7:30 am and reaches Prince Rupert at 10:30 pm and returns to Vancouver Island the next day, maintaining this every-other-day schedule from June to the end of September. The trip is scenic, and the daylight voyage takes 15 hours; the one-way fare for walk-on passengers is C$104. The same ship also makes a stop once a week at the isolated town of Bella Bella in British Columbia.

The easiest way to check current schedules or make reservations is to go to the BC Ferries Web site (www.bcferries.bc.ca). Schedules and reservations can also be obtained by calling or writing BC Ferries (☎ 250-386-3431), 1112 Fort St, Victoria, British Columbia, Canada V8V 4V2. In British Columbia, there is a toll-free number (☎ 888-223-3779).

Once you reach Prince Rupert, the ferry fare to Haines is $122; to Juneau, it's $104.

Hyder If for some strange reason you can't catch an Alaska Marine Hwy ferry at Prince Rupert, there's a last alternative. Make your way east along the Yellowhead Hwy from Prince Rupert and then head north along the Cassiar Hwy. You travel 99mi along the scenic Cassiar Hwy and then turn off at Kitwanga for Stewart. You can either hitchhike this route or catch a Greyhound bus to Kitwanga, basically the junction of Hwy 16 and Hwy 37, an hour's drive from the town of Terrace. At the Petro-Can Service Station, a Seaport Limousine Service bus (☎ 604-636-2622) stops by daily at 4 pm from Monday to Friday and will take you to Stewart for C$21.

Across the border from Stewart is Hyder, a Southeast Alaska hamlet of about 100 people with cafes, bars and gift shops.

During the summer, the Alaska Marine Hwy ferry M/V *Aurora* departs from here on Tuesdays at 3:45 pm, bound for Ketchikan, where you can continue north on one of several other boats. The one-way fare from Hyder to Ketchikan is $40.

It's vital to double-check the departure time for the Hyder ferry, as it may leave on Pacific Time as opposed to Alaska Time.

ORGANIZED TOURS

Many outfitters and companies organize wilderness trips, which include hiking, sea kayaking, rafting or canoeing. Most of the companies are based in Alaska (see Guided Hikes in the Facts for the Hiker chapter) but a few are located in other states.

National Outdoor Leadership School

The National Outdoor Leadership School (NOLS) teaches low-impact camping, survival techniques and environmental awareness through a wide range of activities, including backpacking, sea kayaking and rafting. They sponsor trips that range from two weeks to a month, in the Chugach Mountains, the Brooks and Alaska Ranges and in the Denali area and Prince William Sound.

Their month-long backpacking and rafting trip in the Brooks Range costs $4800, and their 14-day sea kayaking trip in Prince William sound is $2075. Neither trip includes transportation to Alaska. Contact NOLS (☎ 307-332-5300, ☻ admissions@ nols.edu), 288 Main St, Lander, WY 82520-3140, or check its Web site (www.nols.edu).

Natural Habitat Adventures

This tour company specializes in animal-watching adventures around the world, including several in Alaska. Most tour members sign up for the opportunity to photograph the wildlife, which in Alaska could include brown bears, moose, whales, sea lions, caribou and bald eagles. A 13-day tour that includes whale watching in Glacier

Bay, viewing giant brown bears at Katmai National Park and other wildlife at Denali National Park is $4995. All tours include accommodations but airfare to Anchorage is extra. For a catalog, call the company (☎ 303-449-3711, 800-543-8917 in USA and Canada).

North Star

North Star offers a range of sea kayaking, canoeing, trekking and base camp/hiking trips as well as natural history tours where participants stay at remote lodges. Prices range from $1575 for a week of kayaking in Kenai Fjords National Park to more than $1750 for six days of base camp hiking in Lake Clark National Park. Transportation is not included in the price. Contact North Star (☎ 520-773-9917, 800-258-8434, ✉ Northstar@AdventureTrip.com), PO Box 1724, Flagstaff, AZ 86002, or check its Web site (www.AdventureTrip.com) for information.

Getting Around

Travel around Alaska is unlike travel in any other state in the country. The fledgling public transportation system has stabilized and improved remarkably in recent years, but the overwhelming distances between regions make getting around Alaska almost as hard as getting there. Any long visit to Alaska usually combines transportation by car, bus, marine ferry, train and often a bush plane for access to the wilderness. Although the roads in Alaska and the Alaska Marine Hwy system cover only about a quarter of the state, they provide affordable access to an endless number of trails, treks and parks.

AIR
Domestic Air Services

As a general rule, if there is a regularly scheduled flight to your destination, it will be far cheaper than charter flights on the small airplanes known in Alaska as 'bush planes.' This is especially true if Alaska Airlines (☎ 800-426-0333) or its contract carrier, Horizon Air, fly where you want to go. Check out its Web site (www.alaskaair.com).

Alaska Airlines offers these roundtrip economy fares: Anchorage to Fairbanks $140 to $166, Juneau to Anchorage $225 to $260, Anchorage to Nome $352, Anchorage to Kodiak $186, Juneau to Cordova $255, Juneau to Sitka $101 and Juneau to Petersburg $160. Avoid one-way flights if you can; the fares are exorbitant.

Other domestic carriers include Era Aviation (☎ 800-478-1947), which connects Anchorage with Cordova, Seward, Kodiak and Homer; Reeve Aleutian Airways (☎ 800-544-2248) and Peninsula Airways (☎ 800-448-4226), which cover Southwest Alaska and the Aleutian Islands; and Yute Air Alaska (☎ 907-543-3003), which services western Alaska from Bethel.

In Southeast Alaska, Taquan Air (☎ 888-388-1180), a Ketchikan-based air carrier, has recently moved into the Juneau, Sitka and Petersburg markets. Taquan's AirPass ($299) offers you a week's worth of unlimited flights between those cities as well as Wrangell and Klawock. Taquan has a Web site (www.taquanair.com) where you can get more information.

Bush Planes

When you want to see more than the roadside attractions, you go to a dirt runway or small airfield outside town and climb into a bush plane. With 75% of the state not accessible by road, these small single-engine planes are the backbone of intrastate transport. They carry residents and supplies to desolate areas of the Bush, take anglers to some of the best fishing spots in the country and drop off backpackers in the middle of prime, untouched wilderness.

The person at the controls is a bush pilot, someone who might be fresh out of the US Air Force or somebody who arrived in Alaska 'way bee-fore statehood' and learned to fly by trial and error. A ride with such a local offers not only transportation to isolated areas and a scenic view of the state but also an earful of flying tales – some believable, some not.

Don't be alarmed when you hear that Alaska has the highest number of airplane crashes per capita in the country – it also has the largest percentage of pilots. One in every 58 residents has a license, and one resident in almost 60 owns a plane. That's six times more pilots and 16 times more planes per capita than any other state in the USA. Bush pilots are safe flyers who know their territory and its weather patterns; they don't want to go down any more than you do.

A ride in a bush plane is essential if you want to go beyond the common sights and see some of Alaska's most memorable scenery. In the larger cities of Anchorage, Fairbanks, Juneau and Ketchikan, it pays to check around before chartering. In most small towns and villages, however, you'll be lucky if there's a choice. For more information about air-taxi services, see the regional chapters; bush flights are listed under the town or area where they operate.

Bush aircraft include floatplanes that land and take off on water and beach landers with oversized tires that can use rough gravel shorelines as airstrips. Some aircraft may be equipped with skis to land on glaciers, sophisticated radar instruments for stormy areas like the Aleutian Islands and boat racks to carry canoes or hard-shell kayaks.

Fares vary with the type of plane, its size, the number of passengers and the amount of flying time. On the average, a Cessna 185 that can carry three passengers and a limited amount of gear will cost up to $240 to charter for an hour of flying time. A Cessna 206, a slightly larger plane that will hold four passengers, costs up to $300, while a Beaver, capable of hauling five passengers with gear, averages $360 for an hour of flying time. When chartering a plane to drop you off at an isolated USFS cabin or a wilderness trail, you must pay for both the air time to your drop-off point and for the return to the departure point.

Before chartering your own plane, check out all the possibilities. Most air-taxi companies have regularly scheduled flights to small towns and villages in six- to nine-seat aircraft with single-seat fares that are a fraction of the cost of chartering an entire plane. Others offer a 'mail flight' to small villages. These flights occur on a regular basis, with one or two seats available to travelers. Even when your destination is a USFS cabin or some wilderness spot, check with the local air-taxi companies. It's a common practice to match up a party departing from the cabin with another that's arriving, so that the air-charter costs can be split by filling the plane on both runs.

Booking a plane is easy and often can be done the day before departure or even at the last minute, if need be. Double-check all pickup times and places when flying to a wilderness area. Bush pilots fly over the pickup point and if you're not there, they usually return, call the USFS and still charge you for the flight.

When flying in and out of bays, fjords or coastal waterways, check the tides before determining your pickup time. It's best to schedule pickups and drop-offs at high tide or you may end up tramping a half mile through mud flats.

Always schedule extra days around a charter flight. It's not uncommon to be 'socked in' by weather for a day or two until a plane can fly in. Don't panic: they know you're there. Just think of the high school basketball team that flew to King Cove in the Aleutians for a weekend game in the 1960s – they were 'socked in' for a month before they could fly out again.

When traveling to small towns in the Bush, a scheduled flight or mail run is the cheapest way to go. Don't hesitate, however, to charter a flight to some desolate wilderness spot on your own; the best that Alaska has to offer is usually just a short flight away.

BUS

Regular bus services within Alaska are limited, but they are available between the larger towns and cities at reasonable rates. A trip by bus may be difficult to schedule, however, due to frequent turnover in the Alaska bus business. As one bus company goes under, another appears, so the phone numbers, schedules, rates and pickup points change drastically from one summer to the next. It pays to call ahead after arriving in Alaska to make sure that buses are still running to your destination.

The AlaskaPass offers discounts on bus, train and ferry transportation throughout the state. For more information, see Alaska-Pass in the Land section of the Getting There & Away chapter.

Alaskon Express

These Gray Line motorcoaches mainly serve travelers who need a ride along the last leg of the Alcan from Whitehorse in the Yukon to Haines, Skagway, Anchorage or Fairbanks (see Bus in the Land section of the Getting There & Away chapter). You can also travel from Anchorage to Glennallen ($60), from Anchorage to Seward ($40) or from Tok to Fairbanks ($69).

From Haines, Alaskon Express embarks on a two-day run to Anchorage every Tues-

MAJOR ALASKAN & YUKON HIGHWAYS

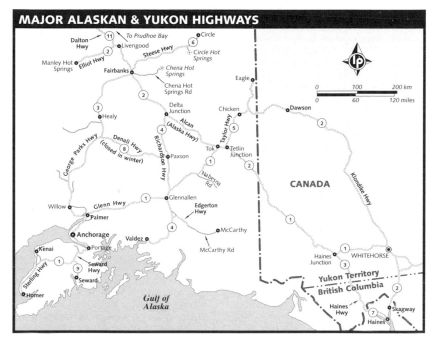

day, Thursday and Sunday at 8.45 am from mid-May to mid-September; the fare is $189, not including overnight lodging at Beaver Creek. An Alaskon Express bus leaves for Skagway at 7:30 am on the same days, overnighting at Beaver Creek and reaching Anchorage at 7:30 pm. You can also travel the reverse routes.

For local passenger boarding points, departure times and phone numbers, see the regional chapters. To make advance reservations, contact Gray Line of Alaska (☎ 800-544-2206), 300 Elliott Ave West, Seattle, WA 98119.

Alaska Direct Bus Line

Alaska Direct offers limited transportation from Anchorage to the rest of the state three times a week; the route ends in Whitehorse. On Sunday, Wednesday and Friday, a bus departs Anchorage at 6 am and reaches Whitehorse at midnight, passing through Palmer, Glennallen and Tok along the way.

There is also daily van service to Skagway. The one-way fare from Anchorage to Glennallen is $37, to Whitehorse $145 and to Skagway $180.

A bus also departs Fairbanks on the same days at 9 am for a similar run to Whitehorse. The one-way fare from Fairbanks to Tok is $40; to Whitehorse, it's $120.

Buses stop at the major hotels in Anchorage, or you can board at the company office at 125 Oklahoma St on the north end of town. Call Alaska Direct Bus Line (☎ 907-277-6652, 800-770-6652) for more information.

Seward Bus Lines

This company provides services between Anchorage and Seward, with a bus leaving Seward daily at 9 am, reaching Anchorage at noon and then departing at 2:30 pm for the return run, which ends in Seward at 5:30 pm; the one-way fare is $30. Board these buses at 1915 Seward Hwy, just north of Seward, or at the company's Anchorage depot, 3339 Fairbanks St. Call ☎ 907-224-3608 for current schedules and rates.

Kachemak Bay Transit

This relatively new company has picked up the Anchorage-to-Homer route that Seward Bus Lines abandoned in the mid-1990s. A KBT van departs Homer between 6:30 and 8:30 am and then begins the return trip from Anchorage between 4 and 6 pm. Hey, this is Alaska, that's the best they can offer in the way of a schedule. The one-way fare between the two cities is $55. Call KBT (☎ 907-399-1378, 907-235-3795) for pickup points and other information.

Denali National Park Van Service

A number of small companies offer van transportation between Anchorage and Fairbanks with a stop at Denali National Park. At times, the drivers can be a little surly, but the regularity of the vans' arrivals and departures make this service an attractive option. Generally these companies offer the cheapest ride to the popular park and usually get you there well ahead of the train, an important consideration if you're hoping to arrange shuttle bus rides, campground sites or backpacking permits.

The Alaska Park Connection shuttle (☎ 907-344-8775, 888-277-2757, ✉ info@alaskacoach.com) offers daily service along the George Parks and Seward Hwys. The Alaska Park Connection took over the popular Backpacker Shuttle runs in 2000. The one-way fare from Anchorage to Denali National Park is $59; to Talkeetna or Seward, it's $39; reservations are required. For more route and fare information, visit their Web site at www.alaska-tour.com.

Parks Highway Express

This company began as a van service to Denali National Park, but in 1999 it expanded to offer service on the three major highways: George Parks Hwy from Anchorage to Fairbanks, Richardson Hwy from Fairbanks to Valdez, and Top of the World Highway from Fairbanks to Dawson City.

Pickups and drop-offs are at popular hostels, and the fares are reasonable. You can go from Anchorage to Fairbanks for $60, Fairbanks to Valdez for $60, Fairbanks to Denali National Park for $25.

Parks Highway Express also offers the only bus pass in Alaska. The $145 pass buys you unlimited travel on any of the routes and is good for the entire travel season, from late May through early September. Contact Parks Highway Express (☎ 888-600-6001, ✉ info@alaskashuttle.com) for current schedules and fares or check its Web site (www.alaskashuttle.com).

TRAIN

In a state the size of Alaska, the logistics of building a railroad were overwhelming at the turn of the century; many private companies tried but failed, leading to federal government intervention in 1912. Three years later, construction began on a route from the tent city of Anchorage to the boomtown of Fairbanks. The line cut its way over what were thought to be impenetrable mountains, across raging rivers and through a wilderness as challenging as any construction crew had faced in the history of American railroading.

No wonder it took them eight years to build the Alaska Railroad. Today, it stretches 470mi from Seward to Fairbanks and provides a good – though not cheap – means of transportation for travelers. The scenery on each route is spectacular. You'll save more money traveling by bus down the George Parks Hwy, but few travelers, even those counting their dimes, regret booking a seat on the Alaska Railroad and viewing one of the world's most pristine wilderness areas from the train's comfortable cars.

The AlaskaPass offers discounts on bus, train and ferry transportation throughout the state. For more information, see Alaska-Pass in the Land section of the Getting There & Away chapter.

Anchorage to Fairbanks

The Alaska Railroad operates a year-round service between Fairbanks and Anchorage, as well as summer services (from late May to mid-September) from Anchorage to Whittier on Prince William Sound and from Anchorage to Seward. Although the 114mi trip down to Seward is a spectacular ride, unquestionably the most popular run is the 336mi trip from Anchorage to Fairbanks with a stop at Denali National Park. Heading north, at Mile 279 the train passes within 46mi of Mt McKinley, a stunning sight from the train's viewing domes on a clear day, and then slows down to cross the 918ft bridge over Hurricane Gulch, one of the most spectacular views of the trip.

North of Denali National Park, the train hugs the side of the Nenana River Canyon, passes numerous views of the Alaska Range and crosses the 700ft Mears Memorial Bridge (one of the longest single-span bridges in the world) over the Tanana River, 60mi south of Fairbanks. Before the bridge was completed, this was the end of the line in both directions, as people and goods were then ferried across the river to waiting cars on the other bank.

From late May to mid-September, two express trains run daily between Anchorage and Fairbanks with stops at Wasilla, Talkeetna, Denali National Park and Nenana. The express trains are geared for out-of-state travelers, as they offer vista-dome cars, reclining seats and a full dining and beverage service. You can also take your own food and drink on board, which isn't a bad idea since dinner on the train can cost between $14 and $17.

The northbound train departs Anchorage daily at 8:15 am, reaching Denali National Park at 3:45 pm and Fairbanks at 8:15 pm. The southbound train departs Fairbanks at 8:15 am, arriving at Denali National Park at noon and Anchorage at 8:30 pm. The one-way fare from Anchorage to Denali National Park is $104; to Fairbanks, it's $154. A ticket from Fairbanks to Denali costs $54. During the railroad's 'Value Season' (from mid-May to early June and the second week of September), you'll save $18 on the Anchorage-to-Denali fare and $34 on the Anchorage-to-Fairbanks fare.

From mid-September to mid-May, the schedule changes to one train per week; it departs Anchorage at 8:30 am on Saturday and then leaves Fairbanks at 8:30 am on Sunday for the return trip.

The Alaska Railroad still makes a 'milk run,' in which a train stops at every town and can even be flagged down by backpackers, anglers and mountain climbers emerging from their treks at the railroad tracks. The run used to extend from Anchorage to Fairbanks but now stretches only from Talkeetna to Hurricane Gulch during the summer. Still, the trip takes you within view of Mt McKinley and into some remote areas of the state. It also allows you to mingle with more local residents than you would on the express train.

From May to October, this diesel train departs Talkeetna at 12:15 pm, reaches Hurricane Gulch at 2:15 pm and then turns around and arrives back at Talkeetna at 5:45 pm. The service is available Thursday through Sunday, and the one-way fare to Hurricane Gulch is $20. The rest of the year, the flag-stop service runs from Anchorage to Hurricane Gulch on the first Thursday of the month. The train departs Anchorage at 8:30 am, and a roundtrip ticket is $88.

There are a few things to keep in mind when traveling by train from Anchorage to Fairbanks. Arrive at the depot at least 15 minutes before departure, as the express trains leave on time. Sit on the east side of the train if you want to see the mileposts. The best scenery is on the west side from Anchorage to Denali National Park and on the east side north of there.

The windows in all carriages are big, but taking pictures through them is less than satisfactory due to their distorting curves and the dust on the glass. Shoot photos from the platform between cars.

Finally, it pays to book early on this popular train; in Anchorage, call ☎ 907-265-2494. Before your trip, you can contact Alaska Railroad (☎ 800-544-0552, fax 907-265-2323, ✆ akrr@Alaska.net), PO Box 107500, Anchorage, AK 99510-7500, or check its Web site (www.akrr.com).

Anchorage to Whittier

Alaska Railroad's newest service is an Anchorage-to-Whittier run with a stop in Girdwood. The train departs Anchorage daily at 9 am, reaches Whittier at 11:30 am and then departs at 5:45 pm for the return trip. The roundtrip fare is $52, and one-way is $26, making it a slightly better deal than purchasing van shuttle service to Portage and a Portage-to-Whittier ticket on the railroad.

Even if you don't plan to take the Alaska Marine Hwy ferry across Prince William Sound, the trip to Whittier can be a fun day trip, as it is a scenic and interesting town. The train ride itself is also interesting, since it includes two tunnels, one of which is 13,090ft long.

Rail service also connects Portage and Whittier during the summer. One run is timed to meet the arrivals and departures of the Alaska Hwy ferry M/V Bartlett, which crosses Prince William Sound to Valdez on a scenic cruise past the Columbia Glacier.

If you don't have a car, you'll have to take a van shuttle from Anchorage to Portage, since the train from Anchorage to Portage only runs once a day. To catch the ferry, you'll need to take the 1:20 pm train out of Portage to arrive in Whittier at 2 pm and board the M/V Bartlett by 2:45 pm. The train then departs Whittier at 3:15 pm. Reservations for the train and ferry are highly recommended, as this is a popular excursion.

The train makes several roundtrips daily; the roundtrip fare from Portage to Whittier is $20 per passenger and $100 for most cars, which includes driver fare.

There are four runs from Portage on Wednesday and Thursday (departing at 10:20 am and 1:20, 4:30 and 7:15 pm) and six trains during the rest of the week (departing at 7:30 and 10:20 am and 1:20, 4:40, 7:30 and 9:35 pm). Tickets can be purchased from conductors at Portage. Although you can't make reservations for the rail service between Anchorage and Whittier, passengers with confirmed ferry tickets enjoy priority boarding on the 1:20 pm train from Portage. Call (☎ 907-265-2607) for pre-recorded information about fares and schedules.

Anchorage to Seward

Some say the ride between Anchorage and Seward is one of the most spectacular train trips in the world, rivaling those in the Swiss Alps and the New Zealand train that climbs over Arthur's Pass in the Southern Alps. From Anchorage, the 114mi trip begins by skirting the 60mi-long Turnagain Arm on Cook Inlet, where travelers can study the bore tides. After leaving Portage, the train swings south, climbs over mountain passes, spans deep river gorges and comes within half a mile of three glaciers: Spencer, Bartlett and Trail. The trip ends in Seward, a quaint town surrounded by mountains on one side and Resurrection Bay on the other.

The service is offered daily from mid-May to early September, with a train departing Anchorage at 6:45 am and reaching Seward at 11:05 am. It departs Seward the same day at 6 pm and reaches Anchorage at 10:25 pm; the roundtrip fare is $86. In 1998, the Alaska Railroad added a baggage car to its Seward run, primarily to accommodate the growing number of kayaks and bicycles being hauled south.

White Pass & Yukon Route

The White Pass & Yukon Railroad, a historic narrow-gauge railroad, was built in 1898 to connect Skagway to Whitehorse. The first railroad to be built in Alaska, it was for a time the most northern line in North America.

The railroad was carved out of the rugged mountains by workers who had to be suspended by ropes from vertical cliffs in order to chip and blast the granite away. The route followed the 40mi White Pass Trail from Skagway to Lake Bennett, where the miners would build rafts to float the rest of the way to Dawson City on the Canadian Yukon River. The line reached Whitehorse in 1900 and by then had made the Chilkoot Trail, a route miners hiked on foot, obsolete.

The railroad also played an important role in the construction of the Alcan during WWII. After that, it transported ore for mining companies in the Canadian Yukon Territory. In 1982, after world metal prices fell and the Canadian mines closed, operation of the White Pass & Yukon Railroad was suspended. But it has always been a popular tourist attraction, especially with travelers on big cruise ships, and in 1988 the railroad resumed limited service under the name White Pass & Yukon Route.

It's still the incredible ride it must have been for the Klondike miners. The White Pass & Yukon Railroad has one of the steepest grades in North America: it climbs from sea level in Skagway to 2885ft at White Pass in only 20mi. The mountain scenery is fantastic, the old narrow-gauge cars intriguing, and the trip is a must for anyone passing through Southeast Alaska.

The train operates from mid-May to late September and offers a one-day summit excursion and a scheduled through-service for travelers who actually want to use it as a means of transportation to Whitehorse and the Alcan. Northbound trains depart Skagway daily at 12:40 pm and arrive in Fraser at 2:40 pm; there, passengers transfer to buses, which arrive in Whitehorse at 5:45 pm (Pacific Time). Southbound buses depart Whitehorse at 8 am (Pacific Time), and the train leaves Fraser at 10:20 am, arriving in Skagway at noon. The one-way fare from Skagway to Whitehorse is $95.

Given the historical allure of this train, reservations wouldn't be a bad idea. Before your trip, contact the White Pass & Yukon Route (☎ 907-983-2217, 800-343-7373, @ info@whitepass.net), PO Box 435, Skagway, AK 99840, or check its Web site (www.whitepassrailroad.com).

CAR
Rental & Purchase
Having your own car in Alaska, as in any other place, provides the freedom and flexibility that public transportation does not. Car rental, however, is a costly way for a single person to travel. But for two or more people, it can be an affordable way out of Anchorage, which has the best car rental rates by far. In Alaska, it isn't the charge per day for the rental but the charge per mile that makes it so expensive. Outside Anchorage and Fairbanks, drivers will find gas 20¢ to 30¢ per gallon more expensive than in the rest of the USA.

The Alaska tourist boom of the 1980s has produced a network of cheap car rental companies that offer rates considerably lower than those of national firms such as Avis, Hertz and National Car Rental. The largest of these is Practical Car Rental (also called Allstar in Alaska; ☎ 800-426-5243), which has offices in seven Alaskan towns but unfortunately not in Anchorage or Fairbanks. It does have branches in Ketchikan, Petersburg, Juneau, Wrangell and Sitka, as well as Klawock on Prince Wales Island. Its rates change from city to city, as its branches are independently owned, but most offices charge around $40 to $50 a day for a subcompact with 100 free miles.

Other companies include High Country Car Rental in Anchorage (☎ 907-562-8078, 888-685-1155), 512 W International Airport Rd, which has subcompacts for $40 a day during the summer. Before June and after August, the rates are considerably lower, sometimes only $30 a day. In Fairbanks, Rent-A-Wreck (☎ 907-452-1606) charges the same rates, with 150 free miles a day for a subcompact.

The downside of car rental is that some of these cars are occasionally stubborn about starting up right away, especially the used models available through the cheaper rental companies. However, if there are three or four people splitting the cost, car rental is far less expensive than taking a bus and allows you total freedom to stop when you want.

All the used-car rental companies are listed in the regional chapters under the towns where they maintain offices. In Anchorage, you can also try Affordable Car Rental (☎ 907-243-3370), Airport Car Rentals (☎ 907-277-7662) or U-Save Rental (☎ 907-272-8728, 800-254-8728).

If you're planning on buying a car in Alaska, be forewarned: The winters are long and the environment is harsh, so used cars are not only expensive but more often than not rust buckets. Purchasing and selling a car for transportation is not a common practice in Alaska. The best place to obtain a used car is Anchorage; begin your search with the classified ads in the Sunday edition of the *Anchorage Daily News*. An even better – and undoubtedly cheaper – strategy is to purchase your car in the Lower 48 and drive it along the Alcan or put it on the ferry.

Motorhome Rental

Want to be a road hog? You can always rent a motorhome (also called a recreational vehicle), as many people do. RVers flock to the land of the midnight sun in numbers that are astounding. There are some roads, like the George Parks Hwy, that look like an endless stream of trailers, pop-ups and land cruisers.

More than a dozen companies, almost all of them based in Anchorage, will rent you a motorhome, ranging from 20 to 35ft in length, that accommodates up to six people. The price can vary from $125 to $175 per day, but again you have to consider all the extra charges. Many places offer 100 free miles per day, then charge 15¢ to 25¢ per mile for any additional mileage.

You also have to pay for insurance and possibly even a 'housekeeping kit' – pots, pans and sheets. It's best to anticipate a daily fee between $150 and $200 and remember that full-hook-up campgrounds cost $15 to $20 a night. Still, when divided between four to six people, the cost comes to around $28 to $35 a day per person for both transportation and a bed – not a bad deal if you can round up several other people who want to share the same itinerary. Other costs include gasoline, food and campsites.

You have to reserve a motorhome four to five months in advance for the summer season. A few of the larger Anchorage rental companies are Great Alaskan Holidays (☎ 907-248-7777, 888-225-2752), which does not charge extra for housekeeping packages, cleaning or insurance and has 20-footers with prices that begin as low as $134 a day (plus 17¢ a mile for a rental of seven days or more); Alaska Motorhome Rentals (☎ 800-254-9929); Alaska Economy RVs (☎ 907-561-7723, @mis@goalaska.com); and Clippership Motorhome Rentals (☎ 800-421-3456).

ABC Motorhome Rentals (☎ 800-421-7456, @ rvalaska@alaska.net) offers units that are totally self-contained; no hook-ups are needed as they are totally battery and propane operated. This means you can stay at small rustic and out-of-the-way places. A camper with a shower runs $150 a day.

BICYCLE

For those who want to bike it, Alaska offers a variety of cycling adventures on paved roads during long days with comfortably cool temperatures. Most cyclists hop on the Alaska Marine Hwy ferries, carrying their bikes on for an additional fee ranging from $7 to $42 for the longest run from Bellingham to Skagway.

From Haines, you can catch an Alaskon Express bus to Tok or Anchorage in the heart of Alaska. There is no charge for carrying the bike, but be prepared to have it stored in the compartment under the bus. You can also take your bike on Alaska Airlines for a $50 excess-baggage fee each way.

Summer cyclists have to take some extra precautions in Alaska. Few towns have fully equipped bike shops, so it's wise to carry not only metric tools but also a tube repair kit, spare inner tubes, brake and shifter cables, spokes, brake pads and any other parts that might be needed during the trip. Due to high rainfall, especially in the Southeast, waterproof saddlebags are useful, as are tire fenders. Rain gear is a must, and storing gear in resealable plastic bags within your saddlebags is advised. Carry warm clothing, mittens and a woolen hat, along with a tent and rain tarpaulin. It's not necessary to weigh yourself down with a lot of food, as you can easily restock on all major roads.

Some roads do not have much of a shoulder – the Seward Hwy between Anchorage and Girdwood, for example – so cyclists should utilize the sunlight hours when traffic is light to pedal in such areas.

Most cyclists avoid gravel, but biking the Alcan (an increasingly popular trip) does involve riding over some short gravel breaks in the paved asphalt. When riding along gravel roads, figure on making 50% to 70% of your normal distance and take spare inner tubes – flat tires will be a daily occurrence on the Alcan.

Mountain bikers, on the other hand, are in heaven on such gravel roads as the Denali Hwy in the Interior, the logging roads on Prince of Wales Island in the Southeast and the park road in Denali National Park. Mountain bikers are even pedaling the Dalton Hwy to Prudhoe Bay.

The Arctic Bicycle Club of Anchorage sponsors a variety of road- and mountain-bike tours during the summer. Call the club's information hot line (☎ 907-566-0177) for a recorded message of upcoming tours, or check its Web site (www.arcticbike .alaska.net) for more information.

You might also consider reading the *Alaska Bicycle Touring Guide* by Pete Praetorius and Alys Culhane, the first guide put This book has been called the 'bicycling equivalent of *The Milepost*' for its thorough description of routes throughout the state, including two that go north of the Arctic Circle.

Another good book is *Mountain Bike Alaska,* by Richard Larson, a guide to 49 trails for mountain bikers. They range from the Denali Hwy and the Denali park road to many of the traditional hiking trails situated on the Kenai Peninsula.

Rental & Purchase

The following cities and towns in Alaska have bike shops that sell bicycles and offer a good selection of spare parts. However, by the end of the summer many are low on, or completely out of, certain spare parts. Mountain bike rentals are also possible in a handful of areas of Alaska, like Denali National Park, and those shops are outlined in the regional chapters.

Anchorage
The Bicycle Shop (☎ 272-5219),
  1035 W Northern Lights Blvd
Gary King Sporting Goods (☎ 279-7454),
  202 E Northern Lights Blvd
REI Co-op (☎ 272-4565),
  1200 W Northern Lights Blvd

Fairbanks
Beaver Sports (☎ 479-2494),
  2400 College Rd

Girdwood
Girdwood Ski & Cycle (☎ 783-2453),
  Alyeska Access Rd

Juneau
Adventure Sports (☎ 789-5696),
  8757 Glacier Hwy
Mountain Gears (☎ 586-4327),
  210 N Franklin St

Sitka
Yellow Jersey Cycle Shop (☎ 747-6317),
  805 Halibut Point Rd

Skagway
Sockeye Cycle (☎ 983-2851),
  5th Ave and Broadway St

FERRY

In the Southeast, the Alaska Marine Hwy ferries replace bus services and operate from Juneau or Ketchikan to Skagway, Haines, Hoonah, Tenakee Springs, Angoon, Sitka, Kake, Petersburg, Hyder and Hollis, with an occasional special run to the tiny fishing village of Pelican (see the Ferry section of the Getting There & Away chapter for more details).

The Alaska Marine Hwy also offers services in Southcentral and Southwest Alaska, where the M/V *Bartlett* and the M/V *Tustumena* connect towns along Prince William Sound and the Gulf of Alaska.

Once a month during the summer, the M/V *Kennicott* sails from Juneau to Valdez and then on to Seward to connect the Southwest ferry with the Southeast line. You can also link the two systems by picking up an Alaska Airlines flight from Juneau to Cordova.

The M/V *Bartlett* sails from Cordova and Valdez to Whittier across Prince William Sound, passing the Columbia Glacier along the way. The M/V *Tustumena* calls at Seward, Homer and Seldovia on the Kenai Peninsula, Port Lions and Kodiak on Kodiak Island and Valdez on the eastern shore of Prince William Sound.

In 1993, the Alaska Marine Hwy instituted a direct service from Whittier to Cordova on the M/V *Bartlett*. From May to September, the ship leaves Whittier at 2:45 pm on Friday, reaching Cordova seven hours later. On Monday, the ship departs Cordova at 7 am and sails to Whittier. This makes the charming town of Cordova a nice three-day side trip from Anchorage.

Also in the summer, the M/V *Tustumena* makes a special run to Sand Point, King Cove, Cold Bay and Dutch Harbor at the end of the Alaska Peninsula. The trip is available five times (in mid-May, June, July, August and September) and takes six days roundtrip from Kodiak. It's clearly the cheapest way to see part of Alaska's stormy arm.

Walk-on passengers can expect to pay the following fares for ferry travel along the Southwest routes: Valdez to Cordova $30; Valdez to Whittier $58; Valdez to Seward $58;

Seward to Kodiak $54; Homer to Kodiak $48; Kodiak to Unalaska $202; Homer to Seldovia $18.

The AlaskaPass offers discounts on bus, train and ferry transportation throughout the state. For more information, see AlaskaPass in the Land section of the Getting There & Away chapter.

LOCAL TRANSPORTATION

The vast majority of towns in Alaska are not large enough to require local transportation beyond taxicabs. The cities that are – Anchorage, Fairbanks, Juneau and Ketchikan – serve that need with a bus system. The largest and most important for travelers is Anchorage's People Mover, an excellent public bus system with reasonable fares ($1 per adult, 10¢ per transfer). See the regional chapters for information on getting to and from the trailheads.

Southeast Alaska

Some of the best hiking in Alaska, and maybe in the USA, is found in Southeast Alaska. Almost every town or village has trails that lead into surrounding mountains, remote valleys or along glaciers. Easy and affordable ferry travel, stunning scenery, excellent wildlife and trails maintained by the US Forest Service (USFS) as part of the Tongass National Forest, explain why some hikers spend their entire summer in the Southeast.

The only drawbacks to hiking in the Southeast are the rainy weather and the lack of long trails. Other than the famous Chilkoot Trail in Skagway, most of the trails in the Southeast are good for day hikes or, at best, overnight hikes. Many hikers, however, are attracted to the idea of spending days in the mountains and nights back at town.

Travel around the Southeast is easy. The Alaska Marine Hwy ferry system connects this region to Bellingham in the US state of Washington and provides transportation around the area, making it the most extensive public ferry system in North America. In the Southeast, the state ferry links 14 ports and serves 66,000 residents, 75% of whom live in Juneau, Ketchikan, Sitka, Petersburg and Wrangell.

Ketchikan Region

Ketchikan is the departure point for a number of wilderness adventures and trails, but most of the trailheads can only be reached by floatplane or tour boat. The trails accessible by road (Ward Lake Nature Walk, Perseverance Trail and Talbot Lake Trail) are under 3mi long. The exception is the Deer Mountain Trail. It can be picked up from downtown and offers an overnight adventure in the mountains surrounding the city.

NATURAL HISTORY

Ketchikan is in the southern end of the Tongass National Forest, the largest national forest in the country. When Tongass National Forest is combined with the coastal forests of British Columbia and the state of Washington, it's part of the largest temperate rain forest in the world. The most common tree along the trails is western hemlock, about 70% of the trees in the forest. Less common is the Sitka spruce, the Alaska state tree, which can grow to heights of 225ft and live for more than 600 years. Western red cedar also grows in the Ketchikan area, and mountain hemlock grows closer to the tree line.

Much of the Deer Mountain trail system is in the beautiful subalpine and alpine world above the tree line. Here you encounter talus slopes (a slope formed by accumulated rock debris), lush meadows, small pothole lakes and stunning views. The lichens, mosses, grasses, sedges and stunted conifers of alpine areas are extremely fragile,

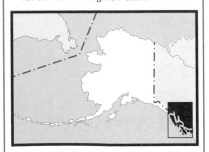

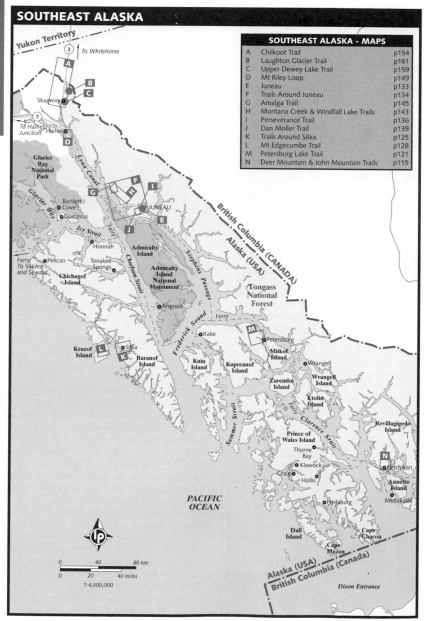

so stay on the trail and select your campsites carefully.

CLIMATE

The region doesn't have ideal hiking weather; more often than not it will be cloudy or drizzly. The Southeast, affected greatly by warm ocean currents, offers warm summer temperatures averaging 69°F (you get the most sun in August), but it also receives a good deal of rain, even in July and August. Annual rainfall in Ketchikan averages 162 inches, but it has been known to exceed 200 inches in some years. The heavy precipitation is responsible for the dense, lush forests and numerous waterfalls that most hikers come to cherish.

INFORMATION

For information about hiking trails or other outdoor opportunities, head to the trip-planning room of the Southeast Alaska Visitor Center (☎ 228-6214), on the corner of Bawden and Mills Sts in Ketchikan. Managed by the USFS, the room contains reference guides, topographic maps and a huge selection of videos to watch. Hours are 8:30 am to 4:30 pm daily in the summer.

KETCHIKAN

The first port of call in the Southeast is Ketchikan (population 8320) on the southwest side of Revillagigedo (ra-vee-ah-ga-GAY-doh) Island, only 90mi north of Prince Rupert.

Naha River Trail

The Naha River Trail is the most interesting hike outside of Ketchikan. The Naha River and its connecting lakes, Jordan and Heckman, can be fished for salmon, cutthroat trout and Dolly Varden. Two USFS cabins – the Jordan Lake Cabin and the Heckman Lake Cabin – can be rented along the trail, and there is a picnic shelter where many backpackers set up camp. Wildlife is plentiful in the area, and in August it's often possible to see bears catching salmon at the small waterfalls along the river.

The only challenge is getting there. The trail is 8mi from the end of N Tongass Hwy, 25mi from the city of Ketchikan. There is not enough demand by hikers to support a water taxi service to the trailhead, so your options at this time are either chartering a floatplane or paddling to the trailhead in a kayak. There are a number of floatplane operators in every Southeast Alaskan town. Island Wings (225-2444, 888-845-2444, ✉ islewing@ktn.net) is but one of them. Kayaks can be rented from Southeast Exposure (☎ 225-8829), 515 Water St. They will also provide transportation to the end of the road for an additional fee. Double kayaks rent for $50 a day, $45 for six days or more. There are also singles available. Southeast Sea Kayaks (☎ 225-1528, 800-287-1607) also rents boats in Ketchikan.

The trailhead is on Naha Bay, which leads into Roosevelt Lagoon through a narrow outlet. Kayakers trying to paddle into the lagoon must enter it at high slack tide, as the narrow pass becomes a frothy, roaring chute when the tide is moving in or out. The current in the salt chuck actually changes directions depending on the tide. Naha River Trail is 6.5mi long, and for the most part, it follows the river past the lakes and two USFS cabins. The trail is a combination of boardwalk, swing bridges and a gentle uphill walk to the higher elevations of Jordan and Heckman Lakes. You begin by skirting Roosevelt Lagoon, a tidal saltwater lagoon that is a haven for waterfowl and shorebirds. The first waterfall, a good spot to see black bear fishing for salmon, is reached 2.5mi from the trailhead. The second is another 3mi up the trail.

The best fishing on the Naha River is during the spring and fall steelhead runs, but anglers can catch Dolly Varden and cutthroat trout on the lower river and lakes throughout the summer. From July through September four species of salmon – silver, chum, sockeye and pink – spawn up the river.

During the summer the cabins ($35 per night) are in heavy demand and must be reserved in advance (see Accommodations in the Facts for the Hiker chapter). For a map, purchase the USGS quad *Ketchikan C-5* at the Southeast Alaska Visitor Center.

SOUTHEAST

The Ketchikan Visitor's Bureau (☎ 225-6166, 800-770-3300), on the city dock, can supply you with general information about Ketchikan and the city bus system. The bureau is open 8 am to 5 pm Monday to Friday and, when the cruise ships are in, on Saturday and Sunday. It also has a Web site (www.visit-ketchikan.com).

Supplies & Equipment

If you're lacking some equipment, need white gas or have a craving for freeze-dried dinners on your hike, the Outfitter (☎ 225-5101), 201 Dock St, has a limited stock of backpacking gear. The best supermarket to stock up on noodle dinners and instant oatmeal is Carrs Quality Center, next door to the Plaza Mall on Tongass Ave.

Places to Stay & Eat

The closest campgrounds to Ketchikan are *Signal Creek* (19 sites, $10), *CCC Campground* (four sites, $10) and *Last Chance Campground* (25 sites, $10), in the Ward Lake Recreation Area. Take N Tongass Hwy 4mi north of the ferry terminal and then turn right onto Ward Lake Rd just before the pulp mill on Ward Cove.

In the center of town is the *Ketchikan HI-AYH Hostel* (☎ 225-3319), in the United Methodist Church at Grant and Main Sts. It's open from Memorial Day to Labor Day and provides kitchen facilities, showers and a space on the floor with a mat to sleep on. The fee is $8 for hostel members, $11 for nonmembers. If you're arriving at night, call the hostel to check whether space is available.

Innside Passage (☎ 247-3700, 114 Elliot St, ✉ raaum@ktn.net), a B&B a half mile north of the city center, has rooms for $65/80 singles/doubles.

The *Gilmore Hotel* (☎ 225-9423, 326 Front St) has rooms for $68/73.

The downtown area has several good restaurants. For breakfast, there is the *Pioneer Pantry (124 Front St)*, which opens at 7 am. Three eggs, potatoes and toast cost $7. Outside the downtown area, there is a *McDonald's* at Plaza Mall on Tongass Ave. Nearby, *Godfather's Pizza*, in the Ketchikan

Entertainment Center at 2050 Sea Level Drive, features medium pizzas with one item for $13 and an all-you-can eat salad bar and lunch buffet specials.

Getting There & Away

Air Alaska Airlines (☎ 225-2145) flies to Ketchikan, with stops at other major Southeast communities, Anchorage, and Seattle. There are several flights between Ketchikan and Juneau, including one that locals call the 'milk run,' as it stops at Petersburg, Wrangell and Sitka and is little more than a series of takeoffs and landings.

Boat It's an exceptional day when there isn't a ferry departing from Ketchikan for other Southeast destinations or Bellingham. The one-way fares from Ketchikan to Wrangell are $24, Petersburg $38, Juneau $74, Sitka $54 and Haines $92.

Deer Mountain & John Mountain Trails

Duration 2 days
Distance 12mi
Difficulty Level Medium to hard
Start Deer Mountain Trailhead
Finish Beaver Falls Hatchery
Cabins & Shelters Yes
Permits Required No
Public Transportation No
Summary The traverse from Deer Mountain to Silvis Lakes is a two-day walk, with much of the time spent above the tree line. The views are excellent, and there are opportunities to climb John Mountain and Mahoney Mountain.

Deer Mountain is the distinctively pointed peak dominating the alpine region above downtown Ketchikan. The 3.1mi trail to the summit is the most popular hike in Ketchikan, and the trailhead is the easiest trailhead in the area to reach. John Mountain Trail is a 4mi hike from the Beaver Falls Hatchery, at the south end of Tongass Hwy, to the 3238ft peak.

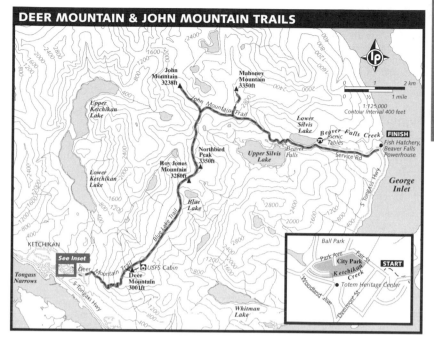

DEER MOUNTAIN & JOHN MOUNTAIN TRAILS

By using the ridge walk known as the Blue Lake Trail to connect the Deer Mountain and John Mountain Trails, you can turn the two trails into a 12mi hike into the mountains that surround Ketchikan. You can spend a night at the USFS cabin (if you have booked it in advance) or camp along beautiful Blue Lake.

Most backpackers walk the traverse in two days. With three days, you can spend another enjoyable night above the tree line and leave the heavy packs in camp for easier climbs of John Mountain and Mahoney Mountain (3350ft). The summit of Deer Mountain makes an excellent day hike.

PLANNING
When to Hike
The recommended season to walk the trail is mid-June through September. Heavy snow lingers well into June. The alpine region comes to life with flowers and blueberries in July and August, the preferred months to

hike this route. The rainy season in Ketchikan often begins by mid-September.

What to Bring
The Deer Mountain Cabin does not have a stove, and it is above the tree line, so bring a backpacker's stove if you plan on staying there and would relish a hot meal at the end of your first day's hike.

Maps
The USGS 1:63,360 quad *Ketchikan B-5* was updated in 1994 and shows the entire alpine route of the Deer Mountain Trail in the best possible detail. You can purchase quads at the Southeast Alaska Visitor Center or the Tongass Trading Company (☎ 225-5101), 201 Dock St.

Cabins & Shelters
The Deer Mountain USFS Cabin, located below the summit, costs $35 a night and should be reserved in advance by calling

National Recreation Reservation Service (☎ 877-444-6777, 515-885-3639 for overseas) or through its Web site (www.reserveusa .com). If you're planning the make the traverse in two days, keep in mind that the cabin is only 2.5mi from the Deer Mountain Trailhead, making the hike from the cabin to the end of the trail a very long one.

GETTING TO/FROM THE HIKE
To the Start

The trailhead for the Deer Mountain Trail can be reached by following the gravel road from the corner of Deermont and Fair Sts (near Ketchikan Creek) and past a subdivision (to the southeast). A trail sign points left, to a side road that leads 100ft to the trailhead and a small parking area.

Getting to the Deer Mountain Trailhead is easy. You can walk to it or jump on a Ketchikan borough bus. The city bus system consists of small buses that hold up to 30 passengers. The buses follow a circular route, from the ferry terminal in the West End to the area south of Thomas Basin, circling back by the Totem Heritage Center and within a half mile of the Deer Mountain Trailhead. Buses run from 5:30 am to 9:30 pm during the week and 8:45 am to 3:45 pm Saturday and Sunday. The fare is $1.

From the Finish

Getting back from Beaver Falls, 14mi from town at the end of the S Tongass Hwy, is much more challenging than getting to the trailhead. Your best bet is to arrange a pickup in town with somebody like a B&B operator, or use the courtesy phone at the Beaver Falls Hatchery to call a taxi company like Alaska Cab (☎ 225-2133), which charges $30 per pickup.

THE HIKE
Stage 1: Deer Mountain Trailhead to Blue Lake

4.6mi, 4 to 5 hours

The Deer Mountain Trail begins with boardwalks that cross a muskeg area then begin to climb the mountain, skirting its western-southwestern slope with a series of switch-

backs through a forest of hemlock and cedar. The first view of the Tongass Narrows pops up within a mile, as you reach 1500ft. The switchbacks continue, and you reach a second viewpoint 2mi from the trailhead, a rock outcropping where a ski hut was built in 1930. Although the hut is no longer there, this is an excellent spot for an extended break. You can enjoy lunch while gazing down on downtown Ketchikan.

The trail climbs from the rest stop, quickly clearing the tree line, to views of **Lower Ketchikan Lake**. Within a quarter mile the trail reaches a posted junction. To the right (east) is the trail to **Deer Mountain**, a 3001ft peak that, on a clear day, provides a 360-degree panorama of Ketchikan, Tongass Narrows and Prince of Wales Island. From there you can descend to the USFS cabin just below the summit on the north side.

The left-hand fork traverses the north slope of the mountain and is also above the tree line, enabling you to look down on Lower Ketchikan Lake or across to the surrounding peaks and ridges. Within a quarter mile, you come to another posted junction. The side trail to the right leads a short way to **Deer Mountain Cabin**, located in a saddle northeast of the summit. The A-frame structure was built in 1962 and at one time was a free-use shelter, but the cabin was constantly being vandalized, forcing the USFS to turn it into a rental unit. The structure sleeps five to six on wooden platforms and a small loft but does not have a stove inside. The maximum stay during the summer is three consecutive nights and, as you can imagine, you must book in advance.

From the spur to the USFS cabin, the trail follows the ridgeline as it heads northeast toward another 3000ft peak. Metal posts mark the route across the open ridgeline and are needed in June when heavy snow is often lingering. This stretch is very steep and difficult in places and offers no protection during foul weather. During such periods of bad weather, the steep drop-offs have claimed lives because of poor visibility. Stay on the trail at all times

Hiking in Wrangell

The next major town north from Ketchikan along the ferry route is Wrangell (population 2549). The community's claim to history is that it was the only Alaskan fort to have existed under three flags – Russian, British and American. When Alaska Pulp Corp closed its Wrangell mill in 1994, the town began to promote tourism, including setting up a hostel, but Wrangell remains off the beaten path for most Alaskan tourists. Unless you rent a car, the hiking opportunities are limited in Wrangell. There aren't any multiday trails on Wrangell Island, but **Shoemaker Bay Overlook** is only 4.5mi from town and makes a delightful overnight trek.

The hike is a 3.5-mile trek from Zimovia Hwy via the Rainbow Falls Trail and the Institute Creek Trail to the overlook, which features a free-use shelter. The trailhead is directly across from the Shoemaker Bay Recreation Area, a small boat harbor and picnic area. Within a half mile of the trailhead, the trail climbs 500ft to arrive at the first viewing deck, which overlooks the falls. Another quarter mile up the trail is a second deck that provides an excellent view of Chichagof Pass.

The posted junction to **Institute Creek Trail** is nearby. This path uses switchbacks to climb through the hemlock-cedar forest and break out into a string of muskeg meadows. Here, the trail crosses the creek, swings west and traverses more meadows via planking before finally reaching the overlook. It's a 1500ft climb from the highway to the overlook, but it's worth it. The shelter sleeps four and overlooks Shoemaker Bay, Zimovia Strait and the surrounding islands. The area also has a picnic table and a vault toilet, but no water. Fill up the water bottles where the trail crosses Institute Creek.

Pack along your insect repellent; it can get buggy here on still nights during the summer. The lower section of the trail can be soggy at times, so wear rubber boots if you have them. A return trip to the ridge takes four to six hours, and the hike is covered by USGS quads *Petersburg B-1* and *B-2*.

If you have a chance, check with the USFS office (☎ 874-2323) in Wrangell, north of town at 525 Bennett St. Plans call for building a 4.5mi trail that would extend from Institute Creek Trail to a trailhead 2mi from the USFS office. To be called North Wrangell Trail, the route would follow the high ridge north of Institute Creek, making the entire system a pleasant three-day hike.

Other trails in Wrangell include the following:

Mt Dewey Trail This half-mile trail winds its way up a hill to an observation point overlooking Wrangell and the surrounding waterways. From Mission St, walk a block and turn left at the first corner, 3rd St. Follow the street past a brown and red A-frame house with a white balcony. The trail, marked by a white sign, begins 50yd past the house on the right. Once you're at the trailhead, the hike is a short one, 15 minutes or so to the top, but it is often muddy. John Muir fanatics will appreciate the fact that the great naturalist himself climbed the mountain in 1879 and built a bonfire at the top, alarming the Tlingits living in the village below.

Thoms Lake Trail At the end of the paved Zimovia Hwy is a dirt road, known officially as Forest Rd 6290, that extends 30mi south along Wrangell Island. On this road, 23mi south of Wrangell, is the Thoms Lake Trail, which leads 1.4mi to a state park recreation cabin and a skiff on the lake. Since there is no state park office in Wrangell, you have to reserve the cabin through the Division of Parks office in Juneau (☎ 465-4563). The second half of this trail isn't planked and can get extremely muddy during wet weather. It is a 1½-hour hike to the cabin (USGS quad *Petersburg A-1*).

Long Lake Trail The trailhead for the Long Lake Trail is 27mi southeast of Wrangell on Forest Rd 6270. This pleasant hike is only 0.6mi long and planked the entire way. It leads to a shelter that sleeps four, a skiff and outhouses on the shores of the lake. Plan a half hour for the hike in to the lake or out (USGS quad *Petersburg A-1*).

Highbush Lake Trail This very short 300ft path leads to a lake where there's a skiff and oars. The fishing is fair, and the surrounding views are excellent. The parking lot for the trailhead is 29mi from Wrangell, off Forest Rd 6265 and Forest Rd 50040.

You ascend to the higher ridgeline and follow it as it skirts high above **Granite Basin** to the west. Within 2.2mi of the cabin junction, the trail descends sharply to the small basin surrounding **Blue Lake**. There used to be a free-use shelter here too, but it was so heavily vandalized that the USFS removed it. Still, the spot is an ideal place to camp.

Stage 2: Blue Lake to Tongass Hwy

6.6mi, 4 to 6 hours

The first half of this day is spent above the tree line in the alpine area. It is a stunning hike if the weather is clear. If it's not, be careful to follow the route correctly, especially on the sharp descent of Northbird Peak.

From Blue Lake, the trail is mostly a marked route with areas of tread here and there. The trail skirts the west end of the lake and continues north along the ridge. Within the first half mile you gently climb **Roy Jones Mountain** (3280ft), descend and then climb **Northbird Peak** (3350ft), which is generally flanked by snowfields throughout the summer. Descend the peak in a northwest direction. The route climbs a 3100ft knob and then descends almost 300ft, to where the ridgeline dips near an alpine pond and a few dwarf hemlocks. Be careful on this stretch, as it is very steep and rocky and marked only by an occasional steel post.

The trail eventually resumes climbing and joins the **John Mountain Trail**, 2mi from Blue Lake at the south end of a basin overlooking another alpine lake. The basin makes a nice spot to camp, enabling you to spend the afternoon climbing John Mountain. The ridgeline and route to the northwest leads to the 3238ft summit, a 1mi climb from the junction in the basin.

To the east, the trail leads gently up a ridge to 3000ft and arrives at a junction with the route to the top of **Mahoney Mountain** (3350ft), a shorter and easier climb than John Mountain. The trail to the Silvis Lakes and Tongass Hwy descends sharply off that ridge into a small bowl at the tree line. Staying well above **Upper Silvis Lake** at first,

you continue down into the forest for the first time, to eventually bottom out at the lake's old dam outlet. The final mile from the tree line to the dam outlet is a steep descent of more than 800ft. Be careful here.

The trail between Upper Silvis Lake and Lower Silvis Lake is another steep descent and used to be a notoriously muddy stretch, but the trail was rebuilt in 1996, making it easier to follow and safer. Within a third of a mile, the trail emerges at the west end of **Lower Silvis Lake**, crosses a stream on a bridge and arrives at a very rocky and rough two-track. You follow the two-track a half mile, as it skirts the south shore of the lake, to a pair of picnic tables and an outhouse at the east end.

The final 2mi of the hike follow a good gravel road that makes a steady descent to Tongass Hwy. The gravel road begins with a gentle descent for a half mile, until you reach an intake station and good views of George Inlet. The final 1.5mi is a fast trip to the bottom. At times the road is so steep you'll practically run down with your backpack. You emerge at Beaver Falls Hatchery, where there is a trailhead sign and a courtesy phone for local calls.

Petersburg Region

The best three hikes in the Petersburg area are a short distance from the town itself. Unfortunately, two of them – Petersburg Lake Trail and Petersburg Mountain Trail – are on Kupreanof Island, requiring a 10-minute boat ride to the other side of the Wrangell Narrows. The third, Raven Roost Trail, is a mile walk from the downtown area.

Because there are no hostel-style accommodations or campgrounds close to town, Petersburg does not draw the number of backpackers that Juneau or Skagway do. Because it lacks a deep-water port for large cruise ships to dock at, there are also significantly fewer tourists. This makes a trip to the town a little more expensive but often much more enjoyable. Once on the trails, you'll encounter only a few other parties, if any at all.

NATURAL HISTORY

Petersburg's temperate rain forests are dominated by hemlock, but along the Petersburg Lake Trail you will encounter some stately groves of Sitka spruce. Mitkof Island also marks the northern end of the range for western red cedar, which can grow to 100ft in height and 4ft in diameter. On the upper slopes of Petersburg Mountain grow mountain hemlock, a species that appears throughout the Southeast beginning at 1500ft.

Along the forest floor, you can easily – and painfully if you are not careful – find devil's club. Almost as prominent is skunk cabbage, which can grow to impressive size in the rain forest. An important food source for both deer and bears, skunk cabbage is a good indicator that the hiking is going to get wetter. Most trails in the area will also cross muskeg bogs, which can be especially sloppy after a recent rainfall, even if the trail is planked.

Petersburg Creek, which runs along the Petersburg Lake Trail, supports large populations of cutthroat, Dolly Varden and rainbow trout, and silver, pink, chum and sockeye salmon runs from mid- to late summer. With so many fish in the river, black bears are plentiful in the area, especially from late August through September. The estuary that the creek flows into attracts a variety of birds, including loons, grebes, geese, bald eagles and even an occasional trumpeter swan.

CLIMATE

Petersburg has the same coastal climate as Ketchikan, only it doesn't rain quite as much. Average rainfall in Petersburg is 110 inches a year, with half falling October through December. The average temperature in July is 56°F.

INFORMATION

For information about hiking, paddling or camping, head over to the US Forest Service office (☎ 772-3871) upstairs in the federal building on Nordic Drive in Petersburg. The office is open 8 am to 5 pm weekdays. You can also write to the Petersburg Ranger District, PO Box 1328, Petersburg, AK 99833.

PETERSBURG

Petersburg (population 3415) is a bustling fishing village located at the northern end of Mitkof Island and surrounded by the Tongass National Forest. The distinctive Devil's Thumb peak looms over this scenic port, and snowcapped mountains surround the town. Le Conte Glacier, the southernmost tidewater glacier in North America, is only 25mi to the east.

For information about lodging, charter boat operators or local floatplane service contact the Petersburg Visitor Center (☎ 772-3646), on the corner of Fram and 1st Sts. The office is open until 5 pm daily during the summer and maintains a Web site (www.petersburg.org).

Supplies & Equipment

For food and general camping gear go to the Trading Union (☎ 772-3881), a supermarket and department store on Nordic Drive.

Places to Stay & Eat

Within town is *LeConte RV Park* (☎ 772-4680), at 4th St and Haugen Drive, which charges $7 for a tent site if there is space. By hiking half a mile beyond the Sandy Beach Park out on Frederick Point, you can camp on the scenic beach. Bring drinking water and pitch your tent above the high-tide line.

There is no hostel in Petersburg but there is *Bunk & Breakfast* (☎ 772-3632, @ ryn@alaska.net). The B&B is a 10-minute walk from the downtown area and has eight bunks for $25 per night, which includes breakfast. You must call in advance for the location and availability of beds.

The *Tides Inn* (☎ 772-4288, 800-665-8433), at the corner of 1st and Dolphin Sts, charges $70/85 singles/doubles, which includes a continental breakfast. Some rooms also have kitchenettes.

Locals eat at *Homestead Cafe* (106 Nordic Drive), which can be a little greasy at times but is open 24 hours and has breakfasts for $6 to $7. The hamburgers ($5 to $8) are served with a huge scoop of potato salad. *Harbor Lights Pizza*, opposite the Sons of Norway Hall on Sing Lee Alley, offers pasta dinners ($7), pizzas ($12 to $15), beer on tap, wine and a good view of the busy boat harbor.

Getting There & Away

The Alaska Airlines (☎ 772-4255) milk run through the Southeast provides a daily northbound and southbound flight out of Petersburg. The airport is a mile east of the post office on Haugen Drive.

The Alaska Marine Hwy terminal (☎ 772-3855) is about a mile along Nordic Drive from the southern edge of town. Northbound and southbound ferries leave almost daily. The one-way fare from Petersburg to Juneau is $44, Ketchikan $38.

Petersburg Lake Trail

Duration 2 to 3 days
Distance 10.5mi one way
Difficulty Level Medium
Start Kupreanof state dock
Finish Petersburg Lake Cabin
Cabins & Shelters Yes
Permits Required No
Public Transportation Yes
Summary This is a two- to three-day hike through the lush rain forest along Petersburg Creek to Petersburg Lake. The area has excellent fishing for trout and salmon, along with opportunities to spot wildlife, including black bears.

A short hop across the Wrangell Narrows is Petersburg's best trail. The well-maintained Petersburg Lake Trail leads into the heart of the Petersburg Creek–Duncan Salt Chuck Wilderness, providing backpackers with a wilderness opportunity and access to a USFS cabin without expensive bushplane travel. The trail is one of the few long, low-elevation hikes in Southeast Alaska, gaining only a 100ft by the time you reach Petersburg Lake.

But it's not an easy hike. The 10.5mi hike from the Kupreanof state dock to the cabin makes for a long day with a backpack on, and good campsites along the way are few and hard to find. You really need three days

for this hike: a day to hike in, a day to spend on the lake or creek enjoying the fruits of your labor and a day to hike out. If you have only two days, give serious consideration to arranging a floatplane to pick you up on Petersburg Lake.

Anglers should schedule at least two spare days. The trail provides access to outstanding fishing. If you pack along a rod and some tackle (see Wilderness Fishing in the Facts for the Hiker chapter), there are good spots in the upper reaches of the creek for Dolly Varden, rainbow trout and cutthroat trout. In August and early September, large coho and sockeye salmon runs throughout the area attract both anglers and bears. Cutthroat trout and sockeye salmon can also be found in the lake.

For the adventurous, it is possible to continue another 7mi from Petersburg Lake to Goose Cove on Portage Bay and then swing southeast and hike to Salt Chuck, site of another USFS cabin. This entire route is known as the Portage Loop Trail. The 11.5mi trail was first blazed by the Civilian Conservation Corps in the 1930s and then re-marked in 1985. But funding shortages have prevented the USFS from finishing the loop back to Petersburg Lake, and maintenance in recent years has been nonexistent. The hike to Portage Bay is very challenging, as the route is hard to follow and involves crossing muskeg areas and stretches often flooded out by beaver dams.

PLANNING
When to Hike

Since it is a low-elevation route, Petersburg Lake Trail can be hiked from April through October. If you're tenting it, remember that in spring and especially in fall Petersburg and much of the Southeast experience heavy rainfall. In October you can count on rain practically every day.

What to Bring

The best footwear for this hike are the brown rubber boots (known as 'Petersburg pumps') that are so common in Petersburg. You can undertake this trail in hiking boots, but make sure they have been recently

PETERSBURG LAKE TRAIL

Route to Portage Bay

FINISH
Petersburg Lake Cabin

Shaky Frank Creek

▲ Del Monte Peak
2700ft

Frederick Sound

Kupreanof Island

Petersburg Creek

Petersburg Lake Trail

High Tide Trailhead

Petersburg Mountain

Petersburg Mountain Trail

Sasby Island

Tidal Flat

Wrangell Narrows

START
State Dock

Ferry Terminal

PETERSBURG

Mitkof Hwy

0   1   2 km
0   ½   1 mile
1:150,000
Contour Interval 400 feet

waxed or your feet will be wet from start to finish.

Maps

The trail is covered on the USGS quads *Petersburg D-3* and *D-4*, with the vast majority of it on *D-4*. You can purchase topographic maps at Diamante (☎ 772-4858), a gift shop at 118 Nordic Drive.

At the forest service office you can purchase a small booklet, *Petersburg Ranger District Hiking Trails* ($3), which describes 25 trails on Mitkof, Kupreanof and Kuiu Islands.

Cabins & Shelters

The trail ends at Petersburg Lake Cabin, a four-bunk cabin that includes a rowboat. Because of the heavy rainfall in the area and the lack of good campsites, the cabin is popular with backpackers and should be reserved in advance. Petersburg Lake Cabin is $35 a night and is booked through the National Recreation Reservation Service (☎ 877-444-6777, 515-885-3639 for overseas callers) or through the reservation service Web site (www.reserveusa.com).

GETTING TO/FROM THE HIKE

The only hitch to this trip is getting across Wrangell Narrows to Kupreanof Island. The USFS office above the post office in Petersburg provides a list of charter-boat operators who will run hikers across. Among them is Petersburg Creek Charters (☎ 772-2425), which charges $20 roundtrip.

The cheapest way to get across Wrangell Narrows is to hitch a ride with one of the boats that cross the narrows every day. Go to the skiff float in the North Harbor (Old Harbor) near the harbormaster's office on the waterfront and ask around for boats crossing. A small population lives on the other side of the narrows, so boats are constantly crossing, though you might have to wait a bit.

You can reduce the walk by 4.5mi by arranging to be dropped off by a charter boat operator at the high tide trailhead, near the mouth of Petersburg Creek. This is also a possibility for those who arrive with their own kayak (a kayak is difficult to rent in Petersburg). Boats need a high tide of at least 14ft to reach the trailhead; kayaks need 12ft.

The quickest and easiest way to reach Petersburg Lake is to charter a floatplane. Kupreanof Flying Service (☎ 772-3396) operates a Beaver floatplane that can take up to five passengers and limited amounts of gear. It is only a 15-minute flight from Petersburg, averaging between $50 and $60 per passenger.

THE HIKE
Stage 1: Kupreanof State Dock to High Tide Trailhead
4.5mi, 2 to 3 hours

The hike begins at the Kupreanof state dock. Nearby is a posted junction. To the right, a trail leads toward **Petersburg Mountain**. Head left for Petersburg Lake. Follow the wide trail east as it curves into the woods and quickly comes to another junction posted 'Kupreanof Trail.' Here you head right and leave the old roadbed, crossing a muskeg area on a series of plank paths. In less than a mile from the dock, the trail returns to the old road and breaks out of the woods at a view of **Petersburg Creek**.

Head right as the trail follows the shoreline. At high tide this portion of Petersburg Creek looks more like a sluggish river. The tidewater arm of the creek is a haven for wildlife, however, especially bald eagles. It pays to stop every once in a while and study the meadows on the opposite shore. Often, you can see black bears and deer feeding. The trail heads northwest along the estuary, meandering in and out of tidewater meadows and forests. Blue diamond markers and blazes keep you on course.

For those who had a late start, the most extensive meadows are reached 2mi from the dock, a suitable place to set up camp. Eventually the trail swings back into the rain forest and, within a mile of the meadows,

makes the only significant climb of the hike. Steps aid you, as the trail climbs into the bluffs to skirt around a private cabin and then descends to a bridge across a stream.

Beyond the climb, the trail remains in the forest but breaks out to an occasional view of the creek before arriving at the well-posted **high tide trailhead**, 4.5mi from the state dock. Just beyond the trailhead, you enter the Petersburg Creek–Duncan Salt Chuck Wilderness. There are a few spots to pitch a tent nearby if you need to.

Stage 2: High Tide Trailhead to Petersburg Lake Cabin
6mi, 3 to 5 hours

The trail continues to follow Petersburg Creek but in the second half of this hike is considerably rougher. In the next 2mi, you will cross three beaver dams (two of them bridged) and then swing away from Petersburg Creek. At times, you might have to search for the next blue diamond. Still, the trail features plenty of planking, log bridges, steps and marking, making it difficult for anyone to get turned around.

The trail crosses an impressive bridge over **Shaky Frank Creek**, the largest stream you will cross all day, 3mi from the high tide trailhead. From the middle of the bridge, you can look up the creek bed and see the ridgeline from which the stream flows. The trail then swings away from Petersburg Creek and enters an extensive muskeg meadow at least a third of a mile wide. The trail is planked through the muskeg, allowing you to keep your boots somewhat dry. This is a scenic spot. The plant life on either side of the planking is intriguing, and **Del Monte Peak** (2700ft) looms to the east.

The trail reenters the hemlock–Sitka spruce forest and returns to the banks of the Petersburg Creek, now a small river of pools and riffles that will entice any angler packing a rod and reel. A mile before the cabin, the trail passes a confluence of an unnamed stream from the south with Petersburg Creek. Some of the best fishing along the creek is in this general area, and up the feeder stream.

The trail continues straight and crosses a **landslide area** a half mile before the cabin. The slide occurred in 1993, creating a landscape of boulders and fallen trees. Most hikers reach this stretch at the end of a long day and need to be careful while walking over or under the trees.

Just beyond the slide, you get your first glimpse of **Petersburg Lake**, and within five minutes you will reach the posted spur to the USFS cabin. **Petersburg Lake Cabin** is a four-bunk structure that was built in 1962 and then moved to its present location in 1973 due to flooding. It has both a wood-stove and oil stove, though oil is not supplied. The cabin overlooks the lake, and a small stream is next to it, where a few sockeye salmon are often spawning in August. The rowboat is a delight, allowing you to fish the lake or just sit out in the middle and enjoy the mountain scenery and wilderness solitude. If you can, book this cabin for at least two nights.

From the cabin, the **Portage Loop Trail** continues north and remains an easy route for the first mile along Petersburg Lake. There are spots here you can make camp, but any site will be brushy. From the lake, the trail continues another 6mi before emerging onto the tidal flats of Goose Cove at the south end of Portage Bay. Backpackers will encounter numerous unbridged streams and areas of muskeg without planking along this stretch.

Stage 3: The Return
10.5mi, 5 to 8 hours
The only way to hike back is the way you came, a long hike that is better broken into two days. Hikers who are short on time might want to arrange ahead of time for a floatplane to pick them up at Petersburg Lake.

Sitka Region

Most trails in the Sitka area are on Tongass National Forest land, which is maintained by the USFS. Along with the usual hand-outs, the forest service office in town sells a useful booklet, *Sitka Trails* ($3), which has information on and rough maps of 30 trails. The trails include beach walks, short hikes to hot springs, and access routes to sub-alpine and alpine areas. Unfortunately, a boat, kayak or floatplane is required to reach most – but not all – of the trails.

Sitka has a number of trails that you can get to on foot. Eight trails, totaling almost 20mi, begin from its roads. Half of the trails are under a mile long, but the Gavan Hill and Harbor Mountain Trails can be combined to form a 5.5mi mountain hike with a night spent camping in the alpine regions.

There's also the Mt Edgecumbe Trail, a 13.4mi climb to the summit crater of the extinct volcano on Kruzof Island. This hike requires boat transportation to the trailhead but features a USFS cabin that can be reserved and a free-use shelter halfway up the mountain.

NATURAL HISTORY
Like the rest of the Southeast, the forests around Sitka are dominated by western hemlock and Sitka spruce. Other species include mountain hemlock, red cedar, red alder, Sitka alder and cottonwood. You'll also find an abundance of edible berries in the Sitka region, including salmonberries, thimbleberries, huckleberries, cranberries and several types of blueberries.

Wildlife that inhabit Baranof and Kruzof Islands include Sitka blacktailed deer, brown bears, mink and martens, as well as bald eagles and an assortment of waterfowl and upland birds. Baranof Island also has a population of mountain goats.

CLIMATE
Like the rest of Southeast Alaska, Sitka lies in the coastal rain forest of the Tongass National Forest. Average precipitation in this region ranges from 80 inches to a soaking 220 inches a year on Baranof, Kruzof and Chichagof Islands, depending on how close to the ocean you are. Sitka itself receives around 100 inches of precipitation a year, the vast majority falling in the form of rain.

Summer temperatures average between 55°F and 60°F, but if the sun is out in July and August, the mercury can easily reach 80°F or even higher. In Sitka, fog can appear suddenly, even on the nicest days. It rolls in from the Pacific Ocean unexpectedly and can reduce visibility to a few feet in no time at all. This is not such a problem on the Gavan Hill or Harbor Mountain Trail, where the paths are well cut and marked, but fog has caused hikers to get lost above the tree line on the Mt Edgecumbe Trail.

INFORMATION

The USFS office (☎ 747-6671), the place to go for trail information and handouts about enjoying the wilderness areas in the Sitka Ranger District, is in a three-story red building on the corner of Siginaka and Katlian Sts in Sitka, across from the Thomas Boat Harbor. The office is open 8 am to 5 pm weekdays.

SITKA

Known best for its beautiful setting and its Russian heritage, Sitka (population 8600) also offers good hiking in the lush forest and high peaks that surround the city. The remainder of Baranof Island and Kruzof and Chichagof Islands also have good hiking.

The Sitka Visitor Bureau (☎ 747-5940) is part of the Isabel Miller Museum, in the Centennial Building off Harbor Drive, next to the Crescent Boat Harbor. It has information about tours, lodging and other attractions. The bureau is open 8 am to 6 pm daily in the summer and has a Web site (www.sitka.org).

Supplies & Equipment

Mac's Sporting Goods (☎ 747-6970), 213 Harbor Drive, has a limited supply of camping and backpacking equipment, including freeze-dried dinners.

Places to Stay & Eat

The *Sitka HI-AYH Hostel* (☎ 747-8661, 303 Kimsham Rd) is in the basement of the Methodist church. Follow Halibut Point Rd

northwest out of town and then turn right onto Peterson Rd, a quarter mile past the Lakeside Grocery Store. Once on Peterson Rd, immediately veer left onto Kimsham Rd. Facilities include a kitchen, lounge and eating area. Open only in the summer, the hostel charges $9/13 for members/nonmembers. Buses from the ferry will drop you right at the doorstep.

There are more than a dozen B&Bs in the Sitka area that offer rooms with a good meal in the morning for around $60/70 a single/double. Stop at the Sitka Visitor Bureau for an updated list of them.

There are five hotels/motels in Sitka. The most affordable is the *Sitka Hotel* (☎ 747-3288, 118 Lincoln St, @ sitkah@ptialaska.net) with 60 rooms at $65/70 for a single/double.

Victoria's (118 Lincoln St) is where locals go for a breakfast ($6 to $10) that is served all day. The biscuits and gravy will stay with you almost to dinner. The *Bayview*, upstairs in the MacDonald Bayview Trading Company building, across from Crescent Harbor, has a variety of hamburgers and fresh seafood dinners for $12 to $16.

Getting There & Away

Air Sitka is served by Alaska Airlines (☎ 966-2422) with flights throughout the Southeast. There are a handful of flights to Juneau during the summer; the one-way fare is $50. The airport is on Japonski Island, 1.8mi west of the town center. The white airporter minibus meets all jet flights and charges $3 for a ride to the city hotels.

Boat The Alaska Marine Hwy terminal (☎ 747-8737) is 7mi north of town on Halibut Point Rd, and there are northbound or southbound departures almost daily.

Passage from Sitka to Juneau is $26, Sitka to Angoon $22, Sitka to Petersburg $26 and Sitka to Tenakee Springs $22. The Ferry Transit Bus (☎ 747-8443) meets all ferries for a trip into town. You can also catch the minibus out to the ferry terminal from the Westmark Shee Atika when it picks up hotel guests. One-way fare to the ferry terminal is $3.

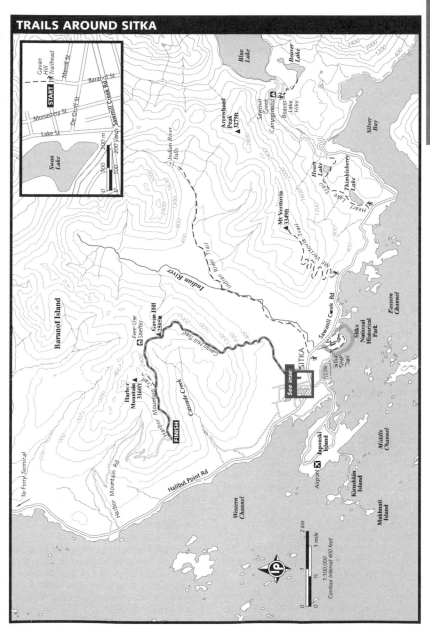

TRAILS AROUND SITKA

Gavan Hill Trailhead
Merritt St
START
Baranof St
Monastery St
De Groff St
Lake St
Swan Lake
Sawmill Creek Rd

200 m
100
200 yards
100

Blue Lake
Beaver Lake
Arrowhead Peak 3275ft
Sawmill Creek Campground
Beaver Lake Hike
Silver Bay
Indian River Falls
Heart Lake
Thimbleberry Lake
Mt Verstovia 3349ft
Heart Lake Trail
Mt Verstovia Trail
Indian River Trail
Free-Use Shelter
Gavan Hill 2505ft
Sawmill Creek Rd
Sitka National Historical Park
Eastern Channel
Gavan Hill Trail
SITKA
Sitka NHP Trail
See inset
Harbor Mountain 3166ft
Cascade Creek
Harbor Mountain Rd
FINISH
Baranof Island
To Ferry Terminal
Halibut Point Rd
Japonski Island
Airport
Middle Channel
Kirushkin Island
Makhnati Island
Western Channel
2 km
1 mile
1/2
1
1:100,000
Contour interval 400 feet

SOUTHEAST

Gavan Hill & Harbor Mountain Trails

Duration 1 or 2 days
Distance 11mi
Difficulty Level Medium
Start Sitka
Finish Harbor Mountain Rd
Cabins & Shelters Yes
Permits Required No
Public Transportation Yes
Summary These trails provide easy access to the alpine country above Sitka. The well-marked route includes a free-use shelter, making the trail an excellent overnight hike.

The only hike in the area that actually begins downtown, Gavan Hill Trail is a 3mi climb to a 2505ft point that is often referred to as Gavan Hill Summit. From the summit, you can continue along the Harbor Mountain Trail, to reach a free-use shelter on an alpine saddle.

The trail ends at Harbor Mountain Rd, the only road in Southeast Alaska that reaches subalpine terrain. Since Harbor Mountain Rd is a winding, gravel road, traffic is light, and many backpackers end up walking the additional 5mi to Halibut Point Rd. This makes the loop an 11mi hike.

PLANNING
When to Hike
The alpine hike is best done June through September, though snow can linger in spots until early July. By mid-September, be prepared for the rainy season.

What to Bring
Bring at least a quart of water per person (2 quarts if you're spending the night in the alpine area), as water is tough to find along most of the route.

Maps
The map in this book (see the Trails Around Sitka map) and those in the USFS booklet

Sitka Trails are not adequate for hiking most of the trails in Sitka. You need USGS 1:63,360 quads *Sitka A-5* and *A-4* for the Gavan Hill Trail. USGS topos can be purchased at Old Harbor Books (☎ 747-8808), downtown at 201 Lincoln St.

Cabins & Shelters
There are no USFS cabins on the Gavan Hill–Harbor Mountain circuit, but there is a free-use shelter halfway along the route. The small, enclosed trail shelter is available on a first-come, first-served basis and doesn't have bunks or heating. In July and August, pack a tent; this is Sitka's most popular trail, and the shelter is often full.

GETTING TO/FROM THE HIKE
To the Start
The Gavan Hill Trailhead is within easy walking distance of the visitor center in the Centennial Building. From Lincoln St, head north up Baranof St for six blocks, past Merrill St to the house at 508 Baranof St. The trail begins just beyond this house and heads to the northeast.

From the Finish
Harbor Mountain Rd is 4mi northwest of Sitka on Halibut Point Rd. Hitching back into town is easy, because of traffic from the ferry terminal and campgrounds at the end of Halibut Point Rd. If you want to arrange a ride back, check with Sitka Tours (☎ 747-8443), which runs the bus out to the ferry terminal. You might also try Harbor Mountain Tours (☎ 747-8294, ✉ h.g.ulrich@worldnet.att.net), which offers a tour to the end of Harbor Mountain Rd from the city center.

THE HIKE
Stage 1: Gavan Hill Trailhead to Free-Use Shelter
3.5mi, 4 to 5 hours
Departing from Baranof St, the trail follows an old pipeline path for the first half mile, through areas of muskeg. The walk is easy, however, as the wettest spots have been planked. Eventually, you enter a forest of spruce and hemlock and begin climbing the southeast side of Gavan Hill. You quickly

pass what used to be the junction with Cross Trail. At one time, Cross Trail skirted Sitka and emerged near the high school, but the trail is no longer maintained and is hard to follow.

Gavan Hill Trail continues as a steep climb up a series of switchbacks, from 500ft to the ridgeline at 2000ft, a two- to three-hour hike from the trailhead. Along the way, a mile from the trailhead, you reach a viewpoint from which you can see Sitka. A nearby stream provides the last reliable source of drinking water. Once on the ridge, you head northeast, first hiking through a stand of stunted trees, then using a series of steps to climb into a subalpine meadow within a quarter mile. That's followed by a short but rocky climb of 200ft to a high point of 2100ft.

From here, the trail follows the Gavan Hill ridge, past great views of the Indian River, the mountainous interior of Baranof Island and Sitka Sound. Within 3mi of the trailhead, the trail swings northwest, and in a quarter of a mile, you climb the 2505ft summit of Gavan Hill. Needless to say, the views from the top of this flat summit are spectacular on a clear day.

The trail descends the west side of the summit, to the subalpine saddle that separates the drainage of Cascade Creek from an unnamed creek to the north. The **USFS free-use shelter** is in the saddle, half a mile from Gavan Hill Summit. The four-sided, 10ft-by-8ft shelter has no source of heat and no bunks. Water is also scarce on the saddle. The alternative is to drop toward Cascade Creek and camp near a feeder stream, but the view there is not nearly as good as the view from the shelter.

Stage 2: Free-Use Shelter to Halibut Point Rd
7.5mi, 3 to 5 hours

A recently cut and upgraded trail continues from the free-use shelter toward Harbor Mountain, where the trail curves almost due west and skirts the steep southern flank of the 3160ft peak. Within 1.5mi of the saddle, the trail climbs several hundred feet, to reach a southwest ridge of the mountain.

This is the route most climbers follow when ascending the peaks of **Harbor Mountain**. The craggy rock encountered during the ascent makes for poor footing and a challenging climb.

The trail heads southwest down the ridge. Within a half mile of the road end, you climb over a **2300ft knob**, where the views of Sitka and the surrounding area are stunning. You can see everything from the ferry terminal to Mt Edgecumbe, and the endless horizon of the Pacific Ocean.

Just before you reach Harbor Mountain Rd, the trail passes a junction. The short spur leads to the top of a **2370ft knob**. The US Army built a lookout and other buildings here during WWII. The military remains are hard to find, but the view is excellent. From the junction, the main trail descends 300ft, with a series of planked switchbacks to the end of Harbor Mountain Rd.

A parking area and an information board are at the trailhead. Head a half mile down the road, and you'll come to a covered picnic shelter and more tables in a subalpine meadow. From here, Harbor Mountain Rd heads steeply down to Halibut Point Rd, reaching it in 4.5mi, after a series of hairpin turns. It's so steep that people pulling trailers or driving RVs are strongly advised not to drive to the end of the road.

Mt Edgecumbe Trail

Duration 2 to 3 days
Distance 13.4mi roundtrip
Difficulty Level Medium to hard
Start/Finish Fred's Creek USFS Cabin
Cabins & Shelters Yes
Permits Required No
Public Transportation Yes
Summary A 3000ft climb to the summit crater of Sitka's extinct volcano, this challenging trail has spectacular views and a free-use shelter.

This 6.7mi trail was originally constructed by the Civilian Conservation Corps in the 1930s; today it is a designated national recreation trail maintained by the USFS. It

SOUTHEAST

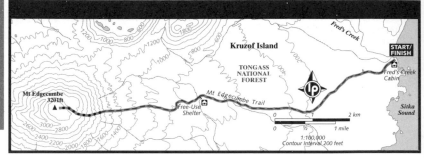

begins at Fred's Creek USFS Cabin and ascends to the summit crater of Sitka's extinct volcano. As you can imagine, the views from the summit are spectacular on a clear day. This is a moderate to challenging hike, as it can be a steep climb at times. The final 2mi to the summit are along a poorly marked route. From Fred's Creek Cabin to the summit crater you climb 3000ft.

The entire hike to the top and back is a 13.4mi walk that takes most people six to eight hours. It's best to spend the first night at the shelter and turn the walk into an overnight hike or even a three-day adventure, since you must spend $160 to be dropped off and picked up.

Beware of being fogged in and getting lost above the tree line (see the earlier Climate section). Carry a roll of bright plastic tape to mark the route once you're above the timber line. Begin the hike wearing rubber boots for crossing the muskeg and muddy sections and then switch to sturdy hiking boots once you're higher. See Gavan Hill & Harbor Mountain Trails for Places to Stay and Getting There & Away information.

PLANNING
When to Hike
Like the Gavan Hill and Harbor Mountain Trails, this hike is best done from mid-June to mid-September.

What to Bring
Wear rubber boots for the first half of this hike, as the trail can be very wet and muddy.

You should also pack along a roll or two of bright plastic tape to flag a route above the tree line, where there is no trail and very few markers. You can purchase this equipment and other gear at Mac's Sporting Goods in Sitka.

Maps
The trail area is split between USGS 1:63,360 quads *Sitka A-5* and *A-6,* which can be purchased at Old Harbor Books (☎ 747-8808), downtown at 201 Lincoln St.

Cabins & Shelters
At the start of the Mt Edgecumbe Trail, there is a USFS cabin, Fred's Creek Cabin. You can book it for $35 a night by calling the National Recreation Reservation Service (☎ 877-444-6777, 515-885-3639 for overseas) or through its Web site (www.reserveusa .com). From the cabin, you can hike to the summit in one day. Halfway up the trail there is a free-use trail shelter.

GETTING TO/FROM THE HIKE
Mt Edgecumbe lies on Kruzof Island, 10mi west of Sitka, and can only be reached by boat because large swells from the ocean prevent floatplanes from landing at Fred's Creek. Charter boat operators will drop off and pick up hikers for around $80, one way, per party. Stop at the visitors bureau for a list of local operators or call Alaska Adventures Unlimited (☎ 747-5576, 800-770-5576), and they will set up the boat charter for you.

Haines Harbor

Historic Iditarod Trail

Crossing a beaver dam on Petersburg Lake Trail

Rabbit Lake

JIM DUFRESNE

JIM DUFRESNE

DEANNA SWANEY

THE HIKE
Stage 1: Fred's Creek Cabin to Free-Use Shelter
2 hours

The trail begins behind **Fred's Creek Cabin**, which, if available, is a wonderful place to end the hike. The 16ft-by-16ft A-frame cabin sits just inside the trees overlooking a scenic beach. The cabin's namesake creek runs along the north side of it. Inside the cabin, you'll find two single bunks and a loft that sleeps four more people, as well as the usual woodstove, table and cooking counter.

The trail departs west into a spruce and hemlock flat, where the hiking is level at first. For the next 2mi, you gain little elevation, alternating between stretches of muskeg and stands of spruce. There is some planking but much of it is deteriorated and never where you really need it. Be ready to do some slogging through the mud.

The trail is not always clearly marked. Be aware of an occasional game trail; Sitka deer and black bears are common here, especially in spring. Generally, however, the main trail is easy to recognize.

At 2.5mi, you run parallel to a stream briefly, and 3mi from Fred's Creek Cabin, at 700ft, you reach the **free-use shelter**. Built by a local conservation group, the shelter is a three-sided structure with no bunks or amenities. It is often littered with the garbage of thoughtless hiking parties. It will keep you dry, however, if a storm rolls off the Pacific Ocean. A stream for drinking water is nearby.

Stage 2: Free-Use Shelter to Summit Crater
4 to 6 hours

The trail immediately crosses the stream in front of the shelter and continues its mild climb through the forest for another mile. When you reach 1000ft, the climb steepens considerably, as you begin to ascend the volcano's east flank.

Within another mile or so, you reach 2000ft and break out of the **tree line**. At this point, the trail ends and the remaining 1.5mi

to the summit is, for the most part, a route of your own choosing. Usually, a flag marks the trail at the tree line, and a few rock cairns mark it on the way up. But most of the cairns are destroyed each winter by the heavy snowfall.

It's important to mark the trail at the tree line with your own plastic tape and take a second to memorize the ridge you are ascending, in case a sudden bank of clouds or fog comes rolling in. Make sure you remove all your flagging on your way down.

Above the trees, the terrain is red volcanic ash. To reach the top, it's a stiff climb straight up, but if the day is clear, you'll be stopping every few feet to admire the views of Sitka and the mountains of Baranof Island. From the rim at the top, you can peer into the **crater**, which is several hundred feet deep. The true summit of Mt Edgecumbe is a **3201ft knob** on the west side of the rim.

Stage 3: The Return
4 to 7 hours

Once you are done playing at the peak, return along the route you climbed up, making sure you pick up the true trail at the tree line. It should take you only half the ascent time to descend to the shelter. A strong hiker could make the return hike in one day, but it is easier to return to the shelter for another night before returning.

Juneau Region

How good is the hiking in Alaska's state capital? The trailhead to one of the best alpine hikes is only a few blocks away from the capitol building. The city's most popular trail system, the Perseverance, is not much farther away and just as easy to reach. Several other trails can be reached on a city bus.

The only thing this area lacks is a long, multiday hike like the Resurrection Pass Trail in the Kenai Peninsula. Although many trails can easily be turned into overnight hikes (including Dan Moller, Perseverance/Mt Juneau circuit, Windfall Lake and Montana Creek Trails) this area is for day hikers. With Juneau's excellent range of accommodations, you can enjoy scenic hikes during the day and a soft bed at night – reach the alpine regions in the afternoon and sip a few with the locals in the Red Dog Saloon at night.

While the city center clings to a mountainside, Juneau actually sprawls over 3100 sq mi, to the Canadian border. Juneau has five sections, and you'll find trailheads in all of them. Beginning in the downtown area are Perseverance and Mt Roberts Trails. In Mendenhall Valley and on the way to it are the Salmon Creek, East Glacier, West Glacier, Nugget Creek and Montana Creek Trails. Beyond Mendenhall Valley, Egan Drive turns into Glacier Hwy, a two-lane road that takes you past the Peterson Lake, Windfall Lake, Herbert Glacier, Amalga (Eagle Glacier) and Spaulding Trails and the trails of Point Bridget State Park. Directly across the Gastineau Channel from downtown Juneau, on Douglas Island, is the Dan Moller Trail, and from Douglas, a small town southeast of Juneau, you can access Mt Bradley and the Treadwell Ditch Trails. In North Douglas, you'll find Cropley Lake Trail, in the Eaglecrest Ski Area.

There are so many trails in the area that the Juneau Parks & Recreation Department (☎ 586-2635) organizes weekly hikes throughout the summer. The city department stages adult hikes every Wednesday and family hikes along easier trails every Saturday. The hikes begin at the trailhead at 10 am; on Wednesday there is often carpooling to the trail, with hikers meeting at Cope Park, a short walk from the Juneau International Hostel. Call for a schedule.

HISTORY

Many trails in the Juneau area are the result of mining activity by prospectors looking for gold or companies servicing their mines. The Perseverance, which began as a trail after Joe Juneau and Dick Harris discovered gold in 1880, was turned into a road in 1889 to reach the mines in Silver Bow Basin. Although only 4mi long, the road required blasting and trestles to bypass the

canyon below Ebner Falls, leading one newspaper to call it 'the longest and best road in Alaska.' Other trails with a mining past include Amalga, Bessie Creek, Montana Creek, Salmon Creek, Sheep Creek and Treadwell Ditch. Lemon Creek Trail was named after John Lemon, a local prospector who was one of the first to cross the Chilkoot Trail – in 1880, almost 20 years before the Klondike gold rush.

NATURAL HISTORY

The highlight of hiking in Juneau is its glaciers. The Juneau Ice Field is a 1500-sq-mi sheet of ice – more than a mile thick in places – that caps the mountains northeast of the city. Snowfall on the ice field often exceeds 100ft a year, resulting in 35 glaciers that spill out of the peaks into the valleys. The most famous glacier is the Mendenhall, one of Alaska's famous 'drive-up' glaciers. The 12mi river of ice attracts thousands of visitors annually who drive to the USFS visitor center and marvel at the glacier's 100ft-high face, which spreads 1.5mi across Mendenhall Lake.

From a foot trail, you can often get a closer and less crowded view of several glaciers. More than 12mi of trails skirt the Mendenhall. The West Glacier Trail is one of the most spectacular hikes in the Southeast. Other glacier walks include the Amalga Trail (Eagle Glacier), East Glacier Trail (Mendenhall Glacier), Nugget Creek Trail (Nugget Glacier), Heintzleman Ridge Route (Mendenhall Glacier) and Herbert Glacier Trail.

CLIMATE

Like Ketchikan and Sitka, Juneau is part of the coastal rain belt of the Tongass National Forest, but it is somewhat drier. The average annual precipitation is 92 inches in the downtown area and only 52 inches in the Mendenhall Valley. The average temperature in Juneau from June through August is 55°F, and in July it's 64°F (often reaching the mid- to high 70s).

INFORMATION

For the status of the trails' condition or information on any outdoor activity in the

Bears of Admiralty Island

To many people the most intriguing area in Tongass National Forest is Admiralty Island, a 1465-sq-mi wilderness area 15mi southwest of Juneau. Admiralty Island has a wide variety of wildlife: Bays like Mitchell, Hood, Whitewater and Chaik contain harbor seals, porpoises and sea lions. Seymour Canal, the island's largest inlet, has one of the highest densities of nesting eagles in the world, and humpback whales often feed in the waterway. Sitka blacktailed deer are plentiful, and the streams choke with spawning salmon during August. But Admiralty Island is best known for its bears. Their numbers are so great that the Tlingit Indians called the area 'Fortress of Bears.' The island has one of the highest densities of brown bears in Alaska, an estimated 1500 to 1700 bruins, or about one per square mile.

One of the best places to view brown bears is at Pack Creek. The creek empties into Seymour Canal on the eastern side of Admiralty Island. Within this area is the Stan Price State Wildlife Sanctuary, named for the pioneering researcher who spent a good part of his life living at Pack Creek. The bears are most abundant in July and August, when the salmon are running. You can watch them from the viewing sand spit or an observation tower along the creek reached by a mile-long trail. The only place to camp in the area is on the east side of Windfall Island, a half mile away, making a boat necessary for those who plan to spend more than a day in the area.

In recent years, Pack Creek has become so popular that the area buzzes with planes and boats every morning from early July to late August. Anticipating this daily rush hour, most resident bears escape into the forest, but a few adult females and cubs hang around to feed on salmon, having long since been habituated to the human visitors. Seeing five or six bears at one time would be a good viewing day at Pack Creek.

The increased number of visitors forced the US Forest Service and Alaska Department of Fish and Game to institute a permit system with a limit on visitors. Only 24 people are allowed per day from July through August. One to three day permits are reserved in advance and are $50 per adult per day. Four guide and tour companies receive 16 of the permits, leaving only eight for individuals who want to visit Pack Creek on their own.

Permits are available from March 1 and are usually gone within two or three weeks. A handful are kept as spares, however, and handed out three days in advance at the monument office. Call the USFS Information Center (☎ 586-8751) in Juneau about obtaining one.

With a permit, you can arrange to be dropped off and picked up by Alaska Seaplane Service (☎ 789-3331, 800-478-3360), which departs Juneau for Pack Creek daily at 8:30 am and returns at 4 pm ($130 roundtrip). If you don't have a permit, then call Alaska Discovery (☎ 800-586-1911), which holds a number of them for its guided trips into the area. The one-day tour includes flying over to Admiralty Island and then kayaking to Pack Creek, where you spend the day watching bears before returning to Juneau. The cost is $450 per person. There is also a three-day trip for $895.

Tongass National Forest, stop at the information center (☎ 586-8751) in Juneau at Centennial Hall, 101 Egan Drive. The center is staffed by both US Forest Service and National Park personnel and is open 8 am to 5 pm daily in the summer. Among the items for sale is the USFS booklet *Juneau Trails* ($3).

For a map of Point Bridget State Park or information on any state park in the Southeast, stop at the Alaska Division of State Parks office (☎ 465-4563), 400 Willoughby Ave on the 3rd floor. It is open 8 am to 4:30 pm weekdays. Current fishing conditions can be obtained by calling the Alaska Fish & Game Department hot line (☎ 465-4116).

SOUTHEAST

JUNEAU

Juneau is a mecca for hikers. The city and the surrounding area offer almost everything you could want: more than 20 trails maintained by the USFS and the state of Alaska, spectacular scenery (mountains, glaciers and the Inside Passage) and a full range of commercial services and stores. It is the most developed city in the Southeast.

The main visitor center for travel information is the Davis Log Cabin (☎ 586-2201, 888-581-2201), 134 3rd St. It's open 8:30 am to 5 pm daily during the summer. The city of Juneau also maintains a Web site (www .juneau.com) with travel information.

Supplies & Equipment

An excellent selection of backpacking equipment, mountaineering tools and just about anything you need on a hike or to climb a glacier can be found at Foggy Mountain Shop (☎ 586-6780), 134 N Franklin St. You might want to invest in rubber boots, or 'Southeast sneakers,' as they are affectionately called by the locals. Many of the trails can be quite muddy, so these brown rubber boots are often more suitable than hiking boots. They can be purchased from several places around town.

If you need to rent overnight equipment – a tent, sleeping bag or a stove – call Gearing Up (☎ 586-2549) or Adventure Sports (☎ 789-5696). For grub on the trail, there's A&P Juneau Market on Willoughby Ave across from the federal building. Also located downtown is Rainbow Natural Foods, at 2nd and Seward Sts, a health food store. In the Mendenhall Valley there is a Carrs supermarket at Egan Hwy and Vintage Blvd.

Places to Stay & Eat

There are some fine campgrounds beyond Mendenhall Valley. **Mendenhall Lake Campground**, 13mi from downtown and 5mi northeast of the Auke Bay Ferry Terminal, is one of the most beautiful USFS campgrounds in Alaska. The recently expanded campground (80 sites) has a separate seven-site backpacking unit on Montana Creek Rd, a dirt road that runs off Mendenhall

Loop Rd. The tent sites are alongside a lake and many have spectacular views of the nearby glacier. The nightly fee is $8 per site. The only drawback of this campground is that sites can be reserved in advance through the National Recreation Reservation Service (☎ 800-280-2267), so it is going to be filled much of the summer.

Eagle Beach campsites, 15mi from ferry terminal on Glacier Highway, are little more than a 5-acre gravel site near the Eagle Beach Picnic Area. You're 28mi from downtown Juneau but the area is very scenic and near several hiking trails. Camping is $3 per night.

The *Juneau International Hostel* (☎ 586-9559), at Harris and 6th Sts, is one of the best hostels in Alaska. The large yellow house has an ideal location – four blocks from the Mt Roberts Trail and two blocks from Basin Rd and the beginning of the scenic Gold Creek area. Fees are $10 a night. For reservations, contact the Juneau International (AYH) Hostel, 614 Harris St, Juneau, AK 99801.

The cheapest hotel is the *Alaskan Hotel* (☎ 586-1000, 800-327-9347, 167 S Franklin St, ✉ akhotel@ptialaska.net), which has rooms without bath for $60/75 singles/doubles. South of there is the *Inn at the Waterfront* (☎ 586-2050, 455 S Franklin St), a small hotel where a single with a shared bath is $60 but includes a light breakfast.

Cheap dinners of pizza or sandwiches can be obtained at *Bullwinkle's Pizza Parlor* (318 Willoughby Ave), across from the State Office Building. Good-sized sandwiches cost $5 to $7, and medium pizzas begin at $11. For hot subs and large salads, try *Rick's Cafe* (730 Willoughby Ave), across from A&P Juneau Market. Of the handful of Mexican restaurants in the city center, the best is the *Armadillo Tex-Mex Cafe* (431 S Franklin St). Two tacos with pinto beans and rice cost $10, a fajita dinner $13.

Getting There & Away

Air Alaska Airlines (☎ 789-5538) has scheduled service to Seattle, all major Southeast communities, Glacier Bay, Anchorage, and Cordova daily during the summer. Recent airfare wars have pushed the one-way fare

JUNEAU

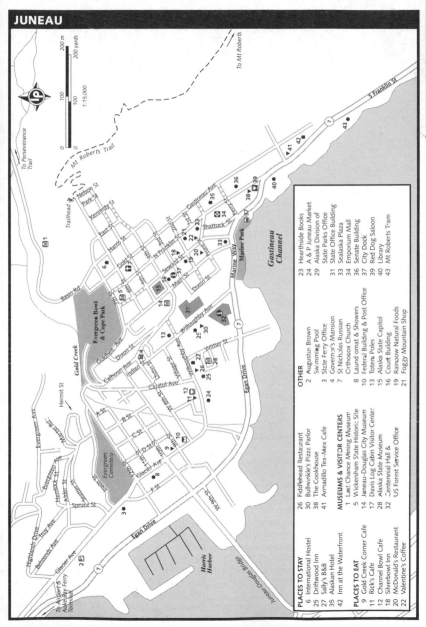

200 m
200 yards

1:15,000

To Mt Roberts

To Perseverance Trail

Mt Roberts Trail

Trailhead

To Mt Roberts

S Franklin St

Gastineau Channel

Gold Creek

Evergreen Bowl & Cope Park

Basin Rd

Evergreen Cemetery

Hermit St

Gold Creek

Capitol Ave

Marine Way

Marine Park

Egan Drive

Harris Harbor

Juneau-Douglas Bridge

To Airport & Auke Bay Ferry Terminal

PLACES TO STAY
6 International Hostel
25 Driftwood Inn
27 Sally's B&B
35 Alaskan Hotel
42 Inn at the Waterfront

PLACES TO EAT
9 Gold Creek Corner Cafe
11 Rick's Cafe
12 Channel Bowl Cafe
18 Silverbow Inn
20 McDonald's Restaurant
22 Valentine's Coffee

26 Fiddlehead Restaurant
30 Bullwinkle's Pizza Parlor
38 The Cookhouse
41 Armadillo Tex-Mex Cafe

MUSEUMS & VISITOR CENTERS
1 Last Chance Mining Museum
5 Wickersham State Historic Site
14 Juneau-Douglas City Museum
17 Davis Log Cabin Visitor Center
28 Alaska State Museum
32 Centennial Hall &
    US Forest Service Office

OTHER
2 Augustus Brown
   Swimming Pool
3 State Ferry Office
4 Governor's Mansion
7 St Nicholas Russian
   Orthodox Church
8 Laundromat & Showers
10 Federal Building & Post Office
13 Totem Poles
15 Alaska State Capitol
16 Court Building
19 Rainbow Natural Foods
21 Foggy Mountain Shop

23 Hearthside Books
24 A & P Juneau Market
29 Alaska Division of
    State Parks Office
31 State Office Building
33 Sealaska Plaza
34 Emporium Mall
36 Senate Building
37 City Dock
39 Red Dog Saloon
40 Library
43 Mt Roberts Tram

SOUTHEAST

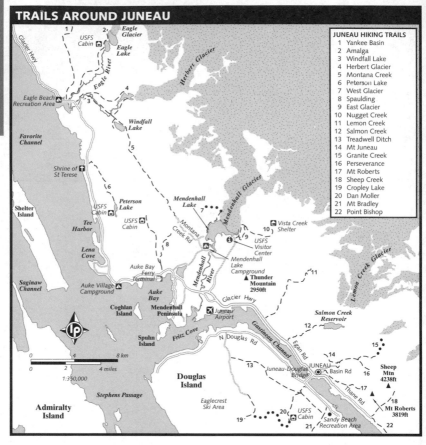

TRAILS AROUND JUNEAU

JUNEAU HIKING TRAILS
1 Yankee Basin
2 Amalga
3 Windfall Lake
4 Herbert Glacier
5 Montana Creek
6 Peterson Lake
7 West Glacier
8 Spaulding
9 East Glacier
10 Nugget Creek
11 Lemon Creek
12 Salmon Creek
13 Treadwell Ditch
14 Mt Juneau
15 Granite Creek
16 Perseverance
17 Mt Roberts
18 Sheep Creek
19 Cropley Lake
20 Dan Moller
21 Mt Bradley
22 Point Bishop

from Juneau to Anchorage to as low as $110. The one-way fare from Juneau to Cordova, which allows you to continue traveling on the state ferries to Valdez, Seward, Homer and Kodiak, is $127 if purchased 21 days in advance. To Ketchikan, the one-way fare is usually about $100. Air North (☎ 800-764-0407) flies three times a week to Whitehorse. There is an airporter bus (☎ 780-4977) that makes hourly runs from major hotels to the airport for $8 a person.

Boat The ferry arrives and departs from the Auke Bay Ferry Terminal, 14mi from the

downtown area. There are daily ferry departures during the summer for Sitka ($26), Petersburg ($44), Ketchikan ($74), Haines ($24), and Skagway ($32). A smaller ferry, the M/V *Le Conte*, connects Juneau to Hoonah, Angoon and Tenakee Springs. During the summer the M/V *Malaspina* makes a North Lynn Canal trip daily, departing Juneau at 7 am and arriving at Skagway at 1:30 pm. It stays in port for two hours then begins a return trip to Juneau, stopping at Haines along the way. The main ticket office for the ferry (☎ 465-3941, 800-642-0062) is at 1591 Glacier Ave.

Late-night arrivals at the ferry terminal should catch the Mendenhall Glacier Transport bus (☎ 789-5460) that meets all ferries and will take you to the airport or downtown for $5.

Perseverance Trail

Duration 1 or 2 days
Distance 11mi
Difficulty Level Medium to hard
Start/Finish Basin Rd
Cabins & Shelters No
Permits Required No
Public Transportation Yes
Summary Juneau's most popular trail system can be a short day hike or a 14-hour hike in the alpine region to the 3576ft peak of Mt Juneau. Mining ruins, waterfalls and spectacular views highlight these trails.

Tucked away behind a mountain are the upper valley of Gold Creek and the city's most popular place to walk and hike, the Perseverance trail system. It's estimated more than 30,000 people hike, jog or mountain bike Perseverance Trail every year. Named after a mine that operated from 1885 to 1895 in the Silver Bow Basin, the 3.5mi trail also provides access to 1.5mi Granite Creek Trail and the 2mi climb to the top of Mt Juneau.

When you combine all three hikes, plus the ridge walk between the Granite Creek Trail and the Mt Juneau peak, you have a 11mi hike that can be done in one long Alaska summer day or be turned into an overnight excursion, with a camp in the upper basin of Granite Creek.

Access to this trail is easy and the scenery is excellent, but in 1996, a violent storm and landslide resulted in a large section of the Perseverance Trail being washed out, including several bridges. Work to repair it began the following summer but as of 1999 hadn't been completed, due to a budget dispute in the state legislature. People are still hiking the trail, but for a few years at least, it won't be the easy walk it once was.

PLANNING
When to Hike
The entire loop is best hiked from mid-June to early September. The Perseverance Trail itself is often hiked earlier in the spring and into October, but keep in mind that the trail traverses active avalanche areas.

Maps
You can purchase USGS quads in the downtown area at the US Forest Service Information Center, in the Centennial Hall on Egan Drive, or Foggy Mountain Shop. In the Mendenhall Valley area, try Hearthside Books (☎ 789-2750) in the Nugget Mall. The entire loop is covered on the USGS 1:63,360 quad *Juneau B-2*.

GETTING TO/FROM THE HIKE
If you are staying downtown, you can easily walk to the trail. Head up Gold St, which leads to Basin Rd. This scenic dirt road will skirt along the steep ravine of Gold Creek and then finally cross the creek itself. After crossing the bridge over Gold Creek, take the left-hand fork and follow it to a posted trailhead.

If you're staying out in the Mendenhall Valley or in Douglas, there's Capital Transit (☎ 789-6901). Juneau's public bus system runs hourly during the week, with alternating local and express services 7 am to 6 pm Monday to Saturday, 9 am to 6 pm Sunday. The main route circles the downtown area, stopping at the city dock ferry terminal, the capitol building and the federal building, then heads out to the Mendenhall Valley and Auke Bay Boat Harbor via the Mendenhall Loop Rd, where it travels close to the Mendenhall Lake Campground. There is also a bus that runs every hour from city stops to Douglas. Fares are $1.25 each way. Grab a map and schedule the first time you board a bus.

THE HIKE
Most of the 1996 storm damage occurred in the first mile of the Perseverance Trail, where it traverses a steep canyon below Ebner Falls. Check with either the USFS Information Center or the Alaska State Park

SOUTHEAST

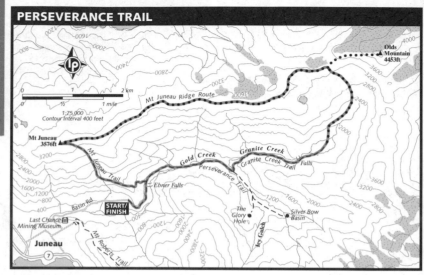

PERSEVERANCE TRAIL

office (see the Information section) for the status of the repairs. If you are contemplating hiking the entire loop in one day, remember that it is a 10-hour hike for experienced hikers carrying a light pack.

Stage 1: Basin Rd to Granite Creek's Upper Basin

4mi, 2 to 3 hours

The loop begins with the Perseverance Trail. From the Basin Rd trailhead, you can view a large air compressor left over from the mining days and then begin the hike with a gentle climb above **Gold Creek**. Within 15 minutes, a half mile from trailhead, you reach a fenced-in lookout high above the stream. On the other side of the ravine, in full view, are buildings and other remains of the Alaska-Juneau Mine. Today, the building is the **Last Chance Mining Museum** (☎ 586-5338), where you can view the impressive complex of railroad lines, ore cars and repair sheds. Hours are 9:30 am to 6:30 pm daily; admission is $3. A trip to the museum before or after your hike is highly recommended.

The worst damage from the storm occurred within 200 yards of the viewpoint.

Here the trail was built into the rock walls of Gold Creek Canyon, with support timbers called 'cribbing' and 'knee braces.' After 30ft of the trail collapsed, what remained was a thin shelf of soil and shale less than a foot wide in places. If the slide area has not been repaired or you feel uncomfortable with the condition of the trail, turn around and choose another trail.

A mile from the end of Basin Rd is the posted trailhead of the **Mt Juneau Trail**, which is reached just before a spur descends in the opposite direction to **Ebner Falls**. Named after a miner who operated a stamping mill here in 1896, the falls are a thundering sight and well worth the extra effort of following the short spur to get to them.

The main trail continues northeast along rushing Gold Creek, skirting the base of the ridge that you will be returning on. In the streams draining this valley, Joe Juneau and Richard Harris turned up flakes of gold in October of 1880 that resulted in a gold rush and the tent city that today is the capital of Alaska. Much of the trail itself is an old wagon road back to the mines in Silver Bow Basin. You cross Gold Creek twice in the next 1.5mi. Just after the second crossing, you arrive at a bridge over **Granite Creek**. Just up the trail is the junction to the **Granite Creek Trail**.

Perseverance heads right and gently climbs along Gold Creek for another mile, until the trail ends at **Silver Bow Basin**, site of the Perseverance Mine, which operated until 1895. In the early 1890s, the complex included a boarding house, a blacksmith shop, a mess hall that could seat 500 men, a compressor plant and even a post office near the end of the trail. Little of the settlement remains today. Less than a half mile from the end of the trail, you pass a well-beaten spur that leads to the Glory Hole, a hard-rock mine shaft almost 300ft deep.

Back at the Granite Creek Trail junction, the Granite Creek Trail heads left and skirts the valley slope along the east side of the creek. Mud and snow will persist late into June. The trail climbs into the first basin, the site of many waterfalls and wildflowers through much of July. From here, follow the creek to reach the upper basin at the base of **Olds Mountain**, 1.5mi from the junction with the Perseverance Trail. You might spot marmots and ptarmigan, and in August you can search for blueberries and salmonberries. Good camping abounds in both basins, but it's best to head to the upper basin and camp well away from this popular trail.

Kayaking in Juneau

If you need a break from hiking while in Juneau or simply want to try something new, consider sea kayaking. Juneau is a mecca for blue-water kayaking, with two places that rent boats, several companies that offer guided trips and a handful of places to kayak. Often, people with experience canoeing undertake their first kayak trips here – unguided – with no problems.

Boats can be rented from Juneau Outdoor Center (☎ 586-3375, @ gokayak@alaska.net), near the Douglas Boat Harbor, or from Adventure Sports (☎ 789-5696), at 8757 Glacier Hwy near the airport. Doubles are $40 to $50 a day, singles $35 to $40. Either outfitter can arrange transportation to any location on the Juneau road system.

If you're unsure about kayaking, Alaska Discovery (☎ 800-586-1911) offers a daily guided day trip in Juneau, giving you a chance to paddle the coastal islands of Lynn Canal. Tours are limited to 10 people, and everything is provided, including boats, lifejackets, rubber boots and transportation from the downtown area. The cost is $95 per person.

The best place in the area to spend a day kayaking is Auke Bay. A paddle out and around its islands makes for an easy but scenic afternoon of kayaking. For something more adventurous, consider a multiday paddle in Tracy Arm. This steep-sided fjord, 50mi southeast of Juneau, is highlighted by a pair of tidewater glaciers and a gallery of icebergs they discharge. You're almost guaranteed to see seals inside the arm, and there's always a possibility of spotting whales on the way there.

Tracy Arm is an ideal choice for novice kayakers. Due to its towering walls and narrow width, calm water is the norm in the 30mi-long arm. It's an easy two- to three-day paddle from one end to the other. Many kayakers spend the first night on a small island deep inside the arm. From the island you can view both glaciers or watch seals haul out on the ice pack.

To avoid the three-day open water paddle to the arm, arrange to be dropped off and picked up by a tour boat that cruises the area. Try Adventure Bound Alaska (☎ 800-228-3875), which charges only $135 per person for drop-off and pickup, or Wilderness Swift Charters (☎ 463-4942, @ tongass@alaska.net).

Tracy Arm Wilderness Area is managed by the USFS. For additional information contact the Forest Service Information Center (☎ 907-586-8751), Juneau Centennial Hall, 101 Egan Dr, Juneau, AK 99801, or the USFS Web site (www.fs.fed.us/recreation/states.ak.html).

Stage 2: Granite Creek to Basin Rd via Mt Juneau

7mi, 6 to 7 hours

Those who detest backtracking more than being swatted by devil's club can return to Basin Rd via a ridge walk and the Mt Juneau Trail. Even without a backpack, this can be a challenging all-day workout. But if the weather is nice, the alpine area is great and well worth all the effort you spend climbing. The alternative, of course, is to leave the equipment at Granite Creek and spend a morning romping along the ridge and then return to hike out the way you came. Either way, make sure your water bottle is filled, because water will be difficult to find once you're on the ridges.

From the upper basin at 2200ft, you access the ridgeline to Mt Juneau by scrambling up the brushy and open grass slopes to the west (left) of Olds Mountain. Once on the saddle to the west side of the distinctively rocky mountain, you can drop the packs for a scramble up the 4453ft peak, but it's not an easy climb.

You continue the hike back by following the ridgeline west. There is no official trail, but the 4mi route is a natural one that climbs over a **4052ft knob** and then follows the ridge. By early July, a snow-free route appears and is marked much of the way by rock cairns. If the weather is nice, you'll enjoy great views of Blackerby Ridge to the north and Mount Roberts to the south. If it's not, then you should avoid the ridge and Mt Juneau Trail.

Eventually you reach **Mt Juneau**. From a point near its 3576ft summit, you get a sweeping panorama that includes downtown Juneau, the Gastineau Channel, Douglas Island and, if the day is clear enough, the north end of Admiralty Island. On the open grassy slopes to the south, the 2mi-long **Mt Juneau Trail**, which leads to the Perseverance Trail, is easy to pick up. It begins with an extremely steep descent of the mountain, dropping almost 2000ft, and passes a small patch of trees.

Eventually the trail skirts the open slopes for almost a mile, crossing one cascading stream after another. In June, this area will often be a series of snowslides that should be avoided or crossed with extreme caution, using an ice axe. If you're traveling in the opposite direction in July or August, gather water here; there is little to be found on top.

Resuming the descent, you pass through a stand of hemlocks, where there is a view of Gold Creek, and then finish off the trail with a series of switchbacks through shoulder-high alder. Mt Juneau Trail joins the Perseverance Trail near the spur to Ebner Falls. Head west (right) on the Perseverance Trail to return to the start at Basin Rd within a half mile.

Dan Moller Trail

Duration 1 or 2 days
Distance 6.6mi roundtrip
Difficulty Level Easy
Start/Finish Pioneer Avenue in West Juneau
Cabins & Shelters Yes
Permits Required No
Public Transportation Yes
Summary This trail features a climb to an alpine bowl in the center of Douglas Island. A USFS cabin can turn this hike into a delightful overnight stay in the mountains.

This is another easy-to-access trail that climbs to a beautiful alpine area overlooking Juneau. The Dan Moller Trail also provides access to the peaks and ridges that make up the backbone of Douglas Island. The trail to the USFS cabin is only a 3.3mi easy hike, but if you're experienced with a map and compass, you could spend an entire day walking the ridges and even return via Cropley Lake and the road to Eaglecrest Ski Area.

This hike takes most hikers five to six hours roundtrip, but it can also be done as an overnight excursion. Either reserve the USFS cabin in advance ($35) or carry up a tent to make camp in Kowee Basin.

PLANNING
When to Hike
The trail is best hiked late May through September. The heavy rains of October make this a slippery hike on steps and planking. In August, pack along a small container; the blueberries and raspberries will be hard to pass up.

Maps
The trail, Cropley Lake and the alpine route to Eaglecrest access road is covered on USGS 1:63,360 quad *Juneau B-2*.

Cabins & Shelters
Four USFS cabins are accessible from the Juneau trail system, including the Dan Moller Trail. All cabins along the trail system can be used by anybody from 10 am to 5 pm as warming shelters and then rented for $35 per night. It's important to reserve the cabins in advance, by calling the National Recreation Reservation Center (☎ 877-444-6777, 515-885-3639 for overseas) or through its Web site (www.reserveusa.com).

The Dan Moller Cabin has a pair of double beds, a pair of single beds and a sleeping loft. There is also a stove with propane furnished by the USFS.

GETTING TO/FROM THE HIKE
The trailhead is 1.5mi from the Juneau International Hostel. You can easily walk to it, or you can catch the minibus to Douglas ($1.25) that runs every hour. Depart at Cordova St, which leads up into a growth of apartments and condominiums known as West Juneau. From Cordova St, turn left onto Pioneer Ave and follow it to the end of the pavement. The trail is well posted, and there is a small parking area.

THE HIKE
Stage 1: Pioneer Ave to USFS Cabin
3.3mi, 1½ to 2 hours
From the trailhead parking area, the Dan Moller Trail begins as an old road and climbs steadily through the lush spruce forest. Within half a mile you break out of the forest

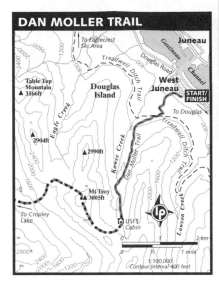

at the first of several muskeg meadows on the way to the cabin. There is a bench and a view of Juneau from here. Most of the muskeg meadows have been well planked, making the hiking considerably easier and allowing you to pause in midsummer to enjoy the abundance of wildflowers. If its been raining or the morning is frosty, be careful. The wood can become extremely slippery.

Shortly after the first meadow, you reach the posted junction with **Treadwell Ditch Trail**. The trail is overgrown, but by heading right here, you will quickly reach a bridge over **Kowee Creek**. The creek is named after the Native chief who lived at the base of it at one time and supposedly led Joe Juneau and Richard Harris up Gold Creek to the precious metal that quickly gave rise to the city of Juneau.

The Dan Moller Trail continues to climb through open meadows and then, 1.5mi from the trailhead, moves into an older forest of spruce and hemlock. Here the trail surface is rocky, the only time it's not heavily planked. You break out into more meadows and then cross to the west side of Kowee Creek and skirt it briefly.

In the final mile, you make two steep ascents toward the higher elevation of the USFS cabin. The first is through a large meadow where the views of the surrounding mountains are superb. You recross Kowee Creek, to its east side, and begin a second climb, through brush and alder before reaching the **USFS cabin** in a beautiful alpine bowl.

Forester Dan Moller was responsible for building the trail in the early 1930s, and by 1936, a warming cabin was constructed in the bowl. Before Eaglecrest Ski Area opened in 1976, this was the place to go downhill skiing. Known as the Douglas Ski Bowl, you would have to hike up here with your skis and then use tow ropes to ski.

Once Eaglecrest was established, the cabin was vandalized periodically, until a local Juneau group, mostly cross-country skiers, donated time and materials and rebuilt it in 1983. Past the cabin the planking leads to an outhouse with a stunning view (if you leave the door open) and a spur to Kowee Creek, which can be used to gather water.

Even if you can't reserve the cabin in advance, the bowl is a wonderful place to camp. The trail to the basin that surrounds the head of Kowee Creek can be very wet at times, but you can find good campsites once you reach it. Arrive in the morning and then spend the afternoon climbing to the saddle in the ridge above Kowee Creek. The ridge forms the backbone of Douglas Island, and views from it include Juneau and Admiralty Island. The distinctive peak just west along the ridge from the bowl is **Mt Troy**, whose 3005ft summit is an easy side trip.

Stage 2: The Return
3.3mi, 1 to 2 hours

For most people, the only way up is also the only way down along this point-to-point trail. But you can deviate near the end, once you reach the junction with Treadwell Ditch Trail in the first meadow. If you head east (right) on the trail, you'll reach the Mt Jumbo trailhead after 5mi, on 5th St in

Douglas. Sections of the trail are overgrown, and at the east end, it can be wet and boggy during the summer.

If you head west (left), the trail leads 7mi to Fish Creek and the access road to Eaglecrest in North Douglas.

West Glacier Trail

Duration 1 to 2 days
Distance 6.8 to 10.2mi roundtrip
Difficulty Level Medium to hard
Start/Finish Mendenhall Lake Campground
Cabins & Shelters No
Permits Required No
Public Transportation Yes
Summary A half-day or overnight hike to the finest viewpoints above Mendenhall Glacier, this trail is one of the most scenic in Southeast Alaska.

This is one of the most spectacular trails in the Juneau area and all of the Southeast. The 3.4mi trail begins off Montana Creek Rd, past Mendenhall Lake Campground, and hugs the mountainside along Mendenhall Glacier, providing exceptional views of the ice falls and other glacial features. It ends at a rocky outcrop but a rough route continues from here to the summit of McGinnis Mountain, another 2mi away. The roundtrip on the West Glacier Trail is 6.8mi; the climb to McGinnis Mountain is 10.2mi. The only downside of the trail is that on any nice day in the summer there will be an endless line of helicopters flying tourists up to the glacier.

For those equipped with crampons, an ice axe and a climbing rope, the West Glacier Trail is the most common route to Mendenhall Glacier. Ice climbers generally hike 1.5mi or so up the trail before cutting over to the glacier.

Plan on four to five hours for the West Glacier Trail, a moderately easy hike that can be done in tennis shoes. If you want to tackle the difficult McGinnis Mountain Route, plan on a long day and wear sturdy hiking boots. Snow persists along this route well into June, but later in the summer you can do an overnight hike and camp above the tree line.

PLANNING
When to Hike
Like the Dan Moller Trail, this hike is best done from late May through September.

Maps
The trail and route to McGinnis Mountain are covered on the USGS 1:63,360 quad *Juneau B-2*. In this book, the trail is shown on the Montana Creek and Windfall Lake Trails map.

GETTING TO/FROM THE HIKE
From Mendenhall Loop Rd, turn north onto Montana Creek Rd and then follow the signs to the campground. Go past the entrance of the campground to a parking area, and you'll find the trailhead at the end of the dirt road. A Juneau city bus ($1.25) will drop you off at the corner of Mendenhall Loop and Montana Creek Rds. From there it's an extra mile to the beginning of the trail.

THE HIKE
Stage 1: Mendenhall Lake Campground to Rocky Outcrop
3.4mi, 2 to 3 hours
From the north side of the parking lot, the trail departs into a stand of willow, cottonwood and alder as it begins to skirt **Mendenhall Lake**. Within a half mile, you cross the first of two bridged streams, but rarely see the lake or the glacier. After crossing the second stream, roughly a mile from the parking lot, the trail begins climbing the eastern flank of **McGinnis Mountain** along a series of switchbacks. Just before the trail starts ascending, look for spurs that will lead you down to the lake and close views of the glacier's face.

The trail climbs up a bluff, and in the next mile, you have spectacular views of **Mendenhall Glacier** from above. The trail then begins skirting the flank of McGinnis Mountain and becomes more challenging to follow. Look for rock cairns if in doubt. Eventually, after

you cross many small streams and climb some steep sections, the **first ice fall**, where the glacier makes a sharp descent toward the valley, appears and is easy to recognize.

The trail ends at the top of a rocky outcrop, where there is a huge rock cairn and spectacular 180-degree views of the glacier and ice pinnacles. Looming above this frozen river are sheer-sided mountains. If the day is nice and the sun is out, cancel the rest of your itinerary and spend an afternoon on this rock ledge. This is one of the most beautiful spots in Juneau. If it's drizzling out, consider yourself lucky. The deepest blues and other shades of glaciers are always better on a cloudy day in light rain.

Stage 2: The Return
3.4mi, 2 hours
For most people, the second stage of this hike is a return to the parking lot and the Mendenhall Lake Campground, a fast hike of two hours or less. A good side trip before returning to the campground, for very experienced hikers who are in good physical shape and don't mind scrambling on loose slopes, is to continue on the McGinnis Mountain Route.

Side Trip: McGinnis Mountain Route
3.4mi, 2 hours
This route is not maintained and is usually only marked with plastic flags. From the rocky outcrop, look for a trail that departs into thick brush and climbs steeply up a forested ridge on the east side of the mountain.

The trail breaks out of the trees at 2300ft and ends at an alpine meadow with a small tarn. From here, you continue west, ascending through alpine meadows to the **4228ft summit**, a 2mi hike from the end of the West Glacier Trail. The views on a clear day are almost infinite and include not only all of Mendenhall Glacier, Auke Bay and the Juneau Ice Field but the distant Fairweather Mountains in Glacier Bay National Park to the northwest. If you haul up a tent and sleeping bags, there are many spots to camp above the tree line.

Montana Creek & Windfall Lake Trails

Duration 1 or 2 days
Distance 11.5mi
Difficulty Level Easy to medium
Start Montana Creek Rd
Finish Mile 27 Glacier Hwy
Cabins & Shelters No
Permits Required No
Public Transportation Yes
Summary This is a long hike that follows two creeks, the Herbert River and Windfall Lake Trail. There is good salmon fishing at times, and the possibility to spot bears.

These two trails connect at Windfall Lake and can be combined for an interesting 13mi overnight trip. Both trails are noted for being extremely wet and muddy at times. On the 9.5mi Montana Creek Trail, hikers used to contend with a rock-slide area, but in the early 1990s the USFS rebuilt the trail and improved the conditions considerably. The trail was improved so much that they held a footrace on it that year, and the winner covered the 13mi in an hour and 10 minutes. Hikers generally take a little longer, anywhere from seven to nine hours to walk from the end of Montana Creek Rd, over a low pass to Glacier Hwy via Windfall Lake Trail.

During July and early August, Montana Creek supports sockeye and silver salmon runs. The fishing for sockeye can be especially good. During this time watch out for bears and hang your food. Also watch out for an occasional mountain biker; cyclists take to this route now that it has been improved.

There are no cabins or shelters, but it's possible to turn this hike into an overnight hike by camping around Windfall Lake.

PLANNING
When to Hike
Since these are basically low elevation trails, you can undertake this hike May through October. In the winter, these trails are a popular route for cross-country skiers.

Maps
Montana Creek Trail is covered on USGS 1:63,350 quads *Juneau B-2* and *B-3*, Windfall Lake Trail on quad *Juneau C-3*.

GETTING TO/FROM THE HIKE
To the Start
The Montana Creek Trail begins near the end of Montana Creek Rd, 3mi from its junction with Mendenhall Loop Rd, where a city bus will drop you off.

From the Finish
The 3.5mi Windfall Lake Trail begins off a gravel spur that leaves the Glacier Hwy just before it crosses Herbert River, 27mi northwest of Juneau. There is no public transportation to this end.

One way to reach Windfall Lake Trailhead is to rent a car. There are almost a dozen car rental places in Juneau. For a $35 special, call Rent-A-Wreck (☎ 789-4111) at 9099 Glacier Hwy, which provides pickup and drop-off service. So do Allstar Rent-A-Car (☎ 790-2414) and Evergreen Motors (☎ 789-9386), which has compacts for around $40 a day.

THE HIKE
Stage 1: Montana Creek Rd to Windfall Lake
8mi, 4 to 5 hours
The Montana Creek Trail was part of a trail system that extended all the way to Echo Cove and was established by territorial Alaska to service mining sites. The first mile follows a portion of **Montana Creek Rd**, now closed to vehicles. From there, a trail heads into the lush rain forest and quickly passes the confluence between Montana and McGinnis Creeks. Within half a mile, you cross a bridge to the east side of the **Montana Creek** and continue upstream into the slide area. There are about a dozen slides above the creek. In 1993, the USFS used the stone to build a trail bed and fill in many of the wet areas. Now the hike up to the pass is easy and, for the most part, dry.

The trail stays close to Montana Creek along a stretch that draws the heaviest runs of salmon, attracting both fly fishers and bears. Beware. Beyond the slide area, you continue a gentle climb along the river and through the woods. A bridge crosses Montana Creek 3mi from the trailhead. Within three hours of the trailhead, you gain over 200ft to reach the **850ft pass**. This low saddle is a series of large, boggy meadows that serve as the headwaters for Windfall and Montana Creeks. From here, experienced hikers sometimes depart for John Muir Cabin in Spaulding Meadows.

The trail continues northwest through the meadows and then begins descending into the Windfall Creek watershed via a series of switchbacks. At first you're above the creek, but after passing through a meadow you reach **Windfall Creek** and cross it 6mi from the trailhead.

You are now only 2mi from the spur to Windfall Lake, and the trail here is easy to follow. The trail swings wide of the marshy south end of the lake and skirts its east side before arriving at the posted spur. The spur trail is well planked and reaches the north end of **Windfall Lake** in a quarter mile and camping spots at the northwest corner in a half mile.

Most of Windfall's shoreline is heavily forested, an angler's worst nightmare, but if you can avoid hanging your lures in branches, the fishing for cutthroat trout and Dolly Varden, as well as silver and sockeye salmon during spawning runs, can be very productive.

Stage 2: Windfall Lake to Glacier Hwy

3.5mi, 2 hours

The walk out to Glacier Hwy is along Windfall Lake Trail, which begins at the junction with Montana Creek Trail and extends 3.5mi northwest. This is an easy hike along a well-maintained trail. Plan on two hours to reach Glacier Hwy, less if you are intentionally hustling along.

From the junction, you skirt around a hill that overlooks the north end of Windfall Lake and then immediately come to a large

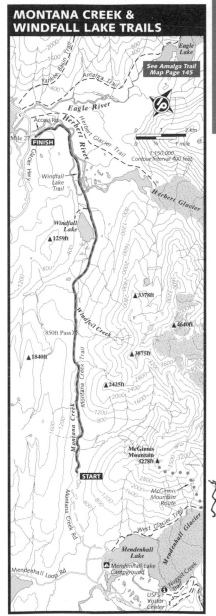

MONTANA CREEK & WINDFALL LAKE TRAILS

See Amalga Trail Map Page 145

1:150,000
Contour Interval 400 feet

FINISH

START

beaver pond. This used to be a wet section of the trail, but the USFS has since installed an elevated boardwalk across the pond, to help you keep your boots dry. The trail continues north, passing several other beaver ponds. At one time, you could pick up a spur that lead to Herbert Glacier from here, but the beavers and their dams have made maintenance of that route impossible.

Within a mile of the junction, you cross a bridge over a stream diverting off nearby Herbert River and then continue into the lush forest of spruce, western hemlock and devil's club. In another mile, you cross the same stream and reach the glacial river.

The final 1.5mi of the trail is a scenic hike that closely skirts the **Herbert River**. You'll have the rushing water at your feet and the peaks that surround Herbert Glacier above you. The trail ends in a parking area. From there, you follow a gravel road for almost a mile out to Glacier Hwy.

Amalga Trail

Duration 1 or 2 days
Distance 15mi roundtrip
Difficulty Level Medium
Start/Finish Mile 28.4 Glacier Hwy
Cabins & Shelters Yes
Permits Required No
Public Transportation No
Summary A trailside USFS cabin near the end of the trail, at the terminus of Eagle Glacier, is one of the most scenic in Southeast Alaska.

Practically next door to Windfall Lake Trail is Amalga Trail. Also known as the Eagle Glacier Trail, this route was extended in 1990 and now ends a quarter mile from Eagle Glacier. There is a USFS cabin on the lake formed by the glacier, and the view is one of the best of any USFS cabin in the area.

Even if you can't secure the unit, don't pass up the trail, as this is a very scenic hike. One option is to camp at nearby Eagle Beach Recreation Area and then undertake a series of day hikes along Amalga, Herbert

Glacier and Windfall Lake Trails, all within walking distance from the campground. As long as you've made your way this far out, you may as well stay and soak up the scenery.

The hike to Eagle Glacier is a 10- to 12-hour hike roundtrip, so many hikers overnight it by camping in a pleasant open area half a mile south of the lake. You can then day hike to the glacier, which has retreated 2mi beyond the lake.

PLANNING
When to Hike
Like the Montana Creek–Windfall Lake Trails, you can undertake this hike from May through October.

Maps
The trail is covered on USGS 1:63,360 quad *Juneau B-3*.

Cabins & Shelters
Eagle Glacier Cabin is a 5.5mi hike from the Amalga Trailhead. The cabin rents for $35 per night, and you can reserve it in advance through the National Recreation Reservation Service (☎ 877-444-6777, 515-885-3639 for overseas) or through its Web site (www.reserveusa.com).

GETTING TO/FROM THE HIKE
The trailhead is at Mile 28.4 of Glacier Hwy, just beyond the bridge across Eagle River and a quarter of a mile past the trailhead for Herbert Glacier Trail. There is no public transportation this far out. For information about renting a car in Juneau see Montana Creek & Windfall Lake Trails.

THE HIKE
Stage 1: Glacier Hwy to Eagle Glacier
7.5mi, 5 hours
From the parking lot off Glacier Hwy, the trail passes underneath Eagle River Bridge and then heads northeast along **Eagle River**. At 1.3mi, you come to a junction with the **Yankee Basin Trail**. This 6mi trail heads due north, following the route of an old tramway to the headwaters of the south fork of Kowee

Creek. In the past, this trail has been in poor condition and nearly impossible to follow in places. There are plans to brush it out and upgrade it. Check with the USFS office in Juneau for the trail's current condition.

The Amalga Trail continues upstream with the Eagle River but, within a quarter mile, veers away to climb up the bordering slopes. Roughly 3mi from the trailhead, you descend to cross **Boulder Creek**, to an area of beaver pools and flooding. At one time, the trail had to be rerouted into the hillsides to the north to avoid the water, and this made it a considerably harder hike. In recent years, the USFS has used boardwalks and fill to return Amalga Trail to its original course in the lowlands of the glacial valley.

In the next 2mi, you swing away from the river again and do some climbing before arriving at an open area and stream near the **old Amalga townsite**. Amalga Mine was actually located 4mi inland, and the trail was originally a horse-tram route. The mine was productive enough to warrant a settlement from 1902 to 1927 and had its own post office. It's now almost impossible to find the mine and little remains of the townsite.

This is a good spot to pitch a tent. You'll find evidence of other backpackers stopping in the open area for the night. From here, it's a half mile to the **Eagle Glacier Cabin** and the lake. The log cabin was purchased by a local conservation group in 1991, and that fall, volunteers renovated it. Right on the lake facing the glacier, the cabin creates a dramatic setting where you can prop your feet and gaze at mountains, ice and a lake. It's rented at night but is open to the public from 10 am to 5 pm daily as a warming hut. The cabin can accommodate as many as 12 people, with a single bunk, a double bunk and a sleeping loft.

From the cabin, the trail continues along **Eagle Lake**. The heavy shoreline thicket of alders and willow has been brushed back, so you can continue another 2mi toward the face of the glacier. After skirting the lake, the trail gains more than 500ft in elevation, climbing up and over a steep rocky moraine. The trail ends a quarter mile from **Eagle Glacier**, on the northwest edge of the lake.

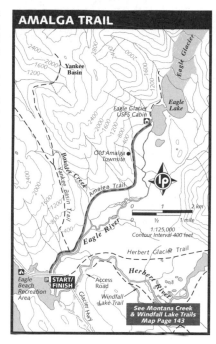

AMALGA TRAIL

From here hikers properly equipped with crampons, ice axes and rope can continue onto the glacier itself to access the Juneau Ice Field.

Eagle Glacier has retreated considerably in recent years, but the view of the surrounding peaks and the lake is still a hard one to match in the Southeast.

Stage 2: The Return
7.5mi, 4 hours

Once at Eagle Glacier, you have little choice but to return the way you came. By camping at old Amalga townsite, you can walk out in less than three hours and get an early start on the next trail.

Haines Region

Haines may lack the touristy charm of Petersburg or Sitka, but it is definitely not lacking hiking opportunities and superb scenery. The town is surrounded by mountains: To the west, the jagged peaks of the Chilkat Mountains loom over Fort Seward (Port Chilkoot). To the east is the Chilkoot Range, and standing guard over Haines is Mt Ripinsky. From the heart of Haines, you can walk to two trails – the challenging Mt Ripinsky Trail to the north and the easier Mt Riley Trail to the south. Farther south on the Chilkat Peninsula is the Seduction Point Trail, in Chilkat State Park. Want more hiking opportunities? You can either jump on the next ferry to Skagway for the Chilkoot Trail or head 120mi north on the Haines Hwy, to Kluane National Park, one of Canada's most spectacular wilderness parks and home of Mt Logan (19,524ft), the country's highest peak. The park visitor center (☎ 867-634-2251), at Haines Junction off the Alaska Hwy, supplies travelers with information on hiking and wilderness trips in the 8649-sq-mi preserve.

NATURAL HISTORY

The flora and fauna around Haines are similar to those in much of Southeast Alaska, with the exception of the extraordinary number of bald eagles that gather in the area. Each year, from October to January, more than 4000 eagles congregate along the Chilkat River to feed on chum salmon. They come because an upwelling of warm water prevents the river from freezing and encourages the late run of salmon. It's the largest known gathering of bald eagles in the world and a remarkable sight. Hundreds of birds, often six or more to a branch, sit in the bare trees.

To protect the migration, the state reserved 75 sq mi of land as Alaska Chilkat Bald Eagle Preserve in 1982. You really have to be here after November to enjoy the birds in their greatest numbers, but even during the summer more than 200 resident eagles can be spotted. The eagles can be seen from the Haines Hwy, where lookouts allow motorists to park and view the birds. The best viewing places are between Mile 18 and Mile 22, where telescopes, interpretive displays and paved walkways along the river were added in 1997.

During the summer, Alaska Nature Tours (☎ 766-2876, @ aknature@kcd.com) conducts daily three-hour tours ($50) that concentrate on the river flats.

Chilkat Guides (☎ 766-2491, @ raftalaska @aol.com) offers a four-hour float down the Chilkat River ($80 for adults) that provides plenty of opportunities to view bald eagles and possibly brown bears; there is little white water. The guide company runs the trip daily, beginning from its shop on Beach Rd in Fort Seward.

You might also want to check out the American Bald Eagle Foundation (☎ 766-3094), near the post office on 2nd Ave. The nonprofit center opened in 1994 and features an impressive wildlife diorama with more than 100 species on display. A tree full of eagles occupies the middle of the hall, and a small video room shows the annual winter eagle congregation on the Chilkat River. Hours are 10 am to 5 pm daily; donation requested.

CLIMATE

Haines is drier than the rest of the Southeast, especially Ketchikan. The average annual precipitation is 53 inches, most of which is winter snow. Still, cloudy conditions are the norm throughout the summer, the reason the average high temperature in July is 65°F. If the sun is out and the wind is down, you can expect those summer temperatures to zoom into the 70s and even 80s at times, especially if you're in the surrounding alpine regions.

INFORMATION

The trails in Haines are either maintained by Haines Borough or the Alaska Division of Parks & Outdoor Recreation. For this reason, the best place for hiking information and trail conditions in Haines is the state park district office (☎ 766-2292), on Main St above Helen's Shop. The office is open 8 am to 4:30 pm Monday to Friday.

HAINES

Haines (population 1775), in the northern reaches of the Inside Passage, is an important access point to the Yukon Territory

(Canada) and Interior Alaska, with a road that actually leads to the 'Outside.'

For travel information, head to the Haines Visitor Center (☎ 766-2234, 800-458-3579, @ hainesak@wwa.com), at 2nd Ave and Willard St. During the summer, the office is open 8 am to 8 pm daily. The center has racks of free information, rest rooms, a small message board, a used-book exchange and a modem line for those who are packing a computer and want to collect their email. The bureau also maintains a Web site (www.haines.ak.us).

Supplies & Equipment

A limited selection of backpacking and camping equipment is available at Alaska Sport Shop (☎ 766-2441), at 4th Ave and Main St. It's far better to purchase what you need in Juneau.

Places to Stay & Eat

Haines has several state campgrounds. The closest to town is *Portage Cove*, on Beach Rd a half mile southeast of Fort Seward. This scenic beach campground is for hikers and cyclists only and features nine tent sites for $6, as well as tables and a water supply. Follow Front St south (which becomes Beach Rd as it curves around the cove near Fort Seward), and the campground is at the end of the gravel road. *Chilkat State Park* (15 sites, $6), 7mi southeast of Haines on Mud Bay Rd, has good views of the Davidson and Rainbow Glaciers spilling out of the mountains into the Lynn Canal. The Seduction Point Trail begins in Chilkat State Park.

Bear Creek Camp & Hostel (☎ 766-2259, *Small Tract Rd; hostel@kcd.com*) is 2.5mi south of town. Follow 3rd Ave south onto Mud Bay Rd near Fort Seward. After a half mile, veer left onto Small Tract Rd and follow it for 1.5mi to the hostel. There is room for 20 people in the hostel's dorms; the cost is $14 per night. There are also tent sites for $12 per night for two people (shower included) and two-person cabins for $38 per night.

Fort Seward Lodge (☎ 766-2009, 800-478-7772, @ *ftsewardlodge@wytbear.com*), the former post exchange in the fort, is the cheapest hotel in town, with rooms beginning at $50/55 singles/doubles. Also in the former fort is *Hotel Halsingland* (☎ 766-2000, 800-542-6363, @ *halsinglan@aol.com*), with rooms for $89/98.

The popular place for breakfast among locals is the *Chilkat Restaurant and Bakery*, at Main St and 5th Ave, which opens at 7 am. A plate of eggs, potatoes and toast is $6, and you can get coffee and a warm muffin for around $2.50. On Friday night, they have an all-you-can eat Mexican dinner for $13.

The *Commander's Room*, in the Hotel Halsingland in Fort Seward, provides a historical setting in which to eat. The cost of breakfast is similar to the Chilkat Restaurant and Bakery, and the portions are filling. At night, the restaurant serves a variety of seafood, with dinners ranging from $14 to $22.

Getting There & Away

Air There is no jet service to Haines, but several charter companies run regularly scheduled northbound and southbound flights. Wings of Alaska (☎ 766-2030), Haines Airways (☎ 766-2646) or LAB Flying Service (☎ 766-2222) all offer daily flights to Juneau. The one-way fare is around $65, roundtrip $130.

Bus From Haines, you can catch buses north to Whitehorse, Anchorage or Fairbanks. Alaskon Express has a bus departing from the Hotel Halsingland at 8:45 am Sunday, Tuesday and Thursday that overnights at Beaver Creek and then continues on to Anchorage, reaching the city at 7:30 pm the following day. The fare from Haines to Anchorage is $195 and does not include lodging.

On the same runs, you can also make connections at either Haines Junction or Beaver Creek for Fairbanks, Whitehorse or Skagway, though why anybody would want to ride a bus instead of a ferry to Skagway is beyond me. The one-way fare to Fairbanks is $182 and Whitehorse $86.

Boat State ferries arrive and depart daily from the terminal (☎ 766-2111) in Lutak

Inlet north of town. The one-way fare north to Skagway is $17 and south to Juneau is $24. Haines Taxi (☎ 766-3138) runs a shuttle bus that meets all ferry arrivals, and for $5 it will take you the 4mi into town. The bus also departs town 30 minutes before each ferry arrival and stops at the Hotel Halsingland and near the visitor center in town before heading out to the ferry terminal.

Another way to reach Skagway is on the Haines-Skagway Water Taxi (☎ 766-3395, @ h2otaxi@kcd.com), which has an 80-passenger boat departing twice daily during the summer ($20 one way).

Mt Riley Loop

Duration 5 to 6 hours
Distance 9 to 10.7mi
Difficulty Level Easy
Start Portage Cove Campground
Finish Fort Seward
Cabins & Shelters No
Permits Required No
Public Transportation Yes
Summary This trail is a moderately easy climb to the excellent views of Mt Riley (1760ft), the highest peak on the Chilkat Peninsula.

The Mt Riley trail system is south of town in Chilkat State Park. All the trails lead to the summit. This 9mi loop is rated easy and provides access to a peak with spectacular views, including Rainbow and Davidson Glaciers.

The three trailheads are a mile beyond Portage Cove Campground, at Lily Lake, and Mud Bay Rd (the steepest and most direct route to the peak). But the loop described here connects the scenic Battery Point Trail with a return on FAA Rd, to eliminate finding a 3mi ride back from Mud Bay Rd. The entire loop is a five- to six-hour day hike for most hikers.

PLANNING
When to Hike
This trail can be hiked any time from June through September, but the ridge to Mt Riley from Battery Point Trail can hold snow well into June.

Maps
The trails are covered on USGS 1:63,360 quads *Skagway A-1* and *A-2*. For USGS quads of the Haines area, stop at Chilkoot Gardens (☎ 776-2226), a gift shop on Main St and Second Ave, or the Babbling Book (☎ 766-3356) on Main St. If you're coming from Juneau, purchase your maps there to avoid missing out in Haines.

GETTING TO/FROM THE HIKE
Mt Riley Loop can easily be reached on foot from the center of Haines. Follow Front St along the waterfront toward Fort Seward and then continue as it becomes Portage Cove Rd to its end. You'll return to Fort Seward on FAA Rd.

THE HIKE
Stage 1: Portage Cove Campground to Battery Point
3mi, 1 to 2 hours
For most hikers, the hike actually begins on Portage Cove Rd, the beach road that heads southeast from Fort Seward to **Portage Cove Campground**. The road continues for another mile beyond the campground, past a handful of private homes, to a trailhead.

For the most part, Battery Point Trail is a level walk near the shoreline, but it first passes a handful of private homes overlooking Lynn Canal. In 1.2mi, just before crossing a small stream, you arrive at a junction. The trail heading west goes to Mt Riley (2.8mi); the other continues to Battery Point.

If you plan to go to Battery Point, cross the stream and follow the trail to the pebbled beach on the west side of **Kelgaya Point**. For the next mile, you can follow the beach and then cut across Kelgaya Point to arrive at **Battery Point**. In the small cove the point forms, you'll find a pleasant beach and a panoramic view of Lynn Canal. People used to camp here and, at one time, there was even an outhouse, but now state park officials strongly discourage camping. In recent years there have been problems with out-of-control campfires and sanitation.

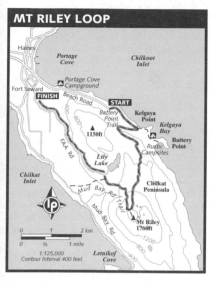

MT RILEY LOOP

Haines
Portage Cove
Chilkoot Inlet
Portage Cove Campground
Fort Seward
FINISH
Beach Road
START
400
800
Battery Point Trail
Kelgaya Point
Kelgaya Bay
1150ft
Battery Point
FAA Rd
Rustic Campsites
Lily Lake
Chilkat Inlet
Chilkat Peninsula
Mud Bay Rd Trail
Mud Bay Rd
Mt Riley 1760ft
1200
0   1   2 km
0   ½   1 mile
1:125,000
Contour Interval 400 feet
Letnikof Cove
400

small stream and ...
with the trail from Fo...
west (left-hand fork), ye...
the trail as it descends to ...
half a mile. The posted trailhead...
parking area are 3mi south of tow...

If you take the right-hand fork a...
junction, you'll reach Fort Seward. In le...
than a quarter mile, the trail arrives at the
water-supply access road, a few hundred
yards from where it ends at **Lily Lake**. Continue north on the road for the next 2mi.
You emerge at **FAA Rd** for the last leg of the
hike. Follow this road for a mile, and you'll
end up at Officer's Row, in the southwest
corner of Fort Seward.

Stage 2: Battery Point to Haines via Mt Riley

7.7mi, 4 to 5 hours

Backtrack to the junction to Mt Riley and
head southwest (left-hand fork). The trail to
the peak begins with a steep climb through
a spruce forest with a heavy undergrowth of
devil's club. Hiking becomes easier within
2mi, when the trail skirts a ridge to **Half
Dome**, a muskeg meadow at about 1000ft
that is loaded with blueberries in August.

From there, you make the final climb up
Mt Riley, through open muskeg meadows,
and emerge at the main trail from Mud Bay
just before reaching the peak, 3.8mi from
Battery Point or 5mi from Portage Cove
Campground. The climb to the summit ends
with a couple hundred yards of planking
along the Mud Bay Rd Trail. Despite Mt
Riley's low elevation, there are excellent
views in every direction, including the entire
Chilkat Peninsula, the city of Haines and
Davidson Glacier across Lynn Canal.

To loop back to town, stay on the Mud
Bay Rd Trail. It descends the west side of
the mountain through muskeg meadows for
the first half mile and then moves into a
spruce forest. Within 1.5mi, you cross a

Skagway Region

Every year, from June through August, thousands of tourists and hikers flood this narrow
valley at the head of Lynn Canal in search of
the gold-rush era. A century ago, Skagway
and neighboring Dyea, now a ghost town,
were the starting points for more than
40,000 gold-rush stampeders who were determined to reach the Yukon and make their
fortune in the Klondike fields.

The actual Klondike gold rush lasted only
from 1896 to the early 1900s, but its legacy
and the Chilkoot Trail that stampeders immortalized have endured, even blossomed,
and are now the basis for Skagway's
economy. Today, most of downtown Skagway and much of the surrounding area are
part of the Klondike Gold Rush National
Historical Park, which extends from Seattle
to Dawson in the Yukon Territory. Not only
is the NPS constantly restoring the historical
buildings to return Skagway to its boomtown appearance, but many of the locals
dress in turn-of-the-century costumes to
welcome the modern-day stampeders from
the state ferry and large cruise ships.

A little touristy for backpackers who come
to Alaska for wilderness solitude? Perhaps,
but the 33mi-long Chilkoot Trail is not so
much a hike in the mountains as it is a walk
through history. The alpine scenery is great,
and you might see some wildlife, but the most

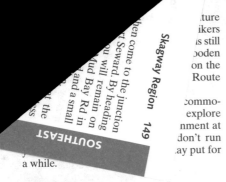

.ture
ikers
is still
ooden
on the
Route

commo-
explore
nment at
don't run
.ay put for

a while.

HISTORY

Even before the Klondike Gold Rush, the Chilkoot Trail was a vital route to the Interior, as one of only three glacier-free corridors through the Coast Range between Juneau and Yakutat. The Chilkoot was first used by Chilkat tribes trading fish oil, clam shells and dried fish with Interior tribes for animal skins and copper. Dyea was originally a small year-round Chilkat-Tlingit village, whose residents jealously guarded access to the pass.

All that changed when the gold rush brought a tide of people, supplies and progress at the turn of the century. In August of 1896, Skookum Jim Mason, Dawson Charlie and George Washington Carmack found gold in a tributary of the Klondike River in Canada's Yukon Territory. The stampede itself was ignited on July 17, 1897, when the steamship *Portland* landed in Seattle with two tons of gold and the *Seattle Post-Intelligencer* bellowed 'GOLD! GOLD! GOLD! GOLD!' in a banner headline. Through the summer and into the winter of 1897–98, thousands of people quit their jobs and sold their homes to finance a trip through Southeast Alaska to the newly created boomtown of Skagway. In the first year of the gold rush, almost 30,000 prospectors tackled the steep Chilkoot Trail to Lake Bennett, where they built crude rafts to float the rest of the way to the goldfields. In all, it was a 600mi journey. Many hopeful gold seekers arrived only to discover most of the good Klondike claims were already staked.

Some miners used the White Pass Trail that departed for Lake Bennett directly out of Skagway. The trail, which was advertised as a 'horse trail,' was brutal. In the winter of 1897–98, some 3000 pack animals were driven to death by overanxious owners. The White Pass became known as the Dead Horse Trail. The Chilkoot Trail was more popular, as it was several miles shorter, but both routes were hard. Stampeders faced murders, suicides, malnutrition and death from hypothermia and avalanches. Until the

Climbing the Chilkoot Pass

Not only was Klondike 'the last great gold rush' in the minds of many people, it was also one of the most photographed, especially when it came to the ordeals of miners struggling up the Chilkoot Trail. Of all the pictures taken along the route, the most amazing one is of the long line of people carrying their heavy loads up the Chilkoot Pass in the winter of 1897–98.

'The final climb produced one of the most moving photographic images in American history,' wrote William Bronson in *The Last Grand Adventure*. 'No staged version of this event could ever match the incredible drama created by the thousands of men and women who struggled up the 30-degree incline to cross the Chilkoot Pass that winter.'

Unless they were rich enough to hire porters, most stampeders would make as many as 40 trips in 40 days before they could get their 'year's worth of supplies' and equipment to the top. On each trip, the miners carried roughly 50lb up the pass, a trek that included 1500 steps carved out of the snow and ice. Most could endure only one climb a day. But, as Bronson noted, 'Whether gold lay at the end of their trails or not, they had crossed the Chilkoot, an achievement that for many was the crowning event in their lives.'

tramways were built along the Chilkoot Trail in late 1897 and early 1898, miners had to carry everything on their backs. The distance from the tidewater to the lake is only 35mi, but stampeders had to trudge hundreds of miles back and forth along the trail, moving a year's worth of supplies from cache to cache.

At the height of the gold rush, Michael J Heney, an Irish contractor, convinced a group of English investors that he could build a railroad over the White Pass Trail to Whitehorse. Construction began in 1898 with little more than picks, shovels and blasting powder, and the narrow-gauge railroad reached Whitehorse, the Yukon capital, in July 1900. The construction of the White Pass & Yukon Railroad was nothing short of a superhuman feat. The railroad made the Chilkoot Pass route unnecessary, sealing the fate of Dyea.

NATURAL HISTORY
Few trails in Alaska offer a more dramatic change in terrain and flora than the Chilkoot Trail. Passing from the USA into Canada, you begin in the coastal rain forest of the Pacific Northwest, featuring dense stands of black cottonwood and alder in the Taiya River floodplain and western hemlock, Sitka spruce and paper birch higher up on the hillsides. You reach stunted mountain hemlock at 1000ft and alpine vegetation of mosses, lichen and dwarf willow as you approach the summit of the Chilkoot Pass (3525ft).

Once across the pass you descend into the drier boreal forests of British Columbia. These forests mainly consist of lodgepole pine, willow and alder.

Wildlife that might be spotted includes hoary marmots, willow and white-tailed ptarmigan and occasionally a mountain goat in the alpine areas. In lower elevations it's possible at times to encounter moose, porcupines, bald eagles and black bears.

CLIMATE
In what up to now might have been a soggy Southeast for many, Skagway is one of the driest places. While Ketchikan gets 154 inches of rain a year and Sitka 100 inches, Skagway averages only 26 inches.

Skagway is also known for its moderate temperatures (the average high in July is 67°F) and high winds. Skagway is occasionally referred to as Home of the North Wind, and strong gusts can blow down out of the mountains and into the valleys to steal your hat on the streets of Skagway.

INFORMATION
In 1997, the National Park Service, Parks Canada and the Alaska Natural History Association teamed up to open the Chilkoot Trail Center (☎ 983-3655) in Skagway. It's located in the restored Martin Itjen House at the foot of Broadway St. The center is a clearinghouse for information on permits and transportation. There is also a 13-minute video on hiking the Chilkoot for those who are not sure if they're up for the adventure. For more information in advance of your trip, contact the National Park Service, PO Box 517, Skagway, AK 99840, or go to its Web site (www.nps.gov/klgo/).

Across the street from the Chilkoot Trail Center, in the White Pass & Yukon Route depot, is the visitor center for the Klondike Gold Rush National Historical Park. This visitor center (☎ 983-2921) is open 8 am to 7 pm daily and features displays, ranger talks and the movie *Days of Adventure, Dreams of Gold,* which is shown every hour. The 30-minute movie is narrated by Hal Holbrook and is the best way to slip back into the gold-rush days. The center also has information on other local trails and camping and leads a 45-minute walking tour of the historic district several times daily.

SKAGWAY
The end of the line for the state ferry in the Southeast is Skagway, a quiet little town of 800 people in the winter, a reincarnated boomtown in the summer.

For general travel information, visit the Skagway Visitor Center (☎ 983-2854, 888-762-1898, ✆ infoskag@aptalaska.net) on 5th Ave just west of Broadway St. Hours are 8 am to 5 pm daily. The center also maintains a Web site (www.skagway.org).

Supplies & Equipment

Packers Expeditions, on 5th Ave off Broadway St, has a limited supply of freeze-dried food and white gas for hiking trips, along with backpacking gear and maps. Fairway Market, at the corner of 4th Ave and State St, has groceries.

Places to Stay & Eat

The city manages two campgrounds that serve RVers and backpackers. *Hanousek Park* (☎ 983-2378), at Broadway St and 14th Ave, provides tables, pit toilets and water in a wooded setting for $8 per tent site. Near the ferry terminal is *Pullen Creek Park Campground* (☎ 983-2768, 800-936-3731), on the waterfront by the small boat harbor. There are 30 sites with electricity and water that cost $20 per night and tent sites for $10. Near the Chilkoot trailhead in Dyea, 9mi north of Skagway, the free *Dyea Camping Area* (☎ 983-2921) is operated by the NPS

on a first-come, first-served basis. There are 22 sites, vault toilets, tables and fire pits but no water.

The *Skagway Home Hostel* (☎ 983-2131), on 3rd Ave near Main St, is a very pleasant place to stay, a half mile from the ferry terminal. Reservations are advised – call the hostel or write to the Home Hostel, PO Box 231, Skagway, AK 99840. Along with a kitchen and baggage storage area, there are laundry facilities and bikes for guests. A bunk is $15; a room for couples is $40 a night.

The recently renovated *Golden North Hotel* (☎ 983-2294, 888-222-1898), at Broadway St and 3rd Ave, has rooms with shared baths that begin at $60.

Corner Cafe, at 4th Ave and State St, has a wide range of seafood and broiled, stuffed, poached or barbecued salmon or halibut dinners for around $15. *Northern Lights Pizzeria*, on Broadway, has pasta,

A Bridge to Dyea

When Skagway was hitting its peak during the Klondike gold rush at the turn of the century, so was Dyea, 9mi away. Located on the tidal flats of the Taiya River, Dyea had long been a camp for Chilkoot Tlingits, who developed the Chilkoot Trail as a trading route into the Interior.

When the stampeders arrived in 1897, Dyea appeared almost overnight. By 1899, it rivaled Skagway, with a population of 8000 and more than 150 businesses, including hotels, saloons, bathhouses and even its own newspaper. Dyea's darkest hour occurred on Palm Sunday in 1898, when an avalanche above Sheep Camp on the Chilkoot Trail claimed 60 victims. But it was the White Pass & Yukon Railroad, which began operations in 1900 and made the Chilkoot Trail obsolete, that sealed Dyea's fate. The town died almost as quickly as it was born. Many buildings were torn down and their lumber shipped for use elsewhere. The only ruins that remain today are a few foundations of buildings, the rotting stubs of the town's Long Wharf and Slide Cemetery.

In the past, visiting this bit of Klondike history meant fording an arm of the Nelson Slough, which was sometimes a bit of a problem. The Dyea Flats have one of the largest tidal ranges in the world, as much as 24ft in six hours. At high tide, the Nelson Slough rises from its normal 18 inches to about 4ft. The problem of access to the ghost town was solved in 1998, when the city of Skagway received a grant and built a bridge over the slough. The US Forest Service provided both the money and the timber, highly prized Alaskan yellow cedar logged from Chichagof Island. The new footbridge is simple, strong, attractive and, being cedar, also aromatic. 'It's probably the best-smelling bridge in Alaska,' said the Juneau engineer who designed it.

Even if you have no intentions of hiking the Chilkoot Trail, Dyea makes an interesting and cheap side trip from Skagway. A number of tour companies will run out to the area for $10 person, and camping at Dyea Campground is free. You can then hike over the historic townsite on your own or join a free walking tour that the National Park Service stages daily during the summer.

Greek or Mexican dinners ($10 to $13) and huge portions.

Getting There & Away
Air There are regularly scheduled flights from Skagway to Juneau, Haines and Glacier Bay with LAB Flying Service (☎ 983-2471), Wings of Alaska (☎ 983-2442), and Skagway Air (☎ 983-2218), which generally offers the cheapest fares. Expect to pay $80 one way to Juneau, $40 to Haines and $85 to Gustavus.

Bus Northbound travelers will find that scheduled buses are the cheapest way to travel. Alaskon Express has a bus departing at 7:30 am daily that arrives in Whitehorse at 11:30 am. On Sunday, Tuesday, and Thursday, you can continue to Beaver Creek, where the bus stops overnight and connections can be made to Anchorage or Fairbanks. Purchase tickets at the Westmark Inn (☎ 983-2241) on 3rd Ave. The one-way fare from Skagway to Whitehorse is $45 and to Fairbanks $206.

Alaska Direct Busline (☎ 800-770-6652) departs from the White Pass & Yukon Route depot at 3 pm daily for Whitehorse ($35). On Sunday, an Alaska Direct bus departs Whitehorse for either Anchorage or Fairbanks. And finally, Alaska Overland (☎ 867-667-7896 in Whitehorse) departs Whitehorse at 8 am (Yukon time) daily, arrives at Skagway at 10:45 am, then departs from the White Pass & Yukon Route depot at 3 pm for the return trip. The one-way fare is only $30.

Train Nowadays, it's possible to travel to Whitehorse on the White Pass & Yukon Route, with a bus connection at Fraser, British Columbia. The northbound train departs the Skagway depot (☎ 983-2217) at 12:40 pm daily during the summer and passengers arrive in Whitehorse by bus at 6 pm. The one-way fare is $95, quite a bit more than the bus, but the ride on the historic, narrow-gauge railroad is worth it.

Boat The Alaska Marine Hwy ferry (☎ 983-2941) departs daily, during the summer,

from the terminal and dock at the southwest end of Broadway St. See the Getting Around chapter for more details. There are lockers in the terminal, but the building is only open three hours prior to the arrival of a ferry and then while the boat is in port.

Haines-Skagway Water Taxi (☎ 888-766-3395) operates an 80-passenger boat that departs the Skagway small boat harbor twice daily for Haines, with the first run at 10:45 am and the second at 5 pm. Roundtrip fare is $32 and one-way is $20; you can purchase tickets on the boat.

Chilkoot Trail

Duration 3 to 4 days
Distance 30 to 35mi
Difficulty Level Medium to hard
Start Dyea
Finish Bennett
Cabins & Shelters No
Permits Required Yes
Public Transportation Yes
Summary The Chilkoot Trail is unquestionably the most famous trail in Alaska. This is a three- to four-day hike along the same route that was used by the Klondike stampeders in the 1898 to 1900 gold rush.

The Chilkoot Trail is not so much a wilderness adventure as it is a history lesson. The well-developed and well-marked trail is littered from one end to the other with artifacts of the era – everything from entire ghost towns and huge mining dredges to a rotting wagon wheel or a rusty coffeepot lying next to the trail. All the artifacts are protected by state, federal and provincial laws that prevent people from stuffing the artifacts in their backpacks. Even so, hikers still need to take great care to avoid inadvertently setting up camp on artifacts, stepping on them or using them as firewood.

The trip is 30 to 35mi long (depending on where you exit) and includes the Chilkoot Pass – a steep climb up loose rocks to 3525ft. Most hikers end up scrambling on all fours to reach the top. The Chilkoot Trail

CHILKOOT TRAIL

can be attempted by anyone in good physical condition with the right equipment and enough time. The hike normally takes three to four days, though it can be done in two days by experienced hikers.

Despite being well marked and well traveled, the trail is rated moderate to challenging. The weather can often turn nasty in the middle of the summer, making the alpine stretch, especially the climb from the Scales to the summit, a wet, cold, even intimidating experience.

The Chilkoot Trail can be hiked from either direction (starting at Skagway or Bennett Lake), but it's easier and safer when you start from Dyea and climb up the loose scree of the Chilkoot Pass rather than down. Besides, there is something about following the footsteps of the Klondike miners that makes this a special adventure.

PLANNING
When to Hike
The best season to hike the Chilkoot Trail is mid-June to mid-September, and it is most crowded from mid-July through mid-August.

Maps
Because the Chilkoot Trail is split between the USA and Canada, four topographical maps are required to cover the entire route. You begin with the USGS 1:63,360 quads *Skagway B-1* and *C-1* for the first half to Chilkoot Pass. Then switch to Canada 1:50,000 quads, produced by the Department of Energy, Mines & Resources; *White Pass 104M/11 East* and *Homan Lake 104M/14 East* cover Chilkoot Pass to Bennett.

That's a steep investment in topos for a three-day hike, so many hikers simply purchase *A Hiker's Guide to the Chilkoot Trail* ($3), which is produced by the Canada Parks Service and sold at the Chilkoot Trail Center. Even better is the *Chilkoot Trail* map by Trails Illustrated ($10).

Permits & Regulations
The Chilkoot Trail has become so popular that a permit and a fee system was set up in 1997. You need to pick up a permit from

both the US National Park Service and Parks Canada, which oversees the northern half. The US permit is free and can be obtained from the Chilkoot Trail Center. Parks Canada charges $24 per adult and $12 per child for its permit and is now limiting its 17mi portion of the trail to 50 hikers per day to protect natural and cultural resources. If you plan to walk the trail during the height of the summer season (July through mid-August), reserve your permit in advance by calling Parks Canada (☎ 867-667-3910, 800-661-0486). There is a $7 reservation fee. Eight permits per day are held out for hikers without reservations, but in the middle of the summer, the demand for them is great.

Hiking the Chilkoot Trail involves crossing the international border into Canada, so if you are beginning your trip in Dyea you must clear Canadian customs before leaving Skagway. You can do this by signing the customs register at the Chilkoot Trail Center. You can also clear customs in Fraser (☎ 867-821-4111). Hikers beginning their trip in Canada must clear US customs. You can do that when you return to Skagway by calling the US customs office (☎ 983-2325) on Klondike Hwy.

GETTING TO/FROM THE HIKE
To the Start
To reach the trailhead from Skagway, make your way to Dyea, 9mi to the northwest. Mile 0 of the Chilkoot Trail is just before the Taiya River crossing. Near the trailhead is an NPS ranger station that is open daily during the summer. It's tough reaching Dyea by hitchhiking, due to steep and narrow roads with blind curves. After the first 2mi, there are few places for motorists to pull over. Frontier Excursions (☎ 983-2517) and the Dyea Shuttle, run by the Skagway Home Hostel (☎ 983-2131), charge $10 for a ride out to the trailhead, which seems to be the going rate. Just about every taxi and tour company in Skagway will run you out there for the same price.

From the Finish
In the past, the highlight of the hike was riding the historical White Pass & Yukon

Route (WP&YR) back to Skagway from Lake Bennett. Much to the joy of backpackers, that service was restored in 1998. The train departs the Lake Bennett depot at 9 am and again and 1 pm daily except Tuesday and Wednesday. The one-way fare to Skagway is $65.

There are cheaper ways to return but don't pass up the train. Experiencing the Chilkoot and returning on the WP&YR is probably the ultimate Alaskan hike, combining great scenery, a firsthand view of history and an incredible sense of adventure.

Another way to return is to hike 6mi south from Bare Loon Lake Campground to the Log Cabin, on Klondike Hwy. An Alaskon Express (☎ 983-2241) bus stops daily at the Log Cabin at 6:30 pm on its way south to Skagway, and a northbound bus reaches the warming hut at 9:30 am on its way to Whitehorse. The one-way fare from Log Cabin to Skagway is $22 and from Log Cabin to Whitehorse is $57. Frontier Excursions (☎ 983-2512) also stops at the Log Cabin, at 11 am and 4 pm, and charges only $20. The company also offers a drop-off in Dyea and pickup at the Log Cabin for $25 total.

THE HIKE
Stage 1: Dyea to Canyon City
7.5mi, 3 to 4 hours
The Alaskan trailhead for the Chilkoot Trail begins at the old Dyea townsite, on the banks of the Taiya River. Dyea grew from a trading post to the largest town in Alaska, at one point rivaling Skagway, Dawson and Seattle. From October 1897 to May 1898, the town held more than 10,000 miners, before a devastating avalanche and the completion of the White Pass Railroad convinced miners to head north on other routes.

Dyea is 9mi from Skagway, over a bridge across the Taiya River. Mile 0 of the Chilkoot Trail is just before the bridge. The route begins with an immediate climb of almost 300ft and then descends to the **Taiya River**, which flows through a flat lowland of willow and brush. Within a mile from the start, the trail merges into an old logging road that provides 3mi of easy hiking.

The old road passes an abandoned sawmill at Mile 3 and then ends at **Finnegan's Point**, the site of the first trailside campground, 4.8mi from Dyea. The point is named after Pat Finnegan, who, with his two sons, maintained a toll bridge over a creek here until he was overrun by stampeders in too much of a hurry to stop and pay the fee. The campground has vault toilets and a nice view of Irene Glacier across the river, but no warming shelter.

The trail leaves the old road and dips to the river, which it follows for a quarter mile. The trail leaves the water to climb over several hills, returns to the Taiya River briefly and then makes one final climb before descending into **Canyon City**, almost 3mi from Finnegan's Point, or 7.5mi from the start.

The Canyon City Campground includes a warming shelter with a woodstove and some interesting literature about the Klondike gold rush. This site, near the mouth of the Taiya River Canyon, was a natural camping spot for Indians long before the stampeders arrived. In 1898, most miners cached their supplies at old Canyon City, which quickly became a permanent settlement of log structures. It became a prosperous settlement after two freight companies built a tramway to transfer gear across the river.

There's not much left of the old city, but you can still visit the townsite by heading a half mile north of the campground and then following a posted side trail across a footbridge. It's an easy 2mi roundtrip from the campground, and some of the ruins, including a boiler from the tramway companies, are interesting.

Stage 2: Canyon City to Sheep Camp
4.3mi, 3 to 4 hours

From the campground the trail heads north, passes the spur to old Canyon City and then begins to ascend steeply as it works its way around the canyon. The climb lasts for more than a half mile and is a knee-bender until the trail reaches the altitude needed to skirt the eastern rim of the can-yon. The hiking is hard, but the views of the glaciers and mountains above the canyon, most notably **Mt Hoffman**, and the rushing water below it are worth it. Within a mile from the campground, you begin descending, passing the first of the occasional telegraph poles (they date back to 1898) on the way to Chilkoot Pass.

You continue to descend until you reach **Pleasant Camp** at Mile 10.4, along the wooded banks of the Taiya River. There is no warming shelter here. The trail stays in the wooded valley for the remaining 2.5mi to Sheep Camp. Within a mile of Pleasant Camp, you cross a suspension bridge and then, just before entering the campground, pass a ranger cabin where park personnel are stationed during the summer.

Sheep Camp, at Mile 11.8, was an important spot for the miners, who cached their year's worth of supplies here during the brutal climb over the Chilkoot Pass. Often, fierce winter storms halted or slowed down traffic across the pass from February to April, making Sheep Camp something of a bottleneck. Sheep Camp's population briefly topped 8000, and it supported a variety of businesses, including general stores, hotels, restaurants and, of course, saloons (three of them to be exact).

Stage 3: Sheep Camp to Deep Lake
11.2mi, 7 to 10 hours

This stage will take all day, so get an early start. You'll climb more than 2500ft before reaching the saddle. The Chilkoot Pass is 4.7mi north of Sheep Camp, and for the most part, the trail makes a gradual but continuous ascent toward it. In 2mi, you'll leave the tree line and quickly pass **Stone House**, a huge, square boulder whose overhanging shelf provides some shelter in an emergency. From this point on, the hiking gets more difficult as you boulder hop toward the pass. Keep an eye out for cairns and other trail markers.

From Stone House, the trail makes a steady half-mile ascent, referred to by the miners as the **Long Hill**. The trail arrives at an old tramway powerhouse 3.7mi from

Sheep Camp. It's another half mile to the next prominent set of ruins along the trail, known as the **Scales**, which are almost at the head of the valley. The Scales, the second of two tramway operations built here, are so called because hired packers reweighed their goods here and charged more before they would head up the pass. In the winter, this was often described as one of the most wretched spots on the trail.

You're now poised to make the final half-mile ascent over the pass. The climb is a steep one – a 45-degree scramble over boulders, lose rock and scree from the Scales at 2600ft to the summit of the pass at 3525ft. Make sure you choose the right route. When facing the pass from the bottom, the Chilkoot route is the left-hand pass, which is posted by metal poles and marked by an old tramway cable. Take extra caution when the weather is bad. The rocks can be slippery, visibility poor due to fog or snow, and the high winds at the top almost unbearable.

The rocky slope you climb was known as the **Golden Stairs** to the miners, who took up to six hours in bad weather to reach the pass. Once at the top, you cross the international border between the USA and Canada. During the gold rush, the royal mounted police established a customs station here to ensure that each miner entered the country with enough supplies to last a year.

From the top of the **Chilkoot Pass**, you begin a rapid descent and cross a perpetual snowfield. Most likely boot prints will lead the way across the snowfield, but keep well to the right. You come to **Stone Crib** 300ft below the pass summit. This was an anchor for the aerial tramway and is now the site of two emergency shelters for those caught on the pass in bad weather.

The route, marked by cairns and poles, continues along the east side of **Crater Lake** through the open country and crosses a handful of streams. Near the northern end of the lake, the trail should be quite visible, as it follows sections of an old wagon road to Lindeman City. From here, the trail continues its gradual descent through the alpine tundra, passing a tarn known as **Morrow Lake** and a small waterfall near

Mile 20.5 as you approach Long Lake. Nearby is **Happy Camp**, a small, sparsely wooded campground 4mi north of the pass summit. Most hikers, however, prefer to push on and stay at Deep Lake.

Past Happy Camp, the trail enters a small canyon, turns right and then climbs 350ft to skirt Long Lake from above, avoiding its rugged east shore. Once beyond the lake, the trail descends, crosses a bridge over a river to the west side of Deep Lake and then arrives at **Deep Lake Campground** at Mile 23. Although you've returned to the tree line here, the forest is still sparse, and the views are excellent from this campground. There is no warming shelter here, but for those who need to dry off, Lindeman City has two shelters and is an easy 3mi hike down the trail.

Stage 4A: Deep Lake to Bennett
10mi, 6 to 8 hours

As the trail leaves the campground, it follows the west side of Deep Lake and continues north. You round the northern end of the lake and then gradually descend the 700ft to Lindeman City by skirting the top of a canyon along the west side of Moose Creek. This is a pleasant stretch, with an occasional view of the surrounding mountains through the fir and lodgepole pine forest. Just before arriving at Lindeman Lake, you pass an old cemetery on top of a hill, where 11 stampeders are buried. The view of the lake and the surrounding peaks is excellent from the hill.

At Mile 26, 3mi from Deep Lake, you reach **Lindeman City**, at the south end of its namesake lake. In the spring of 1898, this was a tent city of 10,000 miners who stopped to build boats for the 600mi journey to Dawson and the Klondike goldfields. Today, Lindeman City is a campground with two warming cabins and a Canadian ranger station.

From the cabins, the trail skirts beneath the hilltop cemetery and then crosses a footbridge over Moose Creek to the remaining 7mi to Bennett. You begin with a gradual climb and then level off for a 2mi forested walk until you break out at a campground at **Dan Johnson Lake**. In another half mile, you reach **Bare Loon Lake**, another camping area at Mile 29 of the trail. Both areas have vault toilets, and often, during July and August, overheated hikers can be seen swimming in Bare Loon Lake.

Here, the trail forks; the left-hand fork heads to Bennett and follows the lake fairly closely, for good views of the water in the remaining 4mi. **Bennett**, with its church on the hill and the old White Pass & Yukon depot, is a picturesque place to camp for a night if you're not in a hurry. At one time, the town boasted a population of 20,000, as stampeders from both the Chilkoot Trail and the route over White Pass gathered here. In May of 1898, more than 7000 boats headed down the lake when the ice broke. The following year St Andrews Church was completed.

In Bennett, you can secure rail transportation along the White Pass & Yukon Route to Fraser on the Klondike Hwy or all the way back to Skagway.

Stage 4B: Bare Loon Lake to Log Cabin
6mi, 3 hours

Just beyond the campground at Bare Loon Lake there is a junction in the trail. The right-hand fork leads to the White Pass & Yukon Route railroad, a 20- to 30-minute hike. Once at the track you can head south. After a gradual 5mi climb, you will reach the Log Cabin, on the Klondike Hwy, to pick up a bus in either direction or the train back to Skagway.

Upper Dewey Lake Trail

Duration 1 or 2 days
Distance 6mi roundtrip
Difficulty Level Easy to hard
Start/Finish Skagway
Cabins & Shelters Yes
Permits Required No
Public Transportation Yes
Summary This series of trails allows you to enjoy lakes, waterfalls and even a night in an alpine area, while escaping the mobs of tourists in Skagway.

Just to the east of Skagway is the Upper Dewey Lake trail system. This series of trails leads to a handful of beautiful alpine and subalpine lakes, waterfalls and historic sites. This popular hiking area has picnic areas, camping spots, even a free-use shelter, enabling you to quickly escape bustling, touristy Skagway for a night in the mountains.

The trail to Lower Dewey Lake is a half-hour stroll, a good way to warm up the legs before hitting the Chilkoot Trail. From here you can continue on to Sturgill's Landing, a 3.5mi hike from town. At Sturgill's Landing, there are campsites and a picnic area. The other overnight possibility is the 3mi climb to Upper Dewey Lake, where there is a free-use shelter. From here, you can hike the alpine area to Devil's Punchbowl before returning along the same route. This is a 9mi roundtrip hike from Skagway.

The hike to Lower Dewey Lake and Sturgill's Landing is rated easy. The climb to the alpine regions of Upper Dewey Lake is challenging, due to a very steep climb.

PLANNING
When to Hike
Being an alpine hike, Upper Dewey Lake is best hiked from mid-June to mid-September. Lower Dewey Lake and Sturgill's Landing can be hiked earlier or later in the season.

Maps
The USGS 1:63,360 quad *Skagway B-1* covers all the trails. The trails are also included on the Trails Illustrated *Chilkoot Trail* map.

Cabins & Shelters
There is a free-use USFS shelter on Upper Dewey Lake. It is in rough but weatherproof condition and does not require advance reservations.

GETTING TO/FROM THE HIKE
The trails are an easy walk from the heart of Skagway. From Broadway St follow 3rd Ave southeast to the railroad tracks. On the other side of the tracks is the posted trailhead.

THE HIKE
Stage 1: Skagway to Upper Dewey Lake

3mi, 3 hours

The trail heads uphill, immediately crosses a stream via a small footbridge and then continues to climb via a series of switchbacks. Within a half mile, you arrive at a junction. The well-beaten right-hand fork is the route along the west shore of Lower Dewey Lake, leading eventually to Sturgill's Landing (See Side Trip: Sturgill's Landing). The left-hand fork leads to Upper Dewey Lake Trail or Icy Lake and Upper Reid Falls.

If you follow the main trail to the left for a couple hundred yards, it crosses **Dewey Creek** and arrives at the posted junction to Upper Dewey Lake. Head right for the climb to the lake, a knee-bender in the first mile. It's easy to follow because it's basically a straight 2mi climb with few switchbacks. The ascent does ease briefly about halfway up, as the trail closely skirts Dewey Creek. Eventually you break out of the tree line in a muskeg opening and cross Dewey Creek again to reach the west side of **Upper Dewey Lake**. This beautiful subalpine lake is right at the tree line, at 3097ft, and surrounded by mountains and peaks. The view of Taiya Inlet is equally impressive.

The **free-use shelter** is an old cabin that is now used by those spending the night in the alpine region. It has bunks for two people, holds maybe four at the most and is a little too rundown for many backpackers. If you hauled up a tent, there are places to set up camp around the lake. Upper Dewey Lake is stocked with rainbow trout, but they can be tough to catch most of the summer.

Side Trip: Sturgill's Landing

3.5mi, 2 to 3 hours

If you head right at the first junction near Lower Dewey Lake, you'll soon come to the reservoir and pass two junctions, one after another. These trails are part of the 2mi loop around **Lower Dewey Lake**. The first fork heads south, where it merges into the trail along the west shore of Lower Dewey Lake, enabling you to continue along the lake to reach a picnic area. At the

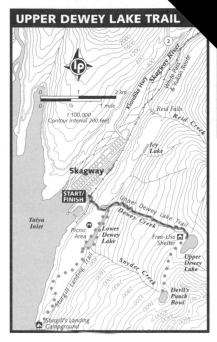

south end of Lower Dewey Lake is the junction with the trail to **Sturgill's Landing**.

Sturgill's Landing is a 2mi hike from Lower Dewey Lake, a 3.5mi walk from town, and features a beach campground, tables and vault toilets. This is the destination for those who want an overnight hike but don't want to endure the hard climb to Upper Dewey Lake. Also, at the south end, you can continue on a trail along the lake's east shore and eventually return to the junction at the reservoir.

Side Trip: Upper Dewey Lake to Devil's Punchbowl

2.5mi, 1 hour

If you are overnighting at the lake, a 2.5mi roundtrip to Devil's Punchbowl is a scenic side trip. Pick up the trail as it heads south from the shelter and quickly emerges from the stunted mountain hemlock to an alpine bench with stunning views of Skagway and the Inside Passage. Rock cairns lead you

the small lake 1.2mi from
e are few, if any, good
ng the rocky shoreline of
l, and at an elevation of
en has ice until August.

Stage 2: The Return
3mi, 2 hours

You can explore the area around the lake
and try the side trip to Devil's Punchbowl,
but the only way back to the trailhead is the
way you came. It should be quicker on the
way down, but take the steep parts slowly to
save your knees.

Laughton Glacier Trail

Duration 1 or 2 days
Distance 3 to 8mi roundtrip
Difficulty Level Easy to hard
Start/Finish White Pass & Yukon Route
Cabins & Shelters Yes
Permits Required No
Public Transportation Yes
Summary This unusual hike includes
glacier walking, dramatic alpine scenery
and flagging down a train on a historic
narrow-gauge railroad.

Glacier Station, at Mile 14 of the White Pass
& Yukon Route, is little more than a sweeping curve in the tracks and a trail sign. But
from there a trail leads into the trees to a
USFS cabin and then into the Laughton
Glacier amphitheater, a dramatic blend of
craggy Sawtooth Range peaks and the
fingers of ice that spill out of them. Combining the train ride and the 1.5mi hike to
stay at the remote cabin makes this an easy
but uniquely Alaskan adventure. Spending
a spare day to follow a moraine to the head
of the glacier and then returning along the
back of it will provide more than enough
wilderness challenge for most hikers.

On Tuesdays and Wednesdays, the railroad has three trips to White Pass Summit,
allowing you to spend most of the day at
Laughton Glacier without staying overnight.
But it is highly recommended that you
spend at least two nights in the area. Even if

you skip the 5mi ridge walk and simply
spend your time soaking up a view of the
glacier from a distance, this outing is still
worth the $52 ticket WP&YR charges to
drop off and pick up hikers.

PLANNING
When to Hike
The White Pass & Yukon Route railroad
operates from mid-May to mid-September.

Maps
The USGS 1:63,360 quad *Skagway C-1*
covers the area, as does Trails Illustrated's
Chilkoot Trail map.

Cabins & Shelters
The Laughton Glacier Cabin ($35) over-
looks the Skagway River from Warm Pass
and is only a mile from the glacier. It has
four bunks that can sleep up to six people.
Reserve the unit by calling the National
Recreation Reservation Service (☎ 877-444-
6777, 515-885-3639 for overseas) or through
its Web site (www.reserveusa.com).

GETTING TO/FROM THE HIKE
The WP&YR has trains passing Glacier
Station daily from mid-May to mid-September. The White Pass Summit Rail Excursion
departs at 8:30 am and 1 pm daily and also
at 4:30 pm Tuesday and Wednesday. The fee
is $52 per person if you only want to be
dropped off and picked up at Glacier
Station.

The WP&YR depot is at the corner of
Broadway St and 2nd Ave in Skagway. When
purchasing your ticket, make sure you find
out what time the train will be passing
Glacier Station on the way back to Skagway
and how to flag the train.

THE HIKE
Stage 1: Glacier Station to
USFS Cabin
1.5mi, 30 to 40 minutes

At **Glacier Station**, the posted trail departs
into the forest and quickly passes a large
display board and outhouse. The first mile
of the trail skirts the **Skagway River** and is
very level. You then swing out of view of the

water, climb a small rise and then resume the level walk until you emerge at **Laughton Glacier Cabin**.

The USFS cabin has four bunks. The two on the bottom are wide enough to handle two people each. The cabin only has an oil stove, which requires carrying in No 1 fuel oil, but the cabin is extremely snug. Operating the stove for only a couple of hours is likely keep the cabin warm for the rest of the night. Even using your backpacker's stove to cook dinner warms the cabin up.

You can't see the glacier from the cabin, but the cabin does have a view of the Skagway River below it. There are some excellent camping spots along it. More sites can be found just upstream, at the river's confluence with Laughton Creek.

Stage 2: USFS Cabin to the Head of Laughton Glacier
5mi, 6 to 7 hours
This is a day-long trip to the head of the valley. Even if you're not up for scrambling over boulders or walking on ice, a short hike into the valley will reveal the stunning scenery that lies just around the corner from the USFS cabin.

Pick up the trail near the outhouse, where the trail winds through the woods and swings south into the valley. Within 10 minutes, you climb a rock outcropping and are rewarded with your first view of a magnificent floe of ice. The 3000ft walls of the **Sawtooth Range** form the head of the valley, and four fingers of nearly vertical ice spill out of the range. **Laughton Glacier** extends from these hanging glaciers for more than a mile. It's the kind of overwhelming scene that you can marvel at for half a day.

From the outcropping, the trail descends into scrub and then emerges at **Laughton Creek**. From the creek, cairns mark the trail. The cairns will lead you down the outwash plain on the west side of the creek and, at times, into the willow and alder scrub along the base of the lateral moraine. In less than a mile from the cabin, the scrub thins out, and you should look for a route to the crest of the moraine.

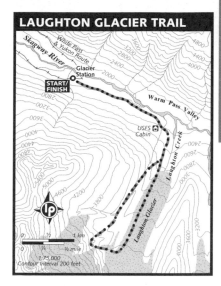

Be careful! Choose your route carefully, as the rocks are large and very loose. Do not climb below somebody; the boulders can easily be dislodged and tumble onto you. The moraine is so steep that you most likely will have to angle up it.

Once you are on top, the hiking is surprisingly easy as you head south toward the head of the valley. Eventually, a narrow path, most likely made by mountain goats, appears on the crest of the moraine. The views from the top are superb. You can gaze down on the entire glacier, study the vertical ice on the walls of the amphitheater or peer east into the upper reaches of **Warm Pass Valley**.

The easy ridge walk lasts for almost a mile. Then the moraine curves past the vertical ice farthest to the west, a hanging glacier that does not extend all the way to the floor of the valley. At this point, you need to leave the moraine and descend toward the ice, but you must be careful. The descent to the hanging glacier is a steep route along loose rocks and gravel. This is followed by another steep stretch along the glacier itself, to the stream that flows from the end of the glacier. Take your time and choose the best route. If you have any doubts about this section, simply backtrack along the moraine.

Once you are at the stream, the hiking becomes much easier, as you follow the stream a short way to the edge of a bluff directly above Laughton Glacier. Again, you are faced with another steep descent along loose gravel and rocks. Pick your route carefully here and then descend one at a time to avoid dislodging rocks on people below you.

At the bottom, it is easy to climb onto Laughton Glacier and along it toward a 20ft-high **rocky knob** protruding from the middle of it. The knob is very visible, and hiking on the glacier is easy; but you must be careful! Stay on the dark bands of rubble that provide good footings and well away from crevasses and other gaps in the ice. If there is snow on the glacier, avoid it completely.

Once you reach the knob, it can be climbed for another view of the amphitheater. Then continue north, following the dark ribbon of rubble to the left until you emerge at the west side of Laughton Creek, about a mile along the back of Laughton Glacier.

Once off the ice, you can follow rock cairns in the outwash plain to return to the cabin.

Other Hikes

KETCHIKAN REGION
Ward Lake Nature Walk
This is an easy trail around Ward Lake that begins near the shelters at the far end of the lake. The trail is 1.3mi of flat terrain marked with information signs. To reach the lake, follow N Tongass Hwy 7mi out of the city, to the pulp mill on Ward Cove. Turn right on Ward Lake Rd and follow it for a mile to reach the beginning of the trail (USGS quad *Ketchikan B-5*).

Perseverance Trail
This is a 2.2mi walk through mature coastal forest and muskeg from Ward Lake Rd to Perseverance Lake. The view of the lake with its mountainous backdrop is spectacular, and the hiking is easy because the trail is mainly boardwalks and steps. The trailhead is 1.5mi from the start of Ward Lake Rd (USGS quad *Ketchikan B-5*).

Talbot Lake Trail
This trail starts from Connell Lake Rd, a gravel road that heads east 3mi from the start of Ward Lake Rd. The 1.6mi trail is a mixture of boardwalk and gravel surface and leads north from the Connell Lake Dam to Talbot Lake, where it ends on private property. The more adventurous hiker, however, can cross a beaver dam at the south end of the lake and hike eastward onto the north ridge of Brown Mountain, to eventually reach its 2978ft summit. This is steep country with no established trail (USGS quad *Ketchikan B-5*).

PETERSBURG REGION
Petersburg Mountain Trail
On Kupreanof Island, this trail ascends 2.5mi from Wrangell Narrows behind Sasby Island to the top of Petersburg Mountain. There are outstanding views from here (the best in the area) of Petersburg, the Coast

Setting out on Laughton Glacier Trail

JIM DUFRESNE

Mountains, glaciers and Wrangell Narrows. Plan on spending at least three hours to get to the top of the mountain and two hours for the return. To get across the channel, see the To/From the Hike section on the Petersburg Lake Trail. From the Kupreanof state dock, head right on the overgrown road that skirts the shoreline toward Sasby Island. Within 1.5mi, you reach a posted trailhead, and from here a trail begins ascending the mountain. It's a steep climb with few switchbacks for the first 1.5mi, until the trail levels off at a saddle. From here to the peak, the trail is less distinguishable but is marked by blue markers (USGS quad *Petersburg D-3*).

Raven's Roost Trail

This 4mi trail begins at the water tower on the southeast side of the airport, which accessible from Haugen Drive. A boardwalk crosses muskeg areas at the start of the trail. Much of the route is a climb – somewhat steep and requiring a little scrambling – to beautiful open alpine areas at 2013ft. A two-story USFS cabin ($35 per night) is above the tree line. Reserve the cabin by calling the National Recreation Reservation Service (☎ 877-444-6777, 515-885-3639 for overseas) or through its Web site (www.reserveusa .com). The area provides good summer hiking and spectacular views of Petersburg, Frederick Sound and Wrangell Narrows (USGS quad *Petersburg D-3*).

Three Lakes Trails

These four short trails, connecting three lakes and Ideal Cove, are off Three Lakes Rd, a forest service road that heads east off Mitkof Hwy at Mile 13.6 and returns at Mile 23.8. A 3mi loop, with boardwalks, begins at Mile 14.2 of Three Lakes Rd, leading to Sand, Crane and Hill Lakes, which are known for their good trout fishing.

Each lake has a skiff and a picnic platform. Tennis shoes are fine for the trail, but to explore around the lakes you need rubber boots. There is a free-use shelter on Sand Lake. From the Sand Lake Trail, there is a 1.5mi trail to Ideal Cove on Frederick Sound (USGS quad *Petersburg C-3*).

Blind River Rapids Boardwalk

Starting at Mile 14.5 of the Mitkof Hwy, this easy mile-long boardwalk winds through muskeg before arriving at the rapids, a popular fishing spot during the summer (USGS quad *Petersburg C-3*).

SITKA REGION

The trails in this region are all on the Trails Around Sitka map in this book.

Indian River Trail

This easy trail is a 5.5mi walk along a clear salmon stream to the Indian River Falls, an 80ft waterfall at the base of the Three Sisters Mountains. The hike takes you through a typical Southeast rain forest and offers the opportunity to view black bears, deer and bald eagles. The trailhead, a short walk from the center of town, is off Sawmill Creek Rd, just east of the Sitka National Cemetery. Pass the driveway leading to the Public Safety Academy parking lot and turn up the dirt road with a gate across it. This leads back to the city water plant, where the trail begins left of the pump house. Plan on four to five hours for a roundtrip to the falls. You can also overnight along the trail by camping where the Indian River forks, a 2mi hike from the trailhead, or at the falls, (USGS quad *Sitka A-4*).

Mt Verstovia Trail

This 2.5mi trail is a challenging climb of 2550ft to the 'shoulder,' a small summit that is the most common end of the trail, although it is possible to climb to 3349ft, the actual peak of Mt Verstovia. The view from the shoulder on clear days is spectacular, undoubtedly the best in the area.

The trailhead is 2mi east of Sitka, along Sawmill Creek Rd. Once you reach Rookies Grill on the left, look for the trailhead marked 'Mount Verstovia Trail.' The Russian charcoal pits (signposted) are reached within a quarter mile and shortly after that the trail begins a series of switchbacks. Plan on a four-hour roundtrip to the shoulder. From the shoulder, the true peak of Mt Verstovia lies to the north along a ridge that connects the two. Allow an extra hour each way to hike to the peak (USGS quad *Sitka A-4*).

Heart Lake Trail

On Sawmill Creek Rd 4mi southeast of Sitka, this mile-long trail winds through hemlock-spruce forest to Thimbleberry Lake and Heart Lake. The trail begins just after you cross Thimbleberry Creek Bridge, where there is a pullout for parking. Conditions on the trail are often slippery and muddy and bears frequent the area (USGS quad *Sitka A-4*).

Beaver Lake Hike

This short trail starts from Sawmill Creek Campground, which is reached from Sawmill Creek Rd, 5.5mi east of Sitka. From Sawmill Creek Rd, you turn left onto Blue Lake Rd for the campground; the trailhead is on the south side of the campground.

Although steep at the beginning, the 0.8mi trail levels out and ends up as a scenic walk through open forest and along muskeg and marsh areas to Beaver Lake, which is surrounded by mountains. Plan on an hour's hike for the roundtrip (USGS quad *Sitka A-4*).

JUNEAU REGION

The trails in this region are all on the Trails Around Juneau map in this book.

Mt Roberts Trail

This is the one of two hikes accessible on foot from downtown. The trail is a 2.7mi ascent to the mountain above the city. The trail begins at a marked wooden staircase at the northeastern end of 6th St and consists of a series of switchbacks with good resting spots. The trail breaks out of the trees at Gastineau Peak, at a wooden cross and good views of Juneau, Douglas and the entire Gastineau Channel. The trail to Mt Roberts summit is a steep climb through the alpine brush to the north of the city. Plan about three hours to hike up and half that time coming back down. The other way to return is on the Mt Roberts Tram. A ride down on the tram to its South Franklin St station is only $5. Purchase $5 worth of

food or drink at the visitor center at the top, and the ride down is free (USGS quad *Juneau B-2*).

Treadwell Ditch Trail

This trail on Douglas Island can be picked up either a mile up the Dan Moller Trail or just above D St in Douglas. The trail stretches 12mi north, from Douglas to Eaglecrest Ski Area, although most people only hike to the Dan Moller Trail and then return to the road, a 5mi trip. The path is rated easy and winds through scenic muskeg meadows and provides views of the Gastineau Channel (USGS quad *Juneau B-2*).

Mt Bradley Trail

Also known as Mt Jumbo Trail, this 2.6mi trail begins in Douglas at a vacant lot behind the 300 block of 5th St and is a much harder climb than the hikes up Mt Roberts or Mt Juneau. Rubber boots and sturdy hiking boots are needed, as the trail can be muddy in the lower sections before you reach the beautiful alpine areas above the tree line. The climb to the 3337ft peak should only be attempted by experienced hikers, as there are dangerous drop-offs near the top. Plan on four hours to the top, even if the weather is good (USGS quads *Juneau A-2* and *B-2*).

Cropley Lake Trail

Also on Douglas Island is the 1.5-mile route to Cropley Lake. The trail was built primarily for cross-country skiing, but in the summer it can be hiked to the alpine lake, which provides good scenery and camping. The trailhead is up Fish Creek Rd, a short way past the Eaglecrest Ski Lodge in a creek gully to the right (USGS quad *Juneau B-2*).

Sheep Creek Trail

Southeast of Juneau along Thane Rd is the very scenic Sheep Creek Trail, a 3mi walk into the valley south of Mt Roberts where there are many historical mining relics. The trailhead is 4mi from Juneau, at a staircase on the gravel spur to a power plant substation. The trail is relatively flat in the valley. From there, you scramble up forested hillsides to the alpine zone. Many hikers follow the power line once they are above the tree line to reach the ridge to Sheep Mountain. From here, it is possible to continue from Sheep Mountain over Mt Roberts and return to Juneau along the Mt Roberts Trail. This is a very long 10- to 12-hour day hike (USGS quad *Juneau B-1*).

Point Bishop Trail

At the end of Thane Rd, 7.5mi southeast of Juneau, is this 8mi trail to Point Bishop, a scenic spot that overlooks the junction between Stephens Passage and Taku Inlet. The trail is flat but can be wet in many spots, making waterproof boots the preferred footwear. The hike makes an ideal overnight trip, as there is good camping at Point Bishop (USGS quads *Juneau A-1* and *B-1*).

Salmon Creek Trail

Just off the northbound lane of Egan Drive, there is access to this 3.5mi trail to Salmon Creek Dam. The trail is reached by heading north 2.5mi on the divided highway and turning right into the Salmon Creek Powerhouse grounds, just past the long retaining wall along Egan Drive. The trail is posted. Hikers used to follow the old tramway and flume up to the reservoir, but for safety reasons, you now must walk along an access road for the first 2mi. Across Salmon Creek, a trail departs into the woods and leads to the foot of the dam. Steep stairways take you up to the dam catwalk and a view of the surrounding mountains (USGS quad *Juneau B-2*).

East Glacier Trail

This trail, one of several near the Mendenhall Glacier, is a 3mi roundtrip that provides good views of the glacier from a scenic lookout at the halfway point. The trail begins off the half-mile nature walk near the Mendenhall Glacier Visitor Center and ends at a junction with the Nugget Creek Trail. Halfway along the trail you pass AJ Waterfalls. Like all the trails at the end of the Mendenhall Valley, the trailhead is rea-sonably accessible on a city bus (USGS quad *Juneau B-2*).

Nugget Creek Trail

Just beyond the East Glacier Trail's scenic lookout is the start of the 2.5mi Nugget Creek Trail to the Vista Creek Shelter, a free-use shelter that doesn't require reservations. The total roundtrip to the shelter from the Mendenhall Glacier Visitor Center is 8mi. Hikers who plan to spend the night at the shelter can continue along the creek toward Nugget Glacier, though the route is brushy and hard to follow at times (USGS quad *Juneau B-2*).

Spaulding Trail

This trail's primary use is cross-country skiing, but it can be hiked in the summer if you're prepared for some muddy sections. The trailhead is at Glacier Hwy, opposite the Auke Bay Post Office, 12.3mi northwest of Juneau. The 3mi trail provides access to the Auke Nu Trail, which leads to the John Muir USFS Cabin (reservations, $35 per night). The Auke Nu Trail is a well planked spur off the Spaulding Trail, about a mile from the trailhead, that leads west to the cabin, a 3mi hike from Glacier Hwy in Auke Bay. The Spaulding Trail continues another 1.5mi from the junction and ends in Spaulding Meadows, an alpine area that is a favorite with cross-country skiers in the winter (USGS quads *Juneau B-2* and *B-3*).

Peterson Lake Trail

This 4mi trail provides access to good fishing in Peterson Creek and Peterson Lake. The trailhead has been moved to avoid private property and is now 20ft before the Mile 24 marker on Glacier Hwy, north of the Shrine of St Terese. Although part of the trail is now planked, wear rubber boots, as it can still be very muddy during the summer. Most of the route is through heavy hemlock forest, but occasionally you hike through open muskeg areas or pass anglers' spurs to fishing holes in the river. A USFS cabin (reservations, $35) is on the southwest corner of Peterson Lake (USGS quad *Juneau B-3*).

Herbert Glacier Trail

This level trail extends 4.6mi along Herbert River to Herbert Glacier. The trail is easy, though wet in some places, and the round-trip takes four to five hours. The trail begins just past the bridge over Herbert River, at Mile 28 of Glacier Hwy in a small parking lot to the left, and skirts the base of Goat Mountain. The trail ends just before the glacier's terminal moraine. By scrambling onto rock piles to the left of the glacier, you can reach an excellent vantage point to view the ice and a spectacular waterfall. Plan on at least five hours for a roundtrip hike to the glacier. This trail is in the same area as Windfall Lake, Amalga (Eagle Glacier) and Yankee Basin Trails. You can spend two or three days out here hopping from one trail to the next (USGS quad *Juneau C-3*).

Point Bridget State Park

Juneau's first state park (2850 acres) was created in 1988. Reached at Mile 39 of Glacier Hwy, only 2mi short of its end at Echo Cove, the park features more than 10mi of trails. These include a stroll along a beach overlooking Lynn Canal, where occasionally you'll spot sea lions or humpback whales. By combining the Point Bridget Trail with the less-developed Cedar Lake and Trappers Trails, you can form a 9mi loop that passes the best scenery of the park, including Point Bridget, Cedar Lake and Camping Cove. This is one of the few trails in the Juneau area where the state park map is adequate for hikers.

The park also features two Division of Parks & Outdoor Recreation cabins. Near Point Bridget Trail is the eight-bunk Blue Mussel Cabin, and on Echoing Creek is Cowee Meadows Cabin. Cowee Meadows is a 2.1mi hike in; Blue Mussel is 3.4mi, and both cabins ($35 per night) are reserved through the Division of Parks & Outdoor Recreation in Juneau (☎ 465-4563). You can also backcountry camp throughout the park, and the beaches overlooking Berners Bay make a particularly pleasant place to set up a tent for a night or two (USGS quad *Juneau C-3*).

HAINES REGION
Mt Ripinsky Trail

Maintained by the city of Haines, this trail system includes a 4.5mi hike to the 3563ft summit of Mt Ripinsky. From there you can continue along a ridge to climb a second peak and emerge at the Haines Hwy. The ridge walk is a challenging 10mi hike that can be turned into an overnighter.

The roundtrip to Mt Ripinsky is a 9mi hike, taking six to eight hours, that rewards you with sweeping views from Juneau to Skagway. Get to the trailhead by following 2nd Ave north to Lutak Rd (the road to the ferry terminal), past the fire station. Leave Lutak Rd when it curves right and head up the hill on Young St. Turn right along an old buried pipeline and follow it for a mile to the start of the trail, just as the pipeline heads downhill to the tank farm.

The trail crosses a pair of streams, passes by an old reservoir and then ascends steadily through spruce and hemlock, reaching open muskeg at 1300ft. After a second climb, you come to Johnson's Creek at 2500ft, where you can fill up on drinking water and impressive views of the Southeast's snowcapped mountains all the way to Admiralty Island. From here, the route goes from dwarfed hemlock to open slope, where there is snow until late summer, and then climbs over Mt Ripinsky's first peak. North Summit is another third of a mile along the ridge.

The longer ridge route is a strenuous 10-hour journey that includes Peak 3920 and a descent from Seven-Mile Saddle to the Haines Hwy. You can make it an overnight trip by camping in the alpine area between Mt Ripinsky's two peaks. The next day, you can descend North Summit and hike west along the ridge to Peak 3920. From here you can descend to Seven-Mile Saddle and then to the Haines Hwy, putting you 7mi northwest of town. This hike is steep in places, and the trail is easy to lose at times, but is the only high elevation hike near Haines. On a clear day it offers some of the best panoramas of any hike in the Southeast (USGS quads *Skagway A-2* and *B-2*).

Seduction Point Trail

This trail begins at Chilkat State Park Campground and is a 6.5mi, one-way hike to the point that separates Chilkoot and Chilkat Inlets. The trail swings between inland forest and beaches and provides excellent views of Davidson Glacier.

It can also be turned into an overnight hike by setting up camp at the cove east of Seduction Point. Carry in water and check the tides before departing, as the final stretch along the beach after David's Cove should be walked at low or midtide. The entire roundtrip takes most hikers nine to 10 hours (USGS quads *Skagway A-1* and *A-2*).

SKAGWAY REGION
AB Mountain Trail

Also known as the Skyline Trail, this route ascends 5.5mi to the 5100ft summit of AB Mountain, named for the 'AB' that appears on its south side when the snow melts every spring. The trailhead is on Dyea Rd, about a mile from Skagway via the Skagway River footbridge off the northwest end of 1st Ave. The trail is very steep and requires a full day to complete (USGS quad *Skagway B-1*).

Denver Glacier Trail

At Mile 6 of the White Pass & Yukon Route, the USFS has renovated a WP&YR caboose into a rental cabin (reservations, $35 per night). From the caboose, an old trail heads up the East fork of the Skagway River for 2mi then swings south and continues another 1.5mi up the glacial outwash to Denver Glacier. Most of the trail is now overgrown with brush and the second half is particularly tough going. It involves more bushwhacking than hiking (USGS quad *Skagway B-1*).

Anchorage Region

From downtown Anchorage, the sight that commands the most attention is the Chugach Mountains looming over the state's tallest buildings. Almost half the state's population looks up at these mountains, one of the most rugged ranges in the country. Hikers can be sipping a latte in a coffee shop downtown and, within 20 minutes, be at a trailhead to an alpine peak. Is this paradise or just another example of Alaska's extremes?

Like Juneau in the Southeast, the Anchorage area offers a fine network of trails, making it possible to hike all day and then return to the city at night. Unlike Juneau, Anchorage has long multiday hikes in the valleys and passes of Chugach State Park. Chugach is one of the most heavily used parks in Alaska, offering a wide variety of developed trails suitable for all levels of hiking. You can join others in climbing Flattop Mountain (the first Alaskan peak for many) or spend a week traversing trail-less areas and exploring one valley and ridgeline after another. Even though this wild area is close to the city, it should not be underestimated; more than one ill-prepared hiker has perished in Chugach State Park and in nearby Chugach National Forest.

NATURAL HISTORY

Chugach State Park is carved from the western climax of the Chugach Range, which stretches 200mi from Anchorage to Canada. At 774 sq mi, Chugach has enough space to contain both New York City and Los Angeles and, by itself, is larger than entire park systems in 47 other states.

Apart from its great size, Chugach also contains an astonishing range of habitats and ecosystems. The park features nine distinct environments, including hemlock-spruce forests, muskeg, alpine tundra, riparian habitats, coastal wetlands and even marine waters, because the park's southern boundary extends halfway across Turnagain Arm. Six conifers – Sitka spruce, white spruce, black spruce, western hemlock, mountain hemlock and mountain juniper – are found here, and paper birch grows throughout the park.

More than 45 species of mammals live in Chugach, including nearly all the terrestrial mammals found in Alaska. Only caribou, musk oxen and polar bears are missing. Brown bears and moose are so numerous that they occasionally wander into Anchorage neighborhoods. Biologists estimate the mammal population includes more than 1000 moose, 40 brown bears and 80 black bears. There are also 2000 Dall sheep, one wolf pack and smaller populations of lynx, beavers, river otters, fox and mountain goats.

Alaska has wilderness areas that are larger and more biologically pristine than Chugach, but no other wildlife-rich habitat on Earth is so close to a major city. It is this

Highlights

- Viewing Mt McKinley from the peak of Flattop Mountain
- Encountering Dall sheep on the Williwaw Lakes Loop
- Spending a night camped in an alpine setting at Rabbit Lake, at the end of McHugh Lake Trail
- Exploring gold mine artifacts along the Historic Iditarod Trail
- Viewing Eklutna Glacier at the end of Eklutna Lakeside Trail

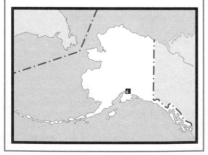

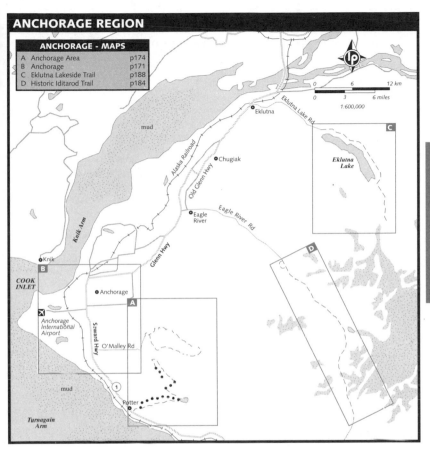

ANCHORAGE REGION

ANCHORAGE - MAPS

ANCHORAGE

amazing accessibility – to 16 trailheads and 110 trails that cover almost 500mi – that makes Chugach so unique and such a favorite among hikers.

CLIMATE

Anchorage has the advantage of being north of the Kenai Mountains, which shield the city from the excess moisture experienced by Southcentral Alaska. The Anchorage Bowl – the city and its surrounding area – receives only 14 inches of rain annually. It also avoids the extreme temperatures of the Interior, due to the moderating effect

of Cook Inlet. The average temperature in January is 13°F, and at the height of summer it's only 58°F.

Spring in Anchorage begins in mid-April, when the longer daylight hours bring out buds on the trees and wildflowers in the mountains. At this time of year, most hikers begin on the trails along the Turnagain Arm. Due to their southern exposure, trails like Indian Valley, Turnagain Arm and Bird Ridge are the first to be free of snow and painted by the colorful blossoms of wildflowers. Throughout most of June and July, you can count on 19 hours of sunlight and

ANCHORAGE

Brown Bear or Black Bear?

In the backcountry, it's easy to get brown and black bears confused from a distance, especially if both species are found in the region you're hiking through. The first thing you should look at to determine whether the animal is a brown bear or a black bear is its profile. A brown bear has a distinct hump on its back that is formed by the muscles in its forelegs. Black bears, on the other hand, have straight shoulders. If you have high-powered binoculars, study the head. The head of a brown bear is massive in relation to its body and its facial profile is concave, or 'dished.' The black bear has a much straighter facial profile, a tapered nose and longer nostrils.

If you come across the tracks of a bear, measure them for size. Brown-bear prints are large, usually ranging from 5 to 10 inches wide; black-bear prints range from 3.5 to 7 inches. The claws on the front feet of a brown bear are long and appear farther away from the toes (which are close together and less arched). Often, you won't see the claw marks on the print of a black bear, but when you do, they'll be shorter, more arched and closer to the toes.

Ironically, the least dependable trait of each species is the color of the fur. A black bear can vary tremendously in color, from blond to brown. Some brown bears can be almost black in color.

temperatures around 65°F. Unfortunately, the area has more than its fair share of overcast days, especially in early and late summer.

INFORMATION

One of the first places to head to after you arrive in Anchorage is the Alaska Public Lands Information Center (☎ 271-2737), in the Old Federal Building at 4th Ave and F St (diagonally opposite the Log Cabin Visitor Information Center). Along with interesting displays on Alaskan wilderness and wildlife, the center has information and handouts on

any national park, federal refuge or state park in Alaska and sells a limited selection of topographic maps and books. Visiting the center is like 'one-stop shopping' for information on outdoor activities and trips; 99% of your questions will be answered here. It is open 9 am to 5:30 pm daily in the summer.

In the city, information on Chugach and other state parks can also be obtained from the Alaska Department of Natural Resources Public Information Center (☎ 269-8400), 3601 C St. Hours are 11 am to 5 pm Monday through Friday. The Chugach State Park headquarters (☎ 345-5014), at Mile 115 of the Seward Hwy in the Potter Section House, has historical displays and a wealth of information on the park. Hours are 8 am to 4:30 pm Monday through Friday. If you plan to spend a great deal of time in the park, pick up a copy of *Ridgelines*, an information newspaper the park puts out.

For information on the Historic Iditarod Trail or other hikes in the Chugach National Forest, call or stop at the ranger office (☎ 783-3242), just off the Seward Hwy on Alyeska Hwy. It's open 7:30 am to 5 pm Monday through Friday.

ANCHORAGE

Anchorage is Alaska's largest metropolitan area, complete with fast-food restaurants, traffic jams and shopping malls, but it lies at the foot of the third largest state park in the USA. Chugach State Park is 774 sq mi of sharp peaks, blue glaciers, pristine alpine lakes and broad valleys.

Due to Anchorage's status as the hub of Alaska's road system and an international air junction, travelers often have to pass through the city at least once, if not several times, during an extended trip. If that's the case, you may as well stay for a few days to restock, rejuvenate, enjoy the city's nightlife and fine selection of restaurants, and take in a few of the local hikes.

There are several visitor centers for general travel information in Anchorage. The main one is the Log Cabin Visitor Center (☎ 274-3531), at 4th Ave and F St, open 7:30 am to 7 pm daily June to August, 8:30 am to 6 pm May and September, and

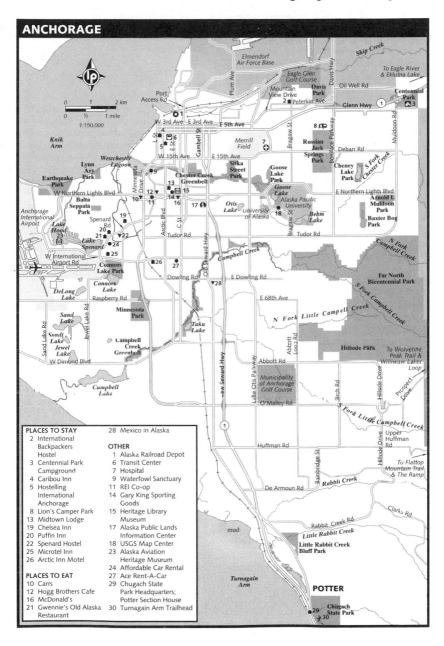

ANCHORAGE

Elmendorf Air Force Base

Eagle Glen Golf Course

Ship Creek

To Eagle River & Eklutna Lake

Mountain View Drive

Davis Park

Oil Well Rd

Peterkin Ave

Port Access Rd

Glenn Hwy

Centennial Park

Knik Arm

W 3rd Ave E 3rd Ave E 5th Ave

Merrill Field

Russian Jack Springs Park

Debarr Rd

Cheney Lake Park

W 15th Ave E 15th Ave

Sitka Street Park

Goose Lake Park

Arnold L Muldoon Park

Westchester Lagoon

Lynn Ary Park

Chester Creek Greenbelt

Goose Lake

E Northern Lights Blvd

Earthquake Park

W Northern Lights Blvd

Balta Seppala Park

Alaska Pacific University

Baxter Bog Park

Anchorage International Airport

Spenard Rd

Otis Lake

University of Alaska

Behm Lake

Lake Hood

Lake Spenard

Tudor Rd

Tudor Rd

W International Airport Rd

Connors Lake Park

Campbell Creek

N Fork Campbell Creek

DeLong Lake

Connors Lake

Dowling Rd E Dowling Rd

Far North Bicentennial Park

Raspberry Rd

E 68th Ave

S Fork Campbell Creek

Sand Lake Rd

Minnesota Park

N Fork Little Campbell Creek

Sundi Lake

Jewel Lake

Taku Lake

Hillside Park

To Wolverine Peak Trail & Williwaw Lakes Loop

W Dimond Blvd

Campbell Creek Greenbelt

Abbott Rd

Campbell Lake

Municipality of Anchorage Golf Course

S Fork Little Campbell Creek

O'Malley Rd

Upper Huffman Rd

Huffman Rd

To Flattop Mountain Trail & The Ramp

De Armoun Rd

Rabbit Creek

Clarks Rd

mud

Rabbit Creek Rd

Little Rabbit Creek

Little Rabbit Creek Bluff Park

Turnagain Arm

POTTER

Chugach State Park

PLACES TO STAY
2 International Backpackers Hostel
3 Centennial Park Campground
4 Caribou Inn
5 Hostelling International Anchorage
8 Lion's Camper Park
19 Chelsea Inn
20 Puffin Inn
22 Spenard Hostel
25 Microtel Inn
26 Arctic Inn Motel

PLACES TO EAT
10 Carrs
12 Hogg Brothers Cafe
16 McDonald's
21 Gwennie's Old Alaska Restaurant

28 Mexico in Alaska

OTHER
1 Alaska Railroad Depot
6 Transit Center
7 Hospital
9 Waterfowl Sanctuary
11 REI Co-op
14 Gary King Sporting Goods
15 Heritage Library Museum
17 Alaska Public Lands Information Center
18 USGS Map Center
23 Alaska Aviation Heritage Museum
24 Affordable Car Rental
27 Ace Rent-A-Car
29 Chugach State Park Headquarters; Potter Section House
30 Turnagain Arm Trailhead

0   1   2 km
0   ½   1 mile
1:150,000

9 am to 4 pm the rest of the year. There is another visitor center (☎ 266-2437) at the Anchorage International Airport, in the baggage claim level of the south (domestic) terminal. It is open 9 am to 4 pm. The Anchorage Convention and Visitors Bureau (☎ 276-4118, @ info@anchorage.net) also maintains a Web site (www.anchorage.net).

Supplies & Equipment

Whatever you need, from crampons to a spare tent stake, you'll find in Anchorage, probably somewhere along Northern Lights Blvd. For backpacking, kayaking or camping gear, there's an impressive REI (☎ 272-4565), 1200 W Northern Lights Blvd, in the Northern Lights Shopping Center, and Gary King Sporting Goods (☎ 279-7454), 202 E Northern Lights Blvd, carries hiking and backpacking equipment. Alaska Mountaineering & Hiking (☎ 272-1811), 2633 Spenard Rd near Northern Lights Blvd, is open daily in the summer and also has an excellent selection.

You can rent equipment such as tents, stoves and sleeping bags at REI (☎ 272-4565). Cheaper rentals are possible at the Campus Center Information Desk at University of Alaska Anchorage (☎ 786-1204) or Moseley Sports Center at Alaska Pacific University (☎ 564-8314), but they can sometimes be hard to deal with if you are not a student or faculty member.

Places to Stay & Eat

The Anchorage Parks and Recreation Department (☎ 343-4474) maintains two parks with overnight camping. *Centennial Park* (☎ 333-9711) has 89 sites, showers and rest rooms but is 4.6mi from the downtown area, on Glenn Hwy. In recent years, theft has also been a problem at the campground. The cost is $15 per night, and there is a limit of seven days. Take the Muldoon Rd exit south of the highway and turn east onto Boundary Ave. Bus No 75, 3 or 4 runs past the corner of Muldoon Rd and Boundary Ave. The city also manages *Lion's Camper Park* (☎ 333-9711), in Russian Jack Springs Park, a wooded area close to town that is ideal for

tent campers. The fee is $15 per night, and bus No 8 takes you within a quarter mile of the park on Boniface Parkway.

The *Hostelling International Anchorage* (☎ 276-3635, 700 H St, @ hipat@servcom .com) is downtown, one block south of the transit center. The cost is $16/19 members/ nonmembers, and there are a few private rooms available for $40. Along with sleeping facilities, the hostel has a common room, kitchen, showers and even double rooms. Laundry facilities are available, and you can store extra bags here for $1 per day. This hostel is busy during the summer, so many travelers reserve a bunk ahead of time by calling in advance and using either a Visa card or MasterCard to secure the reservation.

A smaller but more personal hostel is *Spenard Hostel* (☎ 248-5036, 2845 W 42nd Place, @ spnrdhstl@alaskalife.net), off Turnagain Parkway. You can reach the hostel by Bus No 7. The cost is $15 a night.

B&Bs have blossomed in Anchorage. There are now more than 400 Anchorage residents who have opened up their spare bedrooms to summer travelers. The going rate is a bit steeper in Anchorage than in the rest of the state, generally $85 to $110 per couple a night. Stop at the Log Cabin Visitors Center for an entire rack of B&B brochures, or you can call Alaska Private Lodging (☎ 258-1717, @ apl@alaska.net) to arrange such accommodations.

A surge in the late 1990s has given Anchorage has more than 70 hotels and motels and 6000 rooms for rent. The average rate for a midmarket room is hovering around $90 a night, and trying to find something for under $75 is very challenging. New hotels have popped up primarily around the Anchorage International Airport. *Microtel Inn* (☎ 245-5002, 5205 Northwood Drive) has a free airport shuttle and doubles that begin at $120. *Puffin Inn* (☎ 243-4044, 800-478-3346, 4400 Spenard Rd) has rooms for $99/119, an airport shuttle and complimentary muffins and coffee in the morning.

In the city center avoid the shabby Inlet Inn across from the transit center. A cleaner and safer choice downtown is **Caribou Inn** (☎ 272-0444, 800-272-5878, 501 L St) with 14 rooms that begin at $75/84 with shared bath but include a full breakfast and courtesy pickup from the airport or train station. **Midtown Lodge** (☎ 258-7778, 800-235-6546, 604 W 26th Ave), just off Spenard Rd, has spartan rooms with shared baths, but there is a group kitchen. Rates are only $55/65, which includes a light breakfast, soup and sandwiches later in the day and pickup at the airport.

For those on a strict budget, there's a choice of fast-food places, including **McDonald's**, at W 4th Ave and E St. The most affordable food, however, is at the **Carrs** Aurora Village store, at L St and Northern Lights Blvd, the largest of the Carrs chain. The salad bar is great at $3.50 a pound, and there are also a deli, an Orient Express for stir-fry, a bakery, an espresso shop and seating. **Hogg Brothers Cafe** (1049 W Northern Lights Blvd), at Spenard Rd, is a bizarre restaurant with 'piggy' décor, including a stuffed hog mounted on the wall. Breakfast is served all day and the selection is creative. You could order two eggs, home fries and toast for $4, but why, when more than 20 types of omelets are available?

Also serving breakfast all day is **Gwennie's Old Alaska Restaurant** (4333 Spenard Rd), west of Minnesota Drive. The portions are big, the prices reasonable and the artifacts are so numerous that the place mat doubles as a guide to what's on the walls. Order an omelet ($7 to $9) and then study the baleen sleds that Native Alaskans once used to haul freight, photos of the 1964 earthquake, pieces of the Trans-Alaska Pipeline or the 45,000-year-old bison head found in the Lucky Seven Mine.

The best Mexican dishes are found in South Anchorage at **Mexico in Alaska** (7305 Old Seward Hwy), just south of Dowling Rd. Dinners of traditional Mexican cuisine cost $10 to $13.

Getting There & Away

Air Anchorage International Airport, 6.5mi west of the city center, is the largest airport

Anchorage – A Hiker's Haven

In 1996, the American Hiking Society confirmed what Anchorage residents already suspected: Their city was a paradise for trail users. That year, the society named Alaska's largest city as runner-up in a nationwide list of 'Top Trail Towns.' The honor was credited to Anchorage's 300mi of trails, which include 122mi of paved bicycle trails, 20mi of mountain bike trail in Far North Bicentennial Park and the miles of hiking trails in Chugach State Park on the city's doorstep. The society said that not only did Anchorage have great scenery to go along with its numerous trails, but also plenty of wildlife, noting that the year before, 'a grizzly bear followed a family biking down a trail near Potter Valley.'

The top town was Jefferson County in Colorado, which boasts more than 600mi of trails.

in the state, handling 130 flights daily from more than a dozen major airlines. From Anchorage, you can catch a flight to anywhere in Alaska. Alaska Airlines (☎ 800-426-0333) provides the most intrastate routes to travelers, many of them through its contract carrier, ERA, which services Valdez, Homer, Cordova, Kenai, Iliamna and Kodiak.

The People Mover bus system has restored its service to the airport but operates the route only on weekdays. If you arrive between 7 am and 6:30 pm Monday through Friday, you can pick up Bus No 6 at the domestic terminal and reach downtown Anchorage for only $1. Otherwise call Borealis Shuttle (☎ 276-3600, 888-436-3600). It charges $10 for the ride downtown for one person, $13 for two people and $2 for every additional person.

Bus A variety of bus and van companies operate out of Anchorage and provide service to almost everywhere in the state. You can count on the biggies, like Alaskon

ANCHORAGE AREA

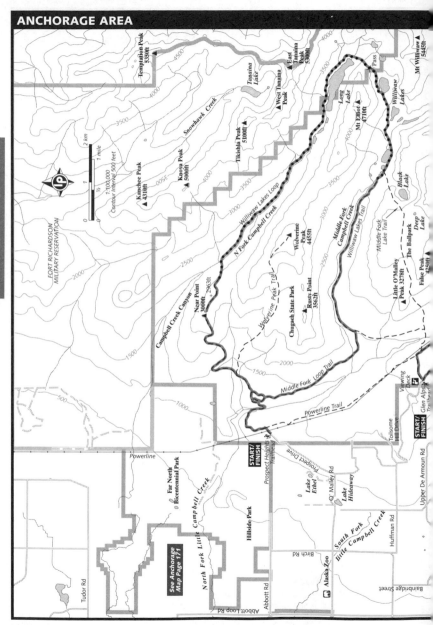

Temptation Peak 5350ft

East Tanaina Peak 5300ft

Mt Williwaw 5445ft

West Tanaina Peak

Tanaina Lake

Snowhawk Creek

Long Lake

Pass

Williwaw Lakes

Thisible Peak 5100ft

Mt Elliot 4710ft

Kamchee Peak 4310ft

Knoya Peak 5000ft

N Fork Campbell Creek

Willwaw Lakes Loop

Middle Fork Campbell Creek

Black Lake

Middle Fork Lake Trail

Deep Lake

Williwaw Lakes Trail

Wolverine Peak 4455ft

The Ballpark

FORT RICHARDSON MILITARY RESERVATION

Campbell Creek Canyon

Wolverine Peak Trail

Chugach State Park

Little O'Malley Peak 3278ft

Fake Peak 4250ft

Near Point 3050ft

Rusty Point 3662ft

2 km

1 mile

1:100,000
Contour interval 500 feet

1/2
1

Middle Fork Loop Trail

Viewing Deck

Glen Alps Trailhead

Powerline Trail

START/ FINISH

Tolsome Hill Drive

Powerline

Far North Bicentennial Park

Campbell Creek

North Fork Little Campbell Creek

Prospect Heights Trailhead

Prospect Drive

START/ FINISH

Lake Ethel

O'Malley Rd

Lake Hideaway

Upper De Armoun Rd

Hillside Park

See Anchorage Map Page 171

South Fork Little Campbell Creek

Huffman Rd

Tudor Rd

Abbott Loop Rd

North Fork Little Campbell Creek

Birch Rd

Abbott Rd

Alaska Zoo

Bainbridge Street

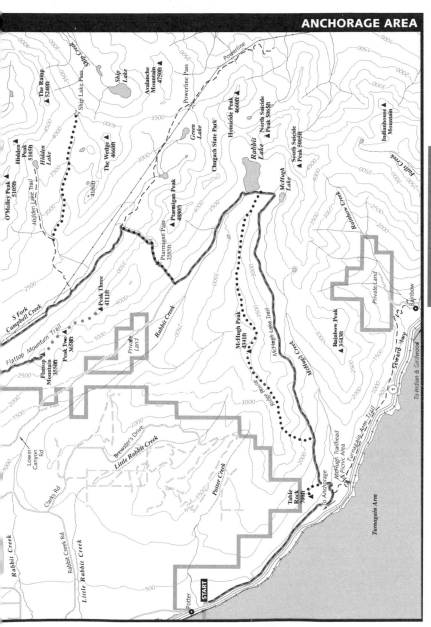

Express, but double-check the smaller companies by making a phone call.

For travelers heading toward Haines or Whitehorse, there are a couple possibilities. Alaskon Express (☎ 227-5581, 800-478-6388) departs from its office on 745 W 4th Ave, and from a handful of major hotels, at 7:30 am on Sunday, Tuesday and Friday for Palmer, Glennallen, Tok and Beaver Creek in the Yukon Territory, where the bus stops overnight. From Beaver Creek, you can make connections to Whitehorse, Haines or Skagway. The one-way fare to Haines is $195 and to Glennallen $61. Alaska Direct (☎ 277-6652, 800-770-6652) has a bus that departs Anchorage at 6 am Sunday, Wednesday and Friday and arrives in Whitehorse at midnight. One-way fare is $145.

Taking a van service to Denali National Park and Fairbanks is the cheapest way to travel the George Parks Hwy, other than hitchhiking. Alaska Park Connection (☎ 907-344-8775, 888-277-2757, @ info@alaskacoach .com) runs a daily shuttle service along the George Parks and Seward Hwys. (This company took over the popular Backpacker Shuttle runs in 2000, but eliminated some routes.) Call for pick-up locations. The one-way fare from Anchorage to Denali National Park is $59; to Talkeetna or Seward, it's $39; reservations are required. For more route and schedule information, visit their Web site at www.alaska-tour.com. Several other companies offer the same service, including Parks Highway Express (☎ 888-600-6001, @ info@alaskashuttle.com).

To get to the Kenai Peninsula, take Seward Bus Line (☎ 224-3608), which departs from 3339 Fairbanks St at 2:30 pm daily for Seward, reaching the town at 5:30 pm. The one-way fare is $30. Also running between Anchorage and Seward is Kachemak Bay Transit (☎ 299-0994, 877-235-9191) and the Alaska Park Connection shuttle (☎ 907-344-8775, 888-277-2757, @ info@ alaskacoach.com). Kachemak Bay Transit departs Anchorage at 8 am from a variety of locations, including the Spenard Hostel, and arrives at Homer between 2:30 and 4:30 pm. One-way fare is $45. Homer Stage Line (☎ 235-7009) also runs the same route,

leaving Anchorage at 3:30 pm and arriving at Homer at 8:30 pm, for the same fare.

Parks Highway Express (☎ 888-600-6001, @ info@alaskashuttle.com) began as van service to Denali National Park, but in 1999, expanded to offer service on the other two major highways, Glenn and Richardson. A bus leaves the Anchorage hostel at 7th Ave and H St at 9 am Wednesday, Friday and Sunday and arrives at Valdez at 4:50 pm. You can also use this service to reach Palmer, Glennallen or other points in between. One-way Anchorage to Valdez fare is $59. The company also has a bus pass ($145) for unlimited travel on any of the routes. It is good for the entire travel season, late May through early September. Alaskon Express also has a bus for Valdez, departing Anchorage at 8 am daily. The one-way fare is $70.

Train The Alaska Railroad (☎ 265-2494, 800-544-0552, @ akrr@Alaska.net) maintains its office in the depot at 421 W 1st Ave and provides services both north and south of Anchorage. The most popular run is the *Denali Express*, which departs Anchorage daily at 8:15 am for Denali National Park and Fairbanks. The one-way fare to Denali is $104 and to Fairbanks $154.

Getting Around

Bus Anchorage has an excellent public bus system in the People Mover. All buses begin at the People Mover's downtown terminal, in the transit center at the corner of 6th Ave and G St. Most buses pass by every half hour, and the schedule is posted at every stop. The fare is $1 a ride or $2.50 for an all-day, unlimited ticket. If the trip requires more than one bus, ask the driver for a transfer, which allows you to ride on the connecting bus for an additional 10¢.

A full service of 17 routes operates 6 am to 10 pm Monday to Friday, with reduced service 8 am to 8 pm Saturday and 9:30 am to 6:30 pm Sunday. People Mover also operates a free bus called DASH, an acronym for Downtown Anchorage Short Hop, that travels between 5th and 8th Aves in the downtown area. For information on any route, call the Rideline at ☎ 343-6543.

The People Mover bus was the cheapest way to get close to some the trails. Unfortunately, in the fall of 1999, the bus system dropped route Nos 90, 91 and 92, which took hikers to within walking distances of the Glen Alps and Prospect Heights parking areas of Chugach State Park. You now have to walk or hitch several miles from bus No 2, rent a car or take a taxi, which from downtown would cost around $17.

Car Rental cars are another way to reach area trails. The cheapest deal is available from Denali Car Rental (☎ 276-1230), 1209 Gambell St, which has subcompacts for $32 a day or $210 a week from June through August. Before or after that, the price is $25 a day. Affordable Car Rental (☎ 243-3370, 800-248-3765), 4707 Spenard Rd, advertises subcompacts for as low as $33 per day. Its compacts are $42 a day. Ace Rent-A-Car in Anchorage (☎ 562-1155, 888-685-1155), 512 W International Airport Rd, has subcompacts for $40 a day. Both Ace Rent-A-Car and Affordable will provide courtesy transportation from your motel or to the airport. Other discounted car rental places include Airport Car Rentals (☎ 277-7662), U-Save Auto Rental (☎ 272-8728, 800-254-8728) and Denali Car Rental (☎ 276-1230).

Flattop Mountain Trail

Duration 3 to 5 hours
Distance 3.4mi roundtrip
Difficulty Level Easy to medium
Start/Finish Glen Alps trailhead
Cabins & Shelters No
Permits Required Yes
Public Transportation No
Summary This is an excellent trail to warm up on after arriving in Alaska and before tackling a multiday hike elsewhere. Flattop Mountain is the most popular peak to climb in Anchorage, with good views of Cook Inlet and the Alaska Range.

Because of its easy access and great views on a clear day, this climb to the peak of Flattop Mountain is the most popular hike in the Anchorage area and probably the most popular in all of Alaska. The trail to the 3550ft peak is easy to follow and not too hard to climb, though there is some scrambling along steep sections near the top. From the summit, there are spectacular views of the surrounding country.

On a Saturday afternoon, the trail is busy with hikers, families and even joggers looking for a challenging run. Occasionally somebody will camp on the flat summit of the mountain, despite the lack of water, just to catch the sunset over the Alaska Range. During Anchorage's annual solstice celebration on June 21, as many as 150 hikers will hike the trail for the sunset, and many will spend the night on the mountain. Others just pack a flashlight and follow the trail back at dusk.

PLANNING
When to Hike
This trail is best hiked June through September. The trail should be avoided in winter and early spring, as the area is prone to avalanches.

What to Bring
Campfires are prohibited along most trails in Chugach State Park. Bring plenty of gorp, or a camp stove if you plan to cook in the park.

Maps
The USGS Earth Science Information Center (☎ 786-7011) sells topographical maps for the entire state. The center, open 8:30 am to 4:30 pm weekdays, is in Grace Hall at Alaska Pacific University, at the east end of Providence Drive. It can be reached on bus No 11 or 45. You can also purchase some maps at the Alaska Public Lands Information Center (see the Information section, earlier) or Maps, Maps, Maps (☎ 563-6277), an excellent store in the Bering Mall, 601 W 36th Ave, which sells USGS topos and a variety of other recreational maps.

The Flattop Mountain Trail is shown on the Anchorage Area map in this book. Most of Chugach State Park is covered on four

USGS 1:63,360 quads – *Anchorage A-6, A-7, A-8* and *B-6* – and Flattop Mountain is covered on *Anchorage A-8*. Only trails that were originally roads are shown on the topos, so pick up a park trail map. The best option is to purchase Alaska Road & Recreation Maps' *Anchorage & Vicinity* ($6). The map is 1:63,360 scale like the USGS topos, but it is updated with trails on it, including Flattop Mountain Trail.

Permits & Regulations
A vehicle entry permit ($5 per day) is required to leave a car at the Glen Alps trailhead parking area.

GETTING TO/FROM THE HIKE
The Flattop Mountain Trail begins at the Glen Alps entrance to Chugach State Park. From the corner of Hillside Rd and Upper Huffman Rd, head 0.7mi east along Upper Huffman Rd and then turn right on Toilsome Hill Drive for 2mi. This switchback road ascends steeply to the Glen Alps park entrance, a parking lot with an information area, vault toilets and a trailhead sign pointing the way to Flattop Mountain.

THE HIKE
Stage 1: Glen Alps Trailhead to Flattop Mountain
1.7mi, 1 to 2 hours
In 1995, the upper portions of Flattop Mountain Trail were extensively rebuilt. Volunteers widened the path and installed stairs and added tread surface material. Still, this stretch is steep and has loose rocks that can be hazardous. When hiking, always be aware of hikers above you and be ready for falling rocks they might kick loose.

From the large parking area, you begin at a well-posted stairway and then climb through a stand of stunted mountain hemlock before breaking out of the trees in the alpine region of the ridge. The trail skirts the side of a 2654ft high point known as **Blueberry Hill** and, in a half mile, reaches a posted junction in the saddle between this hill and Flattop Mountain.

The right-hand fork at the junction is an easy trail to Blueberry Hill that loops back to the parking lot. **Blueberry Loop** is a mile walk and an ideal alternative if you're not up to climbing the mountain. The trail to Flattop is the left-hand fork, which skirts the ridge leading to the peak, following a series of switchbacks in some places to gain elevation. From the side of the ridge, you can see across the valley to the surrounding summits of False and O'Malley Peaks.

The trail along the ridge is narrow and rocky, definitely not a casual stroll for most hikers, yet it's amazing how many children you'll pass here on the weekends. Eventually, the trail makes a sharp 90-degree turn to the right, and you climb steeply to a second saddle. Be aware of those climbing above you and the possibility of falling rocks.

The second saddle provides views into the **Rabbit Creek Valley** on the southwest side of Flattop and is another good spot to take a break. At one point, the state park system had plans for a trail from the southwest side of Flattop Mountain to Rabbit Creek Trail, which is presently closed because it crosses private land, but a budget crunch delayed those plans.

From the saddle, the 3550ft summit of Flattop Mountain is still one more climb away along a boulder-strewn trail. As its name indicates, this popular mountain has a table-top appearance. From its peak, you are rewarded with a spectacular panorama that includes all of Anchorage, Cook Inlet, the Kenai Peninsula and the interior of Chugach State Park. On a crystal-clear day, it's even possible to see Mt McKinley (to the northwest) and Mt Redoubt (to the southwest), the active volcano on the Alaska Peninsula.

Side Trip: Ridgeline
3mi, 2 hours
If you're not satisfied with the climb to Flattop Mountain, you can follow the ridgeline another 3mi to the high point of 4500ft. There is no maintained trail along this stretch, but the crest of the ridge is a natural route that's easy to follow if you're an experienced alpine hiker.

Stage 2: The Return

1.7mi, 1 hour

From the Flattop summit, retrace your steps to the trailhead parking area. It takes much less time than the climb up, but be careful not kick rocks and stones down the slopes, which could hit others below you.

Williwaw Lakes Loop

Duration 2 days
Distance 16mi roundtrip
Difficulty Level Medium
Start/Finish Prospect Heights trailhead
Cabins & Shelters No
Permits Required Yes
Public Transportation No
Summary This loop is an overnight hike to a series of scenic alpine lakes, with opportunities to encounter Dall sheep and climb Wolverine Peak.

A combination of trails and routes, the Williwaw Lakes Loop is the best overnight hike from Anchorage. Many hikers consider it the most scenic outing in the Hillside area of Chugach State Park, and the chances of seeing Dall sheep are excellent. The hike follows Middle Fork Loop Trail to a handful of alpine lakes at the base of Mt Williwaw, an ideal spot to camp for the night. From there, the trail continues as a route across a pass into the drainage of North Fork Campbell Creek and then, at the west end of the valley, climbs Near Point. From this 3000ft peak, you pick up a trail to return to the trailhead. Along the way, you might encounter some mountain bikers in the first 3mi of Middle Fork Trail.

You can also begin the loop from the Glen Alps trailhead, where you pick up the Flattop Mountain Trail. From this trailhead you descend to Powerline Trail, follow it briefly south and then continue east on Middle Fork Loop Trail to Williwaw Lakes Trail. It's a 2mi hike from the Glen Alps trailhead to Williwaw Lakes Trail.

There is less climbing if you begin and end at the Prospect Heights trailhead, due

to its higher elevation. It's also a shorter hike, but don't underestimate this outing. You still need to be well equipped for any type of weather conditions, especially wind. Mt Williwaw was named after a violent thunderstorm with strong winds, known as 'williwaws,' killed three hikers in 1961.

A strong hiker can do the entire loop in a day, but for most people this hike is an overnight adventure. With three days, you can spend a spare afternoon exploring the ridges above Williwaw Lakes.

PLANNING
When to Hike

Like Flattop Mountain, this trail is best hiked June through September.

What to Bring

See the Flattop Mountain Trail section, earlier.

Maps

The hike is covered on USGS 1:63,360 quads *Anchorage A-7* and *A-8,* but the topos do not show the trail system. A better map is Alaska Road & Recreation Maps' *Anchorage & Vicinity* ($6). In this book, the Williwaw Lakes Loop is covered on the Anchorage Area map.

Permits & Regulations

A vehicle entry permit ($5 per day) is required to leave a car in the Prospect Heights parking area.

GETTING TO/FROM THE HIKE

From Hillside Drive and O'Malley Rd, head east on Upper O'Malley Rd for a half mile to a T-junction. Then turn left (north) onto Prospect Drive. After 1.1mi, the road ends at the Prospect Heights entrance and parking area to the Chugach State Park. People Mover used to have a bus that came within walking distance of the trail but dropped the route, No 92, in the fall of 1999 due to budget cuts. Now your choices are to hitch, hire a taxi or rent a car (see the Getting Around section, earlier).

THE HIKE
Stage 1: Prospect Heights Trailhead to Third Williwaw Lake
6.4mi, 4 to 6 hours

From the trailhead, a wide gravel path heads due east and, within 50yd, comes to a junction with **Powerline Trail**. Head left on the old homestead road and follow it as it curves east. Less than a mile from the parking lot, it crosses a bridge over **South Fork Campbell Creek**. On the other side of the bridge is a gentle half-mile climb to a posted junction. Head right on **Middle Fork Loop Trail**.

Middle Fork Loop Trail begins as a narrow path and quickly climbs through stunted spruce to your first views of the day, a glimpse of the Anchorage basin to the west. For the next 2mi, the trail skirts the western flanks of Wolverine Peak, staying above South Fork Campbell Creek, and then descends to cross a bridge over **Middle Fork Campbell Creek**. On the other side of the creek, you climb to a posted junction 3.5mi from the trailhead. Middle Fork Loop Trail continues south and in 2mi reaches the Glen Alps trailhead and parking area. Head east at the junction, on **Williwaw Lakes Trail**.

Within a quarter mile, the trail swings close to Middle Fork Campbell Creek and then climbs a moraine on the south side of the valley. For the next 1.5mi, the trail is a classic hike and easy walk, following the fairly level moraine. The valley is spread out below you, and the amphitheater where the lakes are located is straight ahead. The entire scene is crowned by the pyramid-like peak of Mt Williwaw (5445ft).

Eventually the trail descends to the floor of the valley, and 6mi from the trailhead, you arrive at the first **Williwaw Lake**, a shallow pool at 2600ft. The next two lakes quickly follow. The third one is substantially larger than the other two. There is good camping on the north side of this lake or just east of it on a small bench above it. The bench makes a particularly scenic site, with the small lakes at your feet and peaks all around you. Here you can sit and admire the perfect U-shaped valley that the glaciers scooped out. If you're lucky, a band of Dall sheep will appear in the evening.

Stage 2: Third Williwaw Lake to Prospect Heights Trailhead via North Fork
9.6mi, 5 to 7 hours

The maintained trail ends near the third lake. To continue, you cross over to the north side of the creek feeding the lake and climb out of the brush into the alpine tundra on the side of the ridge. The route to North Fork Campbell Creek heads northeast and is fairly obvious in good weather. Sidle the ridge towards the low point, and eventually you will come to the final **Williwaw Lake** at an elevation of 3250ft. This lake is a stunning alpine scene. Sheer cliffs and bluffs loom over the dark water to the east. On the west side, there are some great campsites, and to the north there is a pass to the North Fork drainage.

The hike to the 3700ft pass is a steady climb, but straightforward and manageable, even with a backpack on. On the steep 600ft descent from the top of the pass to the next valley, however, you should use extreme caution. If you have any doubts about your ability to make this descent, continue east along the crest of the ridge toward the head of the valley until you see a safer, easier route to the pair of alpine lakes below. From the lakes, you continue the gradual descent into the valley, reaching **Long Lake** 1.3mi from the third Williwaw Lake, 7.7mi from the trailhead.

This lake is indeed long – and beautiful, as alpine ridges and peaks surround it. The most distinct peak is Tanaina Peak (5300ft), along the lake's north shore. It's easier to follow the lake's north side, but you will still have to ford a few streams before reaching the outlet of North Fork Campbell Creek, in about a mile. There are several places to pitch a tent along the north shore.

At the outlet of the lake, the **North Fork Campbell Creek** is a small stream just beginning its long journey to Cook Inlet. The valley does not have trails, but the alpine tundra makes hiking easy. You gradually descend with the valley, and within a mile from the west end of Long Lake, you will see Anchorage on a clear day. More importantly, you will see a 2963ft knob on the south side of the ridge that is the key to reaching Near Point Trail.

About 2 miles beyond Long Lake, you need to ford the North Fork, which under normal conditions is easy to do, and begin sidling the ridge towards Near Point. This will make the climb to the 3000ft peak easier, keep you out of Campbell Creek Canyon and put you above the brush on the valley floor. The footing on the ridge is good, but you have to be careful climbing in and out of the ravines along the side.

As you ascend the northwest ridge of Wolverine Peak, aim for a notch just east of the 2963ft knob. Eventually, you will reach a ravine extending from a notch that can be used to ascend to the crest of the ridge. Look for a very rough path on the west side of the ravine that will make the climb easier. Once on top of the 2963ft knob, a very distinguishable path will lead you along the ridge and up the peak called **Near Point** (not labeled on topos).

Near Point is reached 6mi from the third Williwaw Lake, 12.4mi from the trailhead. At the top, it is marked with a large rock cairn, and there are good views of Anchorage, Cook Inlet and even the Alaska Range on a clear day. To the south, you can also see the trail leading to Wolverine Peak (see the Other Trails section at the end of this chapter).

The descent to the trailhead begins on a ridge that gently slopes to the southwest. Quickly, you'll pick up **Near Point Trail**, which will steadily drop toward the tree line. Less than a mile from the peak, you reach the first trees and then, in another quarter mile, a clearing. The clearing was the site of an old homestead. There is a trail sign near here. At this point, the trail merges into an old road. It passes the posted junction to Wolverine Peak less than 2mi from Near Peak and the junction with Middle Fork Loop Trail a half mile beyond that. From there, you retrace the start of the hike, crossing the bridge over South Fork Campbell Creek and ascending to the Prospect Heights trailhead less than 4mi from Near Point, 9.6mi from the third Williwaw Lake.

McHugh Lake Trail

Duration 2 days
Distance 16mi
Difficulty Level Medium to hard
Start Potter Section House on Seward Hwy
Finish Glen Alps trailhead
Cabins & Shelters No
Permits Required No
Public Transportation Yes
Summary This trail is an alpine crossing that includes spending a scenic night on Rabbit Lake. Several area peaks can be climbed to lengthen the hike.

The newest trail in Chugach State Park is the 7mi McHugh Lake Trail. From Seward Hwy, it extends inland to a pair of beautiful alpine lakes, making it ideal for an overnight camp. When McHugh Lake Trail is combined with portions of the Turnagain Arm and Powerline Trails and a climb over Ptarmigan Pass, they form a near loop of roughly 16mi that begins at the Potter Section House along the Seward Hwy and ends at the Glen Alps trailhead in the Hillside area of the state park.

Although the McHugh Lake Trail can be done in two days, you can just as easily spend several days climbing summits like McHugh Peak, Ptarmigan Peak, the Wedge or the Ramp. You could also follow the Powerline Trail east over a low pass and emerge at the Indian Valley Trail and Mile 102 of Seward Hwy.

The first day can be shortened if you begin the hike at McHugh Creek Picnic Area, at Mile 112 of Seward Hwy, and skip the Turnagain Arm portion of the hike, though this is an easy stretch and the views from high above the highway make hiking the extra 2mi well worth it. A strong hiker can hike the 14mi along the McHugh Lake Trail in to and out from the lake in one day.

The hike is rated medium to hard, mainly because the Ptarmigan Pass crossing is a route, not a trail. You'll find the Turnagain Arm and Powerline Trails easy. Powerline Trail is also a popular mountain bike trip.

Birth of a State Park

At 774 sq mi, Chugach State Park is the third largest state park in the USA, surpassed only by Alaska's own Wood-Tikchik (2344 sq mi) and California's Anza-Borrego Desert State Park (938 sq mi). Even more surprising than its size is the fact that Chugach didn't even exist until 1970.

Attempts to preserve portions of the area date back to the 1950s, but it wasn't until 1969, when commercial logging was slated for Bird and Indian Valleys, that momentum for creating a park was successful. Environmentalists and community activists won a lawsuit to stop timber harvesting and then pressured the state legislature to pass a state park bill. In August of 1970, Alaskans had their first state park but no state park system. There was nothing at the time in the way of a management program, permanent staff or even an office. Today, Alaska has the largest system in the country, with a third of all Alaskan lands preserved as state parks. The 120 units include state parks, state historic sites, marine parks and recreation areas that total more 4688 sq mi.

To many, Chugach is still the crowning jewel. The park contains 15 major valleys, 70 lakes and 50 glaciers that represent 10% of the park's area. There are also 70 peaks within the park, with 13 topping 7,000ft. At 8,005ft, Bashful Peak, 5mi southeast of Eklutna, is the tallest.

Perhaps the most telling figure about Chugach is the number of visitors. More than 1.5 million people visit the park annually – almost three times the number of visitors to Denali National Park every year.

PLANNING
When to Hike

Due to the 3585ft elevation of Ptarmigan Pass, it's best not to hike this trail before mid-June or after September.

What to Bring

See the Flattop Mountain Trail section earlier in this chapter.

Maps

USGS 1:63,360 series quads *Anchorage A-7* and *A-8* cover the complete hike, but the trails are not shown on the topos. A better map is Alaska Road & Recreation Maps' *Anchorage & Vicinity* ($6). In this book, the McHugh Lake Trail is covered on the Anchorage Area map.

Permits & Regulations

A vehicle entry permit is not required to leave a car at Potter House but is required ($5 per day) at McHugh Creek Picnic Area.

GETTING TO/FROM THE HIKE

The trail begins at the Chugach State Park headquarters, in the Potter Section House on Mile 115 of Seward Hwy, and ends at the Glen Alps trailhead (see Getting To/From the Hike in the Flattop Mountain Trail section for access information). Alaska Tourquest (☎ 337-4190, ✉ ron@alaskatourquest .com) makes daily runs to Portage and will provide transportation to either Potter Section House or to the McHugh Creek Picnic Area.

THE HIKE
Stage 1: Potter Section House to McHugh Lake
9mi, 5 to 6 hours

From a parking lot across the highway from the Potter Section House, the trail heads uphill for almost a half mile and then levels out as it follows a bluff in a forest of birch, aspen and cottonwood. Originally cut in 1910 as a mail and telegraph route, the trail here is wide enough for a wagon. Most of it is a walk in the forest, but in 2mi you reach a rock outcropping with a viewpoint of Turnagain Arm. From here, the trail begins a gentle descent off the bluff into McHugh Valley.

To the northeast, you can view **McHugh Peak** (4301ft) and, to the east, **South Suicide Peak** (5005ft), just before you arrive at a posted Y-junction 3.2mi from the Potter trailhead. Here, the right-hand fork descends a half mile to the upper parking lot of the **McHugh Creek Picnic Area**, where there are toilets, tables, drinking water and a scenic view of Turnagain Arm. In the lower parking lot of the picnic area is a trailhead for the rest of the Turnagain Arm Trail, to Windy Corner.

To reach McHugh Lake, take the left-hand fork at the junction. The trail heads north, using a series of switchbacks to climb 700ft towards **Table Rock**, an immense rocky outcrop rising above the trail. Follow a spur trail to reach the top of the rock for excellent views of Turnagain Arm. From Table Rock, the trail enters the McHugh Creek drainage area, sidling the sides of the valley high above the creek. About 2mi from the McHugh Creek Picnic Area, you pass a trail that climbs steeply north out of the valley. This is a route to McHugh Peak.

The main trail continues to climb up the valley and, 4mi from the picnic area, emerges from the mountain hemlock and willow to reach the alpine tundra. In another 2mi, the trail closes in on the head of the valley and becomes more of a route marked by rock cairns, before ending at **McHugh Lake**. From here, it's easy to hike over a low ridge to reach the much larger **Rabbit Lake** to the north. The lakes are in a spectacular alpine setting, with the Suicide Peaks looming overhead and Ptarmigan Peak (4900ft) to the north. Good camping spots abound in this area, and a spare day could be spent climbing either one of the Suicide Peaks.

Stage 2: McHugh Lake to Glen Alps Trailhead

7mi, 4 to 6 hours

From McHugh Lake, climb over the low ridge to Rabbit Lake and then follow the lakeshore west to its outlet into **Rabbit Creek**. An old trail can be picked up here and followed up Rabbit Creek Valley. At one time, the trail extended 5.5mi from the lake to Lower Canyon Rd, but it has since been closed to the public because it crosses private property.

Follow the creek 1.5mi, past Ptarmigan Creek to **Ptarmigan Pass**, a 3585ft saddle on

the west side of the peak. Leave Rabbit Creek and the old trail and ascend the ridge into the pass, a climb of more than 700ft. Once on the saddle, you'll see the east-west ridge that most people follow to reach the summit of Ptarmigan Peak.

When descending the north side of the pass, stay west of the stream flowing into South Fork Campbell Creek. This side is considerably steeper than the climb from Rabbit Creek, but in less than half a mile, when you're well above the creek on the south side of the valley, you'll reach **Powerline Trail**, 3mi from Rabbit Lake.

Powerline Trail is an old road closed to vehicles but open to mountain bikes. It's an easy hike out of the valley, as you descend towards the South Fork. A path under the power lines on the other side of the creek also leads through the valley. More mud is normally encountered on this trail.

Within a mile, a trail merges into the road from the valley below. Follow it if you want to climb either **the Wedge** (4660ft) or **the Ramp** (5240ft; see the Other Trails section of this chapter). The Powerline Trail continues its descent, and in 2mi, reaches the half-mile spur that links it to the parking area of the Glen Alps trailhead.

Historic Iditarod Trail

Duration 2 to 3 days
Distance 26mi
Difficulty Level Hard
Start Crow Creek Rd
Finish Eagle River Nature Center
Cabins & Shelters Yes
Permits Required No
Public Transportation No
Summary A route once used by gold miners and mushers, the Historic Iditarod Trail begins in Chugach National Forest, ends at the Eagle River Nature Center in Chugach State Park, and in between passes glaciers and excellent mountain scenery.

Also known as the Crow Pass Trail and the Old Iditarod Trail, this alpine crossing to

ANCHORAGE

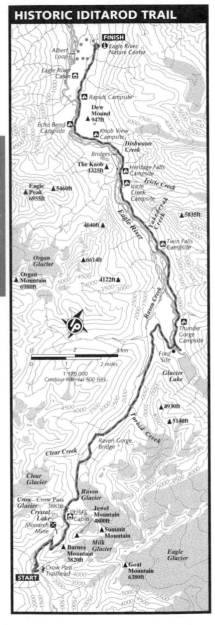

HISTORIC IDITAROD TRAIL

Eagle River Valley is another scenic route in the Anchorage area. The 26mi trail is part of the historic Iditarod route from Seward to Nome that was used by gold miners and dogsled teams until 1918, when the Alaska Railroad was completed to Fairbanks.

Today, the trail is a popular overnight hike through excellent mountain scenery. It begins with the climb to Crow Pass, where you can view nearby Raven Glacier and Crystal Lake. You then hike down into Eagle River Valley and follow the river to the Eagle River Nature Center. The trail is well marked but is still a challenging hike, due to an alpine crossing at Cross Pass and the Eagle River ford.

Because the first portion of trail to Crow Pass lies in the Chugach National Forest and the rest is in Chugach State Park, the trail is maintained by both the Alaska Division of Parks & Outdoor Recreation and the US Forest Service. Over the years, the trail has been improved and well posted. It has been so well improved that a footrace is held on it annually. In 1999, the winner covered the entire 26mi, including the deep ford at Eagle River, in three hours and 15 minutes.

The trail can be hiked in either direction, but by beginning at the Crow Pass trailhead, you start 1000ft higher and have less to climb to reach the highest point of the trail (3883ft). Plus, you'll get all the climbing done in the first few hours, and adrenaline alone will help carry you into the alpine area.

With a light day pack, and in good weather, you can cover the entire length of trail in one long Alaskan summer day. But why rush? The scenery is remarkable, the mining ruins interesting and the hike reasonably challenging. Besides, this is why you came to Alaska – to wander in the mountains.

PLANNING
When to Hike

The traverse is best hiked from mid-June through September. By late June most of the trail is free of snow.

Maps

USGS topos are essential. The route is covered on the 1:63,360 series quads *Anchorage A-7* and *A-6*. All but 3mi of the trail are on *A-6*. You can also use Alaska Road & Recreation Maps' *Anchorage & Vicinity* ($6).

Cabins & Shelters

Crow Pass Cabin ($35 per night) is a US Forest Service rental cabin 3mi from the Crow Creek Trailhead. The cabin is in a stunning alpine setting but must be reserved in advance by calling the National Recreation Reservation Service (☎ 877-444-6777, 518-885-3639 overseas) or through its Web site (www.reserveusa.com).

About 1.2mi from the north end of the trail is the Eagle River Cabin, which sleeps eight and rents for $45 per night. This cabin is managed by the Eagle River Nature Center (☎ 694-2108) and can be reserved a year in advance. There are also a number of backcountry campsites along the trail that feature metal rings for campfires.

NEAREST TOWNS & FACILITIES
Girdwood

A small but charming hostel in the area can be reached by turning right into Timberline Drive before the ski lodge and then turning right again into Alpina Rd. The *Alyeska Hostel* (☎ 783-2099) is in a cabin with wood heating, gas lighting and a kitchen area, and includes the use of a wood-burning sauna. Unfortunately, the hostel only has eight beds, so you might want to call ahead to try to secure space. There is a three-night maximum stay and the nightly fees are $10 for members and $13 for nonmembers. There are also a growing number of B&Bs in Girdwood. *Alyeska View* (☎ 783-2747), on Vail Dr, has three rooms for $75 to $85 per couple. The hosts of Alyeska View, Heinrich and Emmy Gruber, speak German.

There are two good restaurants in Girdwood. *Chair 5 Restaurant* (*5 Lindbald Ave*) is right in town and features gourmet burgers ($7), vegetarian sandwiches, salads, beer on tap and a friendly crew sitting at the bar. *Double Musky Inn* (☎ 783-2822), on Crow Creek Rd, specializes in Cajun dishes and blackened steaks and fish. It's open only for dinner and no reservations are taken, so be prepared for a long wait. Dinners cost $17 to $26, but the food is worth the wait.

Eagle River

Hiland Rd, at Mile 11.5 of Glenn Hwy, is the turnoff for *Eagle River State Campground*, with 58 sites ($15). The campground is in a scenic wooded area on the south bank of the Eagle River but is one of the busiest in the state.

If the public campground is filled and you're too tired to hassle with Anchorage, there's the *Eagle River Motel* (☎ 694-5000), which includes a Laundromat. A room costs $76/$85 singles/doubles.

GETTING TO/FROM THE HIKE
To the Start

The Crow Pass Trailhead is reached by turning onto Alyeska Hwy at Mile 90 of Seward Hwy, 37mi from Anchorage. Within 2mi, veer left onto Crow Creek Rd and then, in 5mi, veer right at the fork immediately following a bridge. Head up the hill, and in a mile, you'll reach the trailhead and parking area.

The Alaska Railroad (☎ 265-2494, 800-544-0552, ✉ akrr@Alaska.net) stops at Girdwood along its Anchorage-to-Whittier run. The train departs Anchorage at 9 am daily, reaches Girdwood at 10:20 am and then returns to Girdwood at 6:35 pm for the return to Anchorage. The one-way fare is $26, the same as the fare to Whittier, and it leaves you near the Seward Hwy, still 7mi from the trailhead.

From the Finish

The Eagle River Nature Center serves as the northern trailhead and is off the Glenn Hwy at Mile 12 of Eagle River Rd. You can hitch from the nature center to the junction of Eagle River Rd and the Glenn Hwy, where People Mover buses Nos 74 and 76 stop on their way to Anchorage. The fare is $1.

ANCHORAGE

THE HIKE
Stage 1: Crow Creek Rd to Crow Pass
4mi, 3 to 4 hours

This leg of the hike is a steep climb of 2500ft to Crow Pass and views of Raven Glacier. Keep in mind that snow will persist in the pass area until mid- to late June. The pass becomes a rainbow of color when tundra wildflowers begin to bloom in July.

From the trailhead parking area at the end of Crow Creek Rd, the trail begins in brush and quickly climbs a series of switchbacks into an alpine region. The trail here is an old miner's road, and it gains more than 1000ft within 1.5mi, before it reaches a posted junction. The left-hand spur continues another half mile to the ruins of **Monarch Mine**, also referred to as Girdwood Mine, on the flanks of Barnes and Jewel Mountains. The hard-rock gold mine was owned and operated by Harry Ingle Staser, a former US Marshall in Alaska, from 1926 until his death in 1940. Today, the mine's remains include an ore-crushing mill and parts of a tram cable. Be very careful when exploring the ruins. A quarter mile beyond the ruins the spur leads west to **Crow Creek Cascade**.

The right-hand fork at the junction is posted 'Crow Pass' and is a narrow trail that departs the old miner's road and sidles the slopes of Barnes and Jewel Mountains as it climbs steeply toward the pass. You top off at Mile 3 and then reach the USFS cabin ($35, reservations) overlooking scenic **Crystal Lake** at 3400ft. The **Crow Creek Cabin** is an A-frame structure with bunks for six people and room for a few more in the loft. There is no stove. The cabin is well above the timber line, and the views are spectacular. Mountain goats and Dall sheep can often be seen on the surrounding ridges. There are camp spots galore surrounding the lake.

From the cabin, follow rock cairns to **Crow Pass** the high point of the trail at 3550ft. It's a little more than a half mile away and a gentle climb. The pass offers a stunning panorama of the surrounding peaks and **Raven Glacier** at your feet. It is a scenic place to set up camp, and there's water nearby. Strong winds can whip through here; stake down freestanding dome tents.

Stage 2: Crow Pass to Thunder Gorge
10mi, 5 to 7 hours

From the pass, a trail well marked by huge cairns descends to the moraine along the southwest corner of Raven Glacier. Follow the moraine for a half mile and enjoy the views of the glacier. Then skirt Raven Creek until Clear Creek merges into it at Mile 6. You ford **Clear Creek** and then, in less than a mile, cross **Raven Gorge** on a bridge, a spectacular spot where the stream thunders through a narrow canyon.

This puts you on the east side of Raven Creek, and for the next 3mi, the trail skirts the hillsides above it. At Mile 9.5, you cross **Turbid Creek** and then begin ascending toward the north end of Raven Ridge. You stop near the ridge's crest, where there are views of **Eagle Glacier** and the lake in front of it. The trail makes a steep descent from the ridge and, at the bottom of the descent, it swings east and heads upstream to the **Eagle River** ford.

The ford, at Mile 13, the halfway point of the hike, is a half mile down from Glacier Lake and well marked and posted along Eagle River. Still, crossing this glacial river should not be taken lightly. Under normal conditions, the water will be almost knee-deep. After a heavy rainfall, it will be even higher, so camp and wait for the water level to drop. A third of a mile upstream from the ford is the glacial lake in front of Eagle Glacier. The lake is easy to reach, and the gravel bars along the river here make scenic campsites.

From the ford, the trail skirts the east bank of the river, as it heads northwest toward the Eagle River Nature Center. The hiking is considerably easier here. Within a mile, you reach **Thunder Gorge**, at Mile 14, where you'll find a backcountry campsite with a metal fire ring. It's not necessary to use the designated campsites, however, and Eagle River Valley is loaded with places to pitch a tent.

Stage 3: Thunder Gorge to Eagle River Nature Center

12mi, 4 to 5 hours

The final leg of the hike is an easy walk through the upper valley of Eagle River to the nature center, 12mi away. From Crow Pass, you will have descended more than 3000ft to Thunder Gorge. To the northern trailhead, you will descend only another 300ft.

The trail continues northwest, staying above the river at first and then swinging close to it just before arriving at Twin Falls at Mile 16.5. Near this stream is a backcountry campsite and fire ring. In the next 3.5mi, you'll cross three streams, all unnamed on the USGS quads. The second, reached at Mile 20, is **Yakedeyak Creek**. You'll come to the third stream, **Icicle Creek**, within a third of a mile. Cross the bridge to the backcountry campsite. Across the river from Icicle Creek is **Heritage Falls**, but the best view of the mountainside cascade is farther up the trail.

Skirting the river, the trail stays on a northerly course until it passes **the Knob**, a distinct 1325ft bluff on the west side of the river. At this point, Eagle River swings almost due west and so does the trail, arriving at a bridge over **Dishwater Creek** at Mile 21.5. Within the next half mile, you pass Knob View Camp and then **the Perch**, which is posted at Mile 22. The Perch is a massive, rocky outcrop. Take a break here to view the mountains and impressive peaks that box in Eagle River Valley.

Heading west, the trail stays close to the river and reaches Echo Bend Campsite at Mile 23. This is a scenic spot for camping by the river, only 3mi short of the visitor center. At Echo Bend, the trail swings away from Eagle River, passes beneath Dew Mound (947ft) and arrives at Rapids Camp, the final backcountry campsite, at Mile 24.5.

In the final 1.5mi, you stay in a birch and aspen forest away from the water, pass the new **Eagle River Cabin** ($45, reservations) and then a posted junction to the **Albert Loop Trail**. If you're not in a rush to reach civilization or a ride back to Anchorage,

Albert Loop is an easy 3mi side trip. It goes through boreal forest to the gravel bars along Eagle River before returning to the nature center.

Just before the nature center, you pass the two posted junctions of the **Rodak Nature Trail**, a 0.75mi loop. If the salmon are spawning, take the time to hike to the viewing deck on this short trail.

Eklutna Lakeside Trail

Duration 1 to 3 days
Distance 25.7mi roundtrip
Difficulty Level Easy
Start/Finish Eklutna Lake Campground
Cabins & Shelters Yes
Permits Required Yes
Public Transportation No
Summary This easy hike or mountain bike ride along an old road provides access to alpine trails, backcountry campsites and a glacier.

At a length of more than 7mi, Eklutna Lake is the largest body of water in Chugach State Park. Surrounded by peaks and towering mountains, it's also one of the most scenic. The lake fills the glacially carved valley, and just beyond the lake's east end is Eklutna Glacier, the ice floe responsible for the sculpture. Chances to spot wildlife are good: Moose are often seen near the lakeshore, Dall sheep frequent the ridges and slopes above the water, and mountain goats and brown bears are found in the more remote regions away from the lake.

At the west end of the lake is the large Eklutna Lake Campground. At the other end are two backcountry campgrounds, and in between, skirting the north shore, is the Lakeside Trail. The trail was originally a road built by the US Army, which conducted training sessions on Eklutna Glacier in the 1960s and 1970s. By 1977, numerous washouts had made the road unpassable for vehicles, so it was designated a route for hikers, horses, mountain bikers and, unfortunately, all-terrain vehicles.

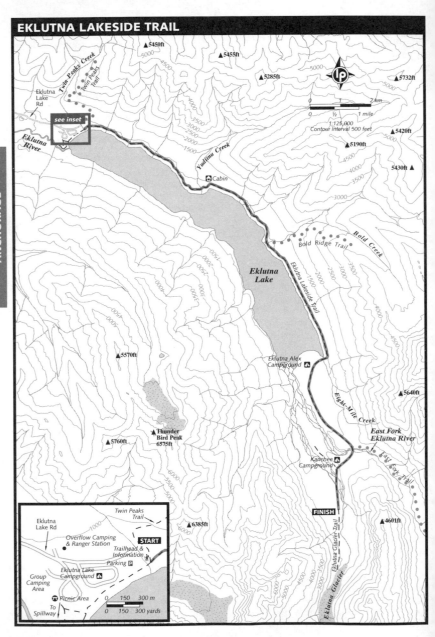

Torrential storms in the mid-1990s again caused severe washouts that made the trail unusable. This time the park staff constructed so many new segments away from the shoreline that there are now two trails along the lake. The original road is posted 'Non-Motorized Trail' and is open only to hikers and mountain bikers. The new road, posted 'Trail,' has mile markers and can be used by ATVs on certain days of the week. The two trails constantly intersect, but for the most part, hikers have their own route for the first 8mi.

The saving grace of the trail, as far as hikers and mountain bikers are concerned, is that off-road vehicles are only permitted on this road from Sunday to Wednesday. Sunday is the busiest day for the gas-guzzling jockeys. Hikers and mountain bikers can use the trail any day of the week.

With three days free of vehicles, you can easily hike to the east end, spend a day exploring the glacier and then return, stopping to enjoy an afternoon in the alpine region. The area is as popular with mountain bikers as it is with hikers. The roadbed makes for easy riding, and by using a bike, you have more time to explore the side trails (see the 'Mountain Biking Eklutna Lake' boxed text).

Lakeside Trail itself is a 12.7mi one-way route to the backcountry campsites and glacier, but several side trips are available. Near the beginning of Lakeside Trail is Twin Peaks Trail, a 3.2mi climb to above the tree line. Just over halfway along the lake is Bold Ridge Trail, another route into the surrounding alpine region. The East Fork and Eklutna Glacier Trails begin near the end of the Lakeside Trail. The hike to the

Mountain Biking Eklutna Lake

The ideal and probably the most popular way to travel the Eklutna Lakeside Trail is by mountain bike. It's a six-hour, 12-mile hike to the east end of the lake, but only a two- to three-hour ride on a mountain bike.

With a mountain bike, Bold Ridge Trail becomes a possible day hike from Eklutna Lake Campground, or you can strap on the backpack and spend the night at Kanchee or Eklutna Alex Campgrounds, free backcountry facilities near the end of the trail.

Lifetime Adventures (☎ 746-4644, 800-952-8624) provides mountain bike and kayak rentals from a visitor center at the trailhead. A full-day bike rental is $35, and rental for a double kayak costs $45. They also offer a paddle/peddle package, in which you kayak to the end of the lake and then pick up a mountain bike to peddle to the glacier. The cost is $65 per person.

You can also rent mountain bikes in Anchorage at Downtown Bicycle Rental (☎ 279-5293), at 4th Ave and C St, which has mountain bikes for $29 a day, or at the Bicycle Shop (☎ 272-5219), 1035 W Northern Lights Blvd, for $20.

Popular trails to mountain bike in Anchorage include Hilltop Ski Area (☎ 346-1446), which rents mountain bikes during the summer for $17 a half day and $26 a full day, and Powerline Trail from the Glen Alps trailhead. For information on organized mountain bike rides with locals call the Arctic Bicycle Club hot line (☎ 566-0177).

backcountry campsites takes five to six hours, two to three hours by mountain bike, but three days are really needed if you want to add on any of the side trips. The shoreline road is a very easy walk, but the climb to the alpine area on Bold Ridge is considerably harder, and Twin Peaks Trail is medium to hard.

PLANNING
When to Hike
The Lakeside Trail is a low elevation route that can be enjoyed May through October, but the alpine routes of Twin Peaks and Bold Ridge shouldn't be attempted before June or after September.

Maps
The entire area is covered on USGS 1:63,360 series quad *Anchorage B-6*.

Information Sources
The Eklutna Ranger Station (☎ 688-0908) is near the campground and open when volunteers are available. You can also get information and trail conditions at Chugach State Park headquarters in the Potter Section House (☎ 345-5014).

Permits & Regulations
For visitors not staying in the Eklutna Lake Campground, there is a separate parking lot for the trailhead which requires a $5-per-day vehicle permit that can be purchased at the ranger station or from a campground volunteer.

Cabins & Shelters
Yuditnu Creek Cabin is a public-use cabin 3mi along the Lakeside Trail. It costs $40 a night and can be rented through the DNR Public Information Center (☎ 269-8400), 3601 C St, Suite 200, Anchorage, AK 99503-5929. The Eklutna Alex Cabin, an old trapper's cabin at the east end of the lake, is no longer rented out.

Lifetime Adventures (☎ 746-4644, 800-952-8624), which runs a visitor center near the Eklutna Lake Campground, also has a wall tent at the east end of the lake that sleeps four to six ($45 a night).

NEAREST TOWNS & FACILITIES
Wasilla
If you're coming from Denali National Park or Fairbanks from the north, Wasilla is the last place for accommodations before reaching the Eklutna Lake area. *Wasilla Backpackers* (☎ 357-3699, 3950 Carefree Drive, ✉ travel@wasillabackpackers.com) is a hostel 2mi south of town, just off George Parks Hwy at Mile 39. Bunks are $22 a night and tent sites $15. Laundry and Internet service are also available. Another convenient place to stay is the *Windbreak Hotel* (☎ 376-4484), a mile south of town on George Parks Hwy. The hotel has rooms for $59/$69 and a good cafe and a bar.

Eklutna Lake
Eklutna Lake State Recreation Area is at the west end of the lake and has 50 sites for $10 a day. This campground is one of Chugach State Park's most popular campgrounds and will often be filled on the weekends during the summer. Sites are available on a first-come, first-served basis.

GETTING TO/FROM THE HIKE
From Anchorage, head north on the Glenn Hwy and take the Eklutna exit at Mile 26. From the service drive, turn right onto the Old Glenn Hwy and then, in half a mile, turn left towards the mountains on Eklutna Lake Rd. Follow the road east for 10mi to the west end of the lake. Park signs will keep you reassured that you're not lost. Any of the Denali Park van services (see the Getting There & Away section and chapter, earlier) will drop you off at the Eklutna exit, but there is no other transportation along the Eklutna Rd, other than hitching.

The trailhead is in the day-use parking area near the campground. Lifetime Adventures, located here, provides a number of services, including mountain bike and kayak rentals. See the boxed text, 'Mountain Biking Eklutna Lake,' for more information. The company also has a 21ft pontoon boat and will do drop-offs and pickups at the other end of the lake. The cost is $15 per person and saves you from having to backtrack the Lakeside Trail.

THE HIKE
Stage 1: Twin Peaks Creek to Eklutna Glacier

13mi, 6 to 7 hours

The day-use area has parking, outhouses, water and an information kiosk with a spotting scope for searching the surrounding mountains for Dall sheep. From here, cross the bridge over Twin Peaks Creek. On the other side is a posted junction. **Twin Peaks Trail** heads west (left). Lakeside Trail heads east (right) as a wide dirt road. If you are used to narrow mountain trails or no trails at all (like in Denali National Park) this route will be an easy walk.

At the beginning, the motorized and nonmotorized trails are the same and skirt the lake close to its edge, providing constant views of turquoise water surrounded by snowy peaks. Near Mile 1 is a rock face that serves as a lambing area in the spring. It is a particularly good place to spot sheep any time of the year. Just past the mile marker, the two trails split. The nonmotorized trail heads right toward the lakeshore. For the next 7mi, the two trails will parallel the lake, merging less than a dozen times. Always take the nonmotorized trail, which is clearly posted. It remains closer to the water, to provide great views.

The trail follows the shoreline, using culverts to cross several creeks and a footbridge to cross **Yuditnu Creek**, almost 3mi from the trailhead. If you're packing along a rod and reel, this is a good place to fish. Eklutna Lake holds populations of rainbow trout and Dolly Varden that range up to 21 inches in length. For the best results from shore, fish where a major freshwater stream, such as Yuditnu, empties into the lake. Other spots that are productive are Twin Peaks Stream near the trailhead, Bold Creek and Eight-Mile Creek. Mepps spinners are the most popular lures.

Beyond the bridge you arrive at a posted junction to the **Yuditnu Creek Cabin**, one of the newest state park cabins. The cabin ($40, reservations) sleeps six and has a three-night limit. From its porch you can view the lake or, at times, spot Dall sheep on the mountain slopes directly behind it.

The trail continues to skirt the shoreline and passes where the northern and southern shorelines pinch the lake to its narrowest width. At this point, you can view the east end of the lake for the first time and spot a hanging glacier among the peaks. About 5mi from the trailhead, the two trails merge briefly, and you cross Bold Creek to arrive at the posted trailhead for **Bold Ridge Trail**, the left-hand spur.

Lakeside Trail continues southeast along the shoreline for the next 1.5mi, until it swings away from the lake 8mi from the trailhead, into spruce and birch forest. Here it becomes a narrow winding road, used by both ATVs and hikers, until it crosses the **Eight-Mile Creek** and begins curving around the east end of the lake. **Eklutna Alex Campground** is just before Mile 9. The facility has four sites, vault toilets, fire rings and picnic tables. Nearby is an old trapper's cabin.

At this point, Lakeside Trail heads toward the narrow, steep-walled canyon from which Eklutna River flows. You reach the posted junction to the East Fork Trail in 1.5mi and then cross East Fork Eklutna River on a wooden bridge where there are excellent views of the canyon. On the other side of the river, at Mile 11, is **Kanchee Campground**. It has four sites and facilities similar to those at Eklutna Alex Campground.

Beyond the campground, the trail reaches the Eklutna River, skirting it briefly before crossing it via another bridge. Once across the river, you reach Mile 12 and the spur that leads to a former camping area. Cottonwood, a walk-in campground in a forested setting, was closed in 1994. Lakeside Trail continues another mile beyond the campground, quickly passing spectacular Serenity Falls before ending 12.7mi from the trailhead.

The final leg to the glacier is along Eklutna Glacier Trail, which is for foot traffic only. Motorized off-road vehicles and mountain bikes are prohibited. It leads 0.75mi farther up the steep canyon along the Eklutna River and across glacial debris. It ends at an interpretive display and viewing area of the Eklutna Glacier.

Side Trip: Twin Peaks Trail

6.4mi roundtrip, 3 to 4 hours

The 3.2mi Twin Peaks Trail is a popular and well-maintained route, starting just over the bridge from the parking area, to the tundra areas surrounding East and West Twin Peaks and Goat Mountain. The trail is an abandoned road but is considered a challenging hike because you climb 1500ft and some sections are steep. For most people, the hike is a three- to four-hour roundtrip. You are rewarded with great views of Eklutna Lake and (possibly) Dall sheep. The trail ends at an alpine bowl with a stream flowing through the middle. You can camp here. More adventurous souls can continue up the bowl to a pass at 4400ft.

Side Trip: Bold Ridge Trail

7mi roundtrip, 6 to 7 hours

Bold Ridge Trail is a one-way hike of 3.5mi to the alpine tundra at the base of Bold Peak. It starts at Mile 5 of the Eklutna Lakeside Trail as a steep climb of switchbacks along an old road. You break out of the brush in less than 2mi, at a 3400ft knob. From there, a trail continues another mile or so up Bold Creek Valley to glacial moraines at the base of Bold Peak (7552ft). You can camp here, but you'll have to search hard for water.

To the south, the valley is boxed in by Bold Ridge, an excellent ridgeline to follow for views of Eklutna Lake, Eklutna Glacier and the Knik Arm of Cook Inlet. To the north, the ridge can be followed to reach a 4800ft pass into the remote Hunter Creek drainage area of Chugach State Park. For those who want to avoid the families and mountain bikers at the east end of the lake, this is an excellent alternate route. Plan on two hours up and an extra day if you want to hike the surrounding alpine ridges.

Side Trip: East Fork Trail

12mi, 6 to 7 hours

This foot trail begins at a posted junction 10.5mi along the Lakeside Trail and winds east along the East Fork Eklutna River to a small knoll overlooking a glacial lake. It's a scenic side trip (13mi if you're staying at Kanchee Campground) but much more difficult than the Lakeside Trail. Rock slides force you to traverse steep slopes of scree at times in order to follow the river. Hiking to the Tulchina Falls is a one-way hike of 2.5mi and continuing beyond that is considerably harder.

The junction to the trail is on the north side of the East Fork. You immediately parallel the river into another steep-sided canyon, traversing steep slopes when necessary. The scenery here is dominated by Baleful, Bold and Bashful Peaks to the northwest. At 8005ft, Bashful is the tallest mountain in Chugach State Park. Within a mile, you'll pass the first waterfall tumbling out of the mountains.

The second cascade, **Tulchina Falls**, is visible from the trail. This one is much more impressive than the first, as it leaps more than 100ft off the side of Bashful Peak before becoming a mountainside stream. The maintained trail ends at the falls, and a rougher route continues upriver. The trail continues its mild climb along the East Fork until the final mile of the route. Here it swings away from the creek and begins a steep climb. You ascend more than 600ft, until the trail tops off near a 2190ft-high knoll in open tundra. The views, needless to say, are stunning. Just east of the knoll is a glacial lake where you can escape the campground crowds for the night. There are also good camping areas at Tulchina Falls and on the gravel bars further upstream.

Stage 2: The Return

12.7mi, 4 to 6 hours

Return the way you came. If you're in a hurry to get back to the Eklutna Lake Campground, you could probably make the hike from Kanchee Campground in four hours. For anything faster, you'd almost have to jog, be on a mountain bike or jump on the Lifetime Adventures pontoon boat.

It's possible to continue from the Lakeshore Trail and traverse Eklutna, Whiteout and Eagle Glaciers, and eventually Raven Glacier, to emerge at the Crow Pass Trail near Girdwood. The Mountaineering Club of Alaska even maintains three huts along the 31mi route for those adventurous souls

Kenai Fjords National Park

Grewingk Glacier Lake

DEANNA SWANEY

Along Glenn Hwy

JIM DUFRESNE

Kenai Fjords National Park

traversing the glaciers. This is a highly technical hike requiring special climbing equipment and mountaineering expertise.

Other Hikes

ANCHORAGE AREA
Wolverine Peak Trail
Part of the Chugach State Park Hillside trail system, this 5.2mi trail ascends to Wolverine Peak (4455ft), the triangular peak that can be seen to the east of Anchorage. It is a strenuous but rewarding full-day trip, with good views of the city, Cook Inlet and the Alaska Range. (See the Anchorage Area map.)

From the Prospect Heights trailhead (see Getting To/From the Hike in the Williwaw Lakes Loop section), the trail begins as an old homestead road. It crosses South Fork Campbell Creek and then passes junctions with Middle Fork Loop and Near Point Trails in the first 2.3mi. Keep heading east, and the old road becomes a footpath that ascends above the tree line and eventually fades out. Make sure to mark the trail's whereabouts in order to find it on the way back. From here, it is 3mi to the Wolverine Peak.

The roundtrip from the corner of O'Malley Rd and Hillside Drive is 13.8mi – a nine-hour hike. Many people just hike to the good views above the bush line, shortening the trip to 7.8mi (USGS quads *Anchorage A-7* and *A-8*).

The Ramp
One of the many alpine summit hikes from the east side of the city, the Ramp is a hike through tranquil tundra valleys, with good chances of seeing Dall sheep during the summer. From the corner of Hillside Drive and Upper Huffman Rd, walk 0.7mi along Upper Huffman Rd and then turn right on Toilsome Hill Drive. Walk 2mi to the Glen Alps trailhead, one of the most popular access points into the Hillside trail system. (See the Anchorage Area map.)

Most people will be heading up to Flattop Mountain, but to reach the Ramp, follow the lower trail in the parking lot for a

half mile, to the Powerline Trail. Turn right and follow the trail for 2mi, past 13 power poles, to where an old Jeep trail crosses over from the left and heads downhill to South Fork Campbell Creek.

Follow the Jeep trail across the creek and continue up the hill beyond it to a valley on the other side. Hike up the alpine valley to Ship Pass, which lies between the Ramp (5240ft) to the north and the Wedge (4660ft) to the south. Either peak can be climbed, though the Wedge is easier. The roundtrip from the Glen Alps trailhead is 11mi, an eight- to 10-hour hike (USGS quads *Anchorage A-7* and *A-8).*

Powerline Trail
This trail, an old road now closed to vehicles, is an easy hike through the heart of the Chugach foothills and over the 3550ft Powerline Pass. You begin at the Glen Alps trailhead and end on the Indian Valley Trail near the Seward Hwy. (See the Anchorage Area map.) This 11mi one-way trip is perhaps the most popular mountain bike route in the park, though cyclists have problems with the steep and rocky descent from the pass to Indian Valley (USGS quads *Anchorage A-7* and *A-8).*

Far North Bicentennial Park
A 4000-acre tract of forest and muskeg in east central Anchorage, this park features more than 20mi of trails for hiking and mountain biking. In the center of the park is the BLM's Campbell Tract, a 700-acre wildlife oasis where it's possible to see moose and bears in the spring. Come back in mid-September, and the fall colors can be brilliant here. To reach the Hilltop Ski Area, take O'Malley Rd east to Hillside Drive and follow the road to the parking area. This is another popular area for mountain biking in Anchorage, and bikes can be rented at the park's Hilltop Ski Area (☎ 346-1446). Pick up a trail guide map in the chalet at the Hilltop Ski Area.

Rendezvous Peak Route
The hike to the Rendezvous Peak (4050ft) is an easy five-hour roundtrip, less from the

trailhead, and rewards hikers with some incredible views of Mt McKinley, Cook Inlet, Turnagain and Knik Arms, and the city far below.

To get there, take the Glenn Hwy northeast from Anchorage 6.5mi, turn off on Arctic Valley Rd (this section is also known as Ski Bowl Rd) and head 7mi to the Alpenglow Ski Area at the end. There is a vehicle fee to park at the ski area during the summer. Bus No 75 from the transit center will drop you off at Glenn Hwy and Arctic Valley Road, but you would have to hitchhike from there. On the weekends there is a steady stream of cars to the trailhead.

From the parking lot, a short trail leads along the right-hand side of a stream up the valley to the northwest. The trail ends at a pass where a short ascent to Rendezvous Peak is easily seen and climbed. The roundtrip from the ski area parking lot is only 3.5mi, but it is a much longer day if you can't thumb a ride up Arctic Valley Rd (USGS quads *Anchorage A-7* and *B-7*).

Ship Creek Valley
Also beginning from the Alpenglow Ski Area is the hike through Ship Creek Valley to Indian Valley. This is a challenging 22mi overnight hike that involves steep, muddy sections and 10mi of unmarked routes with unbridged stream crossings. You pick it up from a pullout on Ski Bowl Rd, across from a gated military road and 0.75mi below the ski area. From here you begin on a trail that descends 3mi into the valley. You end up on the Indian Valley Trail at Indian Pass, which leads you 6mi to the Seward Hwy (USGS quads *Anchorage A-7* and *Seward D-7*).

TURNAGAIN ARM & PORTAGE GLACIER
Indian Valley Trail
This 6mi path to Indian Pass is steep in some places, making it moderately hard, but the trail leads to good views of Turnagain Arm. The trail crosses bridges over Indian Creek and then climbs 2100ft to reach the alpine setting of the pass. The trailhead is at Mile 102 of the Seward Hwy, just west of Turnagain House Restaurant, where you turn toward the mountain and follow a dirt road for 1.4mi. Plan on five to seven hours for the 12mi roundtrip (USGS quads *Anchorage A-7* and *Seward D-7*).

Bird Ridge Trail
This hike is the first snow-free trail in the Anchorage area in spring. The trail begins as an uphill climb to a power line access road, follows it for a third of a mile and then turns left and climbs Bird Ridge, which runs along the valley of Bird Creek. The hike is steep in many places but quickly leaves the bush behind for the alpine beauty above. You can hike over 4mi on the ridge itself, reaching views of the headwaters of Ship Creek below. Viewing points of Turnagain Arm are plentiful. You pick up the trailhead near Mile 102 of Seward Hwy by turning into a large marked parking area to the north. Don't confuse this trail with Bird Valley Trail, which is open to off-road vehicles (USGS quads *Anchorage A-7* and *Seward D-7*).

Falls Creek Trail
This path is only 1.5mi long but follows a scenic stream through a narrow valley and ends above the tree line. From here you can easily spend a long afternoon exploring the open tundra area. The trail is rated moderate because it is steep in some places, as it climbs to 1450ft, and is often confusing due to the many side trails. The main route stays right of the creek until it ends (it does not fork off to the east). The trailhead is a half mile east of Mile 105 of the Seward Hwy and is posted along the highway. You'll find a small parking area near Falls Creek.

Alyeska Glacier View Trail
You begin this hike by taking the chairlift at the Alyeska Ski Resort ($16) to the Glacier Express Restaurant and then scrambling up the knob behind the sundeck. From here, you follow the ridge into an alpine area where there are views of the tiny Alyeska Glacier. The roundtrip is less than a mile. You can continue up the ridge to climb the so-called summit of Mt Alyeska, a high point of 3939ft. The true summit lies farther

Winner Creek Gorge

This is an easy and pleasant hike that winds 3.5mi through a tall spruce and hemlock forest and ends in the gorge itself. The gorge is where Winner Creek flows through a small cleft in the rocks and becomes a series of small falls and cascades on its way to emptying into Glacier Creek. You pick up the trail at Alyeska Ski Resort by parking on Arlberg Rd and walking the bike path past the hotel towards the bottom of the tram. Follow the edge of a ski trail above the tram and look for the footpath heading into the forest.

Byron Glacier Trail

This is an easy mile-long path in the Portage Glacier area to the base of Byron Glacier. Once you reach the permanent snow in front of the glacier, look for the threadlike ice worms, which were immortalized in a Robert Service poem. You reach the trailhead from the road to the boat-tour dock on Portage Glacier Lake.

NORTH OF ANCHORAGE & PALMER
Rodak Nature Trail

The 0.75mi loop begins at the Eagle River Nature Center and passes a series of interpretive panels and an impressive observation deck straddling a salmon stream. The state park visitor center is at Mile 12 of Eagle River Rd, off Glenn Hwy.

Albert Loop Trail

Also beginning from the visitor center, this is a 3mi hike through a boreal forest and along gravel bars of the Eagle River. The hiking is easy, and the views of the glacial river are pleasant. Part of the loop is the end of the Historic Iditarod Trail.

Thunderbird Falls Trail

This mile-long trail is a quick uphill climb to the scenic falls formed by a small, rocky gorge. At the end is a deck with benches overlooking the cascade, a great place to enjoy lunch. At Mile 25 of the Glenn Hwy, depart at the Thunderbird Falls exit and follow the signs north along the Old Glenn Hwy a mile to reach the trailhead parking lot.

Lazy Mountain

The climb to the top of this 3720ft peak is the best hike in the Palmer area. The 2.5mi trail is steep at times but is a pleasant hike that ends in an alpine setting with good views of the Matanuska Valley and its farms below. From the Glenn Hwy in Palmer, head east on Arctic Ave, the third exit into town, which turns into Old Glenn Hwy. After crossing the Matanuska River, turn left onto Clark-Wolverine Rd and then left in a half mile at a T-junction. This puts you onto the unmarked Huntly Rd, which you follow for a mile to the Equestrian Center parking lot at its end. The trailhead, marked 'Foot Trail,' is on the north side of the parking lot. Plan on at least three to five hours for the roundtrip hike (USGS quad *Anchorage C-6*).

McRoberts Creek Trail

This trail is in the same area as Lazy Mountain, and the two trailheads are connected by a 1.5mi spur. McRoberts Creek Trail is a backcountry hike up the creek's valley and provides the best approach to climbing Matanuska Peak (6119ft). The trail reaches the tree line in 2.5mi and Summit Ridge (3880ft) in 9mi. The hike to Matanuska Peak is a challenging 18mi hike. To reach the trailhead, take Old Glenn Hwy from Palmer towards Butte and turn left onto Smith Rd at Mile 15.5. Follow Smith Rd for 1.4mi, until it curves into Harmony Ave. There is no parking at the South Fork trailhead, so leave the car at the bend in the road (USGS quad *Anchorage C-6*).

Pioneer Ridge Trail

This 3mi trail provides access to the main ridge extending southeast of Pioneer Peak. It involves some steep grades until you're above the tree line and then ends at 5330ft. From there, it's another 2mi along the ridge to the 6398ft peak. This alpine section is a route, not a trail. To the southeast, from the end of the trail, an experienced hiker can follow a ridge to a saddle below Bold Peak and then continue on to the Eklutna Lake trail system in Chugach State Park.

Plan on six to seven hours to reach the 5330ft level of Pioneer Ridge, where the views are stunning. To reach the trailhead from Knik River Bridge on Old Glenn Hwy, follow Knik River Rd for 3.6mi. Trailhead parking will appear on the right (USGS quads *Anchorage B-5* and *B-6*).

Gold Mint Trail

Hatcher Pass, a wonderful alpine setting that includes Independence Mine State Historical Park, offers several possibilities for a hike in the mountains. One of the easiest hikes is Gold Mint Trail. It begins from a parking lot across from Motherlode Lodge at Mile 14 of the Fishhook-Willow Rd. The trail follows the Little Susitna River into a gently sloping mountain valley. Within 3mi, you spot the ruins of Lonesome Mine. Keep hiking, and you will eventually reach the head of the river at Mint Glacier (USGS quad *Anchorage D-6*).

Reed Lakes Trail

A mile past Motherlode Lodge at Mile 14 of Fishhook-Willow Rd, a road to Archangel Valley splits off and takes you to the posted trailhead of Reed Lakes. The trail begins as a wide road to an old cabin reached in 2mi. From here, you follow a trail that climbs to the crest of the valley. Lower Reed Lake is found within a quarter mile of reaching the crest, or 3.5mi from the trailhead. Upper Reed Lake, a scenic place to camp, is another mile beyond (USGS quad *Anchorage D-6*).

Craigie Creek Trail

This hike starts off as a road occasionally used by four-wheel drives. It's posted along the Fishhook–Willow Rd, 1.5mi west of Hatcher Pass. The trail follows a valley up to the head of the creek, where it's possible to cross a pass into the Independence Mine Bowl. The road makes a gentle climb for 4mi past several abandoned mining operations and then becomes a very steep trail for 3mi to Dogsled Pass (USGS quad *Anchorage D-7*).

Kenai Peninsula

Just 50mi southeast of Anchorage by road, the Kenai Peninsula is a vast forested plateau bounded to the east by the Kenai Mountains and the Harding Ice Field, to the west by Cook Inlet and laced by hundreds of lakes, rivers and streams. This area is an outdoor paradise; it has an extensive trail system for hikers, long glaciated fjords for kayakers, chains of lakes for canoeists, 80lb king salmon for anglers and a campground around almost every bend in the road.

Most of the peninsula is set aside as Chugach National Forest, Kenai Fjords National Park, Kenai National Wildlife Refuge and Kachemak Bay State Park and Wilderness. Squeezed in between these wilderness preserves are a handful of small towns with supplies and services, paved roads and good public transportation, all within a few hours' drive of Anchorage International Airport.

It's little wonder the Kenai Peninsula is Alaska's top recreational area. It is well serviced, well developed and, unfortunately, well used during the summer. There are times in the middle of the summer when people drive from one public campground to the next, looking for an open site anywhere. In the Kenai, kayakers will see tour boats full of whale watchers, hikers will see mountain bikers on many of the trails and backpackers will see, well, other backpackers.

Despite the crowds, this region of Alaska should not be skipped. The majestic blend of mountains and glaciers can be found along several of the trails covered here, and alpine lakes and meadows beckon you to strap on a backpack and spend a night among the peaks.

From Portage, it's easy traveling down the Seward Hwy into the heart of the Kenai Peninsula. The highway stretches for 127mi and is another scenic gem in the state's fledgling road system.

The campgrounds may be crowded and the highways at times an endless line of RVers, but you can always hike a little longer or climb a little higher to separate yourself from the three-month stampede to this peninsula known as the summer tourist season.

Highlights

- Staying in rustic cabins along the Resurrection Pass Trail
- Fishing for rainbow trout in Upper Russian Lake
- Camping above the tree line along the Primrose & Lost Lake Trails
- Exploring WWII military ruins at the end of the Coastal Trail
- Setting up camp in front of Grewingk Glacier in Kachemak Bay State Park

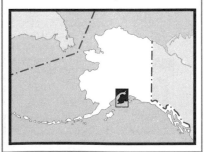

Chugach National Forest

Only a third as large as Tongass National Forest (its counterpart in Southeast Alaska), Chugach is still the second-largest national forest in the USA and an impressive area of forests, rivers, lakes, mountains and glaciers. The 9281-sq-mi national forest spreads from its western boundary in the middle of the Kenai Peninsula to Cordova on the east side of Prince William Sound.

The national forest has more than 200mi of trails, most of which are on the Kenai

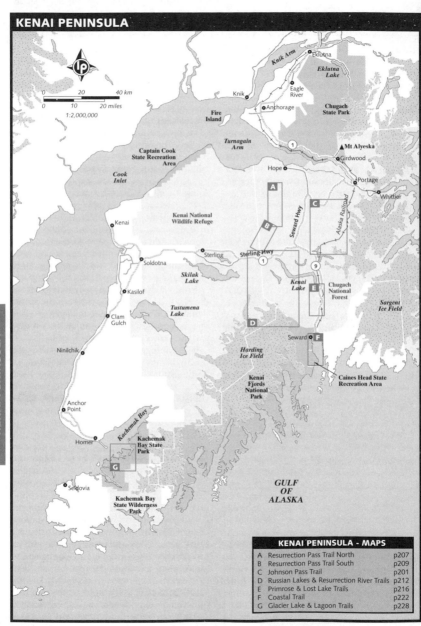

KENAI PENINSULA

Peninsula. Johnson Pass, Resurrection Pass, Russian Lakes Trails and Resurrection River, and Primrose and Lost Lake Trails are described here. These are the longest trails in the national forest, and all of them are overnight treks. The Resurrection Pass, Russian Lakes and Resurrection River Trails are often referred to as the Resurrection trail system, because they can be linked together for a 70mi trek from Hope to Seward.

NATURAL HISTORY

One-third of the national forest is rock (in the form of the Kenai Mountains and the Chugach Range) and glaciers (the most famous being Columbia and Portage). The rest of the land is a rich tapestry of forests, lakes and wildlife. Most trails begin in lush Sitka spruce forests or dense aspen. Almost impenetrable willow and alder take over at about 1000ft, until you reach the alpine tundra.

Wildlife is plentiful for those who make the effort to hike away from the roads and highways. In the alpine region, mountain goats can be found throughout the national forest, and you'll see Dall sheep in the mountains of the Kenai Peninsula. Moose are abundant, and both black bears and, to a lesser extent, brown bears may be encountered. River otters, marmots, porcupines, wolves and more than 200 species of birds also exist in the national forest.

The national forest offers a variety of fishing opportunities; anglers can cast for species like rainbow, lake and cutthroat trout, as well as Dolly Varden, arctic grayling and salmon. However, because the area is easy to get to, roadside lakes and rivers are heavily fished and in most cases not productive if you have limited tackle and no boat. The best waters to concentrate on are the mountain lakes reached on foot, one's that don't have United States Forest Service (USFS) rental cabins. Chugach's most noted fishery, however, is the red salmon run of the Russian River. In July and early August, anglers are often standing elbow to elbow along the riverbank in hope of catching a 60lb trophy.

Ghost Forests

The Good Friday Earthquake, the most powerful ever recorded in North America, shook Alaska on March 27, 1964, and not only killed more than 100 people and destroyed entire towns, it devastated much of Chugach National Forest and the surrounding areas.

The epicenter of the quake, which registered 9.2 on the Richter scale, was in the national forest near Miner's Lake, west of Columbia Glacier. Land to the east rose 6ft and on Montague Island 35ft, resulting in the death of millions of clams and other intertidal life. It also caused the destruction of waterfowl habitat on the Copper River Delta and ruined salmon access to spawning streams.

To the west, land sunk as far as 8ft, and incoming water literally drowned shoreline forests. The trees quickly died in the saltwater, but their trunks remained standing and eventually were bleached by the sun to form 'ghost forests.' Many stands of these stark, lifeless trees can still be seen along Turnagain Arm between Girdwood and Portage. You can also hike through a ghost forest on the Coastal Trail in Caines Head State Recreation Area if you leave the campground at Tonsina Point and begin following the shoreline of Resurrection Bay at low tide.

CLIMATE

The Prince William Sound portion of the national forest has a maritime climate and weather patterns similar to Southeast Alaska. The Kenai Peninsula has cool and often overcast summers but not as much rain as either of those areas. Annual precipitation is 27 to 30 inches. The daytime high in July is 66°F but at night it drops to 40°F. Like in the Anchorage area, you can count on 17 to 19 hours of daylight each summer day.

INFORMATION

In Anchorage, you can pick up information about the national forest and its campgrounds and trails at the Alaska Public

KENAI PENINSULA

Lands Information Center (☎ 271-2737) on 4th Ave and F St or from the USFS district office in Girdwood (☎ 783-3242).

The trails covered here, however, are under the jurisdiction of the Seward Ranger District, making the office in Seward the best source of information. The USFS district office (☎ 224-3374) is at the corner of 4th Ave and Jefferson St and is open from 8 am to 5 pm Monday through Friday. No permits are needed to hike USFS trails, nor are there any fees or special regulations.

Johnson Pass Trail

Duration 2 to 3 days
Distance 23mi
Difficulty Level Medium
Start Mile 64 of the Seward Hwy
Finish Mile 32.5 of the Seward Hwy
Cabins & Shelters No
Permits Required No
Public Transportation Yes
Summary This popular, two-day-long traverse takes you across a 1550ft pass that follows portions of the original Iditarod Trail. Good public transportation to and from both trailheads is an added feature.

This 23mi trail is an overnight trek over its 1550ft namesake pass in the Kenai Mountains. It was built in the 1890s as part of the Iditarod Trail from Seward to the Interior goldfields, and sections of the original route can still be seen. Today, Johnson Pass is as much a trail for mountain bikers as it is for hikers; cyclists have increased traffic on the trail considerably in recent years.

Most bikers can cover the trail in seven to 10 hours, but hikers should plan on two days, with an alpine camp at either Johnson Pass or Johnson Lake. The trail can be hiked in either direction, but you endure less climbing by beginning at the northern trailhead. Johnson Pass is rated moderate, and for the most part, it is a gradual climb to the pass with a few steep sections.

PLANNING
When to Hike
At 1550ft, Johnson Pass is above the tree line, making mid-June through September the best season for this hike.

What to Bring
Because Johnson Lake and Johnson Pass are above the tree line, it is necessary to carry a small stove if you camp there. Purchase all your equipment and supplies in Anchorage, even your noodle dinners and instant oatmeal. One-stop service stations/motels/stores along the highways will be able to supply food and white gas for the stove (at a very steep Alaskan price) but little else.

Maps
The trail is covered on United States Geological Survey (USGS) 1:63,360 series quads *Seward C-6* and *C-7*. A better and cheaper map is *Kenai National Wildlife Refuge* by National Geographic's Trails Illustrated ($10), which is printed on waterproof plastic-coated paper and covers the western half of the Chugach National Forest, including Johnson Pass, Resurrection Pass and Russian Lakes Trails.

It's best to buy your maps in Anchorage (see the Anchorage chapter). Some gift shops and stores along the highway sell maps but never, it seems, the sections you want.

NEAREST TOWNS & FACILITIES
Northern Trailhead
Scattered along the Seward and Sterling Hwys are a number of motels, lodges and, in particular, campgrounds. A mile before the northern trailhead is the ***Bertha Creek USFS Campground***, just past Mile 65 of the Seward Hwy, State Rte 1, with 12 sites ($9) on the banks of the creek. You can spend a day climbing the alpine slopes surrounding the campground here. Less than a mile south of the trailhead is the ***Granite Creek USFS Campground***, at Mile 63 of the Seward Hwy, with 18 sites for $9 per night. (See the Information section earlier in this chapter for USFS contact details.)

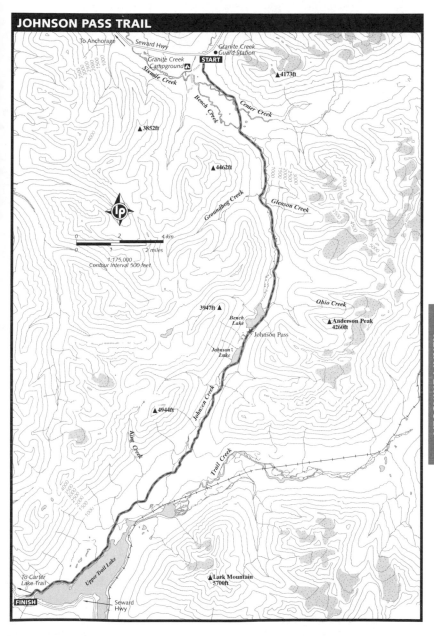

Moose Pass

Less than 3mi from the southern trailhead at Mile 29.4 of the Seward Hwy is the village of Moose Pass (population 200), on the banks of the Upper Trail Lake. Moose Pass has a general store and bar, a handful of B&Bs and *Trail Lake Lodge* (☎ 288-3103). The recently remodeled lodge features a restaurant, 35 rooms that begin at $89 for single or double with a shared bath, showers, Laundromat and a salmon bake on the shores of the lake during the summer. Just down the road is *Moose Pass RV Park* with sites that overlook the lake for $12 a night.

GETTING TO/FROM THE HIKE

Johnson Pass Trail conveniently begins and ends near the Seward Hwy. Just past Mile 64 heading south is the USFS sign pointing to the Granite Creek trailhead at the northern end of Johnson Pass Trail, where a dirt road leads almost half a mile to a parking area. The southern trailhead is at Mile 32.5 of Seward Hwy, near the fish hatchery at Upper Trail Lake. Moose Pass is less than 3mi to the south.

You can reach the trailheads by bus, hitchhiking or renting a car in Anchorage (see the Anchorage chapter). Several bus companies provide transportation along the Seward Hwy, including Seward Bus Lines (☎ 563-0800, 224-3608). In Seward the buses depart the depot at 1915 Seward Hwy at 9 am daily, reaching the Anchorage depot at 3339 Fairbanks St at noon then departing at 2:30 pm for the return trip. One-way fare between the two cities is $30. Departing Anchorage at 8 am for Seward are vans for Alaska Park Connection (☎ 245-0200, 800-208-0200) and Kachemak Bay Transit (☎ 235-3795, 877-235-9101). Both charge about $35 for a one-way trip and will also drop you off at the trailheads along Seward Hwy.

THE HIKE
Stage 1: Granite Creek Trailhead to Johnson Lake

11mi, 6 to 8 hours

From the northern end, Johnson Pass Trail begins as a somewhat level hike through the forest and a few open meadows. Within 2.2mi, after an hour or so of hiking, you cross **Center Creek** on a bridge and then begin climbing. The trail rises steadily, reaches **Bench Creek** and crosses a bridge over it at 3.8mi and then makes a steep ascent up a rocky hill to pass a waterfall 4mi from the Granite Creek trailhead.

You now enter a steep, V-shaped valley where the trail follows Bench Creek on its west side and gains 200ft before crossing **Groundhog Creek** at 5.2mi. Groundhog Creek was the site of an early mining operation, when the route was known as Sunrise Trail. You can still see a bench-cut wagon road here. Beyond Groundhog Creek, the trail crosses to the east side of Bench Creek and continues to climb steadily, reaching **Ohio Creek** at 9mi. At Ohio Creek, you'll pass a stone monument dedicated to Paul Anderson, a forester who died in an accidental explosion while trying to divert a glacial stream from Bench Lake in an effort to improve its fishery.

In the next half mile, you gain 100ft as you climb to the 1500ft high point of the trail and then emerge at the north end of **Bench Lake**. The lake is above the tree line in a mountainous alpine setting where it's easy to scramble the open slopes in almost any direction. You can fish here for grayling or spend the night at a shoreline campsite. Bench Lake makes a much more scenic spot to camp than Johnson Lake.

The trail continues along the east shore of the lake and remains above the timberline to enter **Johnson Pass** and, from there, descends gently to **Johnson Lake** at 1300ft. At the south end of the lake, 11mi from the Granite Creek trailhead, there is a backcountry campsite where the trail returns to the tree line. The lake supports rainbow trout and makes a good base camp from which you can spend a day climbing the surrounding ridges and peaks.

Stage 2: Johnson Lake to Upper Trail Lake Trailhead

12mi, 5 to 7 hours

From Johnson Lake, the trail heads south in a forest setting and steadily loses elevation.

You remain close to **Johnson Creek** along its east side but rarely see the water through the foliage.

After descending more than 400ft, you arrive at the creek, cross it 15.7mi from the northern trailhead and then leave the creek behind for good. Within an hour of steady hiking you cross **King Creek**, and at 19.4mi from the northern trailhead (almost 9mi from Johnson Lake), you break out of the woods at

Iditarod National Historic Trail

Although best known as the route for the world's most famous sled dog race, the Iditarod is actually a network of more than 2,300mi of trails spanning the state from Seward to Nome and recently designated by the US Congress as a National Historic Trail.

Ingalik and Tanaina Indians established the original routes for trade and commerce, but it was gold seekers stampeding to their fortunes in Nome and other places at the turn of the century who turned the trails into a highway through the wilderness. During the summer, the Yukon River teemed with steamers and barges of mining operations, but in the winter, the traffic shifted to the Iditarod. Always seeking the easiest route, miners preferred traveling in the winter when the brush was covered with snow,

the bugs were gone and frozen lakes and rivers made ideal highways. At times these trails were as crowded as a main street in a town. Use of the trail peaked after gold was discovered in 1908 near Iditarod, an Athabascan Indian village on the Iditarod River. The US Army surveyed the trail in 1910, stuck the name of Iditarod on it and used it as a major route until 1924, when the airplanes came into use.

In 1925, the Iditarod captured the attention of the country when a diphtheria epidemic threatened Nome at a time when the community was low on serum to inoculate its residents. Bad weather thwarted plans to send the medical supplies by plane, so instead 20 mushers and a relay of dog teams volunteered. The mushers carried the serum 674mi from Nenana to Nome in just over 127 hours.

Nome was saved; the mushers became heroes; and President Calvin Coolidge awarded medals to everybody. The era of the sled dog went out in a blaze of glory with Balto, the lead dog of the finishing team, immortalized in statues across the country.

The trail was a forgotten part of Alaska's history until 1967, when the first Iditarod sled dog race was staged on 9mi of the original route between Knik and Big Lake. In 1973 the race was expanded to an event between Anchorage and Nome. Since then the 1049mi Iditarod has been held every year in March and has become known around the world as 'the last great race.'

The most popular section of the trail for hikers is the 26mi stretch from Crow Pass in Chugach National Forest to the Eagle River Nature Center north of Anchorage in Chugach State Park. Other sections that can be hiked include Johnson Pass Trail, stretches from Seward to the north and the final 40mi segment from Solomon to Nome.

KENAI PENINSULA

the shores of Upper Trail Lake near its northern end.

The remaining 3.5mi is an easy and pleasant walk along a wide path that skirts the western shoreline of the large lake. Depending on your mood (energetic hiker or gatherer of sunshine), it's a 1½- to two-hour hike along the shoreline to the Upper Trail Lake trailhead near the southern end of the lake on Seward Hwy.

Resurrection Pass Trail

Duration 4 days
Distance 38.5mi
Difficulty Level Easy
Start Hope
Finish Cooper Landing
Cabins & Shelters Yes
Permits Required No
Public Transportation No
Summary Located in the Chugach National Forest, this trail was originally carved by prospectors in the late 1800s and today is the most popular hiking route on the Kenai Peninsula. Highlights are the alpine beauty of the region, a string of rental cabins, and fishing opportunities in Trout, Juneau and Swan Lakes.

What was cut in the 1890s by gold miners trying to find a way from Resurrection Bay to their riches in the Hope goldfields, is today the most popular multiday trail in the Kenai Peninsula. The Resurrection Pass Trail is a 38.5mi trek from the northern trailhead near Hope, across the 3400ft pass and then down along Juneau Creek Valley to the Sterling Hwy near Cooper Landing. The southern trailhead is practically across the highway from the start of the Russian Lakes Trail. The Russian Lakes Trail intersects the Resurrection River Trail, which ends at Exit Glacier near Seward. Together, the three trails provide the hardy trekker with a seven- to 10-day journey on foot from Hope to Seward. (See the Russian Lakes & Resurrection River Trails section

for details on the last two stages of this hike.)

Designated a national recreation trail, the Resurrection Pass Trail is a well-maintained and well-posted path that is also well used. Along with backpackers, you might encounter day hikers, cabin renters who were flown in, mountain bikers and, after June 30, horseback riders (the trail is closed to horses and pack animals from April through June). The popularity of the trail is also evident in how difficult it is to reserve one of the eight cabins along the trail, which can be booked 179 days in advance (see Cabins & Shelters).

Although there are some switchback sections, overall the trail gradually climbs and descends the alpine areas surrounding Resurrection Pass and is rated easy. You can start from either direction, though you save 100ft of climbing to the pass by beginning your trip at Hope. Strong hikers can cover the distance in three days, the average walker in four days. Even families have few problems going from end to end in five days, if the children are properly prepared and equipped.

Staying in the cabins is a pleasant treat during the hike and well worth the effort of reserving them in advance. But there is no lack of camping spots along trail, and the USFS even maintains a series of 13 backcountry campsites that feature a tent pad and fire ring in each. Each site lies off the trail and away from the cabins, for a bit of privacy, and is marked along the route by a four-by-four post. The campsites are posted areas and are maintained by the USFS because they are in a national forest. There are no fees for their use nor can you reserve them in advance (unlike the cabins).

For those hikers wishing to skip the trip to Hope, you can access the Resurrection Pass Trail via Devil's Pass Trail. This 10mi spur begins along Seward Hwy, solving some of your transportation problems, and climbs over a 2400ft gap to reach Resurrection Pass Trail just south of its pass. Devil's Pass is rated medium to hard, and is described in a side trip after stage three of this hike.

PLANNING
When to Hike
Like Johnson Pass Trail, the best season for hiking the Resurrection Pass Trail is mid-June through September.

What to Bring
Despite the fire rings at campsites, you should still pack a stove, especially if you plan to spend a night above the alpine area. Also bring a rod and reel, as most of the lakes have several species of fish.

Maps
Most of the trail is covered on USGS 1:63,360 series quads *Seward C-8* and *D-8*, with the exception of the first 2mi from the southern trailhead, which is on *Seward B-8*. If you plan to enter or depart along Devil's Pass Trail, you'll also need *Seward C-7*. A cheaper alternative is *Kenai National Wildlife Refuge* by Trails Illustrated ($10), which includes Resurrection Pass.

Cabins & Shelters
There are more than 40 cabins in Chugach National Forest, including a series of eight USFS cabins along the route. Devil's Pass, East Creek, Fox Creek and Caribou Creek cost $35 per night; Swan Lake, Juneau Lake, Romig and Trout Lake are $45. They have to be reserved in advance by calling the National Recreation Reservation Center (☎ 518-885-3639, 877-444-6777) or through its Web site (www.reserveusa.com). Don't count on any cabins being empty. The cabins are extremely popular and usually fully booked through the summer.

NEAREST TOWNS
Hope
Hope serves as the gateway to the northern trailhead of the Resurrection Pass Trail. The village maintains an excellent Web site (www.advenalaska.com/hope) that offers additional information on lodging and services.

Hope has a post office, general store, Laundromat and a couple of lodges and cafes. It even has a small mining museum on the main street, Hope Rd. It's better and far cheaper to pick up all your supplies and equipment in either Anchorage or Seward.

Places to Stay & Eat The USFS maintains *Porcupine Campground*, 1.3mi beyond Hope at the end of the Hope Hwy, which has 24 sites for $9 a night. The campground has well-spread-out sites, a scenic overlook to watch the tide roll in and trailheads to Hope Point and Gull Rock. But beware: the place is often full on weekends (and sometimes even in the middle of the week). There is also the *Coeur d'Alene USFS Campground*, 7mi down Palmer Creek Rd, with five free sites, and camping sites around the trailhead on Resurrection Creek Rd.

You can get a meal, beer, shower and room for $60 for two people at *Henry's One Stop* (☎ 782-3222), near town at the junction of Resurrection Creek Rd and the Hope Hwy. Next door is *Bear Creek Lodge* (☎ 782-3141), a scenic resort in the woods with a small restaurant, a scattering of cabins and even a replica of an old log cache. Each of the five restored, hand-hewn log cabins along the creek cost $75 a night. The most affordable accommodations in the area are off Resurrection Rd at *Raven Hill B&B* (☎ 786-3411,) which has a bunkhouse for six people for $16.50 per night. The place is hard to find so call ahead for directions.

Near Porcupine Campground is *Davidson Enterprises*, a general store that sells groceries, gasoline and liquor. At the *Seaview Cafe*, in the heart of Hope, you can get a plate of ribs or chicken for $11 and wash it down with a beer. Hope's favorite restaurant was the *Discovery Cafe* – 'where the goldminers meet and eat' – but it burned to the ground in January 1999. The locals immediately began to rebuild and planned to reopen sometime in 2000.

Getting There & Away The Seward Hwy is the portion of State Rte 1 that runs from Anchorage down to the junction with State Rte 9. At the junction, Rte 1 becomes the Sterling Hwy, which goes west across the entire Kenai Peninsula and ends up at the southern tip, in Homer.

All of Rte 9, which goes south to Seward, is known as the Seward Hwy.

To reach the town of Hope, leave the Seward Hwy/Rte 1 at Mile 56.7, head north on the Hope Hwy, and turn right on Hope Rd at Mile 16.5. There's no public transportation to Hope, but hitchhiking to the town is rarely a problem.

Cooper Landing

Stretched along several miles of the Sterling Hwy (State Rte 1), which was the Seward Hwy until the junction with State Rte 9, this service center at Mile 48.7 is named after a miner who worked the area in the 1880s. Cooper Landing is the main commercial area near the southern trailhead of Resurrection Pass and the trailheads for the Russian Lakes Trail.

Places to Stay & Eat To the west of Cooper Landing is *Cooper Creek USFS Campground*, Mile 50.7 Sterling Hwy, with 27 sites ($9) on both sides of the highway. The final national forest campground is *Russian River USFS Campground*, Mile 52.8 of Sterling Hwy. This is a beautiful spot where the Russian and Kenai Rivers merge, and its 84 sites ($11) are the most popular ones by far. Both the Cooper Creek and Russian River Campgrounds lie on prime red-salmon spawning areas, and the campsites tend to fill up by noon in late summer. A mile along the campground road is the trailhead for the Russian Lakes Trail and practically across the highway is the southern trailhead for Resurrection Pass.

Nearby is *Gwin's Lodge* (☎ 595-1266), Mile 52 of Sterling Hwy, a classic Alaskan roadhouse. The log lodge was built in 1952 and features a cafe, bar and liquor store. Next to the lodge is the old Russian River ferry, preserved like a monument to the red salmon run that draws hundreds of anglers to the Russian River from June through July. The lodge has log cabins at $99/104 singles/doubles at peak season, and rustic fisher's cabins that sleep four and are $40 a night.

Along with a five-building national historic district in Cooper Landing, which includes the colorful Old Cooper Landing Store, there is *Hamilton's Place* (☎ 595-1260). It has rooms for $80, a restaurant, food store and, maybe most importantly, a Laundromat and public showers. There is even a tent area with sites for $10. To the east is *Sunrise Inn* (☎ 595-1222), at Mile 45 of Sterling Hwy, which has a restaurant, bar and RV sites. Motel rooms cost $79 a single/double.

B&B accommodations in the area include the *Kenai River B&B* (☎ 595-1712), Mile 49 of the Sterling Hwy, with two large suites with kitchenettes. A double is $125 per night. *The Hutch B&B* (☎ 595-1270), Mile 48.5 in Cooper Landing, is a 12-room bed and breakfast with doubles ranging from $60 to $75 a night.

Getting There & Away Kachemak Bay Transit (☎ 235-3795, 877-235-9101) has a van that departs Anchorage at 8 am and passes through Cooper Landing at 11:30 am on its way to Homer. In the other direction, the van leaves Homer at 9 am and reaches Cooper Landing at 12:30 am on its way to Anchorage. The one-way fare from Cooper Landing to Anchorage is $40 and to Homer is $30.

Historic buildings in Cooper Landing

KENAI PENINSULA

JIM DUFRESNE

GETTING TO/FROM THE HIKE
To the Start
At Mile 16 of the Hope Hwy, turn left on Resurrection Creek Rd. Four miles down Resurrection Creek Rd, at Resurrection Creek, is the trailhead and parking area. You can also inquire at Hamilton's Place in Cooper Landing (see Places to Stay & Eat) about hiring a local to drive you to the northern trailhead.

The trailhead for Devil's Pass Trail is at Mile 39.4 of the Seward Hwy.

From the Finish
The southern trailhead is a quarter mile west of the Russian River Campground at Mile 52 of the Sterling Hwy. Kachemak Bay Transit (☎ 235-3795, 877-235-9101) provides a drop-off and pickup service at the southern trailhead on its Homer-Anchorage run; see the Getting There & Away section for details.

THE HIKE
Stage 1: Northern Trailhead to Caribou Creek
7.1mi, 4 to 5 hours
In the parking area for the trailhead, there is an information display and a log book where you can write your travel plans. The hike begins with a bridge over **Resurrection Creek** and then skirts the west side of the stream along a mining claim road. Within a quarter mile, you pass a bridge to the east side, where Mountain Bike Alaska (☎ 248-7301) rents bikes for $25 a day.

The first leg of the hike is an easy 2mi stroll through lush spruce forest and tracts of aspen, until the spot where Rimrock Creek flows into Resurrection Creek. Here, the mining road swings right into a private claim, and the trail crosses **Rimrock Creek** on a bridge and continues on the other side as a true footpath. Within a half mile you arrive at the first posted camping area, a pair of sites overlooking the river.

The trail remains on the west side of Resurrection Creek and begins a long steady climb that tops off at a clearing overlooking a stretch of white water. At 5.5mi from the trailhead, you cross **Wolf Creek** and reach

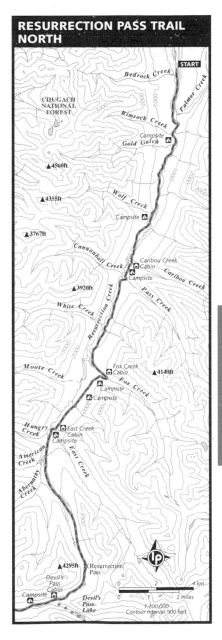

RESURRECTION PASS TRAIL NORTH

KENAI PENINSULA

another set of backcountry campsites. Within a half mile, the trail tops 1000ft, levels out and winds through an area that was the site of a forest fire, with some trees burned pitch black. This scarred area lasts all the way to Caribou Creek and is part of a moose habitat improvement project by the USFS. Interpretive signs will explain why the spruce forest was burned to bring back birch, aspen and willow, the preferred food of moose.

Almost 7mi from the trailhead, you recross Resurrection Creek on a bridge and then quickly reach Caribou Creek and a spur to the first USFS cabin. At 1000ft, **Caribou Creek Cabin** is a 12-by-14ft cabin with bunks for six people and a woodstove. The cabin is still in the tree line but sits on an open bluff overlooking the Resurrection River and the mountains to the west. Just up the trail are the posted campsites on the Caribou Creek itself.

Stage 2: Caribou Creek to Resurrection Pass

12.1mi, 6 to 8 hours

You remain on the east side of the creek and begin the day with a gradual climb up the valley. You gain 1200ft in this stage of the hike, but the majority of the elevation is accomplished in the first 2mi.

Within a mile the trail levels out to cross **Pass Creek** on a bridge then resumes climbing a bit steeper. After you cross a scenic bridge, the hiking gets easier and much more scenic as the trail reaches 1500ft. Here you sidle a bluff above Resurrection Creek, moving from the thinning spruce to the brushy vegetation of subalpine flora. The raspberry bushes that you have been feasting on up to this point give way now to blueberries.

About 7mi from Caribou Creek, or 10mi from the trailhead, you begin a descent as the trail swings east into the Fox Creek Valley. Eventually you reach a bridge over the creek; on the other side are the remains of an old cabin in a setting that makes for a photographer's delight. Resurrection Pass Trail continues south on the other side of the bridge. The spur that continues leading up the creek ends at **Fox Creek Cabin**, reached 11.5mi from the trailhead. Like Caribou Creek Cabin, this cabin has bunks for six people and a woodstove, but it sits 700ft higher. There is also a campsite posted nearby.

The gentle climb up Resurrection Valley continues, and within a mile, you'll pass a pair of posted campsites tucked out of view of the trail. Within the next mile, you descend an unnamed stream, climb steeply out of its ravine and then skirt the ridge above the Resurrection River for the final mile to East Creek. Along the way you pass a pair of old mileage signs, '13' and '14,' and then descend to East Creek, reaching **East Creek Cabin** at 14.4mi. The cabin is identical to the first two and is in a scenic spot near the confluence of Resurrection and East Creeks. At 2200ft, the surrounding trees are sparse and stunted. You'll often see Dall sheep on the ridges above.

The trail quickly crosses **East Creek** via a bridge and passes a series of campsites that line the stream before it makes a short but steep climb. Within 2mi you have climbed 300ft to arrive at the **headwaters of Resurrection Creek**, where American Creek, Abernathy Creek and an unnamed creek merge. Here you clear the last few stunted spruce and enter alpine country where the views of the surrounding mountains improve with every step. You cross the unnamed stream to make the final climb to the pass. On a good day, the next 3mi to the pass is a spectacular stretch. In the beginning, the trail climbs between two streams, and the surrounding tundra will be alive with wildflowers.

Hiking between a pair of 4000ft peaks, you'll reach **Resurrection Pass** 2½ hours from the East Creek Cabin, 19.3mi from the northern trailhead. It is posted. Good camping spots abound in the 2600ft pass, and an extra day could be spent here climbing the surrounding ridges or hiking across a saddle to the southeast to reach the East Creek drainage area. All the whistling you hear is marmots signaling to each other. Sit quietly long enough, and they will eventually come out of their holes out of curiosity.

If you prefer staying at a campsite, the next one is 2.2mi away, or a quarter mile south of Devil's Pass Cabin along the Resurrection Pass Trail.

Stage 3: Resurrection Pass to Swan Lake
6.5mi, 3 to 4 hours

This is a short day of hiking. Either enjoy the morning in the alpine area or make a side trip up Devil's Pass Trail without your pack. From Resurrection Pass, you quickly reach the headwaters of **Juneau Creek** and then skirt the ridge on the creek's west side. Eventually the trail begins to swing to the southwest, and within 2mi, you climb over a low rise to reach the junction with **Devil's Pass Trail**. Nearby is a USFS cabin.

Above the tree line at 2400ft, **Devil's Pass Cabin** is in a spectacular mountain setting. The A-frame unit sits near the confluence of Juneau and Devil's Creeks. It has bunks for six people but can sleep quite a few more in the loft. Unlike the other USFS cabins, it is not stocked with firewood, so there is no woodstove. This is a good place to search for Dall sheep on the surrounding ridges.

From the junction with Devil's Pass Trail, Resurrection Pass Trail continues its gradual descent. Within a quarter mile, you arrive at a set of posted campsites on a knob overlooking a series of beaver ponds. The view is nice because the sites are still above the tree line. You cross Juneau Creek three times in the first 2mi, and after the third time you come into view of Juneau Lake in the valley below. At this point the trail begins a steeper descent into the timberline and to Swan Creek. Just before the descent, you pass a series of posted campsites on an edge of a knob overlooking Swan Lake. There's a great view from any of the sites, but the nearest water is a good walk away.

For 2mi you endure switchbacks as you drop from almost 2500ft to 1400ft. Along the way you pass a pair of junctions to Swan Lake, almost a half mile apart. The second is a half-mile spur that heads to **Swan Lake Cabin**, reached 4.4mi beyond Devil's Pass or 26mi from the northern trailhead. You also pass a backcountry campsite.

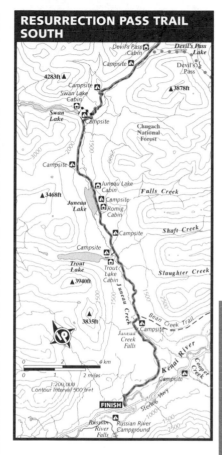

Swan Lake is a six-bunk cabin overlooking the east end of its namesake lake. A boat is provided and the lake is considered fair for rainbow trout, Dolly Varden and, if you can troll deep enough, lake trout.

Side Trip: Devil's Pass Trail
2mi, 1 hour

This trail heads east from Devil's Pass Cabin and leads 10mi to Mile 39 of the Seward Hwy. It can be used to access or depart Resurrection Pass Trail or to explore the surrounding alpine valleys. The trail is well maintained but can be muddy and wet at times due to the creeks and run-off that cross it.

The trail is rated medium to hard in difficulty, and the first 8mi from the Seward Hwy trailhead is a steady climb to Devil's Pass (2400ft).

If you're just sticking to Resurrection Pass Trail, the first 2mi of Devil's Pass Trail from its west end is an easy and interesting side trip. From the cabin, it's roughly a mile to Devil's Pass Lake, where you can fish for Dolly Varden. Continuing east from the lake it's a gradual climb to the pass.

Stage 4: Swan Lake to Sterling Hwy
12.8mi, 6 to 7 hours

From the junction to Swan Lake, the trail stays above Juneau Creek as it makes a very gradual descent, providing sweeping views of the valley. Within 2mi, you quickly descend the ridge to bottom out at a spur that leads to backcountry campsites reached just before the bridge over Juneau Creek. The spur climbs a knoll at the north end of Juneau Lake to a series of sites that overlook the water. From these sites, the sunrise is stunning on a clear morning.

Within a quarter mile from the bridge, or 3mi from the second Swan Lake junction, Resurrection Pass Trail reaches the northern end of **Juneau Lake**. You skirt the edge of the lake for a third of a mile before reaching the first of two USFS cabins. The original **Juneau Lake Cabin** was a classic, complete with moose antlers above the door. It burned down in 1997 but was rebuilt a year later by volunteers. The new structure is the standard 12-by-14ft unit with six bunks, a woodstove and a boat. A quarter mile past Juneau Lake Cabin are a pair of backcountry campsites. The lake has rainbow trout, grayling and lake trout, but the fishing can be spotty at times. A half mile down the shore from Juneau Lake Cabin is **Romig Cabin**, identical to Juneau Lake Cabin. Overlooking the water and surrounding mountains, both cabins are popular and difficult to reserve.

From Juneau Lake, the trail stays on the east side of Juneau Creek and continues down the valley in a spruce and aspen forest, passing a backcountry campsite at **Falls Creek**, a good size stream. The hike remains level and easy, and in less than 2mi from Romig Cabin, you come to the junction with a spur to **Trout Lake**. The half-mile side trail first crosses Juneau Creek, passes a backcountry campsite and then ends at the last USFS cabin. **Trout Lake Cabin** is an A-frame structure with a loft and woodstove. It overlooks a small cove at the eastern end of the lake and has a boat. The fishing is fair for rainbow trout.

The remaining 7mi to Sterling Hwy begins as a level walk through the woods. You remain on the east side of Juneau Creek and pass a pair of backcountry campsites before using a bridge to cross **Shaft Creek**, half a mile past the junction to Trout Lake. Another third of a mile down the trail you cross **Slaughter Creek**.

The easy and scenic hiking continues for the next 2mi as you head south and reach the posted junction with the **Bean Creek Trail**, a primitive route that heads southeast to Slaughter Ridge Rd. Past the junction, Resurrection Pass Trail heads right to quickly descend to Juneau Creek. You cross it on an impressive footbridge and then arrive at **Juneau Falls**. The falls, a five- to six-hour walk of 9mi from Swan Creek, is a roaring cascade at the head of a steep gorge. It's a scenic spot for a long break.

You are now only 4.5mi or 1½ hours from the southern trailhead and the Sterling Hwy. The trail continues south and skirts the gorge for 1.5mi and then swings west. This stretch can be somewhat demoralizing to hikers at the end of a four-day walk. At one point they can see the **Kenai River** and even hear trucks roaring through on Sterling Hwy, leading them to believe the end is near. It isn't. The trail stays on the edge of the bluff above the Kenai River for another 2mi before descending sharply in the final mile via a series of switchbacks.

At the trailhead there are a parking lot, toilets and a large display sign. Less than a mile to the east on the Sterling Hwy is Gwin's Lodge, where you can get a meal or a cold beer.

Russian Lakes & Resurrection River Trails

Duration 2 days
Distance 21.6mi
Difficulty Level Easy
Start Russian River Campground
Finish Snug Harbor Rd
Cabins & Shelters Yes
Permits Required No
Public Transportation Yes
Summary The Russian Lakes Trail is a well-maintained and well-traveled trail that is an ideal alternative for those who do not want to overextend themselves in the Chugach National Forest. Highlights include the possibility of viewing moose or bears, the impressive glaciated mountains across from Upper Russian Lake and the chance for anglers to catch their own dinner.

Practically across the Sterling Hwy from the southern end of Resurrection Pass Trail is the access road to the USFS Russian River Campground and the trailhead to Russian Lakes Trail. For ambitious hikers, this is the second stage of the seven- to 10-day journey from Hope to Seward. You leave the trail 16mi from the western trailhead for the final leg of the journey – a very challenging 16mi hike to Exit Glacier (outside Seward) along the Resurrection River Trail.

For most hikers, however, the Russian Lakes Trail is an easy and pleasant overnight trip, either following it from Russian River to Cooper Lake or using it to reach a USFS cabin or campsite then backtracking to their vehicles. The 21.6mi trail is a well-maintained footpath that receives moderate to heavy use during the summer. You gain 1000ft, but the climb is very gradual and overall this trail is rated easy – an ideal one for families. Much of the time you're hiking in forest, but views of the surrounding mountains, streams and the two Russian Lakes are common along the route.

Keep in mind that Russian River provides the largest sport fishery in Alaska for

sockeye salmon during two runs. In mid-June and again in mid-July to early August, the river will be lined with anglers, many of whom you'll see on the first leg of the trail. Mountain bikers are also common. Along with the salmon, other wildlife that you might see include moose and bears. With a keen eye, or a set of binoculars, you'll also possibly see mountain goats and Dall sheep on the ridges above.

The hiking is actually easier if you begin from the Cooper Lake trailhead at the east end of the trail. The trail, however, will be described in the other direction – by far the most popular route.

PLANNING
When to Hike
A low elevation trail, Russian Lakes can be hiked from late May through early October.

What to Bring
See the Resurrection Pass Trail section earlier in this chapter, as well as the Planning section of the Facts for the Hiker chapter, for general guidelines on what to bring for this hike. If you like to fish, and don't want to rely solely on trout tickling, you should bring a rig for this hike, as there are many good spots to cast your line.

Maps
With the exception of a half-mile section that spills over onto *Kenai B-1*, the entire trail is covered on the USGS 1:63,360 series quad *Seward B-8*. The area featuring Resurrection River Trail is on quads *Seward B-8, A-7* and *A-8*, but the trail itself is not marked on the topos. The entire trail system (except Resurrection Pass Trail) is covered on Trails Illustrated's map *Kenai Fjords National Park and Chugach NF* ($10).

Cabins & Shelters
There are three USFS cabins and some backcountry campsites at Lower and Upper Russian Lakes. Barber Cabin is $45 a night; Aspen Flats and Upper Russian Lake are $35. All of them must be reserved well in advance (see the Cabins & Shelters section of Resurrection Pass Trail).

KENAI PENINSULA

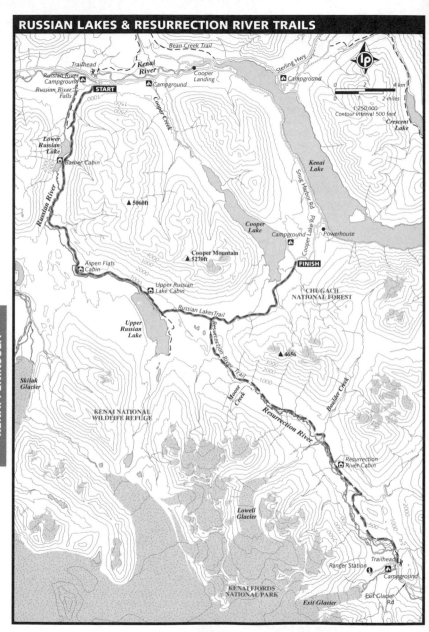

RUSSIAN LAKES & RESURRECTION RIVER TRAILS

Bean Creek Trail

Kenai River

Trailhead

Russian River Campground

Russian River Falls

START

Campground

Cooper Landing

Sterling Hwy

Campground

0   2   4 km
0   1   2 miles
1:250,000
Contour interval 500 feet

Crescent Lake

Cooper Creek

Lower Russian Lake

Barber Cabin

Russian River

▲ 5060ft

Kenai Lake

Snug Harbor Rd

Cooper Lake

Campground

Cooper Lake Rd

Powerhouse

Aspen Flats Cabin

Upper Russian Lake Cabin

Cooper Mountain
▲ 5270ft

FINISH

Russian Lakes Trail

CHUGACH NATIONAL FOREST

Upper Russian Lake

Resurrection River Trail

▲ 4656

KENAI PENINSULA

Skilak Glacier

KENAI NATIONAL WILDLIFE REFUGE

Moose Creek

Resurrection River

Boulder Creek

Resurrection River Cabin

Lowell Glacier

Ranger Station

Trailhead

Campground

KENAI FJORDS NATIONAL PARK

Exit Glacier

Exit Glacier Rd

NEAREST TOWNS & FACILITIES

Cooper Landing is the nearest town; see that section earlier in this chapter for details on Places to Stay & Eat in this area.

GETTING TO/FROM THE HIKE
To the Start

The western trailhead is in the Russian River Campground at Mile 52.8 of the Sterling Hwy, where the Russian and Kenai Rivers merge. A mile down Russian River Campground Rd is the trailhead and parking area for the Russian Lakes Trail.

From the Finish

The eastern trailhead of the Russian Lakes Trail is considerably harder to reach. After crossing the Kenai River bridge, immediately turn south on Snug Harbor Rd at Mile 48 of the Sterling Hwy. Follow this road for 12mi to reach the trailhead and parking area. Most hikers who find themselves at Snug Harbor Rd have little choice but to hitch and hike the 12mi to the trailhead.

After completing the hike, to return to the public bus that runs along Sterling Hwy, follow Snug Harbor Rd (also labeled Cooper Lake Rd) as it heads east for 3mi and then north for 9mi to Sterling Hwy. It can be challenging to thumb a ride on these roads, so you may end up hiking most of this stretch.

For those taking the challenging Resurrection River Trail (see stage 2B of the Russian Lakes Trail), the southern trailhead is posted on Exit Glacier Rd where it crosses the river, 7.4mi from the Seward Hwy. Exit Glacier Rd is 4mi north of Seward. For transportation to and from the southern trailhead of the Resurrection River Trail, see the van services listed under Seward in the Caines Head State Recreation Area section of this book.

THE HIKE
Stage 1: Russian River Campground to Upper Russian Lake

12mi, 7 to 8 hours

From the ranger station in the Russian River Campground, continue on the campground road for almost a mile to the well-marked trailhead. The first 2mi of the trail have been extensively rebuilt in recent years with boardwalks and viewing areas. The route follows the well-forested **Russian River**, but not always directly along the water. It does pass several scenic viewing points of the river, and angler's paths to popular fishing holes are numerous. The main trail, however, is well marked and easy to identify. During the salmon runs from mid-June to mid-July this stretch can be a traffic jam of anglers trying to cash in on the spawning sockeyes.

At 1.7mi from the trailhead, you come to a bridge over Rendezvous Creek and a junction. Here, the half-mile **Falls Trail** swings down to the river and then upstream to a pair of viewing platforms overlooking Russian River Falls. Beginning in mid-July, this is a great place to see spawning sockeye leaping out of the river in an effort to ascend the falls.

The Russian Lakes Trail crosses the bridge over **Rendezvous Creek** and continues south, where it comes to a second junction at 2.6mi. The right-hand fork skirts the shores

---

Tickling a Trout

Some sourdoughs claim you can catch a trout in Alaska even if you're not packing along a rod and reel by using a method called 'trout tickling.'

The object is to seduce the fish until you can grasp it with your hand and toss it onto the bank. The key is locating a trout or chasing one under a deadhead or an undercut bank in a small stream. Then slowly slip your hand into the water and under the trout. Old-timers claim the warmth of your hand on the belly of the trout will lull it into a relaxed state. You can then cup your hand around the fish and ease it out of the stream. When your hand reaches the surface, toss your dinner onto the bank and then grab the trout before it flops back into the water.

Does it work? Who knows. But the Alaska Department of Fish and Game says you still need a fishing license, no matter how you catch that trout.

KENAI PENINSULA

of **Lower Russian Lake** at one point and, 3.5mi from the trailhead, reaches **Barber Cabin**. Situated on the shores of Lower Russian Lake (fair to good for rainbow trout), the five-bunk cabin has a woodstove, wood supply, boat and dock. The cabin, including the vault toilet outside, has wheelchair facilities. Farther down the spur trail are backcountry campsites along the lake.

The main trail continues along the left-hand fork and heads almost due south, passing the southern end of the lake and paralleling **Upper Russian River**. In the next 6mi, you gently gain 200ft and move more into a subalpine setting of birch and hemlock forest. Eventually, 8.7mi from the Russian River trailhead, you reach **Aspen Flats Cabin**, the site of the second USFS cabin. Slightly smaller than Barber Cabin, Aspen Flats is a 12-by-14ft cabin that has six bunks and is reached by a quarter-mile spur off the main trail. Anglers fish this portion of the Upper Russian River for rainbow trout, Dolly Varden and even salmon.

At Aspen Flats, the trail swings to the east with the valley and continues its mild climb around Cooper Mountain (5270ft). The trail closely follows the Upper Russian River for a couple of miles, until you break out at **Upper Russian Lake** and wind along its shoreline briefly before reaching the third USFS cabin, 12mi from the trailhead. **Upper Russian Lake Cabin** is a rustic log cabin overlooking the water, with four bunks and a boat. Nearby are several posted campsites. Upper Russian Lake has excellent fishing; rainbow trout often range in size from 12 to 18 inches.

Stage 2A: Upper Russian Lake to Snug Harbor Rd

9.6mi, 5 to 6 hours

This section of the trail, to the Cooper Lake trailhead, was reworked in 1998. From the USFS cabin the trail continues to skirt the shoreline of Upper Russian Lake for more than a mile, until it reaches a three-way junction. One trail continues south along the lakeshore, but the main trail heads east over a rolling forested terrain. Within 2mi of leaving the lake, or 4mi from the USFS

cabin, you come to a posted junction of the **Resurrection River Trail**.

At the junction, Russian Lakes Trail continues east, winding through the wooded valley at the base of Cooper Mountain as it gradually climbs to the Cooper Lake trailhead (1300ft). A mile west of the junction with the Resurrection River Trail, or 5mi from Upper Russian Lake, you pass a posted campsite on a small lake.

In another mile the trail crosses an unnamed stream and half a mile beyond it swings northeast. In another 3mi you cross a second stream at the southern end of the lake. The final 1.5mi is a well-beaten path to the trailhead, reached 5.6mi from the junction with the Resurrection River Trail, or 10.6mi from the Upper Russian Lake Cabin.

This trailhead is far more isolated than the other the two trailheads, something to consider when planning your route. If you need to overnight here, head west on Snug Harbor Rd to a dispersed camping area on **Cooper Lake**.

Stage 2B: Resurrection River Trail

16mi, 9 to 10 hours

The Resurrection River Trail is, for the most part, a level path with only a gradual descent in the first few miles from its junction with Russian Lakes Trail. In 1995, floods severely damaged the trail from its junction with Russian Lakes Trail up to the USFS cabin, a stretch of 11mi. Due to budget cuts, the US Forest Service has not been able to repair the trail, including removing fallen trees and replacing two bridges that were washed out over Resurrection River and Boulder Creek. The southern half of the trail from the cabin onward has been repaired but still can be quite boggy, and the hiking is sloppy when it's raining. Keep this in mind if you're contemplating following the trail to Seward: It's a challenging hike for even experienced backpackers.

From the junction with Russian Lakes Trail, you begin by gently descending to the river to ford it near its headwaters and then follow the river valley the rest of the way, climbing only when the trail skirts the bordering ridges. Along the way, the trail passes several viewing points of the surrounding mountains before reaching the river near the confluence of **Moose Creek**.

You reach **Boulder Creek** 8.5mi south of the junction with Russian Lakes Trail and, in less than a mile, pass **Resurrection River Cabin**. The 12-by-14ft USFS cabin is one of the newer ones in the Kenai Peninsula and features six bunks and a woodstove. It's an excellent place to spend the night if you can reserve it; good camping spots are limited along the entire length of the trail.

From Boulder Creek, the trail continues parallel to the Resurrection River, though dense forest limits your views. The path is level but extremely boggy in most places, making the hike a slow and laborious process. Within 2mi, you reach the bridge over **Martin Creek**, and 6.5mi from the USFS cabin, you emerge at the trailhead where Exit Glacier Rd crosses the Resurrection River.

The ranger station is another mile west along the road and a free, walk-in campground managed by the National Park Service (NPS) is nearby. Head east on the road, and you'll reach the Seward Hwy in 8mi. During the summer it is fairly easy to hitch a ride into Seward because of the heavy volume of day visitors at Exit Glacier.

Primrose & Lost Lake Trails

Duration 2 days
Distance 15mi
Difficulty Level Medium
Start Primrose Landing Campground
Finish Lost Lake Subdivision
Cabins & Shelters Yes
Permits Required No
Public Transportation No
Summary A great scenic overnight hike to an alpine lake in the Kenai Mountains, this well-developed trail offers the possibility to spend an extra day exploring ridges above the tree line.

Two trails, Primrose and Lost Lake, depart from the Seward Hwy and join at Lost Lake to form one of the best overnight treks in Chugach National Forest. A good slice of this 15mi hike is spent above the tree line, where you can admire the stunning mountain scenery of the surrounding peaks. Camping is excellent at Lost Lake, and a spare day can be spent scrambling the ridges towards Mt Ascension, a 5710ft peak that forms the lake's western border.

You can hike the route in either direction, but the trip is described here beginning with the Primrose Trail, which saves you about 300ft of climbing. The USFS rates the use of these trails as light. Horses are prohibited from April through June, and the Primrose leg is not recommended for mountain bikes. The trails are closed to motorized activity, except to miners with permits; there are still some active mines along the Primrose Trail.

There is public transportation to both trailheads and excellent lodging in Seward.

PLANNING
When to Hike
Since this trail is an alpine traverse, the best season for hiking is late June through September. Snow lingers in the alpine areas into June, sometimes as late as early July if the winter has been especially brutal.

What to Bring
As with all hikes above the tree line, bring a stove and fuel for cooking. Turn to the Planning section in the Facts for the Hiker chapter for complete recommendations on what to bring.

Maps
This route is covered by the USGS 1:63,360 series quads *Seward B-7* and *A-7* and the Trails Illustrated map of *Kenai Fjords National Park and Chugach NF* ($10).

Cabins & Shelters
A spur off of Lost Lake Trail leads to USFS Dale Clemens Memorial Cabin, which rents for $45 a night and must be reserved in advance through the National Recreation Reservation Center (☎ 518-885-3639, 877-444-6777) or through the reservation

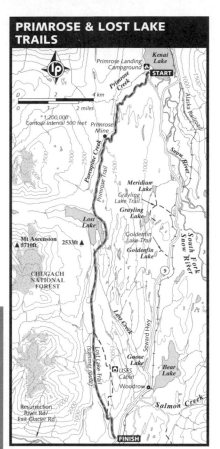

PRIMROSE & LOST LAKE TRAILS

Web site (www.reserveusa.com). There are no cabins along the Primrose Trail or at Lost Lake.

NEAREST TOWNS & FACILITIES

At the northern end of the trail, there is *Primrose Landing Campground* (10 sites, $9); at the southern end, Seward is only 5mi away. For information on Seward see the Caines Head State Recreation Area section later in this chapter. If you need information about the campground, there are a number of places to call, including Seward Ranger District (☎ 224-3374).

GETTING TO/FROM THE HIKE
To the Start

To reach the northern trailhead, turn off the Seward Hwy at Mile 17 and follow the signs for 1.5mi to Primrose Landing Campground. The well-posted trailhead is at the end of the campground access road, away from Kenai Lake. Any of the bus companies that provide service between Anchorage and Seward will drop you off on the Seward Hwy near Primrose Landing Campground. For bus information turn to Seward in the Caines Head State Recreation Area section.

From the Finish

To reach the southern trailhead, turn west into Lost Lake Subdivision at Mile 5.3 of Seward Hwy and drive a quarter of a mile uphill to a T-intersection. Turn left and drive for a quarter of a mile and then right – the trailhead is 100 yards from the end of the road. The trailhead and parking area are on private property but the USFS is negotiating a land swap to preserve access to the trail. Everything is well posted at both ends, but you can call the Seward Ranger District (☎ 224-3374) for the latest information. Other than calling a taxi, there is no public transportation between Lost Lake Subdivision and Seward.

THE HIKE
Stage 1: Primrose Landing Campground to Lost Lake
8mi, 4 to 5 hours

The Primrose Trail follows an old mining road for the first half, making it, for the most part, a wide, easy-to-follow route to the tree line. From the campground it heads southwest, climbing gradually through a thick spruce forest, which limits any views of the mountains that loom overhead. You also stay away from **Porcupine Creek** in the first couple of miles, but eventually the trail swings near it and, less than 3mi from the trailhead, a spur heads right for a short distance to **Porcupine Creek Falls**, an ideal destination for a day hike. The spur is not signposted, but normally you can hear the falls from the main trail.

In the next mile, the trail passes the remains of past mineral exploration, and 3.7mi from the campground, you reach the historic **Primrose Mine**, still active. At this point, the trail heads almost due south and climbs steadily on a ridge above the creek until it reaches the tree line at about 2000ft, less than a mile from the mine site.

To break out of the trees along the Primrose Trail is an unexpected joy. Due west is a 4732ft peak, and to the southwest is **Mt Ascension** (5710ft) with its distinctively sheer north face. The trail continues south by following a subalpine ridge, and in less than 2mi you reach **Lost Lake**. This stretch above the tree line is a beautiful alpine trek unless foul weather or fog create white-out conditions, in which case you'll have to follow a series of 4-by-4-inch posts across the open tundra to the lake.

Once at the lake, Primrose Trail skirts the east shoreline for more than a mile, until it crosses a bridge over Lost Creek. At this point it swings west and ends at **Lost Lake Trail** at the south end of the lake.

Spots to pitch a tent abound in the tundra. The opportunity to sit in the door of your tent and gaze at this pretty little lake and the peaks towering above it is priceless, and it's well worth spending an extra day here. Anglers can fish Lost Lake for rainbow trout, and others can explore the alpine area in almost any direction.

Mt Ascension is a technical climb, requiring mountaineering skills, crampons and an ice axe. However, the ridges reached from the southwest corner of the lake are fun to scramble up and provide wonderful views. You can also hike north along the lake and continue up the valley. It leads west to an impressive view of the mountain's steep north face, and from here it's possible to see mountain goats or even a black bear (if it's early in the summer).

Stage 2: Lost Lake to Seward Hwy
7mi, 3 to 4 hours

To continue south, head to the southern end of the lake, cross **Lost Creek** and end at the junction with Lost Lake Trail. This 7mi trail back to Seward Hwy is actually a pair of trails – a summer-only one for hikers and a winter trail used primarily by snowmobilers. On the Primrose portion, you will have gained 1500ft climbing to Lost Lake; on this leg you'll descend more than 1800ft quite easily.

From the lake, the trail heads almost due south but within a mile climbs a low ridge and skirts the top of it. All of this is above the tree line, and needless to say, the views are excellent on a clear day. Sometimes you can even see Resurrection Bay off in the distance.

Within 2mi from the lake, the trail begins its steady decent and, from here until you reach the tree line, there are extensive thickets of salmonberries, a semisour berry that looks like an overgrown raspberry and ripens in August.

About 3mi into the hike, you descend into the spruce forest, and in another mile or so, you arrive at a posted junction to **Dale Clemens Memorial Cabin**. This trail veers off to the left and returns to the alpine area, where white posts lead you 1.5mi to the cabin. This USFS unit was finished only in 1993 and is designed primarily for winter use. The 14-by-18ft cabin has bunks for four people and a table, cooking counter and even a propane heater for snowmobilers who arrive in the winter. Located at the tree line at 1750ft, the cabin provides spectacular views of Resurrection Peaks, Mt Ascension and also Resurrection Bay.

Within a mile of the junction, the summer trail begins a more rapid descent as it skirts above a stream on the east side of a **forested gorge**. At one point along the gorge, the trees open up to views of the mountains surrounding Resurrection Bay. Eventually, the trail swings away from the ravine and, 5.5mi from Lost Lake, arrives at the south end of the winter trail, though it's hard to pick up during the summer. (Hikers are urged not to follow this route to the cabin as it is steep and wet in areas.) The final leg of the trail is an old road that follows a steady descent to the trailhead in Lost Lake Subdivision.

Caines Head State Recreation Area

Caines Head State Recreation Area is a 6000-acre preserve that lies along the shore of Resurrection Bay, 5.5mi south of Seward. It's the scenic site of an abandoned WWII fort and includes military ruins and 650ft headlands that rise above the water for sweeping views of the bay and the mountains around it. It also features almost 10mi of trails, old military roads and beach and alpine routes that can be combined for a two- or three-day trip out of Seward.

Because it is a favorite with local boaters and kayakers, facilities on the trails around North Beach include shelters, toilets, campsites, rental cabins and a ranger station that is staffed throughout most of the summer. A spare day can be spent exploring the crumbling gun turrets and other army artifacts or following a route into the alpine area above Resurrection Bay.

HISTORY

As the southern terminus of the Alaska Railroad, Seward was the only transportation center available before the construction of the tunnel at Whittier and the Alaska Hwy, and it played a crucial role during WWII. Even before Japan bombed Pearl Harbor, the US Army was busy building a harbor defense system to protect Seward and Caines Head, the key point. At the top of the bluff, they spent $8 million building Fort McGilvray, which boasted two piers, 6.5mi of road, magazine bunkers, a submarine loop station and also an elaborate underground fortress with two massive 6-inch guns, each with a range of 16mi. On South Beach, a self-contained community for 500 men was constructed.

Although the Japanese eventually bombed Dutch Harbor and occupied the Aleutian Islands of Attu and Kiska, Seward was never threatened during the war. Amazingly, two years after breaking ground, the army ordered the cliff-ringed command post to be abandoned.

NATURAL HISTORY

Caines Head is a maritime rain forest featuring spruce and fir trees ranging from 60 to 100ft in height. In some places the forests frame cliffs and headlands that rise almost straight up from shale-covered beaches. Wildlife in the park includes porcupines, brown and black bears and mountain goats and marmots in the alpine regions. Off shore it's possible to see puffins, sea otters and seals.

Seward's most interesting and accessible natural attraction, however, is Exit Glacier, part of the Kenai Fjords National Park. This drive-to glacier attracts more than 100,000 visitors each summer. Most are 10-minute tourists who rush up to the ice, snap a picture then leave. Hikers who have time, however, can view and even experience the Harding Ice Field.

One of the largest ice fields in North America, Harding remained undiscovered until the early 1900s, when a map-making team realized several coastal glaciers belonged to the same massive system. The ice field is 50mi long and 30mi wide and in some places 200 inches deep. Eight glaciers reach the sea from it, and Exit Glacier is a remnant of a larger one that once extended into Resurrection Bay. You can reach the edge of the ice field via the Harding Ice Field Trail (see Other Trails at the end of this chapter). Experienced mountaineers, equipped with skis, ice axes and crampons, often venture onto the icy plateau.

CLIMATE

Unlike Chugach National Park, protected to the north by the Kenai Mountains, Caines Head and Resurrection Bay have a wetter, maritime climate. Annual rainfall in Seward usually exceeds 60 inches and the average high temperature in July is 63°F. July and August are the driest months by far, but you should still bring warm clothes and rain gear for cool, wet weather.

INFORMATION

There is no longer a state park office in Seward. The Alaska Division of Parks and Outdoor Recreation, Kenai/PWS Area

Office (☎ 262-5581) is located across the peninsula at Morgans Landing State Recreation Area near Soldotna and is open 8 am to 5 pm Monday through Friday. You may write them at PO Box 1247, Soldotna, AK 99669.

In Seward there is a USFS district office (☎ 224-3374) at the corner of 4th Ave and Jefferson St; it is open 8 am to 5 pm Monday through Friday. The Kenai Fjords National Park Visitor Center (☎ 224-3175) in the small boat harbor has displays, information and maps for sale on both its park and the surrounding area. The center is open 8 am to 7 pm daily during the summer.

SEWARD

Seward is surrounded by wilderness and rugged land. This town of 3000 people is flanked on one side by Resurrection Bay, on the other by Marathon Mountain and towering overhead is the Harding Ice Field. Just to the north is Chugach National Forest, on its doorstep to the south is Caines Head State Recreation Area and all around is Kenai Fjords National Park. Stay awhile and play.

Within 25mi of Seward to the north there are seven national forest trails: Resurrection River, Lost Lake, Primrose Creek, Goldenfin Lake, Grayling Lake, Victor Creek and

Kayaking Resurrection Bay

Besides hiking, the other way to explore Caines Head State Recreation Area is by kayaking Resurrection Bay. There are now several companies in Seward that rent kayaks and offer guided trips.

Kayaks can be rented from Kayak & Custom Adventures (☎ 224-3960, 800-288-3134, ✆ kayak@arctic.net) at Miller's Landing Campground for $30/55 a day for a single/ double. There is also Sunny Cove Kayaking Company (☎ 345-5339, 800-770-9119, ✆ kayakak@alaska.net), which rents singles and doubles from its office at the Alaska Saltwater Lodge on Lowell Point. Sunny Cove has a three-day minimum with a single/double at $90/165. Each additional day is $25/45.

Both companies offer guided outings to the state recreation area for $95 per person. The six- to seven-hour trips include kayaks and all other necessary equipment, paddling instruction and a shoreline lunch. If you have never kayaked before, this is a great way to get a taste of the sport, view Resurrection Bay's coastal scenery and possibly spot wildlife.

For something more adventurous – and more expensive – consider Kenai Fjords National Park. Experienced kayakers will depart from Resurrection Bay and follow the exposed coastline into the park. Less-seasoned paddlers can arrange a drop-off and pickup on a tour boat into one of the park's protective fjords.

Aialik Bay is the most popular arm for kayakers to paddle in the national park. Tour boats will drop off parties near Aialik Glacier, then pick them up three or four days later in Holgate Arm. The high point of the trip is paddling past Pedersen Glacier and watching Holgate Glacier calve icebergs directly into the bay. Keep in mind, however, that both Holgate Arm and its tidewater glacier also attract visits by most of the boat tours operating in the area.

Remote Northwestern Lagoon is more expensive to reach but is not invaded by nearly as many boats. The wildlife is excellent, especially the seabirds and otters, and there are more than a half-dozen glaciers that can be seen, including three tidewater ones. Plan on three to four days if you are being dropped inside the lagoon.

Either Kayak & Custom Adventures or Sunny Cove Kayaking Company will arrange drop-offs for those who want to skip paddling the Gulf of Alaska. It's $200 to $230 for two people and a kayak to be dropped off and picked up in Aialik Bay and $250 for a round trip into the more remote Northwestern Lagoon.

KENAI PENINSULA

Ptarmigan Creek (see the earlier Chugach National Forest section as well as Other Hikes at the end of this chapter). There is also a limited trail system in Kenai Fjords National Park.

For travel information, the year-round chamber of commerce visitor center (☎ 224-8051) is at Mile 2 of the Seward Hwy. The center has racks of information, brochures on most of the B&Bs in the area and courtesy phones to book rooms or tours. During the summer the office is open 8 am to 6 pm daily. The chamber of commerce also maintains a Web site (www.seward.net/chamber).

There are two banks in Seward, including the National Bank of Alaska (☎ 224-5283), 3rd Ave at D St. The post office is at 5th Ave and Madison St. Email and Internet access is available at the Seward library, at 5th Ave and Adams St. And, if you've been out in the wilderness for a tad too long and need some real cleaning up, Seward Laundry (☎ 224-5727), near the small boat harbor at 4th Ave and B St, also offers showers for $3.50.

Supplies & Equipment

Pick up the equipment you need in Anchorage. Limited camping supplies can be purchased at Western Auto at 5th Ave and Jefferson St near the USFS ranger office.

Places to Stay & Eat

Seward is one of the few towns in Alaska that has an excellent and affordable campground right in the heart of its downtown area. If you are ready for a break from camping, Seward and the surrounding area have a selection of accommodations that ranges from hostels to B&Bs to hotels.

The *Waterfront Campground*, along Ballaine Blvd, is managed by the city's Parks and Recreation Department (☎ 224-3331) and overlooks the bay. Most of it is open gravel parking for RVers, but you'll also find a grassy tent area that even has a few trees and shrubs. There is a day-use area with grills, picnic tables and small shelters and a paved bike path runs through the campground. Best of all is the price: $6 a night for tents, $10 for RVers to park and $15 for full

hook-up. There is also *Miller's Landing* (☎ 224-5739), at Lowell Point, a commercial campground conveniently located near the trailhead for the Coastal Trail in Caines Head State Recreation Area. Tent sites, which include the use of a shower building, cost $20 per night. There is also a small store and a water taxi to North Beach. If you come on the weekend, you might want to make reservations.

The facilities at *Moby Dick Hostel* (☎ 224-7072, 430 3rd Ave), between Madison and Jefferson Sts. are a little shabby, but it does have 18 bunks for $15 a night and small private rooms for $65. *Kate's Roadhouse* (☎ 224-5888), Mile 5.5 Seward Hwy, has a rustic bunkhouse with seven beds for $17 a night as well as rooms ($59 for a double) and four cabins ($29 to $49).

Many of the B&Bs are north of town off the Seward Hwy. Three miles north of town is the *Farm B&B* (☎ 224-5691, ✉ thefarm@ptialaska.net), on Salmon Creek Rd, which has a wide variety of accommodations. Rooms in the remodeled farmhouse range from $85 to $95 a night for two people, but there are also sleeping cottages, complete with decks, for $80 a night and small bungalows that sleep two for $65 a night. At the beginning of Exit Glacier Rd are several inns and B&Bs, including *Creekside Cabins* (☎ 224-3834) which has four cabins that overlook Clear Creek and range in price from $55 to $80 per night. The resort also features a sauna, bathhouse and two secluded tent sites for $15 a night for two people.

None of the hotels in town are cheap. Downtown is *Taroka Inn* (☎ 224-8687, ✉ taroka@arctic net), at 3rd Ave and Adams St, a former officer's quarters during WWII with nine rooms that begin at $85 for a double but include kitchenettes. The nearby *Harborview Inn* (☎ 224-3217), at 3rd Ave and C St, added 13 more rooms in 1998 and now charges $119 for a double in the new section and $109 for one of the eight original rooms.

If you're looking for something to eat in the downtown Seward area, *Don's Kitchen* (405 Washington St) is open 24 hours and probably has the cheapest fare; breakfasts begin at $5, and the Yukon Scrambler for $6 will keep you going until late in the afternoon. A half-pound halibut dinner costs $11.

For something a little healthier, try *Le Barn Appetit*, on Resurrection Rd just off Exit Glacier Rd. Seward's only health-food store is also a restaurant and bakery offering deli sandwiches, crepes, fresh-baked bread and quiche. The vegetarian cuisine costs about $7 for dinner.

As you'd expect, the small boat harbor area features a number of seafood spots. *Smoke'N Alaska Seafood* serves fish and chips, smoked salmon and seafood chowder. The *Depot Grill*, near the small shelter where the train drops you off, has sandwiches and hamburgers that begin at $5 and a pleasant solarium area overlooking the harbor.

For something nicer, try *Legends of the Mountain*, 5th Ave at Washington St, where you can enjoy a view of the bay from any table. Dinners begin at $13, but head over for a late lunch of seafood sauté – halibut, scallops and shrimp sautéed in white wine and herbs – for $10. The *Harbor Dinner Club* (*220 5th Ave*) is another upscale restaurant across from the Hotel Seward. The menu is made up almost entirely of seafood and usually includes an 'inflation-fighter' special for under $11. If fresh halibut cheeks are one of the appetizers, skip dinner and just order these with a few beers.

Getting There & Away

Bus Several bus companies now offer a run between Seward and Anchorage. Seward Bus Lines (☎ 224-3608) provides a service to Anchorage, with a bus departing from a small depot at 1915 Seward Hwy at 9 am daily during the summer. The bus departs Anchorage from 3339 Fairbanks St at 2:30 pm daily for the return trip to Seward; the one-way fare is $30.

Also offering bus service are Kachemak Bay Transit (☎ 235-3795, 877-235-9101), Park Connection (☎ 245-0200, 800-208-0200) and even Alaskon Express (☎ 800-478-6388), though you should definitely call

these companies beforehand to ensure they still serve Seward.

Train From May to September, the Alaska Railroad provides a daily run to Anchorage. Trains leave Seward at 6 pm daily for a spectacular route that includes glaciers, steep gorges and rugged mountain scenery. Even when departing that late, you can still view the scenery thanks to those long Alaskan days. The one-way fare is $50. There's no depot in Seward, the train merely stops at north end of 4th Ave, so call the Anchorage terminal (☎ 800-544-0552) for more information.

Boat In 1995, the ferry terminal (☎ 224-5485) was moved from the downtown waterfront to the Alaska Railroad Dock north of the small boat harbor. From Seward Hwy, head east on Port Ave and follow the signs to the office. Ferries arrive in Seward twice a week, on Thursday and Friday, from Kodiak or Valdez and depart for the same communities before continuing on to other South-central ports. The fare to Valdez is $58, to Kodiak $54 and to Homer $96.

Coastal Trail

Duration 2 to 3 days
Distance 9 to 22mi roundtrip
Difficulty Level Easy
Start/Finish Lowell Point
Cabins & Shelters Yes
Permits Required No
Public Transportation No
Summary This is a popular overnight trek to North Beach, where you can explore the remains of old WWII outposts that were built to protect this strategic area from the Imperial Japanese. A new side trail provides access to alpine areas beneath Callisto Peak.

KENAI PENINSULA

Spanning from Lowell Point to the military ruins at North Beach, the Coastal Trail is a 4.5mi trek into the heart of Caines Head State Recreation Area. The most dominant feature here is Caines Head itself, a massive

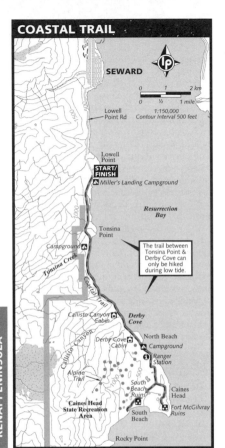

COASTAL TRAIL

SEWARD

0   1   2 km

0   ½   1 mile

1:150,000
Contour Interval 500 feet

Lowell
Point Rd

Lowell
Point

**START/
FINISH**

Miller's Landing Campground

*Resurrection
Bay*

Tonsina
Point

Campground

Tonsina Creek

The trail between
Tonsina Point &
Derby Cove can
only be hiked
during low tide.

Callisto Canyon
Cabin

*Derby
Cove*

North Beach

Derby Cove
Cabin

Campground

Ranger
Station

Alpine
Trail

South
Beach
Ruins

Caines
Head

**Caines Head
State Recreation
Area**

South
Beach

Fort McGilvray
Ruins

Rocky Point

Coastal Trail

Callisto Canyon

KENAI PENINSULA

headland that rises 650ft above the water
against a backdrop of peaks and mountains.
It juts out into Resurrection Bay, forming a
giant breakwater for Seward, and on a clear
day you can see the Pacific Ocean from its
edge.

Caines Head is a popular destination for
boaters and kayakers from Seward who pull
in to picnic or explore the remains of Fort
McGilvray. But the state park also draws the
interest of hikers, as the Coastal Trail and old
military roads make an ideal overnight hike.
Although the Coastal Trail is only 4.5mi one-
way to the campsites on North Beach, if you

add the walk to the trailhead from Seward,
plus the treks to the fort and South Beach
and allow for some backtracking, the trek
becomes close to 22mi long.

The trek is best done as an overnight trip
(or longer) because part of the Coastal Trail
is a beach route that must be walked at low
tide. Tides are mild around Caines Head,
with an average high of 8.3ft. A tide book is
posted at the start of the beach section in
Tonsina Point Campground.

If you're not up to carrying a tent, the
hike to Tonsina Point is a roundtrip of only
3mi and fairly easy. At the point, you can
view the salmon spawning up Tonsina
Creek (July or early August) or hike
through a ghost forest along the bay (the
stark trunks are the result of the Good
Friday Earthquake).

This area has a great deal of natural
beauty and historical significance, but the
highlight of the park for most people is exploring the military ruins. Be aware that
most of the buildings are rotting, especially
those in South Beach, which you should
never enter. Also remember that taking any
historical artifact is strictly prohibited. Part
of the unique aspect of these remnants is
the lack of vandalism due to the remote location of the fort.

PLANNING
When to Hike
The Coastal Trail can be hiked from mid-
May to October. The Alpine Trail shouldn't
be attempted before mid-June, due to lingering snow.

What to Bring
You'll need to know the tide table if you
plan to hike past Tonsina Point on the first
stage of this hike, because you can only hike
it at low tide. You can usually find the
current pages from the Seward tide book
taped to a sign in the Tonsina Point Campground, but it's best to have that information before you leave Seward.

Maps
Caines Head State Recreation Area is
covered on the USGS 1:63,360 series quad

Seward A-7. The Trails Illustrated *Kenai Fjords National Park and Chugach NF* map covers the entire area in smaller detail. If all you're going to do is hike to Fort McGilvray or the South Beach, this is one of the few times in Alaska you can get away with the park brochure, which has a good map on one side. In Seward, maps can be purchased at the Kenai Fjords National Park Visitor Center (☎ 224-3175) in the small boat harbor or at Seward Marine Adventures (☎ 224-3102) at 3rd Ave and D St.

Cabins & Shelters
There are two rental cabins along the Coastal Trail. Callisto Canyon Cabin is located just off the tidal trail a half mile before you reach Derby Cove. It was built in 1998 with funds from the *Exxon Valdez* oil spill settlement and sleeps eight. Derby Cove Cabin is in Derby Cove; it sleeps eight on wooden sleeping platforms and has a wood-burning stove. Either one is $50 per night and is reserved through the Alaska Department of Natural Resources Public Information Center (☎ 269-8400) in Anchorage or the Kenai Area Parks Office (☎ 262 5581) at Morgan's Landing.

GETTING TO/FROM THE HIKE
The trailhead for the Coastal Trail is 3mi down Lowell Point Rd from the Alaska SeaLife Center in Seward. There is no public transportation along Lowell Point Rd (unless you flag a taxi), but the gravel road is a scenic walk along the bay.

One way to avoid backtracking, is to utilize the water taxi service at Miller's Landing (☎ 224-5739). The campground runs a boat shuttle to North Beach daily during the summer, with departures depending on the tides. One-way is $30, roundtrip $40. For another water route, see the boxed text 'Kayaking Resurrection Bay.'

THE HIKE
Stage 1: Lowell Point to North Beach
4.5mi, 2½ to 3 hours
From the trailhead gate and parking area, the first half mile is along a level gravel road

until you reach a posted junction, which points the way to Tonsina Point, a mile away. The trail then indeed becomes a trail and begins a steady climb up a wooded ridge for the next half mile. You eventually top off and break out to a view of Tonsina Point far below and Resurrection Bay all around. From this viewing point to Tonsina Creek it is a rapid descent of more than 200ft.

Tonsina Creek is a river large enough to hold a strong run of silver salmon in July and early August, and occasionally, by hiking upstream, you can see eagles and other wildlife feeding on the spawned-out fish. If the run is on, the mouth of the creek will often be crowded with locals who boat in from Seward.

You cross Tonsina Creek on an impressive footbridge, enter the woods and then cross two more bridges. The third one leads to the walk-in campground on **Tonsina Point**. The facility includes a handful of sites, some with picnic tables (well shaded in the woods), vault toilets, a fire grate and shelter. Use of the campground is on a first-come, first-served basis but camping spots abound in this area.

The next leg of the journey, the 2.5mi stretch from Tonsina Point to Derby Cove, is a beach walk and can only be hiked during low tide. A signpost marks where the trail accesses the beach and usually the current pages from the Seward tide book are taped to the sign.

From the campground, the trail cuts through a ghost forest – trees killed by the 1964 Good Friday Earthquake – and then, at an orange marker, you emerge on the beach, with Resurrection Bay lapping at the shore only a few yards away. The black-sand beach gently curves southeast toward North Beach, and on a clear day, you can see the headland that separates the beach from Derby Cove. Occasionally, you have to clamber over beach boulders, especially if the tide is coming back in, but for the most part, this stretch is an easy and very scenic walk.

A half mile before you reach Derby Cove, a short spur leads from the tidal trail to the new **Callisto Canyon Cabin** located just inside the trees.

In the northwest corner of the Derby Cove a short trail leads to the park's other rental cabin. The **Derby Cove Cabin** is just inside the spruce and hemlock forest above the gravel beach. At the southeast end of the cove the trail to North Beach cuts inland at a well-posted spot.

The final half mile is the climb and descent of the headland that separates the cove from the spot where the US Army arrived in 1941 to build Fort McGilvray. The most visible remains at North Beach are the army dock and pier that somehow survived the 1964 earthquake and tsunami that followed, even though the surrounding land sank 5ft. Over time, however, weather and waves have taken their toll on the pier's decking, so you should stay away from it.

North Beach is a popular spot for recreational boaters to anchor and come ashore for a picnic. There is another campground here with vault toilets, a fire ring and two picnic shelters, and the surrounding beach area provides additional campsites. There is also a ranger station near the north end of the beach, staffed during the summer.

Side Trip: Alpine Trail
6mi, 3 to 4 hours roundtrip

Along the way to North Beach, you pass the posted junction and information display for the new Alpine Trail. The 3mi route was built in 1997 and climbs to the tundra at 1500ft. Almost due west is Callisto Peak (3657ft). This is a moderately challenging trail that takes most hikers two hours to climb. Within 1.5mi of the trailhead is a posted spur that descends to South Beach, allowing you to turn the trail into a loop.

Stage 2: North Beach to Fort McGilvray & South Beach
7mi, 3 to 4 hours

You can spend an afternoon or a whole day exploring the military ruins of this area and enjoying the view from Caines Head. Fort McGilvray boasts more than 6mi of roads, and two roads provide easy access to the ruins. It's a 2mi walk to the fort and 2.5mi to

South Beach, or 7mi to visit both and return to the campground.

From North Beach you head south on the posted roadbed as it heads inland and climbs gently. Within a mile you come to a junction. Head east (left fork) and follow the road as it continues to climb to the top of Caines Head. Along the way you pass the remains of four ammunition magazines and then emerge at **Fort McGilvray** at the edge of Caines Head.

Basically you are on top of a 650ft rocky cliff that offers panoramic views of Resurrection Bay and the surrounding mountains. The excellent condition of the fort is amazing, and there's no doubt its isolated location has kept vandalism to a minimum over the years. You can explore the elaborate underground fortress, but it's best to have a flashlight to find your way around the maze of passages and other rooms. Above ground, take time to examine the two firing platforms. In its effort to defend Seward, the army placed two six inch guns here that had a firing range of 16mi.

Backtrack up the roadbed and at the junction head west on the opposite fork to reach **South Beach**. It's a 1.5mi walk to the beach from the junction along another roadbed that descends to the shoreline of Resurrection Bay. South Beach was where the 500 servicemen who lived here from July 1941 to May 1943 were stationed. Today the state park officials describe the utility buildings and barracks as a 'garrison ghost town.' The buildings are intriguing to look at from the outside, but you should think twice before entering any of the wooden structures, many of which have already collapsed.

Stage 3: The Return
4.5mi, 2½ to 3 hours

Unless you reserved a seat in the water taxi or can hitch a ride with a boater heading back to town, the only way to return is the way you came in. Double-check the tides at the ranger station and then wait for low tide in order to cover the 2.5mi from Derby Cove to Tonsina Point without getting your boots too wet.

Mt Blackburn from the Bonanza Mine

Fording a stream along the Dixie Pass Route

Kennicott and Root Glaciers

Baja Taco Wagon serves espresso in Cordova

Kachemak Bay State Park & Wilderness

Stretching into Kachemak Bay from Homer is a long needle of land known as the Homer Spit. During the summer this 4.5mi sandbar is the heart of the town's fishing industry and the center of activity, drawing thousands of tourists and backpackers every year.

Just a short hop across the bay is Kachemak Bay State Park. This 513-sq-mi wilderness ranges from the Harding Ice Field and 4000ft peaks with glaciers spilling out between them to lush forests of spruce, moss and shoulder-high devil's club. The shoreline is a ragged series of protective coves, bays and lagoons where intertidal zones are alive with starfish, crabs and other marine life. The gravel beaches have long been favorites with Homer's clam diggers.

Visitation of the park is on the rise due in part to better facilities in and around it. Recent developments within the park include an expanded trail system, walk-in campgrounds, additional docks and five rental cabins. Just outside the park boundaries are a number of small wilderness resorts and the community of Halibut Cove. A thriving fishing community from 1911 to 1928, today Halibut Cove is a quaint boardwalk town of art galleries, eateries and a lodge.

The park is only accessible by bush plane or boat from Homer. Most hikers hop on a water taxi and pay the $50 roundtrip fare that includes a swing past Gull Island, the site of hundreds of puffin and other seabird rookeries. Plan on spending at least two nights/three days here to camp near Grewingk Glacier and hike the Alpine Ridge Trail, the two most popular areas of the park. Plan on several more days if you want to escape and explore Wosnesenski River or other trails.

NATURAL HISTORY

Wildlife is plentiful here. The rich lagoons and waters just offshore attract whales, sea otters, seals, dolphins and impressive salmon runs. The seashore and the tidal marshes are teaming with life; mollusks, arthropods and sea stars are just a few of the creatures that can be seen at low tide. In many rivers and streams there are impressive runs of salmon, in particular kings, which gather in Halibut Cove Lagoon in May and June, and pinks, which spawn up Humpy Creek in July and August.

Birders are particularly attracted to the area. A wide variety of seabirds, including horned and tufted puffins, pigeon guillemots, marbled murrelets and common murres, can be seen. Gull Island near Halibut Cove is a rookery for more than 12,000 seabirds, especially puffins. The shoreline habitat attracts bald eagles, loons, and harlequin ducks. Moose and black bears are found in the lowlands; brown bears and mountain goats in the alpine region.

Kachemak Bay's tides are among the largest in the world. The average vertical difference between high and low tide is 15ft, with an extreme seasonal high of 28ft. The tidal currents are so strong that rapids and whirlpools often form in narrow passages.

CLIMATE

Protected from the severe northern cold by the Kenai Mountains, Kachemak Bay has a mild maritime climate with cool, overcast summers typical of the Southeast. Average temperatures in July are in the low 60s (F), and a day above 80°F is rare. Annual precipitation is less than 30 inches, much of it snow, but the area is subject to the severe and unpredictable weather that rolls in from the North Pacific.

The park is often affected by a day breeze. Typically, the seas are often calm until midmorning in the summer, when a breeze from the southwest develops on the bay. This results in 1 to 3ft waves breaking on beaches exposed to the west, making landings more difficult for kayakers and small vessels. By early evening the breeze often dies off and calm conditions return.

INFORMATION

For information on the park in Homer, contact the Alaska Division of Parks &

Outdoor Recreation office (☎ 235-7024) at Mile 168.5 of Sterling Hwy, 4mi north of town. This is a small office, however, and often you end up with the answering machine. If you're passing through Sterling on your way south, you can also stop at the Kenai Area Parks Office (☎ 262-5581) and see if the Halibut Cove Cabin is open. The office is reached by heading south on Scott Lake Loop Rd from Mile 85 of the Sterling Hwy. Within 1.5mi veer right on Lou Morgan Rd; the office is at the end of the road.

More information on hiking and kayaking in the Homer area can be obtained at the Alaska Maritime National Wildlife Refuge Visitor Center (☎ 235-6961), on Sterling Hwy just before entering town. The center also has natural history exhibits, a video theater, and a book and map counter and it hosts guided bird walks throughout the summer. Hours in the summer are from 9 am to 6 pm daily.

Glacier Lake & Lagoon Trails

Duration 3 to 4 days
Distance 16.5 to 30mi
Difficulty Level Easy to hard
Start/Finish Glacier Spit Trailhead/Saddle Trailhead
Cabins & Shelters Yes
Permits Required No
Public Transportation No
Summary This hike through one of the largest coastal parks in the USA features bountiful bird and sea life, glaciers and routes to scenic alpine country.

These two trails stretch from a tour boat drop off at the Glacier Spit trailhead to a dock at the head of Halibut Cove. But because some tour boats do not want to negotiate the strong tides flowing in and out of

Coalition Trail: Saving a Wilderness

The mountains and glaciers that form the east side of Kachemak Bay can be seen from many streets in Homer. With such a magnificent backdrop to their town, it's little wonder locals were eager to preserve this rugged corner of the Kenai Peninsula. So, despite having been a state for less than 15 years, Alaska set aside 391 sq mi as Kachemak Bay State Park in 1970.

The state park designation did not have the immediate result residents had hoped. In 1974, the Alaska Native Claims Settlement Act (ANCSA) allowed the Seldovia Native Association to select 108 sq mi of land, including 47 sq mi in the state park. The ANCSA was the bill that settled land issues with local tribes and allowed oil companies to cross 'Native lands' to build the pipeline to the Prudhoe Bay oil fields. The Seldovia Native Association was one of the 12 regional corporations set up to administer the new Native holdings, and it selected land in the Kachemak Bay area. As a result, logging and mining was slated to take place within the designated state park.

Faced with this possibility, residents formed the Kachemak Bay Citizens Coalition and lobbied the state in an attempt to regain the lost parkland. Ironically, the solution – and necessary money – came from the worst oil spill in US history. The Seldovia Native Association sold the land to the state for $22 million in 1993 when the money became available from the *Exxon Valdez* oil spill criminal penalty fund that had been set up the year before.

In honor of the victory of preservation over development, a new route was built in the state park and named Coalition Trail. The trail begins a half mile south of Halibut Cove Lagoon, with a junction on the China Poot Lake Trail. It extends 1.6mi to China Poot Bay and along the way passes through a portion of the land that had been slated to be logged.

the cove, many hikers end up backtracking a portion of the Lagoon Trail to the trailhead of Saddle Trail to add another 6mi to the hike.

Considering the expense of getting across the bay and the beauty of the park, it's hard to justify only an overnight trip. Throw in a side trip to Alpine Ridge, Poot Peak or the Wosnesenski River and you could easily put together a three- or four-day hike of 20 to 40mi.

An extra day can be spent camped in front of Grewingk Glacier to hike the Alpine Ridge Trail, but you'll find this a popular place during the summer and flightseeing planes abound on any clear day. More than a thousand hikers visit the park every summer, and most spend a night or two at the glacier. Some never go any farther.

You could also extend the hike another day or two by hiking the new trails south of Halibut Cove Lagoon. The Moose Valley Trail/Poot Peak Trail loops 6mi off of China Poot Lake Trail, and the Wosnesenski Trail extends 9mi to the Haystack trailhead on Neptune Bay, where you can arrange a pickup. If you truly want to escape, consider hiking and camping in Halibut Creek. From there you can explore the upper portions of this stream and valley.

The hike to Grewingk Glacier Lake is rated easy, and the Lagoon Trail is moderate to hard. You'll find most hikes that are above the tree line, including Alpine Ridge and Goat Pass, generally challenging.

PLANNING
When to Hike
Glacier Lake and Lagoon Trails can be hiked from late May until mid-October. Alpine routes such Goat Rope Spur Trail, Poot Peak and the Alpine Ridge Trail should be hiked from July through September to avoid snow.

What to Bring
Bring a camping stove and fuel for any hike above the tree line. You might consider binoculars, too, as this is a prime birding and wildlife watching area. The Homer Visitor Center (☎ 235-7740), at 135 Sterling Hwy

can provide tide information, which you'll need when fording Halibut Creek.

Maps
The trail system in Kachemak Bay State Park is split between two USGS 1:63,360 series quads: *Seldovia C-4* and *C-3*. Neither one shows the trails because much of the system is relatively new. An alternative, especially if you plan to stick to the established paths, is the *Kachemak Bay Road & Recreation Map* published by Alaska Road & Recreation Maps. The scale is smaller (one inch to a mile), but the $6 map is updated regularly and shows the entire trail system. In 1999, Trails Illustrated released a *Kachemak Bay State Park* map ($10) that includes the trail system.

You can purchase maps at Alaska Maritime National Wildlife Refuge Visitor Center (see the Information section).

Cabins & Shelters
There are now three state rental cabins in Halibut Cove Lagoon. The original cabin was a bunkhouse for trail crews until it was converted into a three-room facility in 1992. The cabin has a pair of bunk-bed sleeping platforms, as well as electricity and water. It's at the southern end of Halibut Cove and can be reached by boat, water taxi or by hiking along the Lagoon Trail.

There's also Lagoon East Cabin, next door, and Lagoon West Cabin, a half mile west of the public dock. All three have basically the same amenities and are $50 a night. As with all popular USFS cabins, you need to reserve them in advance to ensure getting one during the summer. Make reservations through the Alaska Department of Natural Resources Public Information Center (☎ 269-8400) at 3601 C St in the Frontier Building in Anchorage. Otherwise stop at the Homer Ranger Station (☎ 235-5581) at Mile 168.5 of the Sterling Hwy (if it happens to be open).

NEAREST TOWNS & FACILITIES
Homer
For information on lodging, charter trips into Kachemak Bay or other activities, head

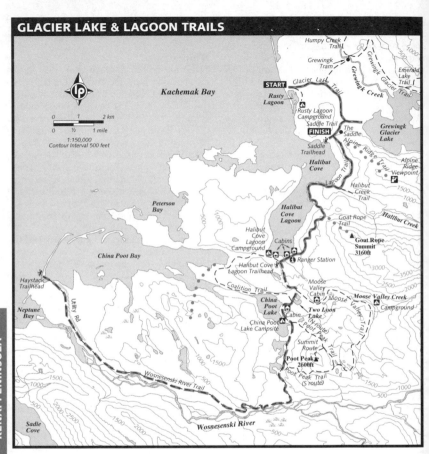

GLACIER LAKE & LAGOON TRAILS

to the Homer Visitor Center (☎ 235-7740) at 135 Sterling Hwy, or what is usually labeled as the Homer Bypass, the area where you'll find banks and the post office. The center is open until 8 pm Friday through Sunday during the summer and has racks of information, free coffee and courtesy phones to book rooms or tours. The center also maintains a Web site (www.xyz.net/~homer).

Supplies & Equipment Rain gear, boots or outdoor clothing such as Polar Fleece can be purchased at NOMAR (☎ 235-8363, 800-478-8364), at 104 E Pioneer Ave. More spe-

cialized backpacking equipment has to be picked up in Anchorage.

Places to Stay & Eat Beach camping is allowed in designated areas of the west side of Homer Spit, a beautiful spot to pitch a tent. The nightly fee is $3 if you camp in the city-controlled sections near the end of the spit; there are toilets next to the harbormaster's office, and a shower costs $3 at the *Homer Spit Campground* (☎ 235-8206). Keep in mind the spit can get rowdy at times.

The *Karen Hornaday Memorial Campground* (follow signs north on Bartlett St) is on a wooded hill with an impressive view of the town and bay below, making it considerably more private than the Spit. This city campground also has a $3 nightly fee for tenters and a 14-day limit. You can take a shower ($3) and wash your clothes at Washboard Laundromat (☎ 235-6781) at 1204 Ocean Drive, passed on your way to the Spit.

There's no official youth hostel in Homer, but there is *Seaside Farm (☎ 235-7850, 235-2670)*, 5mi from Homer out on East End Rd. The working farm has a variety of accommodations, including a backpacker hostel with bunks for $15 and rustic cabins for $55 a double, or you can also pitch your tent for $6 in a grassy pasture overlooking Kachemak Bay. The farm has an outdoor kitchen area for campers, and showers and laundry facilities.

Like everywhere else in Alaska, Homer has an ever growing number of B&Bs; at last count there were more than 40. Check with the tourist office for a list of all of them. Above the city is *Skyline B&B (☎ 235-3832, 60855 Skyline Dr)* with a beautiful view of Grewingk Glacier, four rooms for $60/65 singles/doubles and a bunkroom with beds for $20 a night.

There are almost a dozen hotels/motels in the area with mostly single rooms costing from $60 to $70. All of them are heavily booked during the summer. A delightful, small hotel is the *Driftwood Inn (☎ 235-8019, 800-478 8019, @ driftinn@xyz.net)* at Main St and Bunnell Ave, near Bishop Beach. Rooms without a view or bath are $46/56 singles/doubles, and its ship quarters accommodations, small rooms with a bath, begin at $54/74.

Within walking distance of downtown Homer is *Ocean Shores Motel (☎ 235-7775, 800-770-7775, 3500 Crittenden Dr)* with a variety of rooms. Doubles begin at $95, and new bayview rooms with kitchenettes are $140 a night.

Homer's assortment of cafes and bakeries includes a handful of espresso shops. The most interesting is *Cafe Cups (162 W Pioneer Ave)*, with its bizarre coffee-cup exterior and its pleasant interior; each wall is an art gallery. Huge sandwiches, made with thick cuts of bread, are $6 and include several veggie options, and homemade soup is $5. The cafe opens at 7 am and serves several unusual egg dishes.

Neon Coyote (435 E Pioneer Ave) is an interesting and affordable diner that specializes in Southwest cooking. At dinner, the grande burrito filled with chicken and black beans will fill you up for $7, or you can order shrimp enchiladas for $16.

The best vegetarian spot is *Smoky Bay Natural Foods (248 W Pioneer Ave)*. This co-op is Homer's health-food store, which includes a small kitchen that serves filling vegetarian dishes at lunch for under $7 and soups and sandwiches for even less. There's limited seating inside. Carnivores in search of the best baby-back ribs should go to the nearby *Pioneer Barbecue (270 W Pioneer Ave)*.

On the way to the Spit, you'll pass *Eagle Quality Center (90 Sterling Hwy)*, the best place in town for groceries, fresh baked breads, deli sandwiches and salads ($3.50 per pound). The supermarket is open 24 hours.

Getting There & Away Homer is the jump-off spot for Kachemak Bay State Park and can be reached from Anchorage by air, ferry, bus or rental car (see the Getting Around section of the Anchorage chapter for details).

ERA Aviation (☎ 235-7565, 800-426-0333), the contract carrier for Alaska Airlines, provides eight daily flights between Homer and Anchorage from the Homer airport, 1.7mi east of town on Kachemak Dr. The one-way fare is $98; a roundtrip, advance-purchase ticket is $140.

Kachemak Bay Transit (☎ 235-3795, 877-235-9101) provides bus service between Homer and Anchorage and points in between along the Sterling Hwy. A bus departs Homer at 9 am and arrives at Anchorage at around 5 pm. One-way fare is $45. Running the same route for the same fare is Homer Stage Line (☎ 235-7009). Both buses will arrange pickups at any hotel or B&B in town as well as at the ferry terminal. Kachemak Bay Transit also picks up at the Lakeside Mall on Lake St. Homer

KENAI PENINSULA

Stage Line picks up at Quicky Mart, 1242 Ocean Dr.

The ferry M/V *Tustumena* provides service twice a week from Homer to Seldovia and three times a week to Kodiak, including one run that continues on to Seward and the rest of the Southcentral ports. The ferry terminal (☎ 235-8449) is at the end of Homer Spit. The one-way fare from Homer to Seldovia is $18 and from Homer to Kodiak $48.

Halibut Cove

If you become enchanted with the south shore of Kachemak Bay, you might want to extend your stay with a night in Halibut Cove. This small village of 50 people began as a fishing port and in the early 1920s supported 42 herring salteries and a population of more than 1000. Today, this boardwalk community is best known as a side trip out of Homer where you can view art galleries, dine at the noted Saltry Restaurant or spend a night in a cabin.

The **Quiet Place Lodge** *(☎ 296-2212)* has cabins for $182 per couple, which includes the breakfast. There is also the **Country Cove Cabins** *(☎ 296-2257, 888-353-2683, ✉ ctjones@xyz.net)*. The cabins are $95 per night for two people, but there is a discount if you arrive with a sleeping bag. Many who come to Halibut Cove stop to dine on the outdoor deck of the **Saltry Restaurant** (☎ 296-2223), an excellent spot for seafood and vegetarian cuisine. Dinner at the Saltry starts at about $16, and it's well worth it.

Danny J is the ferry that will run you across the cove from the Spit. It departs at noon, swings past Gull Island and then at 1:30 pm arrives at Halibut Cove, where you have 2½ hours to explore the 12 blocks of boardwalks and galleries or have lunch. The ferry returns to the Spit by 5 pm and then makes an evening run to the cove for dinner at the Saltry, returning to Homer at 10 pm. The noon tour costs $35 per person, the evening trip is $17.50. Book the ferry through Kachemak Bay Ferry (☎ 296-2223) or Central Charter Booking Agency (☎ 235-7847, 800-478-7847), which has an office on the Spit.

GETTING TO/FROM THE HIKE

A number of tour boats drop off and pick up at Halibut Cove. St Augustine's Charters drops off hikers at Glacier Spit in the morning and picks them up at Saddle Trailhead in the afternoon. Roundtrip fare is $50. Book them through Inlet Charters (☎ 235-6126, 800-770-6126) on the Spit. You can also try Mako's Water Taxi (☎ 235-9055), Bay Excursions (☎ 235-7525, ✉ bay@xyz.net) or Homer Ocean Charters (☎ 235-6212, 800-426-6212, ✉ hoc@xyz.net).

To avoid backtracking you need to be picked up at the public dock in Halibut Cove Lagoon, which has to be prearranged and carefully timed around the tides. Plan on paying $60 to $70 for a drop off at Glacier Spit and a pick-up in the Lagoon.

The other way to avoid backtracking is by hiking the Wosnesenski Trail to the Haystack trailhead on Neptune Bay. Call Tutka Bay Taxi (☎ 235-7166) to arrange a pick up from Haystack trailhead.

Whatever tour boat you choose, make sure the operator swings past Gull Island on the way to the cove. This group of bare rock islets, halfway between the Spit and Halibut Cove, is the site of thousands of nesting seabirds: tufted puffins, black-legged kittiwakes, cormorants, common murres and many more species, so many that you can usually photograph the birds up close without a telephoto lens.

THE HIKE
Stage 1: Glacier Spit Trailhead to Grewingk Glacier Lake
3.5mi, 1½ to 2 hours

Most water taxis prefer to drop you off a quarter mile or so down the Glacier Spit. From the landing site, you head north on the sloping gravel beach, passing a fair amount of driftwood and sea life washed up by the high tides, until a large orange triangular sign marks the start of the Glacier Lake Trail.

From the posted trailhead, the route heads east into a lush forest and, after a quarter mile, arrives at a well-posted junction to the **Rusty Lagoon Campground**, a rustic camping area that is a 10-minute hike down the spur. The campground features picnic tables, fire grates and vault toilets. The main trail continues in the lush forest for a spell and then breaks out to the glacial outwash, which is rocky and dotted with young stands of cottonwood.

At 1.2mi is the junction with the new **Grewingk Glacier Trail** (see 'Grewingk Glacier Trail' boxed text). At this junction, the Glacier Lake Trail swings southeast and skirts the edge between the forested ridge and the bushy growth of the level outwash. Hiking is easy, and 3mi from Glacier Spit, you reach the posted junction with the **Saddle Trail**. Ascend the Saddle Trail a hundred yards or so to refill your water bottles from a clear running stream. This water is much better than the silt-filled lake in front of the glacier.

The final leg of the trail is a hike across rocky terrain to the lake; it's marked by a series of cairns, though they are hardly needed. You might have spotted the glacier earlier from a distance, but emerging from the bush and seeing it properly for the first time is like Dorothy and the scarecrow seeing the emerald city of Oz – it takes your breath away.

This giant river of ice spills gracefully out of the mountains into Glacier Lake, sending wave after wave of icebergs to litter the shoreline where you pitch your tent. This is a gorgeous spot to camp for a day or two. There are lots of fire pits around, so use an old one or destroy your fire pit before you move on, as this scenic spot surely doesn't need another one.

Side Trip: Alpine Ridge Trail
4mi roundtrip, 3 to 4 hours
This a great side trip but it's a steep climb of 2mi to the alpine area. Picked up along the Lagoon Trail (see stage 2), the first half of the Alpine Ridge Trail is a series of switchbacks through the lush spruce forest. The second half is above the tree line, but the alder here is often at eye level. The alpine region is reached at 2000ft, and once you're on top, the views of the surrounding area, including **Grewingk Glacier**, are stunning. From here you can climb along the ridge to

---

Grewingk Glacier Trail

Built in 1997, Grewingk Glacier Trail heads northeast from Glacier Lake Trail, crosses Grewingk Creek, climbs steeply over Foehn Ridge and, in 5.1mi, ends at a tarn lake. From there it is easy to hike to the face of Grewingk Glacier.

Unfortunately, a hand-operated tram that was set up over Grewingk Creek to assist hikers fell into disrepair in 1998, and Grewingk Creek is not fordable. State park officials are unsure when or if the tram will be replaced. Until it is, Grewingk Glacier Trail can only be accessed from the Humpy Creek Trailhead north of the creek.

If the tram is operating, you can also use it to head north and add two more days to the hike. Grewingk Glacier Trail, Humpy Creek Trail and Emerald Lake Trail – all new trails in 1997 – can be linked to form a 15mi loop. You could overnight at campsites at Humpy Creek Trailhead or above the tree line along Emerald Lake. Emerald Lake Trail's long, steep climbs can be a moderately challenging hike but very scenic, with sweeping views of Kachemak Bay once you clear the tree line 2mi north of its junction with Grewingk Glacier Trail.

get better views of the glacier. You'll reach the **3647ft peak** 1.5mi after emerging in the tundra. It's an 11 to 12mi roundtrip if you spend a spare day at the glacier.

If you're just dropping your packs at the junction, plan on at least an additional three hours for the side trip up to the alpine region and back. By hauling your packs up, however, you can spend a memorable night in the mountains, as there are places to camp. Pack water in case the snow patches have melted.

Stage 2: Grewingk Glacier Lake to Halibut Cove Lagoon
7mi, 6 to 7 hours
The easy trekking is over. On the leg to Halibut Cove Lagoon there is much more

KENAI PENINSULA

climbing as you skirt the side of the shoreline mountains. You begin by backtracking to the Saddle Trail junction then following the trail for almost a mile as it climbs the saddle between Halibut Cove and Grewingk Glacier. It then levels out, and you'll pass a small creek along the way.

Just before it makes its steep descent to Halibut Cove, you pass a posted junction with the **Lagoon Trail**. This trail continues the steep climb until it reaches the posted junction with the **Alpine Ridge Trail**.

Lagoon Trail levels out somewhat after the junction with the Alpine Ridge Trail and hugs the steep side of the coastal ridge for more than a mile. You descend sharply to cross a creek, regain some of the elevation and then cross a bog before emerging at the junction with **Halibut Creek Trail**.

Halibut Creek Trail is a half-mile trail that briefly follows the ridgeline above the creek and then descends sharply into the valley. It's not hiked nearly as much as the other trails, and it has great spots to pitch a tent and escape the crowds at Grewingk Glacier.

From the junction with Halibut Creek Trail, Lagoon Trail descends sharply to bottom out at the mouth of the creek and the delta it forms in **Halibut Cove**. More orange triangles lead you across the gravel delta to the creek, which has to be forded. It's considerably easier at low tide, when you can go to the braided section at the mouth and ford relatively low channels. Otherwise, be prepared to get your boots wet. Don't ford just before or after high tide, as the water will be swift, cold and often waist deep.

On the other side, orange trail markers lead you up the creek 100yd or so to where the trail resumes in the spruce forest. You quickly pass a junction to a trailhead spur on the cove and then begin a steep climb via a series of switchbacks. The climb is steep until it reaches almost 1200ft, the highest point of Lagoon Trail. Here you arrive at the posted junction of the **Goat Rope Trail** (see Side Trip: Goat Rope Trail).

From the junction, Lagoon Trail descends 800ft and then levels out for half a mile before making a final and steep descent to the bottom where it passes **Halibut Cove Ranger Station** (staffed two or three days a week) and **Lagoon Overlook Cabin** within 100yd.

This public-use cabin, which at one time housed trail crews, overlooks the lagoon and has a stairway that leads to an interesting floating dock and small raft. It features two bedrooms with bunk-bed sleeping platforms and a main room with a cooking counter, table and chairs. The unit is equipped with electricity, water and a purifying filter. A boardwalk leads to nearby **Lagoon East Cabin**.

A stairway takes you down to **Falls Creek** and the end of the trail at its junction with **China Poot Lake Trail**. To the north is **Lagoon West Cabin** and campsites at the end of Halibut Cove Lagoon with picnic tables, fire rings and vault toilets. Hemmed in by mountains, you'll find the scenery at the end of the lagoon spectacular, making this area another excellent choice for a spare day. Day hiking opportunities here are numerous and Falls Creek has good fishing when the king and pink salmon runs are on.

Side Trip: Goat Rope Trail
3mi, 2 to 3 hours
This trail is a one-way spur that continues the steep ascent for another half mile through a notch to the alpine area at 2700ft. From here, rock cairns continue another mile up an open alpine ridge to a 3160ft summit. There are no developed campsites along the route, but good backcountry camping exists above the tree line.

The climb is challenging, but the views are great. The 3160ft summit rivals Poot Peak for its panoramic views, but without the loose scree and hazardous climb. Plan on an additional two hours if you add this trail to your itinerary.

Stage 3A: Halibut Cove Lagoon to Saddle Trailhead
6mi, 3 to 4 hours
Unless you have arranged a pickup in Halibut Cove Lagoon or Haystack trailhead (see Getting To/From the Hike), you're going to have to backtrack along Lagoon Trail to catch the afternoon ferry departing Saddle Trailhead. It's a challenging 5.5mi

hike, with a steep climb from the ranger station to the posted junction with the Saddle Trail. Remember to time the hike so you are fording Halibut Creek near low tide.

From the junction with the Saddle Trail you head south for a very steep descent to the **Saddle Trailhead** on the upper portion of Halibut Cove. The trailhead is flanked to the north by private property and a dwelling; on the south side is a small beach area with the piled remains of an old cannery. Occasionally, this is the preferred pick-up point, especially in bad weather, as it offers considerable protection from the wicked surf off Kachemak Bay.

Stage 3B: Halibut Cove Lagoon to Haystack Trailhead

9mi, 5 to 6 hours

An alternative to backtracking Lagoon Trail is to hike to the Haystack trailhead via China Poot Lake and Wosnesenski Trails. From Halibut Cove, **China Poot Lake Trail** extends south 2.6mi past three lakes to a campsite on its namesake lake. The trail is an easy hike, but the first half mile is an uphill walk of almost 500ft to the first lake and the junction with **Coalition Trail** (see the boxed text 'The Coalition Trail: Saving a Wilderness').

China Poot Lake Trail then levels out through a spruce forest and muskeg area and in a mile reaches **Two Loon Lake** and a junction with Moose Valley Trail. Built in 1998, **Moose Valley Trail** is a 6mi loop off of China Poot Lake Trail that connects with the Poot Peak Trail. It first extends east to a campsite on Moose Valley Creek and then turns south to connect with the Poot Peak Trail, a 6mi loop off of China Poot Lake Trail.

In its final mile to China Poot Lake, the China Poot Lake Trail levels off and then passes a **rental cabin** on the lake and then a campsite just before crossing a bridge over **Moose Valley Creek**. It ends at a posted junction with Poot Peak Trail and Wosnesenski Trail. For rental information, see the Cabins & Shelters section, earlier.

Poot Peak Trail is a 4.6mi loop with a spur route that climbs to the 2600ft summit. This trail is not maintained and is very challenging. Plan three to four hours if following the

North Poot Peak Route from the China Poot Lake campsite. To climb the peak at the end involves scrambling up loose scree and fractured rock with poor handholds. Think twice before undertaking it in threatening weather.

Wosnesenski Trail, often called 'the Woz' by locals, begins with a 2.3mi segment that heads south along the shoreline of three lakes formed by a geological fault. For the most part, the trail is an easy walk along level terrain, but near the end you climb over a low saddle and descend to Wosnesenski River, draining from its namesake glacier 5mi to the east. There are good camping areas on the open gravel flats surrounding the river.

You can explore the valley, but heading east towards the glacier you soon run into cliffs on the north side. It's far easier to reach the glacier on the south shore, but that means fording Wosnesenski River. This glacial river is very difficult to ford and should be attempted only at low levels.

In 1998, the Wosnesenski Trail was extended west along the river and now reaches the Haystack trailhead at the mouth of the Wosnesenski River in Neptune Bay. It's a 9mi trek from the China Poot Lake campsite to the trailhead where you can prearrange to be picked up by boat (see Getting To/From the Hike, earlier).

Other Hikes

CHUGACH NATIONAL FOREST
Crescent Creek Trail

Half a mile beyond Crescent Creek Campground, this trail leads 6.5mi to the outlet of Crescent Lake and a USFS cabin ($35 per night). Crescent Lake Cabin can be reserved in advance by calling the National Recreation Reservation Center (☎ 518-885-3639, 877-444-6777) or through its Web site (www.reserveusa.com). The trail is an easy walk, and the fall colors are beautiful in September. From the cabin, there is access to the high country, and anglers can fish for arctic grayling in the lake during summer and fall (USGS quads *Seward B-7, C-7* and *C-8*).

Carter Lake Trail

At the east end of Crescent Lake is Carter Lake Trail. Beginning at Mile 33 of the Seward Hwy, this 3.5mi trail provides quick but steep access into the subalpine area. It begins as an old Jeep trail and, from the parking area on the west side of the highway, ascends almost 1000ft to Carter Lake in 2.3mi, where there are scenic camping spots.

From the lake, a trail continues another mile or so around the west side of the lake to Crescent Lake. Carter Lake and Crescent Creek Trails are connected by Crescent Lake Trail, a minimally maintained trail that follows the south shore for 9mi. The trail passes through alder thickets, grassy openings and small spruce forests and halfway along reaches the USFS Crescent Saddle Cabin (see the previous hike for reservation information). You might encounter mountain bikes on the two trails but not usually on the route in between (USGS quads *Seward B-7* and *C-7*).

Ptarmigan Creek Trail

Beginning in the USFS Ptarmigan Creek Campground (26 sites, $6; see Crescent Creek Trail for contact information), this 7.5mi trail leads to Ptarmigan Lake, a beautiful body of water that reflects the mountains surrounding it. From the campground, the trail follows a creek and, in 3.5mi, reaches the lake. A 4mi trail continues around the north side of the lake, which offers good fishing for Dolly Varden at its outlet to the creek. Plan on five hours for a return hike to the lake, as some parts of the trail are steep. The campground and trailhead are at Ptarmigan Creek Bridge, Mile 23 of the Seward Hwy (USGS quads *Seward B-6* and *B-7*).

Victor Creek Trail

Farther south on the Seward Hwy at Mile 19.7 is the trailhead for this fairly difficult path. In 3mi Victor Creek gains 1100ft (most of it in the first mile) to reach the alpine area with good views of the surrounding mountains, including Andy Simons Mountain and Sheep Mountain. Plan on at least two hours to reach the end of the trail. From there it's often possible to see mountain goats on the slopes above (USGS quad *Seward B-7*).

Grayling Lake Trail

This is an easy 2mi hike to Grayling Lake and the side trails to Meridian Lake and Leech Lake (a beautiful spot with good views of Snow River Valley). All three lakes can be fished for grayling and there are high-bush cranberries in the open meadows. The fishers' trail to Leech Lake is along the eastern shore of Grayling Lake, half a mile from where the main trail reaches the lake's north end. The trailhead is in a paved parking lot at Mile 13.2 on the west side of the Seward Hwy. This trail is shown on the Primrose & Lost Lake Trails map in this book (USGS quad *Seward B-7*).

Goldenfin Lake Trail

This family hike is only 0.6mi (one way) from the trailhead at Mile 11.6 of Seward Hwy to the small lake. It's about a 30-minute hike, and the trail can be wet and muddy at times. The lake can be fished for Dolly Varden, and blueberry picking is excellent from mid- to late August. This trail is shown on the Primrose & Lost Lake Trails map in this book (USGS quad *Seward B-7*).

Gull Rock Trail

This is a fine hike for those spending an extra day or two in Hope. From Porcupine Campground, this trail is an easy 5.1mi one-way walk to Gull Rock, a rocky point 140ft above the Turnagain shoreline. The trail follows an old wagon road built at the turn of the century, and along the way there are the remains of a cabin and a sawmill to explore. You also get an occasional view of the Turnagain Arm and even Mt McKinley on a clear day during this extremely scenic trek.

It's possible to camp at Gull Rock if you pack water, but it's better to return to Porcupine Campground to spend the night. The trip to Gull Rock and back takes four to six hours (USGS quad *Seward D-8*).

Hope Point

Another good choice if you're spending extra time in Hope, this is more a route than a trail. It follows an alpine ridge, giving incredible views of Turnagain Arm. Begin at the entrance sign to Porcupine Campground, where the trail is posted, and follow a path along the right-hand side of small Porcupine Creek. After 0.3mi, the trail leaves the side of the creek and begins to ascend a bluff to the right, reaching an outcrop (offering good views of Turnagain Arm) in 45 minutes or so. From here, you can follow the ridge above the tree line to Hope Point (3708ft). Other than an early summer snowfield, there is no water source after Porcupine Creek (USGS quad *Seward D-8*).

CAINES HEAD STATE RECREATION AREA
Race Point Trail

The most popular trail near Seward is the trek towards the top of Mt Marathon, the mountain that sits behind the city. The route is well known throughout Alaska. In 1909, two sourdough miners wagered how long it would take to run to the top and back and then dashed off for the peak. After that, it became an official event at the Seward Fourth of July celebrations, and today the race attracts hundreds of runners and an equal number of spectators. The fastest time is 43 minutes and 23 seconds, set in 1981. Most runners come down the mountain in less than 10 minutes, usually by sliding halfway on their behinds.

Hikers, on the other hand, can take their time and enjoy the spectacular views of Seward and Resurrection Bay. The hikers' trail begins at the end of Monroe St where a yellow gate blocks vehicle access on an old road. Follow the road and head left at the first fork. At one point a spur departs for the runners' route, but the hikers' trail is the main one. After skirting a creek, it arrives at Race Point.

The runners' trail begins at the west end of Jefferson St (also known as Lowell St) and heads up Lowell Canyon Rd to a picnic area, where the trailhead is posted just past a pair of water tanks. Scramble up the ridge to the right of the gully; for fun return through the gully's scree. You never really reach Mt Marathon's 4603ft summit – that's left to climbers with mountaineering equipment. Race Point, a high point of 3022ft on the broad east shoulder, is still a good afternoon hike though. Plan on three to four hours for the 3mi roundtrip (USGS quad *Seward A-7*).

Iditarod National Historic Trail

Although most of the world knows the Iditarod as a sled-dog race from Anchorage to Nome, the legendary trail actually begins in Seward. There is a historical marker in Hoben Park at the foot of 4th Ave to mark Mile 0; from there a paved bike path heads north along the beach.

A far more interesting segment for hikers, however, is reached by heading east on Nash Rd just after the Seward Hwy crosses the Resurrection River. Within 2mi you'll cross Sawmill Creek and arrive at a gravel parking lot on the north side of the road. From here you can follow the Iditarod Trail through the woods for the 4mi hike to Bear Lake. The best map is *Kenai Fjords National Park* by Trails Illustrated.

Two Lakes Trail

This easy, 1mi loop goes through a wooded area and passes two small lakes at the base of Mt Marathon. Begin the hike near the first lake behind the Alaska Vocational & Training Center at 2nd Ave and B St. Near the start of the trail is a scenic waterfall.

Exit Glacier Nature Trail

The NPS maintains a series of trails at Exit Glacier, reached from Exit Glacier Rd at Mile 3.7 of Seward Hwy. The first is a half-mile nature trail that departs from the ranger station and winds through cottonwood forest, alder thickets and along old glacial moraines before emerging at the information shelter. It's a great way to return from the glacier if you're not up to facing the mass of humanity on the paved trail.

Other Exit Glacier Trails

A network of loops provides close access to the ice itself from the information center. The Lower Loop Trail is an easy half-mile walk to the outwash plain in front of the ice. All around there are warning signs advising you to stay away from the face due to the danger of falling ice.

The Upper Loop Trail departs off the first loop and climbs steeply to an overlook at the side of the glacier before returning. Combined, the trails are not much more than a mile long; sections may be closed at times because of falling ice. Don't skip the short spur to Falls Overlook, a scenic cascade off the upper trail.

Harding Ice Field Trail

Besides the trails from the ranger station to Exit Glacier, the only other developed hike in the glacier area is the trek to Harding Ice Field. The hike to the ice field is a challenging ascent that follows a steep, roughly cut and sometimes slippery route on the north side of Exit Glacier, beginning at its base. It's a 5mi, one-way hike to the ice field at 3500ft for reasonably fit hikers, a good four-hour hike/climb.

The all-day trek is well worth it for those with the stamina, as it provides spectacular views of the ice field and Exit Glacier and the valley below. The upper section of the route is snow covered for much of the year.

You pick up the trailhead at the start of the Lower Loop Trail, and within 30 minutes, you'll see the glacier. Above the tree line the trail is not the well-cut path it is in the beginning, and at times you will have to look twice to see it. Near the ice field, the NPS maintains an emergency shelter. If you want some company on this challenging hike, a ranger leads an all-day hike to the ice field every Saturday at 8 am (USGS quad *Seward A-7*).

KENAI NATIONAL WILDLIFE REFUGE

Most of the trails on the western half of the Kenai Peninsula are in the Kenai National Wildlife Refuge and administered by the US Fish & Wildlife Service (USF&WS).

Stop at the refuge visitor center (☎ 262-7021) for information on hiking or to pick up the booklet *Kenai National Wildlife Refuge Hiking Trails*. The center is reached from the Sterling Hwy just south of Soldotna by turning east on Funny River Rd and then turning immediately south onto Ski Hill Rd for a mile. Along with a good series of wildlife displays, daily slide shows and wildlife films in its theater, the center has naturalist-led outdoor programs on the weekends. Hours are 8 am to 4:30 pm weekdays and 10 am to 6 pm weekends.

Fuller Lake Trail

This 3mi trail begins at Mile 57.2 of the Sterling Hwy and ends at Upper Fuller Lake just above the tree line. The trail, an old road blocked by logs, climbs rapidly in the first half until you reach Lower Fuller Lake. Here, you cross a stream and move into dwarf willow and birch to continue over a low pass to Fuller Lake.

There are several backcountry campsites along the trail between the two lakes, but the best place to spend the night is at Upper Fuller Lake, where you'll enjoy spectacular views of the surrounding mountains.

A spare day can be spent scrambling up the nearby ridges or fishing for grayling in Lower Fuller Lake or Dolly Varden in the upper lake. The trail is rated moderate; plan on two to three hours to reach Fuller Lake (USGS quads *Kenai B-1* and *C-1*).

Skyline Trail

Near Fuller Lake Trail, this 1.2mi climb begins on the north side of the Sterling Hwy at Mile 61. It is a challenging climb of 1800ft that provides quick access to Mystery Hills. From the forest, the trail emerges above the tree line in 0.75mi and ends in the alpine area where there are views of the Kenai Mountains in one direction and Cook Inlet in the other.

It's also possible to form a loop from the Skyline and Fuller Lake trails. Just beyond Fuller Lake (see previous hike) is a junction; the left-hand fork leads up a ridge to the Skyline Trail. It is an alpine route that should only be attempted by experienced hikers. The entire loop is 12mi, and reaches the high point of 3520ft (USGS quad *Kenai C-1*).

Kenai River Trail

This 5.5mi trail provides access to the lower Kenai River. The upper portion of the trail is a 3mi hike from Skilak Lake Rd past good views of Kenai River Canyon. It ends at a fork with either branch continuing to the lower section of the trail. Continue on the left-hand fork, and you'll reach the river in half a mile. Follow the river closely until the trail reaches a dead end after 1.5mi.

There are two trailheads; the first is less than a mile west on Skilak Lake Rd from its junction with the Sterling Hwy at Mile 58. The second is 2.4mi from the junction, at a USF&WS Visitor Center (USGS quad *Kenai B-1*).

Hidden Creek Loop

This easy walk along level terrain begins a mile west of Hidden Lake Campground. In less than a mile, the trail divides: The right-hand fork heads directly to the shores of Skilak Lake, and the other fork first swings past Hidden Creek. Along this branch it's possible to pick up a spur that crosses the creek and joins the Kenai River Trail. Hidden Creek Trail is a 3mi roundtrip involving little climbing. It's possible to camp along the shores of Skilak Lake (USGS quad *Kenai B-1*).

Skilak Lookout Trail

Beginning at Mile 5.5 of Skilak Lake Rd, Skilak Lookout Trail ascends 2.6mi to a knob at 1450ft with excellent views of the surrounding mountains and lakes. Plan on four to five hours for the roundtrip and bring water, as there is none on the trail. Campgrounds nearby include Upper Skilak Lake, 3mi to the west on Skilak Lake Rd, and Hidden Lake Campground, 2mi to the east. Reservations can't be made for these campgrounds. The camping fee at each is $10 a night. For information contact the Kenai National Wildlife Refuge office in Soldotna (☎ 262-7021; USGS quad *Kenai B-1*).

Seven Lakes Trail

This point-to-point trail is a 5mi hike to the Sterling Hwy from Skilak Lake Rd. The southern trailhead is at the end of a spur to Engineer Lake at Mile 9.7 of Skilak Lake Rd. The trail is an easy walk over level terrain and passes Hidden and Hikers Lakes before ending at Kelly Lake Campground on a side road off the Sterling Hwy. Be prepared for wet and muddy sections in the middle, especially between Hidden and Engineer Lakes (USGS quads *Kenai B-1* and *C-1*).

HOMER AREA
Bishop Beach Hike

For all the natural beauty that surrounds it, the city of Homer lacks good public trails. The best hiking is along the beaches, because most trails off the road system are private paths that usually lead to somebody's homestead or cabin. This hike begins at Bishop Park and makes either an excellent afternoon stroll or a 10mi trek north of Homer. The views of Kachemak Bay and the Kenai Mountains are superb, and the marine life you'll see scurrying along the sand at low tide is fascinating.

Check a tide book, available from most gasoline stations or sports stores, and leave before low tide and return before high tide. High tides cover most of the sand, forcing you to scramble onto the base of the nearby cliffs. Within 3mi of the park you'll pass a sea otter rookery a few hundred yards offshore, and in 7mi, you'll reach Diamond Creek. Head south on Main St, then left on Bunnell Ave and right on Beluga Ave to reach Bishop Park (USGS quad *Seldovia C-5*).

Homestead Trail

This trail, developed by the Kachemak Heritage Land Trust (KHLT), is a 6.7mi trek from Rogers Loop Rd to the city reservoir just off Skyline Dr on Crossman Ridge Rd. From Rogers Loop Rd it's a 2.5mi walk to Rucksack Drive, which crosses Diamond Ridge Rd. Along the way you pass through open meadows where there are panoramic views of Kachemak Bay and Mt Iliamna and Mt Redoubt on the other side of Cook Inlet. The hike continues another 4.2mi by following Rucksack Dr and Crossman Ridge Rd to the reservoir. Cars are banned from both of these dirt roads.

To reach the west of the trail, head out of town on the Sterling Hwy and then turn right on Rogers Loop Rd across from Bay View Inn. The trailhead will be a half mile on your right. For an interpretive brochure on the trail stop at the Kachemak Heritage Land Trust office (☎ 235-5263) at 395 E Pioneer Ave.

Grace Ridge Trail

Built in 1998, this 7mi trail stretches from a campsite at Kayak Beach Trailhead to deep inside Tutka Bay in Kachemak Bay State Park. Much of the hike is above the tree line along the crest of Grace Ridge where, needless to say, the views are stunning. You could hike the trail in a day, but it makes a great two-day hike with an overnight camp in the alpine. Tutka Bay Taxi (☎ 235-7166) will provide transportation from Homer to Kayak Beach and then pick you up at the South Grace Ridge Trailhead for the return trip for $45 per person.

Copper River Region

The Copper River originates in the Wrangell Mountains and empties into the Gulf of Alaska, forming the western boundary of Wrangell–St Elias National Park at one end and supporting Cordova, with its rich salmon fishery, at the other end. This chapter covers hiking in both the national park and outside the fishing town. These are isolated areas of Alaska. Cordova can only be reached by air or on board an Alaska Marine Hwy ferry, and only two rough roads provide passage into Wrangell–St Elias.

Wrangell–St Elias National Park

The road to McCarthy, the main access road to Wrangell–St Elias National Park, begins with a highway sign informing you that the vehicle bridge at the end is washed out. Then it warns you to watch out for loose spikes. Finally, it sends you off with this blessing: *Drive At Your Own Risk.* From the end of the Edgerton Hwy to the historical mining town of McCarthy, it's 62mi of dust and flying stones, a 25mph-drive over a surface that resembles grandma's washboard, with potholes that would be legendary if this were any state other than Alaska. Built on the abandoned bed of the Copper River & Northwestern Railway, the road is littered with railroad artifacts. Iron rails line the shoulders, and railroad ties are still half buried in the road. Then there are the railroad spikes. Six inches long, sharp at one end, blunt at the other – they used to hold the rails in place, but now the spikes chew tires like a three-year-old eats candy on Easter morning.

The road ends at the Kennicott River, across from McCarthy, a beautiful mountainous hamlet with a year-round population of eight to 20 people, depending on who's staying for the winter. What's amazing isn't that this century-old town can

only be reached by a footbridge. What's truly amazing is that McCarthy Rd, without guardrails, pavement or a single gasoline station, is the main access route to the largest national park in the USA. Created in 1980 as part of the Alaska Lands Bill, Wrangell–St Elias National Park & Preserve sprawls across 20,625 sq mi in the Southcentral region of the state. The park abuts Canada's Kluane National Park, and together their 31,250 sq mi represent one of the largest wilderness areas left in the world, the reason the two parks have been recognized by the United Nations as a world heritage site.

There are few, if any, maintained trails in this park that are of the same standard as those in Chugach National Forest, but Wrangell–St Elias is laced with old mining roads, historical horse-packing trails and

COPPER RIVER

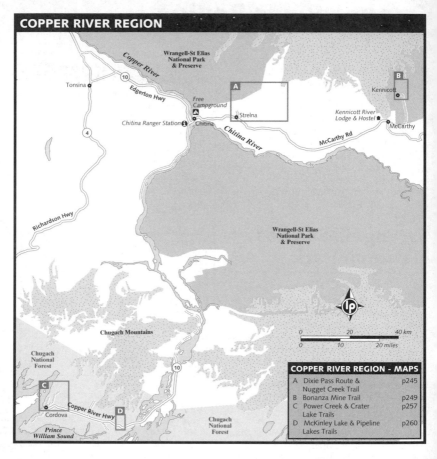

COPPER RIVER REGION

Wrangell-St Elias National Park & Preserve

Copper River

Tonsina

Edgerton Hwy

Free Campground

Chitina Ranger Station

Chitina

Strelna

Chitina River

McCarthy Rd

Kennicott

Kennicott River Lodge & Hostel

McCarthy

B

A

Richardson Hwy

Wrangell-St Elias National Park & Preserve

Chugach Mountains

Chugach National Forest

Cordova

Copper River Hwy

Prince William Sound

Chugach National Forest

C

D

0   20   40 km
0   10   20 miles

COPPER RIVER REGION - MAPS

A	Dixie Pass Route & Nugget Creek Trail	p245
B	Bonanza Mine Trail	p249
C	Power Creek & Crater Lake Trails	p257
D	McKinley Lake & Pipeline Lakes Trails	p260

COPPER RIVER

other avenues to its interior. Many trails require bush-plane travel to reach their remote locations, but the three routes described in this section – Dixie Pass, Nugget Creek and Bonanza Mine – can be reached from McCarthy Rd, thus eliminating the expensive air-taxi charter cost.

Even with public transportation to McCarthy, the Wrangell–St Elias area is still not a quick side trip or a spur-of-the-moment outing. This is not Denali by any stretch of the imagination. There is no park bus, elaborate visitor center or easy access to campgrounds. In fact, the park has few campgrounds. Although the number of visitors to McCarthy and Kennicott is increasing by leaps and bounds every year (more than 30,000 made their way to the historic towns in the late 1990s), the logistics of putting a hike together here are far more difficult than in almost any other area covered in this book.

NATURAL HISTORY

Wrangell–St Elias is characterized by its high peaks and massive glaciers. Four great ranges, Chugach, Wrangell, St Elias and the eastern end of the Alaskan Range, converge in an area the size of six Yellowstones. The St Elias Range merges with the Wrangells in the heart of the park and then arcs eastward past the Canadian border, where it forms the highest coastal range in the world.

Alaska's highest peak, Mt McKinley (20,320ft), may be in Denali National Park, but within the borders of Wrangell–St Elias are nine of the 16 highest peaks in the country, including the second highest, Mt St Elias (18,008ft), Mt Bona (16,500ft), Mt Blackburn (16,390ft) and Mt Sanford (16,237ft). And then there's the Bagley Ice Field, the largest subpolar ice field in North America. It spawns such giant glaciers as the Malaspina Glacier complex, an ice floe bigger than the state of Rhode Island.

From its glaciated roof of mountains and peaks, the terrain in the park descends to the north as treeless tundra and then boreal-forested uplands. To the south, the glaciers extend from the mountains almost to the tidewaters of the Gulf of Alaska.

Dall sheep and mountain goats live in the alpine region, caribou around the Wrangell Mountains to the north and moose in the bogs and brushy areas of the lowlands. Bison were released in Copper River Valley in 1950 and along the Chitina River in 1962, and remnants of those herds remain today. Black and brown bears roam throughout the park.

CLIMATE

The park has a rainy maritime climate in the south along the coast, and farther north, you can enjoy the dry summers of Interior Alaska. Kennicott and the areas off McCarthy Rd, for the most part, are shielded by the Wrangell Mountains to the north and by the Chugach Mountains to the south. During much of the summer, this topography creates a pattern of warm, dry weather. Even so, the range of temperatures between day and night is remarkable. In July, it's not unusual to experience a string of 80°F afternoons and have the temperatures drop to the 40s (F) or even the 30s at night.

Like high, mountainous topography elsewhere, the Wrangell and Chugach Mountains create weather that can change suddenly and often. Enjoy the sun, but keep your rain gear handy. By mid- to late August, expect cool and cloudy days, as well as rain. Annual precipitation is 17 inches, much of it falling as rain in late August and September.

INFORMATION

The park's main headquarters (☎ 822-5234), PO Box 439, Copper Center, AK 99573, is at Mile 105 of Richardson Hwy, 10mi before the junction with the Glenn Hwy. The office is open 8 am to 6 pm daily during the summer, and rangers can answer questions about the park and supply various handouts and rough maps of the area. This is also the best place to leave your trip itinerary. The national park also maintains a Web site (www.nps.gov/wrst).

During the summer, rangers are stationed in a log cabin visitor center (☎ 823-2205), in Chitina at the end of Edgerton Hwy, that is open during the summer from 10 am to 6 pm.

In Anchorage, head to the Alaska Public Lands Information Center (☎ 271-2737), 605 W 4th Ave, for information on the park.

GETTING THERE & AWAY

Most visitors to the park enter via Edgerton Hwy and McCarthy Rd, arriving from either Glennallen or Valdez. These two roads provide a 92mi route into the heart of the park, ending at the footbridge that crosses the Kennicott River to McCarthy. The 32mi Edgerton Hwy, fully paved, begins at Mile 82.6 of Richardson Hwy and ends at Chitina. The town, which has 40 or so permanent residents, is the last place you can purchase gas and get a reasonably priced meal.

From Chitina, McCarthy Rd – a rough dirt road that is not regularly maintained – leads 60mi to the Kennicott River. Your $40-a-day Rent-A-Wreck can usually travel this stretch during the summer, but plan on three to four hours for the trip. If it has been raining hard, don't attempt it at all.

Air

Several small air companies fly daily service between McCarthy and Glennallen. Ellis Air (☎ 822-3363, 800-478-3368 in Alaska) departs the Gulkana airstrip at 10 am on

Wednesday and Friday, arrives in McCarthy at 11 am and then turns around and heads back. The one-way fare is $62. Wrangell Mountain Air (☎ 554-4440, 800-478-1160) has service between McCarthy, Glennallen and Chitina. A roundtrip flight between Chitina and McCarthy is $130 and doubles as a flightseeing trip that includes five glaciers and the mountaintop mines on Bonanza Peak.

Bus

Backcountry Connection (☎ 822-5292, 800-478-5292 in Alaska) provides transportation out of Glennallen to the McCarthy footbridge. The small tour company departs from Caribou Motel on Glenn Hwy at 7 am Monday through Saturday, reaching Chitina at 8:30 am and the McCarthy footbridge at noon. After a five-hour layover, enough time to see McCarthy and the ruins at Kennicott, the van backtracks to Glennallen, reaching the crossroads town at 8:30 pm. The roundtrip fare, if you return on a different day, is $105 and one-way is $70. The roundtrip fare is slightly less if you return on the same day as you arrive.

Dixie Pass Route

Duration 4 to 5 days
Distance 22mi roundtrip
Difficulty Level Hard
Start/Finish Nugget Creek/Kotsina Rd
Cabins & Shelters No
Permits Required No
Public Transportation Yes
Summary The Dixie Pass Route is a popular wilderness adventure into the interior of Wrangell–St Elias National Park that doesn't require bush-plane travel. Dixie Pass offers superb scenery, good camping and opportunities to spend an extra day or two hiking the ridges.

Easily accessed by McCarthy Rd, Dixie Pass is probably the most popular hike for backpackers looking for a multiday adventure in Wrangell–St Elias National Park. The fact

that no bush-plane travel is required is what attracts most hikers to this route, but once the hikers are on the trail, it doesn't take long for the mountain scenery, remoteness of the wilderness and the wildlife to replace the savings on airfare as the highlight of the trip.

Initially, the trail is easy to identify, but for much of the 11mi hike to the pass, you'll follow streambeds or use game trails to make your way up the valley. The trip is rated hard, but it is certainly within the ability of most hikers who have experienced the trail-less areas of Denali National Park and, of course, can use a map and compass. For hikes like these, being able to look at mountains, streams and ridges and relate them to your topographical map is the key to successful hiking.

Most people take two days to climb to Dixie Pass, where they spend a spare day and then backtrack to the trailhead, making this a four- to five-day, 22mi hike. The 11mi return from Dixie Pass to the trailhead makes for a long day but can be done by hikers who are in good shape.

Be aware that bears can be encountered anywhere along the route. Keep your camp clean.

PLANNING
When to Hike

The best time of year for this hike is mid-June through mid-September. In July and August, however, don't be surprised if you encounter other hiking parties in the area.

What to Bring

The route to Dixie Pass requires numerous bridgeless stream crossings. Either bring a spare pair of shoes or accept that you'll be hiking in soggy boots for most of the second half of the trail. Also carry head nets and some potent bug repellent. The mosquitoes can be murderous in the beginning, when you are hiking through spruce and willow lowlands. Often, you'll get relief from them only after you climb close to the tree line.

Maps

It is unthinkable to enter this park without the proper USGS 1:63,360 series quads.

COPPER RIVER

Unfortunately, none of the hikes discussed in this section are conveniently covered by just one sheet. Dixie Pass is covered on USGS 1:63,360 quads *Valdez C-1* and *McCarthy C-8*. The best place to purchase the maps is at the park headquarters (see the Information section, earlier) in Copper Center. Then get a ranger to outline the hike on your map and ask how the trailhead on Nugget Creek/Kotsina Rd is marked. The map *Wrangell–St Elias National Park and Preserve*, by Trails Illustrated, does not provide enough detail to make it suitable for hikers.

NEAREST TOWNS & FACILITIES

Pick up food, white gas or other supplies in Valdez, Glennallen or Copper Center, which has a gas station, a small grocery store and a post office. In Chitina, there is also a grocery store, post office and two restaurants; the *Chitina Cafe* is a good place to stop for your 'last supper' before the hike.

Copper Center

Copper Center, off the Richardson Hwy near Mile 101, is not only home for the park headquarters but also an interesting village with a touch of Alaskan character that is lacking in Glennallen to the north. At the turn of the century, Copper Center was an important mining camp and today it's still a logical place to gather information and supplies for a journey into the park.

Places to Stay & Eat Historic and affordable lodging is available at *Copper Center Lodge (☎ 822-3245)*, which began in 1897 as the Blix Roadhouse and was the first lodge built north of Valdez. Don't pass up its breakfast of sourdough pancakes, reputedly made from century-old starter. Rooms with shared bath/private bath are $84/94 for two people.

The nearest campground to Edgerton Hwy is *Squirrel Creek State Campground (Mile 79.4 of Richardson Hwy, 3mi south of the junction)* with 14 sites for $10 per night. The scenic little camping area is on the banks of the creek and is often filled with anglers and others trying to catch grayling and rainbow trout.

Getting There & Away Any Alaskon Express bus (☎ 277-5581, 800-478-6388) making the Valdez-Anchorage run can drop you off in Glennallen or near Copper Center. The one-way fare is $61 to Glennallen. If you're already in Glennallen, at least one Alaskon Express bus passes through daily in the early afternoon heading south to Valdez, skirting the park and passing the start of the Edgerton Hwy. Gray Line picks up passengers and sells tickets at the Caribou Cafe (☎ 822-3656) on the Glenn Hwy.

Even better and cheaper is Parks Highway Express bus (☎ 888-600-6001). On Wednesday, Friday and Sunday from either Fairbanks or Anchorage, the van passes through Glennallen and then reaches the Wrangell–St Elias National Park Headquarters in Copper Center at 2:50 pm. One-way fare to Copper Center from Anchorage or Fairbanks is $45.

Edgerton Hwy & McCarthy Rd

Within Chitina, at the end of the Edgerton Hwy, backpackers can camp along the 3mi road south to O'Brien Creek or beside Town Lake. The best spot, however, is *Liberty Falls State Recreation Site*, 10mi before you reach Chitina. The campground has only three, maybe four sites for RVers, but it has another half a dozen spots for tents, including four tent platforms right along rushing Liberty Creek. There is no piped-in water here, but thundering Liberty Falls is within the campground. The fee is $10 per night.

There is also a *small campground* with eight free sites next to the Copper River Bridge. It is maintained by the Alaska Department of Transportation and used primarily by dipnetters who descend on Chitina in July and August to scoop up red and king salmon. At Mile 11 of McCarthy Rd is *Silver Lake Campground* (no phone), a commercial facility with very limited services (gas is not one of them).

At Mile 14.5, you come to the access road to the trailheads for Dixie Pass and Nugget Creek Trail. By heading up the access road a couple miles, you'll reach *Strelna Zephyr Bunkhouse*. Sandy Casteler and her family run the quaint log-cabin accommodations. Inside, they have four bunks and a woodstove but no running water or electricity. Don't worry about advance reservations, the family has no phone.

GETTING TO/FROM THE HIKE
From Chitina, follow McCarthy Rd for roughly 14.5mi to the Strelna airstrip, a grass airstrip on the south side of the road. On the north side is Nugget Creek/Kotsina Rd, marked by a painted white rail wheel with 'Nugget Creek' written on it in red letters (it can be tough to spot in the tall brush at times). Follow this road northwest, and in 2.5mi you will reach the intersection of Nugget Creek Rd, which crosses the creek (see Nugget Creek Trail later in this chapter), and Kotsina Rd. If your car has low clearance, high mileage or a loose bumper, park here and walk the rest of the way. Continue on Kotsina Rd, and in 1.3mi you will come to the trailhead on the right. Generally, a stick or pile of rocks marks the trail, but don't bet on it.

If you're without a vehicle, make arrangements with Backcountry Connection (☎ 822-5292) to be dropped off and picked up at McCarthy Rd. Then just add 4mi to your hike on the first and last day.

THE HIKE
Stage 1: Kotsina Rd to Strelna Creek Confluence
6mi, 4 to 6 hours
From the Dixie Pass trailhead, if you can call it that, the initial 2mi is on a well-defined trail along a level bench area forested in paper birch, spruce and willow. The hiking is easy, and within a mile, you break out of the trees to your first glimpse of the mountains.

Eventually, you sharply descend a riverbank to arrive at **Strelna Creek**, a fast-flowing stream at this point, where the current is rippling around a series of boulders. The trail swings northeast and follows the west bank of the stream, but first makes a very steep climb and an equally steep descent to bypass a narrow gorge.

For the next 3mi, you stay along the west bank of the stream; the trail is fairly easy to

recognize. You reach the **first confluence** of Strelna Creek approximately 6mi from the trailhead, where a tree trunk allows you to cross the river without getting your boots wet.

After crossing Strelna Creek, continue northeast along the stream that drains the Dixie Pass area. Once along the new drainage creek, you'll immediately begin passing gravel bars where you can camp. You'll find more gravel bars a half mile upstream. The farther you hike upstream, the higher you'll climb, and the more the bugs will diminish.

Stage 2: Strelna Creek Confluence to Dixie Pass
5mi, 5 to 7 hours
Remain on the northwest side of the drainage creek, where there are easy-to-follow animal trails along the banks. Eventually, a sheer cliff forces you to ford the river back and forth, following game trails, dry streambeds or gravel bars.

Within one to two hours, approximately 2mi from Strelna Creek, you reach the **second confluence**. Ford to the westerly channel and choose a side to travel on. I found the west side had a well-developed animal trail almost halfway to the gorge, but that can change from season to season. At this point, the brush begins to thin out, and bashing through the waist-high willow is no longer a painful experience.

Within a mile upstream, you can spot Dixie Pass if the day is clear. You also pass numerous gravel bars that make excellent campsites if you got an early start the first day. After several fords, you round a huge and distinctive rock bluff and then enter a gorge. The short gorge has impressive walls on both sides, and if the water is low, you can practically skip through it. When the stream is at its normal level, you can slosh your way through it to reach the west end, but if the stream is high, it's best for hikers to climb the easterly ridge and avoid the gorge completely.

The valley broadens out on the other side of the gorge, and good camping spots abound on wide gravel bars. Many people

DIXIE PASS ROUTE & NUGGET CREEK TRAIL

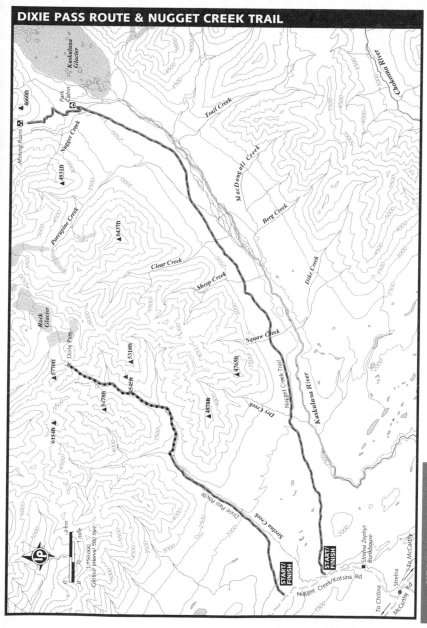

set up camp here and continue on to Dixie Pass with only a day pack.

After reaching the **third confluence** at the end of the gravel bars, you begin the final leg to the pass. This 2mi hike climbs a ridgeline between the two streams. Within a mile, you emerge in the alpine tundra and then begin the final climb to **Dixie Pass**, along an apparent route. Enough hikers trek to the pass every summer that there is now something of a beaten path to it. This climb is steep but is often done with heavy backpacks.

Needless to say, the views from the 5100ft pass are spectacular if the weather is clear. You can see the Strelna Creek area and also Rock Creek Valley on the north side. On top, you'll find camping spots for two or three small tents and ridge lines to follow for more adventure. For the best views, climb to the high point of 5770ft on the ridge to the northeast. Water is available from a nearby snowfield runoff, making it possible to spend a comfortable night or two at the pass.

Stage 3: The Return
11mi, 8 to 12 hours

Most hikers who walk to Dixie Pass simply turn around and return along the side route they hiked in on. This makes a 22mi, three- to five-day hike into the heart of Wrangell–St Elias National Park.

Nugget Creek Trail

Duration 3 to 4 days
Distance 29mi roundtrip
Difficulty Level Medium
Start/Finish Nugget Creek/Kotsina Rd
Cabins & Shelters Yes
Permits Required No
Public Transportation Yes
Summary Nugget Creek Trail is a two-day walk along an old mining pack trail to mining ruins, a cabin and mountain scenery, with a return along the same route.

Nugget Creek is a considerably easier hike than Dixie Pass, as it follows an old mining road most of the way, gradually climbing 1000ft to a park cabin and views of Kuskulana Glacier. For those not comfortable with the trail-less, backcountry travel to Dixie Pass, Nugget Creek Trail is a suitable alternative. This trail is also open to mountain bikes.

Unlike Dixie Pass, you spend the entire hike in the forested lowlands, where bugs persist throughout much of the summer. There are eight major streams to ford, and stretches in the beginning can be muddy. As always, bears can be encountered almost anywhere along this route. Also keep in mind that off-road vehicles can be driven here. All a driver needs is a permit from the park headquarters, which is relatively easy to get. Fortunately, the road is much too rugged and rutted for anything but a four-wheel all-terrain vehicle (ATV). Chances are you'll only encounter miners heading off to their private claims.

Most hikers cover this 29mi roundtrip in three to four days. The trip can be lengthened by spending another day or two at the end, exploring mining ruins or ridge walking in the alpine areas above Nugget Creek. By bringing in some extra supplies and caching them near the start of the Nugget Creek Trail, you could easily do Dixie Pass and Nugget Creek Trail back-to-back before heading on to a cold beer and well-deserved rest in McCarthy. The trailheads are only 1.3mi apart on Nugget Creek/Kotsina Rd and are covered by the same USGS quads.

PLANNING
When to Hike
This trip can be enjoyed June through September. From late August to early September would be an especially nice time, as bugs begin to diminish and fall colors set in.

What to Bring
See the Dixie Pass Route section earlier in this chapter.

Maps
The route is covered on the USGS 1:63,360 quads, *Valdez C-1* and *McCarthy C-8*. The map *Wrangell–St Elias National Park and Preserve,* by Trails Illustrated, does not

provide enough detail to make it suitable for hikers.

Cabins & Shelters

At the end of Nugget Creek Trail, there is an old miner's cabin owned by the NPS and available as a shelter to anybody: hikers, mountain bikers or others who arrive on an off-road vehicle. No fee or reservations are required, but the cabin is not maintained. Mining ruins are scattered through the park, including old bunkhouses, but you should think twice before entering them, much less spending a night in the dilapidated structures.

NEAREST TOWNS & FACILITIES

See the Dixie Pass Route section earlier in this chapter.

GETTING TO/FROM THE HIKE

The trailhead to Nugget Creek Trail is considerably easier to spot along Nugget Creek/Kotsina Rd than the Dixie Pass trailhead. From McCarthy Rd, follow the rough dirt road northwest past the log cabins, which belong to a handful of homesteaders. Within 2.5mi, the road arrives at a small clearing overlooking Strelna Creek. Kotsina Rd continues north and Nugget Creek Trail crosses the stream, the start of the hike. There is parking here for up to six cars.

THE HIKE
Stage 1: Kotsina Rd to Sheep Creek
8mi, 5 to 6 hours

From the parking area, you immediately cross **Strelna Creek**, the first of eight creeks you have to cross to reach the NPS cabin. Strelna is manageable most of the time, but high water can mean a quick end to this adventure. On the other side, you climb up the bank and enter the forest along an old miner's pack trail that today also accommodates mountain bikers and even off-road vehicles occasionally. You will have little difficulty following the trail.

The beginning of the trail can be wet and quite boggy in places; be prepared to get your boots muddy negotiating a route through the ooze. The worst section is reached a half mile into the hike, and you really don't escape it for good until the trail starts climbing gently, 3.5mi from the trailhead. Eventually, you reach 2000ft and cross **Dry Creek**.

At this point, the trail becomes a rolling wooded miners' road through the forest as it heads northeast along a low bench above the Kuskulana River. You don't actually see the river. In fact, you don't see much of anything, because you never leave the forest, even when you cross Nugget Creek toward the end of the trail. You reach **Squaw Creek** 2mi from Dry Creek, or 6mi from the trailhead, and will find camping spots on the banks of this small but clear stream.

From there, it's less than 2mi to **Sheep Creek**. Just after fording Sheep Creek, you will find the best spots to set up camp. Sheep Creek is also a clear-running stream.

Stage 2: Sheep Creek to NPS Cabin
6.5mi, 4 to 5 hours

The second day is a considerably drier, easier hike. Within 1.5mi of Sheep Creek, you cross the appropriately named **Clear Creek**, descend slightly and then, 3mi into the hike, cross **Porcupine Creek**. In another mile, the trail swings to its closest point with the Kuskulana River, though you still remain in a forested setting, and then begins a wide swing to the northeast.

The final leg is a 3mi march along a trail that gently climbs a couple hundred feet and ends when you break out of the trees at the banks of **Nugget Creek**. The creek itself is a silty, braided glacial runoff that can usually be easily forded but may give you problems immediately after a heavy rainstorm or in early summer.

On the other side of the creek is an **old miners' cabin** that is owned by the NPS. The rustic log structure is not maintained, but it is bearproof, will keep you dry during a storm and has three bunks and a woodstove. If there are too many mice running around the cabin for your taste, campsites abound in this area. It's even possible to set up the tent within view of Kuskulana

COPPER RIVER

Glacier, a gravel-covered ice floe. As inviting as it may seem, it's best to stay off the glacier unless you have the knowledge, expertise and equipment to hike on ice.

A better adventure is to continue along the trail as it leaves the cabin and steeply climbs almost 1000ft in its final 2mi, terminating at 4000ft, well above the tree line. Along the way, you pass a few historical **miners' buildings** and even an old horse stable. The trail ends near a private mining claim. From here, it's easy to access the surrounding alpine area for day hikes along the ridgelines.

Stage 3: The Return
14.5mi, 6 to 7 hours

Since the Nugget Creek Trail is a one-way trail, when you leave, you must backtrack to where you started. If you are fit and have a light load you can probably cover the entire 14.5mi in under seven hours, cutting a day off the return and using it for day hiking in the alpine areas at the end of the route. On a mountain bike you'd cover the route in under three hours.

Bonanza Mine Trail

Duration 7½ to 11½ hours
Distance 8mi roundtrip
Difficulty Level Easy to medium
Start/Finish Kennicott
Cabins & Shelters No
Permits Required No
Public Transportation Yes
Summary The best hike from Kennicott is this alpine trek to Bonanza Mine. It's a steep climb, but the views are wonderful and the mining history intriguing.

Out of all the hiking possibilities in the Mc-Carthy/Kennicott area, Bonanza Mine Trail offers the most developed route to the alpine region and spectacular views of the surrounding mountains and glaciers. Even more intriguing for many hikers are the mining artifacts that litter this trail from beginning to end. It's a delightful hike when the weather is pleasant; haul up a tent and

you can camp among the peaks above the tree line. But even when the skies are blue and the sun is shining, it's a hard climb to the historic mine at the top.

You gain 4500ft in the 4mi, one-way hike. A good portion of it is a heart-pounding climb on a moderately steep slope. The trail is actually a rough dirt road, picked up just west of the Kennicott ruins, to the tree line. Once you are above the brush (a three- to four-hour climb for most hikers), the views are stunning.

Like the Chilkoot Trail, this is a hike into history. The best way to begin is to stop at the McCarthy & Kennicott Museum – an old railroad depot that features faded photographs and dusty artifacts dating back to the days when Kennicott was the world's greatest producer of copper. The museum's brochure, *Walking Tour of Kennicott Alaska* ($1), describes the buildings in Kennicott that you'll pass through.

Pack extra water; there isn't any along the trail till near the end. And pack extra time if at all possible. The hike requires at least a full afternoon, and after working so hard to reach the area, it's a shame to have to rush back down. You could easily spend a whole day examining what the miners left behind or enjoying the mountain-top panoramas.

The hike is rated moderate because, though it is a steep climb, it is easy to follow. Arrange a ride to the tree line (see Getting To/From the Hike) and it becomes an easy hike.

PLANNING
When to Hike
Because the trail is a climb into the high alpine country, Bonanza Mine Trail should not be attempted before mid-June or after September.

Maps
The area is covered on USGS 1:63,360 quads *McCarthy B-5*, *B-6* and *C-5*, though this is one of the few hikes on which the quads are not really necessary – just follow the road. If you need quads for the national park while in McCarthy, Willow Herb Mountain Depot, reached 2.5mi before the

footbridge on McCarthy Rd, sells USGS maps. Hopefully, they will have the ones you need. They even take Visa and MasterCard.

NEAREST TOWNS & FACILITIES
McCarthy

Supplies & Equipment It is best to pick up food, white gas or other supplies in Valdez, Glennallen or Copper Center. If you must, you can pick up food, a cold beer and even limited camping supplies from McCarthy Gift Shop and Groceries, near the McCarthy Lodge in McCarthy.

Places to Stay & Eat The cheapest option is camping along the west side of the Kennicott River. A mile before the end of the road, the National Park Service maintains a free camping area. At the end of the road, camping is on private land, and a $5 fee is charged. There are vault toilets but not piped-in water. On the weekends, it can get crowded and dusty here. It's hard to camp around either McCarthy or Kennicott, because most of the land is privately owned.

There is now a hostel in the area. ***Kennicott River Lodge & Hostel*** (☎ 554-4441), at Mile 58 of McCarthy Rd, is a short walk from the end of the road. The two-story log lodge includes a common kitchen, lodge and large porches overlooking the Kennicott Glacier. Accommodations are bunkrooms in the lodge, cabins or wall tents. The rate is $25 per night.

Accommodations options in McCarthy change almost seasonally, so it pays to walk around to see if anybody is renting out a cabin or has started up a B&B. ***McCarthy B&B*** (☎ 554-4433), on McCarthy Rd a half mile from the Kennicott River, has four cabins for $85 for a double without a bath. In the morning, you can enjoy an all-the-pancakes-you-can-eat breakfast in the home of the host, John Adams.

In the heart of McCarthy is the ***McCarthy Lodge*** (☎ 554-4402), which is full of mining relics and photographs of the era, the place to get a bed, meal, shower or a cold beer in a frosty mug. The main lodge has a dining room where full dinners cost $17 to $22 and a lively bar with $3 to $4 beers. Showers are

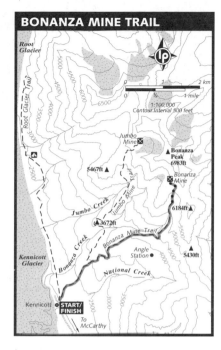

$5, so skip the shower and have a beer. Across the street, the lodge runs ***Ma Johnson's Hotel***. Built in 1916 as a boarding house, and today it is totally renovated. Rooms begin at $95/110 singles/doubles, more if you want your meals included.

Next door to Ma Johnson's Hotel is ***Tailor Made Pizza***, where a pizza costs $15 and can be enjoyed with beer and wine.

Getting There & Away For bus information along the Edgerton Hwy and McCarthy Rd from either Glennallen or Valdez, see Getting There & Away at the beginning of this chapter.

Once you've crossed the footbridges over the glaciated Kennicott River and then the McCarthy River, a road leads a half mile to a junction at the former railroad depot. To reach the town of McCarthy, take the right-hand fork. To continue on to Kennicott and the Bonanza Mine Trailhead, take the left-hand fork.

The McCarthy Tram

The footbridge across the Kennicott River to McCarthy was opened in 1997, and when it did, a colorful bit of Alaskan history vanished with the tram it replaced. The first bridge across the Kennicott was built by the Copper River & Northwestern Railway in 1911, to haul out the copper from the Kennecott Mines. This gave rise to McCarthy, a wild little railroad junction of saloons and bordellos.

In 1974, the state built a pair of bridges across the river's two channels, and for a year, you could actually drive to McCarthy, but high water partially destroyed the bridges the following spring, reducing them to rickety pedestrian crossings that were totally washed away in 1981. Two years later, a tram was installed.

The tram was an open, two-seat affair that hauled passengers over the river. Although the tram was designed to hold two passengers, as many as four or five locals, including two with mountain bikes, would jump on it to cross the river. The tram had to be pulled the 100yd across the river by hand, making It cumbersome and slow. During the summer, 30 minutes was a normal waiting time, and on the Fourth of July weekend, you could easily wait several hours.

Because McCarthy has no government, the tram had no agency responsible for it. It's the Alaskan way of handling liability: Nobody acknowledged it, so nobody could get sued if a tourist fell off the platform into the glacial waters below. Maintenance was spontaneous at best and usually done late at night.

Despite the tram's dangers, tourists loved it. After surviving the dusty drive in to McCarthy and crossing on the tram, you truly felt as if you had stepped back in time. Some residents also saw it as an effective way of preserving their isolated lifestyle in McCarthy.

By the early 1990s, with McCarthy attracting more than 30,000 visitors a summer, it was evident the beloved tram would have to go, but the small town became angrily divided over the type of replacement crossing during a series of public hearings in 1995. Some wanted another tram, others a vehicle bridge, a few nothing at all. One person wanted a bridge with a gate that they could lock to keep 'outsiders away.' This idea prompted a resident at a meeting to call out, 'Give the key to someone in McCarthy, and you'll have a gunfight.'

The state finally decided to build a modern, steel-and-girder footbridge, and construction began in the fall of 1996. When the bridge became fully operational the next year, use of the tram was discontinued. In so doing, McCarthy lost a little bit of its character, but hopefully not its way of life.

Kennicott

Places to Stay & Eat In Kennicott, *Kennicott Glacier Lodge* (☎ 800-582-5128 outside Alaska, 800-478-2350 in Alaska) offers beds, running water and electricity, but no private bath, for $149/169. It also has a dining room. For $255 per couple, you can get a bed, six meals and a guided walk of the mines. Even if you don't stay here, hike up in the morning and have breakfast on the long front porch. The meal is $12 and includes eggs, sourdough pancakes and sausage, along with pitchers of juice and coffee, all enjoyed with a spectacular view of peaks and glaciers.

There are also *campsites* overlooking the end of Root Glacier, a mile west of the lodge (see the Root Glacier Trail section under Other Hikes at the end of this chapter).

Getting There & Away Kennicott can be reached from McCarthy by either walking the railroad grade, now the main road, or by hiking Old Wagon Rd. Old Wagon Rd is more of a trail for hiking and mountain bikes than a road. You pick it up from the main road at a junction marked with a 'To Glacier' sign. Either way it's a 5mi hike. You can also hitch a ride up from McCarthy during the summer, as there is a trickle of traffic between the two towns.

Wrangell Mountain Air and McCarthy Air run vans between the two towns, charging $5 one-way. Pick up the van at their log cabin offices in McCarthy or at the Kennicott Glacier Lodge at Kennicott. You can also pedal to Kennicott; mountain bikes are the transportation of choice for most of the locals. You'll be amazed how many zip past you in the morning as riders hurry off to work. If you didn't haul your own bike here, you can rent a mountain bike from St Elias Alpine Guides (☎ 888-933-5427, ✉ stelias@ ptialaska.net) for $35 per day.

GETTING TO/FROM THE HIKE

From the Kennicott Glacier Lodge, walk past the huge red concentration mill and out of town, heading west on Old Wagon Rd. The first junction is Silk Stocking Rd, where you turn right and follow it briefly as it curves back towards town. The next junction is Bonanza Mine Trail. Hang a left and start climbing.

If you want to skip the long haul up but still enjoy the alpine portion of the hike, Kennicott–McCarthy Wilderness Guides (☎ 554-4444, 800-664-4537) uses a 4WD

vehicle to take hikers above the tree line for $25 roundtrip, with a minimum of four passengers. From there, it's still a good 90-minute hike to the mine.

THE HIKE
Stage 1: Kennicott to Bonanza Mine
4mi, 5 to 7 hours

In a quarter mile from the trailhead, the road passes underneath the **Jumbo Tramway** and, in another mile or so, passes the junction to Jumbo Mine itself. The mine is not marked, or even well defined, and most hikers miss it. If you can find the start of the overgrown road to Jumbo Mine, you can follow it, roughly 3mi, to the ruins of Jumbo Mine, situated on a glacier below Bonanza Peak (6983ft). The road crosses Bonanza Creek within a mile and then reaches the alpine tundra at 3700ft.

There's no losing the Bonanza Mine Trail, however. It continues to climb steeply along a series of switchbacks, and soon spruce gives way to alder, which gives way to lower brush and, finally, your first views of the surrounding mountains. Once you are above the tree line, you are generally greeted with a 180-degree panorama of Mt Blackburn,

Imported Chihuahua for Dinner

An adult bald eagle is Alaska's largest resident bird of prey, weighing up to 14lb and boasting a wingspan of up to 7 ½ft. Such a large bird has a big appetite. Fish, particularly salmon, are the main diet of bald eagles, but when fish are in short supply an eagle will consume waterfowl, small mammals, carrion, clams, crabs, sea urchins and, once in a while, somebody's pet.

Such was the case in 1993, at the Chevron station in Valdez, when two tourists from Georgia pulled in to wipe off the windshield of their camper. They let their Chihuahua out for a quick run, unaware that a bald eagle was sitting in a tree nearby. The little yapper was only 5ft from the camper when the eagle swooped down.

According to the local paper, the Georgia tourists 'looked on in shock as the great bird snared the dog, crushing the life out of the squirming animal almost instantly. Before the couple could react, the eagle circled up and away, the family dog gripped firmly in its razor-sharp talons.'

'It was the damnedest thing I ever saw,' a service station attendant was quoted in the *Valdez Star*. 'The dog gave one yelp and that was it.'

The horrified RVers could only watch as the eagle and their dog disappeared, soaring over Prince William Sound. Welcome to Alaska. Next time leave the pet at home.

COPPER RIVER

The Green Grass of Copper

The world's richest copper mine began as a patch of grass in 1900, when a pair of sourdough miners named Jack Smith and Clarence Warner spotted a large green spot on the mountain between Kennicott Glacier and McCarthy Creek. After climbing the east side of the glacier, the prospectors were dumbfounded to discover that the grass was actually huge chunks of almost pure copper. The entire mountainside, in fact, held some of the richest copper ever uncovered. In the Lower 48, mines were operating on ore that contained only 2% copper. Here, the veins that miners eventually uncovered contained on the average 13% copper, and some contained as much as 70%.

Eventually, a group of East Coast investors bought the existing stakes and formed the Kennecott Copper Corp, named after a clerical worker misspelled 'Kennicott.' The first major hurdle was transporting the copper ore from the mines to the coastal town of Cordova, where it would be shipped to Tacoma, Washington, for smelting.

For this task, the syndicate called on Michael J Heney, the legendary railroad builder who was responsible for laying down the tracks of the White Pass & Yukon Railroad during the height of the Klondike gold rush. In the spring of 1908, construction began on the Copper River & Northwestern Railway. Most observers doubted that the 196mi line through the wilderness could ever be built. To many, CR&NW stood for 'can't run and never will.' The amazing Heney proved them wrong by building a $23 million railroad that included Cordova's famous Million Dollar Bridge around Childs Glacier and, in the process, cutting the bed for what is now the McCarthy Rd.

Next, the syndicate built the company town of Kennicott, a sprawling complex that included offices, the crushing mills, bunkhouses for the workers, company stores, a theater, wooden tennis courts and a school, all perched on the side of a mountain above Kennicott Glacier. From 1911 until 1938, the mines operated 24 hours a day, produced 591,000 tons of copper and reported a net profit of more than $100 million.

But in November 1938, faced with falling world prices for copper, uncertainty over how long the veins would pay out and, most of all, a possible labor strike, the company managers decided to close the operation. They made the decision, and the next morning, told the workers that the mine was shut down and that the miners could stay or leave, but in two hours the last train out of Kennicott was leaving. The disgruntled miners left in what was one of the greatest exoduses of a US town.

the Kennicott and Root Glaciers and the Kennicott River.

From the start of the mining road, most hikers take three hours or more to reach a short spur where 4WD pickups drop off their passengers and park for the day. At this point, you're still a good 90 minutes to two hours from the mine, but it's by far the most enjoyable stretch of the hike.

The road becomes a narrow footpath that first follows a ridgeline and then skirts the slope of a small rock knob. As you circle the knob into the final valley, all of the glory of the Kennicott mining era becomes apparent. At one point, you can look down and see

the **tram station**, where miners switched trams, and then follow the cables up the mountain until they cross the trail.

The final leg of the hike enters the valley. Here the trail clings to the valley's steep edge as it heads straight for the mine at the head of the valley. Halfway up, you come to the only source of water on the hike, a small mountain creek. The area where you cross the creek is littered with mining artifacts: engines, wheels, parts of a building, the chassis of an old truck etc. A wooden platform here appears to be the floor of an old building. Use it as a convenient campsite for a free-standing dome tent.

The Green Grass of Copper

What was left behind was a perfectly preserved slice of US mining history. Despite pillaging by thoughtless tourists after the McCarthy Rd opened up in the 1970s, Kennicott is still an amazing sight. The mill where the ore was crushed and where the copper was concentrated towers above the surrounding buildings. Tram cables still lead up the mountain to the Bonanza and Jumbo Mines. The rest of the buildings, including the bunkhouses, train depot, workers' cottages and power plant, sit perched above the Kennicott Glacier, surrounded by mountain peaks.

In 1998, the NPS purchased the mill, power plant and many of the buildings from private owners, as the first step to restoring Kennicott. Saving this unique piece of Alaskan history will undoubtedly take years. Until then, you have to be content with strolling through the center of town and peeping through the windows. Also keep in mind that many of the buildings are still privately owned, and it is illegal to enter them.

Kennicott was a company town, self-contained and serious. McCarthy, on the other hand, was created in the early 1900s as a place of 'wine, women and song' for the miners. In its heyday, McCarthy featured several saloons, restaurants, a red-light district, several hundred residents, its own newspaper and a school. Today, both O'Neill's Hardware Store and Mother Lode Power House, the site of St Elias Alpine Guides, have been listed on the National Register of Historical Places.

For a guided walk through Kennicott, search out Chris Richards, the town's only legally registered voter. The colorful, year-round resident lives across the street from the Kennicott Glacier Lodge and offers historic tours as Kennicott–McCarthy Wilderness Guides (☎ 554-4444, 800-664-4537). He provides a colorful 2-hour tour ($25) that includes going inside some of the buildings, as well as giving you an idea of what it's like to live in a one-person town in the winter (he reads a lot). Richards also offers half-day glacier treks.

If the day is clear, splurge on a flightseeing tour of the surrounding mountains and glaciers. Both McCarthy Air (☎ 554-4440) and Wrangell Mountain Air (☎ 554-4400, 800-478-1160) offer a wide range of scenic flights. A 30-minute flight begins at around $50, but if you do fly, invest in an hour flight, at $100 per person, giving you enough air time to fly around Mt Blackburn (16,390ft) and volcanic Mt Wrangell.

From the stream, the trail continues to climb, ending in an amphitheater with the **Bonanza Mine** perched up on one side. At the mine, there are a handful of old buildings, including bunkhouses and a tram station. The final climb to the site is a hard one across a steep slope of loose rock and scree. You should avoid entering the buildings or structures, as they have long passed the stage of being safe to enter.

It's possible to camp in the high alpine area of the Bonanza Mine, and if the weather is clear, such an evening would be far more enjoyable than battling the hoards of RVers at the end of McCarthy Rd. Keep in mind that the surrounding ridges are not the best for day hiking, as they are composed of loose scree, commonly referred to as 'rotten rock.'

Stage 2: The Return

4mi, 2½ to 4½ hours

The only way to return is the way you came up. If it took you five hours to climb to the mine site, you can make it down in half the time, but you should avoid the urge to run down the trail, even though gravity is pulling at you. Rest often on the way down, or you'll pay a heavy price the next morning, with aching knees and ankles.

COPPER RIVER

Cordova Region

The Copper River originates on the north side of the Wrangell Mountains, swings south where it forms the western boundary of Wrangell–St Elias National Park and finally empties into the Gulf of Alaska after a journey of 287mi. This was the pipeline that the Kennecott Mining Co used in the early 1900s to connect the Wrangell Mountains to Cordova. The company built a railroad where the Copper River had sliced through the rugged terrain and used it to transport copper from the mines near McCarthy to ships docked at Cordova.

Today Cordova (population 2435) is isolated again, even from McCarthy. You have to hop a ferry or board a plane to reach this beautiful little fishing village on the east coast of Prince William Sound, but the effort is well worth it as Cordova, in the shadow of Mt Eccles, is the center of an outdoor paradise. Although outside the borders of Wrangell–St Elias National Park, much of the land surrounding Cordova is part of the Chugach National Forest, making the town a staging area for 14 USFS cabins; some good alpine hiking; and the Copper River Delta, a nesting area for millions of birds each year. Copper River Hwy is your avenue to adventures. At the end of the highway is Childs Glacier, perhaps Alaska's most active and spectacular glacier accessible by road.

More than 35mi of trails depart from the Cordova road system, several leading to USFS cabins. Both hikes described in this section, McKinley Lake & Pipeline Lakes Trails and Power Creek & Crater Lake Trails, feature rental cabins. As in much of the Southeast, the hiking in this area is excellent, combining a lush forest with alpine terrain, great views and glaciers.

NATURAL HISTORY

The Copper River Hwy provides access to the Copper River Delta, a 60mi arc formed by six glacier-fed river systems. Stretching for more than 1094 sq mi, the delta is the largest continuous wetland on the Pacific Coast of North America. The delta's myriad tidal marshes, shallow ponds and outwashes are used by millions of birds and waterfowl as staging areas during the spring and fall migrations and as nesting areas in the summer.

May is the prime month for birders, a period when as many as 20 million shorebirds rest and feed in the tidal flats, including seven million western sandpipers and the entire population of West Coast dunlins. Other easily seen species are arctic terns, dusty Canada geese, trumpeter swans, great blue herons and bald eagles. A drive along the highway at dawn or dusk can also provide you with views of moose, brown bears, beavers and porcupines and, on rare occasions, a lynx or wolverine.

The wildlife is so abundant in this area that, in 1962, the USFS, the US Department of Fish & Wildlife and the state agreed to manage 52 sq mi of the delta as a game and fish habitat. The refuge has since been enlarged to 3594 sq mi and, in 1972, the delta on the east side of the Copper River Hwy was closed to off-road vehicles.

The streams and rivers along the highway are renowned for their fishing. Sockeyesalmon fishing begins in mid-June and peaks around July 4. Coho salmon run from August to September, and cutthroat trout and Dolly Varden can be caught throughout the summer and fall.

CLIMATE

Cordova has a maritime climate similar to Southeast Alaska. While most of Prince William Sound averages 100 inches of precipitation a year, Cordova gets more than 165 inches. Pack along good rain gear and a pile sweater for warmth. Summers tend to be cool. The average temperature in July is 54°F. In January temperatures average 21°F.

INFORMATION

Before venturing into the surrounding area, hikers should first stop at the USFS office (☎ 424-7661) at Browning Ave and 2nd St to pick up an assortment of free trail maps. Hours are 8 am to 5 pm Monday through Friday.

CORDOVA

General information about Cordova can be obtained from the Chamber of Commerce (☎ 424-7260) on 1st St. It's open 8 am to 4 pm Monday to Friday. It also has a Web site (www.ptialaska.net/~cchamber). The best place for travel information is the Cordova Museum (☎ 424-6665) at Adams Ave and 1st St. The center maintains a brochure rack and a very helpful traveler's information notebook with listings and prices for hotels, restaurants, bike rentals and tours and will let you store a bag in the lobby for a few hours.

Supplies & Equipment

The best place to pick up your own supplies and general camping equipment is AC Value Center on Nicholoff Way, across from the small boat harbor.

Places to Stay & Eat

The closest campground is the **Odiak Camper Park** *(☎ 424-6200)*, a half mile from town on Whitshed Rd. The city campground is little more than a gravel parking lot with a rest room and some play equipment. It has an excellent view of Cordova, with Mt Eyak looming overhead, but the smell of fish is often so strong you have to think twice about pitching a tent here. The tent rate is $3 per night and includes water, showers and rest rooms.

A dozen B&Bs operate in and around town. Check with the visitor center for a current list of B&Bs. The **Northern Nights Inn** *(☎ 424-5356)*, at 3rd St and Council Ave, has four rooms, with rates beginning at $65 for a double. Just up the hill towards Mt Eyak Ski Hill is the **King's Chamber** *(☎ 424-3373)*, on Fourth St, with five rooms in two houses. Singles/doubles are $65/75.

Of the four hotels in town, the **Alaskan Hotel & Bar** *(☎ 424-3299)*, on 1st St, is the cheapest. A room with a shared bath costs $40 a night a double or single, and rooms with a private bath are $60. The Alaskan, like all hotels in Cordova, is booked solidly through most of the summer. Avoid the seedy Cordova Hotel on 1st St, and instead, book a room at the **Cannery Bunkhouse**

(☎ 424-5920), above the Cookhouse Cafe on Orca Inlet. Rooms cost $45/50.

The AC Value Center also has an espresso bar, bakery and deli. True to its name, the **OK Restaurant**, close to the museum on 1st St, has okay Chinese food, with an $8 lunch special and dinners that range from $11 to $14. If the weather is nice, head to the **Baja Taco Wagon**, a converted school bus on Nicholoff Way near the small boat harbor. You can sit outdoors with a view of the harbor or the mountains and feast on a taco plate ($7.50) or an order of nachos ($5).

The **Ambrosia** *(413 1st St)* specializes in pizza and Italian food, with pasta dinners from $11 to $14, medium pizzas for $16 and soup and subs for $9.

Getting There & Away

Air Alaska Airlines (☎ 424-7151) makes a daily stop at Cordova on its run to Seattle, and its contract carrier, ERA, flies twice daily from Anchorage. An advance-purchase ticket is generally around $80 one-way and $160 roundtrip.

All jets arrive at and depart from Cordova's airport, 12 miles from town on the Copper River Hwy. The airport shuttle (☎ 424-3272) greets all arrivals and charges $10 for the trip into town. For the return trip to the airport, you can catch the shuttle at the major hotels in town.

Boat During the summer, the M/V *Bartlett* stops at Cordova on Monday, Wednesday and Friday en route from either Valdez or Whittier. The fare from Cordova to Valdez is $30; it's $58 to Whittier. The ferry terminal (☎ 424-7333) is 1.5 miles north of town on Railroad Ave.

Getting Around

If you have the time, an excellent way to explore the Copper River Hwy is by mountain bike. You can arrange to be dropped off at the end and then spend three or four days pedaling back to town, breaking up the ride with hikes on trails like McKinley Lake. Cordova Coastal Adventures (☎ 424-3842, 800-357-5145) has mountain bikes for rent at

$15 a day, with your helmet, water bottles and a small rack for gear. They will also provide transportation to the end of the highway for $75 per trip for up to three persons with gear. The van holds seven, and they charge $5 for each additional passenger.

Power Creek & Crater Lake Trails

Duration 2 to 3 days
Distance 12 to 15mi
Difficulty Level Medium to hard
Start Mile 7 of Power Creek Rd
Finish Mile 2 of Power Creek Rd
Cabins & Shelters Yes
Permits Required No
Public Transportation Yes
Summary An alpine traverse from the Power Creek Basin to Crater Lake and then into the town of Cordova, the hike offers mountain scenery on a clear day and the opportunity to stay in a trail shelter or USFS cabin.

Power Creek Trail was first started in 1919, to provide access to a potential hydropower site, and finally finished in 1986 by the US Forest Service (USFS) and volunteers. The Crater Lake Trail was built in 1938 by the Civilian Conservation Corps (CCC), and today the two routes can be combined to form the best overnight hike in Cordova.

The scenery along the traverse is stunning and includes alpine lakes, hanging glaciers and views, on a clear day, that extend to the Copper River Delta, the Chugach Mountains to the north and various islands in Prince William Sound. You have a reasonable chance to spot bears, mountain goats and trumpeter swans, and you might even catch a cutthroat trout in Crater Lake. The free-use shelter is in an ideal spot to overnight and, best of all, transportation to the trailheads is cheap and relatively easy to arrange.

Crater Lake and Power Creek are well-developed trails that make excellent day hikes. The ridge walk between the two trails is a route marked with cairns, requiring map-and-compass skills. The entire traverse is a two- to three-day hike for most backpackers. Being so close to town, the trails do attract heavy use but, nonetheless, always keep an eye out for bears during the berry season from July through August.

PLANNING
When to Hike
The alpine traverse is best hiked from late June to mid-September, to avoid heavy spring snow and the rainy fall weather.

Maps
The USGS quad *Cordova C-5* covers the area but does not show the Power Creek Trail. Trails Illustrated's *Prince William Sound East* map ($10) does show the trail, but the detail is too small for most hikers. Purchase maps in town at the USFS office or at Orca Book & Sound Co (☎ 424-5305), 507 1st St.

Cabins & Shelters
Several of the trails accessible from the Cordova road system lead to USFS cabins, including Power Creek Trail, which has a cabin at the end, 4.2mi from the trailhead. There is also a trail shelter halfway along the traverse to Crater Lake.

The shelter is free and used on a first-come, first-served basis, but the Power Creek Cabin (and all the area cabins) costs $35 a night and must be reserved in advance through the National Recreation Reservation Service (☎ 877-444-6777, 518-885-3639 international) or on the NRRS Web site (www.reserveusa.com).

GETTING TO/FROM THE HIKE
To the Start
If you are anticipating walking the entire loop, it's easier if you are first dropped off at the Power Creek Trailhead at the end of Power Creek Rd, 7mi northeast of town. Copper River/Northwest Tours (☎ 424-5356) offers drop-offs and pickups for $1 a mile. You could then hike all the way back into town via the Crater Lake Trail and Power Lake Rd or the Mt Eyak Trail.

COPPER RIVER

Mt McKinley

Denali State Park rental cabin

Charter plane in Denali National Park

Packing a bear-resistant container

Boarding the Alaska Railroad at Denali NP

From the Finish

The Crater Lake Trailhead is at Mile 2 of Power Creek Rd, about a half mile beyond the municipal airfield on Eyak Lake, across from Skaters Cabin.

THE HIKE
Stage 1: Power Creek Trailhead to Free-Use Shelter

6.5mi, 6 to 7 hours

Power Creek Trail begins by skirting a narrow valley along the north side of the creek and steadily climbs toward Power Creek Basin. Within a mile, you reach im-pressive **Ohman Falls** thundering below you in a rocky gorge. The falls is named after Oscar Ohman, who, in the 1920s, began digging a tunnel from a pond above the cascade, as a way to produce hydropower. The project was never finished.

Above the falls, the trail enters the wide Power Creek Basin, known by locals as **Surprise Valley** because the sudden beauty of it is captivating. You remain on what is now the west side of the creek, skirting the base of the ridge, easily viewing the braided channels and sandbars. The trail passes several beaver ponds, dams and lodges

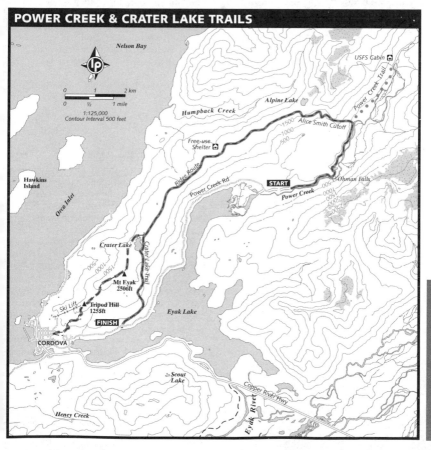

POWER CREEK & CRATER LAKE TRAILS

before arriving at the **Alice Smith Cutoff** 1.3mi from Ohman Falls, 2.3mi from the trailhead.

Power Creek Trail continues east to a USFS cabin (see Side Trip: Power Creek Cabin). Those hikers headed for the traverse to Crater Lake take the Alice Smith Cutoff. The trail angles west, climbing steadily from 500ft in the basin to 1700ft, where it leaves the subalpine mountain hemlock and reaches the crest of the ridge. Once you are on the ridge, the views are mind-boggling if the weather is good. The trail passes an **alpine lake** that, on a calm day, will mirror Snyder Mountain (3432ft) to the northeast. Take time to scan the slopes here; this is mountain goat country.

The trail runs out just beyond the lake, a 2mi climb from the Power Creek Trail. A route marked with cairns replaces the trail and leads southwest along the ridgeline. If the weather is fair, enjoy the scenery. If clouds have created whiteout-like conditions, then the cairns may be difficult to follow and extreme caution must be used if you continue.

After skirting the top of a 2175ft knob, the route descends to 1900ft and reaches the **free-use shelter** located on the north side of the ridge, 4mi from the junction with the Power Creek Trail. The shelter is enclosed to provide protection from wind and rough weather but has no other facilities. The only water sources nearby are snow patches that could disappear by the end of the summer.

Side Trip: Power Creek Cabin
2mi, 1 hour

From the junction with Alice Smith Cutoff, Power Creek Trail continues northeast up the basin until it ends at the USFS cabin, 4.2mi from the trailhead. Built in 1991, Power Creek Cabin is a single-room structure with six bunks, a woodstove and a sleeping loft. It also has a large covered porch with a spectacular view of the valley, the surrounding mountains and their hanging glaciers. This is a place where you could easily hang out for a couple of days.

The traverse from Power Creek to Crater Lake via the Alice Smith Cutoff is a 12mi hike. If you continue up the Power Creek to the USFS cabin and then backtrack to the cutoff the trip is close to 16mi.

Stage 2A: Free-Use Shelter to Power Creek Rd via Crater Lake Trail
5.5mi, 4 to 6 hours

The alpine traverse continues the second day. From the shelter, the route climbs more than 300ft, to the top of a 2180ft knob, descends and then begins ascending the next knob along the ridgeline. This time, you climb 700ft before reaching a pair of knobs a half mile apart along the ridge. The second knob is higher and, at 2300ft, is the highest elevation reached during the traverse.

At this point, some 2.5mi from the shelter, the route begins a steady descent toward **Crater Lake**, which is clearly visible to the southwest. The 800ft descent can be steep in places, and caution must be used in choosing the right route. The southern end of the lake, where you pick up **Crater Lake Trail**, is roughly a mile from the second knob, 3.5mi from the shelter.

You can pitch a tent in a handful of spots around the lake, and spending another night in this picturesque alpine bowl is not a bad idea. The USFS says there are cutthroat trout in the lake, if for some reason you're packing along a rod and reel.

The most common return route is via Crater Lake Trail. The trail quickly enters the tree line and begins a steep descent, much steeper than Alice Smith Cutoff, which was used to reach the ridge. Switchbacks make the hike easier on the knees, and logs cross many of the numerous streams, but this can still be a slick and muddy hike at times.

Views are limited, due to the mature Sitka spruce and western hemlock forest the trail winds through, but 1.2mi from the lake, a short spur leads to an overlook with a bench. It's a good place for an extended break, as you can gaze over Eyak Lake and the mountains that surround it. The trail continues its steady descent, and 2.4mi from

COPPER RIVER

the lake arrives at **Power Creek Rd**, just east from the airstrip and 2mi from town.

Stage 2B: Free-Use Shelter to Cordova via Mt Eyak

6.5mi, 5 to 6 hours

The alternate route back to town from Crater Lake – for the adventurous – is to scale Mt Eyak. There is no maintained trail to the 2506ft peak, but from the southwest corner of the lake you can access the north ridge, which is the easiest route to the top. From the peak, a trail descends the western ridge to the Mt Eyak Ski Hill, which you can easily descend to the ski hut at the end of 6th Ave, a hike of at least 3mi from Crater Lake.

McKinley Lake & Pipeline Lakes Trails

Duration 1 day
Distance 6mi
Difficulty Level Easy to medium
Start/Finish Mile 21.6 of the Copper River Hwy
Cabins & Shelters Yes
Permits Required No
Public Transportation No
Summary This is a day hike to the ruins of the Lucky Strike Mine that can be turned into an overnight adventure by reserving a USFS cabin in advance.

The McKinley Lake Trail begins at Mile 21.6 of Copper River Hwy and leads to the head of McKinley Lake and the remains of the Lucky Strike gold mine, 2.5mi from the trailhead. Along the way, you skirt the west side of McKinley Lake. The lake is the site of an impressive sockeye salmon run in August and can be fished for Dolly Varden and cutthroat trout throughout the summer. Lucky Strike Mine is an ideal half-day hike. You can turn it into a pleasant overnight adventure by reserving the McKinley Lake Cabin, which is located near the end of the trail. Finding a level and dry spot to pitch a tent anywhere along the route is a challenge.

Departing from the McKinley Lake Trail is the Pipeline Lakes Trail, which loops back to Mile 21.4 of the Copper River Hwy. This 2mi trail turns the hike to McKinley Lake into a 6mi loop and provides access to several small lakes that can be fished for grayling and cutthroat trout. The Pipeline Lakes Trail also provides excellent views of the surrounding Chugach Mountains, but is not nearly as well maintained as McKinley Lake Trail, and the muskeg areas can be very wet in places.

The McKinley Lake Trail is an easy hike, but the Pipeline Lakes is rated medium.

PLANNING
When to Hike

Either trail can be hiked from May through October, though the Pipeline Lakes Trail, which crosses a great deal of muskeg, would be a soggy struggle during the heavy rains in the spring and fall.

What to Bring

If you're planning to hike the Pipeline Lakes Trail, rubber boots are highly recommended. This can be a wet hike almost any time of the year.

Maps

The entire hike is covered by the USGS quad *Cordova B-4*, which was updated in 1994 and has both trails and the cabins on it.

Cabins & Shelters

There are two USFS cabins along the McKinley Lake Trail. The first, McKinley Trail Cabin, is only a short way up the trail. The second, McKinley Lake Cabin, overlooks the north end of the lake, a 2.2mi hike in. The cabins cost $35 a night and must be reserved in advance through the National Recreation Reservation Service (☎ 877-444-6777, 518-885-3639 international) or on its Web site (www.reserveusa.com).

GETTING TO/FROM THE HIKE

There are two main trailheads for this system. The posted trailhead for the McKinley Lake Trail is at Mile 21.6 of the Copper

COPPER RIVER

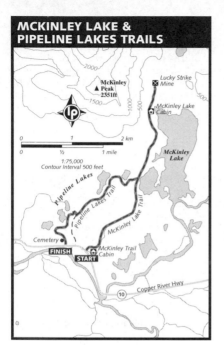

MCKINLEY LAKE & PIPELINE LAKES TRAILS

River Hwy. Just to the west, at Mile 21.4, is the trailhead for the Pipeline Lakes Trail. It is not marked as well as the McKinley Lake Trailhead.

The only problem with this trail or any trail along the Copper River Hwy is transportation. Hitching is possible, though slow at times, and the number of rental cars in Cordova is limited. Cordova Car Rentals (☎ 424-5982) is located at the airport and has vehicles for $65 a day with unlimited mileage. You can also try the Reluctant Fisherman Hotel (☎ 424-3272, 800-770-3272), which has cars for $75 a day.

Copper River/Northwest Tours (☎ 424-5356) offers a six-hour tour out to the Million Dollar Bridge for $35 per person, with a minimum of four people per trip, and is by far the most reasonable way to see this road. The company uses a 25-passenger bus and will work with backpackers who want to be dropped off at the trailhead and picked up on another day.

THE HIKE
Stage 1: Copper River Hwy to Lucky Strike Mine

2.5mi, 2 hours

It's a gentle climb of only 100yd from the Copper River Hwy to **McKinley Trail Cabin**. The six-bunk cabin has a woodstove, an outdoor grill and, most unusual, skylights in its roof. The only drawback is that the structure sits right on the trail, allowing every hiker passing through to peek through the windows.

Beyond the cabin, the trail swings north and winds through lush Sitka spruce and western hemlock forest. Every rock and fallen trunk is carpeted here in a thick layer of moss. Within a half mile, you use a footbridge to cross a stream and, 1.2mi from the trailhead, see the southern end of **McKinley Lake** just before you arrive at a posted junction with the **Pipeline Lakes Trail**.

The next mile is a very gentle climb that crosses two streams on the way to McKinley Lake Cabin. This section can be extremely sloppy after a rain but is well planked over the wettest sections.

McKinley Lake Cabin has six bunks, usually a couple of plastic gold pans inside and something of a wraparound porch overlooking the lake. Anglers can fish the lake for trout and Dolly Varden, and the sockeye run from late July to mid-August is impressive. Just remember that when there are salmon spawning, there are often bears feeding.

Mining artifacts are scattered around the cabin, but **Lucky Strike Mine** is another quarter mile to the north, at end of the trail. The remains consist of a collapsed horizontal shaft in the side of the hill, much fallen timbers and ironwork rails and pipes and a unique-looking tractor. The mine was operated in the 1920s without much success. In 1927, the Lucky Strike Mine Co cut the first trail to McKinley Lake, but the trail was gone when the USFS rebuilt it in 1934. Use extreme caution when poking around the ruins or the shafts.

The lack of campsites makes this a difficult overnight hike if you haven't reserved the cabin. The best places to search for a level tent spot are uphill from the cabin.

Stage 2: Lucky Strike Mine to Copper River Hwy via Pipeline Lakes Trail

3.5mi, 3 to 4 hours

Backtrack 1.2mi to the junction with the Pipeline Lakes Trail. If it's been raining, muskeg is something you try to avoid. Skip the Pipeline Lakes route and remain on McKinley Lake Trail to return to Copper River Hwy.

The Pipeline Lakes picked up their name because they were used to provide water to the steam locomotives operating on the Copper River & Northwestern Railway from 1911 to 1938. The original trail was built by the mining company as a route for the pipelines that carried the water to the tracks. Segments of rusting pipes are still visible today along the lower portions of the trail.

The first quarter mile from the junction remains in the forest and climbs away from McKinley Lake. Exposed roots and running water make this section difficult at times. You top off at the **first Pipeline Lake**. Fishing is only fair here, but the setting is stunning. The lake is surrounded by mountains to the north, and on a calm day you can see the reflection of McKinley Peak (2351ft) in the lake's surface.

You continue to climb and, in another quarter mile, reach the **second and largest Pipeline Lake**. This one presents the best fishing opportunities, including cutthroat trout. At the lake, the trail swings south and begins crossing large stretches of muskeg that make this a wet and more challenging hike. Poles with orange diamonds mark the trail, but a few of the markers are missing, and there will be times when you will have to search for the right route. The payoff for all this effort is constant views of the Chugach Mountains.

You reach a posted junction 1.25mi from the McKinley Lake Trail. To the south is a direct but very wet route to Copper River Hwy. The main trail heads north and quickly reaches the **third Pipeline Lake**. This stretch can be confusing but keep an eye out for those orange diamonds. Beyond the **fourth Pipeline Lake**, you move into the forest. The

trail is easier to identify but remains wet almost to the end.

The trail passes near the **fifth Pipeline Lake** and then begins a steady descent toward Copper River Hwy in the final quarter mile. Right before breaking out at the road, you pass a small **cemetery**. Copper River Hwy is reached in little more than 2mi from the junction with McKinley Lake Trail. Head east on the road, and you'll reach the McKinley Lake Trailhead in a quarter mile.

Other Hikes

WRANGELL–ST ELIAS NATIONAL PARK

If you want to do more than just view the glaciers in this area, check in with St Elias Alpine Guides (☎ 554-4445, 888-933-5427, ℮ stelias@ptialaska.net), at the historic Mother Lode Powerhouse in McCarthy. The longtime Alaskan guiding company offers a variety of day hikes on glaciers, including a full-day's hike along the alpine ridges to the mining ruins at the base of Castle Mountain for $95 per person. A four- to six-hour hike on Root Glacier is $55 and includes crampons and other equipment. For $125, the outfitters will fly you in for a stunning four- to six-hour hike higher on the glacier.

Root Glacier Trail

From Kennicott Glacier Lodge, the Root Glacier Trail is a 2.5mi roundtrip past the mine ruins to the sparkling white-and-blue floe of ice. In this book, the trail is shown on the Bonanza Mine Trail map. Hike west of the town and continue past an unmarked junction to Bonanza Mine, reached in less than a quarter mile. Along the way, you cross Jumbo Creek; a plank upstream makes fording this creek easy in normal water conditions. In another half mile, campsites overlook the end of Root Glacier. The sites have a storage bin to keep the bears out of your food and an outhouse nearby.

You can climb the glacier, but you should be extremely careful walking on the ice if you are inexperienced and lack the proper equipment (crampons, ice axe, etc). A safer alternative is to follow the rough trail that skirts the lateral moraine along the glacier. It continues another 1.5mi, providing excellent views of the ice (USGS quads *McCarthy B-6* and *C-6)*.

Worthington Glacier Trail

The Worthington Glacier is not within Wrangell–St Elias National Park but southwest of the park along the Richardson Hwy. For most people, it's a drive-in glacier, like Portage Glacier near Anchorage and Mendenhall Glacier outside Juneau. You drive in, look at it and take off, hurrying to get somewhere else.

That's a shame. This 2mi roundtrip is well worth the one or two hours you spend on the trail, as it provides the best vantage points to view this beautiful ice floe. The hike is short and rated easy. It begins with a stiff climb and then follows a narrow trail along a moraine that skirts steep drop-offs to the glacier. You could spend an entire day in this area, however, beginning with this hike and continuing with a romp in the tundra at Thompson Pass, less than 3mi south along the Richardson Hwy.

Reached at Mile 26, Thompson Pass is an alpine area at 2771ft, where it is easy to pull off the highway and hike through the heather into meadows filled with wildflowers in early summer. Another 2mi south along the highway is *Blueberry Lake State Recreation Site*, an alpine campground that borders two small lakes. This is a great place to spend a day almost entirely in the mountains above the tree line (USGS quad *Valdez A-5)*.

VALDEZ REGION

Because Valdez is in an area surrounded by mountains and glaciers, you would expect good hiking. This is not the case. Though many trails have been proposed, and a new route has been cut to within view of Shoup Glacier, the town has far fewer hiking trails than Juneau or Anchorage. There is also no USFS office in Valdez and no nearby cabins.

Mineral Creek Trail

The best walk away from town is the old road along Mineral Creek and the 1mi trail from its end to the old Smith Stamping Mill. The road can be in poor condition at times, but most cars can usually manage it without bottoming out too many times.

To reach the trailhead, follow Hazelet Ave north 10 blocks from Egan Drive to Hanagita St and turn left (west); then turn right (north) onto Mineral Creek Rd. The road bumps along for 5.5mi and then turns into a mile-long trail to the stamping mill. Built by WL Smith in 1913, the mill required only two men to operate it and used mercury to remove the gold from the ore.

Following the trail beyond the mill at Brevier Creek requires considerable bush hacking. If you are hiking the entire road, the trip up the lush green canyon can be a pleasant 13mi adventure that requires five to six hours. It is also a popular place for mountain biking (USGS quad *Valdez A-7)*.

Shoup Glacier Trail

Built in 1999, Valdez's newest trail begins at the west end of town and skirts Port Valdez for 12mi. It crosses Gold Creek along the way and ends up in Shoup Bay, where there are views of Shoup Glacier. To reach the trailhead, follow Egan Drive west across Mineral Creek and into the Cottonwood subdivision. The trail begins from a parking lot at the end of the street (USGS quad *Valdez A-7)*.

Solomon Gulch Trail

Another relatively new trail is located across from the Solomon Gulch Fish Hatchery on Dayville Rd, off the Richardson Hwy. This 1.3mi trail is a steep, uphill hike that quickly leads to splendid views of Port Valdez and the city below. It ends at Solomon Lake, which is the source of 80% of Valdez's power. Along the way is some excellent berry picking (USGS quad *Valdez A-7)*.

Goat Trail

The oldest trail in the area is Goat Trail, which originally was a Native Americans' route and then was discovered by Captain

Abercrombie in his search for safe passage to the Interior. Today, you can pick up the posted trailhead at Mile 13.5 of the Richardson Hwy, just past Horsetail Falls in Keystone Canyon. The trail twists and turns for 2.5mi as it follows the Lowe River, until it stops at the original bridge over Bear Creek (USGS quad *Valdez A-6* and *A-5*).

CORDOVA REGION
Sheridan Mountain Trail

This trail starts at the end of Sheridan Glacier Rd, southeast of town at Mile 13 of the Copper River Hwy. The road leads 4.3mi to the north, ending at a picnic table with a partial view of the ice floe. Near the end of the road is the trailhead for the Sheridan Mountain Trail. Most of the 2.9mi, one-way trail is a moderate climb that passes through mature forests before breaking out into an alpine basin. The view of mountains and Sheridan and Sherman Glaciers from the basin is a stunning sight, and it only gets better when you start climbing the surrounding rim. During a dry spell, hiking boots are fine for the walk; otherwise, you might want to tackle this one in rubber boots.

There are places to pitch a tent along the stream at the north end of Sheridan Glacier Rd. Beyond the trailhead, it's easy to walk the rest of the road – badly eroded at this point – to gain access to the dirt-covered glacial moraines at the snout of Sheridan Glacier, reached in about a mile. The view is excellent from the top of these gravel hills. You can also access the glacier here but need to be extremely careful when hiking on a glacier without crampons or ice axes (USGS quad *Cordova C-4*).

Saddlebag Glacier Trail

This trail is accessed via a firewood-cutting road, at Mile 25 of the Copper River Hwy. It's an easy walk of 3mi through cottonwoods and spruce until you emerge at the outlet of Saddlebag Lake. The view is outstanding, as the namesake glacier is at the far end of the lake and has littered the lake with icebergs. The lake and glacier are surrounded by peaks and cliffs where you can

often spot mountain goats. If you're mountain biking the highway, this is one of the few trails dry enough to be followed on a bike (USGS *Cordova B-3*).

Childs Glacier Trail

Just before Copper River Hwy crosses the Million Dollar Bridge, 48mi from Cordova, there is a short side road that ends at the Childs Glacier Recreation Area. It's common for people to camp overnight here, and the area has picnic benches and rest rooms. Near the parking area is a 15ft-high viewing platform with interpretive displays and one end of the Childs Glacier Trail. The 1.2mi trail follows an old road along the Copper River, passing superb views of

---

Deadly Glaciers

With its 300ft-high face only 1200ft from the observation platform (or less if you stand on the banks of the Copper River), Childs Glacier is one of the closest tidewater glaciers you can view. It's so close that every year icebergs calving into the river cause swells to reach the opposite bank.

It is estimated that 20 to 50 times a year, a berg creates a 10ft wave that's high enough to cross the river and sweep through the day-use area. Every two years, a glacial calving produces a 20ft wave, and in 1993, when a piece of ice half the size of a football field broke off, a monstrous 40ft wave resulted.

The wave was so powerful that it hurled picnic tables more than 50ft and swamped the people standing on the 15ft-high observation deck. Slabs of ice the size of cars littered the day-use area after the water retreated, and two women who were standing on the beach admiring the glacier were seriously injured.

If that wasn't enough of a reminder of how dangerous glaciers can be, in the same month a 36-year-old Anchorage man was killed when a chunk of ice fell on him while he was kayaking around Blackstone Glacier near Whittier.

COPPER RIVER

the glacier. It ends at another observation platform overlooking the Million Dollar Bridge. Though severely damaged by the 1964 earthquake, the bridge has been jury-rigged to allow an occasional brave soul, mostly rafters looking to put in upstream, to drive across it. By all means, walk to the middle of it for its million-dollar view. Less than a mile downstream is Childs Glacier, and 5mi upstream is Miles Glacier. More amazing then the view is the fact that, when they built the bridge in 1910, the north lobe of Childs Glacier was only 1500ft away.

Childs Glacier is the most impressive glacier along the Copper River Hwy. The 3mi-wide glacier sits perched right above the Copper River. The ice moves forward 500ft a year and is constantly calving icebergs into the river. It's especially active in late spring and summer, when the Copper River rises above the glacier's rocky bed, undercutting its icy blue face to halt any further advance. The discharging ice is an incredible, noisy show, because the 300ft face of the glacier lies only 1200ft from the observation platform (USGS quad *Cordova C-3*).

Denali

Once you give a mountain a name it's hard to take it back. In 1896, gold miner William Dickey named what he was sure was the tallest mountain in Alaska, Mt McKinley, in honor of the Ohio governor. A year later William McKinley became the 27th US president, and the name stuck, even though he never saw the peak that honors him or even set foot in the land it crowns.

This irked many Alaskans, who protested angrily in 1980. As part of the battle over the Alaska National Interest Lands Conservation Act, Alaskans wanted to change the name back to Denali, the original Athabascan name, which meant 'the high one.' But Ohio has a lot more political muscle than Alaska, and the highest peak in North America remains named in honor of McKinley.

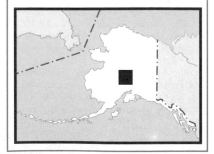

Highlights

- Viewing Mt McKinley from the end of Mt Healy Overlook Trail

- Camping overnight among the multi-colored mountains of Polychrome Pass

- Sighting caribou and Dall sheep while hiking the East Branch of the Toklat River

- Hiking the open tundra around Mt Eielson in Denali National Park and Preserve

- Setting up camp with a view of Mt McKinley along the Kesugi Ridge in Denali State Park

As a result of the 1980 Alaska Lands Bill, however, what was then called Mt McKinley National Park was enlarged to 9375 sq mi (larger than the state of Massachusetts) and redesignated as Denali National Park and Preserve. Ironically, today it's 'Denali,' not 'McKinley,' that conjures up the most vivid images among trekkers in the USA and around the world. For them it is the ultimate wilderness destination, where they can throw on a backpack and follow treeless valleys and experience the wonders of subarctic wildlife.

Since the passage of the Alaska Lands Bill, this huge slice of Interior Alaska has been managed as three distinct units by the National Park Service (NPS); the entire area was formally established in 1980 and is known as Denali National Park and Preserve. Denali Wilderness is the original national park. The Denali National Park & Preserve lands practically surround the original park. Denali Wilderness is administered as a wilderness area: Fires and pets are prohibited and strict regulations for backcountry use and travel are enforced; traditional subsistence use by local rural residents is allowed. Denali National Preserve – large tracts in the northwest and southwest corners of the park – allows sport hunting, trapping and fishing.

Denali National Park & Preserve

Denali Wilderness, with its park road, campgrounds, visitor center at Eielson and easy access to the backcountry, draws the attention of both tourists and trekkers. Few backpackers enter the new national park land, with the exception of a trickle through Cantwell. Virtually no visitors explore the national preserve areas.

Despite the size of the park tripling, hikers are still concentrated in what is a

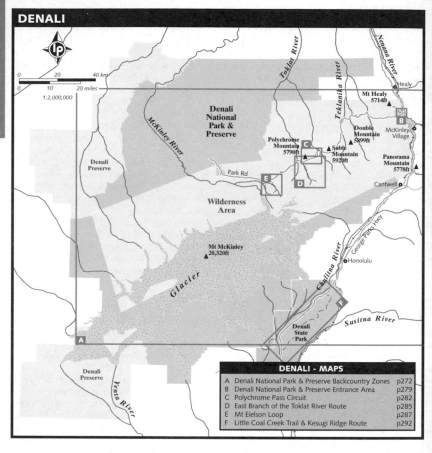

DENALI

Denali
National
Park &
Preserve

Denali
Preserve

Park Rd

Wilderness
Area

Mt McKinley
20,320ft

Glacier

Denali
Preserve

Denali
State
Park

Toklat River

McKinley River

Polychrome
Mountain
5790ft

Sable
Mountain
5920ft

Teklanika River

Nenana River

Healy

Mt Healy
5714ft

Double
Mountain
5899ft

McKinley
Village

Panorama
Mountain
5778ft

Cantwell

George Parks Hwy

Chulitna River

Honolulu

Susitna River

Yenta River

0   20   40 km
0   10   20 miles
1:2,000,000

DENALI - MAPS

A	Denali National Park & Preserve Backcountry Zones	p272
B	Denali National Park & Preserve Entrance Area	p279
C	Polychrome Pass Circuit	p282
D	East Branch of the Toklat River Route	p285
E	Mt Eielson Loop	p287
F	Little Coal Creek Trail & Kesugi Ridge Route	p292

relatively small section. In a modern day paradox, we're so eager to 'get away from it all' that we're overrunning Denali. In 1995, with the park attracting more than 300,000 visitors a year, the National Park Service instituted the most sweeping change in the history of its management of the wilderness by allowing a concessionaire to implement fees for the shuttle buses that traverse the wilderness and a reservation system for both a seat on the shuttle and sites in the campgrounds. Backcountry bus fees now range as high as $31, and 65% of the seats can be reserved in advance; 100% of four

popular campground areas can be reserved in advance.

Combine the park's easy viewing of wildlife and the grandeur of Mt McKinley with its wilderness reputation throughout the world, and suddenly the crowds are easy to understand. During the peak of the summer tourist season Denali National Park and Preserve is a busy and popular place. Riley Creek Campground overflows with camper vans; nearby Morino Campground is crowded with backpackers; and the park's hotel is bustling with large tour groups. The pursuit of shuttle-bus seats, backcountry permits and campground reservations at the Visitor Access Center often involves long Disney World–type lines.

The new fees have reduced the maddening crowds from the early 1990s peak, and many people prefer to visit the park in early June or September to avoid the summer rush. September can be particularly pleasant, for not only are the crowds thinning out but so are the bugs. This is also when the area changes color. Valleys go from a dull green to a fiery red, and the willows turn shades of yellow and gold. But the shuttle buses (your ticket into the backcountry) stop running in mid-September. A four-day vehicle lottery follows, when 400 private cars a day are allowed into the park, and then the road is closed to all traffic until the next May. By late September, the snow has usually arrived for the winter, and another backpacking season is over.

Without advance reservations, you have to include extra days for your trip. It's hard to get around it: You'll waste one day alone on the outside of the park waiting to get into the Riley Creek area. Another two days can be used up waiting for a campground or backcountry area to become available. Even if all you want to do is camp at the entrance and take the shuttle bus out along the road one day, a minimum of four days is needed at the park at the height of the season. If you want to spend three days backpacking or staying in the interior campgrounds, it's best to schedule seven to 10 days.

If you can plan your trip in advance or have the patience to wait for permits and bus seats on a first-come, first-served basis, Denali National Park and Preserve is still the great wilderness that awed so many of us 10 or 20 years ago. The entrance has changed, but the park itself hasn't, and a brown bear meandering on a tundra ridge still provides the same quiet thrill it did when Denali first opened in 1917.

HISTORY

Although generations of Athabascans had wandered through the area that the national park now encompasses, no one ever set up permanent settlements. This changed in 1905

when gold was discovered and a miners' rush resulted in the town of Kantishna. A year later, naturalist and noted hunter Charles Sheldon was stunned by the beauty of the land and horrified at the reckless abandon of the miners and others in hunting the caribou and other big game. Sheldon returned in 1907 and, with guide Harry Karstens, traveled the area in an effort to set up boundaries for a proposed national park.

Sheldon then launched a campaign for a Denali National Park, but politics being politics and Ohio having a particularly strong delegation of senators, it emerged as Mt McKinley National Park. Karstens became the park's first superintendent, and in 1923, when the railroad arrived, 36 visitors enjoyed the splendor of Denali.

The first attempt to scale Mt McKinley was undertaken by James Wickersham, the US district judge in Alaska. After moving his court from Eagle to Fairbanks in 1903, the judge took a couple of months off that summer and trekked overland more than 100mi to reach the 7500ft mark of the 20,320ft peak. Though his party was unsuccessful in its bid to be the first on top, it created a summit fever that would rage on for more than a decade until the peak was finally conquered.

In 1906, Dr Frederick Cook made what was his second attempt at the peak, this time from the south. His party disbanded after a month of slogging through the heavy brush and tussock, but then in September, Cook and a companion sent a telegram to New York claiming that they had reached the peak and even sent along a photo showing the good doctor holding a flag at the top. The climbing world immediately disputed the claim, and four years later, Belmore Brown located the false peak and duplicated Cook's photo. Not only was the 8000ft peak a lot shorter than Mt McKinley, it was more than 20mi from the true summit.

The next serious attempt came in 1910, when four Fairbanks miners decided Alaskans should be the first to conquer the peak, not Outsiders. Dubbed the Sourdough Expedition, they headed straight for the peak visible from Fairbanks. Remarkably, they climbed the final 11,000ft and returned to their base camp in 18 hours. Even more remarkably, they carried only a thermos of hot chocolate, a bag of donuts and a 14ft spruce pole. Imagine then their shock when they reached the top of the North Peak, only to realize that it was 850ft lower than the South Peak and thus not the true summit.

Success finally came in 1913, when an expedition of Hudson Stuck, Henry Karstens, Robert Tatum and Walter Harper reached the top on June 7. The foursome would have made it in May, but they spent three weeks hewing a 3mi staircase through a mass of jumbled ice caused by the 1912 eruption and earthquake of Katmai 300mi away. When they reached the top they saw the spruce pole on the North Peak, verifying the claims of the Sourdough Expedition.

Today, roughly 1300 climbers attempt the peak each year, spending an average of three weeks on the mountain. Expeditions carry roughly 120lb of food and gear per person for the ascent. Ironically, due to the multiple trips required to shuttle gear to higher camps, successful climbers actually climb the mountain twice. In a good season, when storms are not constantly sweeping across the range, 50% of those attempting the summit will be successful.

NATURAL HISTORY

Situated on the north and south flanks of the Alaska Range, 237mi from Anchorage and about half that distance from Fairbanks, Denali is the nation's first subarctic national park and a wilderness that can be enjoyed by those who never want to sleep in a tent. Within it roam 37 species of mammals, ranging from lynx, marmots and Dall sheep to foxes and snowshoe hares, and 130 different bird species have been spotted, including the impressive golden eagle. Most visitors, however, want to see four animals in particular: moose, caribou, wolves and brown bears. If you see all four from the shuttle bus, you will have scored a rare 'grand slam,' according to the drivers.

There are an estimated 200 brown bears in the park and another 200 black bears, most of them west of Wonder Lake. Everybody's favorite, the brown, or grizzly, bear, is almost always seen while you're on the shuttle bus. Since Denali's streams are mostly glacially fed, the fishing is poor, and consequently, the bears' diet is 85% vegetable materials. This accounts for their small size. Most males range from only 300 to 600lb, while their cousins on the salmon-rich coasts can easily top 1000lb.

All the caribou in the park belong to the Denali herd, one of 13 herds in Alaska, which fluctuates in size between 2500 and 3000 animals. Since the park has been enlarged, the entire range of the herd, from its calving grounds to where it winters, is now in Denali. The best time to spot caribou is often late in the summer, when the animals begin to band into groups of six to a dozen in anticipation of the fall migration. The caribou is easy to spot, as the racks of a bull often stand 4ft high and look out of proportion with the rest of its body.

Most visitors will sight their moose on the eastern part of the park road, especially along the first 15mi. Moose are almost always found in stands of spruce and willow shrubs (their favorite food) and often you have a better chance of seeing a moose while you're hiking the Horseshoe Lake Trail than you do in the tundra area around Eielson Visitor Center. There are roughly 1500 moose on the north side of the Alaska Range, and the most spectacular scene in Denali comes in early September when the bulls begin to clash their immense racks over breeding rights to a cow.

The wolf is the most difficult of the 'grand slam' four to see in the park. There is a stable population of 150 wolves, and during much of the summer, when small game is plentiful, the packs often break down and wolves become more solitary hunters. The best bet for most visitors is witnessing a lone wolf crossing the park road.

There are more than 1000 Dall sheep in the park. An average ram weighs around 160lb, the ewe around 110lb. Dall sheep forage predominantly on grasses, stunted willow and sedge on rugged hillsides. They winter in the foothills north of the park road, and in early summer, many move south, often crossing the road, to feed near the headwaters of streams and rivers that drain the Alaska Range. Trekking around Polychrome Pass has always been one of the best places to spot Dall sheep. Bands of Dall sheep are often seen grazing on the slopes of Igloo and Cathedral Mountains near Igloo Creek Campground.

Trekkers who take to the ridges will inevitably encounter a hoary marmot, a cousin of the groundhog. Often when you're taking a break on a ridge, the marmots' curiosity will bring them out of their holes for a peek at you. At times like these, marmots are interesting, almost comical animals. In Denali, most of the marmots sport a gray-and-brown coat that blends into the talus slopes where they make their home. Marmots are social animals, so if you see one, chances are there are more in the area. Being a favorite food of brown bears and wolves, they often produce a shrill whistling sound to alert other marmots of approaching danger.

Because hunting has never been allowed in the wilderness area, professional photographers refer to animals in Denali as 'approachable wildlife.' That doesn't mean you can actually approach them, though every year visitors and photographers alike try to in an effort to get that photo of a lifetime. It means bears, moose, Dall sheep and caribou are not nearly as skittish as in other regions of the state and tend to continue their natural activities despite 40 heads with camera lenses hanging out of a bus 70yd away on the park road. This trait and the park road, which was built to maximize the chances of seeing wildlife by traversing high, open ground, makes Denali an excellent place to see a variety of animals.

CLIMATE
The Alaska Range causes Denali's weather to change often and rapidly, sometimes from hour to hour, making it very hard to predict. Mt McKinley is such a massive mountain that it literally creates its own weather on the north side where most of the trekking takes place. Annual precipitation is 15 inches, with rain in June, July and August accounting for more than half that. On average, it will rain half of the days during the summer, much of it light showers or drizzle. In other words, be prepared for cool and cloudy conditions.

High temperatures in July average 66°F, in August only 63°F and in September 52°F. It's important to remember that it has snowed or dropped below freezing in the summer, and any given day might be very cold. Wildflowers, always a beautiful sight in the park, generally peak from mid-June to the end of July, when the area enjoys 18 to 19 hours of sunlight each day. Snow almost always closes the park road for good in September, usually by the third week.

INFORMATION
The Visitor Access Center, or VAC for short, near the entrance of the park is the place to organize your trip into Denali, pick up permits and purchase topographic maps and books. The center is open 7 am to 8 pm daily during the summer.

Within the VAC there is a bookstore; staffed counters for backcountry permits, shuttle buses and campsites; a video theater with shows 10 and 40 minutes after the hour; and rest rooms. There is also an information area on other parks in Alaska, in case the Denali hassle is too much for you. Outside there are storage lockers that are big enough to handle a backpack. The VAC also offers daily nature walks and longer hikes throughout the park, and the auditorium behind the park hotel features slide or film programs at 1:30 and 8 pm daily. These cover the history, wildlife or mountaineering aspects of the park.

Eielson Visitor Center is a smaller center at Mile 66 of the park road that features displays, a small bookstore and a great observation deck overlooking Mt McKinley. There are also bathrooms, drinking water and a picnic area, but the center sells no supplies or food. Nor can you arrange backcountry permits here. Eielson is open 9 am to 7 pm daily during the summer.

When to Hike
The best time to hike in Denali National Park and Preserve is in the summer. The

A New Denali National Park

In 1997, the National Park Service (NPS) released its *Entrance Area and Road Corridor Development Concept Plan* for Denali National Park and Preserve, and by the end of the century, the NPS had already begun implementing some of the recommendations. But many more changes for Alaska's best-known park are scheduled to take place in the near future.

The most significant one will be the closing of the Denali National Park Hotel. By 2002, this hotel will be adapted into an environmental education and science center, and no accommodations other than campsites will be available inside the national park.

The plan calls for expanding the existing Visitor Access Center into an interpretive center and building a new VAC and parking lot nearby. Other changes include an additional 50 campsites at Riley Creek, new campgrounds in the Nenana River Corridor and the Kantishna area, a bicycle permit system for the park road and permanent rest areas and interpretive facilities at Savage and Toklat Rivers. Eventually, the NPS plans to develop a South Side Denali Entrance, which will include a visitor center and a campground.

One change that has already taken place is the construction of additional trails. As far as backpackers are concerned, Denali will still be a 'trail-less park,' but there are now a growing number of footpaths along the park road that are designed for the casual day hiker. The NPS is building interpretive loops of a mile or less at the Primrose pullout, Savage, Toklat and Teklanika rest areas and from the Eielson Visitor Center north to a ridge.

There will also be several trails departing from near Wonder Lake Campground. The main one, McKinley Bar Trail, has already been relocated and upgraded. This 2mi trail descends from the campground access road south to the McKinley River flats. Plan on a half day for the roundtrip hike on the McKinley Bar Trail.

hikes listed in this chapter are possible whenever the shuttle bus operates, from late May or early June to mid-September.

What to Bring

A bear-resistant food container is required and is lent free of charge at the backcountry desk of the VAC. You'll also need to bring a stove, fuel and cooking equipment, as campfires are not permitted in the Denali Wilderness. White gas is available at the Denali National Park Hotel store.

Rain gear is a good idea in this part of Alaska, no matter the season. Mt McKinley creates its own weather patterns, and it can rain or even snow at any time. Weather is unpredictable and changes rapidly. The NPS recommends that you have a sleeping bag and pad with protection to 20°F for any overnight summer trip.

Finally, the park service recommends that you bring some insect repellent (or even a head net!) and an emergency signaling device, such as a flare, even on short day hikes in the backcountry. For more detailed information on what to bring, turn to the Planning section of the Facts for the Hiker chapter.

Maps

Because the park is without trails or markers of any kind, a set of USGS 1:63,360 series quads is crucial. The necessary quad for each hike is given in the information for that hike. The USGS has a park map with a scale of 1:250,000, and Trails Illustrated sells *Denali National Park & Preserve*, with a scale of 1:200,000, for $10. With detail at this scale, the maps are good for an overview of the park but should not be used for an extended trek in the backcountry. Maps can be purchased at the VAC.

Books

For the best overview of the different zones in the park, purchase the book *Backcountry*

Companion for Denali National Park by Jon Nierenberg (Alaska National History Association). It's available at both the VAC and park hotel gift shop.

Information Sources

For information in advance of arriving, call the VAC (☎ 683-2294, 683-1266 in the summer, 800-622-7275 for recorded information), check the park's excellent Web site (www.nps.gov/dena) or stop in at any of the Alaska Public Lands Information Centers in Anchorage, Fairbanks or Tok, or the Southeast Alaska Discovery Center in Ketchikan. You may also write to Denali National Park & Preserve, PO Box 9, Denali Park, AK 99755.

Permits & Regulations

Head to the Visitor Access Center, or VAC, to organize any overnight trek into the park and pick up permits. The center is open 7 am to 8 pm daily during the summer, and lines begin forming outside before the doors are unlocked.

A free backcountry permit is required for any overnight trek in the park and must be arranged at the VAC. The park is divided into 43 zones, and in 37 of them only a regulated number of backpackers is allowed into each section at a one time. You have to obtain a backcountry permit for the zone you want to stay overnight in. Behind the Backcountry Desk are two wall maps with the zone outlines and a quota board indicating the number of vacancies in each zone, or unit. (See the Denali National Park & Preserve Backcountry Zones map.) Backcountry permits are issued only a day in advance, and at first glance backpackers are horrified to find most units full for two or three days in a row. Be prepared to wait two days at Riley Creek until something opens up, but once you've arranged for one overnight into the park, you can then arrange all your subsequent overnights at the same time, without having to abide by the 'one day in advance' rule.

For many, the reason to come to Denali and endure the long lines at the VAC is to escape into the backcountry for a true wilderness experience. Unlike many parks in the Lower 48, Denali's rigid restrictions ensure that you can trek and camp in a piece of wilderness that you can call your own, even if it's just for a few days. You can hike virtually anywhere in the park that hasn't been closed because of visitors' impact on wildlife.

Like getting into the campgrounds, the hard part of obtaining a permit is first getting into the backcountry. Once you're in, you can book a string of other units throughout the park for the next 14 days. Units that are easier to obtain include Nos 1, 2, 3 and 24, because they surround the park entrance and are heavily wooded. Spend a night or two here and then jump on a camper bus for a more favorable place deeper in the park. Or try for any of the more than a dozen units that don't abut the park road, such as Nos 37–41. Reserving your first night in such a zone means you'll have to start off early in the day and hike longer before stopping, but at least you're in the backcountry.

At the west end of the park are the zones with unlimited access. These tend to be areas of extensive tussock where the trekking is extremely difficult or involves a major fording of the McKinley River, a difficult feat even when the river is low. Again, by camping here, you can enter the backcountry immediately and then book other units as they open, bypassing the one-day-in-advance restriction.

Although any regulated zone can be filled, you'll generally find the more popular ones to be Nos 12, 13 and 18 in the tundra area south of Eielson Visitor Center; in fact, in the middle of the summer these may be almost impossible to get in without spending a week or more elsewhere in the backcountry. You will also find it challenging to get a permit for Nos 8, 9, 10 and 11, which include both branches of the Toklat River and tundra area south of Polychrome Pass; No 27, north of Sanctuary Campground; and No 15, the unit just west of Wonder Lake.

The first step in the permit process is to watch the Backcountry Simulator Program

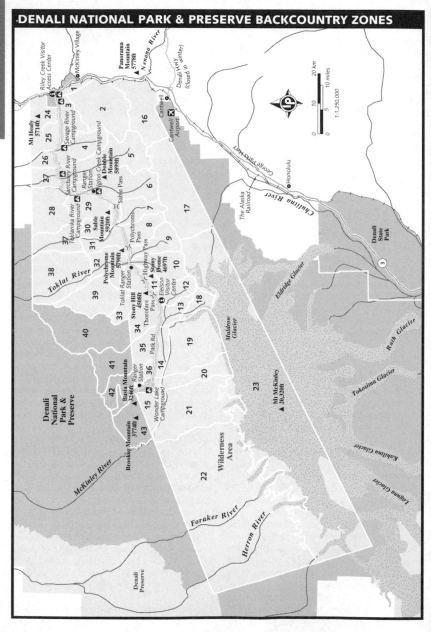

DENALI NATIONAL PARK & PRESERVE BACKCOUNTRY ZONES

in a video booth in the VAC. It's an interactive video that covers such topics as dealing with bears and backcountry travel. Then check the quota board for an area that you can access within a day and finally approach the ranger behind the desk to outline your entire backcountry itinerary.

Along with your permit, you'll receive a bear-resistant food container, free of charge, for food storage in the backcountry. The containers are bulky, but they work. Since they were first introduced in 1986, bear encounters in the park have dropped by 90%. Next, shuffle over to the shuttle bus counter and purchase a camper bus ticket ($15) and finally head over to the bookstore to purchase whatever topographic maps ($4) you will need.

There is also an admission fee, though it should hardly stop anybody from visiting the park. A $5 per person or $10 per family fee is charged to all visitors traveling beyond the checkpoint at Savage River Campground. The fee is good for seven days in the park and is collected when you obtain a shuttle bus ticket at the Riley Creek Visitor Access Center. Keep in mind that this is an entrance fee and you will still have to pay to stay in the park's campgrounds.

Warnings

It's important to realize that Denali is a trail-less park and the key to successful backcountry travel is being able to read a topographic map. You must be able to interpret the contours (elevation lines) on the map into the land formations in front of you. Riverbeds are easy to follow and make the best avenues for the backpacker, and wildlife for that matter, as they provide mild grades, unobstructed views and solid footing. But they almost always involve fording a river. Pack a pair of tennis shoes or sport sandals for this.

Ridges are also good routes to hike if the weather is not foul. The tree line in Denali is at 2500ft, and above that you usually will find tussock or moist tundra – humps of grass and willow hummocks with water between that make for sloppy hiking. In extensive stretches of tussock, the hiking has

been best described as 'walking on basketballs.' Above 3400ft, you'll encounter alpine or dry tundra, which generally makes for excellent hiking. Avoid scree-covered slopes if you can, however, as footing here will inevitably be loose.

Regardless of where you are headed, 5mi of backcountry hiking in Denali is a full day for the average backpacker. The NPS suggests that if there are three or four people in your party, try to stick to riverbeds, spread out, and avoid following each other, as you will heavily damage the frail ground vegetation. Everybody in the backcountry should avoid camping in the same spot for more than two nights.

Three of the treks described here are in Denali's backcountry and are routes, not trails by any means. They involve following rivers or passes and are only described here to help you envision what the outing will involve. Mileage given is only a rough estimate; your exact distance will depend on your line of travel, where you choose to ford the river, etc. The routes – Polychrome Pass Circuit, East Branch of the Toklat River Route, and Mt Eielson Loop – also follow some of the best areas for hiking in the park, thus there will be a heavy demand for the limited number of permits in their zones. You most likely will have to explore a different zone in the backcountry before being able to obtain a permit to explore an area like the East Branch of the Toklat River Route.

GETTING THERE & AWAY

The entrance to Denali National Park and Preserve is at Mile 237.3 of George Parks Hwy, and close to the highway are the VAC and Riley Creek Campground. Thanks to the popularity of Denali, the highway before and after the park entrance has become a tourist strip of private campgrounds, lodges, restaurants and other businesses, all feeding off Alaska's most famous drawing card. Hitchhiking to the park is considerably easier than hitchhiking out of it.

Bus

Both northbound and southbound bus services are available to Denali National Park

DENALI

and Preserve from several companies. From Anchorage, you can take the Alaska Park Connection shuttle (☎ 907-344-8775, 888-277-2757, ✉ info@alaskacoach.com), which offers daily service along the George Parks Hwy. The Alaska Park Connection took over the popular Backpacker Shuttle runs in 2000. The one-way fare from Anchorage to Denali National Park is $59; call for pick-up locations. Parks Highway Express (☎ 888-600-6001) leaves Fairbanks at 9 am and the Anchorage Hostel on 7th Ave and H St at 6:15 am. One-way fare from Anchorage to Denali is $35 and from Fairbanks $25.

Train

The most enjoyable way to arrive or depart from the park is aboard the Alaska Railroad (see the Getting Around chapter) with its viewing-dome cars that provide sweeping views of Mt McKinley and the Susitna and Nenana River valleys along the way. All trains arrive at the train station between the Riley Creek Campground and the park hotel, and only stay long enough for passengers to board.

The northbound train arrives in Denali at 3:45 pm and reaches Fairbanks at 8:15 pm. The southbound train arrives in Denali at noon and in Anchorage at 8:15 pm. Tickets are not cheap; a one-way fare from Denali National Park to Anchorage is $102, to Fairbanks $54.

GETTING AROUND
Shuttle Bus

What makes the park and its wildlife so accessible is the park road that runs the length of the preserve and the shuttle buses that use it. The shuttle bus service began in 1972 after the George Parks Hwy was opened and attendance in the park doubled in a single season. Park officials put a ban on private vehicles to prevent the park road from becoming a highway of cars and RVers, and today the wildlife is so accustomed to the rambling buses that the animals rarely stop their activities when one passes by.

The buses also provide access for day hiking, for which backcountry permits are not needed. Once in the backcountry, you

can stop a bus heading east on the park road by flagging it down for a ride back. Some photographers ride the bus only until wildlife is spotted. Changing buses several times each day is a practice commonly referred to as 'shuttle bus surfing.' By all means get off the buses, as it's the only way you will truly see and experience the park, but remember, you can only get back on if there is an available seat. No one is ever left out in the backcountry against their will but it's not too uncommon at the height of the season to have to wait two or three hours because the first four buses that pass you are full.

While riding the buses, passengers armed with binoculars and cameras scour the terrain for wildlife. When something is spotted, the name of the animal is called out, prompting the driver to slow down and most often stop for viewing and picture taking. The driver also doubles as a park guide and naturalist for a more interesting trip.

In 1995, 25 buses were added and buses now leave the VAC for Eielson Visitor Center every half hour from 6:30 am until 2 pm, when the last bus departs. There are also several buses that go all the way to Wonder Lake. It's an 11-hour trip to ride out to the end of the road and back, which makes for a long day. The ride to Eielson is an eight-hour roundtrip journey and passes the most spectacular mountain scenery by far. The only exception to this is when Mt McKinley is visible: Then, the ride to Wonder Lake is 11 of the most scenic hours you'll ever spend on a bus of any kind.

Technically, you pay for for the shuttle ride west on the park road and get a free ride back to the Riley Creek area. The single-trip fare to Toklat is $12.50, to Eielson $21 and to Wonder Lake $27. There are youth fares, and multiple-trip tickets allow one person to ride the bus for several days. The three-day ticket costs $42 to Eielson and $54 to Wonder Lake.

Tickets are available by phone up to the day before you travel. To book bus seats in advance call Denali National Park Reservation Service (☎ 272-7275, 800-622-7275). You can also print out the reservations forms from the Denali National Park and Preserve Web site (www.nps.gov/dena) and send them in via a fax to ☎ 907-264-4684, but you must pay with a credit card. Reservations can be made for the buses beginning in late February for that year.

If you don't have a reservation, you most likely will have to wait two days to obtain a bus ticket. One way around this is to stop at the park and reserve one and then keep heading north to spend a few days in Fairbanks, backtracking to Denali when your reservations kick in.

Camper Bus

Due to the popularity of the shuttle buses, the park has set up a camper bus system. They're the same buses, but a third of the seats have been removed to make room for backpacks and mountain bikes. Four camper buses leave the VAC several times a day and charge $15.50 per trip. If you get a campsite or backcountry permit, there is no hassle or wait for a ticket for the camper bus.

Car

If you arrive by car, you can drive to the VAC and the first 14mi of the park road without having to obtain a road pass or permit. At Mile 14 there is a ranger booth that turns back all vehicles without a permit. You can drive to three campgrounds, Riley Creek, Savage River and Sanctuary River, without a road permit, but you still must obtain a campground reservation from the VAC (see Campgrounds later in this chapter). You can also drive to Teklanika Campground, but you need to secure both a reservation and a road permit that will allow you to drive beyond Mile 14 from the VAC. Park your car in the overflow parking lot at the Riley Creek Campground if you're entering the backcountry for the day or longer. Both the camper bus and the shuttle bus swing through to pick up passengers.

For a very small number of people who want to drive their own vehicles all the way into the park, a road lottery takes place each fall. Contact the NPS Denali National

Driving the Denali Park Road

Feeling lucky? If so, then try the Denali park road lottery staged by the National Park Service. Every year when the shuttle buses stop service in mid-September, the NPS allows 400 lucky visitors to drive the park road during a four-day period – all the way to Wonder Lake at Mile 84. That includes stopping as often as you like to check out the wildlife.

Each of the 400 permits is good for one day only, and they are handed out in a special lottery, usually held at the end of July. There is a limit of one entry per person into the lottery, which, for obvious reasons, is heavily dominated by Alaskans.

If you are interested, the first step is calling the park headquarters (☎ 907-683-2294) to find out when the road is going to be open and the date of the lottery. Then send a self-addressed, stamped envelope to Road Lottery, PO Box 9, Denali Park, AK 99755. Include your first and last name and your choice of the four days in order of preference. A letter is unnecessary; just mark the order of the dates you prefer on the lower, left-hand corner of the self-addressed envelope.

Park Reservation Service or see the boxed text 'Driving the Denali Park Road' for more about this rare opportunity.

Mountain Bike

An increasingly popular way to explore the park road is on a mountain bike. No special permit is needed to ride your bike on the road, but you are not allowed to leave the road at any time. Most bikers book a campsite at the VAC and then carry the bike on the camper bus, using it to explore the road from there. You can even book sites at a string of campgrounds and ride with your equipment from one to the next. You can rent a bike from Denali Outdoor Center (☎ 683-1925, 888-303-1925, ✉ docadventure@hotmail.com) for $40 a day, $37 per day for two- to four-day rentals and $35 if you rent it longer. The center is at Mile 238.6 of the George Parks Hwy, next to Northern Lights Gift Shop, but runs a free shuttle from the train station in the park.

Guided Hikes

There are numerous guided walks in the park for those unsure of entering the backcountry on their own. The best is the Discovery Hike that departs at 8 am daily for a moderately strenuous, three- to four-hour hike in the park's backcountry. The location of this trail-less adventure changes daily, and you must sign up one to two days in advance. The Visitor Access Center (see the Information section earlier in this chapter) will have a list of all ranger-led hikes.

NEAREST TOWNS & FACILITIES

You would be wise to purchase most of your supplies at the last major town you depart from, whether it is Anchorage, Wasilla or Fairbanks. You'll have a better selection, and you'll save yourself some money.

Inside the Park

Supplies & Equipment Within the park, McKinley Mercantile, a block from the hotel, sells a variety of foods, including dried items, some canned goods and white gas in small quantities ($2 per quart). But the fact that it has a larger selection of wine than it does freeze-dried dinners should tell you something. It's open 8 am to 11 pm during the summer, and showers are available for $5 per person.

Places to Stay & Eat There are seven campgrounds in Denali National Park, and sites in them are always in high demand. As with the shuttle bus seats, you can reserve a campsite in advance for a $4 reservation fee. All the sites in Riley Creek, Savage River, Teklanika and Wonder Lake Campgrounds are available by advance reservations. The sites in Morino, Sanctuary River and Igloo Creek are available only by walk-in requests at the VAC. If you can plan the exact days you will be in the park, reserving campsites saves an awful lot of hassle. To arrange a reservation, call Denali National

Park Reservation Service (☎ 800-622-7275). You can also print out the reservation forms from the Denali National Park Web site (www.nps.gov/dena) and send them in via a fax to 907-264-4684, but you need to have a credit card. Campground fees are $6 to $12 a night.

The key to getting into the campground of your choice, like Wonder Lake, is just getting into a campground, any campground, including either Morino or Riley Creek. Once in, you can secure a guaranteed site for the next 14 days wherever there is an opening. With this system, you can still get to Wonder Lake, even during the busiest time of the year, if you are willing to camp elsewhere in the park for four or five days. The limit on staying in one campground or a combination of them is 14 days.

At the main entrance of the park is **Riley Creek Campground**, the largest and nicest facility in Denali as well as the only one open year-round. A quarter mile west of George Parks Hwy, Riley Creek has 102 sites, piped-in water, flush toilets and evening interpretive programs. Popular with RVers – in fact overrun by RVers – sites cost $12 per night.

Near the train station, **Morino** is a walk-in campground for backpackers without vehicles. It provides only two metal caches to keep your food away from the bears, piped-in water and vault toilets. There are around 40 sites, but it has to be awfully crowded for the rangers to begin turning people away. First pick out a site at the campground, then return to the VAC to register and pay for it ($6 per night per site).

Despite its name, **Savage River Campground** ($12) is a mile short of the actual river. It is only one of two campgrounds with a view of Mt McKinley. It has 33 sites that can accommodate both RVs and tents and has water, flush toilets and evening interpretive programs. Campers with a vehicle can drive to this campground.

Sanctuary River is the next campground down the road, at Mile 23 of the park road on the banks of a large glacial river. There are seven sites for tents only, and they can't be reserved in advance. There is no piped-in water. Sanctuary River is a great area for day hiking. You can either head south to hike along the Sanctuary River or make a day out of climbing Mt Wright or Primrose Ridge to the north for an opportunity to see and photograph Dall sheep.

At Mile 29, *Teklanika River Campground* has 53 sites ($12) for either RVs or tents, piped water and evening programs. Unlike other Denali campgrounds, you must book this one for a minimum of three days (due to the fact that you are allowed to drive to it). Registered campers are issued a road pass for a single trip to the facility. You must leave your vehicle parked at Teklanika for the duration of your stay there, but with a campground reservation you also get a shuttle bus pass, so you can see the rest of the park from a shuttle bus while staying in the campground. When moving to another campground, you must first take your car back to the parking lot at Riley Creek.

Located at Mile 34, *Igloo Creek Campground* ($6) is another waterless facility. The seven sites cannot be reserved in advance and are limited to tents. The day hiking in this area is excellent, especially the numerous ridges around Igloo Mountain, Cathedral Mountain and Sable Pass that provide good routes into the alpine area.

The jewel of Denali campgrounds is *Wonder Lake*, at Mile 85 of the park road, with immense views of Mt McKinley. The facility has 28 sites for tents only ($12) but does feature flush toilets and piped-in water. If you are lucky enough to reserve a site, book it for three nights and then pray that the mountain appears during one of

Wilderness with Class

If money is no option and you're fed up with the crowded nature of the Denali National Park entrance area, consider a side trip to the resorts at the end of the road.

The Denali park road ends at the historic district of Kantishna, at Mile 91. The settlement was founded in 1905 as a gold mining camp at the junction of Moose and Eureka Creeks and was originally outside the national park boundary. But in 1980, after the park was expanded to its present size of 9375 sq mi, it became an island of private holdings.

Today Kantishna is the home of three places that are as close to wilderness lodges as you'll ever find on a road. Their rates tend to shock most budget-conscious backpackers but include roundtrip transportation from the train station, meals and guided activities.

The best known is *Camp Denali* (☎ 683-2290, PO Box 67, Denali National Park, AK 99755, ✉ dnpwild@alaska.net). The camp offers several different types of accommodations, most with fixed arrival and departure dates. The camp is a resort – not just a place to sleep – and offers a wide range of activities, including wildlife observation and photography, rafting, fishing, gold panning and, of course, hiking. Plus, your best view of Mt McKinley is obtained from here. Rooms at both Camp Denali and it's North Face Lodge are $335 per person per night, and a two- or three-night minimum is required.

Nearby is the *Kantishna Roadhouse* (☎ 683-1475, 800-942-7420, PO Box 81670, Fairbanks, AK 99708, ✉ kantshna@ptialaska.net). Established in the early 1900s, the roadhouse has 28 cabins that cost $280 per person per night. Activities range from gold panning and hiking to photographic activities, and at night you can soak your worries away in a hot tub or sauna.

Also at the end of the road is the *Denali Backcountry Lodge* (☎ 783-1342, 800-841-0692, ✉ denalibl@pobox.alaska.net), with 30 cabins for $300 per person based on double occupancy and $249 per person for a quad.

Keep in mind that these places will most likely be booked long before you arrive in Alaska. If you want to treat yourself, you must email or write to the lodges in advance, as many visitors book reservations here six months ahead.

the days you are there. Also pack plenty of insect repellent and maybe even a head net. In midsummer, the bugs are vicious.

Travelers opposed to sleeping in a tent have few alternatives inside the park. The *Denali National Park Hotel* (☎ 683-2215 in the summer) is the only lodging available here and rooms cost $159 for two people per night. For being the official lodge of one of the best-known national parks in the country, this hotel is sadly lacking.

There are two restaurants and one bar in the park, all off the lobby of the Denali National Park Hotel. The *Denali Dining Room* serves full meals in pleasant surroundings but is overpriced for most budget travelers. Breakfast after 7 am, however, can be a leisurely and reasonable $6 to $8 affair. The *Whistle Stop Snack Shop*, also off the lobby, opens at 5:30 am to provide early shuttle-bus passengers with breakfast or a box lunch. Egg breakfasts start at $5, and hamburgers and sandwiches cost less than $7. Surprisingly, the shop serves garden burgers and veggie sandwiches. The *Gold Spike Saloon*, two lounge cars side by side, is the hotel's bar.

Unfortunately, the National Park Service has decided to close the Denali Park Hotel permanently in September of 2001. There are no plans to open any other hotels within Denali National Park, as the goal is to maintain the wilderness setting within the park boundaries. If you visit after 2001, you'll have to look outside of the park entrance for dining and hotel accommodations. For more about the NPS's changing plans for Denali, see the boxed text 'A New Denali National Park' earlier in this chapter.

Entrance Area
Supplies & Equipment Outside the park you can find limited groceries and supplies at Lynx Creek Park Mart at Mile 238.5 of the George Parks Hwy, just over a mile north of the entrance. They use the same phone number as Lynx Creek Pub (☎ 683-2547). You can purchase stoves and other equipment at Denali Mountain Works (☎ 683-1542) at Mile 239 of the Parks Hwy. The shop also rents out tents, sleeping bags

and other equipment, and is the home of Too-loo-uk River Guides, which runs multi-day rafting trips on various rivers inside and outside Denali.

Places to Stay & Eat For a park of 9375 sq mi, Denali occasionally stuns visitors who arrive late in the afternoon or the early evening to find that there is no place to stay. They are informed by National Park Service rangers of individuals offering private accommodations outside the park, and these people can make a living just from the overflow.

Included among these are several private campgrounds where you can expect to pay from $15 to $20 for a campsite. Three miles north of the park is *Denali Riverside RV Park* (☎ 888-778-7700, ✉ rvalaska@aol.com), Mile 240 of the George Parks Hwy, with tent sites for $10 and RV sites for $25. This campground is basically a gravel parking lot squeezed in between the highway and the Nenana River. Much nicer but farther away is the *Denali Grizzly Bear Campground* (☎ 683-2696), at Mile 231 of the George Parks Hwy, 6mi south of the park entrance, which offers wooded campsites for $17 a night, platform tents for $23, and 20 well-spread-out cabins, with a couple of small ones for $50 for two people and the rest in the $70 to $100 range.

If there are three or four in your party, consider booking a cabin in advance. Across the highway from Grizzly Bear Campground is *Denali River Cabins* (☎ 683-2500, 800-230-7275, ✉ denali@polarnet.com), Mile 231, with cedar cabins for two ($99) and for four ($156). The cabins are 6mi south of the park but there is a free shuttle service to the entrance. Even farther south of the entrance at Mile 224 is *McKinley Creekside Cabins* (☎ 683-2277, 888-533-6254, ✉ cabins@mtaonline.net), and across the street, the *Carlo Creek Lodge* (☎ 683-2576). Both have cabins in the $90 to $110 range for two people, but those at Carlo Creek are in a much nicer setting along the creek. There is also a wooded campground at Carlo Creek. This is a great area to stay at; you can escape the park crowds here, but you need

DENALI

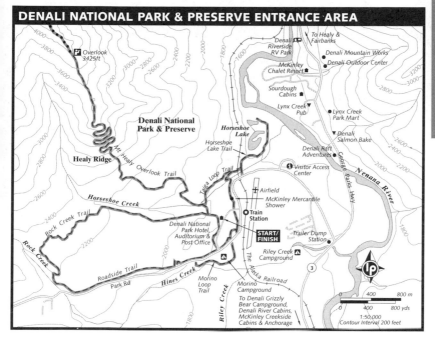

DENALI NATIONAL PARK & PRESERVE ENTRANCE AREA

Overlook 3425ft

Denali National Park & Preserve

Healy Ridge

Mt Healy Overlook Trail

Horseshoe Creek

Rock Creek Trail

Rock Creek

Roadside Trail

Park Rd

Hines Creek

Horseshoe Lake

Horseshoe Lake Trail

Taiga Loop Trail

Morino Loop Trail

Morino Campground

Riley Creek

The Alaska Railroad

To Healy & Fairbanks

Denali Riverside RV Park

Denali Mountain Works

McKinley Chalet Resort

Denali Outdoor Center

Sourdough Cabins

Lynx Creek Pub

Lynx Creek Park Mart

Denali Salmon Bake

Denali Raft Adventures

Visitor Access Center

Airfield

McKinley Mercantile Shower

Train Station

START/FINISH

Trailer Dump Station

Riley Creek Campground

George Parks Hwy

Nenana River

Denali National Park Hotel, Auditorium & Post Office

To Denali Grizzly Bear Campground, Denali River Cabins, McKinley Creekside Cabins & Anchorage

3

0   400   800 m
0   400   800 yds
1:50,000
Contour Interval 200 feet

a vehicle. Neither lodge supplies transport to the park.

There are cabins closer to the entrance that do offer van transport, but keep in mind that space is at a premium just north of the park. Cabins here are small and usually crammed together. Places include **Sourdough Cabins** (☎ 683-2773, 800-354-6020, @ denalisourdough@hotmail.com), at Mile 238.8, where rates begin at $150 per night for a double.

For the best pizza outside the park, try the **Lynx Creek Pub** (☎ 683-2548), Mile 238.6 of the Parks Hwy, north of the park entrance. The log-cabin restaurant also has vegetarian specials, a lunch buffet and an impressive selection of beer.

Closer to the park entrance, on the other side of the highway, is **Denali Salmon Bake**, where $20 buys you the usual Alaskan salmon dinner. You get a single serving of salmon, but everything else is all-you-can-

eat. Also located here is **Lynx Creek Park Mart**, offering the best selection of groceries and liquor in the area.

Getting There & Away Many of the accommodations outside the park run van transport to the VAC or the train station and are often there waiting for guests when the train pulls in. To reach the business area a mile north of the entrance, you can also hop on the courtesy bus for the McKinley Chalet Resort.

Healy

Healy is a small town and service center 11mi north of the park entrance, where gas, limited supplies and lodging are available.

Places to Stay & Eat There is an excellent backpacker's hostel just south of Healy. **Denali Hostel** (☎ 683-1295), on Otter Lake Rd, has bunks for $24 a night along with kitchen facilities, showers and transport back to the park – even as early as 6 am to catch the first shuttle bus! If you arrive on the train, there will be a Denali Hostel van at the depot.

In Healy is *McKinley RV & Campground* (☎ *800-478-2562 or 683-2379, 800-478-2562),* Mile 248.4 on the George Parks Hwy, a wooded facility with tent sites ($18), RV sites ($20 to $28) and bus transportation to the VAC. There are also a handful of motels and B&Bs within town. *Totem Inn* (☎ *683-2420),* at George Parks Hwy and Healy Spur Rd, has a variety of accommodations from deluxe ($101 for a double) to economy rooms that are located in what is basically an elongated trailer ($74 for a double). The best B&B is *Denali Dome Home* (☎ *683-1239,* @ *denalidome@alaskaone.com),* on Healy Spur Rd, a geodesic house with doubles for $90. Probably the best place to eat in Healy is at Totem Inn Café (☎ 683-2420).

Getting There & Away For transportation between Denali National Park and Healy, either make arrangements with one of the van shuttle services that go to Fairbanks (see Bus under Getting There & Away earlier in this chapter) or call Caribou Cab (☎ 683-5000).

Mt Healy Overlook Trail

Duration 3 to 4 hours
Distance 5mi
Difficulty Level Medium
Start/Finish Denali National Park Hotel
Cabins & Shelters No
Permits Required No
Public Transportation Yes
Summary This well-maintained trail climbs steeply to offer views of the Alaska Range, including Mt McKinley if the weather is clear. It's a good warm-up before venturing into the Denali National Park and Preserve backcountry.

Even for those who have neither the desire nor the equipment for an overnight trek, hiking is still the best way to enjoy the park and obtain a personal closeness with the land and its wildlife. The simplest way to undertake a day hike is to ride the shuttle bus (see Getting Around earlier in this chapter) and get off at any valley, riverbed or ridge that takes your fancy. Best of all, no backcountry permit is needed for day hiking.

The only maintained trails in Denali National Park and Preserve are in the entrance area. Of the handful of trails there, only the climb to Mt Healy Overlook truly lets you escape the crowds and the bustle of this area. It's a 5mi roundtrip from the park hotel that climbs 1700ft. No camping is allowed anywhere along the trail because the route is within the day-use area of the park entrance.

The uphill effort will reward you with excellent views of the Nenana River valley, Healy Ridge and other ridgelines. The entire hike takes most people from three to four hours, so after spending a frustrating morning at the VAC, you have ample time to get this hike in before dinner.

PLANNING
Maps
The area of the Mt Healy Overlook Trail is covered on USGS 1:63,360 series quad *Healy C-4,* although the trail is not shown. In this book, the trail is shown on the Denali National Park & Preserve Entrance Area map.

Permits & Regulations
A backcountry permit is not needed for any day hike in the park. There is an admission fee to Denali, but you only pay that when you use the shuttle or camper bus to enter the backcountry (see Permits & Regulations earlier in this chapter). You can drive into the entrance area and hike this trail without paying the $5 admission fee.

GETTING TO/FROM THE HIKE
Mt Healy Overlook Trail begins near the Denali National Park Hotel at the start of the park road, a five-minute walk from Morino Campground. There is free transportation into and around the park entrance. The Front-Country Shuttle Buses run every half-hour, beginning at the VAC.

THE HIKE
Stage 1: Denali National Park Hotel to Mt Healy Overlook
2.5mi, 2 to 3 hours

The hike begins near the guest parking lot west of Denali National Park Hotel at the Taiga Loop Trailhead. This trail loops behind the hotel, passes a junction to Rock Creek Trail and then comes to a service road, immediately followed by another one. At the second service road turn left and follow the road for about 50yd to the trailhead of the Mt Healy Overlook Trail.

Once on the trail, you'll quickly cross a bridge over **Horseshoe Creek** and then continue a moderately steep climb through a forest of spruce mixed with aspen and alder. A mile from the hotel, you reach the scenic viewpoint where you can gaze upon Mt Fellows to the east and the Alaska Range to the south. At this point the trail moves from stunted spruce into thickets of alder and at the base of a ridge begins to follow a series of switchbacks as it heads for Mt Healy Overlook. You reach **Halfway Rock**, a 12ft boulder, at 1.2mi, which provides an opportunity for you to catch your breath.

The steep climb continues, with the switchbacks becoming shorter, and at 1.6mi you move from a taiga zone of alder to the alpine tundra: a world of moss, lichen, wildflowers and incredible views. Keep an eye out for the large hoary marmot, a northern cousin of the groundhog, and the pika, a small relative of the rabbit. Pikas will often sit motionless on the large stones of a rock slide.

In the final 0.4mi, the trail emerges below **Mt Healy Overlook**. You then curve steeply around the ridge to emerge at the rocky bench that is the overlook. The trail actually ends at a rock pile, 2mi from the hotel.

The view from the overlook is excellent. Sugar Loaf Mountain, at 4450ft, dominates the horizon to the east, and above the overlook to the northwest is the actual summit of Mt Healy. If you have a pair of binoculars, search the slopes to the north for Dall sheep. If the weather is clear, look to the southwest for the Mt McKinley massif, some 80mi away.

Stage 2: The Return
2.5mi, 1 to 2 hours

The overlook (3425ft) is a rocky shoulder of the Healy Ridge, a climb of more than 1700ft from the hotel. You can continue up the ridge on a more gentle climb for another mile to reach the high point of 4217ft. The summit of Mt Healy (5700ft) is still another 2mi to the northwest.

To return, you have little choice but to retrace the route that you just climbed. Take heart, however, in the knowledge that it will take far less time, perhaps half the hiking time, to go downhill than it did to go up.

Polychrome Pass Circuit

Duration 1 to 2 days
Distance 8mi
Difficulty Level Medium to hard
Start Mile 42.7 of the Park Road
Finish Polychrome Pass Rest Area
Cabins & Shelters No
Permits Required Yes
Public Transportation Yes
Summary This is a day hike or overnight trek into one of the most scenic sections of the park, where brilliantly colored rocks and multicolored mountains are the backdrop to this 8mi loop off the park road.

The Polychrome Pass Circuit is a one- or two-day hike into one of the most scenic sections of the park. The brilliantly colored rocks of Polychrome Pass are the result of volcanic action some 60 million years ago. Today, the multicolored hills and mountains here, including Polychrome Mountain (5790ft) and Cain Peak (4961ft), are a stunning sight in the low-angle light of a clear Alaska summer day.

The first leg of this trek, following the East Fork of the Toklat River north from the park road, is a challenging hike over rough tundra that may include climbing around cliffs. There is also a narrow canyon to bushwhack through at one point, giving this 8mi loop off the park road a rating of medium to hard. You have a good opportunity to spot

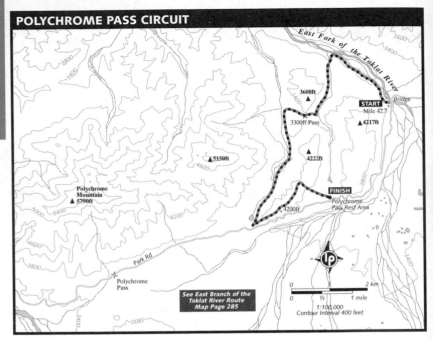

wildlife in the Polychrome Pass area, especially Dall sheep in early summer. Bears are also found here in good numbers.

This circuit can be a long day hike for experienced backcountry travelers or an overnight trek for everybody else. The advantage of doing the circuit as a day hike is that a backcountry permit is not required.

PLANNING
Maps

The entire Polychrome Pass Circuit is covered on USGS 1:63,360 series quad *Healy C-6* and lies in backcountry zone No 31. The best place to purchase your maps is at the VAC after consulting rangers about your itinerary and obtaining a backcountry permit.

Although trail-less, for the most part much of Denali is also treeless, allowing for far easier orientation than if you were hiking down a wooded trail in the Kenai Peninsula.

The tree line at Denali is at 2500ft; if you get lost, simply climb the nearest ridge for an overview of the area you are in.

Permits & Regulations

Unless you are fit and experienced enough to complete this hike in one day, you will need to get a backcountry permit for an overnight hike from the Visitor Access Center near the park entrance. See the Permits & Regulations section of Denali National Park & Preserve earlier in this chapter for complete details.

GETTING TO/FROM THE HIKE

Depart the shuttle bus or camper bus at Mile 42.7 of the park road, just after it crosses the bridge over the East Fork of the Toklat River. (Park shuttle information is discussed in detail in the Getting Around section earlier in this chapter.) Normally, there is a bus stop at the west side of the river.

THE HIKE
Stage 1: East Fork River Bridge to 3300ft Pass
3.5mi, 4 to 5 hours

The loop begins on the west side of the park road bridge across the **East Fork of the Toklat River**. Downstream, or north from the bridge, the East Fork flows as a braided river across a wide gravel bar for almost 8mi until it enters a 7mi-long canyon. During periods of low to medium water levels, there are enough braids in the river for a safe crossing.

At other times its volume is too high to cross; that's when you might run into problems. While you are following the river along its west bank, it's possible that deep channels may force you to climb up and around the bordering cliffs to bypass a stretch of steep banks.

It's 1.5mi along the gravel bars from the park road to the first major tributary flowing out of the hills south of Polychrome Mountain. Head upstream (south) along the unnamed tributary for another 1.5mi, fording to its west side at the best possible crossing. Just before the stream enters a mile-long canyon, a low pass will appear to the west. It's a 200ft ascent to the pass that forms a saddle between a 3608ft peak to the north and a 4222ft peak to the south.

From the top of the pass, it's an easy stroll into the next valley where two streams converge. For those wanting to spend a night in the backcountry, the pass or the bench on its west side are the best places to set up camp. The confluence of the two streams to the west is also a possibility but keep in mind that the valley forms a natural route for wildlife that includes, of course, brown bears.

If you arrive in the morning and have an afternoon to kill, it's possible to climb the 4222ft peak. The easiest route is from the pass along the ridgeline that heads almost due south. Be cautious near the top, however, as the rock and scree slopes here can be loose and hazardous. If the day is clear the views of Mt McKinley are stunning from near the peak.

Stage 2: 3300ft Pass to Polychrome Pass Rest Area
4.5mi, 4 to 5 hours

Descend to the confluence and hike down the valley along either side of the creek. The scenery will be dominated by the northern slopes of **Polychrome Mountain**, whose colors, especially in late August and early September, justify its name. In early summer, search the slopes for Dall sheep.

Within half a mile upstream from the confluence, the stream enters a narrow canyon that will be filled with willow, dwarf birch and alder. Search for animal trails to follow for easier hiking through the narrow area. Most likely, however, you'll have to ford the stream a few times. Be wary as you travel through the canyon. Your visibility will be limited by the brush, and bears often pass through here. Clap your hands, sing songs, argue loudly about politics. Do anything to make noise.

It takes a mile of bushwhacking through the canyon before the stream breaks out into a wide area of the valley. Travel is far easier now, though at times it can be boggy and wet. Within another mile you arrive at the source of the stream, a small lake often frequented by waterfowl. The lake is less than a quarter mile north of the park road.

The easiest way to return to Polychrome Pass Rest Area is to hike the road, enjoying the views to the south of Toklat River, other valleys and, if you're lucky, Mt McKinley. At the rest area you'll find vault toilets and covered benches, but no source of water.

For those who want one last climb, skip the easy road route and climb the 4000ft ridge due east of the lake. It's manageable at first, steep and loose at the end. Eventually you reach the 4200ft high point and from there follow the ridge line to a low saddle at its north end. Head east from this pass, cross the bushy ravine and then climb a final hill where on the other side is **Polychrome Pass Rest Area**. You'll most likely see people on top of the hill, viewing Polychrome Mountain during their short bus stop.

DENALI

East Branch of the Toklat River Route

Duration 2 to 3 days
Distance 12 to 16mi
Difficulty Level Medium to hard
Start/Finish Mile 52.4 of the Park Road
Cabins & Shelters No
Permits Required Yes
Public Transportation Yes
Summary This hike takes you up the valley of the East Branch of the Toklat River and does not require fording a major river or stream. Highlights include the possibility of seeing caribou and Dall sheep.

Flowing north from glaciers in the Alaska Range are the West and East Branches of the Toklat River, which merge at Mile 52.5 of the park road. Both are in classic U-shaped glacially carved valleys where the rivers become braided channels across wide rocky bars. The East Branch is a particularly good area for hiking if you are new to Denali, because you don't have to ford the Toklat River or any other major glacial streams to travel up the valley. There is also good visibility in all directions thanks to the surrounding vegetation of dry tundra and sparse willow, and the rocky riverbed provides sure footing.

The trek can be either a day hike or an overnight hike where you could go 6mi or so up the valley and then spend a morning or a day exploring the area before returning along the same route. This would make a roundtrip of 12 to 16mi and provide you with a reasonably good chance of seeing wildlife. Small bands of caribou are often viewed on the riverbeds throughout the summer, and Dall sheep can be spotted on the ridges and slopes above. Grizzlies travel the route as well, to feed on the soapberry crop.

PLANNING
Maps
The required USGS 1:63,360 series topos are *Healy C-6* and *B-6* and *Mt McKinley C-1*,

although all but the first mile falls on *Healy B-6*. This trip is rated moderate in difficulty and falls into backcountry zone 9, a tough one to secure a permit in.

Permits & Regulations
If you plan to complete this hike in one day, you don't need a backcountry permit. Otherwise, you will need to get one from the VAC near the park entrance. See the Permits & Regulations section of Denali National Park & Preserve earlier in this chapter for more about Denali's regulations.

GETTING TO/FROM THE HIKE
Ask the driver of the shuttle or camper bus (see the Getting Around section earlier in this chapter) to let you out at the bridge over the Toklat River, Mile 52.4 of the park road.

THE HIKE
Stage 1: Toklat River Bridge to Upper Toklat Valley
6mi, 5 to 7 hours
The **Toklat River Bridge**, located just before the Toklat Ranger Station, marks where the East Branch and the main branch of the Toklat River merge. After departing the bus at the bridge, you'll soon realize the East Branch here is too deep and cuts too close to the road to cross before you enter the valley. Head east along the park road, for a half mile to a mile and look for a suitable place to descend the steep bank through the willows to where the Toklat River opens up into the broad valley.

The East Branch of the Toklat River is highly braided, which has resulted in an open terrain of broad gravel bars and channels, the reason for its popularity among hikers. It is also a popular place to see brown bears, so keep an eye on the surrounding landscape. Two miles from the bridge, the East Branch completes its wide curve south into a valley that is walled in on the west side by **Divide Mountain** (5195ft) and on the east by an unnamed 5000ft peak.

From this point on, the valley becomes narrower with every step you take toward the glaciers. Travel, however, is easy along the gravel bars. Search the mountain slopes

EAST BRANCH OF THE TOKLAT RIVER ROUTE

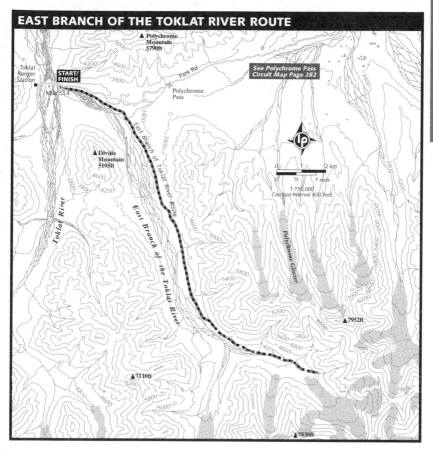

See Polychrome Pass
Circuit Map Page 282

to the east in the beginning for the best chances to spot Dall sheep. The East Branch is a glacial river with mud-gray water, but 5mi after leaving the bridge, you reach the first clear-water stream that flows out of the mountains to the east.

In another mile, or 6mi from the bridge, you should reach a second stream flowing out of the steep mountain walls of the valley. This general area makes a particularly good campsite, providing a source of clear water, a scenic backdrop of the surrounding peaks of the Alaska Range and a good dose of back-country solitude.

Stage 2: The Return
6 to 10mi, 8 to 9 hours

You return the way you came. It's the same route but the view is different as you hike out of the widening valley with the colorful slopes of the Polychrome Pass area rising above the park road to your north.

Before heading back, adventurous hikers can take a side trip to one of the glaciers at the head of the valley. From the second stream, the steep walls of the valley close in on the east side, forcing the river to hug a cliff. This forces you to scramble up the slope and follow the river from above for a mile or so.

You'll bypass where the East Branch splits into two main channels before being able to descend back to the valley floor. The channels head in opposite directions to glaciers of their own. The stream and small valley to the left as you face south is the easiest to explore. It's also another good place to search for Dall sheep.

You can follow the rocky terrain on either bank of the stream, and the south side might even be a bit easier. Be especially cautious whenever you're fording glacially fed streams.

Mt Eielson Loop

Duration 2 days
Distance 14mi
Difficulty Level Medium
Start/Finish Eielson Visitor Center
Cabins & Shelters No
Permits Required Yes
Public Transportation Yes
Summary This loop traverses the most popular areas to hike in Denali National Park and Preserve and, on a clear day, offers stunning views of Mt McKinley and Muldrow Glacier.

This is perhaps the most natural loop off the park road. It conveniently begins and ends at the Eielson Visitor Center, offers stunning views of Mt McKinley and Muldrow Glacier, and gets you far enough into the backcountry for a good sense of being in the wilderness area.

Needless to say, it's a popular area, and the greatest demand for permits in the park is probably for backcountry zones 12 and 13 (where the loop falls). It's debatable which is harder: winning the New York lottery or getting these permits without first spending a week somewhere else in the backcountry.

Backpackers are often discouraged by the park staff from attempting this route. Either you'll be frustrated at the inability to get permits or once out there dismayed to see that in areas a footpath is developing due to the popularity of the loop. That's a shame,

for this is still one the most scenic areas in the park to explore on foot. Sighting wildlife, especially grizzly bears, is likely, and if Mt McKinley appears, the sight of it will overwhelm you for a day…if not a lifetime. Even if you are unable to obtain the backcountry permits – and I can't stress enough how hard it is to arrange them – portions of the loop make for an interesting day hike.

The trip is rated moderate because it involves fording the Thorofare River, twice – always a challenging crossing. A strong, experienced backcountry traveler can cover this 14mi loop in a day, others can easily walk it in two days. But if you can obtain the permits, by all means spend three days or even longer in this special area of the park.

PLANNING
Maps
The entire route is covered on the USGS 1:63,360 series quad *Mt McKinley B-1*.

Permits & Regulations
If you plan to complete this hike in one day, you don't need a backcountry permit. Otherwise, you will need to get one; for information about obtaining permits see the Permits & Regulations section of Denali National Park & Preserve earlier in this chapter.

GETTING TO/FROM THE HIKE
Take the camper bus or shuttle bus to Eielson Visitor Center at Mile 66 of the park road (for details, see the Bus section of Getting Around, earlier in this chapter).

THE HIKE
Stage 1: Eielson Visitor Center to Pass Summit
5.2mi, 4 to 6 hours
This loop is described in a clockwise direction, the easiest way to follow the route. But if the weather is especially clear and Mt McKinley is out, you might consider following the route in the opposite direction. The best views of the mountain are obtained while hiking stage 2 of the loop.

From **Eielson Visitor Center**, there is a trail that drops down a steep ridge to Gorge

MT EIELSON LOOP

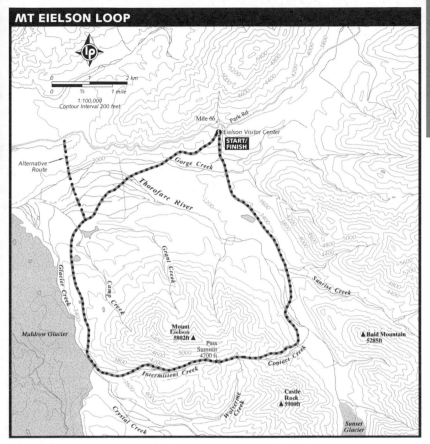

Creek. The creek is reached within a mile and is generally an easy ford; sometimes you can even leap across it. Once across, climb the bluff on the south side to an obvious bench of rolling tundra. This is open terrain, so visibility will be good. Head south for 2mi, passing a small lake within a mile (if you are not too far off course).

Once past the lake, you'll mostly likely be able to pick up an animal trail that will lead you to the edge of the bench. Follow it until you come to where **Sunrise Creek** flows into **Thorofare River**. Ford Sunrise Creek and

then cross Thorofare River. Be cautious at the river, however. Take time to carefully scout it to find the most braided section and then unhook your hip straps and cross diagonally, heading downstream.

Once on the west side of the river, head upstream until you are directly west of a 5285ft peak known as Bald Mountain and look for **Contact Creek**, a clear-water stream that flows into the Thorofare River. This is your route to Pass Summit. Either follow the creek or the ridgeline just north of it to climb more than 1000ft in the next mile. It's hard work with a backpack but a manageable climb for most hikers. Eventually, 5.2mi or so from Eielson Visitor Center, you should reach the pass.

At 4700ft, **Pass Summit** is a scenic place to spend the night if the weather permits. Views of Mt McKinley to the southwest are possible on a clear day, and to the north is Mt Eielson, a 5802ft peak. It's a spectacular spot if it's calm. The pass funnels storms and strong winds, so you may have to continue through it and drop to a more sheltered location at a lower elevation. Water is usually available near the pass from Wolverine Creek to the south.

Stage 2: The Return
8.8mi, 6 to 8 hours

Those with an extra day in their itinerary might want to spend it at the pass to scale Mt Eielson. The most obvious route is a talus and rocky slope due north of Wolverine Creek that provides easy access to the ridge line. From here it is a pleasant trek to the 5600ft summit where views of Mt McKinley, Muldrow Glacier and the

Alaska Range are stunning on a clear day. To reach the true summit at 5802ft requires more scrambling and rock climbing. The mountain is also very accessible from its west side. If you climb that side, you might want to camp on a bench above Glacier Creek.

From the pass, hike west towards **Intermittent Creek**. This route is so popular something of a footpath has begun to appear. You then descend the slope to its confluence with Glacier Creek. It's approximately 3.5mi from the pass to Glacier Creek; on the other side is the rubble-covered ice of Muldrow Glacier.

Head north along **Glacier Creek** and in the beginning you can follow the gravel bars. Eventually you're forced to climb the bench along its east side. The alternative is to climb the bench a half mile before the confluence of Glacier and Intermittent Creeks. Either way you end up following the rolling flanks of the mountain for almost 2mi until you descend to the flood plains of Thorofare River. Heading northeast away from Glacier Creek, you will first ford

A Wild Ride on the Nenana River

While waiting for your backcountry zone to open up, you can spend a thrilling afternoon floating the Nenana River. Thanks to its location on the edge of Denali National Park and Preserve, the Nenana River and the impressive gorge it carves are the most popular white-water rafting trip in Alaska. The most exciting stretch begins at the park entrance and ends 10mi north near the town of Healy. Here the river is rated Class III, as rafters sweep through standing waves, rapids and holes with names like 'Coffee Grinder,' 'Razorback' and 'Royal Flush' that are situated in sheer-sided canyons. South of the entrance, the river is much milder, but to many it's just as interesting as it swings away from both the highway and the railroad, increasing your opportunity to spot wildlife.

Several rafting companies offer daily floats during the summer. Denali Raft Adventures (☎ 683-2234, 888-683-2234, ✉ denraft@mtaonline.net) has been around the longest and seems the most organized. Its office is at Mile 238 of the highway, but it will provide free transportation from the train station inside the park. Both its Canyon Run through the gorge and the milder McKinley Run cost $50 per person and are offered three or four times daily. The four-hour Healy Express is a combination of both for $70. It departs daily at 7:30 am and 12:30 pm.

Just up the George Parks Hwy at Mile 238.6 is the Denali Outdoor Center (☎ 888-303-1925), which runs the river in inflatable kayaks as well as rafts. These trips are one person per kayak, putting you more in the middle of the action as opposed to just holding on to the side of a raft. The guided kayak tours depart at 8:30 am and 2 pm daily and cost $75 per person.

Along the road to Fairbanks

Free-use shelter, Granite Tors Trail

Backpacker sporting head netting

The top of Chena Dome Trail

Camp Creek and then Thorofare River, taking time to choose the best spot possible along the braided river.

At this point you can head due north to reach the park road and bus transportation in a little over a mile, or continue northeast to Eielson Visitor Center, reached in another 3mi. Keep in mind that Thorofare River is a natural route for brown bears.

Denali State Park

They share the same name and border but there could hardly be two more different parks than Denali National Park & Preserve and Denali State Park. The national park is world renowned, heavily developed at its entrance and a 'must see' on everybody's Alaskan itinerary.

Denali State Park, on the other hand, has no hotel, no shuttle-bus service and no park road (unless you count George Parks Hwy, which divides the park in half from north to south). In recent years the state has made a series of improvements to the park, including adding another campground and building its first visitor center, but these are pale compared to the kind of development encountered in and around the national park.

There are also no stunning peaks in Denali State Park. The tallest peak in North America doesn't lie here, but the best views of it do. The state park has superb vantage points to view both Mt McKinley and the mountains that surround it in the Alaska Range. Many say the best roadside view of 'the High One' anywhere in the state is from Mile 135.2 of George Parks Hwy, just inside the state park's southern boundary. Here, motorists pull off at South Denali Viewpoint to gaze upon Ruth Glacier less than 5mi to the northwest and Mt McKinley, Mt Hunter and Moose Tooth. Hikers who climb Kesugi Ridge are stunned by the view of the Denali massif on a clear day. Earlier in the century it was the views from Peters Hills in the southwest corner of the park that Alaskan painter Sydney Laurence studied to capture the beauty of McKinley on his large canvases.

But the main difference between the two parks is the number of people visiting them. There is no comparison. Many travelers rushing up George Parks Hwy to get to the national park are oblivious they are passing through one of the largest state parks in Alaska. There are no crowds in the state park, no lines of people waiting for a permit and no need for backcountry zone quotas.

That could change some day, as more and more people, especially hikers, discover this gem of a state park. The reality is that Denali State Park is among the most accessible of all Alaskan parks. It's bisected by the Parks Hwy and less than a three hour drive for half the population of the state. Still, it's hard to imagine this area ever getting as overrun as its counterpart to the north.

NATURAL HISTORY

This 507-sq-mi park is the fourth-largest state park in Alaska, behind Wood-Tikchik, Chugach and Kachemak Bay. Denali State Park is 160mi north of Anchorage by road and situated between the Talkeetna Mountains to the east and the Alaska Range to the west. This makes the park the transition zone from low, coastal environment to the spine of the Alaska Range. Its terrain ranges from heavily forested steams and river valleys to the alpine tundra of the Curry and Kesugi Ridges, which make up the 35mi-long backbone of the park.

The timberline within the park is at 2500ft, and alpine areas, featuring moss campion and many wildflowers, are found on both the Curry and Kesugi Ridges. Below the tree line, the park is dominated by spruce and paper birch forests and patches of dense birch-alder-willow thickets that crowd the trails and make off-trail hiking nearly impossible in these transitional zones. You'll find black spruce around the many bogs and beaver ponds and abundant crops of wild berries above the tree line, where you can eat blueberries to your heart's content.

Kesugi – its name is a Dena'ina Indian word meaning 'the Ancient One' – is a ridge 4 to 6mi wide that parallels George Parks Hwy. Composed of volcanic sediments and granite, Kesugi and neighboring Curry Ridge reach heights of only 4500ft and lack the jagged spires, rock walls and knife-edged ridgelines that are the trademarks of Mt McKinley and the Alaska Range to the west. Instead, you find gently rolling tundra at the top of the ridges that's much more conducive to hiking.

Wildlife in the state park is similar to that found in the national park. The park, roughly half the size of Rhode Island, is home to both brown and black bears, moose and marmots – found above the tree lines of the Curry and Kesugi Ridges. In the lower areas, you'll encounter muskrats, beavers, possibly red foxes, and porcupines. On the west side of the park, the rivers are of glacial origin and are often clouded with pulverized rock known as 'glacial flour.' This makes them a poor habitat for fish. But on the east side, the streams are clear and support populations of arctic grayling, Dolly Varden, rainbow trout and all five species of Pacific salmon. In Byers Lake, anglers concentrate on both lake trout and whitefish.

CLIMATE

Thanks to the Alaska Range, Denali State Park is much more temperate and doesn't suffer from the temperature extremes that often occur in the national park and the rest of Interior Alaska. In the summer, the temperatures are usually around 60°F, with highs exceeding 80°F rare. The park receives 30 inches of precipitation annually. Much of it falls as snow, which begins accumulating in October, or as showers from late August through September.

INFORMATION

A visitor center has been built at the Alaska Veterans Memorial at Mile 147 of George Parks Hwy just north of the Byers Lake Campground. Along with displays and videos, the center sells topographical maps, books and even bear spray. Hours are 9 am to 6 pm daily during the summer. Another place for information is the Mat-Su area office of the Division of Parks & Outdoor Recreation (☎ 745-3975, fax 745-0938), HC 32, Box 6706, Wasilla, AK 99654-9719.

GETTING THERE & AWAY
Bus

Any bus company that makes a run to Denali National Park (see Getting Around in the Denali National Park & Preserve section, earlier in this chapter) will drop you off along the highway in the state park.

Train

The Alaska Railroad (☎ 265-2494 in Anchorage) forms the eastern border of the state park, and on Thursday, Friday, Saturday and Sunday during the summer, self-propelled rail diesel cars provide local 'flag stop' service to Hurricane Gulch, just north of the park. This train departs Talkeetna at 12:15 pm and will stop anywhere along the tracks.

This sounds ideal for hikers, but the trailheads are all along the highway. Even those travelers interested in off-trail travel in the east side of the park would first have to find some way to cross the Susitna River, which can't be forded, and then contend with thick willow and alder, bushwhacking their way up the ridge.

It wasn't always so difficult to access the trails from the train. In the early 1900s, when it took two days to travel from Seward to Fairbanks, train passengers would often lay over in Curry for an extra day to climb the east side of Curry Ridge and view Mt McKinley. The small hexagonal-shaped building at Curry Lookout is still there, but the cable for safe transportation across the river is long gone.

Car

You can drive to Denali State Park from Anchorage in a few hours on George Parks Hwy (State Rte 3). Trapper Creek is a small service center at Mile 115.5 of the George Parks Hwy and the last place to purchase gas before heading north into the state park. You enter Denali State Park when you cross the southern boundary at Mile 132.2. The Little Coal Creek Trailhead is at Mile 163.9, where there is a parking area off the highway. The state park extends north to Mile 169.2, just south of Hurricane.

Little Coal Creek Trail & Kesugi Ridge Route

Duration 2 to 4 days
Distance 6.2 to 27.4mi
Difficulty Level Medium to hard
Start Mile 163.9 of the George Parks Hwy
Finish Byers Lake Campground at Mile 147 of the George Parks Hwy
Cabins & Shelters No
Permits Required No
Public Transportation Yes
Summary This two- to four-day hike along Kesugi Ridge rewards you with stunning views of Mt McKinley if the weather is clear.

Little Coal Creek Trail features a well-defined path and is the easiest climb into the alpine area of Kesugi Ridge. From its trailhead just off the George Parks Hwy, you emerge above the tree line in less than 3mi. It's a steady climb, especially with a backpack on, but not nearly as steep as the hike up Kesugi Ridge from the Byers Lake Campground.

The trail also serves as the first leg of the Kesugi Ridge Route – a route that parallels the crest of the ridge south to reach Byers Lake State Campground in 27.4mi or the trailhead of Troublesome Creek Trail in 36.2mi. It's not a maintained trail, rather a worn path in some places of the tundra and little more than a series of cairns in others.

Park rangers stress that the Kesugi Ridge Route is a challenging trek that requires you to know how to use maps and a compass properly. Above the tree line, snow can reach depths of more than 6ft during the winter and often lingers into July. On the ridge, you're also exposed to foul weather and high winds that can appear quickly and last for days. Poor visibility due to whiteouts and inclement weather are common problems.

If you are unsure about your ability to traverse the entire ridge, plan to enter and leave the park from the trailhead of Little Coal Creek Trail. The trail will lead you to excellent camping areas in the alpine area but will also provide you with quick access out of the high country if foul weather moves in suddenly. Hiking and then backtracking the first two stages would be such a trek, and you would end up with a 16mi roundtrip overnight hike into the alpine area that would be rated moderate in difficulty. Traversing the entire ridge is rated as a hard hike.

There are no permits or fees needed for this hike.

PLANNING
When to Hike
Due to the high elevation, this hike is best done from mid-June to early September. It's important to remember that late August into September is often a rainy period in the state park, and after September the snow begins to stick and temperatures really drop.

What to Bring
Fires are not allowed in the backcountry, other than on the gravel bars of Chulitna, Susitna and Tokositna Rivers, so you must pack a stove. The Alaska Veterans Memorial Visitors Center also has bear-resistant food containers that hikers can use. There is no charge for using a container, but you must leave a $25 deposit. For more advice on what to bring, turn to the Planning section of the Facts for the Hiker chapter.

Maps
The park's main trail system, including Troublesome Creek Trail, Byers Lake Loop, Little Coal Creek Trail and the Kesugi Ridge Route are covered on USGS 1:63,360 series quads *Talkeetna C-1*, and *Talkeetna Mountains C-6* and *D-6*. The map for Little Coal Creek Trail only is *Talkeetna Mountains D-6*. Topos can be purchased at the Alaska Veterans Memorial Visitors Center at Mile 147.

Cabins & Shelters
There are no cabins or free-use shelters along Little Coal Creek Trail or Kesugi Ridge, but there are two state park cabins overlooking Byers Lake. One can be driven

DENALI

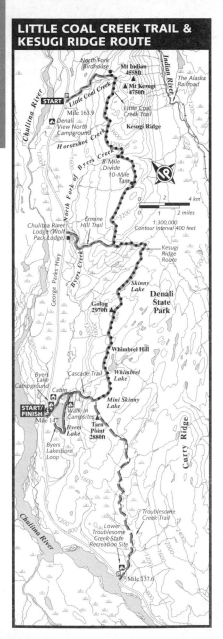

LITTLE COAL CREEK TRAIL & KESUGI RIDGE ROUTE

to; the other is a 0.3mi hike in. Either one would make for a pleasant end to the Kesugi Ridge traverse. The maximum stay at one of the public-use cabins is five consecutive nights. Each costs $35 a night and should be reserved in advance through the DNR Public Information Center (☎ 269-8400) in Anchorage or the state park office in Wasilla (☎ 745-3975).

NEAREST TOWNS & FACILITIES
Inside the Park
Other than backcountry camping, accommodations within the park consist of three public campgrounds and a lodge with cabins. ***Lower Troublesome Creek State Recreation Site*** at Mile 137.3 of the George Parks Hwy has 20 sites for $6 a night and ***Byers Lake State Campground*** at Mile 147 has 68 sites for $12 a night. Byers Lake Campground also has six walk-in sites located 1.8mi along the loop trail around the lake.

At Mile 162.7 of George Parks Hwy is ***Denali View North Campground***, with 20 sites for $10 a night. With the exception of some charming walk-in sites, the campground is basically a parking lot, but the views are stunning from here. You overlook the Chulitna River while Mt McKinley overwhelms you from above. Interpretive displays and a spotting scope help you enjoy the panorama.

At Mile 156 is ***Chulitna River Lodge*** (☎ 242-5060) (also known as Wolf Pack Lodge), the only commercial facility within the park. The lodge has a small cafe, gas, limited supplies and log cabins for $50 to $80 a night.

Trapper Creek
Trapper Creek is a small service center at Mile 115.5 of the George Parks Hwy and the last place to purchase gas, lodging or a meal before heading north into the state park. Among the handful of businesses is the ***Trapper Creek Trading Post*** (☎ 733-2315), which has tent sites for $5 a night and cabins for $50 for two people. It also sells groceries and gas and has showers, a Laundromat and a café.

GETTING TO/FROM THE HIKE

The Little Coal Creek Trailhead is at Mile 163.9, where there is a parking area off the highway. Byers Lake Campground is at Mile 147. Many hikers opt to be dropped off at the trailhead and then picked up a few days later to continue on to Denali National Park and Preserve; any of the van services to Denali National Park will drop off and pick up hikers at the trailheads, and you can schedule it in advance.

THE HIKE
Stage 1: George Parks Hwy to North Fork Birdhouse
3.1mi, 2 to 3 hours

The trailhead for Little Coal Creek Trail includes a large parking area, vault toilets and an information board with warnings, suggestions and a topographical map with the entire Kesugi Ridge route drawn in. Copy the information but don't steal the map.

From here the trail immediately heads into the spruce-and-birch woods and heads for Little Coal Creek. You can hear the water rushing below you at times, but you never really see it, as the trail quickly swings to the southeast and remains in the forested edge above the rugged ravine. In less than a mile, the trail skirts a beaver pond, passes the remains of a 6ft-high dam and a quarter mile beyond that emerges at an opening where it is possible to see the creek below.

From that point, or 1.8mi from the trailhead, the trail begins to do some serious climbing. In less than half a mile, you're going to gain 1000ft, climbing above the tree line, crossing a creek at 2mi and then hiking through some thick alder. Along the way the brush will thin out, and you'll be able to view **Little Coal Creek** and the canyon it has cut both directions.

The climbing tops off at a 3100ft rocky knob unofficially known as **the Lunch Spot**. The knob is well named; the views on a clear day are excellent here and allow you to munch on lunch in view of Mt McKinley. The knob also marks where you move from subalpine willow and alder into an alpine tundra setting of grassy meadows that are loaded with ripe blueberries in August.

The trail is still easy to recognize as it continues across the rolling meadows to the headwaters of Little Coal Creek. At 3.1mi from Parks Hwy you reach what is referred to as the North Fork of Little Coal Creek and an area that is known as the **North Fork Birdhouse**. There is a posted topographical map where you cross the creek. If you had a late start, there are places nearby to set up a tent and spend the night.

Stage 2: North Fork Birdhouse to 8-Mile Divide
5mi, 3 hours

What makes Kesugi Ridge such a natural route is a rolling plateau at the 3000ft level on its western side. To reach it, you ford the North Fork of Little Coal Creek and then follow the trail as it enters an amphitheater and becomes obscured in a rock slide. Somewhere in these boulders is Little Coal Creek.

Carefully make your way across the boulders to ascend to the tundra meadow on the south side, where you'll see the South Fork of Little Coal Creek following through. You should also be able to pick up the trail here as it crosses the creek and then climbs a ridge at 3500ft. The trick here is getting through the bog around the creek without soaking your boots.

Once you climb the ridge, the natural route along the bench is very apparent if the weather is clear. And if it is, the views will be outstanding. You'll be hypnotized by Mt McKinley and the Alaska Range to the west, the broad valley of the Chulitna River seemingly lying at your feet and, if you look carefully, even the George Parks Hwy, where the RVers look like ants scurrying from a picnic table.

The route up here is a mix of well-beaten segments of path with other stretches merely marked by rock cairns. From the ridge you descend gently to a pair of small pools, reached 1.2mi after crossing the North Fork, and then to a third pool that is tucked away in the base of the high alpine ridge you're skirting.

Within another mile you pass another group of alpine pools from where two creeks begin their fast journey down Kesugi Ridge into the Chulitna River. The first is labeled **Horseshoe Creek** on park maps. This spot, 2.3mi from the North Fork, or 5.4mi from the trailhead, is a good spot to set up camp for the night if you want to take an additional day to hike the ridge. You have water, magnificent views and enough flat terrain to handle a number of tents.

The next reliable source of water on the ridge, the **North Fork of Byers Creek**, is another 2mi south, or 7.5mi from the trailhead. You gently descend to cross the creek and then climb out of it on the other side, skirt a knob and descend to **8-Mile Divide**. This is an area of small pools and tarns where it's possible set up camp.

Stage 3: 8-Mile Divide to Skinny Lake
9mi, 5 to 7 hours
From the divide, the route continues to head south, meandering across the crest of the ridge with stunning views of the mountains to the west. Within 2mi you come to a large tarn, referred to as **10-Mile Tarn**, and then immediately skirt a distinctive rock formation that some people call Stonehedge.

You remain above 3000ft for the next 2.5mi, until the trail descends to cross a stream and continues to drop off the ridge, moving into thicker willow and alder brush. At times the route will be flagged in this stretch. At 13.6mi from the trailhead of Little Coal Creek Trail, you cross another stream and come to the junction with the **Ermine Hill Trail**.

This 3.1mi route heads west to Mile 156 of the George Parks Hwy, the location of Chulitna River Lodge (see Places to Stay, earlier), near Ermine Lake. It was originally an emergency escape route for anybody caught on the ridge during foul weather, and for the most part, it was a very steep descent off the ridge. But in 1999 and 2000 the park recut the trail and added numerous switchbacks to make it an easier hike.

The Kesugi Ridge Route continues southeast and also makes a rapid descent back into the forest. You descend 1000ft in the next 2mi before bottoming out. Other

than at the beginning and the final descent to Byers Lake, this is the only other time you dip below the timber line. At this point, roughly 7mi from 8-Mile Divide, the trail crosses what is often referred to as **Bitch Creek** (probably so-called because it can be such a boggy area) and then swings southwest and resumes climbing again. The east end of **Skinny Lake** is 1.5mi away.

The trail reaches the well-named lake 17.2mi from the trailhead of Little Coal Creek Trail and skirts its north side. You'll find a few camping areas here among the willow, alder brush and the few spruce trees that border it.

Stage 4: Skinny Lake to Byers Lake
10.3mi, 6 to 8 hours
The walk along Skinny Lake lasts almost a mile, until you cross a stream at its west end and then resume climbing. You climb 700ft in the next mile, topping off at **Golog**, a 2970ft peak that is labeled on the USGS topos, 19mi from the trailhead of Little Coal Creek Trail. There are sweeping views from the top of the knob.

The route descends off the south side of Golog, dropping several hundred feet to cross a stream, climbs **Whimbrel Hill** (2500ft) on the other side and then gently drops to reach the west end of what is referred to as Whimbrel Lake. At this point, the trail is much more developed and easier to follow. It continues its southwest course, skirts **Mini Skinny Lake** and then 2mi from Whimbrel Lake, or roughly 24mi from Little Coal Creek Trailhead, arrives at a junction.

The left-hand fork is Troublesome Creek Trail, which leads 11mi along the stream to end at Mile 137.6 of the highway. Keep in mind that through much of the summer this trail is often closed due to large numbers of bears feeding on the salmon run.

The right-hand fork is **Cascade Trail**, which heads northwest for Byers Lake State Campground. It begins with a very steep descent, by far the steepest anywhere along the route. In the next 1.5mi, you'll drop 1500ft in leaving Kesugi Ridge, much of it in the first half mile. Just before bottoming out, or 1.6mi from the trailhead in the campground, you pass the **cascades** where the creek from Whimbrel Lake thunders down the ridge.

You bottom out at the junction with **Byers Lakeshore Loop**, a 4.8mi walk around the lake. Head left to reach a series of **walk-in campsites** along the lake, which make for a much nicer place to spend the night than the campground itself. Head right to reach the **Byers Lake State Campground** in 1.5mi. Within a half mile you'll cross a suspension bridge over a stream and then emerge at a trailhead located on the east side of the campground.

Other Hikes

DENALI NATIONAL PARK & PRESERVE

The best maps for this area are in the booklet *Denali National Park Entrance Area Trail Guide,* sold at the VAC, but really you can get away with the maps in the free park handout called *Denali Alpenglow.* It would be hard to get lost on these trails. In this book, the maps in this section are on the Denali National Park & Preserve Entrance Area map.

Horseshoe Lake Trail

This trail is a leisurely 1.5mi walk through the woods to an overlook of the oxbow lake and then down a steep trail to the water. The trailhead is on Mile 0.9 of the park road, where the railroad tracks cross. Follow the tracks north a short way to the wide gravel path.

Morino Loop Trail

This leisurely walk of 1.3mi can be picked up at the back of Morino Campground, as well as from the park hotel parking lot. It offers good views of Hines and Riley Creeks.

Taiga Loop Trail

This is another easy hike that begins off the parking lot of the park hotel and loops 1.3mi through the taiga forest.

Rock Creek Trail

This moderate 2.3mi walk connects the hotel area with the park headquarters and dog kennel area. The trail begins just before the park road crosses Rock Creek but doesn't stay with the stream. Instead it climbs a gentle slope of mixed aspen and spruce forest, breaks out along a ridge with scenic views of Mt Healy and the Parks Hwy and then begins a rapid downhill descent to the service road behind the hotel and ends on the Taiga Loop Trail. It's far easier hiking the trail to the hotel, as all the elevation is gained with the drive up the park road.

DENALI STATE PARK

In this book, the Troublesome Creek Trail and Byers Lakeshore Loop are shown on the Little Coal Creek Trail & Kesugi Ridge Route map.

Troublesome Creek Trail

The trailhead is posted in a parking area at Mile 137.6 of the George Parks Hwy. The trail ascends along the creek until it reaches the tree line, where you move into an open area dotted with alpine lakes and surrounded by mountains. From here, it becomes a route marked only by rock cairns as it heads north to Byers Lake.

The hike to Byers Lake State Campground is a 14.2mi backpacking trip of moderate difficulty. Keep in mind that numerous black bears feeding on salmon are the reason for the creek's name and that the trail is often closed to hikers in July and August. Call the ranger office in advance (see Information in the Denali State Park section, earlier) about possible closures due to bears. Otherwise you risk arriving at a trailhead that will clearly be posted 'No Hiking' (USGS quad *Talkeetna C-1).*

Byers Lakeshore Loop

This is an easy 4.8mi trek around the lake. It begins at the Byers Lake State Campground and passes six hike-in campsites on the other side of the lake that are 1.8mi from the posted trailhead. Although there is boat access onto the lake at Byers Lake

DENALI

State campground, Byers is closed to gasoline motors, ensuring you a quiet evening at the walk-in sites (USGS quad *Talkeetna C-1*).

Peters Hills Trail

Petersville Rd leads from Mile 115 of the George Parks Hwy 40mi northwest, passing some homes and the historic Forks Roadhouse, and finally crosses over Peters Hills. The trail never enters the Denali State Park Boundaries, but it provides access close to the remote western section. The foothills of the Alaska Range are known for their magnificent views of Mt McKinley only 40mi to the north.

The road to Forks Roadhouse can be handled by most cars, but it quickly deteriorates after that. Continue 13mi west of the roadhouse, past the Petersville Placer Mine, to an all-terrain vehicle track on the north side of the road. This hike begins on the ATV track but, within a mile, departs as a narrow footpath. Viewpoints of Mt McKinley are reached within another mile, or you can hike 7mi to Long Point, the place where painter Sydney Laurence used to set up his canvases. The views of the mountain from here are breathtaking, and the surrounding tundra makes an ideal spot to camp for a day or two (USGS quad *Talkeetna C-2*).

Fairbanks Region

This far north the tree line is lower, the days longer, the tundra peaks and domes more rounded. All this adds up to classic ridge walking in which you can quickly ascend to the alpine area and then use the rolling ridges as your path into the wilderness. If the day is clear, you will enjoy an endless view with almost every step.

The biggest challenge to hiking this far north is getting to the trailhead. Unlike Anchorage or Juneau, Fairbanks does not have trails at its doorstep. The region's best hikes lie an hour or more from the city, often along lightly traveled gravel roads. Public transportation has improved in recent years but is still thin this far north, and many car rental places stipulate that their vehicles may not be driven on remote dirt roads. Hitchhiking

is always possible, but you'll find traffic is light, even by Alaskan standards.

Thus, hiking in the Fairbanks area requires more time and patience than in other regions, along with a strong desire to explore the land that borders the Arctic Circle. The logistics can be a headache at times, but the trails are worth it, very much so. The scenery is unusual, especially if you come from the Southeast or the Kenai Peninsula. The crowds found in places like Denali National Park and Preserve are absent, and often at the end of the hike you can spend a day recuperating with a soak in a natural hot spring.

Of the three ridge walks described here, Granite Tors and Chena Dome Trails are the easiest to reach. Both trailheads are located along Chena Hot Springs Rd, a paved road with a steady stream of traffic and good public transportation. At the end of the hike you can continue east for a soak at Chena Hot Springs.

The other hike, Pinnell Mountain Trail, is more difficult to reach but not impossible. This three-day walk is one of the great hiking trails in Alaska, on par with the Chilkoot Trail and Resurrection Pass in terms of scenery. This wonderful adventure is enhanced even more if you continue east along the Steese Hwy to visit the remote town of Central and soak at Circle Hot Springs.

Highlights

- Experiencing the midnight sun from the Pinnell Mountain Trail
- Searching valleys for caribou or brown bears along the Pinnell Mountain Trail
- Exploring the unusual rock formations along the Granite Tors Trail
- Viewing the plane wreck on the Chena Dome Trail
- Enjoying a soak in a hot spring after Pinnell Mountain or Chena Dome Trails

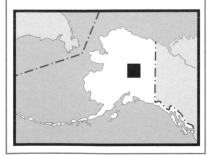

NATURAL HISTORY

The Chena River State Recreation Area lies east of Fairbanks and covers 397 sq mi that include forests, tundra uplands and the streams of the Chena River watershed. To the north is the 1875-sq-mi Steese National Conservation Area, which straddles the Steese Hwy. Managed by the Bureau of Land Management (BLM), this area protects a portion of the rolling Tanana-Yukon uplands that the Pinnell Mountain Trail traverses.

Together these recreation areas are home to a wide range of wildlife. Moose are frequently spotted near beaver ponds and sloughs where they feed on shrubs and aquatic plants. Black and brown bears also inhabit the area, and backpackers occasionally encounter grizzlies feeding on berries in the treeless uplands. Other large mammals include wolves, caribou, beavers and red foxes, and the Chena River is renowned for its grayling fishing.

The drawback of ridge walks is that encounters with wildlife are greatly reduced when you're hiking above the tree line. Black bears and moose, which favor the abundant vegetation of the lowlands and river valleys, are rarely seen on these trails. By packing a pair of compact binoculars you can search the surrounding valleys and occasionally spot wolves, bears and even small groups of caribou from your high vantage point. But on the trails themselves, wildlife is limited more times than not to hoary marmots, pika or 'rock rabbits,' and a variety of migratory birds like Lapland longspurs, northern wheatears, lesser golden plovers and golden eagles. Rock ptarmigan, year-round residents on the alpine ridges, might also be encountered.

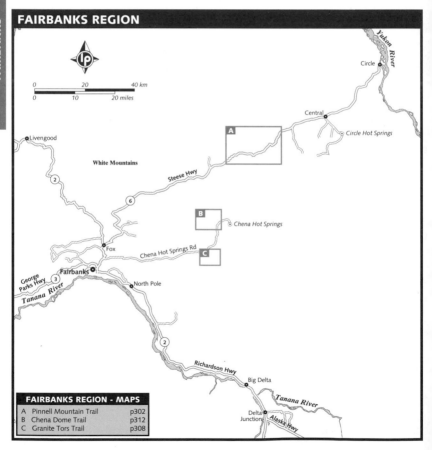

FAIRBANKS REGION

Livengood

White Mountains

Steese Hwy

Yukon River

Circle

Central

Circle Hot Springs

A

Chena Hot Springs

B

Fox

Chena Hot Springs Rd

C

George Parks Hwy

Fairbanks

Tanana River

North Pole

Richardson Hwy

Big Delta

Tanana River

Delta Junction

Alaska Hwy

0   20   40 km
0   10   20 miles

FAIRBANKS REGION - MAPS

A	Pinnell Mountain Trail	p302
B	Chena Dome Trail	p312
C	Granite Tors Trail	p308

CLIMATE

Like the rest of the Interior, Fairbanks has excellent hiking weather during the summer. From mid-June to mid-August it is often pleasantly warm, with an average temperature of 70°F and an occasional hot spell in August when the temperature closes in on 90°F. The days are long, with more than 20 hours of light each day from June to August, peaking at almost 23 hours on June 21. Generally, the trails are clear of snow from June through September.

You must be prepared with rain gear and warm clothing, however, because winds in these alpine areas can be strong, sometimes exceeding 50 mph in places where there is little protection. Winds can also lower the temperature significantly during the summer. On the Pinnell Mountain and Chena Dome Trails low-lying clouds can also create white-out conditions, making travel much more challenging.

Before setting out on a hike, call the local National Weather Service (☎ 452-3553) for a prerecorded local forecast.

INFORMATION

The best place to get hiking information anywhere in the Fairbanks area is the Alaska Public Lands Information Center (☎ 456-0527) on Cushman St, two blocks south of the Chena River, in downtown Fairbanks. You'll find local trail information at the center along with brochures on state and national parks, wildlife refuges and recreation areas elsewhere in Alaska. Hours for the center are 9 am to 6 pm daily during the summer.

Information on Pinnell Mountain Trail or the White Mountain trail system can also be found at the BLM office (☎ 474-2200) at Airport Way and University Ave. Practically next door to the BLM office, at 3700 Airport Way, is the Public Information Center of the Alaska Department of Natural Resources (DNR; ☎ 451-2705, fax 451-2706) with information on the Chena River State Recreation Area. For trail conditions contact the State Parks Office (☎ 451-2695) at the same location.

Diamonds in the Willow

One of the most prized woods in Alaska is diamond willow, so-called because the grain of the wood has a distinctive diamond pattern. There are 33 species of willow in the state, and at least five of these can develop diamond patterns, which are easy to see when you strip the bark.

The diamond-shaped markings on the tree are caused by a fungal infection that attacks the joints between branches and the trunk. Once the fungi invade, the tree becomes stunted and grows in no specific direction, often curving downward or twisting several times at the trunk.

Woodcarvers love diamond willow for both its unusual pattern and curvaceous nature. Under the bark, the willow's natural cream-colored wood contrasts beautifully with the reddish, diamond-shaped depressions, which can be over 5 inches long. Diamond willows can be found growing throughout Alaska, particularly in river valleys. You'll also see hand-crafted art in gift shops – in the form of walking sticks, furniture and lamp bases – carved from diamond willow.

FAIRBANKS

Fairbanks is Alaska's second-largest city (population 84,000) and the gateway to the Arctic.

The main source of travel information in Fairbanks is the Convention & Visitors Bureau Log Cabin (☎ 456-5774, 800-327-5774, @ fcvb@polarnet.com), which overlooks the Chena River near the corner of 1st Ave and Cushman St. The log cabin is open 8 am to 8 pm daily during the summer and also has a Web site (www.fairbanks .polarnet.com) with tourist information.

Supplies & Equipment

By all means, stock up on your Lipton noodle dinners, instant coffee and jars of peanut butter before heading out on any trail. Fairbanks has lots of grocery stores,

FAIRBANKS

but Fred Meyers, just west of Alaskaland on Airport Way, has a great selection of food and a limited selection of camping equipment. It's open to 10 pm daily. Near the downtown area, head to Carrs on Gaffney Rd near Cushman St. It has loads of freshly baked goods, gorp, dried fruit and nuts by the pound. You'll also find an excellent salad bar ($3.50 a pound), homemade soups ($3 a pound) and a deli. It's open 24 hours. Right across the street is a Laundromat.

For a more serious selection of backpacking gear, or for freeze-dried dinners, go to Beaver Sports (☎ 479-2494), at 3480 College Rd on the north side of town. It's open to 7 pm Monday through Friday, until 6 pm Saturday and until 5 pm on Sunday. Downtown, Big Ray's (☎ 452-3458), at Lacey St and 2nd Ave, has rain gear, camping equipment and white gas.

Places to Stay & Eat

The only public campground in the Fairbanks area is the *Chena River State Campground* on University Ave just north of Airport Way, which has 57 sites for $10 a night for walk-in tents and $15 for RVs. The other campgrounds in the city are private and charge from $15 to $25 per night to camp when you have a vehicle. They include *River's Edge RV Park* (☎ 474-0286, 800-770-3343, 4140 Boat St), on the Chena River near the corner of Airport Way and University Ave, which has showers, laundry facilities, shuttle service and access to the city's bike trail system.

One of the best things to happen to Fairbanks in a long time is the arrival of backpackers' hostels that offer inexpensive, bunkroom lodging. *Billie's Backpackers Hostel* (☎ 479-2034, 2895 Mack Rd, ✉ akbillie@ aol.com), at Westwood Way, has a common kitchen, lounge area, a sundeck and an optional $7 breakfast that includes homemade sourdough bread or pancakes. *Fairbanks Shelter & Shower* (☎ 479-5016, 248 Madcap Lane, ✉ brob@alaska.net) is just north of UAF and has tent space, bunks and rooms. A tent space is $10, dorm room $15 and a private room $18.

Fairbanks has more than 100 B&Bs and most of them have a brochure in the visitors bureau downtown. A courtesy phone there lets you check who has a room and who's filled for the night. If you're arriving by train or bus, *Ah, Rose Marie* (☎ 456-2040, Cowles St and 3rd Ave) is within easy walking distance of the depot, has singles/doubles that start at $50/75.

Most hotel/motel rooms in Fairbanks are not as expensive as those in Anchorage, but be prepared to pay $80 per night during the summer, especially when you add the 8% city bed tax. If you've just spent 10 days in the Bush and want to splurge, check into the *Bridgewater Hotel* (☎ 452-6661, 800-528-4916, 723 1st Ave) downtown. The hotel is one of the nicest in Fairbanks and certainly has the best location, overlooking the Chena River. Singles/doubles cost $140/150 a night.

A relatively inexpensive breakfast of two eggs and toast ($4.25) is available at *Co-op Diner*, in the Co-op Plaza at 3rd Ave and Cushman St. The 1950ish diner also has hamburgers and sandwiches ($6 to $7) and Thai specials that begin at $7. *Gambardella's Pasta Bella* (706 2nd Ave) has homemade pasta dinners for $10 to $17 and some of the best pizza in the Interior ($10 to $12). Its outdoor cafe is a delight during Fairbanks' long summer days. *Plate & Palette Gallery Cafe*, at 1st Ave and Noble St, has vegetarian dishes on the menu and local artwork on the walls. Sandwiches are $4 to $7, dinners $13 to $18. By walking south on Cushman St, you'll reach several more restaurants. *Cafe Latte*, at 6th Ave and Lacy St, offers good espresso drinks, bagels, Internet access and outdoor seating.

Hungry souls should take in the *Alaskaland Salmon Bake* (free shuttle bus from major hotels, including the Bridgewater), out toward the airport, where, for $20, you not only get grilled salmon but halibut, spareribs and salad.

Getting There & Away

Air The Fairbanks International Airport serves as the gateway for supplies and travelers heading into the Brooks Range and

Arctic Alaska. The airport is almost 4mi southwest of the city off Airport Way.

Alaska Airlines (☎ 474-0481) provides eight daily flights to and from Anchorage, where there are connections to the rest of the state. The one-way standard fare to Anchorage is normally around $100 to $150, but airfare wars have pushed it to as low as $50 at times, making it cheaper than taking the train or bus. Delta Air Lines (☎ 800-221-1212) also offers a handful of flights between the two cities, while Air North Canada (☎ 800-764-0407 in Alaska) provides service from Dawson City with connecting flights from Whitehorse. A roundtrip advance-purchase ticket costs $160 to Dawson City and $270 to Whitehorse.

Bus Alaskon Express (☎ 451-6835) provides service to Fairbanks from Haines, Skagway, Whitehorse, Tok and Delta Junction on a run that departs from Beaver Creek Monday, Wednesday and Friday at 8:45 am. In Fairbanks, buses depart from the Westmark Hotel at 820 Noble St in the city center at 8 am Sunday, Tuesday and Friday during the summer for the return trip. The one-way fare to Fairbanks from Delta Junction is $56, from Tok $70 and from Haines $182.

If you're coming up from Anchorage or Denali National Park, Parks Highway Express (☎ 888-600-6001) offers van service during the summer. The van departs Anchorage at 9 am and Denali at 3:15 pm. On the return trip, Parks Express departs Fairbanks at 9 am and charges $20/55 for Denali/Anchorage.

Parks Highway Express also provides service to Glennallen ($45 one-way) and Valdez ($59), with a bus departing Fairbanks at 8:30 am Wednesday, Friday and Sunday.

Train The Alaska Railroad (☎ 456-4155) has an express train to Fairbanks that departs Anchorage daily at 8:15 am from late May to mid-September, stops at Denali National Park and then reaches Fairbanks at 8.15 pm. One way costs $154; the railroad depot is at 280 North Cushman St, a short walk from the Chena River.

Pinnell Mountain Trail

Duration 3 days
Distance 27.3mi
Difficulty Level Medium to hard
Start Eagle Summit at Mile 107.3 of the Steese Hwy
Finish Twelvemile Summit, closer to Fairbanks at Mile 85 of the Steese Hwy
Cabins & Shelters Yes
Permits Required No
Public Transportation Yes
Summary A three-day walk along tundra ridgetops, this hike includes great mountain scenery, the midnight sun in June and lots of marmots to entertain you.

The first national recreational trail to be established in Alaska was Pinnell Mountain Trail, a 27.3mi hike that follows a serpentine route along treeless, alpine ridges. Located in the 1875-sq-mi Steese National Conservation Area and managed by the BLM, this trail climbs over or around several high passes and peaks, including Porcupine Dome (4915ft) and Pinnell Mountain, the high point of the hike at 4934ft. There are stunning views almost every step of the way as you gaze down upon valleys and rivers or out at the White Mountains, Tanana Hills and Alaska Range on the horizon.

For many, the most outstanding sight on the trail is the midnight sun. From June 18 to 25 the sun never sets on the trail, giving hikers 24 hours of light each day. The polar phenomenon of the sun sitting above the horizon at midnight can be viewed and photographed at several high points on the trail, including the Eagle Summit trailhead. June is also an excellent time to view the wildflowers that carpet the arctic-alpine tundra slopes from late May. In August, you can feast on blueberries, low-bush cranberries and other wild berries.

The trail winds along tundra ridges that lie above 3500ft, and at times, the hiking can be steep and rugged. It is well marked with both cairns and mileposts, and on a clear day, it's easy to follow, as the next cairn or

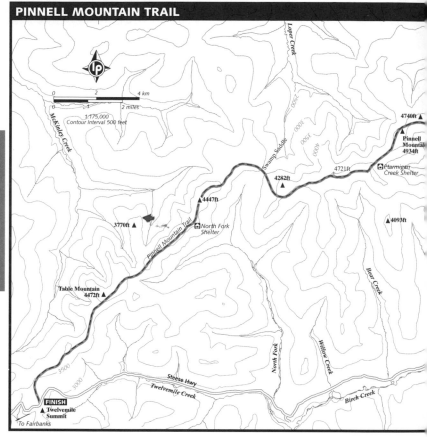

PINNELL MOUNTAIN TRAIL

milepost is almost always in sight. But during foul weather, low clouds lead to white-out conditions, which obscure the trail and make following the right route much more challenging. If the weather is bad, don't hesitate to sit out a day playing cards in the emergency shelter. The weather will eventually improve.

Pinnell Mountain Trail is a natural three-day adventure, with backpackers covering 8 to 10mi a day. If you're not up for the entire route, the first few miles from either trailhead make excellent day hikes. Within 2mi of Twelvemile Summit are spectacular views

of the alpine area and some unusual rock formations. A climb of less than a mile from the Eagle Summit trailhead leads to the top of the 3624ft peak. This is the highest point along the Steese Hwy and a place where the midnight sun can be observed skimming the horizon.

PLANNING
When to Hike

Expect snow cover in May and mid-September. The best time to hike is June, when you can use the remaining snow patches as a good source of water. You can hike the

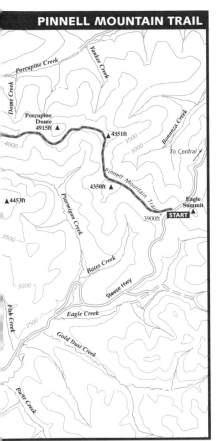

PINNELL MOUNTAIN TRAIL

a windscreen for your camp stove. Otherwise, cooking dinner can become a long ordeal.

Maps
Do not depend on the free trail map that the BLM publishes. Purchase and carry the proper USGS 1:63,360 series topos, *Circle B-3, B-4, C-3* and *C-4*. The trail is labeled on most of them.

The Public Lands Information Center sells USGS topos for the Fairbanks region. You also can pick up topographic maps for anywhere in Alaska at the Geophysical Institute Map Office (☎ 474-6960) on the UAF campus. Hours are 8 am to 5 pm Monday to Friday.

Cabins & Shelters
The Pinnell Mountain Trail has two free-use shelters, strategically placed at Mile 10 and Mile 17 of this 27mi hike. You should still pack a tent, however. These small four-sided shelters are designed as cooking areas or for emergency accommodations during foul weather. They should not be monopolized by two or three people trying to sleep in them.

NEAREST TOWNS & FACILITIES
There are two public campgrounds along the Steese Hwy. The first is the *Upper Chatanika River State Recreation Site* at Mile 39, which has 25 sites on the river for $8 a night. Water and firewood are usually available, but have your bug dope handy – this is mosquito country. The next is the *Cripple Creek BLM Campground* at Mile 60, with 21 sites for $10 a night.

Central & Circle Hot Springs
From Eagle Summit, the eastern trailhead of the Pinnell Mountain Trail, it's just 20mi along the Steese Hwy to Central, a colorful town of hard-core miners, and the turnoff for Circle Hot Springs. In Central (population 800 in the summer), you'll find gasoline, groceries, a post office and the *Central Motor Inn* (☎ 520-5228). This motel has it all – rooms, campsites, showers, cafe and gas. Double rooms are $50/60 for shared/private bath and showers are $3 per person.

trail until early September, but keep in mind that during a dry summer water might be hard to find from mid- to late August.

What to Bring
Water is scarce on this trail. Start the hike with 2 to 3 quarts of water per person and then refill your supply at either snow patches, springs or tundra pools at every opportunity. Boil or filter all standing water from pools and slow-running springs.

The winds can be brutal in this barren region, as there are no trees to slow the gusts that can come howling over the ridges. Bring

Just beyond Central, the Circle Hot Springs Rd heads south and, in 8mi, ends at *Circle Hot Springs Resort* (☎ 520-5113). Now listed on the National Register of Historic Places, the hotel is a classic. Hotel rooms with shared baths begin at $100 for doubles and on the 3rd floor are five sleeping cubby holes for $20/35 for singles/doubles. The rustic cabins, some with no running water, and other more deluxe cabins with kitchens and hot tubs, go for around $110 for two people.

The hot springs are piped into an Olympic-sized pool in which 139°F mineral water is pumped through at a rate of 231 gallons per minute. Spend 20 or 30 minutes soaking here, and you won't have sore muscles or a care in the world. If you're camping down the road, it's $5 to soak in the pool; it's open until midnight.

GETTING TO/FROM THE HIKE

Most hikers begin at the Eagle Summit trailhead on Mile 107.3 of the Steese Hwy, the higher end of the trail. The western end lies at Twelvemile Summit, closer to Fairbanks at Mile 85 of the Steese Hwy. Traffic on the Steese Hwy is light this far out of Fairbanks, but there is still a steady trickle. Hitchhiking is possible if you are willing to give up a day getting out there and back. Even with a car, most hikers also end up hitching back to the trailhead where they began.

There is now van transportation along the road to Central, and even the town of Circle on request. Steese Highway Stage Line (☎ 520-5610, @ loki@xyz.net) makes the run Monday, Wednesday and Friday, departing Circle Hot Springs at 9 am for Fairbanks. The van then departs Fairbanks at 2 pm for the return run. Roundtrip drop-off and pickup at the Pinnell Mountain trailheads from Fairbanks is $100. Hopefully this company will stay in business, but it would be wise to double-check its status early in the summer.

For two or three travelers, splitting the cost of a used rental car is the best and cheapest way of getting to outlying areas such as Chena Hot Springs. What many operators won't let you do, however, is drive

the rough Steese, Elliott or Dalton Hwys to reach such hikes as the Pinnell Mountain or Summit Trails. If that's your destination, look around for an agency in Fairbanks that lists 'gravel road permission,' such as Aurora Rental Car (☎ 459-7033, 800-653-3300) at 1000 Cadillac Court.

If you can drive a stick shift, Rent-A-Wreck (☎ 452-1606, 800-478-1606), at 2105 Cushman St, has compacts for $37 per day. The first 100mi are free, and every mile after that is 30¢ (ouch!). Affordable Car Rental (☎ 800-471-3101), at 3101 Cushman St south of Airport Way, has some small compacts for $40 a day with 150 free miles or $45 a day for unlimited mileage. Also check with Arctic Rent-A-Car (☎ 479-8044) at the airport, which has some 'gravel road permission' vehicles.

THE HIKE
Stage 1: Eagle Summit to Ptarmigan Creek Shelter
10.2mi, 5 to 6 hours

From the Eagle Summit parking area, you begin to climb immediately and ascend 180ft before the trail swings to the northwest. A short spur completes the climb to the top of the 3900ft knob from which the first of many great views along this route is enjoyed.

The Pinnell Mountain Trail, meanwhile, descends to a pass along the ridge where it reaches Mile 1 and then skirts the east side of a **4350ft peak**. Perched on the side of this knob you enjoy good views of the Bonanza Creek valley and Porcupine Creek in the distance. Sit for a while with a pair of high-powered binoculars, and you might spot a bear or other wildlife crossing the creeks.

The trail descends to another low point in the ridgeline and then reaches Mile 3, which marks the first steep climb of the day. In the next mile you ascend 700ft with the help of a series of switchbacks. Along the way you pass a huge boulder that will offer a bit of shade if it's one of those sunny, 90°F days in the Interior. You top off at the ridge's high point of 4351ft and are immediately rewarded for all your efforts. The views from here are excellent. On a clear

The Midnight Sun

Although some tour-group operators will fly you north from Fairbanks to see the Arctic Circle, the circle is actually an imaginary line that circumscribes the earth at latitude 66° 32', parallel to the equator. This is the point where the sun does not set for an entire day on June 21 (the summer solstice) and does not rise for an entire day on December 21 (the winter solstice).

This is where you can experience the strange polar phenomenon of the midnight sun. At the witching hour the sun is still above the horizon. Go north of the Arctic Circle to Barrow, and you'll find the sun doesn't dip for 84 days, from May 10 to August 2. That's because the earth is tilted and, during the summer, the northern frigid zone leans towards the sun. It doesn't make any difference where the earth is in its 24-hour rotation, north of the Arctic Circle the sun will always be shining.

Although the Pinnell Mountain Trail is south of the circle, due to the refraction of the sun's rays, the sun does not set on it from June 17 to June 24. The refraction effect this close to the North Pole is so great that it causes the light to linger and makes the sun appear as if it hasn't set at all. It's something of an optical illusion.

The Pinnell Mountain Trail, with its high points and open tundra, is a great place to watch the sun at midnight. Don't bother lathering on the suntan lotion – the rays strike the earth at such a low angle in Alaska they have lost much of their intensity. Also, because of the angle, the sun appears to skim the horizon throughout much of the day, never setting but never getting very high in the sky either.

The best thing about this slanting Arctic light is the warm colors and shades it produces throughout the summer, especially in late August and early September. A clear day is a photographer's dream, when every hour is like the golden hues of late afternoon elsewhere. If you're on the Pinnell Mountain Trail on a clear day, plan on burning up some film. The blue sky, white clouds, the golden tundra of fall or the wildflowers of early summer will be painted in deep, rich colors that have never looked so good.

day it's possible to see in every direction, including to the Eagle Summit parking lot, your starting point 4mi away. You can also gaze down on the Ptarmigan Creek drainage area for the first time. All around you ancient rocks are perched in unusual upright positions and piles. The rocks, some of the oldest in Alaska, dating back 500 billion years, look like headstones, prompting a few backpackers to refer to this as the 'graveyard stretch' of the hike.

The trail follows the high ridgeline, descends sharply to another pass where it reaches Mile 5, then climbs halfway up **Porcupine Dome** before it begins skirting its south side. At this point it's easy to drop the packs and scramble up the loose talus slope for the remaining 400ft to the top of the 4915ft peak. Along the south side, you begin 'bouldering,' stepping from one large rock to

the next. You pass Mile 6, halfway around, and finally descend to a pass in the ridgeline.

You bottom out at Mile 7 and then begin the final and hardest climb of the day, actually accomplished in two stages. First you climb close to the ridge's high point of 4740ft, bouldering along the north side, from where views of Porcupine Creek are possible. The second stage, beginning at Mile 9, is **Pinnell Mountain** itself. It's a 300ft climb along a series of rock switchbacks and, considering it's at the end of your first day out, a heart-pounder for most people. But the 4934ft peak is a beautifully rounded dome with views everywhere, including your starting point almost 10mi away. Stay a while if the weather is nice, there is no need to rush down to the shelter.

The last leg of the day is the sharp descent off the peak. On the way down you'll spot

FAIRBANKS

The Habits of the Hoary Marmot

Though most hikers want to see bears, moose, Dall sheep and possibly even wolves, the animal many of them get to know best is the hoary marmot. The marmot is the largest member of the squirrel family – some tip the scales at 30lb in midsummer. They are usually found above the tree line in mountainous areas throughout Alaska, from Barrow to Bristol Bay, including Denali National Park and the ridge trails around Fairbanks such as Pinnell Mountain, Chena Dome and Granite Tors.

JIM DUFRESNE

The marmot is easy to encounter and watch because it's diurnal, rising at the crack of dawn and leaving its burrow to feed or to just sun itself. Marmots are also naturally curious and very social animals that live in communities on rocky but open ridges.

Among the most comical things to witness is the meeting of two marmots. They often will touch muzzles and then may stage what appears to be a wrestling match, with the pair tumbling down the rocky slope. Biologists believe this nuzzling is used to identify members of a community, and the wrestling may help to establish male dominance.

The other noticeable trait of the marmot is its whistle. Produced by internal cheek pouches, a marmot whistle is so loud at times that it can be heard 2mi away. Whistling is an alarm system that protects other marmots from approaching predators. At times, a marmot will also bark, yip and even yell.

It's hard to sneak up on a marmot, but there is no better way to spend a warm afternoon in the mountains than watching a community of marmots feeding, sunning and wrestling each other.

the **Ptarmigan Creek Shelter** in the saddle below and possibly a few tents. You pass Mile 10 a quarter mile before reaching the shelter. The camping is excellent here, with views off both sides of the pass. Often there are small pools of water on the south side of the pass.

Stage 2: Ptarmigan Creek Shelter to North Fork Shelter
7.5mi, 4 to 5 hours

The route is marked in the pass and begins with an immediate climb up a ridgeline. Once on the ridge hikers tend to head south toward a 4595ft knob. But the route continues to climb and then heads west along a ridge that features another set of ancient rocks. Many are pinnacles that have been carved into unusual shapes by wind, rain and other elements of nature. One, positioned just after Mile 11, looks like a profile of former US president Richard Nixon.

There, in the middle of the Alaskan wilderness, is Tricky Dick greeting you.

You skirt the high point of 4721ft along the south side, pass Mile 12 and then descend more then 400ft to a low point in the ridgeline. The route then begins to climb toward a 4282ft dome but swings toward the north side before reaching the top. After bouldering around the side of the peak, you emerge to the view of **Swamp Saddle**.

It sounds uninviting – and Swamp Saddle *can* be in early July if the flies and other bugs overpower you – but in late summer this can be a delightful area. You descend to Mile 14 where more than a mile of planking leads across the boggy area. The wild berries here are as thick and sweet as anywhere along the trail and include blueberries and low-bush cranberries. Small pools, within reach of the planked trail, exist through most of the summer and can be used to refill your water bottles.

The planking descends the saddle, crosses it and then heads up a ridge on the other side, extending a short way past Mile 15. Eventually the planking stops, and soon you top off on a ridge where the route begins a wide curve to the southwest. At Mile 16 you make the final climb on the way to the second shelter. The first 300ft are covered in a series of switchbacks, but it is still a knee-bending climb. Gradually the route levels out, passes Mile 17 and reaches the high point of 4447ft.

The descent on the other side is just as hard and even more disconcerting to many backpackers when they can't see the shelter in the saddle below. That's because it's off the trail to the south. **North Fork Shelter** is a classic log structure pitched on the edge of the ridge, with a sweeping view of its namesake river below. There are places to camp on the saddle, and usually a few pools of water can be found here as well.

Many hikers will pass up the North Fork Shelter and continue on the trail to reduce the walk on the final day. The next spot to camp is at the next saddle, 2mi farther, and 3mi to the one beyond that, where you would reduce your final trek to less than 7mi.

Stage 3: North Fork Shelter to Twelvemile Summit Trailhead
9.6mi, 5 to 6 hours

From the shelter, you resume climbing and then skirt the north side of a pair of 4300ft knobs before descending to the next saddle, passing Mile 19 on the way down. Blueberries abound here, as do the places to pitch a tent. You leave the area with a brief climb and then undertake a long descent 300ft into the saddle at the foot of Table Mountain.

If it's still the second day, camp here. **Table Mountain** is a hard climb to undertake at the end of long day of hiking. You begin with a series of steep switchbacks that take you 600ft to the top of the mountain's flat, table-like ridgeline, where you pass Mile 22.

The trail never does reach the mountain's true 4472ft peak but instead departs Table Mountain from its southeast corner and begins a long descent. You'll drop more than 700ft in the next 1.5mi, before passing Mile

24 and climbing a 3865ft knob. At the top you'll pass Mile 25 and a **surveyor's marker** implanted in the ground. Important to many hikers is the view of the Steese Hwy, which from here looks incredibly close.

The last leg of the journey is a climb around one more knob of 4100ft and through another gallery of impressive rocks and stone pinnacles. Just beyond Mile 26 the trail begins descending and eventually curves to the south toward the highway and trailhead parking area. Much of the final mile is wet muskeg, but planking makes it a pleasant end to the three-day hike.

Granite Tors Trail

Duration 2 days
Distance 15mi
Difficulty Level Medium
Start/Finish Tors Trail State Campground at Mile 39.5 of Chena Hot Springs Rd
Cabins & Shelters Yes
Permits Required No
Public Transportation Yes
Summary This 15mi loop in the Chena River State Recreation Area provides access to an alpine area and a series of unusual granite rock formations.

What began as a rock climbers' route to a series of pinnacles in the alpine area east of Fairbanks, became a backpackers' destination when the Youth Conservation Corps (YCC) constructed a trail in the early 1980s to the granite tors of Chena River State Recreation Area. Today, this 15mi loop provides easy access to the tundra world above the tree line, where you can hike and camp among these unusual rock formations.

Tors are large granite outcrops that were formed 60 to 80 million years ago when molten rock pushed upwards but cooled before reaching the surface. When the surrounding area eroded, the large hard-rock pinnacles remained, inviting rock climbers to scale them and trekkers to hike between them. The pinnacles range in size from boulders to rock outcrops up to 200ft high. Most are above the tree line.

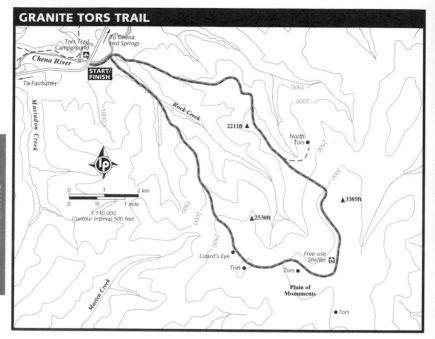

GRANITE TORS TRAIL

For the most part, Granite Tors Trail is a very well-marked and easy-to-follow trail that gains 2700ft from Chena Hot Springs Rd to the tors. This trail is used much more than the Pinnell Mountain Trail, especially on any nice weekend in the summer when there's an influx of locals. The loop makes an ideal overnight outing for most people or a long day hike for strong hikers. The west side of the loop offers a shorter (7mi) but steeper route to the tors. The trail features mileposts that begin along the east side, but don't be surprised if a few are missing.

You can camp anywhere along the trail, and you'll see many areas that are obviously favorites among backpackers. One of the best places to stay for the night, however, is on the east edge of the Plain of Monuments, where a free-use shelter was erected in 1994. Like on the Pinnell Mountain Trail, you should pack a tent on the Granite Tors Trail, as the shelter is small and heavily used

on the weekends. From the shelter, the tors are less than a mile away.

PLANNING
When to Hike
This trail can be hiked any time from June through mid-September. After that chances are good you will encounter snow.

What to Bring
At times water can also be scarce on this trail, though not to the degree that it is on Pinnell Mountain or Chena Dome Trails. Start with at least 2 quarts of water per person and then refill your supply at every opportunity. Also, bring a camp stove, because open fires are prohibited along the trail, and pack a tent in case the shelter is being used.

Maps
The area is covered by the USGS 1:63,360 series quad *Big Delta D-5*, but the trail itself

is not marked on it so it's necessary to pick up the *Granite Tors Trail* leaflet from the Public Lands Information Center, the state park office or – when they are in stock – from a box at the trailhead. See Maps in the Pinnell Mountain Trail section earlier in this chapter for where to buy topos in Fairbanks.

Cabins & Shelters

There is a free-use shelter halfway along the Granite Tors Trail, reached about 7mi from the trailhead when hiking the east half of the loop first.

NEAREST FACILITIES

The facilities in the area are all located along or off of Chena Hot Springs Rd, which extends 56mi east off the Steese Hwy. At Mile 24 of Chena Hot Springs Rd, before you come to the state recreation area, is Pleasant Valley Plaza, which includes Soapy's Suds, a Laundromat with showers, and across the road, Tack's General Store, with a limited supply of groceries.

Located between the two Chena Dome trailheads near Mile 50 of Chena Hot Springs Rd is *Angel Creek Lodge* (☎ 369-4128), which has cabins ($50 per double), the only local restaurant and a bar.

Chena River State Recreation Area

There are three campgrounds along Chena Hot Springs Rd; each has sites for $8 per night. The first is *Rosehip State Campground*, at Mile 27, whose large, flat gravel pads make it a favorite with RVers. There are 37 sites. Farther to the east is *Tors Trails State Campground* at Mile 39.5, with 24 sites. Across the highway is the trailhead for the Granite Tors Trail. The third is *Red Squirrel*, at Mile 42.8, with 12 sites.

There are also five rental cabins in the Chena River State Recreation Area. The *North Fork Cabin* ($35 per night) is at Mile 47.7 of Chena Hot Springs Rd and can be reached by vehicle. The rest can only be accessed on foot or by mountain bike or all-terrain vehicle (ATV). The closest is *Lower Angel Creek Cabin* ($25 per night), which is 3.6mi along an ATV trail from Mile 50.5 of Chena Hot Springs Rd, which is also the

Chena Dome Trailhead. Stop at the Alaska DNR (☎ 451-2705) on Airport Way in Fairbanks to check availability.

Chena Hot Springs Resort

Chena Hot Springs Resort (☎ 452-7867, 800-478-4681, @ vhenahs@polarnet.com) is at the end of Chena Hot Springs Rd, at Mile 56. The springs are at the center of a 40-sq-mi geothermal area and produce a steady stream of water that's so hot (156°F) it must be cooled before you can even think about a soak. The most popular activity is hot-tub soaking, done both indoors and outdoors. There are three Jacuzzis, a pool and a hot (very hot) tub. This fine resort is a perfect way to end an overnight hike. It has a good restaurant, a lively bar and even a masseur in case the hot tubs don't soothe your aching muscles. Hotel rooms begin at $105 per couple per night; rustic cabins begin at $65. There are also large cabins with sleeping lofts that hold six for $110. If there are only one or two of you, head for the campground, where a wooded site along a creek is $15 per night. The use of the hot tubs costs extra for campers: $8 for unlimited day use, $6 after 7 pm.

GETTING TO/FROM THE HIKE

The trailhead is marked with an information bulletin board in the parking area of Tors Trail State Campground at Mile 39.5 of Chena Hot Springs Rd. The trail actually begins on the other side of the road and is well posted. Hitchhiking is not the grand effort it is on the Steese Hwy because of the heavy summer usage of the Chena River State Recreation Area. You can also call Chena Hot Springs Resort (☎ 452-7867, 800-478-4681, @ vhenahs@polarnet.com), which has a shuttle van service to the end of the road; there are usually two runs per day and roundtrip fare is $30 per person.

THE HIKE
Stage 1: Tors Trail State Campground to Free-Use Shelter
7mi, 5 to 6 hours

From a bulletin board in the parking area of Tors Trail State Campground, a trail climbs to the highway bridge over the

Chena River and crosses it on a walkway. From here you cross Chena Hot Springs Rd to a posted path on the other side and follow it to the river itself.

You briefly skirt the river and then arrive at a split in the trail. The left-hand fork leads off to the East Trail, the right-hand fork to the West Trail. The easiest way to hike the loop is to begin with the East Trail, which leads across a boardwalk through black spruce and bog areas before crossing Rock Creek a half mile from the trailhead.

At this point the trail swings southeast and skirts the creek. You head upstream briefly through a forest of white spruce before moving into stands of birch and aspen where, a mile from the trailhead, the climbing begins. The ascent is steady but not steep, and the forest is beautiful. For the next 3mi you continue to gently climb through white birch and are occasionally rewarded with a view though the trees of the Chena River and even the bridge where the trailhead is located.

Just past Mile 4 you break out to an open knob where you can see the ridgeline that you'll be walking that afternoon and the next morning. The view of the tors scattered along the ridge is impressive and makes the knob a popular place to camp for those who get a late start. A descent back to a saddle and the tree line follows, and then you begin climbing Munson Ridge. Just past Mile 6 is a posted junction. To the left is a half-mile spur to the North Tors, a small group of tors that is below the timberline. The main trail heads right, and a short way from the junction, a spring bubbles out sweet and cold, the finest water on the trail. Top off those water bottles, especially if you are overnighting at the Plain of Monuments.

Eventually you begin to traverse the talus slope across the face of Munson Ridge. The trail is well above the tree line at this point, so the views are spectacular. On a clear day you can see Chena Dome to the northwest, which at 4421ft is the highest point in the state recreation area. The climb is steady until Mile 7, where you top off and descend to an alpine meadow. After passing through

a small stand of stunted spruce, you emerge at the free-use shelter on the east edge of the Plain of Monuments. The well-named spot is where three ridges merged. Spread out before you is an open tundra plain with clusters of tors less than a mile away.

The free-use shelter, built by the Boy Scouts in 1994, features a woodstove, benches and a porch where you can sit and admire the scenery. Four can sleep inside, and nearby in the tundra are pools of water. Some backpackers stay at the shelter, others hike to the nearest cluster of tors and camp there. From either spot, the plain can be an impressive sight at sunset.

Stage 2: The Return
8mi, 5 to 6 hours

From the shelter, you head southwest across the Plain of Monuments. For the most part, the East Trail ends at Mile 7, and the West Trail isn't picked up until Mile 9. In between is a much less developed route through the tundra muskeg marked by rock cairns and wooden tripods. On a clear day, you will have no problems following the trail, but if the weather is poor, take your time searching for the next marker. The hiking can be wet. In less than a mile, the trail swings past a cluster of four tors. There are good camping spots (but no water), and it's easy to climb one of the tors for an overview of the plain and even the Alaska Range to the south. The main gathering of tors is a half mile east, but there is no trail to it. The Granite Tors Trail heads west at this point and climbs to its highest point, 3346ft. This is the most spectacular stretch of the trail. As you climb the ridge, there are clusters of tors all around you, and on the horizon is the Alaska Range. In this treeless terrain the view seems to extend forever.

The trail tops off at a prominent tor and arrives at the edge of a steep drop. On the way down, you pass Mile 9 and continue on the well-developed West Trail. You bottom out at a saddle of alder and spruce and then resume climbing, topping off at 3000ft and the last group of tors, known as the Lizard's Eye, reached near Mile 10. This is a popular place to set up camp.

From here, you endure the longest and steepest descent – or ascent depending on your direction of travel – of the hike. Within a mile, the trail drops more than 1000ft. At Mile 11 the descent becomes more gradual and then levels out briefly at Mile 12. You eventually resume descending until you bottom out in the muskeg that surrounds **Upper Rock Creek**. Extensive planking helps you keep your boots dry, and at Mile 14, you use a bridge to cross a small feeder stream.

More extensive planking follows, with one stretch more than a quarter mile long, until you arrive back at the junction between the East Trail and West Trail on the banks of the Chena River. Head left to follow the levee back to Chena Hot Springs Rd and the bridge over the Chena River.

Chena Dome Trail

Duration 3 to 4 days
Distance 29.5mi
Difficulty Level Hard
Start Mile 50.5 Chena Hot Springs Rd
Finish Mile 49.1 Chena Hot Springs Rd
Cabins & Shelters Yes
Permits Required No
Public Transportation Yes
Summary Most of this three- to four-day loop around the Angel Creek drainage is in the open tundra. The views are good throughout the summer and include Mt McKinley on a clear day.

Also in the Chena River State Recreation Area is the Chena Dome Trail, a 29.5mi loop that circles the entire Angel Creek drainage area. The first 3mi of the trail cuts through forest and climbs to the timberline. It ends that way as well, but in between the hike follows tundra ridges where the route has been marked by rock cairns and mileposts.

For those who enjoy romping in the alpine, this route is a treat. Four times you reach summits that exceed 3000ft, and in between, you are challenged with steep climbs and descents. One summit is Chena Dome, the highest point in the state recreation area. The flat-topped ridge rises to 4421ft and, on a clear day, provides views of Mt McKinley.

The loop is usually walked in three or four days. It's hard to make use of the free-use shelter at Mile 17 unless you take four days to cover the trail or endure a 12.5mi hike the final day. The easiest direction of travel is by beginning at the trailhead at Mile 50.5 of the Chena Hot Springs Rd. The northern trailhead is also the start of a scenic day hike. Within a mile you pass a overlook of Angel Creek and in 3mi reach the tree line.

PLANNING
When to Hike
The trail can be walked June through early September. Water in the form of snow patches and pools is most plentiful in June. Snow can be encountered after mid-September.

What to Bring
Like Pinnell Mountain, water can be scarce here in August or during a dry summer. Start off with at least 3 quarts per person and then replenish every chance you get from small pools in the tundra. Mosquitoes and gnats can be bad from June through early August so bring powerful insect repellent. Also pack a stove; open fires are not permitted in the area.

Maps
USGS quads *Big Delta D-5* and *Circle A-5* and *A-6* cover the area, but the trail is not shown. Also carry along the *Chena Dome Trail* leaflet, available at the Alaska State Parks office, the Public Lands Information Center in Fairbanks or from a box at the trailhead (when in stock).

Cabins & Shelters
Near Mile 17 is a free-use shelter that has space for up to four people, and future plans call for a second free-use shelter to be built in the saddle at Mile 7.5.

There is also a spur trail at Mile 23 that descends 1.5mi and 1900ft from the ridge to Upper Angel Creek Cabin ($25 per night).

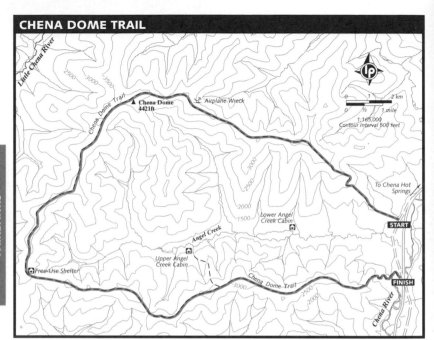

CHENA DOME TRAIL

You need to reserve the cabin in advance through the Alaska DNR (☎ 451-2705, fax 451-2706) at 3700 Airport Way, Fairbanks, AK 99709-4699.

GETTING TO/FROM THE HIKE

Most hikers begin from the upper trailhead at Mile 50.5 of Chena Hot Springs Rd, finishing at the lower trailhead at Mile 49.1 Chena Hot Springs Rd. When traveling west, the upper trailhead is 0.7mi past Angel Creek Bridge on the left side of the road. If you leave a vehicle here, add another 1.4mi to the trek for the walk along Chena Hot Springs Rd.

If you need transportation call Chena Hot Springs Resort (☎ 452-7867, 800-478-4681, ❷ vhenahs@polarnet.com), which has shuttle service to the end of the road. The roundtrip costs $30 per person. Pickup is usually at 5 pm for the resort or 6 pm for a trip back to Fairbanks.

THE HIKE
Stage 1: Northern Trailhead to Mile 9

9mi, 8 to 9 hours

At the northern trailhead you'll find outhouses, an information board and parking but no water. If you need some, Chena Hot Springs Rd crosses the Chena River a half mile to the north. There are two trails that depart from the trailhead: the ATV two-track to the two state park rental cabins (see the Granite Tors Trail section, earlier, for more information about the cabins) and the Chena Dome Trail. Both are well posted.

The hiking trail also begins as a two-track, quickly crosses the ATV trail at a posted junction and then narrows and begins climbing. The climb is steady but not steep, and within a mile, you break out to an impressive view of the Angel Creek valley. If you started out late, it's possible to camp here.

The climb becomes steeper after Mile 2 and remains that way until you clear the tree line of birch, spruce and alder past Mile 3. Take a break at the rock outcropping here. The views are wonderful and a steeper climb lies just ahead. The trail is now a route marked by rock cairns that continues the steep ascent until you reach a 3700ft dome. You are now well above the tree line and will remain there until the final 3mi of the trek.

From the dome you descend past Mile 4 and then begin another climb. This is classic ridge walking, and for the next 3mi, you climb a series of domes, including one that rises to 3400ft at Mile 5. On a clear day the views are endless in almost every direction; in poor weather take your time to find the next cairn.

Just before Mile 7 you begin a major descent, passing the milepost on the way down. You bottom out at a boggy saddle where there should be **pools of water**. This is the best source of water on your first day, so fill up. The spring that is past Mile 8 is often dry in late summer. From the saddle you're faced with an incredible climb: 900ft within a half mile. This intimidating slope occurs near the end of a long day, making it an especially brutal climb for most backpackers. Grit your teeth and bear it. On the way up, the route levels out briefly twice before you reach Mile 8. Just beyond the milepost is the **plane wreck**.

The plane was a WWII surplus military C-46 that was returning from flying supplies to Barrow. It crashed in the early 1950s when, in the heavy fog, the pilot misjudged the top of the ridge by 10ft. Two people died, and today the plane's wreckage is spread across the ridge. There are pieces of aluminum everywhere. The main body and wings are actually on the north side of the ridge. Thirty yards from there is the propeller and engine. Another 100yd away is the pilot's seat. A quarter mile away is a piece of chain. Amazing.

From the wreck you sidle the left side of a rocky peak where there might be a spring running, but don't count on it in late summer. The trail then descends to a saddle where Mile 9 is located. This is a scenic spot to camp, but there is no water nearby.

Stage 2: Mile 9 to Free-Use Shelter
8mi, 6 to 7 hours

The day begins with a quick scramble over a rocky knob and then a descent to the saddle at the base of Chena Dome. From the knob, the hike to the top of the dome looks imposing, but it's not nearly as hard as the 900ft climb the day before. The ascent is much more gradual, and in the middle you get a reprieve with a bit of level ground. Eventually you reach the table-top peak of **Chena Dome**, hike across it and reach a communications relay station in the middle, just past Mile 10. The Alaska Range is clearly visible to the south, including Mt McKinley to the southwest if the day is clear.

Cairns descend the dome to a wide, flat saddle and then cross it to Mile 11. The hiking becomes easy for the next 2mi as you first skirt the left side of a rocky peak, then the right side of the next one and finally the left side of the third one for a level stretch. Just past Mile 12, near the middle peak, are often **pools of water**. Look for them near the edge of the ridge: They are the most reliable source of water since the saddle before Mile 8.

After a noticeable climb past Mile 13, you top off to another stretch of easy ridge walking. What little climbing there is in the next 2mi is hardly noticeable because the views are so expansive. That all changes a half mile past Mile 16, where there is a 700ft descent along a steep slope. At the bottom is the **free-use shelter**.

Built in 1998–99, the shelter is located in a saddle and has two benches, a woodstove and room for four people to sleep at night. Blueberries and low-bush cranberries abound on the saddle, but there is no water. If you're dry, there might be pools past Mile 18, a climb of more than 700ft.

Many backpackers planning to cover the trail in three days push on past the shelter to shorten their final day of hiking. There is

Hiking to Hot Springs

One of the most pleasant aspects of backpacking in the Fairbanks area is ending a long hike with a soothing soak at a hot spring. On Pinnell Mountain, Chena Dome and Granite Tors Trails, it's a short ride from the trailhead to the nearest hot tub or heated pool. But only one hiking route – the new Angel Rocks–Chena Hot Springs Traverse – actually ends where you go to take a soak.

This 8.3mi route begins at Mile 48.9 of Chena Hot Springs Rd and traverses a series of ridges to the Chena Hot Springs Resort. The trail could be undertaken as a separate hike or as a way to add more days to the Chena Dome Trail. The Angel Rocks trailhead is located almost across the road from the lower end of the Chena Dome Trail.

The hike begins on the well-maintained Angel Rocks Trail (see the Other Hikes section), which skirts the Chena River and then climbs a ridge past granite outcroppings, called 'tors.' In 2.2mi from the trailhead you reach a marked junction. To the east, the traverse continues as a climb above the tree line, becoming a route marked by cairns along the open ridgeline.

Once on the ridge, you'll enjoy views of the Alaska Range and Granite Tors to the south, Chena Dome to the north and Far Mountain to the west. Five miles from the trailhead you reach a free-use shelter, an excellent place to overnight. The next day would be a quick 3.3mi hike to **Chena Hot Springs Resort** (☎ 452-7867, 800-478-4681, ✉ vhenahs@polarnet.com).

Within minutes you could have your boots off and your toes soaking in one of a series of hot tubs and pools at the resort. Ahhhh! Or leave your boots on and head straight for the bar, where you can sample the microbrew beers on tap. Afterwards, either make arrangements to stay at the resort that night in its campground or lodge (see Granite Tors Trail) or catch the Chena Hot Springs Resort van that departs daily at 6 pm for Fairbanks.

good camping and water a half mile past Mile 20. Just keep in mind that this 3mi stretch involves a pair of 700ft climbs and a steep descent.

Stage 3A: Free-Use Shelter to Southern Trailhead

12.5mi, 10 to 12 hours

If you're covering this stage in one day, start early! This is true especially if you have made arrangements to be picked up by the Chena Hot Springs shuttle at the trailhead (see Getting To/From the Hike, earlier).

From the shelter you begin with an immediate climb to a dome at 3195ft then pass Mile 18 and a series of small pools just beyond the mile marker. Don't be surprised if these are dry late in the summer. The route then descends to 2600ft before beginning the next climb, this time to a 3348ft dome. The climb can be a knee-bender but the view from the top is excellent. Almost due north is Chena Dome, and with a small twist of the head, you can see the entire 8mi

you covered the day before. To the southeast are the Granite Tors (see Granite Tors Trail), and on the horizon to the southwest, you can see Mt McKinley – if the gods are smiling on you with clear weather.

The following descent is steep, but you bottom out at 2400ft in a saddle where there should be **tundra pools**. These are good sources of water, and sometimes the last sources on the ridge before the end of the hike, if the summer has been dry. Three more **domes** follow in the next 3mi, a stretch that will test your resolve. Just past Mile 22, you top off on the second dome at 3200ft and can clearly see the Upper Angel Creek Cabin in the valley to the north. From here you descend 400ft past a large granite outcropping to a saddle at Mile 23, where there is a **posted junction** with the spur to the rental cabin (see stage 3B).

The third dome is the last major climb of the hike and a steep one. From the saddle, you ascend 600ft in a half mile to top off on a rounded dome at 3400ft. The view, needless to say, is outstanding. The route descends gently off the east side of the dome and near Mile 24 passes some small pools just before skirting the left side of a rocky knob.

You descend to a bushy saddle and then make the final ascent of the trip along a narrow ridge, really the first one of the hike, where you can look down into valleys on both sides of you. The ridge tops off to a 180-degree view east where you can see the Angel Rock tors, the Chena River and even the bridge near the northern trailhead.

At this point you begin your descent to the Chena River Valley. The route heads northeast and begins on a slope of dwarfed birch, where at times you have to search for the next cairn. At Mile 27, however, a well-beaten path appears and continues the descent with a series of switchbacks.

You reenter the tree line, pass Mile 28 and in another half mile come to a junction. Continue straight for another 20yd to see an unusual **rock drinking fountain** that has been set up next to a small stream. The main trail curves left and continues with switchbacks. You bottom out beyond Mile 29, cross several small creeks and then arrive at the banks of the **Chena River**. The southern trailhead is just a short walk away and includes an outhouse, information display and hand pump for water.

Stage 3B: Mile 23 to Northern Trailhead via Upper Angel Creek Cabin
8.2mi, 5 to 6 hours

An alternate way to return to the northern trailhead at Mile 50.5 of Chena Hot Springs Rd is to depart Chena Dome Trail at a junction in a saddle at Mile 23. The junction is posted for 'Angel Creek Cabin' and is a descent of 1400ft in 1.5mi to the rental unit. The start of the spur is little more than a series of rock cairns that drop steeply out of the saddle. Within a half mile you reach the tree line and continue along a well-defined path that follows a gently sloping ridge.

You emerge at Upper Angel Creek Cabin, which has bunks for four people, a wood-burning stove, an outhouse and even

a lantern. The cabin must be reserved in advance (see Cabins & Shelters earlier). Nearby is Angel Creek, a small and very cold stream where occasionally somebody catches a grayling.

The northern trailhead is then reached via an ATV trail that departs from the cabin, crosses Angel Creek on a bridge and heads east the length of the valley. The trail appears as an old two-track and is a considerably easier hike then returning to the Chena Dome Trail. But keep in mind the ATV trail rarely swings past Angel Creek and the views are not nearly as good from the bottom of the valley as they are from the top of the ridge. Plan on an hour to descend from the ridge to Angel Creek and four to five hours to hike the 6.7mi to the trailhead along the ATV trail.

Other Hikes

Creamer's Field Trail
A self-guided, 2mi trail winds through Creamer's Field Migratory Wildlife Refuge, an old dairy farm that has since become a bird-lover's paradise, where more than 100 species of bird pass through each year. The refuge is at 1300 College Rd in Fairbanks, and the trailhead is in the parking lot adjacent to the Alaska Department of Fish & Game office (☎ 452-1531), where trail guides are available. The trail is mostly boardwalk, with an observation tower along the way and lots of bugs. The flocks of geese, ducks and swans move onto nesting grounds by late May, but sandhill cranes can be spotted throughout the summer.

Chena Lakes Recreation Area
This facility opened in 1984 as the last phase of an Army Corps of Engineers flood control project prompted by the Chena River's flooding of Fairbanks in 1967. Two separate parks, Chena River and Chena Lakes, make up the recreational area, which is 18mi southeast of Fairbanks past North Pole, off the Laurance Rd exit of the Richardson Hwy. The Chena River park contains a 2.5mi self-guided nature trail.

Between the two parks there are three campground loops providing 78 sites ($6 per night).

Angel Rocks Trail

This 3.5mi loop leads to Angel Rocks, large granite outcroppings near the northern boundary of the Chena River State Recreation Area. It's a moderate day hike, with the rocks less than 2mi from the road. From the first set of rocks, the trail makes a moderately steep ascent of several hundred feet as it weaves through many granite tors before emerging at a rock ridge.

The posted trailhead is just south of a rest area at Mile 49 of the Chena Hot Springs Rd. Practically across the street is the southern trailhead for the Chena Dome Trail (USGS quads *Big Delta D-5* and *Circle A-5*).

Summit Trail

The BLM, which maintains the Pinnell Mountain Trail, also administers the White Mountains trail network, which includes the Summit Trail. This 18mi, one-way route was especially built for summer use and has boardwalks over the wettest areas. The route winds through dense spruce forest, traverses scenic alpine ridges and arctic tundra and ends at a junction with Wickersham Creek Trail. From there you can continue east for 2mi to reach scenic Beaver Creek, an outstanding grayling fishery. On the other side is Borealis-LeFevre Cabin, but it is usually not possible to safely ford Beaver Creek.

Hiking in for a bit of fishing on Beaver Creek is a five-day adventure. Even stopping short of it, the hike still takes two or three days to reach the highest point along

the route – the 3100ft ridgeline, 10mi from the Elliott Hwy. The highlight of the hike is the view from the top of Wickersham Dome, which includes Mt McKinley, the White Mountains and the Alaska Range.

The last 2.5mi of this trail drop off the ridgeline and descend into a muskeg area where hikers must ford up to four streams. Most parties end the day camping above the tree line instead of dealing with the low-lying swamp.

The trailhead is at Mile 28 of the Elliott Hwy, 31mi north of Fairbanks. Don't confuse the Summit Trail (also called the Summer Trail), which was made for hikers, with the Wickersham Creek Trail, which departs from the same trailhead. Both the Summit Trail and the Wichersham Trail begin at Mile 28 of the Elliot Hwy. They immediately split off and merge back together 2mi from Beaver Creek. The Wickersham Creek Trail, like most of the trail system in the White Mountains, leads through swampy, muskeg lowlands, making hiking extremely challenging.

There is now public transportation on a portion of the Elliott Hwy and the Dalton Hwy that will provide drop-off service to the trailhead. Dalton Highway Express (☎ 452-2031) makes the run twice a week and charges $70 for roundtrip to the Summit Trail. The BLM District Office in Fairbanks (☎ 474-2200), at 1150 University Ave, has a useful *Trip Information Planning Sheet* (TIPS) on this trail and other trails in the recreation area. You can also pick them up at the Public Lands Information Center (☎ 456-0527) on Cushman St in downtown Fairbanks (USGS quads *Livengood A-3, B-2* and *B-3)*.

Glossary

Alcan or **Alaska Hwy** – the only overland link between the state and the rest of the country
aurora borealis or **northern lights** – mystical snakes of light – possible at almost any time of the year – that weave across the sky from the northern horizon as a result of gas particles colliding with solar electrons

backcountry – the area of a park not accessible by vehicle or road
backcountry camping – setting up camp in a wilderness area where there are no designated sites
backcountry campsite – a designated camping area near the trail
bidarka – a skin-covered sea kayak used by the Aleuts
BLM – Bureau of Land Management (sometimes referred to as the Bureau of Logging & Mining), which oversees a wide range of preserves and recreational areas, including the Pinnell Mountain Trail
boardwalk – boards or planks used to cross a bog, muskeg or other wet area along a trail; also referred to as 'planking'
bouldering – hopping from one boulder or rock to the next, often along a river or shoreline where there is no trail
braided stream – a stream or river with many shallow channels, broken up by bars of gravel; the safest place to ford a river
bug dope – slang term for insect repellent

cairn – a pile of rocks used to mark a route
circuit – a loop trail or route that brings the hiker back to the trailhead without covering the same ground
cirque – an alpine basin carved by a glacier, usually at the head of a valley
confluence – where two rivers or streams merge
contour lines – the elevation lines on a topographical map

crampons – a set of spikes attached to the bottom of boots, allowing hikers and climbers to cross snowfields and glaciers

DNR – Alaska's Department of Natural Resources, which oversees state parks and state recreation sites
Dolly Varden – a species of freshwater fish that resembles rainbow trout
drop-off – a steep descent along a slope, ridge or mountain

fire ring – a designated area for campfires in a campsite
flashlight – torch
ford – to cross a stream or river without the aid of a bridge
fork – a junction where two trails head in different directions

glacial outwash – the gravel debris left behind by a retreating glacier
gorge – a narrow ravine, often where a river or stream flows through in a series of rapids

hemlock – a species of pine tree native to Alaska

milepost – mile markers found along Alaskan highways and some hiking routes, for example, the Chena Dome Trail
moose nuggets – hard, smooth little objects dropped by moose after a good meal
moraine – an accumulation of debris pushed into a mound by a glacier, called 'terminal,' 'lateral' or 'medial,' depending on its position within the glacial valley
muskeg – a bog in Alaska, with layers of matted plant life floating on top of stagnant water

no-see-ums – slang term for the tiny gnats found throughout much of the Alaska wilderness

NPS – National Park Service, the federal agency that oversees national parks

outcrop – a bare rock face or pinnacle

pepper spray – an aerosol spray derived from the capsicum pepper, designed as a defense against bear attack

permafrost – permanently frozen subsoil that covers two-thirds of the state

planking – see 'boardwalk'

quadrangle number – number used to identify a USGS topographical map

quads – short for 'quadrangle,' used by hikers in reference to a USGS topographical map

ridgeline – crest of a ridge, often used for travel through alpine areas

ridge walking – to follow the crest of a ridge in an alpine area

route – a natural direction of travel, such as along a river or ridgeline, but not a developed path

runoff – the melted ice of a glacier

RVers – the drivers of large recreational vehicles, motor homes or trailers pulled by cars

saddle – a low place on a ridge or between two peaks, which provides the easiest access from one valley to another

scat – animal droppings, usually used to describe bear droppings

scree – steep slopes covered in loose rock, found in alpine areas

sidle – to walk around or along the side of a hill

slips – areas where huge volumes of earth and rock have 'slipped' from the hillside, obliterating parts of a track; also called 'landslides'

solstice – the first day of summer, on June 21, and the first day of winter, on December 21

spur – a small ridge that leads up from a valley to the main ridge; also a side trail

summer solstice – on June 21, the first day of summer and the longest day of the year (with 21 to 22 hours of daylight in the Interior and around Fairbanks)

switchbacks – the section of a trail that weaves back and forth, allowing hikers to ascend a ridge or slope in a gradual manner

talus – a slope formed by accumulated rock debris

tarn – a small alpine lake, often nestled in flat ridges

tent pad – a posted and elevated area to pitch a tent

topo – a slang term for USGS topographical maps

tor – natural column of rock

trail – a footpath or track built for hiking

trailhead – the posted starting point of a trail

traverse – to move horizontally across a slope

tree line – boundary between the last patches of trees and the alpine area

true left/right – the left/right side of a river as seen when facing downstream

tundra – vast, treeless Arctic plains

two-track – also known as 4WD track; a rough road used by all-terrain or four-wheel-drive vehicles to reach remote areas

USFS – US Forest Service, which oversees Tongass and Chugach National Forests in Alaska

USF&WS – US Fish & Wildlife Service, the federal agency that oversees wildlife preserves in Alaska

USGS – US Geological Survey, the federal agency that produces topographical maps

vault toilet – outhouse, nonflushing loo, pit toilet

LONELY PLANET

You already know that Lonely Planet produces more than this one guidebook, but you might not be aware of the other products we have on this region. Here is a selection of titles which you may want to check out as well:

Alaska
ISBN 0 86442 754 9
US$18.99 • UK£12.99 • 149FF

Hiking in the USA
ISBN 0 86442 600 3
US$24.99 • UK£14.99 • 179FF

The Arctic
ISBN 0 86442 665 8
US$19.95 • UK£12.99 • 160FF

Canada
ISBN 0 86442 752 2
US$24.95 • UK£14.99 • 180FF

Available wherever books are sold.

Index

Text

A

AB Mountain Trail 167
accommodations 70–3. *See also individual locations*
B&Bs 71
cabins 24, 72–3
camping 70, 71–2
hostels 59, 70–1
hotels & motels 71
wilderness lodges 71
acute mountain sickness (AMS) 79–80
Admiralty Island 131
Aialik Bay 219
AIDS 81
air travel 88–92, 101–2
airlines 88, 89
airports 68, 88–9
bush planes 101–2
tickets 89–90
Alaska Chilkat Bald Eagle Preserve 146
Alaska Direct Bus Line 93–4, 103
Alaska Discovery 17, 49
Alaska Hwy. *See* Alcan
Alaska Marine Hwy 96–9, 109–10
Alaska National Interest Lands Conservation Act 16, 17, 23
Alaska Native Claims Settlement Act 15, 16, 26, 226
Alaska Natural History Association (ANHA) 56
Alaska Railroad 104–7
Alaska Range 18
Alaska Wilderness Recreation and Tourism Association (AWRTA) 21
AlaskaPass 96
Alaskon Express 93, 102–3
Albert Loop Trail 187, 195
Alcan 15, 92, 94
alcoholic drinks 75. *See also* bars

alder 30
Aleutian Range 18
Aleuts 13, 25
Alpine Ridge Trail 231, 232
Alpine Trail 224
altitude sickness 79–80
Alyeska Glacier View Trail 194–5
Amalga Trail 144–5, **145**
AMS 79–80
Anchorage region 168–96, **169, 171, 174–5**
accommodations & food 172–3
climate 20, 169–70
hikes 177–96, **184, 188**
natural history 168–9
supplies & equipment 172
transportation 173, 176–7
Angel Rocks Trail 316
Angel Rocks–Chena Hot Springs Traverse 314
Aniakchak National Monument & Preserve 22
ANWR. *See* Arctic National Wildlife Refuge
Arctic Bicycle Club 56, 109
arctic char 55
Arctic National Wildlife Refuge (ANWR) 16–7, 20
Ascension, Mt 217
Athabascans 13, 25
ATMs 61
Auke Bay 137

B

backpacks 46
Bagley Ice Field 241
bald eagles 38, 146, 251
B&Bs. *See* accommodations
baneberry 31, 83
Baranov, Aleksandr 14
Bare Loon Lake 157
bargaining 62
bars 75

Bean Creek Trail 210
bears
avoiding 84–5
encountering 85–6
species of 32–3, 170
watching 131, 268
Beaver Lake Hike 164
beavers 36
Bellingham, Washington 98
belugas 37, 39
Bench Lake 202
Bennett 158
Bering, Vitus 13
Bering Glacier 19
Bering Land Bridge National Preserve 22
berries 30–1
bicycling 108–9. *See also* mountain biking
guidebooks 66, 109
rental & purchase 109
birch 30
Bird Ridge Trail 194
birds. *See also* bald eagles
guidebooks 67
species of 38–9
watching 38–9, 56, 254
Bishop Beach Hike 237
black bears 32–3, 170
blackflies 82
blanket toss 26
Blind River Rapids Boardwalk 163
blisters 77–8
BLM. *See* Bureau of Land Management
Blue Lake 118
Blueberry Loop 178
boats. *See* ferries
Bold Ridge Trail 192
Bonanza Mine Trail 248–53, **249**
books 64–7
guidebooks 65–6
health guides 76
natural history 67
survival manuals 84

Bold indicates maps.

Boxed Text

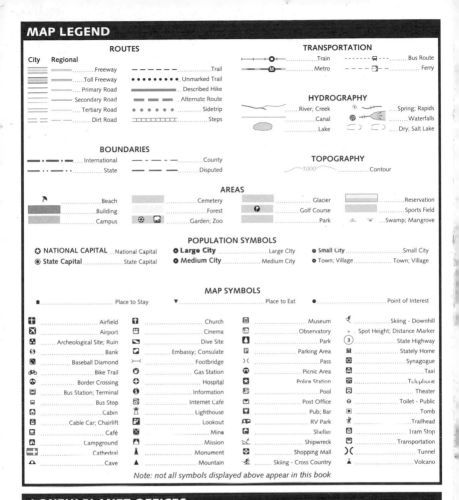

MAP LEGEND

ROUTES

City **Regional**

Freeway
Toll Freeway
Primary Road
Secondary Road
Tertiary Road
Dirt Road

Trail
Unmarked Trail
Described Hike
Alternate Route
Sidetrip
Steps

TRANSPORTATION

Train
Metro
Bus Route
Ferry

HYDROGRAPHY

River; Creek
Canal
Lake
Spring; Rapids
Waterfalls
Dry; Salt Lake

BOUNDARIES

International
State
County
Disputed

TOPOGRAPHY

1000 .... Contour

AREAS

Beach
Building
Campus
Cemetery
Forest
Garden; Zoo
Glacier
Golf Course
Park
Reservation
Sports Field
Swamp; Mangrove

POPULATION SYMBOLS

NATIONAL CAPITAL ... National Capital
State Capital .... State Capital
Large City .... Large City
Medium City .... Medium City
Small City .... Small City
Town; Village .... Town; Village

MAP SYMBOLS

Place to Stay
Place to Eat
Point of Interest

Airfield
Airport
Archeological Site; Ruin
Bank
Baseball Diamond
Bike Trail
Border Crossing
Bus Station; Terminal
Bus Stop
Cabin
Cable Car; Chairlift
Café
Campground
Cathedral
Cave

Church
Cinema
Dive Site
Embassy; Consulate
Footbridge
Gas Station
Hospital
Information
Internet Café
Lighthouse
Lookout
Mine
Mission
Monument
Mountain

Museum
Observatory
Park
Parking Area
Pass
Picnic Area
Police Station
Pool
Post Office
Pub; Bar
RV Park
Shelter
Shipwreck
Shopping Mall
Skiing - Cross Country

Skiing - Downhill
Spot Height; Distance Marker
State Highway
Stately Home
Synagogue
Taxi
Telephone
Theater
Toilet - Public
Tomb
Trailhead
Tram Stop
Transportation
Tunnel
Volcano

Note: not all symbols displayed above appear in this book

LONELY PLANET OFFICES

Australia
PO Box 617, Hawthorn 3122, Victoria
☎ 03 9819 1877 fax 03 9819 6459
email talk2us@lonelyplanet.com.au

USA
150 Linden Street, Oakland, California 94607
☎ 510 893 8555, TOLL FREE 800 275 8555
fax 510 893 8572
email info@lonelyplanet.com

UK
10A Spring Place, London NW5 3BH
☎ 020 7428 4800 fax 020 7428 4828
email go@lonelyplanet.co.uk

France
1 rue du Dahomey, 75011 Paris
☎ 01 55 25 33 00 fax 01 55 25 33 01
www.lonelyplanet.fr

World Wide Web: www.lonelyplanet.com *or* AOL keyword: lp
Lonely Planet Images: lpi@lonelyplanet.com.au